TERRORIST EVENTS WORLDWIDE 2023-2024

EDWARD MICKOLUS, PHD

WANDERING WOODS PUBLISHERS

Terrorist Events Worldwide 2023-2024

By Edward Mickolus, PhD

ISBN: 978-1-949173-21-5

Published in the United States by
Wandering Woods Publishers
EdwardMickolus.com

Book Design, Cover and Typesetting by
Cynthia J. Kwitchoff (CJKCREATIVE.COM)

DISCLAIMER

All statements of fact, opinion, or analysis expressed are those of the author and do not reflect the official positions or views of the Central Intelligence Agency (CIA) or any other U.S. Government agency. Nothing in the contents should be construed as asserting or implying U.S. Government authentication of information or CIA endorsement of the author's views. This material has been reviewed by the CIA to prevent the disclosure of classified information. This does not constitute an official release of CIA information.

ABOUT THE AUTHOR

Edward Mickolus, PhD, is the President of Vinyard Software, Inc. He served a 33-year career with the Central Intelligence Agency, has written 50 books, and has taught intelligence tradecraft courses at numerous federal agencies.

Vinyard Software's International Terrorism Data Center provides universities, research institutions, governments, the media, and others interested in international terrorism the best publicly-available data on terrorists and events around the world. His terrorism books include:

Terrorism Events Worldwide 2022

Terrorism Events Worldwide 2021

Terrorism Events Worldwide 2019-2020

Terrorism Worldwide 2018

Terrorism Worldwide 2017

Terrorism Worldwide 2016

Terrorism 2013-2015: A Worldwide Chronology

Terrorism 2008-2012: A Worldwide Chronology

Terrorism, 2005-2007

with Susan L. Simmons Terrorism, 2002-2004: A Chronology, 3 volumes

with Susan L. Simmons Terrorism, 1996-2001: A Chronology of Events and a Selectively Annotated Bibliography, 2 volumes

with Susan L. Simmons Terrorism, 1992-1995: A Chronology of Events and a Selectively Annotated Bibliography

Terrorism, 1988-1991: A Chronology of Events and a Selectively Annotated Bibliography

with Todd Sandler and Jean Murdock International Terrorism in the 1980s: A Chronology, Volume 2: 1984-1987

with Todd Sandler and Jean Murdock International Terrorism in the 1980s: A Chronology, Volume 1: 1980-1983

with Peter Flemming Terrorism, 1980-1987: A Selectively Annotated Bibliography

International Terrorism: Attributes of Terrorist Events, 1968-1977, ITERATE 2 Data Codebook

with Susan L. Simmons The 50 Worst Terrorist Attacks

with Susan L. Simmons The Terrorist List: North America

with Susan L. Simmons The Terrorist List: South America

with Susan L. Simmons The Terrorist List: Eastern Europe

with Susan L. Simmons The Terrorist List: Western Europe

with Susan L. Simmons The Terrorist List: Asia, Pacific, and Sub-Saharan Africa

The Terrorist List: The Middle East, 2 volumes

The Literature of Terrorism: A Selectively Annotated Bibliography

Transnational Terrorism: A Chronology of Events, 1968-1979

Combatting International Terrorism: A Quantitative Analysis

TABLE OF CONTENTS

Introduction   1

Overview of 2023   2

Overview of 2024   6

Worldwide   13

Africa   13

Asia   37

Australia/Oceania   64

Europe   67

Latin America   112

Middle East   123

North America   222

Updates of pre-2023 incidents   267

Bibliography   321

Find the Author at:

Books: EdwardMickolus.com

Terrorism Data: VinyardSoftware.com

INTRODUCTION

This book uses the same **definition** of terrorism as found in its predecessors, allowing comparability across decades. Terrorism is the use or threat of use of violence by any individual or group for political purposes. The perpetrators may be functioning for or in opposition to established governmental authority. A key component of international terrorism is that its ramifications transcend national boundaries, and, in so doing, create an extended atmosphere of fear and anxiety. The effects of terrorism reach national and worldwide cultures as well as the lives of the people directly hurt by the terrorist acts. Violence becomes terrorism when the intention is to influence the attitudes and behavior of a target group beyond the immediate victims. Violence becomes terrorism when its location, the victims, or the mechanics of its resolution result in consequences and implications beyond the act or threat itself.

The book is divided into a region-by-region (and within each, a country-by-country) look at terrorist incidents and a separate section updating events that occurred prior to 2023. The Incidents section is based solely on publicly available sources. This section is not intended to be analytical, but rather comprehensive in scope. As such, the section also includes descriptions of non-international attacks that provide the security and political context in which international attacks take place. In some cases, the international terrorists mimic the tactics of their stay-at-home cohorts. Often, these are the same terrorists working on their home soil against domestic, rather than foreign, targets. Domestic attacks often serve as proving grounds for techniques later adopted for international use. The section discusses major technological, philosophical, or security advances, such as: the use of letter bombs; food tampering; major assassinations; attempts to develop, acquire, smuggle, or use precursors for a chemical, biological, radiological, or nuclear weapon; key domestic and international legislation and new security procedures; key arrests and trials of major figures; and incidents involving mass casualties. Non-international entries do not receive an eight-digit code.

The section also provides follow-up material to incidents first reported prior to January 1, 2023. For example, updates include information about the outcome of trials for terrorist acts occurring prior to 2023 and "where are they now" information about terrorists and their victims. The update is identified by the original incident date, and includes enough prefatory material to give some context and to identify the original incident in the earlier volumes.

The international terrorist incidents and airline hijackings are identified by an eight-digit code. The first six digits identify the date on which the incident became known as a terrorist attack to someone other than the terrorists themselves (e.g., the date the letter bomb finally arrived at the recipient's office, even though terrorists had mailed it weeks earlier; or the date on which investigators determined that an anomalous situation was terrorist in nature). The final two digits ratchet the number of attacks that took place on that date. In instances in which either the day of the month or the month itself is unknown, "99" is used in that field.

The information cutoff date for this volume is December 31, 2024.

The Bibliography includes references drawn from the same public sources that provide the incidents, literature searches, and contributions sent by readers of previous volumes. It does not purport to be comprehensive. The citations are grouped into topic areas that were chosen to make the bibliography more accessible, and includes print and web-based material. The Bibliography gives citations on key events and may be referenced for more detail on specific attacks described in the Incidents section.

Overview of 2023

Innovations in Terrorist Methods

Early trends in 2023 were shattered in the last quarter of the year, when Hamas engaged in the largest complex terrorist attack on record.

Terrorist attacks—international and domestic—were down from previous years' tallies. Major terrorist leaders remained quiet, possibly hiding from rivals and/or government agencies attempting to bring them to justice, either in the courts or on the battlefield.

The long arm of the law caught up to several prominent, albeit ancient, cases.

European governments led the way in coming to closure with complex prosecutions of terrorists whose depradations occurred years earlier; similar prosecutions of age-old cases were held in Latin America, the Middle East, and the United States.

- In Belgium, on July 25, a Brussels court convicted six out of ten suspects guilty of "terrorist murder" in the March 22, 2016 ISIS suicide attacks at Brussels Zaventem Airport and the Maelbeek metro station that killed 36 and injured more than 300.

- In France, authorities convicted right-wing Barjols terrorists who planned operations against officials, migrants, and the assassination of President Emmanuel Macron.

- Germany prosecuted right-wing Reichsbürger (Citizens of the Reich) movement adherents who plotted to kidnap Health Minister Karl Lauterbach and subject him to a show trial, blow up power infrastructure, stir civil unrest, and violently overthrow the government.

- In February, Chris Heaton-Harris, the secretary of state for Northern Ireland, told Parliament that the British government would launch an independent investigation into the Omagh car bombing that killed 29 people and injured 220 in Northern Ireland in August 1998.

- In February, Libyan man Abu Agila Mohammad Mas'ud Kheir al-Marimi pleaded not guilty to three federal charges brought against him in Washington, D.C. regarding making the bomb that destroyed Pan Am Flight 103 over Lockerbie, Scotland, on December 21, 1988.

European governments also repatriated numerous spouses and children of ISIS terrorists; Germany prosecuted repatriated ISIS wives for crimes against women in ISIS-run territory. Germany banned the Hammerskins Germany neo-Nazi organization and far-right anti-Semitic Artgemeinschaft group. Dissident Irish republican paramilitary groups reappeared in Northern Ireland. The continuing Russian occupation of Ukrainian territory led to bombings in both countries that could be attributed to the combatants or like-minded sympathizers. Radicalized loners, often armed with simple knives, conducted attacks in France, Germany, Portugal, Spain, and the United Kingdom.

Similarly, the **United States** successfully prosecuted scores of January 6, 2021 insurrectionists, but was not as successful in finding solutions to the Guantánamo Bay cases, many of which dragged into their third decade. The U.S. repatriated some of the Guantánamo Bay detainees who were believed affiliated with al-Qaeda, but still was faced with individuals whom no government would take, and no U.S. state wanted on its soil, much less in its courts. Federal officials underscored the growing threat posed to the country by various groups and individuals espousing anti-Semitic, Islamophobic, racist, neo-Nazi, and other extremist right-wing ideologies. The Department of the Treasury issued economic and financial sanctions against dozens of suspected supporters and practitioners of international terrorism. Attacks and threats were reported against election officials, elected officials, schools, and places of worship. Prosecutors obtained convictions against terrorists of all stripes, particularly those attempting to provide material support to ISIS and right-wing extremists. While lone nuts used firearms in a spate of attacks, others tried ricin and razor blades taped to gas pumps.

African terrorists—among them Islamist adherents to ISIS and al-Qaeda, as well as irredentists, separatists, and secular extremists—conducted numerous multi-casualty attacks, some which neared the total of the Hamas October 7 campaign, but generated little Western media coverage. The Congo's ISIS-linked Allied Democratic Forces (ADF) were especially active, sometimes crossing borders to harass civilians and officials in Uganda. China, attempting to expand its economic foothold in the region, found its workers coming under attack in the Central African Republic, Congo, and Ethiopia. Al-Shabaab similarly made forays outside of its Somali homeland, conducting attacks in Kenya and Ethiopia, when it was not fleeing from U.S. Africa Command airstrikes. Nigeria remained plagued by ISIS affiliate Islamic State—West Africa Province gunmen and a host of kidnappers with religious, political, or simply monetary motivations. Jihadi gunmen continued to threaten civilians and governments throughout eastern Africa.

In **Asia**, ethnic and religious tensions continued to lead to armed attacks in India against civilians and government forces. Kashmiri separatist violence somewhat ebbed from previous years. Tehreek-e-Taliban Pakistan and Baluch separatists battled Pakistani forces and conducted numerous attacks against diverse targets. A

suicide bombing against a mosque in Peshawar, Pakistan in January killed 101 people and injured 221. A newly-formed Tehreek-e-Jihad announced its presence with a bombing and ISIS-K claimed a suicide bomber crossed the border with Afghanistan to kill 63 and injure 123 in Khyber Pakhtunkhwa Province in July.

In **Latin America**, in January, thousands of election-denying supporters of former Brazilian President Jair Bolsonaro, an ally of former U.S. President Donald Trump, took over the Brazilian Congress building, the Supreme Court, the Planalto Presidential Palace, and areas surrounding the Plaza of the Three Powers in Brasilia. Numerous rioters clashed with police. The parallels with the January 6, 2021 attack on the U.S. Congress were striking. Police cleared the buildings and arrested 1,500 people. Colombian terrorists, including FARC dissidents and ELN adherents, continued to pose threats against the government, which raided numerous rebel safehouses and confiscated arms and ammunition. The ELN and government, however, agreed on a six-month cease-fire in August. Ecuador was the scene of extensive violence aimed at derailing the presidential election, topped by the assassination of presidential candidate Fernando Villavicencio, 59, at a political rally at a school north of Quito. Gangs in Haiti were responsible for numerous acts that would constitute terrorism if they had a political bent.

In the **Middle East**, the U.N. Security Council indicated that many countries suggested that former Egyptian army special forces lieutenant colonel Mohammed Salahuddin Zeidan, alias Saif al-Adel (sword of justice), believed to be hiding in Iran, was the new "de facto and uncontested" leader of al-Qaeda, which otherwise had little activity in the area. The ruling Afghan Taliban continued to be harried by ISIS-K, which conducted numerous mass casualty events. Individuals opposed to girls' education poisoned possibly thousands of schoolchildren in Afghanistan and Iran. Terrorists crossed several borders into Iran, conducting harassing operations against government and religious leaders. Iran continued to allow al-Qaeda leaders to reside on its turf, and was suspected of providing support to numerous other terrorist groups around the world.

Palestinian terrorists, particularly Hamas and to a lesser extent Islamic Jihad in the Gaza Strip, lobbed rockets into Israeli territory, leading to retaliatory airstrikes. Hizballah conducted similar actions from Lebanon. Palestinians used such weapons as firearms, knives, and vehicles to conduct low-level attacks in Israel and Israeli-occupied territories. Israeli settlers often struck back against perceived Islamic enemies with similar deeds. The conflict in Syria dragged on, with the U.S. conducting airstrikes against ISIS and netting several of its leaders. Türkiye's National Intelligence Organization (MIT) claimed it had killed the suspected leader of ISIS, Abu Hussein al-Husseini al-Qurashi. Some of the countries that had led the world in earlier years as sites for attacks were quiet, Algeria, Egypt, and Libya among them.

The exceptional quiet of the first three quarters of the year was shattered with the October 7 attack on Israel by hundreds (or possibly thousands) of Hamas terrorists arriving from Gaza by sea, ground, and even air gliders with mounted machine guns. The terrorists attacked nearly two dozen locations in Israel. While members of the Israeli Defense Forces, police, and volunteers ultimately killed hundreds of the invaders, Hamas slew 1,200 Israelis at two dozen sites and kidnapped more than 230 people, including 135 holding foreign passports. The hostages were believed to have been hidden in the miles of tunnels Hamas maintains in the Gaza Strip.

Israeli retribution was immediate and sustained, ultimately involving a ground incursion into Gaza that killed more than 21,000 Palestinian civilians, including possibly 5,000 children, according to Palestinian health services. As of this writing, the numbers continue to rise.

The Israeli intelligence services were critiqued for two major intelligence failures:

- The attack, which appears to have been planned for more than a year, caught the IDF by complete surprise. Despite the vaunted intelligence successes by Mossad and others in penetrating Palestinian circles with human sources, plus other technical intelligence collection means, no indicators of an impending attack were gleaned. The at-tack was the most complex, coordinated terrorist incident in history, arguably even surpassing the 9/11 hijackings. While Hamas had conducted occasional forays into Israel, no intelligence service had credited it with such extensive intelligence collection capabilities or military order-of-battle insights.

- The attackers had developed detailed information on the location of specific targets within Israeli bases, including communications hubs, which were quickly destroyed by the terrorists. Such a counterintelligence failure was especially disturbing to Israeli authorities which had been aggressive in ferreting out potential threats.

Mediation by Qatar, Egypt, and the United States led to a weeklong pause in the fighting in late November, during which humanitarian aid poured into Gaza, Israel freed 180 jailed Palestinians, and Hamas freed more than 60 hostages, most of them women and children. Negotiations to continue the agreement collapsed on December 1, when Israel resumed military operations.

The extent of the attack and its surprise nature was too much for conspiracy theorists to not comment on, featuring suggestions that the news media, or even the highest levels of the Israeli government, were tipped off.

Threats of violence and actual attacks, particularly in the U.S. and Western Europe, ramped up, especially against Jewish and Muslim interests. Arab terrorists, anti-Semites, white supremacists, lone wolves, and others came out of the woodwork to conduct numerous incidents against Jews and Arabs alike. U.S. troops, particularly those in Syria and Iraq, experienced dramatic upticks in attacks on their facilities and personnel. Houthis uncharacteristically expanded their area of operations, normally confined to Yemen, to fire missiles at Israeli shipping, foreign commercial carriers, and U.S. warships in the Red Sea.

Fates of Key Terrorists

The several prequels to this volume suggested that terrorism-hunters concentrate on several key terrorists, including lone wolves, who popped up throughout the world. Security forces stopped many, but not all, before they could attack. Lone nuts with political grievances were mixed in with more recognized radical organizations for a spate of incidents.

Senior Terrorists Killed in 2023

The year 2023 continued the litany of misfortunes for ISIS leaders, with Turkish forces claiming to have killed the most recent successor to emir al-Baghdadi in April. The short tenure of Abu Hussein al-Husseini al-Qurashi (who replaced al-Baghdadi's immediate successor, who was also killed by counterterrorist forces) ended at an abandoned farm that was being used as an Islamic school in Jindires (variant Jandaris), in the northwest region of Afrin in Syria. Al-Qurashi was always on the run, and never had time nor opportunity to give a public address.

Palestinian Islamic Jihad leaders were also harried by counterterrorist forces, with the two leaders of Gaza Strip-based rocketeers "neutralized" by Israeli Defense Force airstrikes in May.

This list includes those killed by coalition and Russian forces, including by airstrikes, and by rival terrorist groups, plus those who died of natural causes.

Although not a member of a formal terrorist group, imprisoned Unabomber Ted Kaczynski, 81, committed suicide in prison while serving a life term.

Al-Qaeda in the Arabian Peninsula (AQAP)

- Hamad bin Hamoud al-Tamimi, alias Abdel Aziz al Adani, a Saudi who served as president of the consultative council and judge.

ISIS

- Abu Hussein al-Qurashi, variant Abu al-Hussein al-Husseini al-Qurayshi, ISIS emir

- Abu Zacharia, Jer Mimbantas, and Faharudin Hadji Benito Satar, who headed the Dawlah Islamiya Maute (DI-Maute), the Philippines affiliate

Palestinian Islamic Jihad

- Khader Adnan, PIJ leader, from a three-month hunger strike in Israeli prison

Other Terrorists Killed in 2023

Allied Democratic Forces

- Musa Kamusi, a unit commander

ISIS

- Hamza al-Homsi, a senior leader in Syria
- Khalid 'Aydd Ahmad al-Jabouri, who planned attacks into Europe
- Abu Morsid, logistics chief of the Dawlah Islamiya Maute (DI-Maute), known as the ISIS in Southeast Asia
- Usama al-Muhajir, an ISIS leader in eastern Syria
- Ibrahim al-Qahtani, who was associated with planning ISIS detention center attacks in Syria
- Bilal al-Sudani, an Islamic State leader operating in northern Somalia
- Shafi Ullah, an ISIS commander in Bajur in Pakistan

Hamas

- Rifaat Abbas, one of the three seniormost commanders of Hamas's key Daraj Tuffah Battalion
- Shadi Barud, Hamas's deputy chief of intelligence, who Israel said planned Hamas's October 7 attacks
- Ebrahim Biari, the head of Hamas's Jabalya battalion and a leader of the October 7 massacre
- Ibrahim Jadba, one of the three seniormost commanders of Hamas's key Daraj Tuffah Battalion

- Tarek Maarouf, one of the three seniormost commanders of Hamas's key Daraj Tuffah Battalion
- Ayman Nofal, Hamas military commander

Al-Shabaab

- Moalim Ayman, who led the Jaysh Ayman al-Shabaab unit responsible for terrorist attacks in Kenya and Somalia, and was accused of masterminding a January 5, 2020 attack on a military base in Kenya that killed three Americans

KEY TERRORISTS CAPTURED/ SURRENDERED IN 2023

Allied Democratic Forces (operating in Congo and Uganda)

- Njovu, leader of the ISIS-linked ADF believed responsible for killing two foreign tourists and their local guide in a national park on October 17

ISIS

- Batar, an ISIS Syria Province official believed planning attacks on detention centers guarded by the Syrian Democratic Forces (SDF) and manufacturing IEDs
- Abu Halil al-Fad'ani, an operative in Syria
- Hudayfah al-Yemeni, an ISIS attack facilitator in Syria

Baluch Nationalist Army

- Gulzar Imam, alias Shambay, founder and leader of the BNA

OVERVIEW OF 2024

ACTIVITIES OF KEY TERRORIST GROUPS

In the Middle East, Israel's gloves-off approach to its campaign to rid Gaza of Hamas included a raid on a hospital, which it claimed was used as a hideout for Hamas and the Palestinian Islamic Jihad, in which a joint counterterrorist team killed three terrorists in their beds. Fortunes for Hamas turned downhill dramatically in mid-October, when the IDF killed Hamas leader Yahya Sinwar, architect of the October 7, 2023 massacre of 1,200 Israelis.

The IDF onslaught against Gaza Strip targets caused a massive humanitarian crisis, with a million Palestinians displaced and, according to Gaza Health Ministry figures, roughly 46,000 Palestinians killed. More modest airstrikes against West Bank teargets and Hizballah in Lebanon logged thousands of additional casualties.

Israel hacked into pagers, Lebanese Hizballah's preferred means of communication, and set them to explode, injuring 2,800 people and killing nine. The next day, Israel detonated walkie-talkies, killing 20 and injuring 450. Hizballah had shunned cell phones, believing the IDF could monitor them.

Numerous tertiary actors offered their services in harassing Israelis, attempting to extend the war to a region-wide conflagration.

- Hizballah lobbed missiles and drones from Lebanon into Israeli territory.
- Yemen's Houthi rebels continued the campaign against shipping in the Red Sea, expanding ino the Gulf of Aden, Gulf of Oman, Indian Ocean, and other nearby waterways. They even fired a few missiles at Israeli territory, to little effect aside from plenty of publicity. The Houthis claimed that they were trying to interfere with Israeli-involved and Israel-bound vessels, but the attacks extended to ships with no clear Israeli ties. American and British naval

forces shot down most, but not all, Houthi missiles and the U.S. conducted air strikes against Houthi bases in Yemen. Houthis were undaunted, continuing to lob missiles, particularly at Israeli targets toward the end of the year.

For its part, Israel struck back with numerous aerial sorties, and also focused on successful decapitation operations against Hizballah and Hamas, killing their senior leadership on their turf in the West Bank, Gaza Strip, Lebanon, and Iran. Israel decimated on-the-ground capability of Hizballah and Hamas to conduct operations locally and out-of-area as well. Anti-Israel actors threatened retaliation, but were unable to develop spectacular operations after weeks of saber-rattling.

Iran's Axis of Resistance, already reeling from leadership and order-of-battle losses by key proxies Hizballah and Hamas, was further devastated by the overthrow of the 50-year-old al-Assad regime in Syria in December. While it is too early to evaluate the composition and direction of the successor regime, many of the rebellion's leaders had ties to ISIS and al-Qaeda. The erstwhile rebel leadres, despite ties with al-Qaeda-linked Hay'at Tahrir al-Sham, initially appeared willing to cooperate with the West.

Africa-based terrorism continued to get little coverage in the Western media, despite major terrorist insurgencies and mass casualty attacks, most notably in Congo and Somalia. Congo was a hotbed of terrorist activity, with 120 rebel groups active in the area, led by Allied Democratic Forces jihadis.

In Latin America, fragile truces with the Revolutionary Armed Forces of Colombia (FARC) were often shattered by uncooperative splinter groups, while peace talks continued fitfully with the country's second-largest rebel group, the National Liberation Army (ELN).

In the Caribbean, Haitian armed gangs roamed freely as the country had no government in place.

Europe was the site of increasing threats and attacks by right-wing terrorists and lone actors inspired by white supremacists and other extremists.

South Asia saw extensive attacks across borders and inside Aghanistan, Pakistan, and India, with governments charging each other with supporting domestic terrorist movements. Pakistan in particular was hit hard, with the Islamabad-based Center for Research and Security Studies reporting that 2,526 people were killed in attacks in 2024, including nearly 700 security personnel, more than 900 civilians, and circa 900 armed fighters. These deaths represent a nine-year high, exceeding the record of 2,432 deaths in 2016. Khyber Pakhtunkhwa Province was especially plagued by attacks. Pakistan saw expansion of operations by Baloch separatists as well as a continuation of Pakistani Taliban operatives.

India was likewise beset by terrorist attacks, mainly by Kashmiri separatists.

INNOVATIONS IN TERRORIST METHODS

Some terrorists looked into going for mass publicity and mass casualties by targeting venues with tens of thousands of people.

- Olympics organizers were especially sensitive to the possibility, fielding circa 70,000 law enforcement and security personnel to protect the athletes and spectators. No attacks were recorded, but secondary targets, such as the French train system, were hit by saboteurs and arsonists.

- ISIS, or its Afghanistan affiliate ISIS-K, conducted a mass casualty terrorist attack in the Moscow suburbs on March 23. Four terrorists killed at least 133 concertgoers and injured another 185 while destroying a large auditorium/mall. The attack came days after President Vladimir Putin secured a fifth term in a questionable election. The U.S. had provided intelligence a fortnight earlier warning of a likely major terrorist attack on a public venue in Moscow, but Putin brushed aside the warning as provocative and mere propaganda.

- It remains unclear whether the individual who missed by an inch assassinating former President Donald Trump at a campaign rally intended to kill just him or conduct a mass casualty attack. Fanciful conspiracy theories arguing that the attack was staged ignored that the shooter had never shown such precision in his earlier target practice. Conspiracy theories continued to swirl in the wake of a second assassination attempt, this time while Trump was playing golf at his Florida golf course.

- Taylor Swift canceled three concerts for 200,000 fans in Vienna, Austria after authorities received intelligence suggesting that the venues had been targeted.

FATES OF KEY TERRORISTS

A festering sore in terrorism—what to do judicially with the incarcerated "high value" al-Qaeda terrorists and sympathizers, including the 9/11 planners—looked to be coming to resolution with reports of a plea agreement for five 9/11 leaders, including Khalid Sheikh Mohammed. Secretary of Defense Lloyd Austin revoked the agreement, however, saying that such a momentous decision should be taken at his level, not the prosecution. As of this writing, the Guantánamo cases drag on, although the Biden administration was able to export several Gitmo alumni to various countries during the first few days of 2025.

SENIOR TERRORISTS KILLED IN 2024

This list includes those killed by coalition forces, including by airstrikes, and by rival terrorist groups, plus those who died of natural causes.

Al-Aqsa Martyrs Brigades

- Ibrahim al-Nabulsi, head of the al-Aqsa Martyrs Briagdes

AQAP

- Khalid al-Batarfi, AQAP leader

Bangsamoro Islamic Freedom Fighters

- Mohiden Animbang, alias Karialan, BIFF leader

HAMAS

- Azzam al-Aqra, alias Abu Abdullah, 54, a leading commander of the Qassam Brigades' military operations outside Gaza

- Saleh al-Arouri, Deputy Head of the Political Bureau of Hamas, and a founder of the group's military wing, the Izz ad-Din al-Qassam Brigades

- Samir Fendi, alias Abu Amer, a senior leader of the Qassam Brigades and its top commander in southern Lebanon.

- Hazem, Amir, and Mohammed Haniyeh, sons of Hamas leader Ismail Haniyeh. The IDF said Mohammed and Hazem were Hamas military operatives and that Amir was a cell commander.

- Ismail Haniyeh, political chief of Hamas

- Marwan Issa, the group's #3 and deputy to Mohammed Deif, the head of Hamas's military division. Issa was one of the planners of the October 7 attack.

- Izz al-Din Kassab, politburo member

- Rafe Salama, head of the Khan Younis brigade

- Fatah Sharif, a senior commander in Lebanon

- Yahya Sinwar, the group's leader and architect of the October 7, 2023 massacre of 1,200 Israelis

- Ra'ad Thabet, one of the group's ten senior commanders, responsible for research and development, strengthening systems, and headed the group's production unit

ISIS

- Ahmad Hamid Husayn Abd-al-Jalil al-Ithawi, head of all ISIS operations in Iraq

- Jassim al-Mazroui Abu Abdul Qader, ISIS leader in Iraq

Lebanese Hizballah

- Mohammed Afif, head of media relations

- Ahmad Moustafa al-Haj Ali, commander of Hizballah's Houla Front

- Ibrahim Aqil, who sat on the military Jihad Council and was part of the Radwan Force

- Mohammad Ali Hamdan, commander of Hizballah's anti-tank unit in the Meiss El Jabal area in southern Lebanon

- Ali Hussein Hazima, head of intelligence
- Suhail Hussein Husseini, military commander of Hizballah's headquarters in Beirut, who oversaw logistics, budget, and management
- Ali Karaki, a senior Hizballah leader
- Ibrahim Kobeisi, responsible for rocket launches towards Israel
- Hassan Nasrullah, the group's leader
- Mohammad Naameh Nasser, alias Abu Naameh, who headed the group's Aziz Unit, one of three regional divisions in southern Lebanon
- Sheikh Nabil Qaouk, head of Hizballah's Preventive Security Unit and member of Hizballah's central council
- Nasser Rashid, deputy commander in Bint Jbeil, Lebanon
- Hashem Safieddine, the group's leader in October 2024
- Mohammed Qassem al-Shaer, a commander of the elite Radwan Force
- Fu'ad Shukr, Hizballah's seniormost military commander
- Muhammad Hussein Srour, head of the group's Aerial Command
- Ahmed Wahbi, a senior commander in Hizballah's military wing

Nusra Front of Syria, renamed Hayat Tahrir al-Sham

- Maysara al-Jubouri, alias Abu Maria al-Qahtani, co-founder of the Nusra Front

OTHER TERRORISTS KILLED IN 2024

Abu Sayyaf

- Nawapi Abdulsaid, alias Khatan, who had been implicated in 15 beheadings

Bangsamoro Islamic Freedom Fighters

- Saga Animbang, brother of Mohiden Animbang, the group's leader, who was killed in the same firefight

Harakat al-Nujaba, an Iraqi militia

- Mushtaq Talib al-Saidi, variant Abu Taqwa al-Saidi, deputy commander of operations for Baghdad

Kurdish Workers' Party (PKK)

- Faik Aydin

Horas al-Din (Guardians of Religion) AQ-affiliate in Syria

- Abu Abdul Rahman Makki, a senior Saudi leader

ISIS

- Abu Hammam, who oversaw all operations in western Iraq
- Shakir Abud Ahmad al-Issawi, who led all military operations in western Iraq
- Usamah Jamal Muhammad Ibrahim al-Janabi, a senior member in Syria
- Abu Ali al-Tunisi, who oversaw technical development
- Abu Yusif, a commander in Syria

Islamic State in the Greater Sahara/Sahel Province

- Abu Huzeifa, alias Higgo, a commander wanted for the deaths of four American soldiers and four Nigerien troops killed in an attack in 2017 in Tongo Tongo, Niger

Dawlah Islamiyah (of the Philippines)

- Abdul Hadi, a bomb maker
- Saumay Saiden

Hamas

- Saeed Atallah Ali, a senior commander of the Hamas military wing
- Arafat Amer, a gunman in Jenin
- Majdi Aqilan, commander of the Hamas Shatti Battalion
- Abu Etewi, believed to have led an October 7, 2023 attack on a bomb shelter in Re'im, southern Israel
- Hassan Hakashah, a central figure in firing rockets from Syria toward Israel

- Wassem Hazem, head of Hamas in Jenin
- Mohammed Jalamneh, spokesperson for Hamas's military wing in the Jenin refugee camp, who allegedly communicated with Hamas officials in other countries and had been injured in preparing a car bomb attack
- Mehdoh Mahana, a senior member of Hamas's Gaza Brigade tunneling unit
- Muhammad Masek, Izzedine al-Qassam Brigades gunman
- Maysara Masharqa, gunman in Jenin
- Hadi Mustafa, a member of the Qassam Brigades, the Hamas military wing. The IDF said Mustafa was directing cells to attack "Israeli and Jewish targets" in different parts of the world.
- Zahi Yaser Abd al-Razeq Oufi, commander in the West Bank
- Sharhabil Ali al-Sayyid, alias Abu Amr, a senior commander of the Jamaa Islamiya in Lebanon who cooperated with Hamas against Israel, according to the IDF
- Mahmoud Zaki Shaheen, Mohammed al-Rayes, Mohammed Bashasha, and Ahmed Hamoud, killed in a drone strike in Beirut on January 2, 2024
- Ahmed Suidan, a Shatti Battalion company commander

Lebanese Hizballah

- Taleb Sami Abdullah, alias Abu Taleb, commander of the Nasr Unit that is in charge of parts of south Lebanon close to the Israeli border.
- Ali Muhammad Aldbas, a senior commander of Hezbollah's elite Radwan Force
- Ali Barakat, a senior member of Hizballah's Aerial Unit
- Ali Hussein Barji, variant Burji, who was in charge of Hizballah's drones in southern Lebanon
- Ali Hudruj, a commander in Lebanon
- Ali Ahmad Hussein, a commander of Hizballah's elite Radwan Force

- Ibrahim Issa, a deputy commander of Hezbollah's elite Radwan Force
- Abu Ali Rida, commander for the Baraachit area of southern Lebanon
- Fadel Shaar, a Hizballah member
- Wissam al-Tawil, a commander in the secretive Radwan Force that operates along the border
- Ismail al-Zin, a commander in the anti-tank missile unit of Hizballah's Radwan Forces
- al-Jamaa al-Islamiya (Islamic Group of Lebanon)
- Musab Khalaf, who was behind attacks on Israeli troops in the disputed Chebaa Farms that Israel captured from Syria

Kataib Hizballah of Iraq

- Wisam Mohammed Saber al-Saedi, a commander who was responsible for attacks on American forces in the region

Pakistani Taliban

- Abdul Rahim, a commander

Palestinian Islamic Jihad

- Ahmed al-Dalu, a member of the Islamic Jihad's Military Intelligence Unit who participated in a massacre of the kibbutz community of Kfar Aza during the October 7 attacks
- brothers Basel and Mohammed Ghazawi, PIJ members. The IDF said that Muhammad Ghazawi had shot at Israeli troops in the West Bank.
- Ahmed Aish Salame al-Hashash, head of PIJ's rocket unit in Rafah in the Gaza Strip
- Muhhamad Jabber, alias Abu Shujaa, commander of the Tulkarem Battallion of the al-Quds Brigades
- Islam Khamaysa, a leader of the Jenin Brigade
- Mamdoh Lulu, an assistant to the heads of the northern region of the Gaza Strip in the Palestinian Islamic organization, and was in contact with senior officials of the organization's headquarters abroad

West Papua Liberation Army military wing of the Free Papua Movement

- Abubakar Kogoya, alias Abubakar Tabuni, a regional commander
- Damianus Magay, alias Natan Wanimbo, a regional commander

East Asia Anti-Japan Armed Front

- Satoshi Kirishima, who died in a Tokyo-area hospital 50 years after he became one of Japan's most wanted fugitives

ADDITIONAL RESEARCH SOURCES

For those who prefer to run textual searches for specific groups, individuals, or incidents, a computer version of the 1960-2024 ITERATE (International Terrorism: Attributes of Terrorist Events) textual chronology is available from Vinyard Software, Inc., 502 Wandering Woods Way, Ponte Vedra, Florida 32081-0621, or e-mail via edmickolus@hotmail.com

The data set comes in a WordPerfect and Word textual version and looks remarkably like the volumes in this series of hardcopy chronologies. A numeric version offers circa 150 numeric variables describing the international attacks from 1968-2023 (and soon 2024). The data sets can be purchased by specific year of interest. See www.vinyardsoftware.com for further details.

Vinyard also offers the Data on Terrorist Suspects (DOTS) project, where you will find a detailed biographical index of every terrorist suspect named in this and previous volumes of this chronology.

Comments about this volume's utility and suggestions for improvements for its likely successors are welcome and can be sent to edmickolus@hotmail.com. Please send your terrorism publication citations to ensure inclusion in the next edition of the bibliography.

2023 - 2024 INCIDENTS

WORLDWIDE

November 16, 2023: The *Washington Post* reported that numerous postings on *TikTok, Instagram,* and *X* had publicized Osama bin Laden's "Letter to America" to millions online.

December 25, 2023: *Fox News* reported that al-Qaeda released a video in which it threatened an "open-source Jihad" against Western and Jewish targets, including airlines. *Atlas News* added that the video called for increased attacks on U.S., UK, and French airlines, among others, such as American Airlines, United Airlines, Delta Airlines, British Airways, EasyJet, Air France, and KLM Royal Dutch Airlines.

AFRICA

BURKINA FASO

January 1, 2023: *UPI* reported that the civilian Collective Against Impunity and Stigmatization of Communities (CISC) said that 28 people were killed in Nouna by a group claiming to be part of the government-supported Homeland Defense Volunteers, who said they thought the victims were jihadis. The bodies were found over the weekend.

January 12-13, 2023: *NPR, AP,* and *CNN* reported on January 16 that gunmen took hostage 50 women and girls gathering wild fruits in the Sahel region in two incidents on January 12 and 13. Some were kidnapped 15 kilometers from Arbinda, while others were taken elsewhere in Soum Province. *Al-Jazeera* reported on January 18 that some of the women escaped after being forced to walk through the jungle for a day.

January 26, 2023: *Al-Jazeera* and *AFP* reported that gunmen killed ten civilians in two attacks in Dassa.

January 29-30, 2023: *Al-Jazeera* reported that gunmen conducted two attacks, killing 28 people, including soldiers and civilians. In an attack on January 29, authorities found the bodies of 15 men in the Cascades region near the border with Ivory Coast. In a January 30 incident, gunmen attacked a combat unit in Falagountou, near the border with Niger, killing 10 soldiers, two fighters of the volunteer force, and a civilian. The army claimed it found the bodies of 15 terrorists. Gunmen had stopped two transport vehicles carrying eight women and 16 men. The women and one man were freed.

February 8, 2023: *USNWR* and *Reuters* reported that two staffers of Medecins Sans Frontieres were killed. The charity suspended operations to conduct a risk assessment.

February 17, 2023: *USNWR* and *Reuters* reported that gunmen ambushed an army unit in Oudalan Province in the Sahel region, near the border with Mali, killing 51 soldiers. The armed services reported that some 160 "terrorists" died in a counter-offensive air strike.

February 20, 2023: *USNWR* and *Reuters* reported that jihadis killed 19 soldiers at a military camp in Tin-Akoff in Oudalan Province. Several soldiers were missing. Hundreds of civilians fled the area.

April 15, 2023: *Al-Jazeera* reported that gunmen killed 40 people and wounded 33 others in a 4 p.m. attack on army and volunteer defence forces near Aorema village the Ouahigouya governorate. The gunmen killed 34 auxiliaries from the Volunteers for the Defence of the Fatherland (VDP) and six soldiers. A security source told *AFP* that security forces had "neutralized" dozens of terrorists.

April 27, 2023: *Al-Jazeera* reported that gunmen attacked a military base in Ougarou in the Est region, killing 33 soldiers and wounding 12. The soldiers killed 40 terrorists.

September 4, 2023: *Al-Jazeera* reported that rebels killed 17 soldiers and 36 volunteers assisting the military in Koumbri commune in Yatenga Province. Seven dozen rebels were killed and their combat equipment destroyed.

November 26, 2023: *AP* and state-run *RTB Television* reported on November 29 that al-Qaeda-linked rebels killed 40 civilians and wounded 42 by trying to take control of the besieged town of Djibo near Mali's border. Rebels had blockaded the town for more than a year. The JNIM was believed responsible for torching three camps for internally displaced people.

February 25, 2024: Gunmen attacked Catholic worshippers in Essakane as they gathered for Sunday prayers, killing 15 and injuring two. Jihadis were suspected.

Al-Jazeera and *AFP* added that at 5 a.m., gunmen attacked a mosque in Natiaboani, killing several dozen people, most of them Muslim males. The gunmen also fired at soldiers and members of the Volunteers for the Defence of the Fatherland (VDP), a civilian force that supports the military.

Al-Jazeera and *AFP* reported on March 4 that 170 people were killed and several others wounded in attacks on Komsilga, Nodin, and Soroe villages in northern Yatenga Province.

Gunmen also attacked a military detachment in Tankoualou in the east, a rapid response battalion in Kongoussi in the north, and soldiers in the northern region of Ouahigouya.

June 11, 2024: *Al-Jazeera* reported on June 16 that Jama'at Nusrat al-Islam wal-Muslimin (JNIM) claimed responsibility for a June 11 attack that killed 107 Burkinabe soldiers in the Mansila area near the border with Niger. The group took seven soldiers hostage.

August 9, 2024: An assessment by French government security officials reported that jihadis killed 150 soldiers in an ambush of a convoy in Tawori.

August 24, 2024: *AP* and *al-Jazeera* reported that the Jama'at Nusrat al-Islam wal-Muslimin (JNIM) killed 200 villagers and soldiers and injured another 140 in a raid on the Barsalogho commune in Kaya. Terrorists shot people digging trenches designed to protect security outposts. Several soldiers were missing after the attack. The attackers stole weapons and a military ambulance. *Reuters* reported that JNIM claimed it killed 300 people, but had targeted militia members affiliated with the army. *CNN* reported on October 4, 2024 that a French government security assessment estimated that 600 people had died at the hands of the motorcycle-riding terrorists in the 11 a.m. raid. Many of the dead were women and children.

BURUNDI

December 11, 2023: The RED-Tabara rebel group exchanged fire with the military in northwestern Burundi. The group is based in the Democratic Republic of the Congo.

December 22, 2023: *Al-Jazeera, AFP,* and *AP* reported that government spokesperson Jérôme Niyonzima said that during the night, gunmen attacked nine homes in Vugizo close to the Lake Tanganyika border with the Democratic Republic of the Congo (DRC), killing 20, including 12 children, two pregnant women, and a police officer, and wounding nine others. The RED-Tabara rebel group, considered a "terrorist" group by the Burundian authorities, claimed credit. The attackers appeared to be wearing Burundian Army uniforms. The military and police fled. Grocery shop owner André Kabura was wounded in both legs in the gunfire. A senior official said the attackers retreated to the DRC.

February 25, 2024: Rebels firing rifles killed nine people, including six women and a soldier, and wounded five others in a nighttime attack in Gihanga in Bubanza Province. The government accused Rwanda of supporting the RED-Tabara, which claimed credit. The group, based in Congo's South Kivu Province, said it killed six Burundian soldiers.

CAMEROON

February 25, 2023: *Reuters* reported that the armed wing of the separatist Ambazonia Governing Council claimed credit for setting off several small explosions in Buea in South-West Region while 529 athletes were running up the highest mountain in West and Central Africa as they competed in the Mount Cameroon Race of Hope. Nineteen athletes, including a Gabonese citizen, were treated for blast injuries. AGC spokesperson Capo Daniel said, "Our primary target was the Cameroon elite forces... that were providing security for the athletes. We will not allow Cameroon to continue its occupation." Participants came from East, Central, and Northern Africa and France.

November 6, 2023: *Al-Jazeera* reported Anglophone separatist gunmen killed 20 people and injured another 10 in a dawn raid on the village of Egbekaw, a neighborhood in the town of Mamfe in western Cameroon. They torched several homes.

CENTRAL AFRICAN REPUBLIC

March 18, 2023: *Reuters* reported that at 5 a.m., gunmen killed nine Chinese citizens and wounded two others at a gold mine run by the Gold Coast Group outside Bambari. The Chinese Embassy issued a travel advisory against

going outside the city. Bambari Mayor Abel Matchipata blamed the Coalition of Patriots for Change, an alliance of rebel groups formed before the 2020 presidential election to oppose President Faustin-Archange Touadera. CPC denied responsibility and condemned the attack.

July 10, 2023: *UPI* reported that gunmen attacked a U.N. peacekeeping unit patrolling around the town of Sam-Ouandja. Peacekeepers killed three attackers, but a Rwandan peacekeeper was killed. The 18,486 U.N. MINUSCA peacekeepers in the Central African Republic serve as police and troops.

May 12, 2024: Rebels from the Coalition of Patriots for Change, an alliance of rebel groups aligned with former President Francois Bozize, attacked the Chinese-run gold mining town Gaga, killing four people and injuring several others.

November 26, 2024: Gunmen tied up then killed six motorcycle taxi drivers and four of their clients near the central diamond mining town of Bria. The ten were driving back from a religious ceremony in Ippy to Bria, the capital of the central Haute-Kotto Prefecture. The terrorists set the victims' motorcycles on fire. The Coalition of Patriots for Change, an anti-government militant group, was suspected.

CHAD

February 28, 2024: *AP, Reuters, AFP,* and *al-Jazeera* reported that members of the opposition Socialist Party Without Borders arrived in more than ten vehicles and attacked the N'Djamena headquarters of the National State Security Agency. During the gun battle, several people were killed, including the group's leader, Yaya Dillo, current transitional president Mahamat Deby Itno's cousin and a strong contender in the scheduled May 6 election. Authorities arrested two dozen people. Authorities separately arrested the opposition party's finance secretary for allegedly trying to assassinate the president of the country's supreme court.

March 25, 2024: A bomb killed seven soldiers during a patrol near Lake Chad. Authorities suspected Boko Haram.

October 27, 2024: The office of the presidency announced that a nighttime attack on a military base in the west killed 40 soldiers.

November 9, 2024: Boko Haram attacked a military base in the Lake Chad region, killing 17 Chadian soldiers. Troops fought back, killing 96 terrorists.

COMOROS

September 13, 2024: President Azali Assoumani, 65, was slightly injured in a kitchen knife attack while attending the funeral of a religious leader in Salimani, a Moroni suburb. A civilian was injured while attempting to protect the president. The suspect, Ahmed Abdou, 24, a male soldier, was found dead in a police cell on September 14.

CONGO

January 15, 2023: *NPR, UPI,* and *al-Jazeera* reported that the ISIS-linked Allied Democratic Forces (ADF) claimed credit when ten people were killed and 39 wounded in a bombing during Sunday services of the parish of the 8th Community of Pentecostal Churches of Congo in Kasindi in North Kivu Province near the Uganda border. Masika Makasi, 25, reported that her leg was injured and her sister-in-law died instantly.

March 12, 2023: *VOA* reported that the ADF was suspected of attacking civilians in Kirindera in North Kivu Province, killing 19 people and setting fire to a health center and houses. ISIS said on *Aamaq* that it had killed more than 35 "Christians" and wounded dozens in eastern Congo the previous week.

June 12, 2023: *DW* and the *New York Times* reported that gunmen carrying machetes attacked the LALA camp the U.N. MONUSCO peacekeeping mission runs for internally displaced people in Ituri Province, killing 45 civilians and wounding ten. The Cooperative for the Development of Congo (CODECO) militia, which claims to represent Lendu farmers against Hema herders, was suspected. Several people were burned alive after their tents were set on fire.

July 19, 2023: *Al-Jazeera* and *AFP* reported that an explosive accidentally went off during the evening in a field in Lubwe Sud in North Kivu Province's Rutshuru territory, killing nine and wounding 16. A civilian had picked up a bomb in a field and gave it to a militiaman; it subsequently exploded.

August 27, 2023: *Al-Jazeera* reported that Lendu militia gunmen from CODECO attacked Gobu during the evening, killing nine civilians and a Congolese soldier and wounding two soldiers and two civilians. Four gunmen died.

September 1, 2023: *Al-Jazeera* reported that gunmen attacked a four-vehicle TSM Mining convoy that was carrying gold from a site near the Kimbi River in the Fizi region of South Kivu Province. Four people were killed, including two Chinese citizens, a soldier, and a Congolese driver. A Chinese mine employee, a soldier, and a Congolese mine worker were injured. The attackers were from the neighboring Maniema region.

October 23, 2023: ISIS-affiliated ADF gunmen killed 26 people in Oicha in North Kivu Province. Beni Charles Ehuta Omeonga, the military administrator for the area, added, "Among the victims were seven members from the same family killed by the assailants in their home." Nicolas Kikuku, a deputy governor in the region, said most of the victims were shot in their homes.

November 12, 2023: *Al-Jazeera* reported that the ADF was suspected when gunmen killed 19 bound villagers with machetes and other weapons in Mukondi during the night. Maurice Mabele Musaidi told *Reuters* that other people were missing and might have drowned while crossing the Lamia River into Uganda. The army said it killed six terrorists.

January 25, 2024: The Army blamed M23 rebels for firing mortars at the town of Mweso in North Kivu Province during the evening, killing 19 and injuring 27 other civilians.

January 30, 2024: The Allied Democratic Forces (ADF) attacked three villages in the Beni territory of North Kivu Province, killing 12 people. Two people died in Mangazi-Kasongo, five in Matadi-Beu, including the village chief, and five in Mamove.

February 12, 2024: M23 rebels were suspected of bombing the Zaina displacement camp in North Kivu Province, killing three civilians and injuring eight others.

February 13, 2024: *Al-Jazeera* reported that the Cooperative for the Development of the Congo (CODECO) militia was suspected of an attack on mining sites in Djugu, killing seven panners.

February 14, 2024: Two South African National Defence Force soldiers died and three were injured when a mortar hit their base in North Kivu Province.

AP and *al-Jazeera* reported that CODECO rebels attacked a gold mine near Djugu district in Ituri Province, killing 12 and kidnapping 16.

February 17, 2024: *Al-Jazeera* reported that the CODECO militia ambushed people on a road near Tali in Ituri Province, stopping and killing 15 people, including a woman, during the afternoon. Jules Tsuba, a civil society leader in Djugu, added that the terrorists tied them up and undressed them before killing them. Some "had their throats cut, others were shot dead". The victims' bodies had the marks of torture.

February 2019, 2024: ADF rebels with machetes and guns killed 11 people in Beni territory in North Kivu Province.

February 20, 2024: *Al-Jazeera* reported that the United Nations Security Council sanctioned the leaders of six armed groups fighting in the Democratic Republic of the Congo. The committee imposed an arms embargo, travel ban, and asset freeze on two leaders of the ADF, one leader from the Twirwaneho armed group, one from the National Coalition of the People for the Sovereignty of Congo (CNPSC) rebels, the military spokesperson for the M23 Tutsi-led rebels, and a leader with the Democratic Forces for the Liberation of Rwanda (FDLR), founded by Hutus who fled Rwanda.

ADF rebels killed 13 people in Mambasa territory of Ituri Province; most died in their homes.

March 5, 2024: Following days of fighting with government troops, M23 gunmen seized Nyanzale in North Kivu Province, killing ten people, burning down homes, looting shops, and displacing thousands.

April 2, 2024: The ADF was suspected when gunmen killed 12 people, torched a local hospital, and kidnapped several people in North Kivu Province. The army killed four attackers and rescued four hostages. Local civilian leader Kakule Mwendapeke said 17 people died.

April 8, 2024: *BBC* reported that a mortar attack killed three Tanzanian soldiers from a southern African military force and wounded three other people.

April 13, 2024: ADF gunmen attacked four sites in the commune of Mulekera, near Beni in North Kivu Province, killing 11 people, torching vehicles, and stealing possessions.

April 30, 2024: *BBC* reported that M23 rebels claimed to have seized the town of Rubaya, a coltan mining town in the Masisi district. Coltan is used in manufacturing batteries for mobile phones and electric vehicles.

May 3, 2024: M23 was suspected when a bomb exploded at Mugunga refugee camp in North Kivu Province, killing five people, including two children and their mother, and wounding 20. By May 10, the death toll in the bombings of Mugunga and Lac Vert camps had reached 35, with two more people in critical condition.

June 7, 2024: *Al-Jazeera* reported that ADF terrorists used guns and machetes to kill 38 people in an overnight attack on a village in Beni territory in North Kivu Province. The ADF was believed behind another village assault that killed 16 people earlier in the week. *AP* later added that the government claimed that the ADF killed 41 people in the villages of Masala, Mahihi, and Keme in North Kivu Province. Local civil society members said 80 died.

June 30, 2024: Gunmen attacked a Tearfund foreign aid convoy in Butembo in North Kivu Province, killing two staff members.

Al-Jazeera reported that during its raid on Kanyabayonga in Lubero territory in North Kivu Province, M23 lynched two people. Hours earlier, they had attacked a convoy of five vehicles carrying a dozen humanitarian workers that had left Lubero territory for Beni, killing two Congolese aid workers with the UK-based NGO Tearfund, including John Nzabanita Amahoro, 37, who had worked for the charity for 10 years as a water, sanitation, and hygiene technician. M23 also torched five cars and seven motorcycles.

July 3, 2024: CODECO claimed responsibility for attacking a gold mine in the village of Gambala and the nearby Camp Blanquette gold mine in Ituri Province, killing six Chinese miners and two Congolese soldiers and kidnapping two other miners. The mine is guarded by the Zaire Militia, a CODECO dissident faction.

July 9, 2024: *Al-Jazeera* reported that the United Nations Office for the Coordination of Humanitarian Affairs (OCHA) announced that more than 170 security incidents directly targeted humanitarian workers in the DRC in the first half of 2024, killing four, injuring 20, and kidnapping more than a dozen humanitarian workers.

July 13, 2024: *AP* and *Radio Okapi* reported that members of the Mobondo militia, claiming to be defenders of the Yaka people, who were in a two-year conflict with the Teke community, attacked Kinsele in Kwamouth territory in Kwango Province, killing 72 people, including nine soldiers and a soldier's wife. The militia had tried to attack the village the previous day.

July 15, 2024: *Al-Jazeera* and *AFP* reported that M23 bombarded Bweremana in North Kivu, killing two children from the same family and two other teenagers. The dead were aged two, three, 16, and 18. Bweremana Police Commissioner Paulin Ilunga added that a mother and her four-year-old child were wounded. Five people were hospitalized with serious injuries.

August 8, 2024: *Al-Jazeera* reported that a military court sentenced 26 people accused of involvement in armed groups, including the M23, to death. Corneille Nangaa, Alliance Fleuve Congo (AFC) leader, was found guilty of war crimes, participation in an insurrection, and treason. Nangaa and 20 other defendants were sentenced to death in absentia. The five accused who were present for the trial had five days to appeal the sentence. Nangaa, former president of the DRC's electoral commission, launched the AFC political-military movement in December 2023. The coalition includes the M23 armed group accused of mass killings. M23 figures on trial included its president Bertrand Bisimwa, military chief Sultani Makenga, and spokespeople Willy Ngoma and Lawrence Kanyuka.

August 10, 2024: ADF gunmen attacked several villages, including Mukonia, in North Kivu Province, killing a dozen people. Several villagers were missing.

August 14-16, 2024: The ADF attacked farmers and villagers in Mambasa territory in Ituri Province, killing 16 and kidnapping 20, including the mother and sister of local government official Gilbert Sivamwenda.

November 15, 2024: The ADF attacked Mabisio village in North Kivu Province during the evening, killing 13 people, including women, kidnapping others, and burning and looting homes.

November 20, 2024: Minister of the Interior Jacquemain Shabani accused the Rwanda-backed March 23 Movement (M23) rebel group of "ethnic cleansing" in Rutshuru and Masisi in North Kivu Province.

December 3, 2024: The ADF attacked civilians in Tenambo in North Kivu Province during the evening, killing nine people, including an 8-month-old baby and a 14-year-old girl, and kidnapped three others.

ETHIOPIA

January 30, 2023: *Reuters* reported that during the evening, gunmen attacked nine Chinese citizens in Gebre Guracha, a town in northern Oromiya, killing one.

The previous week, gunmen briefly held dozens of workers of Nigeria's Dangote Cement in Oromiya region. They were later released unharmed.

April 9, 2023: *Reuters* and *AP* reported that gunmen shot to death two Catholic Relief Services (CRS) workers identified as Chuol Tongyik, a security manager, and Amare Kindeya, a driver, near Kobo in the Amhara Region while returning to Addis Ababa.

June 7, 2023: *Al-Jazeera* reported that Ethiopia claimed it foiled an al-Shabaab suicide attack at Dollo near the border with Somalia. Al-Shabaab said that it conducted two suicide bombings at an Ethiopian military base on the Somali side of the border. One group attacked "the headquarters of the local military command" while the second hit a weapons and ammunition warehouse. "The two operations resulted in heavy casualties in deaths and injuries."

April 12, 2024: A shootout between Fano militiamen and police officers who tried to apprehend them near Millennium Hall in downtown Addis Ababa killed three people, including a bystander. Two police officers were injured. Police said the trio were "on a mission to carry out a terrorist attack." Police killed two gunmen and arrested the third.

July 3, 2024: *BBC* reported on July 10, 2024 that dozens of bus passengers, mostly students from Derbak University, were believed kidnapped by gunmen. A man thrice called the Bekeles, the family of one of the students, demanding a 700,000 Ethiopian birr ($12,000; £9,400) ransom. Some hostages escaped; three told *BBC* they believed that 100 were still being held. The convoy consisted of three buses, en route to Addis Ababa from Derbak University in the Simien Mountains. They were stopped near Garba Guracha, a small town in Oromia. The kidnappers forced their captives to a remote rural area where the Oromo Liberation Army (OLA) rebel group is believed to operate. One captive student snuck a phone call to her family, saying she saw the terrorists killing some of the students.

GUINEA

November 4, 2023: *CNN* reported that around 4 a.m., gunmen freed from the Central House prison in Conakry's Kaloum administrative district the former head of Guinea's 2008 military junta, Moussa Dadis Camara, and three other high-ranking officers. The four had been on trial since 2022, accused of orchestrating a stadium massacre and mass rape by Guinean security forces in which 150 people were killed during a pro-democracy rally on September 28, 2009. Later that day, Camara was recaptured along with two of the three officers—Moussa Tiegboro Camara and Blaise Gomou. The third officer, Colonel Claude Pivi, remained at large.

KENYA

January 3, 2023: *CNN, The Standard, The Daily Nation,* and *Reuters* reported that motorbike taxi riders alerted Kenyan police that they had discovered the body of prominent LGBTQ rights campaigner Edwin Chiloba, stuffed inside a metal box near Eldoret in Uasin Gishu County. The riders saw the box dumped by the roadside from a vehicle with a concealed license plate. Chiloba ran a fashion business.

January 17, 2023: *Al-Jazeera* reported that a rocket-propelled grenade hit a vehicle in a convoy in Garissa County, killing one person.

January 18, 2023: *Al-Jazeera* reported Kenyan security forces killed 10 al-Shabaab terrorists and recovered rocket-propelled grenades and improvised explosive devices in Galmagalla in Garissa County.

April 24, 2023: *Reuters, Kenya Broadcasting Company,* and the *Washington Post* reported that police recovered 101 bodies, mostly of children, from mass graves in the Shakahola forest of Kilifi

County. The victims were thought to be followers of Good News International Church, a Christian cult who believed they would go to heaven if they starved themselves. Authorities arrested cult leader Paul Mackenzie on April 14 on a tip that shallow graves contained the bodies of at least 31 of his followers. Three more suspects were arrested; another 14 cult members were in police custody. *NTV* reported that one was a close associate of Mackenzie. The group had been living in several settlements in an 800-acre area. The Directorate of Criminal Investigations tweeted that 33 people had been rescued, but many were refusing food.

Mackenzie was arraigned on April 15 at Malindi Law Courts. He was refusing food and water. He had preached that education is evil and that people should stop working as the Second Coming would be soon.

A survivor told authorities that children were to die in March, women in April, and men in May.

The *Straits Times* and *Reuters* reported on May 1, 2023 that the bodies of several exhumed children showed signs of starvation and asphyxiation.

The Kenyan Red Cross reported that more than 300 people were reported missing.

AP reported on May 3, 2023 that the number of deaths had risen to 110. *Reuters* reported on May 13, 2023 that the death toll had reached 201. By early June, 250. On June 14, 2023, *Reuters* reported that the death toll had reached 300.

On January 16, 2024, *AP* reported that Mulele Ingonga, Kenya's director of public prosecutions, ordered that 95 people from a doomsday cult led by Paul MacKenzie be charged with murder, manslaughter, radicalization, cruelty, and child torture, among other crimes, over the deaths of 429 people believed to be members of the church in Kilifi County in April 2023. Mackenzie was serving a one-year prison sentence for operating a film studio and producing films without a valid license.

January 15, 2024: Al-Shabaab was suspected when five police officers were wounded when their truck was hit by a roadside bomb in Lafey Mandera County.

January 18, 2024: A donkey cart carrying a suspected bomb exploded past the Somali checkpoint of Bula Hawa on the Kenya-Somalia border, killing a Kenyan police officer and critically wounding four others. The cart was pulled by two donkeys and ridden by one man. Kenyan authorities at a Mandera border post stopped the cart to check the load after it entered Kenyan territory. The rider jumped off and ran back into Somalia. Moments later, the bomb went off. Somali police arrested the driver. The Mandera county security team asked the Bula Hawa police to hand him over to Kenyan authorities. Al-Shabaab was suspected.

April 29, 2024: Al-Shabaab was suspected when a bomb on a donkey cart exploded in El Wak in Mandera County, near the border with Somalia, killing five people.

Earlier in April, suspected al-Shabaab gunmen entered the village's hospital and injured guards while asking about the whereabouts of doctors. No arrests were made.

June 5, 2024: Police at the Mandera border point with Somalia recovered a bomb that was about to detonate. Al-Shabaab was suspected.

Also that week, gunmen killed two herders at a watering point in the Mandera area by gunmen.

June 8, 2024: Gunmen fired on eight construction workers, killing four at a hospital construction site near Kenya's largest refugee camp, Dadaab, in Garissa County and the border with Somalia. Al-Shabaab was suspected.

August 8, 2024: *BBC* reported that Kenya deported to the UK British terrorism suspect Jermaine Grant, 41, after completing a lengthy prison sentence in Kenya. London Metropolitan Police detained him upon arrival at Heathrow under the Terrorism Act. In 2011, authorities found bomb-making equipment in his apartment in Mombasa. He was believed to have shared the apartment with Samantha Lewthwaite, alias White Widow, who is wanted in connection with London's July 7 bombings. Upon his 2011 arrest, Kenyan police accused him of plotting to bomb tourist hotels. In 2019, a court convicted him of possessing bomb-making materials but acquitted him of conspiracy over the alleged plot. He was also arrested on suspicion of being a member of al-Shabaab. He was believed to have become radicalised after spending time in prison with would-be shoe bomber Richard Reid, who was serving a life sentence in the United States.

Muslim convert Lewthwaite was nicknamed the White Widow following her marriage to London suicide bomber Germaine Lindsay. She spent her childhood in Aylesbury, Buckinghamshire. She was wanted in Kenya and the UK for suspected links to al-Shabaab and several attacks.

October 18, 2024: *BBC* reported that at 7:30 a.m., eight masked men in two vehicles kidnapped a Briton and several Turkish citizens in Nairobi. The next day, four of the Turkish citizens were missing. Necdet Seyitoğlu, an 18-year resident of the UK who moved to Kenya two years ago was released after eight hours when he showed his captors a copy of his British passport. Yusuf Kar, a British national of Turkish origin, identified the kidnapped men as Hüseyin Yeşilsu and Necdet Seyitoğlu, 49, an education consultant. Seyitoğlu said the Swahili-speaking kidnappers dropped him off at a place he did not recognize and gave him 1,000 shillings ($7.50; £6) for transport back home. They refused to return his phone and laptop.

MALI

January 10, 2023: *Al-Jazeera* reported that two Malian military vehicles hit mines in separate incidents, killing 14 soldiers and injuring 11. The military responded, killing 31 rebels with ties to al-Qaeda and ISIS. No one claimed credit.

June 9, 2023: *Al-Jazeera* reported that gunmen attacked a patrol of the United Nations Multidimensional Integrated Stabilization Mission in Mali (MINUSMA) in Ber in Timbuktu region, killing a U.N. peacekeeper and seriously injuring four others. The terrorists first set off a bomb and then fired on the patrol.

September 7, 2023: *Al-Jazeera* and *AFP* reported that at 11 a.m., gunmen fired three rockets at the engines of a COMANAV ferry boat on the Niger River between Abakoira and Zorghoi, in the territory of Rarhous, and attacked an army base in the Bourem Circle, part of the Gao region, killing 49 civilians and 15 soldiers. The al-Qaeda-affiliated Group for the Support of Islam and Muslims (JMIN) claimed credit for both attacks.

Since August 13, JMIN had blockaded Timbuktu.

September 12, 2023: Gunmen from the Permanent Strategic Framework for Peace, Security and Development claimed credit for an armed attack on soldiers in Bourem in Gao region that killed ten government soldiers and wounded 13. The government said the terrorists employed "booby-trapped vehicles by several terrorists aboard several vehicles and motorcycles". Colonel Souleymane Dembelé, a spokesman for the Malian Armed Forces, said 46 attackers were killed.

September 17, 2023: *Al-Jazeera* reported that the Coordination of Azawad Movements (CMA) attacked two military camps in Lere in the Timbuktu region, killing five soldiers. Eleven other soldiers were missing. The government said it had "neutralized" 30 terrorists.

September 22, 2023: *Al-Jazeera* reported that artillery hit Timbuktu in the afternoon, killing two people and wounding five. The government suspected the al-Qaeda-linked Support Group for Islam and Muslims (GSIM) and had warned supply trucks from neighboring regions not to enter the city.

November 1, 2023: *Al-Jazeera* reported that eight U.N. peacekeepers were injured by explosives while withdrawing from Gao.

November 3, 2023: *Al-Jazeera* reported that seven U.N. peacekeepers were injured by improvised explosive devices while withdrawing from Gao.

November 4, 2023: *Al-Jazeera* reported that 22 United Nations peacekeepers were injured in Anefis in northern Mali after their convoy was hit by two improvised explosive devices as they continued to withdraw from the country. This was the sixth incident since the U.N. troops left their base in Kidal on October 31; the six incidents injured 39 peacekeepers.

November 7, 2023: Drone strikes around Kidal killed 14 people in the rebel stronghold. Kidal Mayor Arbakane Ag Abzayack said that the town's deputy mayor and a local councilor were among the victims. The first strike injured children who had gathered in front of the former U.N. peacekeeping camp that was vacated a week earlier. A second strike hit near an auction site.

January 25, 2024: *Al-Jazeera* and *Reuters* reported that military government spokesperson Colonel Abdoulaye Maiga announced the immediate cancellation of the 2015 Algiers Accord peace deal with CMA separatist rebels, mostly semi-nomadic Tuaregs, after months of fighting, other signatories not keeping their commitments, and hostility by chief mediator Algeria.

April 28, 2024: *AP,* Malian state television, and *BBC* reported that Malian, Nigerien, and Burkinabe soldiers killed Moroccan national Abu Huzeifa, alias Higgo, a commander in the Islamic State in the Greater Sahara/Sahel Province wanted for the deaths of four American soldiers and four Nigerien troops killed in an attack in 2017 in Tongo Tongo, Niger. The U.S. Department of State had offered a $5 million bounty. Moussa Ag Acharatoumane, leader of a Tuareg armed group allied with the state, said his forces participated in the operation in Indelimane in the Menaka region in northern Mali.

June 21, 2024: The International Criminal Court in The Hague unsealed an arrest warrant, originally issued under seal in 2017, for Iyad Ag Ghaly, alias Abou Fadl, a Malian accused of war crimes and crimes against humanity in Timbuktu in 2012-13, where he is suspected of leading Ansar Dine, an al-Qaeda-linked Islamic extremist group. The warrant charged him with crimes including murder, rape, sexual slavery, and persecution of women and girls on gender grounds. In one attack on a military base, the terrorists executed more than 40 Malian soldiers who were not taking part in hostilities, including some who had surrendered and others who were in the base's hospital.

June 26, 2024: The International Criminal Court in The Hague convicted Al Hassan Ag Abdoul Aziz Ag Mohamed Ag Mahmoud, who is accused of being a key member of the al-Qaeda-linked Ansar Dine, to war crimes, crimes against humanity, torture, and cruel treatment between 2012 and 2013. The court noted that he abused prisoners as the de facto chief of the Islamic police in the historic desert city of Timbuktu. He faced life in prison. He was represented by attorney Melinda Taylor.

July 1, 2024: *Al-Jazeera, AFP,* and *Reuters* reported that gunmen killed 40 people in Djiguibombo village in the Mopti region during a three-hour raid. Some of the victims were attending a wedding.

July 21, 2024: Gunmen attacked villagers working in their farmlands in Dembo during the evening, killing 26. The JNIM was suspected.

July 26, 2024: The pro-independence CSP-DPA coalition in the Tuareg north and the al-Qaeda affiliate in the Sahel, Jama'at Nusrat al-Islam wal-Muslimin (JNIM), claimed credit for killing dozens of government soldiers and Russian mercenaries from the Wagner group on the outskirts of Tinzawaten village near the border with Algeria. JNIM said 50 Russians and several Malian soldiers were killed. The Malian army said two soldiers had been killed and 10 wounded in a rebel attack that also disabled two armored vehicles and two pickup trucks. The army claimed its troops killed 20 rebels and destroyed several vehicles. *CNN* reported that the rebels released videos showing white victims. Some unofficial Russian *Telegram* channels said 80 Russians, including military blogger Nikita Fedyanin, were killed and 15 captured. A Wagner channel said commander Sergei Shevchenko was killed.

September 17, 2024: *AP, Reuters, AFP,* and *al-Jazeera* reported that in the morning, JNIM gunmen attacked the Faladie gendarme school and a military base near Bamako airport, causing significant damage. *AFP* added that 77 people were killed and 255 injured, although other reports said 100 died. An *AP* reporter heard two explosions; witnesses heard gunshots. Hospitals ran out of beds to treat the victims. Authorities arrested 15 suspects. JNIM claimed that a few dozen gunmen killed and wounded "hundreds", including members of the Russian mercenary group Wagner. National Airways Corporation, the South African aviation company that owns a plane used for humanitarian work by the World Food Programme (WFP), was one of those damaged while on the ground.

September 19, 2024: Authorities in Bamako closed seven livestock markets that typically are run by the Fulani/Peuhl semi-nomadic ethnic group that officials associate with the al-Qaeda-linked JNIM.

November 20, 2024: *AP* and *BBC* reported that the International Criminal Court in The Hague sentenced al-Qaeda-linked Ansar Dine extremist leader Al Hassan Ag Abdoul Aziz Ag Mohamed Ag Mahmoud, 48, to 10 years in prison for war crimes and crimes against humanity carried out when he headed the Islamic police in Timbuktu in 2012. Judges in June 2024 found him guilty of torture, overseeing public amputations by machete, brutal floggings of residents, including children, religious persecution, and other inhumane acts. He was acquitted of several charges regarding the abuse of women and of destroying Timbuktu's ancient mausoleums. The three-judge panel found that rape and sexual slavery occurred while his group controlled Timbuktu, but that he could not be connected to those crimes. He was represented by attorney Melinda Taylor. He was granted time served. He was in ICC custody since March 2018, leaving him with around 3.5 years remaining.

November 21, 2024: The al-Qaeda-linked JNIM ambushed a convoy of Russian Wagner Group mercenaries in the Mopti region, killing six Russians and burning vehicles.

December 1, 2024: *AP* and *ORTM TV* reported that government drone strikes killed eight Tuareg Azawad separatist leaders, including Fahad Ag Al Mahmoud, Secretary General of the Gatia, a Tuareg armed group, in Tinzaouatine. The previous day, armed groups in the north announced they were merging into a single political-military Azawad Liberation Front.

MOZAMBIQUE

April 24, 2023: *UPI* reported that the 27-member European Union's council sanctioned ISIS-Mozambique and two of its leaders—Abu Yasir Hassan and Bonomade Machude Omar. The U.S. had previously designated all three as terrorists. The ODNI website indicated that ISIS recognized the affiliate in 2019, citing Hassan as its overall leader and Omar being a senior military commander and attack coordinator.

March 6, 2024: *AP* and *Lusa* reported that 72 children were missing after attacks by the Islamic State Mozambique on 27 villages in Cabo Delgado Province in late February. Thirty families sought shelter in Nampula Province and asked for help in finding their children. During the first weekend of March, Islamic State Mozambique occupied the coastal town of Quissanga, one of Cabo Delgado's district capitals. *AP* added that the following day, terrorists beheaded three members of the security forces on a nearby island.

May 10, 2024: *Al-Jazeera* and *Reuters* reported that President Filipe Nyusi announced that at around 10 a.m., the army was fighting hundreds of ISIS-linked gunmen who were attacking Macomia in Cabo Delgado Province.

October 18, 2024: *AP, al-Jazeera, Carta de Moçambique,* and *BBC* reported that just before midnight, gunmen in two vehicles fired on the dark grey BMW SUV of Venâncio (Elvino) Dias, a lawyer and advisor to opposition presidential candidate Venancio Mondlane, and Paulo Guambe, the spokesperson for the opposition PODEMOS party, killing them on Joaquim Chissano Avenue near the Russian Embassy in Maputo. The two men were preparing to challenge the results of the October 9 presidential election that drew allegations of vote rigging and clamping down on dissent against the governing Front for the Liberation of Mozambique (FRELIMO) party, which has been in power for 49 years since obtaining independence from Portugal. Police said a woman who was in the car was hospitalized with injuries. Police spokesperson Leonel Muchina said the victims had earlier been at a local bar and were followed from there.

NIGER

August 15, 2023: *Al-Jazeera* reported that gunmen killed 17 Nigerien Armed Forces (FAN) soldiers and injured 20 soldiers moving between Boni and Torodi at Koutougou near the border with Mali. The army said more than 100 assailants were "neutralized".

September 28, 2023: *Al-Jazeera* reported that several hundred suspected rebels attacked soldiers in Kandadji in Tillaberi region, killing seven; five others died in a traffic accident while trying to respond to the assault. Seven people were hospitalized.

October 2, 2023: *ABC News* reported that the junta announced that more than 100 jihadis killed 29 Nigerien soldiers near the border with Mali. Several dozen terrorists were killed, 15 motorcycles were destroyed, a large quantity of weapons and ammunition was seized.

March 19, 2024: Jihadis were blamed when during the night, gunmen on motorcycles ambushed Nigerien soldiers in a border region near Mali and Burkina Faso, killing 23 soldiers. The army returned fire, killing 30 attackers.

June 25, 2024: Terrorists ambushed Nigerien soldiers near the Burkina Faso border, killing 21 troops.

The previous week, the Patriotic Liberation Front, led by Salah Mahmoud, attacked a Chinese-backed pipeline and threatened future attacks if the $400 million agreement was not cancelled. 24069902

July 8, 2024: *BBC* reported that 14 soldiers were killed and 11 others wounded in an ambush by suspected jihadist groups linked to al-Qaeda between the villages of Ila Fari and Djangore in the Tillaberi region. Another 24 soldiers remained missing as of July 11.

July 11, 2024: *AP* and *BBC* reported that during the night, inmates, including suspected jihadis, escaped from Koutoukale Prison in the Tillaberi region. Authorities declared a curfew.

August 2, 2024: A local al-Qaeda affiliate, JNIM, released a video on *az-Zallaqa* of two men claiming to be Russians who said they were kidnapped while working in Baga in northeastern Niger. Yury said he is a geologist and was working for a Russian company. The other man said he was in Niger for a month. The duo spoke in English. It was the first known sighting of the men and the first Russian hostages of jihadis. They might have been taken during a July 19 clash between the jihadis and Nigerien military forces in Baga.

NIGERIA

April 7, 2023: *Reuters* and the *Irish Times* reported gunmen kidnapped 80 people, mostly women and children, in Wanzamai village in Tsafe local government area of Zamfara State. Musa Usman said his son, Ibrahim, 14, was among those abducted. He added that children and women from the village were clearing land for farming and collecting firewood when the victims were taken by gunmen and marched into a nearby forest. Another parent, Haruna Noma, said some of the hostages were from two nearby villages of Kucheri and Danwuri who had gone to Wanzamai to clear land to farm. Amina Tsafe said her daughter, 17, was abducted and that most of the children taken were between 12 and 17 years old.

May 17, 2023: *NPR* and *Politico* reported that in the afternoon, gunmen ambushed two U.S. Embassy vehicles in the Ogbaru Local Government Area of Anambra State, located in southeastern Nigeria, killing four people. *UPI* reported that five other people were missing. The motive was to be determined. It was possible that the Embassy was not targeted directly. The convoy included five employees of the U.S. Embassy in Nigeria and four members of the Nigerian Police Force en route to Anambra in advance of a planned visit by mission personnel to a U.S.-funded flood response project. *AP* reported that two of the Embassy's local workers and two police officers were killed. The *Washington Post* reported that

National Security Council communications co-ordinator John Kirby said no U.S. citizens were involved.

July 5, 2023: *Daily Post Nigeria* reported that the Nigerian Air Force (NAF) killed more than a dozen Islamic State West Africa Province (ISWAP) terrorists in an airstrike near the Marte Local Government Area of Borno State. A counter-insurgency expert in the Lake Chad region, Zagazola Makama, tweeted, "The insurgents were neutralized in a precise, intelligence-led air strike carried out by the Air Component command, Operation Hadin Kai in Tumbum SHITTU" after surveillance detected a large gathering of terrorists in the region.

July 24, 2023: *Reuters* reported that gunmen killed 34 people, including seven soldiers and 27 villagers, in an ambush in the Dan Gulbi district of the Maru local government area of Zamfara State.

August 14, 2023: *Reuters* reported that bandits fired on a Nigerian Air Force helicopter, causing it to crash near Chukuba village in the Shiroro local government area of Niger State. The helicopter was sent to evacuate victims of an attack on August 13 that killed 10 soldiers in an ambush.

August 28, 2023: The government announced the rescue of 25 captives, mostly women and children, held by jihadis in Borno State's Gwoza district.

September 26, 2023: *Al-Jazeera* reported that security forces rescued 14 of 20 students and some workers abducted from Federal University Gusau in Zamfara State's Bungudu district the previous week. It was the first mass school abduction in Nigeria since President Bola Tinubu took office in May. Two other people were also rescued.

December 12, 2023: Gunmen ambushed a convoy escorting two South Koreans on a work trip in the Ahoada East council area Rivers State. Four Nigerian soldiers were killed and the two South Korean oil workers were kidnapped.

December 23-25, 2023: The *Guardian, AP, al-Jazeera,* and *AFP* reported that during the three-day weekend gunmen killed 160 people and wounded more than 300 in Plateau State in attacks on 20 villages. The local Red Cross reported 104 deaths in 18 villages in the Christian-dominated Bokkos region. Some 50 people were killed in several villages in the Barkin Ladi area. At least 27 people were killed in Mbom Mbaru village. Fulani herders were suspected.

On December 24, *Reuters, AFP*, and *Arab News* reported that around midnight, 16 people died in an attack in Mushu in Plateau State.

January 22-23, 2024: *AP, AFP,* and *al-Jazeera* reported that gunmen attacked villages in Plateau State's Mangu district for two days, killing 50 villagers, injuring more than 100, and torching homes. No group claimed credit; locals blamed Fulani Muslim herders for attacking ethnic Mwaghavul Christians. Gunmen returned and attacked Kwahaslalek, raising its total casualty figure to 35.

February 1, 2024: The *Daily Beast* and *P.M. News* reported that during the night, gunmen shot to death Segun Aremu, a retired army general and traditional monarch whose title is the Olukoro of Koro, in his palace and kidnapped his wife and three other people. As of February 2, no ransom was demanded.

The *BBC* reported that also that night, a senior government official was kidnapped Wednesday night outside the capital, not far from the home of six sisters who were abducted for ransom—with one killed after loved ones did not pay up fast enough.

Earlier in the week, gunmen killed two traditional rulers in the nearby Ekiti State and abducted five schoolchildren, demanding more than $100,000 for their return.

March 6, 2024: *BBC* reported that authorities believed Boko Haram within the past few days had kidnapped between 50 to more than 300 displaced people, mostly women who lived in a camp in Gamboru Ngala in the northeast and had gone to collect firewood to use for cooking or to sell. *AFP* reported that anti-jihadist militia leader Shehu Mada blamed the Islamic State of West Africa Province (ISWAP).

March 7, 2024: *CNN, Reuters,* and the *Washington Post* reported that during an 8:30 a.m. assembly, dozens of gunmen on motorcycles kidnapped more than 300 school children between the ages of eight and 15 at the LEA Primary and Secondary School in the Kuriga village of Kaduna's Chikun district in Kaduna State. Some were rescued but 287, one hundred from the primary side and 187 from the secondary school, remained with the kidnappers. A member of the community who confronted the abductors during the attack was killed.

BBC reported on March 9 that 28 of the kidnapped schoolchildren escaped. One pupil, believed to be age 14, died in a hospital of gunshot wounds.

BBC reported on March 12 that Musa Garba (an alias to protect him), 17, camouflaged by his school uniform as he hid in a heap of cut grass, slithered on the ground and escaped through the bush. Sadiq Usman Abdullahi (an alias), 10, was among those still being held hostage.

CNN added on March 14 that the kidnappers demanded a ransom of 1 billion naira ($621,848) and threatened to kill all of the students if their demands were not met within 20 days of the kidnapping. *AP* reported that day that President Bola Tinubu ruled out paying ransoms for the schoolchildren. Murtala Ahmed Rufa'i, an associate professor of peace and conflict studies at Usmanu Danfodiyo University in Sokoto State said the mastermind of the kidnapping was known, as were other bandit leaders.

BBC, al-Jazeera, and *AP* reported that on the morning of March 24, 2024 that 137 of the child hostages were freed unharmed in a forest, days before a $690,000 (£548,000) ransom deadline. *BBC Hausa* reported that one of the teachers died in captivity. Military spokesman Maj. Gen. Edward Buba said 76 girls and 61 boys had been rescued from Zamfara State.

March 16-17, 2024: *AP, AFP,* and *al-Jazeera* reported that gunmen wearing army uniforms attacked two communities in Kaduna State's Kajuru council area, kidnapping 100 people. The

kidnappers attacked the Dogon Noma community on the morning of March 16, abducting 14 women, and the Kajuru-Station community at 10:30 p.m. on March 17, kidnapping 87 people. Eight of the hostages were relatives of Madaki Tanko Aridu in Dogon Noma. *Reuters* reported that five people escaped and returned home. Aruwa Ya'u said he was captured but released because he struggled to walk due to his poor health. Haruna Atiku said his wife and two daughters were missing.

May 10, 2024: Gunmen attacked the Confluence University of Science and Technology in Osara in Kogi State during the night and abducted at least nine students.

May 15, 2024: *AP* and the *Daily Trust* newspaper reported that a male, 38, resident of the area, injured 24 worshippers when he set off a bomb during an attack on a mosque in Kano State during morning prayers. Police spokesman Abdullahi Haruna said he attacked the mosque in Gadan village "purely in hostility following prolonged (a) family disagreement". Haruna said preliminary forensic analysis suggested a gasoline explosion. The suspect had attacked people in the area earlier regarding the sharing of an inheritance.

May 20, 2024: The Nigerian Army announced the rescue during a days-long military operation of 350 hostages, among them 209 children, 135 women, and six men, who were held captive for months or years by Boko Haram extremists in the Sambisa Forest. Hostage Hajara Umara had seven children. Some extremists were killed and their makeshift houses were destroyed.

May 24-25, 2024: *CNN* reported that Boko Haram was suspected when ten people, including members of a local vigilante group who confronted the attackers, were killed and 160 others, including children, were abducted during a 5:30 p.m. raid by 300 gunmen on motorbikes in Kuchi village, Munya district, in Niger State, that lasted until 4:00 a.m. the next day. The gunmen took over residences, making a fire to get warm, cooked Indomie (instant noodles) and spaghetti, and made tea before escaping with their hostages. A local resident said it was the fifth attack on Kuchi. The kidnappers had not made demands as of May 27.

May 30, 2024: *Al-Jazeera* reported that the Nigerian military said that Indigenous People of Biafra (IPOB) separatists killed six civilians and five soldiers in a "surprise" assault on a checkpoint at the Obikabia junction in the city of Aba in Abia State.

June 9, 2024: *BBC* and *Reuters* reported that during the night, dozens of gunmen on motorbikes attacked Yargoje in Kankara State, looting shops, killing 25 people, and abducting others. A resident claimed 50 villagers died and 30 were hospitalized.

June 10, 2024: Amnesty International claimed that dozens of women and young girls who had escaped from Boko Haram were unlawfully detained and abused in Nigerian military detention facilities. Some of the women were detained with their children for years. AI conducted 126 interviews, mostly with survivors.

June 22, 2024: *Al-Jazeera* and *Reuters* reported that in a nighttime raid, gunmen on motorbikes killed seven people and kidnapped 100 at Maidabino village in the Danmusa local government area of Katsina State. Many women and children were missing.

June 29, 2024: *CNN* and *AP* reported that female Boko Haram suicide bombers hit a 3 p.m. wedding, the General Hospital Gwoza, and a funeral, killed 18, including men, pregnant women, and children, and wounded 48, including 19 seriously, in Borno State.

A bomber was believed to be in Pulka, two kilometers away.

July 31, 2024: A bomb planted in a café went off at 8 p.m. at a tea shop popular with locals in Kawori in the Konduga area of Borno State, killing 16 people and seriously wounding 24 others, many critically.

August 15, 2024: *AP* and *This Day* reported that during the evening, gunmen ambushed two buses carrying eight University of Maiduguri students and a dozen University of Jos students

along Benue State's Otukpo road near Otukpu. *Al-Jazeera* reported that the attackers kidnapped 20 students and a doctor who were traveling to the south for a Federation of Catholic Medical and Dental Students conference in Enugu. The kidnappers demanded a ransom. A student reported that they were held in the Oglewu Ehaje area in Benue State. *Al-Jazeera* and *AFP* reported that on August 23 the police chief said that in an operation by a tactical squad, the medical students were "rescued tactically and professionally" without payment of a ransom.

September 1, 2024: More than 50 Boko Haram terrorists on motorcycles fired on a market in the Tarmuwa council area of Yobe State during the evening, killing 102 villagers and torching buildings. BH said it was a reprisal against villagers informing security operatives about their activities.

September 14, 2024: Soldiers rescued 13 hostages who were kidnapped by an extremist group in Kaduna State, killing several kidnappers, capturing others, and seizing weapons, ammunition, solar panels, and cash.

November 18, 2024: Some 200 Boko Haram terrorists ambushed a convoy of 80 security operatives tasked with protecting the power network in Shiroro in Niger State during a patrol mission. Seven members of the Nigeria Security and Civil Defence Corps were missing two days later and 50 Boko Haram gunmen were killed in the clash.

December 8, 2024: *Al-Jazeera* reported that gunmen carrying rifles went door to door and abducted dozens of women and children in Kafin Dawa in Zamfara State. Resident Hassan Ya'u, who escaped, said "We found out that they kidnapped more than 50 women, including married women and girls," including his younger sister. Nigeria's *Daily Trust* news site reported 43 people were kidnapped.

SOMALIA

January 17, 2023: *Al-Jazeera* and *Reuters* reported that al-Shabaab attacked a military base in Hawadley with a suicide car bomb, then opened fire, killing seven soldiers, including the base commander. The military had recaptured the base in October 2022.

January 20, 2023: *CNN* reported that a U.S. Africa Command airstrike in support of Somalia National Army forces killed 30 al-Shabaab fighters near Galcad.

January 22, 2023: *Al-Jazeera, Reuters,* and *NPR* reported that a suicide car bomb exploded at a perimeter wall of the Mogadishu mall next to the Banadir administration headquarters and the mayor's office, injuring five people and damaging nearby buildings. Gunfire was heard.

January 25, 2023: *Military Times, NBC, UPI, Reuters,* and *al-Jazeera* reported that U.S. special operations forces killed Bilal al-Sudani, an Islamic State leader operating in the northern mountains, and 10 ISIS associates. The U.S. said al-Sudani was a key figure in funding ISIS cells around the globe. The U.S. Department of the Treasury sanctioned him in March 2022 for facilitating financing for foreign fighters to travel to an al-Shabaab training camp.

The *Washington Post* reported on February 3, 2023 that al-Sudani had been of interest to U.S. counterterrorism experts since 2012, when the U.S. imposed sanctions on him under his real name, Suhayl Salim Abd el-Rahman, for his role in facilitating the entry of foreign fighters into Somalia for al-Shabaab. In 2015, a small group, including al-Sudani, split off from al-Shabaab and pledged allegiance to ISIS. Al-Sudani had worked in al-Shabaab's media department and his brother was active with ISIS. In August 2016, Somali and Puntland special forces conducted a raid to try to capture him and his al-Karrar supporters. Al-Sudani's office financed the jihadi Allied Democratic Forces in the Congo beginning in late 2017, sending hundreds of thousands of dollars in concert with Meddie Nkalubo, alias The Punisher, ADF's external operations coordinator. Al-Sudani was also believed linked to al-Shabaab (no relation) terrorists in Mozambique and to the Islamic State in South Africa.

February 10, 2023: *CNN* and *Task and Purpose* reported that a U.S. Africa Command airstrike killed 12 al-Shabaab fighters in a remote area in support of the federal government and army 28 miles southwest of Hobyo, 290 miles northeast of Mogadishu.

February 21, 2023: *Task and Purpose* reported that a U.S. Africa Command airstrike near Galmudug killed seven al-Shabaab terrorists.

February 22, 2023: *AFP, Reuters,* and the *Defense Post* reported that at noon, al-Shabaab attacked a house in Mogadishu's northern Abdiaziz district, killing 10 civilians and wounding three. Soldier Mohamed Ali said the attackers set off explosives at the main gate, then attacked the house.

April 1, 2023: *Task and Purpose* reported that U.S. Ambassador to Somalia Larry André told *Voice of America* that al-Shabaab had lost a third of the territory it had earlier held.

May 24, 2023: The U.S. Department of the Treasury's Office of Foreign Assets Control (OFAC) announced sanctions against several individuals and entities, including financial facilitators and operatives, supporting al-Shabaab. Treasury designated:

- **Hasaan Abshir Xuuroow**, an AS intelligence and finance officer who led AS associates to collect mandatory "donations" from civilians in Kismayo. Xuuroow took livestock from owners as donations for AS, later auctioning them off to make a profit for personal financial gain.

- **Aadan Yusuf Saciid Ibrahim**, an AS mandatory donations collector in Lower Shabelle. Ibrahim enforced the collection of fees associated with livestock and market sales. Ibrahim levied heavy charges on behalf of AS but retained some of those profits for his own personal enrichment

- **Mumin Dheere**, as of early 2022, was the deputy emir of Wayanta, Lower Juba. Dheere coordinated retaliatory attacks for al-Shabaab by targeting Somali and African Union Mission in Somalia (AMISOM) security forces, and planned to use vehicle-borne improvised explosive devices (VBIEDs) and mortars in the attacks. Dheere also planned to attack Kismayo International Airport.

- **Macalin Burhan** was appointed AS Hisbah Commander of the Wayanta area in Lower Juba in late 2021. By mid-2022, AS had imprisoned more than 80 civilians in the Wayanta area. Burhan refused to release the civilians.

- **Ali Ahmed Hussein**, an AS emir in the Lower Shabelle region, who demanded payment from local clans, assisted in the movement of AS fighters who kidnapped citizens in Lower Shabelle, and purchased and stored weapons for AS militants in the region.

- **Maxamed Cali**, an al-Shabaab company commander in charge of 100 fighters. Cali reported to Dheere and regularly associated with Roobow, Burhan, and Xuuroow.

- **Ahmed Kabadhe**, AS emir in Jubaland who ordered AS fighters under his command to attack and continually harass local security forces. In late 2022, AS members Kabadhe, Dheere, Cali, and Burhan plotted an attack using VBIEDs and suicide bombers.

- **Siyaat Ayuto** was appointed in mid-2021 as the AS Hisbah commander for the Wiliyat area, Lower Juba, Somalia. Ayuto earlier served as the Hisbah commander of Beer Xaani, Somalia. Ayuto also served as the AS emir for Kismayo operations.

- **Mohamed Abdullah Hirey**, AS Governor of the Juba Region who participated in pro-AS propaganda.

- **Cabdi Roobow** as of early 2022 was a mid-level AS commander in charge of the Wayanta area in Lower Juba, Somalia. Roobow, with Dheere and another AS official, planned attacks against Abdi Biroole, Lower Juba.

- **Hassan Yariisow Aadan**, an AS commander who collected fees from locals in the Lower Shabelle area to support AS.

- **Siciid Abdullahi Aadan**, an AS member who operated as an IED expert and facilitator. Aadan also extracted fees from the local population on behalf of AS.

- **Shiek Aadan Abuukar Malayle**, an AS leader who oversaw the collection of fees from the local population in Lower Shabelle, Somalia. The money collected by AS was used to purchase weapons, ammunition, and supplies for the group.

- **Aadan Jiss** served as a Hisbah commander for AS. Jiss also managed a detention center and handled detainments for AS's "courts".

- **Cumar Guhaad**, an AS commander in the Lower Shabelle who ordered clans in the region to pay large sums of money to support the terrorist group.

Hasaan Abshir Xuuroow, Aadan Yusuf Saciid Ibrahim, Mumin Dheere, Macalin Burhan, Ali Ahmed Hussein, Maxamed Cali, Ahmed Kabadhe, Siyaat Ayuto, Hassan Yariisow Aadan, and Siciid Abdullahi Aadan were designated pursuant to E.O. 13224, as amended, for having acted or purported to act for or on behalf of, directly or indirectly, AS.

Mohamed Abdullah Hirey, Cabdi Roobow, Shiek Aadan Abuukar Malayle, Aadan Jiss, and Cumar Guhaad were designated pursuant to E.O. 13224, as amended, for having materially assisted, sponsored, or provided financial, material, or technological support for, or goods or services to or in support of, AS.

May 26, 2023: *DW, Reuters, al-Jazeera,* and *AFP* reported that al-Shabaab attacked an African Union Transition Mission in Somalia (ATMIS) base in Bulo Marer, variant Bulamarer, 75 miles southwest of Mogadishu, and an adjacent one housing Somali troops. A Somali military commander said both sides suffered large casualties. AS claimed its suicide bomb attack killed 137 soldiers. *Reuters* reported on May 28 that Ugandan President Yoweri Museveni announced that there had been casualties during an attack by al-Shabaab on a military base manned by Ugandan peacekeepers in Somalia.

ATMIS includes 22,000 soldiers from Uganda, Burundi, Djibouti, Ethiopia, and Kenya. It replaced the AU Mission in Somalia (AMISOM) in 2022.

June 9, 2023: *UPI* and the *Somali National News Agency* reported that at 7:55 p.m. terrorists attacked Mogadishu's luxury Pearl Beach Hotel resort, killing six civilians and three police officers and injuring ten others. Authorities killed all seven al-Shabaab gunmen after a seven-hour siege. *Xinhua* added that two suicide bombers set off their explosive vests near the entrance of the resort where hundreds of people had gathered. Authorities evacuated 84 people, including two children.

June 10, 2023: *UPI* reported that a discarded bomb exploded during a recreational soccer game on an open public field in Janaale in Lower Shabelle region, killing 27 people, including 22 children, and injuring 53. *Xinhua* reported that all of the dead children were boys aged between 10 and 15.

June 17, 2023: *Shabelle Media Network* reported that al-Shabaab publicly executed via firing squad five men, aged between 28 and 52, on espionage charges. Hundreds of residents watched the murders in the Lower Shabelle region after an al-Shabaab "court" convicted them of spying for the Somali government and foreign intelligence agencies, and providing intelligence on the terrorists.

July 7, 2023: *Stars and Stripes* reported that a U.S. convoy hit a roadside bomb near Kismayo, causing no casualties.

July 10, 2023: *Stars and Stripes* reported that three U.S. Africa Command airstrikes 65 miles north of Kismayo killed ten al-Shabaab terrorists.

July 20, 2023: *CNN* reported that a U.S. Africa Command airstrike, conducted at the request of the Federal Government of Somalia, killed five al-Shabaab terrorists in a remote area near Hareeri Kalle, 15 kilometers south of Galcad.

July 24, 2023: Al-Shabaab claimed credit when a suicide bomber targeted the Jalle Siyad military training academy in Mogadishu, killing 25 soldiers and wounding more than 40 others.

July 27, 2023: *UPI* reported that the U.S. Departments of State and Treasury announced that sanctions were imposed on Specially Designated Global Terrorist Abdiweli Mohamed Yusuf, a Somali accused of being the financier of ISIS-Somalia since late 2019. He was believed to be in his early 40s. He was accused of delivering foreign fighters, supplies, and ammunition on behalf of the terrorist organization, which generated $2 million in 2022 via extortion payments.

August 10, 2023: *Garowe Online* reported that the National Intelligence Security Agency (NISA) tweeted that it had intercepted a vehicle carrying explosives destined for al-Shabaab along the Elasha-Biyaha Road in Mogadishu. The driver died in a shootout.

August 21, 2023: *Al-Jazeera* reported that Somalia's Minister of Communications Jama Hassan Khalif banned *TikTok, Telegram,* and online betting website *1XBet* over "horrific" content and misinformation posted by al-Shabaab.

August 26, 2023: *Voice of America* reported that U.S. Africa Command (AFRICOM) announced that a "collective self-defense" airstrike killed 13 al-Shabaab terrorists near Seiera, 45 kilometers northwest of Kismayo.

VOA and *SONNA* reported that in a morning attack, al-Shabaab using car bombs raided the recently (August 22) liberated village of Cowsweyne in Galmudug State, killing government soldiers. Al-Shabaab claimed it killed 178 soldiers and captured prisoners.

September 23, 2023: *Al-Jazeera, AP, AFP,* and *Reuters* reported that a truck bomb being pursued by a pick-up owned by security personnel exploded at a checkpoint in a residential area in Beledweyne in Hiran region, killing 13 and hospitalizing 45 others. No one claimed credit. *Al-Jazeera* reported on September 24 that Abdirahman Dahir Gure, the interior minister of Hirshabelle state, put the death toll at 18.

September 29, 2023: *Al-Jazeera* reported that a suicide bomber attacked a shop selling tea in Bar Bulsho Mogadishu near the presidential palace, killing seven people. Al-Shabaab claimed credit in a statement on its Arabic media unit *Shahada News Agency*, saying 11 died and 18 were wounded.

December 17, 2023: The *Washington Post* reported on December 22 that on December 17, a U.S. Africa Command drone strike in Jilib killed Moalim Ayman, who led the Jaysh Ayman al-Shabaab unit responsible for terrorist attacks in Kenya and Somalia, and was accused of masterminding a January 5, 2020 attack on a military base in Kenya that killed three Americans. A U.S. contractor and two other U.S. service members were injured. Six U.S. aircraft were destroyed. In 2015, the unit attacked Garissa University, killing 148 people. The U.S. Rewards for Justice Program offered a $10 million bounty for him.

January 10, 2024: *AP, Reuters, al-Jazeera,* and the *Washington Post* reported that al-Shabaab attacked a United Nations helicopter that made an emergency landing due to engine failure in Xindheere near Gadoon village in Galmudug State, variant Galgaduud, in territory controlled by the extremists in Somalia. The terrorists killed one passenger and abducted five or six others. The minister of internal security of Galmudug State in central Somalia, Mohamed Abdi Aden Gaboobe, said six foreigners and a Somali were on board. One was shot dead while trying to escape. One or two went missing. The terrorists burned the helicopter, which had been headed to Wisil for a medical evacuation. Most of the passengers were medical professionals and soldiers. The *Post* quoted a Mogadishu-based official who said four Europeans and five Africans were on board. No Americans were believed on board. *AP* reported that on January 12, Oleh Nikolenko, spokesman for Ukraine's foreign affairs ministry, said that four of its citizens were among those captured. He added that the helicopter belongs to a Ukrainian private company, which executed a contract for transport for the United Nations.

January 11, 2024: Al-Shabaab fired mortars inside the Aden Adde International Airport, where the United Nations Assistance Mission in Somalia (UNISOM) compound is located, killing a member of the U.N. Guard Unit and damaging infrastructure.

January 11, 2024: *Reuters* reported that two U.S. Navy sailors were missing at sea while conducting operations off the coast of Somalia the previous evening. U.S. Central Command said they were forward-deployed to the U.S. 5th Fleet (C5F) area of operations supporting a wide variety of missions.

CNN reported on January 21, 2024 that CENTCOM announced that the two SEALs were dead. Teams from the US, Japan, and Spain searched more than 21,000 square miles to try to locate the two sailors, who were boarding an unflagged vessel in search of illicit Iranian weapons bound for Yemen. One fell into the water due to eight-foot swells; the second jumped in to rescue him.

CNN reported on January 22 that the Naval Special Warfare Command identified the SEALs as

- Navy Special Warfare Operator 1st Class Chris Chambers, 37, from Maryland, who enlisted in the Navy in May 2012 and had served with SEAL units on the West Coast since 2014. His awards and decorations included four Navy/Marine Corps Achievement Medals, one with the Combat Action Ribbon, the Army Achievement Medal and more. The Pentagon announced on January 31 that Chambers, while boarding the board, slipped into the gap the high waves had created between the vessel and the SEALs' combatant craft.

- Navy Special Warfare Operator 2nd Class Gage Ingram, 27, from Texas, who enlisted in September 2019, immediately going into pre-special warfare training after completing boot camp at Recruit Training Command Great Lakes, Illinois. He completed SEAL qualification training in 2021. His awards and decorations included the Navy "E" Ribbon, Global War on Terrorism Expeditionary Medal and Service Medal, and National Defense Service Medal. He had jumped into the water to save Chambers.

Both were assigned to a Naval Special Warfare unit on the West Coast of the U.S.

Military Times reported that federal prosecutors in Richmond, Virginia on August 8, 2024 indicted two Iranian brothers, Shahab Mir'kazei and Yunus Mir'kazei, plus Pakistani boat captain Muhammad Pahlawan, with providing material support to Iran's weapons-of-mass-destruction program. The Iranians linked to Iran's Revolutionary Guard faced terrorism charges in the U.S. in connection with the interception of a vessel in the Arabian Sea that resulted in the deaths of two Navy SEALs. The brothers are at large. Pahlawan and three of his crew members have been in custody since the Navy SEAL team intercepted their dhow in January 2024. The new indictment alleges the two brothers who work for the Revolutionary Guard Corps paid Pahlawan 1.7 billion rials (US$40,000) to conduct smuggling operations from Iran to the Somali coast near Yemen.

January 16, 2024: *Al-Jazeera* reported that following a police chase, an al-Shabaab terrorist set off his explosives outside an Indian restaurant in Mogadishu's Hamar Weyne district, killing three and injuring two. Al-Shabaab claimed he was targeting local security officials.

February 6, 2024: *Al-Jazeera* and *Reuters* reported that four explosions inside four well-known electronic shops at the crowded Bakara market in Mogadishu killed 10 and hospitalized 20. Al-Shabaab was suspected.

February 10, 2024: *AP* reported that al-Shabaab claimed credit for an attack at the General Gordon Military Base in Mogadishu. *Reuters* initially reported that five people, including Somali military officials and a United Arab Emirates (UAE) soldier, were killed when a soldier opened fire at a military base. *Al-Jazeera* and *WAM* reported that the UAE's defence ministry clarified that three members of its armed forces and one Bahraini officer were killed in a "terrorist act" while they were training Somali armed forces; a fourth died en route to the UAE. *WAM* identified the dead as a colonel, two warrant officers and a corporal. Two more were injured.

February 29, 2024: A military court in Puntland sentenced to death by firing squad six Moroccans believed to be foreign fighters for ISIS. Mohamed Hassan, Ahmed Najwi, Khalid Latha, Mohamed Binu Mohamed Ahmed, Ridwan Abdulkadir Osmany, and Ahmed Hussein Ibrahim can appeal. An Ethiopian and a Somali were each sentenced to 10 years in prison. Another Somali defendant was acquitted due to lack of evidence. The Moroccans were accused of receiving training at the ISIS base in the Cal-Miskaat Mountains in northeastern Somalia. The Moroccans were apprehended in the mountain range to the east of Bosaso.

March 10, 2024: *Voice of America* reported that a U.S. Africa Command (AFRICOM) "collective self-defense" airstrike at the request of Somalia's federal government in the vicinity of Ugunji in Lower Shabelle region killed three al-Shabaab terrorists.

March 11, 2024: *UPI* reported that the U.S. Department of the Treasury announced sanctions against an international network of money launderers and facilitators of al-Shabaab, blacklisting eight people and eight entities in the Horn of Africa, the United Arab Emirates, and Cyprus. Treasury said that al-Shabaab generates more than $100 million annually via extorting local businesses and individuals and through its financial support network. Among those listed was the Dubai-based Haleel Group, which the Treasury deemed "a key financial facilitator for al-Shabaab". Five of the Haleel Group's subsidiaries were listed, along with Kenya-based Crown Bus Services on accusations on money laundering and supporting al-Shabaab's logistical operations.

March 14, 2024: Al-Shabaab said on its *Telegram* channel that its fighters had entered the SYL Hotel, near the presidential palace in Mogadishu. *DPA* reported that a suicide bomber set off his car bomb in front of the hotel, killing three hotel security officers and two members of the security services. Witnesses heard a loud explosion and gunfire during the night. *AFP, BBC,* and *al-Jazeera* added that police officer Abdirahim Yusuf announced that the 13-hour siege ended after security forces killed all five terrorists. *Reuters* reported that three soldiers were killed and 27 people, including three members of parliament and the government spokesperson, were wounded. Al-Shabaab attacked the Syl Hotel in 2019.

May 31, 2024: *Task and Purpose* reported that U.S. Africa Command announced that an air strike killed three ISIS members near Dhaardaar.

June 10, 2024: *CNN* reported that U.S. intelligence had determined that Houthis were discussing with al-Shabaab how to provide weapons to the Somali group.

July 13, 2024: Prisoners tried to break out of a Mogadishu jail in the morning but failed. Five prisoners and three soldiers died and 21 people were wounded. Some inmates had obtained small arms and hand grenades, exchanging fire with guards before an elite police unit intervened. The prisoners involved in the attempted jailbreak were believed to be members of al-Shabaab.

July 14, 2024: *AP, al-Jazeera, AFP,* and *BBC* reported that a car bomb exploded at 10:28 p.m. at Mogadishu's Top Coffee café where people were watching the Euro 2024 soccer final between Spain and England, killing nine and injuring 20. Al-Shabaab claimed credit, saying it hit a place where security and government workers meet at night. The bomb destroyed ten cars and damaged several buildings near the presidential palace.

August 2, 2024: The *New York Times, CNN, AFP, BBC, Reuters,* and *SONNA* reported that six al-Shabaab gunmen attacked a restaurant at the Beach View Hotel in Mogadishu's Abdiaziz district. Some 37 people were killed and 63 injured when a suicide bomber set off his explosives. Five terrorists also died in the four-hour assault. Police said that the sixth attacker was captured alive. Al-Shabaab said it was targeting Somali officials and officers.

AP added on August 5 that the dead included Abdikani, son of Adar Sabriye.

September 14, 2024: Al-Shabaab was suspected when a bomb planted in a street where youths were taking photos exploded in Mogadishu's

Kahda district. A second bomb went off minutes later, victimizing rescuers and causing most of the five deaths and eight injuries.

October 17, 2024: *Al-Jazeera* reported that an al-Shabaab suicide bomber hit a café outside the General Kaahiye Police Academy training school in Mogadishu, killing seven and wounding six people drinking tea. Officers and civilians were among the victims.

SOUTH AFRICA

March 12, 2024: Police arrested a man, 35, after three Egyptian monks (Monk Hegumen Takla el-Samuely, Monk Yostos ava Markos, and Monk Mina ava Markos) belonging to the Coptic Orthodox Church were fatally stabbed in an attack at the Saint Mark the Apostle and Saint Samuel the Confessor Monastery in Cullinan, a town east of Pretoria. A fourth person was beaten with an iron rod before escaping and hiding in a room at the monastery. The Coptic Orthodox Church of South Africa said that el-Samuely was the deputy of the local diocese.

May 27, 2024: The *Washington Post* reported 40 political assassinations, mostly against local officials, politicians, and activists, since the beginning of 2023. They included Ntombenhle Mchunu, 75, a town councilor, in August 2023; the husband of Senzeni Zulu, killed shortly thereafter; Ayanda Ngila; Nokuthula Mabaso; and Lindokuhle Mnguni. The Global Initiative Against Transnational Organized Crime into assassinations in South Africa logged 166 political killings since 2019. Some 25 members of the Abahlali Mjondolo squatters movement were killed.

SOUTH SUDAN

December 31, 2023: *Al-Jazeera* reported that during the evening, armed men killed six people, including a senior local administrator, in the Abyei region, claimed by both Sudan and South Sudan. Rival factions of the Dinka ethnic group—Twic Dinka from South Sudan's neighboring Warrap State, and Ngok Dinka from

Abyei—disagree on the location of an administrative boundary. The gunmen ambushed Abyei Deputy Chief Administrator Noon Deng and his team along the road from Abyei to Aneet town when they were returning from an official visit to Rummamer County. Tereza Chol, a South Sudanese lawmaker, told *Reuters* that "His driver and two bodyguards plus two people of national security were all killed."

January 27, 2024: *Al-Jazeera* and *AP* reported that in the evening, gunmen attacked villagers in the Nyinkuac, Majbong, and Khadian areas in the oil-rich Abyei region, claimed by Sudan and South Sudan, killing 52, including a Ghanaian United Nations Interim Security Force for Abyei (UNISFA) peacekeeper in Agok, and wounding 64. The motive was believed related to a land dispute over the Aneet area pitting Twic Dinka tribal members from neighboring Warrap State and Ngok Dinka from Abyei, located at the border. Authorities suggested that the actual attackers were armed youth from the Nuer tribe who migrated to Warrap State in 2023 because of flooding in their areas.

February 3-4, 2024: Fighting over a land feud during the weekend in Rum-Ameer, Alal and Mijak counties in Abyei killed 37 people. Some 19 people were killed and 18 injured on February 3, with another 18, including four women and three children, killed on February 4. Gunmen stole 1,000 head of cattle.

Sudan

April 15, 2023: *UPI* reported that the U.N. World Food Program suspended operations in Sudan after three staff members were killed and two injured in Kabkabiya in North Darfur region.

A U.N. aircraft for humanitarian aid was "significantly damaged" by gunfire at the Khartoum International Airport.

April 17, 2023: *Reuters* reported that the paramilitary Rapid Support Forces was believed behind an attack on a U.S. diplomatic convoy.

June 14, 2023: *Sudan Tribune* and *UPI* reported that gunmen killed Khamis Abdullah Abakar, governor of West Darfur. The Sudanese Armed Forces and the breakaway paramilitary Rapid Support Forces blamed each other.

July 20, 2023: *Al-Jazeera* reported that gunmen attacked 18 Doctors Without Borders workers trying to deliver medical supplies to the Turkish Hospital in Khartoum. The attackers briefly detained the driver and stole his vehicle.

November 2, 2023: *Al-Jazeera* reported on November 10 that on November 2, the Rapid Support Forces (RSF) attacked a camp for displaced people after hitting a nearby army base in West Darfur. During three days, the terrorists killed 1,300 people and injured 2,000. Another 310 people were missing. RSF and its allied militias aim to eradicate the non-Arab Masalit tribe from West Darfur. Six tribal leaders and their families were killed in the attack on the camp in Ardamata in West Darfur. The RSF killed Mohamad Arbab, 85, his son, and eight grandchildren. Masalit tribal leader Abdelbasit Dina was killed with his wife, son, and 50 other residents in their community.

December 10, 2023: *Al-Jazeera* reported that an attack in Khartoum on an International Committee of the Red Cross (ICRC) convoy of three ICRC vehicles and three buses killed two people and injured seven, including three ICRC staff members. The ICRC said the convoy was due to evacuate more than 100 vulnerable civilians, including foreign nationals, from St Mary's Church in Khartoum to Wad Madani. 23121002

July 31, 2024: *AP* and *al-Araby TV* reported that President of the Sovereign Council and Commander-in-Chief General Abdel-Fattah Burhan was not hurt in a drone attack on an army officer graduation ceremony he was attending in Gebeit. The two drones killed five people after the ceremony had concluded.

September 8, 2024: *Reuters* reported that the paramilitary Rapid Support Forces fired artillery at Sennar in the southeast, killing 31 people and wounding 100.

October 21, 2024: *BBC* and *Sudan Tribune* reported Russia's embassy was investigating reports that a Russian-made Iyushin Il-76 cargo plane with a Russian crew on a mission to deliver equipment and medicine to the army-held city of el-Fasher was shot down in Darfur. The opposition RSF said it had downed a Russian-made Antonov flown by the Egyptian military that it accused of bombing civilians. The *Sudan Tribune* claimed that all members of the crew, among them three Sudanese nationals and two Russians, were killed in the crash in the Malha area, near the border with Chad. *BBC Verify* reported that the RSF claimed it had recovered documents, including a Russian passport, a job identification card from Manas airport in Kyrgyzstan, and two South African driving licenses (with different expiry dates), for one individual who may have graduated from a Russian military academy and may have been a resident in South Africa.

December 13, 2024: *Al-Jazeera* reported that the Federal Ministry of Health blamed the paramilitary Rapid Support Forces (RSF) for a drone strike on the Saudi hospital in el-Fasher in the Darfur region that killed nine people and injured 20 others. The group also fired four RPGs.

TANZANIA

September 6, 2024: Gunmen kidnapped Ali Kibao, a secretariat member of the CHADEMA party, from a bus traveling from Dar es Salaam to the port city of Tanga. The next day, he was found dead with signs of beatings and acid poured on his face.

TOGO

July 2024: *CNN* reported that the Jama'at Nusrat al-Islam wal-Muslimin (JNIM) attacked a military base.

UGANDA

June 16, 2023: *CNN*, the *New York Times, AP,* and *NTV Uganda* reported that between five and 20 ISIS-linked Allied Democratic Forces (ADF) gunmen armed with machetes attacked the Lhubirira secondary school in Mpondwe in Kasese District at 10:40 p.m., killing 41 people, including 38 students, a guard, and two residents, and abducting six others, whom they used as porters of food they had stolen. Several died when their dormitories were set on fire. The Uganda Peoples' Defense Forces military chased the suspects a mile into the Congo and believed the gunmen had holed up in Virunga National Park. The *Washington Post* and *Reuters* had the death toll at 37 with eight wounded by five gunmen. *New Vision* reported 42 deaths, some of whom died when a terrorist bomb went off as they fled.

The *Washington Post* reported on June 21, 2023 that the Ugandan military announced that it had rescued three students abducted in the attack. An army spokesman added, "They were rescued in Virunga National Park… There was a fight between the army and the terrorists. During the fight, the young men were able to escape." He said a woman and two children abducted in a separate operation were also rescued. He added that two of the terrorists were "put out of action".

Among the dead was Mbusa Zephanius, 37, the school's gatekeeper on duty the night of the attack, Florence Masika, and Elton Masereka, 17, a student at the school. Brian Musoka, 17, was among the missing. The ages of the dead ranged from a 12-year-old female student to a 70-year-old man. 23061601

October 2023: *Al-Jazeera* reported that the government claimed to have foiled several other planned ADF attacks in 2023, including a plot to blow up churches in Kibibi in October.

October 12-13, 2023: *Reuters* reported that the Congo-based ISIS-affiliated ADF killed one man and injured another in an overnight ambush of a truck in western Uganda.

October 17, 2023: *Al-Jazeera* reported that the government blamed the ADF for killing a honeymooning couple—David Barlow from the UK and Celia Barlow from South Africa—and their Ugandan guide Eric Ayai while on a safari in

Queen Elizabeth National Park near the Congo border. ISIS claimed credit the next day for killing "three Christian tourists" with machine guns.

October 30, 2023: *Al-Jazeera* reported that the ADF was blamed for a machete attack in Oicha, which killed 26 people.

November 2, 2023: *Al-Jazeera* and *AFP* reported that Uganda announced the capture of Njovu, leader of the ISIS-linked ADF believed responsible for killing two foreign tourists and their local guide in a national park on October 17. Six ADF terrorists were killed in the raid.

December 18, 2023: *Al-Jazeera* reported that at 10 p.m., the ADF attacked Kyabandara parish in Kamwenge district in western Uganda, killing a local councillor whom they found in a small roadside restaurant she operated, alongside four of her clients who had just sat down for a meal. They burned the restaurant and looted items from nearby stores, then fled.

December 28, 2023: *Reuters* and *BNN* reported that army spokesman Deo Akiiki said the army killed Musa Kamusi, a commander of a unit of the Islamist ADF, in Kibale National Park, a rainforest in western Uganda near the border with the Democratic Republic of Congo. His unit was believed behind several violent attacks on civilians and public institutions, including murdering 37 students at a boarding school and killing a British and South African couple, along with their Ugandan guide. The group also killed ten farmers and bar customers.

August 13, 2024: A panel of the High Court in Gulu convicted Thomas Kwoyelo, a former commander of the Lord's Resistance Army rebel group, on 44 of the 78 counts he faced for crimes against humanity, including murder, pillaging, enslavement, imprisonment, rape, and cruelty, committed between 1992 and 2005. His trial began in 2019; he had been in detention since 2009 when he was captured in Congo. Kwoyelo held the military rank of colonel within the LRA and ordered violent attacks on civilians, many of them displaced by the rebellion. Kwoyelo asserted that he was abducted as a young boy to join the LRA.

October 25, 2024: A panel of the High Court in Gulu sentenced LRA Colonel Colonel Thomas Kwoyelo—a child soldier turned rebel commander in the Lord's Resistance Army—to 40 years in prison for brutal crimes, including multiple counts of murder, rape, pillaging, and enslavement, committed by the group during its insurgency that started in the 1980s.

ZAMBIA

July 23, 2024: *BBC* reported that Guntila Muleya, newly-named director general of the Independent Broadcasting Authority, was kidnapped after leaving work. His bullet-riddled body and two bullet cartridges were discovered on the outskirts of Lusaka. He was previously the general manager in Zambia of South African pay TV firm *MultiChoice*.

December 20, 2024: Police spokesperson Rae Hamoonga announced the arrests of Jasten Mabulesse Candunde, 42, and Leonard Phiri, 43, who were allegedly hired by Nelson Banda, the younger brother of fugitive lawmaker Jay Banda, to bewitch Zambian President Hakainde Hichilema. Jay Banda escaped from police custody in August 2024 while facing charges of aggravated robbery. The two suspects faced charges of practicing witchcraft, possession of charms, and cruelty to animals. The police spokesperson said the suspects disclosed that they had agreed to a payment of $7,400 for their witchcraft services.

ZIMBABWE

November 11, 2023: *UPI* reported on November 15 that Zimbabwe Citizens Coalition for Change opposition party activist and pastor Tapfumaneyi Masaya was kidnapped while campaigning ahead of a special election and was later found dead on a roadside near Harare.

ASIA

ARMENIA

March 24, 2024: Three men tried to storm a police station in Yerevan, setting off grenades that injured two attackers. A third man stood in the entrance of the station for an hour threatening to detonate another grenade. Police units headed by Deputy Internal Affairs Minister Aram Hovhannisyan detained the attacker, who was held in the Nor-Nork police station. No other injuries were reported. Armenian media outlets reported that the trio wanted to free members of the Combat Brotherhood organization, who were being held at the station after being detained earlier that day. The group opposes the planned transfer of several villages in the Tavush region to Azerbaijan.

BANGLADESH

March 7, 2023: *Reuters* reported that a bomb exploded in a crowded market inside a seven-story building in Dhaka, killing 15, wounding several others, and heavily damaging two floors and a nearby bus. Among the injured was Kamal Ahmed, who was shopping on the sidewalk.

January 5, 2024: *Reuters* reported that 14 arsons hit polling booths, eight educational institutions, and a Buddhist monastery two days before the general elections.

Four people, including two children, were killed and eight passengers were injured at 9 p.m. in an arson that spread to four compartments of the Benapole Express headed for Dhaka. Police arrested a senior Bangladesh Nationalist Party (BNP) leader from Dhaka and seven others from the party's youth wing.

October 31, 2024: During the night, arsonists torched the Dhaka headquarters in the Bijoy Nagar area of the Jatiya Party that supported ousted leader Sheikh Hasina. No one claimed credit.

CHINA

July 10, 2023: *UPI*, the *Washington Post*, *AFP*, *BBC*, *al-Jazeera*, the state-run *Global Times*, and the state-owned *China Daily* reported that at 7:40 a.m., a man with a knife attacked people at a kindergarten in downtown Lianjiang's Hengshan Township in southeastern Guangdong Province, killing six people, including three children, two parents, and a teacher, and injuring one person. Authorities apprehended the attacker, a Lianjiang man surnamed Wu, 25, for "intentional assault".

October 13, 2023: The *Times of Israel* and *Reuters* reported that an Israeli embassy staffer in Beijing was in stable condition after being hospitalized following an attack not at the embassy. Hamas had called for a "day of rage".

May 7, 2024: *Red Star News*, *Guizhou Province Television*, state media outlet *The Paper*, *CNN*, and *AP* reported that before midday, a man from a village in Zhenxiong slashed people at Zhenxiong County People's Hospital (variant Chengnan) in Yunnan Province, killing two and injuring 21. At least one doctor was injured. Police detained the attacker, whose motives were unknown.

May 20, 2024: *BBC* reported that a woman, 45, armed with a fruit knife, killed two people and injured ten others in a noontime attack at a primary school in Guixi in Jiangxi Province.

June 10, 2024: The *Washington Post*, *CNN*, and *Reuters* reported that in the morning, four instructors from Cornell College in Mount Vernon, Iowa were stabbed while in Beishan Park during a teaching visit to their partner Beihua University in Jilin. Iowa state Representative Adam Zabner (D) said on Instagram that his brother, David, was wounded in the arm. David is a PhD student at Tufts University and was in China as part of a program with Cornell College and Beihua. *Al-Jazeera* reported that China detained a man, 55, surnamed Cui, suspected of stabbing the four plus a Chinese person who tried to intervene.

June 25, 2024: A man with a knife stabbed a mother and her child at a school bus stop run by a Japanese school in Suzhou. He then attacked a woman who tried to stop him from getting on the bus, seriously injuring her. Police detained him.

October 1, 2024: *Al-Jazeera* and *UPI* reported that police from the Songjiang police branch arrested Lin, 37, after he was believed to have killed three people and injured 15 in a 10 p.m. knife attack at a suburban supermarket on Songhui Middle Road in Shanghai. Police said early investigations indicated he had travelled to Shanghai to "vent his anger" following a personal financial dispute.

November 16, 2024: *Al-Jazeera, AP, BBC,* and *UPI* reported that at 6:30 p.m., police detained Xu, 21, a male former student at Wuxi Vocational Institute of Arts and Technology (*BBC* translated it as the Wuxi Yixing Arts and Crafts Vocational and Technical College) in Yixing, a smaller city within Wuxi, who had stabbed to death eight people and injured 17. Wu had failed his examinations and could not graduate. He also was dissatisfied about his pay at an internship. The suspect confessed.

INDIA

April 12, 2023: *U.S. News and World Report* and *Reuters* reported that the Indian Army announced that it had located an assault rifle believed to have been used to kill four soldiers at a military base in Punjab State in a 4:35 a.m. attack. Senior police officer S.P.S. Parmar said the attack in the barracks was "not a terror attack". Two people were believed involved.

April 20, 2023: *Al-Jazeera* reported that suspected rebels opened fire and threw explosives at an army truck, killing five soldiers of the Rashtriya Rifles Unit deployed for counterterrorist operations in the southern Rajouri sector in disputed Indian-administered Kashmir. Another soldier was hospitalized and an army vehicle set was on fire on a highway in the mountainous area.

April 28, 2023: *Al-Jazeera* reported on May 5, 2023 that five Indian soldiers were killed and several wounded during an army operation against armed groups in the Rajouri sector of Kashmir. The terrorists, when cornered, set off a bomb. Two soldiers died and another three succumbed to their injuries.

May 3-6, 2023: The *New York Times* reported that several days of clashes between ethnic groups in remote Manipur State killed 54. The groups were attempting to claim a special tribal status with extra privileges. Homes, vehicles, churches, and temples were torched.

July 31, 2023: *USNWR* and *Reuters* reported that Hindus and Muslims clashed 30 miles south of New Delhi. Five people, including two members of the home guard, a voluntary group that assists police to control civil disturbances, were killed after a Hindu religious procession passed through the Muslim-dominated Nuh region in Haryana State. In the evening, a mosque was torched, killing the cleric and injuring another person in neighboring Gurugram. Sixty people, including ten police, were injured. Five cars were set on fire and several shops were damaged. Nishant Kumar Yadav, deputy commissioner of Gurugram, said "Five people involved in the incident have been rounded up and the others are being identified."

October 29, 2023: A bomb exploded at the Zamra International Convention Center in Kalamassery in Kerala State, where hundreds of Jehovah's Witnesses were gathered for prayer, killing one person and injuring 36.

December 21, 2023: *Al-Jazeera* reported that in the afternoon, rebels ambushed two Indian military vehicles—a mini-truck and a gypsy—carrying nine soldiers in the southernmost border district of Rajouri in Indian-administered Kashmir, killing four Indian soldiers and injuring three others. The attackers hid in the dense forest area. The little-known People's Anti-Fascist Front, which officials have said is the proxy of the Pakistan-based armed group Jaish-e-Muhammad, claimed responsibility.

December 26, 2023: *Reuters* reported that a bomb went off near the Israeli Embassy in New Delhi at 5:20 p.m., causing no injuries.

December 29, 2023: The United Liberation Front of Asom (ULFA), led by Arabinda Rajkhowa, which fought for decades to free India's northeastern state of Assam from New Delhi's rule, signed a peace accord with the government pledging to end the insurgency in the region. A hard-line faction, led by Paresh Baruah, is not part of the agreement. The *Press Trust of India* news agency reported that he was believed to be hiding along the China-Myanmar border.

March 1, 2024: *Al-Jazeera* reported that a bomb hidden in a bag exploded at 1 p.m. at Rameshwaram Cafe in eastern Bengaluru, India's tech capital, injuring eight.

April 16, 2024: *AP* and *BBC* reported that police killed 29 suspected Maoist Naxalite rebels in the Kanker district of Chhattisgarh State. Three security officers were wounded near Bastar, a rebel stronghold. Police seized several weapons. Authorities believed that two senior members of the CPI (Maoist) were killed.

June 9, 2024: *Al-Jazeera* and *AP* reported that nine people were killed and 33 others injured after a bus carrying Hindu pilgrims returning from the popular base camp of the Hindu temple Mata Vaishno Devi in the area fell into a ravine after suspected separatists conducted a shooting attack near Reasi in Indian-administered Kashmir. No one claimed responsibility for the shooting. A police officer said some of the victims had gunshot wounds and blamed the attack on Muslims.

July 7, 2024: *Al-Jazeera* and *AFP* reported that two soldiers and six rebels died in two gun battles in Modergram and Frisal Chinnigam villages in the Kulgam district in Indian-administered Kashmir. Authorities said they retrieved the bodies of two terrorists from Modergram, and four others from Frisal Chinnigam.

Gunmen fired at an army camp in the Rajouri district, wounding a soldier.

July 8, 2024: Rebels were suspected in an ambush of an army vehicle on a routine patrol in the Kathua district of Indian-controlled Kashmir that killed five Indian soldiers and wounded five others.

July 14, 2024: *Al-Jazeera* reported that the Indian Army killed three fighters trying to cross from the Pakistan-controlled side of the Line of Control in Kashmir's Kupwara district.

July 15, 2024: *Al-Jazeera* and *AFP* reported that during the night, rebels ambushed Indian troops in the forests of Doda district in Jammu division in Indian-administered Kashmir, killing four soldiers. The Kashmir Tigers claimed credit for the 20-minute attack.

October 4, 2024: *NPR* and *AP* reported that Indian soldiers killed 31 Naxalite rebels in a nine-hour clash after counterinsurgency troops, acting on intelligence, cornered 50 suspected Maoists in the Abhujmaad forest area along the border of Narayanpur and Dantewada districts in Chhattisgarh State. Troops recovered arms and ammunition, including automatic rifles.

October 12, 2024: *AP* and *BBC* reported that during the night, a gunman shot to death senior politician Baba Siddique, 66, outside the Mumbai office of his son, who is also a politician. Siddique had close ties with Bollywood, throwing lavish parties, and was associated with the Indian National Congress party for decades. In February 2024, he joined a regional party that rules Maharashtra State. The *Press Trust of India* reported that police arrested two suspects and were searching for a third. *NDTV* said the two suspects claimed they were part of a crime gang run by Lawrence Bishnoi that has carried out multiple killings. Bishnoi was serving a jail sentence for his involvement in several high-profile murder cases, including the killing of the Indian rapper Sidhu Moose Wala in 2022. Siddique had recently received death threats.

October 14-15, 2024: *BBC* reported that bomb hoaxes were called within 48 hours against ten Indian flights. On October 14, threats were posted on *X*; police detained a teen. An Air India plane from Delhi to Chicago landed at Canada's Iqaluit airport as a precautionary measure. *Al-Jazeera* reported that later that day, Singapore scrambled two F-15SG fighter jets to an Air India Express flight AXB684 away from populated areas before it landed at Changi airport at 10:04 p.m. following a bomb threat. The plane was en route from Madurai, India, to Singapore. IndiGo, SpiceJet, and Akasa Air flights also received threats.

On October 15, seven flights, including two Air India planes, were threatened on a now-suspended *X* account.

October 18, 2024: Police blamed militants following the discovery of the body of a worker from eastern Bihar state, riddled with bullet wounds, in a maize field in Shopian district.

October 20, 2024: Gunmen killed seven people—five non-local laborers and officials, a Kashmiri worker, and a Kashmiri doctor—and wounding five who were working on a strategic tunnel project in Sonamarg in Kashmir. No one claimed credit. Police blamed militants for the nighttime attack on the camp for construction workers.

October 24, 2024: Rebels fired on an army vehicle carrying troops close to the line of control near Gulmarg during the night, killing three Indian soldiers and their two civilian porters.

November 2, 2024: Soldiers intercepted a group of rebels in a forested area in Anantnag district in Indian-controlled Kashmir, killing two rebels. Later in Srinagar, police and paramilitary soldiers killed a militant after troops cordoned off a neighborhood on a tip that he was hiding in a house. Two soldiers and two police were injured. The troops torched the home where the rebel was trapped.

November 3, 2024: A terrorist threw a grenade from a flyover bridge at a busy marketplace in Srinagar, wounding nine people.

November 7, 2024: In a clash with soldiers and police in a village near Sopore in Indian-controlled Kashmir, two suspected militants were killed.

Gunmen killed two members of the government-sponsored Village Defense Group militia in the remote southern Kishtwar area in Kashmir. The duo, one Hindu and one Muslim, were abducted from a forested area where they had gone to graze cattle. The Kashmir Tigers, an offshoot of the Pakistan-based Jaish-e-Mohammad militant group, claimed responsibility.

December 19, 2024: Following up on a tip that rebels were hiding in a village in Kulgam district in Indian-controlled Kashmir, soldiers and police killed five gunmen. Two soldiers were injured.

INDIAN OCEAN

November 24, 2023: The Hizballah-affiliated *al-Mayadeen* pan-Arab satellite channel and *AP* reported that during the night, a suspected Iranian triangle-shaped Shahed-136 bomb-carrying drone attacked the Malta-flagged container ship *CMA CGM Symi*, owned by an Israeli billionaire, while in international waters. The ship was damaged but no injuries were reported. CMA CGM is based in Marseille, France. Symi is owned by the Singapore-based Eastern Pacific Shipping, which is controlled by Israeli billionaire Idan Ofer.

December 23, 2023: *Reuters* and *CNN* reported that at 10 a.m., a drone caused a fire on the *MV Chem Pluto*, an Israel-affiliated, Japanese-owned, Netherlands-operated, Liberian-flagged chemical products tanker en route from Saudi Arabia southwest of Veraval off India's west coast. No one was injured among the 20 Indian and one Vietnamese crew on board the merchant ship. Western authorities said the drone came from Iran.

March 14, 2024: *U.S. Naval Institute News* reported that Houthi spokesmen Brig. Gen. Yahya Sare'e and Mohammed Abdulsalam individually posted on *X* threats to target merchant ships in the Indian Ocean on their way to the Cape of Good Hope.

April 24, 2024: *Al-Jazeera* reported that Houthi military spokesman Yahya Saree said the group targeted the Israeli ship *MSC Veracruz* in the Indian Ocean and launched projectiles at a U.S. warship.

May 9, 2024: Houthis claimed they had attacked the *MSC Vittoria* container ship.

INDONESIA

February 2023: On February 15, 2023, *Reuters* and *CNN* reported that Papua separatists released images of New Zealand pilot Philip Mehrtens, who had been taken hostage the previous week after he landed a commercial Susi Air charter flight at Paro Airport in the remote Nduga region. West Papua National Liberation Army (TPNPB) rebels demanded that authorities acknowledge the independence of the area. The rebels said they had burned the plane.

August 14, 2023: *Reuters* reported that Indonesia's Densus 88 counter-terrorism unit arrested an ISIS loyalist suspected of planning an attack on the headquarters of the police's security division. During the raid on his house outside Jakarta, authorities found an ISIS flag, ammunition, and 16 weapons, mostly handguns and modified air rifles. The suspect worked for a state railway company. He had posted pro-ISIS content on social media and sought to raise funds for extremism via *Telegram*.

September 21, 2023: *Reuters* reported that a bomb squad was dispatched following an explosion at the Eika Hospital in the Serpong area of Jakarta. *Detik.com* quoted police who suggested an overheated power supplier in the radiology unit was the cause.

October 16, 2023: Indonesian security forces on October 27 recovered the bodies of six traditional gold mining workers who had been missing since a separatist attack at their gold panning camp in the Yahukimo district of Highland Papua Province on October 16. During the attack, gunmen killed seven workers and torched three excavators and two trucks. A two-hour shootout followed between the rebels and joint security forces of police and military. Rebel spokesman Sebby Sambon of the West Papua Liberation

Army, the military wing of the Free Papua Organization, claimed responsibility. Eleven workers hid in the jungle. One body was found before October 27. Two of the bodies were charred and the four others had gunshot and stab wounds.

October 31, 2023: *Al-Jazeera* reported that the government arrested 59 people, including members of Jemaah Islamiyah (JI) and Jamaah Ansharut Daulah (JAD), for plotting to disrupt the 2024 presidential election. A spokesperson for Indonesia's Counterterrorism Special Detachment 88 unit added that police seized weapons, propaganda material, and bomb-making chemicals. Nineteen were from the al-Qaeda-linked JI network; 40 suspects were from the ISIS-affiliated JAD.

April 4, 2024: Free Papua Movement independence rebels clashed with a joint police and military force near the gold mining town of Tembagapura in Central Papua Province, killing two Papuan separatist leaders, identified as West Papua Liberation Army regional commanders Abubakar Kogoya, alias Abubakar Tabuni, and Damianus Magay, alias Natan Wanimbo. Several other rebels were wounded but escaped into the jungle. The gunmen were armed with military-grade weapons, axes, and arrows.

April 16-18, 2024: Indonesia's elite counter-terrorism police conducted raids in Central Sulawesi Province over three days and arrested eight members of a new cell linked to Jemaah Islamiyah. Five suspects were arrested in Palu, two in Sigi, and one in Poso. Police seized two laptops, several cellular phones, and documents, including jihadist books. National Police spokesperson Trunoyudo Wisnu Andiko credited information obtained from 59 suspected militants detained in October 2023.

June 30, 2024: *Al-Jazeera* reported on July 5, 2024 that 16 senior members of Jemaah Islamiyah announced via online video the dissolution of the group.

August 5, 2024: *AP* and *BBC* reported that Free Papua Organization (OPM) gunmen attacked a helicopter and killed its New Zealand pilot, Glen Malcolm Conning, 50, who flew for the

Indonesian aviation company PT Intan Angkasa Air Service, shortly after it landed in Alama village in the Mimika district of Central Papua Province. The members of the West Papua National Liberation Army, the armed wing of the Free Papua Movement, released two local health workers and two Indigenous Papuan children the aircraft was carrying. They then set fire to the helicopter.

JAPAN

January 7, 2023: *CNN* and *NHK* reported that at 6 a.m., a man phoned Jetstar to say that he had put a bomb on an A320 en route from Tokyo's Narita airport to Fukuoka. The plane made an emergency landing at Chubu Airport. One person was injured.

April 15, 2023: The *Japan Times, NHK,* and *Washington Post* reported that Prime Minister Fumio Kishida was evacuated after a loud explosion was heard just before he began a stump speech in Wakayama. Authorities believed a smoke bomb was thrown at him. Police officers subdued a man, 24, at the scene. Two minor injuries were reported. Kishida was campaigning for a candidate of the ruling Liberal Democratic Party before local elections scheduled for April 23. The *Florida Times-Union* reported that on September 6, 2023, prosecutors indicted Ryuji Kimura, 24, for attempted murder and other charges. He underwent a three-month psychiatric evaluation to determine his fitness for trial.

June 14, 2023: *UPI, AP,* the *Washington Post,* and *NHK* reported that at 9 a.m., a Japanese Ground Self-Defense Force recruit, 18, fired an automatic rifle at three instructors, killing two Japanese soldiers, aged 25 and 52, and injuring the third, 25, at the Hino Kihon shooting range in the central prefecture of Gifu. He was arrested on the scene for attempted murder and admitted to the shooting. He had joined the SDF in April.

June 15, 2023: *UPI* reported that Yokota Air Base, regional headquarters of the U.S. Air Force and headquarters for Japan's Air Defense Command, in western Tokyo was evacuated and locked down for three hours after a bomb

threat was posted on *Facebook* at 10:20 a.m. No bomb was found. Personnel from the 374th Airlift Wing command post, including a residential tower and several nearby buildings, were evacuated. No injuries were reported.

October 19, 2024: *AP* and the *New York Times* reported that police arrested masked suspect Atsunobu Usuda, 49, in the morning after he threw several firebombs into the headquarters of Japan's governing Liberal Democratic Party in Tokyo, then crashed his car into the fencing of Prime Minister Shigeru Ishiba's residence, causing no injuries. He was charged with obstructing the performance of official duties. Usuda lived in Saitama Prefecture near Tokyo.

KYRGYZSTAN

August 30, 2023: *Al-Jazeera* reported that Kyrgyzstan repatriated 95 ISIS wives and children (31 women, 64 children) from Syrian internment camps with the help of the U.S., the U.N., and the Red Cross. The country repatriated 59 nationals in February 2023 and 79 from camps in Iraq in March 2021.

MALAYSIA

May 2, 2024: Faisal Halim, who plays winger for the Malaysian national soccer team and Malaysian club Selangor, sustained fourth-degree burns following an acid attack by two assailants at a shopping mall. He was in critical condition, with limited movement and speech. Two people were initially detained; one was later released.

May 7, 2024: *AP* and *The Star* reported that during the night, two assailants on a motorbike tailed former Malaysian national soccer team captain Safiq Rahim after a training session in southern Johor State. They later threatened him with a hammer and smashed his car's rear window.

May 17, 2024: *Al-Jazeera, Bernama, AP,* and the *New Straits Times* reported that in the morning, a masked man suspected of membership in the al-Qaeda-affiliated Jemaah Islamiyah rolled up on a motorcycle, took out a machete, and stormed a police station in Ulu Tiram in Johor State, killing two police officers and injuring another. He hacked to death a constable, grabbed the officer's service revolver, and shot dead a second officer. An injured officer shot the attacker to death. Police believed the terrorist planned to seize weapons for a "yet to be determined agenda". Police raided the suspect's nearby house and found "numerous JI-related paraphernalia". The suspect had no criminal record. Police arrested five members of his family, including the suspect's father, 62, who police said was a "known JI member". The *Malay Mail* reported that police were rounding up 20 other JI members in Johor.

AP reported on June 19 that Radin Imran Radin Mohd Yassin, 62, the father of the attacker, Radin Luqman, 21, was charged on four counts, including inciting terrorism in his family. His Singaporean wife and three other children also appeared in a Johor court to face charges.

Charge sheets showed that Radin Imran, who is unemployed, was accused of supporting terrorist acts by keeping four homemade air rifles in his home for ISIS activities. He allegedly pledged allegiance in 2014 to ISIS's then-leader, Abu Bakr al-Baghdadi. Police found a book linked to ISIS in his possession.

Eldest son Radin Romyullah, 34, faced two separate charges of pledging loyalty to al-Baghdadi and of possessing an external hard drive containing materials related to ISIS. Both father and son faced life imprisonment, which in Malaysia is up to 40 years, and a fine.

Radin Imran's Singaporean wife, Rosna Jantan, 59, and two daughters aged 19 and 23, were charged with the omission of information related to the spread of terrorism.

The family offered no plea and had no attorneys. Their next hearing was scheduled for July 31, 2024.

Maldives

July 31, 2023: *UPI* reported that the U.S. Departments of State and Treasury imposed economic sanctions against 20 people accused of financially supporting the operations of ISIS and al-Qaeda in the Maldives. They included key leaders and financial facilitators of the terrorist organizations active in the South Asian archipelago nation, such as an ISIS-affiliated terrorist cell in Addu City, ISIS-aligned criminal gang Kuda Henveyru, al-Qaeda operatives, and associates of Mohamad Ameen, an ISIS operative who was sanctioned by the United States in 2019. The administration charged that the Addu City ISIS cell had plotted terrorist attacks involving bombs and drones since at least 2018. The group's leader, Jinaau Naseem, who turns 29 in early August, was among those sanctioned. The administration accused Kuda Henveyru of organizing large robberies to generate funds for Maldivian ISIS foreign terrorist fighters in Syria. Twenty-nine companies associated with those sanctioned were also designated.

Myanmar

April 13, 2023: *AFP* reported that four car bombs exploded at midday at the Yan Taing Aung pagoda in Yangon where a crowd had gathered for the Thingyan festival that marks the start of the Buddhist new year, killing four people, injuring 12 people, two seriously, and destroying three vehicles in eastern Shan State's Lashio Township. A three-year-old was wounded. The ruling junta blamed anti-coup fighters. No group claimed credit.

May 7, 2023: *Reuters* and *VOA* reported that gunmen fired on Association of Southeast Asian Nations (ASEAN) officials delivering humanitarian aid in Hsi Hseng Township in western Shan State.

November 11, 2023: *USNWR* and *Reuters* reported that the Karenni Nationalities Defence Force (KNDF) claimed that using heavy machine guns, it downed a government fighter jet in Kayah State in eastern Myanmar during clashes with the military near the border with Thailand. Junta spokesperson Zaw Min Tun told state-run *MRTV* that the jet crashed due to a technical problem.

January 3, 2024: The Kachin Independence Army claimed it shot down a helicopter believed to be on a resupply mission in a combat zone in the northern state of Kachin. It had taken off from the Nahpaw army outpost close to Nam San Yang village in Waing Maw township, to return to its base in Myitkyina township, the state's capital, around 11:50 a.m. *Khit Thit Media* reported that six soldiers aboard the aircraft had been killed and one survived; other reports said seven had died.

March 7, 2024: The Kachin Independence Army attacked more than ten outposts controlled by the army and army-affiliated militia in several townships along the main road to the state capital of Myitkyina in Kachin State. Three civilians, including a child living in Laiza town, were killed. Fighting was reported in Laiza, Bhamo, Waingmaw, Momauk and Myitkyina townships.

August 5, 2024: *AP* reported on August 10, 2024 that an artillery and drone attack killed 150 civilians from Myanmar's Muslim Rohingya minority in the western state of Rakhine. The Arakan Army, the military wing of the state's Rakhine ethnic group, denied responsibility. The Rohingya were trying to flee fierce fighting in Maungdaw by crossing the Naf River into Bangladesh.

October 18, 2024: *AP*, the *Irrawaddy*, and *Khit Thit* reported that a bomb exploded in the afternoon near the Chinese Consulate in Mandalay's Chanmyathazi township, causing some damage to roof tiles but no casualties.

December 20, 2024: Khaing Thukha, a spokesperson for the Arakan Army, said the rebels had captured the army's western command headquarters in Ann township in Rakhine State. The headquarters' deputy commander, Brig. Gen. Thaung Tun, and its chief operating officer, Brig. Gen. Kyaw Kyaw Than, were taken prisoner.

PACIFIC OCEAN

May 6, 2024: *Business Insider* and *AP* reported that South African citizen Ntando Sogoni, 35, a new *Norwegian Encore* cruise ship worker was accused of using scissors to stab a female passenger and two crew members on its voyage to Alaska from Seattle. The attacker was arrested and charged with assault with a dangerous weapon.

He allegedly stabbed the passenger several times in her arm, hand, and face; a security guard in the head; and a second security guard in the back and shoulders. Sogoni faced ten years in prison and a $250,000 fine.

PAKISTAN

January 14, 2023: *UPI* and *Anadolu* reported that around midnight, six or seven Tehreek-e-Taliban Pakistan gunmen armed with grenades, sniper rifles, and automatic weapons attacked the Sarband police station outside Peshawar, killing three police officers, including a senior officer.

January 30, 2023: The *Washington Post, NPR, Dawn, CNN, AP, Reuters,* and *UPI* reported that a suicide bomber attacked during afternoon prayers in the Police Lines Mosque inside a police compound in Peshawar, killing 101 people, including prayer leader Noor-ul-Amin, and injuring 250, some critically. Roughly 90% of the casualties were police officers. The mosque's roof and the main hall of the building collapsed. Sarbakaf Mohmand, a commander for the Pakistani Taliban, and spokesman Umar Mukarram Khorasani tweeted responsibility, saying the bomber was avenging the killing of Abdul Wali, alias Omar Khalid Khurasani, who died in Afghanistan's Paktika Province in August 2022. Another spokesman denied involvement, saying it was un-Islamic to attack a mosque packed with men at prayer. *Reuters* and *NPR* reported on February 2 that Pakistan announced that the bomber arrived on a motorcycle and was wearing a police uniform.

On November 12, 2024, provincial police chief Akhtar Hayyat announced the arrest the previous day of police constable Mohammad Wali for facilitating the attack. Wali allegedly shared a map of the compound with the suicide bomber. He had joined the outlawed Jamaat-ul-Ahrar, a breakaway faction of the Pakistani Taliban, which orchestrated the attack, in 2023. Police earlier released CCTV images showing the suicide bomber in a police uniform approaching the site pushing a motorcycle. Hayyat said Wali allegedly provided the uniform.

February 17, 2023: *USNWR* and *Reuters* reported that the Pakistani Taliban attacked a Karachi police station, killing two people and wounding 11 before security forces killed the three terrorists in an hours-long siege.

March 6, 2023: *Al-Jazeera, AP,* and *UPI* reported that in the morning, a suicide bomber on a motorcycle crashed into a police van in the Kambri Bridge area of Kachhi district in Balochistan Province, killing 10 people, including a civilian, and wounding 12. Agha Samiullah, the deputy commissioner of Balochistan's Kachhi district, said the van was carrying 21 members of the Balochistan Constabulary, a wing of the provincial police force, from Sibi city to Quetta. The newly-formed Tehreek-e-Jihad claimed credit.

April 1, 2023: *Al-Jazeera* and the Pakistani military's media wing *ISPR* reported that gunmen attacked soldiers on patrol along the Pakistan-Iran border, killing four soldiers: Sher Ahmed, Muhammad Asghar, Muhammad Irfan, and Abdur Rasheed. No one claimed credit for the attack in the Jalgai sector of Kech district. Baluch nationalists were suspected.

April 5, 2023: During a nighttime raid on a militant hideout in Shin Warsak in South Waziristan near the Afghan border, Pakistani security forces killed eight gunmen. One soldier was killed and four wounded.

April 7, 2023: The intelligence service arrested Gulzar Imam, alias Shambay, founder and leader of the banned Baluch Nationalist Army, formed in a merger of the Baluch Republican Army and United Baluch Army. He had visited India and Afghanistan and was believed to have links with hostile intelligence agencies.

April 24, 2023: *NPR* and *al-Jazeera* reported that two explosions at a Counter-Terrorism Department (CTD) facility in Kabal in Khyber Pakhtunkhwa Province's Swat Valley in the northwest killed 12, many of them police counterterrorism officers, along with a mother and her child who were passing by, and injured more than 50 people, some critically. The bombing was similar to earlier TTP attacks. The building complex also houses the Kabal district police station and headquarters of a reserve police force. Provincial police chief Akhtar Hayat said there was an old ammunition store in the office.

May 12, 2023: *Al-Jazeera* reported that in the early morning, gunmen attacked a Frontier Corps camp in the Muslim Bagh area of northern Balochistan, killing 7 people, including six soldiers and a civilian. The six gunmen were killed. Six people, including a woman, were wounded. The armed forces were conducting a hostage rescue operation in the area.

June 28, 2023: The Pakistani military announced that it had killed Shafi Ullah, an ISIS commander, and two other terrorists in a raid on a hideout in Bajur district in the Khyber Pakhtunkhwa Province bordering Afghanistan.

July 5, 2023: *Reuters* reported that three soldiers and several civilians died when a suicide bomber blew up a vehicle close to a military checkpoint in North Waziristan district near the Afghan border. No one claimed credit.

July 6, 2023: *Reuters* reported that the Pakistani Taliban claimed credit for killing Pakistani Army Major Abdullah Shah, 33, who was leading an operation in the Khyber tribal area when his unit came under fire. The Army said three "terrorists and their facilitators" were taken prisoner.

July 12, 2023: *Al-Jazeera* and *Reuters* reported that in the early morning, gunmen armed with guns, hand grenades, and rockets attacked a military base in Northern Balochistan's Zhob district, killing four soldiers and critically injuring five soldiers. Three terrorists were killed; two others escaped. The newly-founded Tehreek-e-Jihad Pakistan (TJP) said it would release pictures and videos of their fighters who took part in the attack. Saeed Ahmad, a senior government official, said all five terrorists were killed.

July 18, 2023: *Al-Jazeera* and *Reuters* reported that a suicide bomber set off his explosives near a truck carrying paramilitary Frontier Corps forces on a busy road in Hayatabad, a suburb of the capital of Khyber Pakhtunkhwa Province, which borders Afghanistan, injuring eight people and badly damaging the truck and nearby civilian vehicles. The attacker was killed. Tehreek-e-Jihad Pakistan claimed credit.

July 30, 2023: *Al-Jazeera, AP, Reuters,* and *CNN* reported that a suicide bomber set off his explosives jacket under a traditional shalwar kameez at a rally of the workers' convention of Maulana Fazlur Rehman's Jamiat Ulema-e-Islam-Fazl (JUI-F) party on the outskirts of Khar, capital of Bajur district in Khyber Pakhtunkhwa Province, which borders Afghanistan, killing 63 and wounding 123, some 17 critically. TPP was suspected; it condemned the bombing. The *Daily Beast* reported that ISIS was also suspected. The *Washington Post* reported that ISIS-K claimed credit. *Al-Jazeera* added on July 31 that local police chief Nazir Khan said three suspects were arrested overnight. Sultan Zeb said that his nephew, Saeed Anwar, 18, had died; Anwar's wife was pregnant. JUI-F worker Mumtaz, 46, was treated for shrapnel in her foot and a burst eardrum. *Al-Jazeera* added on August 3, 2023 that Prime Minister Shehbaz Sharif said "Afghan citizens" had been involved in recent attacks.

August 7, 2023: *Al-Jazeera* reported that a roadside bomb hit a vehicle carrying Ishaq Yaqub—a local politician from the Balochistan Awami Party—and his friends in Kech in Balochistan Province, killing him and six others.

A suicide bomber prematurely set off his explosives in North Waziristan in Khyber Paktunkhwa Province, killing a married couple in a nearby car. The Tehreek-e-Taliban Pakistan (TTP) was suspected.

August 13, 2023: *Al-Jazeera* and China's state-run *Global Times* newspaper reported that Gawadar Deputy Superintendent of Police Chakar Baloch announced that security forces killed two Balochistan Liberation Army (BLA) Majeed Brigade gunmen who attacked a convoy of three SUVs and one van carrying 23 Chinese engineers in Gawadar in Balochistan Province. No one else was injured. The terrorists had small arms and hand grenades. 23081301

August 16, 2023: *Al-Jazeera* reported that hundreds of people armed with batons and sticks torched the Salvation Army Church and the Saint Paul Catholic Church in Jaranwala in Faisalabad District in Punjab Province following allegations of blasphemy by two Christian residents. Another mob torched private homes in a Christian colony. The *Washington Post* and *al-Jazeera* reported that Pakistani police arrested 146 suspects for attacking at least five churches and dozens of homes. Among the victims was Masih, 47, whose home was burned down; it was home to 19 people.

August 20, 2023: *Al-Jazeera* and *Reuters* reported that a roadside bomb exploded under a truck carrying laborers to an army construction project in Waziristan district in North Waziristan's Shawal Valley in the Khyber Pakhtunkhwa Province, near the Afghan border, killing 11 workers. No group immediately claimed credit.

August 31, 2023: *Al-Jazeera* and *AFP* reported that a motorcycle-riding suicide bomber crashed into a truck that was part of an army convoy in the Bannu district of Khyber Pakhtunkhwa Province, killing nine soldiers and injuring five.

September 6, 2023: *Al-Jazeera* reported that Tehreek-e-Taliban Pakistan gunmen attacked two military checkpoints in the Chitral district of Khyber Pakhtunkhwa Province. Four soldiers and a dozen TTP terrorists were killed. The armed forces claimed that the attacks were coordinated from the Kunar and Nuristan Provinces of Afghanistan.

September 9, 2023: *Al-Jazeera* reported that Pakistan deployed paramilitary forces to rescue six soccer players, all between the ages of 17 and 23, who were abducted in Dera Bugti district in Balochistan Province. The players were kidnapped around 9 a.m. en route to Sibi town to participate in a local football tournament organized by the provincial government. Among those kidnapped were Babar Ali Ditta and Muhammad Yasir, 23. No group immediately claimed credit or made demands.

September 29, 2023: *Al-Jazeera, CNN,* and *Voice of America* reported that in the Mastung District of Balochistan Province, a bomb killed 59 people and wounded 50. Mastung's Assistant Commissioner Atta Ul Munim claimed a senior police officer, who was killed in the explosion, was the target of the attack.

A bomb went off in a mosque in Hangu in Khyber Pakhtunkhwa Province, killing five people and injuring ten. Guards fired on two attackers on bikes who tried to enter a police station near the mosque. People were gathering for an Eid Milad-ul-Nabi procession to mark the birthday of the Prophet Muhammad.

Amir Rana, director of the Islamabad-based Pakistan Institute of Peace Studies, blamed ISIS. TTP denied involvement. Pakistan blamed India's Research and Analysis Wing intelligence service.

November 2, 2023: *Al-Jazeera* and *Dawn* reported that gunmen fired on a police camp in Dera Ismail Khan, killing one police officer.

November 3, 2023: *Al-Jazeera* reported that gunmen set off a bomb near a police patrol in Dera Ismail Khan, killing five and injuring 21.

November 3, 2024: *Al-Jazeera* reported that gunmen ambushed a military convoy in Baluchistan Province, killing 14 soldiers.

November 4, 2023: *Al-Jazeera* and the *New York Times* reported that at 3 a.m., gunmen used a ladder to scale a wall and attacked an air force training base in the Mianwali area in the morning. Troops killed nine Tehreek-e-Jihad Pakistan (TJP) terrorists. Three grounded aircraft and a fuel tanker were damaged.

November 10, 2023: The *Washington Post* reported that the Pakistan Institute for Conflict and Security Studies indicated that terrorist attacks throughout the country were up 80 percent in the first six months of the year. Most were attributed to the Pakistani Taliban. Pakistani officials claimed that 14 of 24 major terrorist attacks carried in 2023 in Pakistan were by Afghan nationals, a charge Kabul denied.

November 18, 2023: *AP* and *al-Jazeera* reported that Pakistan security forces killed four militants, including most wanted militant commander Ibrahim, in a shootout during an overnight raid

in the Khaisoor area of North Waziristan district near the border with Afghanistan. Troops seized weapons, explosives, and ammunition.

November 19, 2023: *AP* reported that a remotely-detonated roadside bomb planted on a dirt road in the Balgatar area of Kech district killed three men, including two brothers, on their way to a family gathering in Baluchistan Province. Baluch nationalists were suspected.

Police in the Rajanpur district of Punjab Province arrested four militants during a raid, seizing explosives and weapons.

December 2, 2023: *Al-Jazeera* and *DPA* reported that at 6:30 p.m., gunmen attacked a bus travelling the Karakoram Highway near Chilas in the mountainous region of Gilgit Baltistan in northern Pakistan, killing 10 bus passengers, including two soldiers, and injuring 26 others, including the driver. The bus collided with an oncoming truck. No group claimed credit.

Al-Jazeera added on December 8 that among the 45 passengers were Ismaili family Shah Bulbul, 35, his wife, Bibi Roshan, and two children Umaima, 5, and Arsalan, 2, who left his hometown of Ghizer, en route to Karachi, 30 hours away. Roshan was hit by six bullets.

December 5, 2023: *Al-Jazeera* reported that a roadside bomb exploded in the middle of a road near a school in Peshawar in the morning, injuring seven people, including four children. An eight-year-old child was seriously injured. The youngest of the injured children is six; the others are 14 and 17 years old. No one claimed credit.

December 12, 2023: *Al-Jazeera*, the *Washington Post,* and *AP* reported that a Tehreek-e-Jihad Pakistan (TJP) suicide bomber crashed his truck into the main gate of a police station used as a military post in Daraban, 37 miles from Dera Ismail Khan in Khyber Pakhtunkhwa Province. Gunmen then poured in, sparking an hours-long shootout, killing 23 people, and injuring 34, several critically. The building collapsed and several businesses and shops were damaged, with windows shattered. Six terrorists were killed. The army said it killed 27 terrorists in several operations in the same region. Mohammed Qassim, TJP spokesman, claimed credit, saying, "Our suicide bombers attacked a military compound at 2:30 a.m. and started killing soldiers one by one. An army camp is set up in a school. More than 20 soldiers were killed in the attack."

December 15, 2023: *Al-Jazeera, DawnNewsTV,* and *Reuters* reported that in the morning gunmen attacked a police station in the Tank district of Khyber Pakhtunkhwa Province's Dera Ismail Khan division, killing two police officers and wounding three others. Three terrorists died; two were killed by police, the third set off a suicide bomb. Police found an unexploded suicide jacket. Ansar-ul-Islam called *Reuters* to claim responsibility. *Dawn* reported that Ansarul Jihad claimed credit.

Gunmen attacked a military outpost in the morning, killing two soldiers and wounding five.

Late December 2023: On January 1, 2024, counterterrorism police announced they had arrested 21 Pakistani Taliban members in the eastern Punjab Province over the past two weeks. They included Mohammad Arshad, an alleged chief commander of the banned Baluch Nationalist Army which mostly operates in southwestern Baluchistan Province.

January 5, 2024: Gunmen killed Sunni Muslim cleric Masoodur Rehman Usmani and wounded his driver in Ghauri Town, an Islamabad suburb. Thousands attended his funeral in a busy commercial area in Islamabad. No one claimed credit. Usmani was a deputy secretary at the Sunni Ulema Council.

January 8, 2024: *Al-Jazeera* reported that in the early morning, a bomb targeted a police vehicle during a polio vaccination drive in Bajaur tribal district in Khyber Pakhtunkhwa Province, killing five police officers and wounding nearly two dozen, five critically. The Pakistani Taliban claimed responsibility, as did ISIS.

January 10, 2024: At dawn, a dozen gunmen attacked the Lachi checkpoint along the Indus Highway in Kohat district in Khyber Pakhtunkhwa Province bordering Afghanistan, killing three police officers and a civilian before fleeing. The Pakistani Taliban was suspected. No one claimed credit.

January 13, 2024: A bomb went off under the vehicle of security forces during an operation in Kech District in Baluchistan Province. Gunmen then fired on the troops, killing five Pakistani soldiers, aged between 23 and 25. Authorities killed three terrorists. No one claimed credit.

Security forces killed four suspected terrorists in Khyber Pakhtunkhwa Province and seized weapons, ammunition, and explosives. The army claimed they had conducted terrorist attacks against security forces, and extorted and killed civilians.

January 16, 2024: *CNN* and *Tasnim* reported that Pakistani authorities charged that an Iranian air attack on two strongholds of the Sunni separatist group Jaish al-Adl (Army of Justice), known in Iran as Jaish al-Dhulm, in the Kouh-Sabz (green mountain) area of Pakistan's southwest Balochistan Province killed two children and injured two women and a teenage girl. Jaish al-Adl claimed that Iran's Revolutionary Guards fired six attack drones and several rockets to destroy two houses where the children and wives of its fighters lived.

January 18, 2024: *CNN* and *Tasnim* reported that Pakistan conducted military strikes against what it said were separatist militant hideouts inside Iran's southeastern Sistan and Baluchistan Province in Operation Marg Bar Sarmachar (Death to Guerrilla Fighters), killing several terrorists. *IRNA* reported that Sistan and Baluchistan Province Deputy Governor Alireza Marhamati said nine people were killed in the 4:30 a.m. strikes, including three women and four children. Another explosion took place near Saravan, causing no casualties.

January 22, 2024: Security forces killed seven gunmen in a shootout in Zhob district in southwestern Baluchistan Province near the border with Afghanistan. The military recovered munitions after the shootout.

January 29, 2024: At 9 p.m., the Baluchistan Liberation Army fired rockets in retaliation for strikes by Pakistan on insurgent hideouts in Iran, killing a police officer and wounding 15 members of the Pakistani security forces. Six gunmen died in the ensuing 12-hour shootout in the Mach district of Baluchistan. *Al-Jazeera* reported that four security officials died.

January 30, 2024: A roadside bomb killed three supporters of former Prime Minister Imran Khan, who is serving a prison term for graft. Five others were injured in the Sibi district of Baluchistan Province. Khan supporters on motorcycles were passing through a bazaar to attend an election rally. No one claimed responsibility.

February 5, 2024: *AP* and *al-Jazeera* reported that at 3 a.m., gunmen fired rockets, guns, and grenades at a police station in the Chodwan area of Dera Ismail Khan district in Khyber Pakhtunkhwa Province, killing 10 officers and wounding six, including police officer Naseeb Khan, who sustained bullet injuries in his hand, and officer Sharaf Khan, before fleeing. Tehreek-e-Taliban Pakistan (TPP) claimed responsibility for the hours-long attack.

February 7, 2024: Bombs hit two political offices in Baluchistan Province, killing 29 people and wounding more than two dozen, a day before scheduled parliamentary elections. Some 17 people died and more than 20 were wounded, some critically, in an attack at independent candidate Asfandyar Khan's election office in the Pashin. A second bombing killed 12 people at the office of a leading radical Islamist party in Qilla Saifullah, about 130 kilometers (80 miles) away. Eight people were wounded.

February 27, 2024: During a morning gun battle in Mardan in Khyber Pakhtunkhwa Province, two wanted Pakistani Taliban members and police superintendent Ijaz Khan, who was leading the raid on a militant hideout, died. Two other police officers were wounded. The dead Taliban were wanted for more than 20 attacks on security forces.

March 10, 2024: *Al-Jazeera, Geo News TV,* and *AP* reported that a motorcycle carrying between nine and eleven pounds of explosives prematurely blew up near the Board Bazaar area of Peshawar, killing two people and critically wounding one man, who was admitted to Lady Reading Hospital. The suspected bomber was also killed.

March 16, 2024: *AP, al-Jazeera,* and *Reuters* reported that a suicide truck bomber crashed into a sprawling military post in in North Waziristan district in Khyber Pakhtunkhwa Province, killing five soldiers. A portion of a military post collapsed. Another two soldiers died in an ensuing shootout. Responding troops killed six more attackers, some of whom were wearing suicide vests. The newly-formed Jaish-e-Fursan-e-Muhammad claimed credit.

March 20, 2024: *AP* and *al-Jazeera* reported that security forces killed eight separatists as they repulsed an attack on a sprawling government building outside the Chinese-funded Gwadar port in Baluchistan Province. Three security forces were killed and two injured. All Chinese nationals working at the port were reported safe. At 4 p.m., a suicide bomber set off his vehicle bomb near a complex of the Gwadar Port Authorities. Terrorists with hand grenades then attacked security forces, who fired back during the two hours of fighting. The Majeed Brigade, the armed wing of the separatist Baluchistan Liberation Army, claimed credit.

March 21, 2024: A roadside bomb hit a security convoy in Dera Ismail Khan in Khyber Pakhtunkhwa Province, killing two soldiers and wounding 15 others. The Pakistani Taliban was suspected.

Security forces killed an insurgent commander and wounded two others in an operation in Panjgur district in Baluchistan Province.

March 25, 2024: Gunmen from the outlawed Baluchistan Liberation Army tried to sneak into the Siddiqui navy air base in Turbat district in Baluchistan Province. A soldier and four attackers were killed.

March 25-26, 2024: Security forces killed four insurgents in an overnight raid on a militant hideout in Dera Ismail Khan district in Khyber Pakhtunkhwa Province. Troops found a cache of weapons, ammunition, and explosives.

March 26, 2024: *Reuters* and *AP* reported that a suicide bomber crashed his vehicle into a convoy of Chinese engineers working on the Dasu Dam project in Balochistan Province, killing five Chinese nationals and a Pakistani driver. Regional police chief Mohammad Ali Gandapur said that the engineers of the construction firm China Gezhouba Group Company (CGGC) were en route from Islamabad to their camp at the dam construction site in Dasu in the Khyber Pakhtunkhwa Province. No one claimed responsibility for the attack in Shangla. The Pakistani Taliban denied involvement. Pakistan announced the next day that investigators would perform DNA testing on the bomber's remains.

AP reported on April 1, 2024 that Pakistani counterterrorism police in multiple raids arrested 12 suspects who helped those who orchestrated the bombing. Some of them had links with Pakistani militants. Officials said some of the detainees transported an explosive-laden car to Shangla.

AP reported on May 24, 2024 that Pakistan announced that it would pay $2.58 million in compensation to the families of the five Chinese engineers. The family of the Pakistani driver who was killed would receive $8,950. The Taliban denied Pakistan's claims that the attack was planned in Afghanistan and the bomber was an Afghan citizen.

March 30, 2024: A bomb killed one person and wounded 14, including three soldiers in Hernai district in Baluchistan Province when a team from Mari Petroleum Company was conducting a gas exploration survey. No one claimed credit.

April 2, 2024: *Al-Jazeera* reported that envelopes containing a suspicious white powder were sent to the eight judges of the Islamabad High Court, with a note in English criticising the "justice system of Pakistan" and mentioning bacillus anthracis, a bacteria that can cause anthrax, which can be fatal if not immediately treated.

April 3, 2024: *Al-Jazeera* reported that envelopes containing a suspicious white powder were sent to four Supreme Court judges, including Chief Justice of Pakistan Qazi Faez Isa, and five judges of the Lahore High Court. Police said the lesser-known Tehreek-e-Namoos Pakistan claimed responsibility.

April 5, 2024: Security forces killed eight militants in Dera Ismail Khan district in Khyber Pakhtunkhwa Province during the night. Authorities recovered weapons, ammunition, and explosives.

April 6, 2024: Gunmen fired on a police vehicle, killing a deputy superintendent and a constable and injuring another two people in Lakki Marwat district in Khyber Pakhtunkhwa Province. Umar Marwat, a TTP commander from the district, claimed responsibility for the attack and alleged the deputy superintendent had been active in operations against the TTP in the area.

Security forces killed eight militants in Dera Ismail Khan district in Khyber Pakhtunkhwa.

April 7, 2024: A motorcycle bomb in Khuzdar, Baluchistan Province, killed two people and wounded five including a woman and two police officers. No one immediately claimed responsibility.

April 12, 2024: Masked gunmen killed two people and wounded six in a car that blew past a blockade they had erected. Down the road near Nushki, they stopped a bus carrying 70 people en route from Quetta to Taftan and went through passengers' IDs. They kidnapped nine people from Punjab Province, fled into the mountains of Baluchistan Province, and killed them. Police found the nine bodies under a bridge three miles from the highway. The killers escaped. There was no immediate claim of responsibility and no ransom demand.

April 17, 2024: Security forces killed seven militants trying to sneak into the country from Afghanistan. Authorities found them near the Ghulam Khan border town in Khyber Pakhtunkhwa Province.

April 18, 2024: During the evening, gunmen ambushed a vehicle carrying officials from the customs department in Dera Ismail Khan district in Khyber Pakhtunkhwa Province, killing four of them before fleeing. No one immediately claimed responsibility.

Gunmen killed Afghan Taliban religious scholar Mohammad Omar Jan Akhundzada inside a mosque in Quetta. No one claimed responsibility. Chief Afghan Taliban spokesperson Zabihullah Mujahid said he taught at a jihadi seminary in Afghanistan's Kandahar Province and was a member of the Taliban oversight committee of Islamic scholars.

April 19, 2024: *AP, al-Jazeera,* and *Los Angeles Times* reported that a suicide bomber on a motorcycle set off his suicide vest near a bullet-proof van carrying Japanese auto workers in Karachi, killing a bystander and injuring three passers-by—one later died. The Japanese were unharmed. Police escorting the van killed a second attacker. Police corrected their earlier claim that the five worked at Pakistan Suzuki Motors, clarifying that it was another factory. No one immediately claimed responsibility.

April 20, 2024: During the late night, gunmen ambushed customs officials at a checkpoint in Dera Ismail district in Khyber Pakhtunkhwa Province, killing two and wounding three others. No one claimed credit.

April 22, 2024: Pakistani security forces killed ten militants in a raid in Dera Ismail Khan district in Khyber Pakhtunkhwa Province.

Another militant was killed in a second raid in a former stronghold of the Pakistani Taliban in the North Waziristan district in the northwest.

April 27, 2024: Fifteen gunmen on motorbikes intercepted Judge Shakirullah Marwat's vehicle as he was travelling toward Dera Ismail Khan district in Khyber Pakhtunkhwa Province, set his car on fire, and kidnapped him. His driver was unharmed. The kidnappers released a video showing the judge saying that the Pakistani Taliban would not release him until their demands were met. *AP* reported on April 29 that police freed him in a late-night operation.

April 30, 2024: Gunmen fired at a police team protecting polio vaccination workers in Bajaur district in Khyber Pahktunkhwa Province, killing a police officer. No one immediately claimed responsibility.

May 2, 2024: A land mine detonated under a truck passing through a valley in coal-rich Duki district in Baluchistan Province. A second one exploded when counter-terrorism officials and civilians responded. One person died and 18 were wounded. The next day, Baloch Liberation Army separatists claimed credit.

May 3, 2024: In the afternoon, a motorcyclist attached a sticky bomb to a car then rode off. The bomb exploded when the vehicle reached Chamrok Chowk, killing three people, including prominent journalist Muhammad Sadique Mengal, president of the Khuzdar Press Club and a member of the religious JUI-F political party, and wounding seven in Khuzdar in Baluchistan Province. No one claimed credit.

May 8, 2024: Terrorists set off a bomb during the night at the private Aafia Islamic Girls Model School, the only girls school in Shawa in the North Waziristan district of Khyber Pakhtunkhwa Province, badly damaging the structure but causing no injuries. There was no immediate claim of responsibility. Police said the attackers first beat up the school guard.

May 9, 2024: Before dawn, gunmen shot to death seven barbers in a home near the port city of Gwadar in Baluchistan Province. The barbers hailed from Punjab Province and lived and worked together. No one immediately took credit.

May 14, 2024: A drone fired a missile at a house in South Waziristan in Khyber Pakhtunkhwa Province before dawn, killing four villagers, including children. The civilians had no known link to insurgents.

May 16, 2024: During the night, a bomb exploded at a girls' school in South Waziristan district in the Khyber Pakhtunkhwa Province, destroying the structure but causing no injuries. No one claimed credit. The Pakistani Taliban was suspected.

May 27, 2024: Shootouts with suspected Pakistani Taliban gunmen killed seven soldiers and 23 terrorists.

In an overnight clash outside Peshawar, capital of Khyber Pakhtunkhwa Province, six terrorists and two army officers died. Another confrontation in Tank district killed ten gunmen. Five soldiers and seven gunmen died in Khyber district.

May 29, 2024: During the night, terrorists used kerosene to set alight a girls' school in North Waziristan in Khyber Pakhtunkhwa Province, destroying furniture, computers, and books, but causing no injuries. No one claimed credit.

June 3, 2024: Gunmen fired on a team of polio workers in the Wargari area of Lakki Marwat district in Khyber Pakhtunkhwa Province, killing a police officer assigned to protect them. An attacker died; the others fled. No one claimed credit.

June 8, 2024: District police chief Ghulam Moinuddin said a person shot and killed two Ahmadis hours apart in Mandi Bahauddin, a district in the eastern Punjab Province. The next day, police arrested a man who confessed to killings under questioning. He faced murder charges. Amir Mahmood, spokesperson for the Ahmadi community, said the attacker was a student at a seminary, and that a campaign against the Ahmadiyya community is on the rise.

June 9, 2024: A roadside bomb exploded near a security convoy in Lakki Marwat, a district in the Khyber Pakhtunkhwa Province, killing seven soldiers, including an army captain. The Pakistani Taliban was suspected.

June 10, 2024: During the night, security forces raided a terrorist hideout in the Lakki Marwat district in Khyber Pakhtunkhwa Province, killing 11.

June 19, 2024: The separatist Baluchistan Liberation Army claimed credit for kidnapping 10 people from Harnai district in Baluchistan Province.

June 21, 2024: A roadside bomb went off near a security convoy in Kurram district in Khyber Pakhtunkhwa Province, killing five soldiers and wounding two others. The Pakistani Taliban was suspected.

June 26, 2024: Ziaullah Langau, Baluchistan Province's Interior Minister, announced the arrests of Pakistani Taliban senior officers Commander Nasrullah and Commander Idress. The government released a video in which Nasrullah

said he had been a TTP member for 16 years, and that he spent several years in Afghanistan hiding from Pakistani military operations.

July 1, 2024: Baluch separatists were suspected when a roadside bomb exploded among four people walking in Turbat district in Baluchistan Province, killing a woman and two children.

An overnight rocket attack on a security post in Jamrud district in Khyber Pakhtunkhwa Province killed two security personnel. The Pakistan Taliban was suspected.

July 3, 2024: A roadside bomb hit a vehicle in Bajur district in Khyber Pakhtunkhwa Province, killing five people, including former senator Hidayatullah Khan, who was traveling in a convoy to attend an election rally. The Pakistani Taliban denied involvement.

Security forces killed militant commander Irfan Ullah in Bajur. The military said he was involved in numerous past "terrorist activities" and was behind targeted killings of civilians.

July 3, 2024: A roadside bomb hit a vehicle in Bajur district in Khyber Pakhtunkhwa Province, killing five people, including former senator Hidayatullah Khan, who was traveling in a convoy to attend an election rally. The Pakistani Taliban denied involvement.

Security forces killed militant commander Irfan Ullah in Bajur. The military said he was involved in numerous past "terrorist activities" and was behind targeted killings of civilians.

July 5, 2024: A roadside bomb planted on a bridge hit a speeding rickshaw in Mardan district in Khyber Pakhtunkhwa Province, killing three people and wounding seven others. Police believed that a police vehicle crossing the bridge was the target. The Pakistani Taliban was suspected.

July 10, 2024: During a government raid on a Pakistan Taliban hideout in suburban Matni outside Peshawar, three officers and three insurgents, including commander Abdul Rahim, were killed.

July 15, 2024: A suicide car bomber detonated his explosives and at least one accomplice set off his vest near the outer wall of a military facility in Bannu in Khyber Pakhtunkhwa Province in the morning, wounding eight civilians and several soldiers and damaging nearby homes. Security forces stopped insurgents from entering the sprawling military facility. A Pakistani Taliban splinter group, led by commander Gul Bahadur, claimed credit. The Pakistani military said the next day that it had killed all ten attackers in an 18-hour operation.

July 19, 2024: The deputy inspector general of police, Usman Gondal, announced that the Counter-Terrorism Department in Punjab Province arrested near Jhelum Afghan citizen Amin ul Haq, an al-Qaida leader who was a close aide to Osama bin Laden. He was accused of working as a financer for al-Qaida and supplying arms to insurgents.

A roadside bombing in South Waziristan killed two people.

July 29, 2024: Police in Okara in Punjab Province arrested Zaheerul Hassan Shah, deputy chief of the radical Tehreek-e-Labaik Pakistan Islamist party, on the charge of offering 10 million rupees ($36,000) to anyone who beheads Qazi Faez Esa, the Chief Justice at the Supreme Court over his alleged support to the minority Ahmadi community. The previous day, a video showed him making the offer to his followers.

July 30, 2024: Gunmen fired on a bulletproof vehicle carrying local staff working for the United Nations Office for Project Services development agency in Dera Ismail Khan district in the Khyber Province. No one was harmed. The Pakistani Taliban denied involvement.

Clashes between two tribes over a property dispute in the Kurram district killed 49 people.

August 2, 2024: Gunmen ambushed police officers escorting a vehicle that was carrying three judges in Dera Ismail Khan district in Khyber Pakhtunkhwa Province, killing two officers. The judges were unharmed. The judges were hearing multiple cases, ranging from robbery to acts of terrorism in the region.

August 9, 2024: The Gul Bahadur breakaway faction of the Pakistani Taliban claimed credit

for three attacks against army posts in the Tirah Valley in Khyber Pakhtunkhwa Province. Three soldiers and four jihadis died in the ensuing clashes.

August 12, 2024: Baloch Liberation Army gunmen ambushed a vehicle carrying deputy commissioner Zakir Baloch in Mastung district of Baluchistan Province, killing him and wounding two other people before fleeing. No one claimed credit.

On August 20, 2024, *AP* reported that Pakistani security forces shot and killed three gunmen in Mastung who were involved in the killing. The military said the trio were involved in other attacks.

August 13, 2024: The Baloch Liberation Army claimed credit for throwing hand grenades at a house and a store selling Pakistani national flags in Quetta in Baluchistan Province, killing three people and wounding six. Days earlier, the group asked shop owners not to sell the flags. It also warned people not to celebrate the August 14, 1947, date of Pakistan's independence from British colonial rule.

Jihadis killed four security forces in South Waziristan district in Khyber Pakhtunkhwa Province. Troops returned fire, killing six insurgents.

August 15, 2024: During the night, Baluch Liberation Army (BLA) gunmen threw a grenade at people sitting in front of a hotel in Quetta, killing one person and wounding ten.

August 19, 2024: Security forces killed five militants trying to sneak into the country from Afghanistan. Three soldiers were killed in the clash in Bajur district in Khyber Pakhtunkhwa Province.

August 22, 2024: *AP, DPA,* and *al-Jazeera* reported that in the morning, gunmen fired on a school van in Attock in Punjab Province, killing two children and wounding six other people, including five children and the driver, who seemed to be the target of the attack. Local police official Mohammad Shakil said, "Our initial investigations indicate that the driver had an enmity with someone." The children were as young as five.

The attack might have stemmed from a feud between two families, but police were "looking into the possibility of terrorism".

August 22, 2024: During the night, bandits armed with guns and rocket-propelled grenades killed 12 police and wounded eight officers in the Kacha area in Rahim Yar Khan district of Punjab Province. Police killed bandit leader Bashir Shar and wounded five others as they pursued the gang. The officers were trying to fix their vehicle, which had broken down while passing through farm fields flooded by monsoons.

August 24, 2024: *Al-Jazeera, Dawn,* and *Reuters* reported that a remotely-detonated bomb attached to a parked motorcycle went off near a police office in Pishin district, killing two children and injuring 16 people.

August 26, 2024: *Al-Jazeera, AFP, BBC,* and *AP* reported that gunmen in Baluchistan Province killed 38 people, including 14 security forces, in three attacks. Security forces killed 21 insurgents.

During the night, Baluch Liberation Army (BLA) attackers pulled people from 22 buses, vehicles, and trucks in Musakhail, variant Musa Khel, district, checked their identification documents, and shot to death 23 people identified as from Punjab Province. One of them was the husband of Sakina Nazir. They burned ten vehicles, then fled.

In Qalat district, gunmen killed ten people, including five police officers and five passersby, in attacks on a police station and a highway.

Authorities found the bodies of six people in Bolan, where insurgents blew up a railway track.

Gunmen attacked a police station in Mastung district and attacked and burned vehicles in Gwadar district, but caused no injuries.

Hours earlier, the BLA had warned people to stay away from highways in Baluch Province.

In Khyber Pakhtunkhwa Province's North Waziristan district, a roadside bomb killed four people and wounded 12.

Al-Jazeera reported that 70 people died in four assaults. Provincial chief minister Sarfraz Bugti said 53 people, including security forces, were killed in the attacks.

The military said 14 soldiers and police, plus 21 gunmen, were killed in fighting after the largest of the attacks, which targeted vehicles on a major highway in Bela in Lasbela district.

Bombs went off on a rail bridge in Bolan and a rail link to Iran. Police found six bodies near the site of the attack on the railway bridge.

The next day, the BLA claimed credit for the attacks, warning of "even more intense and widespread" attacks. It asserted that it did not harm civilians and claimed that 800 of its fighters took part in the shootings and bombings.

August 28, 2024: Jihadis were suspected of kidnapping Army Lt. Col. Khalid Khan, his two brothers who are also government officers, and one of his nephews, who were sitting in a mosque to receive mourners after attending Khan's father's funeral in Dera Ismail Khan district in Khyber Pakhtunkhwa Province. No one claimed credit. In video statements released hours after they were kidnapped, two of the abductees said they were in the custody of the Pakistani Taliban. Tribal elders secured the release of the four on August 31.

August 29, 2024: Security forces killed 37 insurgents in multiple raids since August 20 on jihadi hideouts in a former stronghold of the Pakistani Taliban. More than a dozen gunmen died in an overnight clash in Tirah Valley in Khyber Pakhtunkhwa Province, which borders Afghanistan. Troops also killed five insurgents in three operations in Balochistan.

September 9, 2024: A roadside bomb hit a vehicle carrying officers assigned to protect health workers conducting a polio immunization drive in South Waziristan district in Khyber Pakhtunkhwa Province, wounding six officers and three civilians. No polio workers were hurt; police appeared to be the target. No group claimed responsibility.

September 11, 2024: Gunmen on motorcycles shot at police escorting a team of polio workers during a door-to-door vaccination campaign in Bajur district in Khyber Pakhtunkhwa Province, killing an officer and a polio worker. No one immediately claimed responsibility.

A roadside bomb hit a vehicle carrying officers assigned to protect health workers conducting polio immunization in South Waziristan district in Khyber Pakhtunkhwa Province, wounding six officers and three civilians. ISIS claimed credit.

September 14, 2024: ISIS claimed credit for setting off a bomb against a Pakistani police vehicle on a highway in Kucklak near Quetta, killing two officers and wounding two others.

September 18, 2024: Police shot to death Shah Nawaz, a doctor in the Umerkot district in Sindh Province, who went into hiding two days earlier following accusations of insulting Islam's Prophet Muhammad and sharing blasphemous content on social media. Local police chief Niaz Khoso said officers signaled two men riding on a motorcycle to stop in Mirpur Khas in Sindh province. Rather than stop, the men opened fire and tried to flee. The police returned fire, killing Nawaz. The other fled on the motorcycle. Local clerics threw rose petals at police and praised officers for killing the blasphemy suspect. A mob had burned Nawaz's clinic that day as well.

September 20, 2024: The Pakistani Taliban was suspected when gunmen killed nine Pakistani troops in separate attacks in the tribal districts of North and South Waziristan in Khyber Pakhtunkhwa Province, which borders Afghanistan. After midnight gunmen hit a military post in Misha, South Waziristan, killing six troops and injuring 11. Gunmen hit a patrol in North Waziristan, killing three security forces.

September 22, 2024: The Pakistani Taliban denied involvement when a convoy escorting foreign ambassadors and their family members was bombed in Malam Jabba, one of Pakistan's two ski resorts in Khyber Pakhtunkhwa Province's Swat Valley. A police officer was killed and four others were wounded. No envoys were hurt. The convoy included ambassadors and officials from Indonesia, Portugal, Kazakhstan, Bosnia and Herzegovina, Zimbabwe, Rwanda, Turkmenistan, Vietnam, Iran, Russia, and Tajikistan.

September 28, 2024: Gunmen raided a rented house in Panjgur in the Punjab area, killing seven male workers from Punjab, all from the same family of Muhamad Mubashir and aged between 20 and 40, and injuring another. Baloch separatists were suspected.

September 29, 2024: In a morning raid, gunmen attacked a camp in Musa Khel district in Balochistan Province and kidnapped 20 laborers who worked for a private energy company. No one claimed credit.

October 2, 2024: In a raid on an insurgent hideout in Harnai district in Balochistan Province, Pakistani security forces killed six members of the Baloch Liberation Army.

October 5, 2024: *Al-Jazeera* and *AP* reported that in an overnight shootout in North Waziristan in Khyber Pakhtunkhwa Province, six Pakistani soldiers, including Lieutenant Colonel Muhammad Ali Shoukat, and six jihadis died.

Another army operation killed two militants in Swat in Khyber Pakhtunkhwa. One terrorist was involved in an attack on a convoy of foreign ambassadors in the area in September.

October 6, 2024: *Al-Jazeera, Geo News,* and *AP* reported that the Junaid Baloch (Baloch Liberation Army) claimed credit for the 11 p.m. suicide bombing of a convoy of Chinese engineers and investors outside Karachi's Jinnah International Airport, killing two Chinese workers and wounding eight people, including a Chinese national and police officers who were escorting the convoy in Sindh Province. Chinese staffers working at the Port Qasim Electric Power Company, which is owned by PowerChina Resource Ltd., a subsidiary of Power Construction Corporation of China, were in the convoy. Four vehicles were destroyed in the bombing. *Geo News* claimed ten people were injured. *Dawn* reported that ten vehicles were damaged. 24100601

October 10, 2024: Suspected jihadis riding a motorcycle shot at a vehicle carrying police officers in Tank in Khyber Pakhtunkhwa Province, killing two of them and wounding two others.

AP and *al-Jazeera* reported that the Baloch Liberation Army was suspected when gunmen killed 21 miners and wounded six others in a raid on miners' quarters at the small private Junaid Coal mine in Duki (variant Dukki) district in Balochistan Province during the night. The attackers shot miners, fired rockets, threw grenades at the mine, damaged machinery, then fled. Most of the casualties were from Pashto-speaking areas of Balochistan. Three of the dead and four of the wounded were Afghan. 24101002

Counterterrorism police announced that gunmen attacked a van transporting two suspects linked to a 2021 bombing that killed nine Chinese nationals and four Pakistanis working on a dam in the northwest. Two suspects who were being moved to a prison in Sahiwal in Punjab Province were killed. No officer was harmed.

October 12, 2024: Tribal clashes in the Kurram district of Khyber Pakhtunkhwa Province killed 11 people and injured eight, including women and children, after two people were critically injured in a shooting incident between rival tribes.

October 20, 2024: In a nighttime attack, two men armed with daggers killed two transgender women at their home in Mardan in Khyber Pakhtunkhwa Province, then fled.

October 24, 2024: Security forces killed nine insurgents in an overnight shootout in Bajur district in Khyber Pakhtunkhwa Province. Troops seized weapons and ammunition. Troops killed another ten gunmen in Mianwali in eastern Punjab Province.

Gunmen used assault rifles and grenades in attacking a security post during the night in Draban in Dera Ismail Khan district in Khyber Pakhtunkhwa Province, killing ten security forces and wounding three. The assailants fled with their dead and wounded.

October 25, 2024: Gunmen ambushed a police vehicle, killing a local police chief and another policeman. No one claimed credit. The Tehrik-e-Taliban Pakistan was suspected.

Gunmen in the Islamabad suburbs fired on three prison vans and briefly freed some supporters of imprisoned former premier Imran Khan. They were being transported to the Attock jail after their appearance in city court. Dozens of other inmates on trial were also in the vans. Police arrested all those trying to escape and later nabbed some of the attackers.

October 26, 2024: A suicide car bomber set off his explosives at a checkpoint in the Mir Ali area of North Waziristan, Khyber Pakhtunkhwa Province, killing four Pakistani security personnel and critically injuring five. TTP was suspected.

A remotely-detonated bomb hit a military convoy in Tank district in Khyber Pakhtunkhwa Province. No casualties were reported.

October 28, 2024: During the night, gunmen killed five construction workers assigned to repair a dam in Banjgur district in Balochistan Province.

October 29, 2024: A small militant group led by Gul Bahadur said that a few days earlier, it had captured a Russian national in Dera Ismail Khan district in Khyber Pakhtunkhwa Province. The group released a photo showing a man sitting with two bearded men. 24102901

Gunmen attacked a health center used in an anti-polio effort in Orakzai district in Khyber Pakhtunkhwa Province, sparking a shootout that killed three terrorists and two police officers. No one immediately claimed responsibility for the morning attack. No polio worker was harmed.

Gunmen attacked a health center in North Waziristan in Khyber Pakhtunkhwa, stole guns from officers, and warned health workers who had gathered there not to take part in the anti-polio campaign.

November 1, 2024: *Al-Jazeera, Reuters, AFP,* and *AP* reported that a bomb attached to a parked motorcycle exploded near a vehicle carrying police officers assigned to protect polio workers in Mastung district in Balochistan Province, killing nine people and wounding 17 others. The bomb hit a motorized rickshaw carrying schoolchildren nearby, killing five children, a police officer, a shopkeeper, and two passersby. No one claimed credit. The Pakistani Taliban was suspected.

November 4, 2024: Pakistani forces killed an insurgent commander in an overnight raid in North Waziristan district in Khyber Pakhtunkhwa Province.

In a second raid, Pakistani forces killed five Pakistani Taliban terrorists trying to sneak from Afghanistan into Pakistan's South Waziristan district. Three insurgents were wounded.

November 6, 2024: A bomb hit a vehicle carrying security forces in South Waziristan district, killing four officers and wounding five others. The bomb also killed five Khwarij (the military's term for the Pakistani Taliban).

Later that day, two schoolchildren walking to school were killed when a mortar exploded near them on a road in the Tirah valley in Khyber Pakhtunkhwa Province.

November 9, 2024: *AP, UPI,* the *New York Times,* and *NPR* reported that at 8:45 a.m., a suicide bomber disguised as a passenger hit a rail station in Quetta, capital of Balochistan Province, killing 26 people, including more than a dozen soldiers and six railway staff, and wounding 62 others, some critically. Nearly 100 passengers were waiting for a train to travel to Rawalpindi from Quetta. The Balochistan Liberation Army claimed credit, saying the attacker targeted troops at the station.

November 13, 2024: Pakistani security forces killed four insurgents in a raid in Kech in Balochistan Province.

Security forces killed eight terrorists and wounded six others in a morning raid on a Pakistani Taliban hideout in North Waziristan.

November 14, 2024: At dawn, a car bomb accidentally detonated at the house in Mir Ali in Khyber Pakhtunkhwa Province of a Pakistani Taliban terrorist, killing two children and five suspected militants. Police official Irfan Khan said that local TTP commander Rasool Jan was fitting a bomb in a car at his house, which collapsed in the explosion. The bomb badly damaged several nearby homes and wounded 14 people, including women.

Security forces raided a hideout of insurgents in Harnai district in Balochistan Province,

sparking a shootout in which a soldier and three insurgents were killed. An army major was killed when a roadside bomb exploded near his vehicle.

A suicide bomber riding a motorcycle set off an explosive device prematurely on a deserted road in Charsadda district in Khyber Pakhtunkhwa Province, killing himself but harming no one else.

November 19, 2024: A suicide bomber set off an explosives-laden vehicle at a perimeter wall of a security post in Bannu district in Khyber Pakhtunkhwa Province during the evening, killing 12 members of the security forces and wounding several others. The military said six "khwarij" (Pakistani Taliban) were killed in a gun battle at the scene. The Hafiz Gul Bahadur breakaway faction of the Pakistani Taliban claimed credit.

November 21, 2024: Gunmen shot at a convoy of 100 vehicles in Kurram district in Khyber Pakhtunkhwa Province carrying Shi'ite Muslims from Parachinar to Peshawar, killing 42 people, all Shi'a, including six women, and wounding 20 others, ten critically. No one immediately claimed credit. Witness Mir Hussain, 35, said he saw four gunmen emerge from a vehicle and open fire on buses and cars for 40 minutes.

November 22, 2024: During a nighttime clash between armed Sunni and Shi'ite groups in Kurram, 37 people were killed and 25 injured. Station house police officer Saleem Shah said gunmen in Bagan and Bacha Kot torched shops, houses, and government property during the battle between the Alizai and Bagan tribes in the Lower Kurram area.

BBC added that by November 24, more than 80 people were killed and 156 wounded in three days of fighting in Kurram. A local administration official told *AFP* that the tallies were 82 dead, including 16 Sunnis and 66 Shi'ites, and 156 injured.

December 7, 2024: Gunmen attacked a Frontier Corps checkpoint in Bagam in the Kurram district, killing six Pakistani security personnel and wounding seven. There was no immediate claim of responsibility.

The military said it had killed 22 Pakistani Taliban in the districts of Tank, North Waziristan, and Thal in Khyber Pakhtunkhwa Province in the previous 24 hours. Six soldiers died in a clash in Thal.

December 17, 2024: Gunmen on a motorcycle fired at a police post in Shangla in Khyber Pakhtunkhwa Province, killing two officers and wounding three others before fleeing. No one claimed credit. Interior Minister Mohsin Naqvi blamed "khwarij" — a term used for Pakistani Taliban.

December 21, 2024: The Pakistani Taliban claimed responsibility in a *WhatsApp* chat group for an early morning attack on a military checkpoint in South Waziristan in Khyber Pakhtunkhwa Province in which it used heavy weapons to kill 35 soldiers and injure 15 others before seizing weapons and a night vision device.

The *New York Times* reported that the Pakistani Interior Ministry had announced earlier in the month that 924 people had died in 1,566 terrorist attacks in the last 10 months. Some 341 terrorists also died. The figures compared with 2,451 people killed in 1,717 attacks in 2013 and 220 dead in 146 attacks in 2020.

Papua New Guinea

February 7, 2023: On February 15, 2023, *Reuters* and *CNN* reported that Papua separatists released images of Christchurch, New Zealand pilot Philip Mark Mehrtens, who had been taken hostage the previous week after he landed a commercial Susi Air charter flight at Paro Airport in the remote Nduga region. His five passengers were released. West Papua National Liberation Army (TPNPB) rebels demanded that authorities acknowledge the independence of the area. The rebels said they had burned the plane.

Reuters added on March 10 that Mehrtens appeared in three videos put out by the armed wing of Free Papua Movement (OPM) separatists calling for the United Nations to mediate in the conflict in the resource-rich region. Rebel spokesman Sebby Sambom said the videos were shot on March 6. Mehrtens said in one video,

"Try not to worry about me I am being taken care of as well as can be expected given the situation... Hopefully we can be together soon." In one video, a separatist called on New Zealand, Australia, the U.S., UK, France, China, and Russia to stop military cooperation with Indonesia.

In April 2023, gunmen attacked Indonesian troops deployed to rescue the pilot, killing six soldiers.

AP reported on April 26, 2023 that West Papua Liberation Army rebels released a video of hostage Mehrtens, saying that recent Indonesian military attacks threatened his safety. He said in the video, "It's almost three months since OPM kidnapped me from Paro. As you can see, I'm still alive and I'm healthy and eating well... Indonesia has been dropping bombs in the area over the last week... Please, there is no need. It's dangerous for me and everybody here."

AP reported on February 7, 2024 that independence rebels led by Egianus Kogoya, a regional commander in the Free Papua Movement Indonesia, expressed their readiness to release Mehrtens. Kogoya said the Indonesian government must allow Papua sovereignty. Terianus Satto, a leader of the Free Papua Movement's armed wing, countered that the West Papua Liberation Army (TPNPB), was willing to let Mehrtens go without preconditions and expected the United Nations to facilitate. The rebels released videos of Mehrtens, who said the date was December 22.

On September 17, 2024, the gunmen said they were willing to talk about a release involving media coverage.

AP reported on September 20, 2024 that independence fighters led by Egianus Kogoya warned that recently increased Indonesian military attacks to rescue Mehrtens from his captors could threaten his safety.

AP and *BBC* reported on September 21, 2024 that the rebels freed Mehrtens, now 38, in Yuguru in the Maibarok district. He was then flown to Timika.

February 19, 2023: *VOA* and *Reuters* reported on February 26 that Australian archaeologist Professor Bryce Barker and Papua New Guinea female researchers doctoral student Teppsy Beni from the University of Southern Queensland,

and Papua New Guinea National Museum researcher Jemina Haro were released after a ransom payment to 20 armed men who had kidnapped them a week earlier in Fogomaiyu village in a remote area of Mount Bosavi. The kidnappers remained at large. The kidnappers had demanded a ransom of 3.5 million kina ($960,000).

Cathy Alex had been captured with the others but released on February 22. She was on leave from her job as a project coordinator for the PNG Women Leaders Network in Port Moresby.

Police initially said the criminals were from Komo in Hela and had a grievance over logging operations. 23021901

February 18, 2024: *Al-Jazeera* reported that tribal violence involving the Ambulin and Sikin tribes armed with AK47 and M4 rifles killed 64 people in the northern highlands. Police told the *Post-Courier* newspaper that the killings began at dawn in the Wapenamanda District of Enga Province. The *Australian Broadcasting Corporation (ABC)* said violence between the same tribes killed 60 in Enga Province in 2023. *AFP* reported that the military deployed 100 troops to the area. *AP* reported that at least 26 combatants and an unconfirmed number of bystanders were killed.

July 16-18, 2024: A gang of 30 young men attacked three remote northern villages, killing 26 people in Angoram district on the crocodile-infested Sepik River. Another eight people were missing. Authorities attributed the violence to contested land ownership and sorcery allegations. U.N. Commissioner for Human Rights Volker Turk said the dead included 16 children.

September 15, 2024: During several days of tribal violence pitting illegal miners in the Porgera Valley near the New Porgera gold mine in Enga Province, 35 people were killed. A UN humanitarian adviser for PNG, Mate Bagossy, said up to 50 people died. The *Post-Courier* newspaper reported that homes and businesses in Suyan were razed.

PHILIPPINES

March 4, 2023: *AP, Manila Times,* and *UPI* reported that six gunmen wearing military camouflage uniforms and bulletproof vests killed Roel Degamo, governor of Negros Oriental Province, and five others while he was meeting villagers in the morning at his home in Pamplona. The *New York Times* reported that authorities arrested three suspects, all aged between 40 and 50, hours later; two were former soldiers. Police seized a .45-caliber pistol and ammunition.

AP reported that on March 21, 2024, East Timor police in Dili, relying on an Interpol Red Notice, arrested former Filipino congressman Arnolfo Teves, Jr., who is accused of masterminding the killings of a provincial governor and several others. Philippine Department of Justice officials said he would be deported to the Philippines. He had tried to seek asylum in East Timor. He faced murder charges in connection with the killings by six men armed with assault rifles and wearing military camouflage and bullet-resistant vests of Roel Degamo and eight other people, including some seeking aid at his home in Pamplona town, in March 2023. Police said 17 others, including a doctor and two army soldiers, were wounded in the attack on Degamo's residential compound. The gunmen fled in three SUVs. Teves claimed that he was set up.

Teves was also implicated in the killings of three people in 2019 in Negros Oriental and violations of the country's gun and explosives law. Authorities found assault weapons and ammunition in his family's residential compound.

June 14, 2023: *Al-Jazeera* reported that more than 100 officers from five Philippine army and police battalions killed regional ISIS leader Abu Zacharia, aliases Jer Mimbantas and Faharudin Hadji Benito Satar, who was known as the Emir of ISIL in Southeast Asia and headed the Dawlah Islamiya Maute (DI-Maute), and Abu Morsid, the DI-Maute group's logistics mastermind, in an early morning raid that lasted five hours on two rented flats in Marawi on Mindanao island. One soldier was wounded in the leg.

Abu Zacharia was a nephew of Alim Abdul Aziz Mimbantas, vice chairman for military affairs with the Moro Islamic Liberation Front.

Abu Zacharia split from his influential family in 2012, when the MILF signed a preliminary peace agreement and called for autonomy via political means vice violence. He joined DI-Maute with brothers Omar and Abdullah Maute. In 2016, Abu Zacharia helped DI-Maute seize control of his birthplace, Butig in Lanao del Sur, and in 2017, the group attacked Marawi city. In 2022, he succeeded Owaida Marohombsar (Abu Dar) as DI-Maute's leader.

October 4, 2023: *Bloomberg* and the *Voice of America* reported that the Philippines Air Traffic Service put 42 airports on "heightened alert" after receiving an e-mailed bomb threat against airplanes from Manila bound for the tourism hubs of Puerto Princesa, Palawan, Cebu, Bicol, and Davao.

December 3, 2023: *AP* and *CNN* affiliate *CNN Philippines* reported that an explosion at a Sunday morning Catholic Mass service being held in a Mindanao State University gymnasium in Marawi, a predominantly Muslim city on the southern island of Mindanao, killed four people and injured 50. Philippine President Ferdinand Marcos, Jr., blamed unnamed "foreign terrorists". Police said the bomb was made from a 60 mm mortar round. The explosion hit students and teachers. Two days earlier, military airstrikes and artillery fires killed 11 suspected ISIS-affiliated Dawlah Islamiyah terrorists near Datu Hoffer in Maguindanao Province.

Al-Jazeera and *CNN* added that ISIS posted on *Telegram*, "The soldiers of the caliphate detonated an explosive device on a large gathering of Christian disbelievers… in the city of Marawi." *GMA News* quoted police as saying that they were investigating two people of interest.

January 25, 2024: Philippine troops killed nine suspected Dawlah Islamiyah jihadis in the hinterland village of Taporug near Piagapo town in Lanao del Sur Province, including two key suspects in a bomb attack on December 3, 2023 that killed four Christian worshippers and wounded dozens. Four army scout rangers were slightly wounded in the clashes with 15 gunmen. Eight bodies were identified, including those of Saumay Saiden and Abdul Hadi, who were among the suspects in the bombing during Sunday Mass in a state-run university gymnasium in southern Marawi city. Hadi allegedly assembled the bomb, which police investigators said consisted of a 60 mm mortar round and a rifle grenade.

February 18, 2024: A gun battle between Philippine troops and Dawlah Islamiyah terrorists killed seven soldiers and two rebels and wounded four other soldiers near Munai in Lanao del Norte Province.

April 22, 2024: During an hour-long firefight in a marshy hinterland in Datu Saudi Ampatuan in Maguindanao del Sur Province, Philippine troops killed Mohiden Animbang, alias Karialan, leader of the small Bangsamoro Islamic Freedom Fighters; his brother, Saga Animbang; and ten of his men blamed for past bombings and extortion. Authorities recovered a dozen firearms. Seven soldiers were wounded.

April 24, 2024: Philippine police, backed by military intelligence agents, killed Abu Sayyaf terrorist Nawapi Abdulsaid, alias Khatan, who had been implicated in 15 beheadings, including of 10 Filipino marines in al-Barka in 2007 and two of six Vietnamese sailors kidnapped from a passing cargo ship near Sumisip town in 2016, in a nighttime clash in Hadji Mohammad Ajul on Basilan island. Abdulsaid was also involved in attacks against government forces in 2022 and a bombing in November 2023 that killed two pro-government militiamen and wounded two others in Basilan.

June 28, 2024: Philippine soldiers battled 20 New People's Army gunmen, killing ten, including three commanders, near a village in Pantabangan town in Nueva Ecija Province. The army seized 13 rifles and a pistol.

October 17, 2024: During the night, gunmen armed with M-16 rifles and disguised as police officers kidnapped Vermont resident and U.S. citizen Elliot Onil Eastman, 26, in Sibuco in Zamboanga del Norte Province, shooting him in the leg as he tried to resist. They threw him into a speedboat and sped away toward Basilan or Sulu Province. Sibuco resident Abdulmali Hamsiran Jala told to police that four black-clad gunmen armed with M16 rifles took Eastman.

On October 29, 2024, Philippine police arrested three suspects and believed Eastman was alive. Two suspects surrendered separately and pointed to a third suspect, who was arrested in Sibuco. Three other suspects were at large. Authorities filed criminal complaints of abduction against the six suspects. The suspects belonged to a criminal group and not to any armed Muslim rebel group.

Eastman had lived in Sibuco for five months and recently returned to attend the graduation of his Filipino wife.

Three suspects were killed in a gun battle with police in the south in November 2024.

AP reported on December 5, 2024 that police officials were checking reports Eastman died after being shot twice in the thigh and abdomen while resisting. A relative of a kidnapper said they decided to throw Eastman's body into the sea after he died. The next day, *Philippines News Agency* and *CNN* reported that a witness claimed he was shot during a struggle with his captors.

October 30, 2024: A clash regarding a dispute regarding 716 acres of agricultural land between two commanders of the Moro Islamic Liberation Front in Kilangan village in Pagalungan town in Maguindanao del Sur Province killed 14 people and wounded dozens.

November 23, 2024: *AP* and *UPI* reported that Philippine Vice President Sara Duterte, 46, announced that she had hired an assassin to kill President Ferdinand Marcos, Jr., 67, his wife Liza Araneta-Marcos, and House of Representatives Speaker and the president's cousin Martin Romualdez if she herself is killed, in a public threat that she warned was not a joke. Duterte resigned from the Marcos Cabinet in June 2024 as education secretary and head of an anti-insurgency body. She is the daughter of former President Rodrigo Duterte, who told a public Philippine Senate inquiry in October that he had maintained a "death squad" of gangsters to kill other criminals when he was mayor of Davao. Marcos, Jr. is the son of Ferdinand Marcos, who was president from 1965 to 1986.

SOUTH KOREA

January 17, 2023: *Yonhap* reported on February 16, 2023 that an Uzbek man, 31, and a Kazakh man, 29, both residing in South Korea, were arrested for funding the al-Qaeda-linked terrorist group Katibat al-Tawhid wal Jihad using cryptocurrency. The National Office of Investigation of the National Police Agency sent them to the Supreme Prosecutor's Office on January 17 on charges of breaking the anti-terrorism and anti-terrorist funding acts. The U.N. designated KTJ as a terrorist group in March 2022. Seven other foreigners who funded KTJ with the two suspects were deported in December 2022. The Uzbek was suspected of collecting 10 million won (U.S.$7,770) from other foreigners in Yeongam, South Jeolla Province, since August 2021. The Kazakh allegedly sent 1 million won worth of cryptocurrency to KTJ.

August 3, 2023: The *Washington Post, al-Jazeera, CNN, Reuters,* and *KBS* reported that a man, 22, rammed a car into pedestrians, hitting five, then stabbed nine people near Seohyeon subway station in Seongnam. Police Commissioner General Yoon Hee-keun said authorities were treating the incident as a "terror act" and an indiscriminate attack on civilians. Police arrested the attacker.

August 4, 2023: *Al-Jazeera* and *UPI* reported that Daejeon Metropolitan Police Agency police arrested a man in his late 20s who stabbed a high school teacher, 49, in the face, chest, and arm at 10 a.m. with a knife in Daejeon. The individual waited for the teacher to step out of a classroom at Songchon High School before stabbing him and fleeing. The teacher underwent surgery and was reported in critical condition. Police arrested a man carrying a knife near a bus terminal in Seoul's Gangnam area.

August 5, 2023: The *New York Times* reported that authorities detained seven people on suspicion of threatening to conduct stabbings similar to those experienced in the previous two days. Some people turned themselves in. Authorities arrested a boy, 14, in the Seoul suburb of Hanam in Gyeonggi Province. He posted that he would kill people outside a subway station the next day. Police arrested him on August 4 while he was walking around the station. He claimed he was "just bored and posted it as a joke". The threats specified times and locations, including other Seoul subway stations and an amusement park south of Seoul. One threat was for Seoul's Gangnam area in the Seongdong district, and another in the Gwanak area. Yoon Young-joon, head of the Seoul Metropolitan Police Agency, said five people were arrested in Seoul. The threats were posted on social media between July 24 and August 5.

October 31, 2023: *Al-Jazeera* and *Yonhap News Agency* reported that police arrested a man, Park, 77, who stabbed two police officers who asked him to move past the Ministry of National Defense, which houses the presidential compound. He stabbed one in the abdomen and the other in the left arm.

January 2, 2024: *CNN, Politico, Insider, Yonhap,* and *YTN Television* reported that South Korea's main opposition Democratic Party leader Lee Jae-myung, 59, was attacked with a knife while speaking to reporters during a tour of the construction site of the Gadeokdo New Airport in Busan. He was stabbed on the left side of his neck, damaging his jugular vein. *UPI* reported that Lee was airlifted to a hospital in Seoul, where doctors performed a revascularization. *AP* reported that the attacker appeared to be seeking an autograph. Democratic Party officials subdued the attacker before police detained him. Videos showed the suspect wearing a paper crown reading "I'm Lee Jae-myung". The suspect, Kim, 66, told investigators that he bought the seven-inch knife online. *AP* reported that police were expected to request that the suspect be formally arrested for alleged attempted murder because he told investigators he intended to kill Lee. Lee lost the 2022 presidential election to now-President Yoon Suk Yeol by 0.7 percentage point, the narrowest margin recorded in a South Korean presidential election. Lee faced a series of corruption allegations and other criminal charges, including the allegation that he gave private developers illegal favors while he was mayor of Seongnam. He also served as governor of Gyeonggi Province.

AP reported on January 10 that the suspect told investigators that he wanted to kill Lee to prevent him from becoming the country's president and was dissatisfied with authorities' failures to punish Lee for corruption. Lee was released from the hospital after eight days of treatment, including surgery. The suspect left an eight-page note regarding such motives. Police said the suspect bought an outdoor knife in April 2023 and followed Lee to five events since June 2023. A Busan court approved an arrest warrant for him for attempted murder.

AP, al-Jazeera, and *Yonhap* reported on July 5, 2024 that the Busan District Court sentenced Kim, 67, to 15 years in prison.

Sri Lanka

October 23, 2024: *CNN* and *The Guardian* reported that the U.S. and Israel warned of a potential terrorist attack on tourist locations in the Arugam Bay coastal area. Israel's National Security Council directed Israeli citizens to "immediately leave Arugam Bay and the south and west coastal areas of Sri Lanka…The travel alert for Arugam Bay and the coastal areas in south and west Sri Lanka (including for the cities Ahangame, Galle, Hikkaduwa and Weligama) has been raised to level 4… We recommend leaving these areas immediately. For those currently in these areas, we recommend leaving the country or at least traveling to the capital city Colombo, where there is heavier presence of local security forces." Israeli citizens should "avoid openly exhibiting anything that could identify you as Israeli, such as t-shirts with Hebrew writing, or any symbol that discloses your religion or nationality." The UK and Australia also updated their travel advisories. *AP* reported the next day that Sri Lankan police arrested three people.

Thailand

April 22, 2023: *AP* and *al-Jazeera* reported that gunmen fatally shot former lieutenant colonel Sai Kyaw Thu, deputy director-general of the military-appointed Union Election Commission, in his car in eastern Yangon's Thingangyun

Township. He was hit numerous times in the chest, neck, and head. For The Yangon, possibly part of the People's Defense Force urban guerrilla group, the armed wing of the pro-democracy National Unity Government, claimed credit. The Yangon posted on *Facebook* "Mission: Accomplished" along with three photos of their target. For The Yangon claimed Sai Kyaw Thu had been a plaintiff in the election fraud case against Nobel winner Aung San Suu Kyi, who was sentenced to three years in September 2022. A member of the group texted that Sai Kyaw Thu was assassinated "for being the deputy director-general of the illegal election commission of the military council, which disrespected the votes of the people in 2020 general election and abused the people unjustly, and also for being the one who falsely prosecuted President Win Myint and Aung San Suu Kyi as an accessory of the military council".

October 3, 2023: *UPI* and *Channel News Agency* reported that a gunman, 14, killed three people and injured four at the four million square foot upscale Siam Paragon shopping mall on Rama Road in central Bangkok's Pathum Wan district at 4:20 p.m. One non-Thai was hurt. The gunman surrendered. Police recovered a hand gun from the scene.

July 16, 2024: The *Washington Post, CNN, BBC,* and *UPI* reported that cyanide poisoning was suspected when six people of Vietnamese descent, two of them U.S. citizens and four with Vietnamese citizenship, were found dead on the fifth floor of the five-star Grand Hyatt Erawan hotel in Bangkok at about 4 p.m. The three men and three women were believed to have been dead for 24 hours. There was no immediate sign of robbery or assault. Police were looking for a seventh person who is said to be part of the hotel booking. Cups of coffee and tea with traces of white powder were found in the room. *CNN* reported that there was a dispute linked to bad investments. Traces of cyanide were found in the teapot, all six coffee cups, and the blood of the victims.

November 20, 2024: *BBC* reported a court in Bangkok sentenced Sararat Rangsiwuthaporn, alias Am Cyanide, 36, for putting poison in

the food and drink of Siriporn Khanwong, 32, a wealthy friend while they were on a trip to a Buddhist protection ritual at a river in Ratchaburi Province in April 2023. An autopsy found traces of cyanide in the victim's body. She was accused of murdering 14 friends with cyanide since 2015. Thai media quoted police as indicating that she had a gambling addiction and targeted friends she owed money to, then stole their jewelry and valuables. Her former husband, Vitoon Rangsiwuthaporn, an ex-police officer, and her lawyer, were sentenced to one year and four months, and two years, respectively, for hiding evidence. Police said the ex-husband most likely helped Sararat poison an ex-boyfriend, Suthisak Poonkwan.

Sararat was also ordered to pay Siriporn's family two million baht ($57,667; £45,446) in compensation.

December 13, 2024: *AP, AFP, Bangkok Post, al-Jazeera,* and *BBC* reported that police arrested two suspects—a Thai youth and a man belonging to the Karen National Union (KNU) rebel group—after a bomb was thrown into a crowded dance floor at 11:30 p.m. during an outdoor performance at an annual Red Cross Doi Loyfa festival in Umphang district in Tak Province that killed three and injured 48, six critically. Defense Ministry spokesperson Thanathip Sawangsang said that there was a fight between rival groups of men before the explosion and that there was no wider security threat. Tak police chief Major-General Samrit Ekamol said the Myanmar suspect threw the bomb after encountering a "rival gangster" he had previously fought with. A senior KNU official denied involvement.

AUSTRALIA/OCEANIA

AUSTRALIA

July 29, 2023: *UPI*, the *Washington Post*, and *CNN* reported on November 2, 2023 that Victoria Police announced that Australian woman Erin Patterson, 49, was charged with three counts of murder and five counts of attempted murder for a July 29, 2023 incident in which three people died after consuming a beef Wellington lunch made with allegedly poisonous death cap mushrooms (*Amanita phalloides*), and for a series of incidents between 2021 and 2022 in which a 48-year-old Korumburra man became ill after eating meals she allegedly served. She was the only adult at the lunch who did not fall ill. She was amicably separated from her husband. *Nine News* reported that she was arrested in her home on Gibson Street in Leongatha in southern Victoria.

Gail Patterson, 70, and Don Patterson, parents of Erin Patterson's ex-husband, died in August 2023 while being hospitalized after her July meal. Gail Patterson's sister, Heather Wilkinson, 66, also died. Wilkinson's husband, Reverend Ian Wilkinson, 68, became critically ill but survived and needed a liver transplant. He was released from Melbourne's Austin Hospital in September. Simon Patterson, Erin Patterson's ex-husband, nearly died from stomach issues in 2022. Erin Patterson was expected to appear on November 3, 2023 in the La Trobe Valley Magistrates' Court in Morwell.

November 1, 2023: *UPI* reported that the Australian High Court voted 6-1 to invalidate an anti-terror law used by then Home Affairs Minister Peter Dutton to strip Algerian-born cleric Abdul Nacer Benbrika, who was found guilty on terrorism charges in 2008 for leading a terror cell that targeted Australian landmarks, of his citizenship. Benbrika could possibly be released from prison within weeks. Dutton deprived Benbrika of his citizenship in 2020 just before he was due to be released from a 15-year prison sentence. Benbrika was held in custody since under a post-sentence detention order due for renewal on December 24, 2023.

January 8, 2024: The *Washington Post* reported that the government banned displays of Nazi salutes and symbols, including the Hakenkreuz (swastika) and the double-sig rune associated with the SS; lawbreakers faced a year in prison.

April 13, 2024: *AP, Australian ABC News, NBC News,* and *7News* reported that a homeless man, Joel Cauchi, 40, stabbed five women and one man (Faraz Tahir, a Pakistani refugee who worked at the mall as an unarmed security guard) to death and wounded 12 people, mostly women, including a nine-month-old, at Westfield Shopping Centre in Bondi Junction in the eastern Sydney suburbs before female police inspector NSW Police Inspector Amy Scott fatally shot him. Cauchi's father Andrew, 76, blamed his son's frustration at not having a girlfriend. Cauchi had a history of schizophrenia.

AP, Radio FiveAA, and *Nine Network Television* reported on April 24 that Prime Minister Anthony Albanese made French construction worker Damien Guerot, alias Bollard Man, 31, an Australian permanent resident for his heroism during the attack. Security camera footage showed him standing at the top of an escalator and warding off Cauchi with a plastic barrier post. Guerot's temporary Australian work visa was due to expire in July. Work colleague Silas Despreaux had chased Cauchi and threw a barrier post at the killer. Albanese floated citizenship for Pakistani security guard Muhammad Taha, who was stabbed in the stomach.

On November 12, 2024, *BBC* reported that an inquest determined that Cauchi fatally stabbed six people and injured ten in less than six minutes. Fourteen of those stabbed were female. Cauchi had been off his psychotropic medication since 2019. After sleeping rough in the Maroubra suburb, he entered the mall around 3:30 p.m. He then stabbed, in order, Dawn Singleton, 25; Jade Young, 47; Yixuan Cheng, 25; and Ashlee Good, 38. Good saw Cauchi stabbing her nine-month-old baby girl in her pram, and was further wounded trying to save her child. He next stabbed Faraz Tahir, 30, who died "trying to save others". Cauchi fatally stabbed Pikria Darchia, 55, before being shot dead. No alarm had sounded.

April 15, 2024: *AP, NBC News, 9News,* the *Daily Beast,* and *BBC* reported that during televised 7 p.m. services, a man stabbed Orthodox Assyrian bishop H. G. Mar Mari Emmanuel, 53, at the altar and three congregants at Christ the Good Shepherd Church on Welcome Street in Sydney's Wakely suburb. The injured men were aged between 20 and 70. Parish priest Father Isaac Royel was also injured. One man, 39, was injured in the shoulder while trying to intervene. Police arrested the attacker. In a May 2023 video by the *Australian Broadcasting Corporation* about a campaign targeting the LGBTQ+ community, the bishop said in a sermon that "when a man calls himself a woman, he is neither a man nor a woman, you are not a human, then you are an it. Now, since you are an it, I will not address you as a human anymore because it is not my choosing, it is your choosing." He had also been critical of vaccine mandates and lockdown restrictions. *Reuters* reported that he was ordained a priest in 2009 and a bishop in 2011.

Hundreds of people rioted, turning on police, throwing bricks, concrete, and palings at police, police equipment, and police vehicles. Twenty police vehicles were damaged; 10 were unusable. Some 51 police officers were injured.

CNN and *UPI* reported the next day that police deemed the attack a "terrorist act" by a boy, 16, who himself was injured severely in the hand. *AP* reported on April 19 that police charged the boy with terrorism offenses because of his suspected religious motivation and that the boy traveled up to 90 minutes from his home. He spoke in Arabic about the Prophet Muhammad being insulted. He faced a life sentence. He had a history of knife-related offenses and had seen three psychologists and a school counselor. He was represented by attorney Greg Scragg in child's court. He noted that the boy had a "long history of behavior" consistent with a mental illness or intellectual disability. He was remanded to a children's detention center once released from the hospital. His next court hearing was scheduled for June 14.

Sydney mosques received firebomb threats.

UPI reported that on April 23, 2024, police arrested seven male juveniles in raids executed at 13 locations in Sydney and Goulburn across New South Wales. *AFP* noted that another two men and three juvenile males were assisting authorities with their inquiries regarding possible radical religiously-motivated terrorist attack planning. The seven, aged 15 to 17, were part of a network that included the 16-year-old charged in the stabbing.

AP reported on April 29, 2024 that police told the court that four teenagers plotted to buy guns and attack Jewish people days after the stabbing. Attorney Ahmed Dib represented two of the boys.

May 4, 2024: *CNN, BBC,* and *AP* reported that Australian police shot to death a Caucasian male, 16, after he stabbed with a large kitchen knife and seriously injured in the back a man in his 30s in a nighttime attack that had the "hallmarks" of terror in the parking lot of a hardware store in suburban Willetton, a suburb of Perth, Western Australia. Local police at 10 p.m. received a call from a male indicating that "he was going to commit acts of violence." Three police officers ordered him to put down the knife, but the suspect refused, and rushed the police. Two tasers did not subdue him, and a third officer fired a single shot. Police said the teen was "part of a program about online radicalization for the last couple of years." He had been in the Countering Violent Extremism program but had no criminal record.

AP reported on May 6 that police determined that the 16-year-old had no links to an alleged network of teen extremists in Sydney.

June 10, 2024: After 3 a.m., a vandal wearing a dark hoodie used a small sledgehammer to smash nine holes in the reinforced glass windows of the U.S. Consulate building in North Sydney, New South Wales State. Someone painted two inverted red triangles, seen by some as a symbol of Palestinian resistance but by others as supporting Hamas, on the front of the building.

August 5, 2024: The government raised the nation's terrorism threat alert level from "possible" to "probable".

October 19, 2024: Air New Zealand flight 247 stayed on the Sydney Airport tarmac during an hours-long bomb scare in the cabin.

December 6, 2024: *UPI, AP, CNN,* the *Washington Post, Reuters,* and *ABC Melbourne* reported that Victoria Police were searching for two suspected arsonists who torched Adass Israel on Glen Eira Avenue in Melbourne at about 4:10 a.m. Prime Minister Anthony Albanese deemed it "an act of hate" and anti-Semitism. A male witness, who was there to attend morning prayers, sustained minor injuries to his hand. He said the mask-wearing suspects spread an accelerant on the floor. The synagogue, in the Ripponlea suburb, suffered extensive damage. The synagogue was built by Holocaust survivors. The Victoria government offered 100,000 Australian dollars (US$64,300) to help repair the synagogue.

AP reported on December 9 that law enforcement authorities declared the attack to be a terrorist act, thereby increasing resources, information, and legal powers available to the investigation, which was taken over by the Victorian Joint Counter-Terrorism Team which involves Victoria state Police and Australian Federal Police as well as the Australian Security Intelligence Organization. Authorities continued searching for three suspects.

Australian Federal Police announced the formation of Special Operation Avalite to target antisemitism around the country.

NEW CALEDONIA

September 18, 2024: During a police raid in the Saint Louis area near the capital, Nouméa, to apprehend ten indigenous Kanak activists suspected of involvement in deadly unrest, including arson and looting, over attempts by Paris to amend the French constitution and change voting lists in the French Pacific territory, two people were killed. The activists faced charges of complicity in attempted murder, organized theft with a weapon, organized destruction of private property while endangering people, and participation in a criminal group with an intent to plan a crime.

NEW ZEALAND

June 19, 2023: *UPI* reported that a Chinese male, 24, swinging an ax, entered three Chinese restaurants—Zhang Liang Malatang, Yue's Dumpling Kitchen, and Maya Hotpot—on Corinthian Drive in Albany, a suburb of Auckland's North Shore, at 9 p.m. and attacked diners, injuring several of them. Three were hospitalized. He was arrested near the scene and was to appear in North Shore District Court on charges of wounding with the intent to cause grievous bodily harm. He faced 14 years in prison. Police said there was no evidence of a racial motivation.

August 14, 2024: Auckland City Mission, a charity working with homeless people in Auckland, unknowingly distributed pineapple candies filled with a potentially lethal dose of methamphetamine in its food parcels to 400 people after the sweets were donated by a member of the public. Solid blocks of methamphetamine were enclosed in candy wrappers with the label of Malaysian brand Rinda. Three people were hospitalized after consuming them, but were later discharged. The New Zealand Drug Foundation tested the candies and concluded that the amount of methamphetamine in each candy was up to 300 times the level someone would usually take and could be lethal. Foundation spokesperson Ben Birks Ang explained that disguising drugs as innocuous goods was a common cross-border smuggling technique. The candies had a high street value of NZ$ 1,000 ($608) per candy, which suggested the donation was accidental rather than a deliberate attack. Officers recovered 16 of the candies. Eight families, including a child, had reported consuming the contaminated candies.

EUROPE

November 19, 2024: *CNN* reported that European officials suggested Russian responsibility after two submarine Internet cables in the Baltic Sea were suddenly disrupted in an apparent sabotage operation. *Telia Lithuania*, the telecommunications company that runs the link, reported that a cable between Lithuania and Sweden was cut on November 17. The state-controlled Finnish telecoms company *Cinia* said a cable connecting Finland and Germany was disrupted on November 18.

Russia was also suspected of recent arson attacks against a bus garage in Prague, the Museum of Occupation in Riga, Latvia, a warehouse of a Ukrainian company in London, and a shopping center in Warsaw, Poland.

AUSTRIA

March 15, 2023: *USNWR and Reuters* reported that Vienna police bolstered armed patrols at sensitive sites, including churches and other places of worship, after the domestic intelligence agency received information suggesting jihadis were planning an attack.

May 16, 2023: The *Washington Post* reported that the intercom on an Austrian ÖBB national railway train headed toward Vienna ran the voice of Adolf Hitler, delivering a speech and seeming to shout "Sieg Heil!" The firm tweeted that "two unauthorized persons"—neither of whom were members of its staff—were involved. An ÖBB spokesman told *Der Standard* that the duo appeared to have used a key that rail employees have to access the intercom and played the recordings from a cellphone.

June 18, 2023: *Reuters* reported that Omar Haijawi-Pirchner, Austria's domestic intelligence chief, said that security services had thwarted a planned attack on the previous day's Vienna Pride parade. Three suspects between the ages of 14 and 20 were arrested on suspicion of planning to attack the parade, which attracted some 300,000 people. The suspects, all Austrian citizens with Bosnian and Chechen roots, sympathize with ISIS.

August 7, 2024: *CNN* reported that three Taylor Swift Eras Tour concerts were cancelled after authorities arrested two suspects planning an alleged explosives and knives attack in the Vienna region. She was scheduled for three shows at Ernst Happel Stadium in Vienna between August 8-10, averaging 65,000 concertgoers per night, along with 20,000 standing outside the stadium. Police arrested an Austrian male, 19, with North Macedonian roots, believed to be an ISIS sympathizer in Ternitz and another person in Vienna. Authorities said the duo had undertaken "concrete preparatory measures" for a terrorist attack after police suspected explosives were stored at the home of the suspect in Ternitz. Police found chemical substances in the Ternitz resident's home.

CBS News reported on August 8 that authorities found ISIS and al-Qaeda material at the home of the second suspect, an Austrian, 17, with Turkish and Croatian roots. Security officials said the duo wanted to conduct an attack outside the stadium and kill "as many people as possible."

Authorities said the 19-year-old was "clearly radicalized in the direction of the Islamic State and thinks it is right to kill infidels." Franz Ruf, Austria's director general for public security, said that the 19-year-old quit his job on July 25, saying he had "something big planned" and that he planned to detonate a device within the concert venue. Authorities found explosive devices, detonators, extensive ISIS propaganda material, 21,000 euros in counterfeit money, machetes, knives, and anabolic steroids at his home. Prosecutors said he confessed that he had been planning the attack in July.

The other suspect, 17, was employed a few days earlier by a facility company providing services at the venue during the concerts. He had recently broken up with his girlfriend.

Recent ISIS-K propaganda called for attacks on targets in Europe, particularly sports stadiums.

CNN reported on August 9 that Austrian authorities arrested an Iraqi, 18.

A 15-year-old was held and questioned but was soon released.

On August 13, Werner Tomanek, a lawyer for the 19-year-old, said that his client appeared to have mental problems and described him as "a lone wolf without social contacts."

The *New York Times* and *CNN* reported on August 28, 2024 that David S. Cohen, Deputy Director/CIA, said at the annual Intelligence Summit outside Washington, D.C., that the Agency and other U.S. intelligence agencies provided intelligence to Austrian law enforcement authorities regarding four ISIS-connected people who were planning an attack. Some of those arrested had bomb-making material and access to the concert venue. The plot could have killed tens of thousands.

September 10, 2024: Security forces raided 72 alleged Islamic extremists during the week.

BELARUS

March 19, 2023: *Ukrainska Pravda* and *Bel-TA* reported that the Belarusian State Security Committee (KGB) claimed to have killed a foreigner planning a terrorist act on Kurchatov Street in Grodno. He allegedly entered Belarus illegally. The KGB said he battled KGB special unit group 'A' using automatic weapons and detonating combat grenades. No one else was injured.

BELGIUM

May 3, 2023: *Reuters* reported that Belgian police arrested an Iraqi on suspicion of having taken part in a series of bombings in Baghdad as part of an al-Qaeda cell. Prosecutors said he was believed to be partly responsible for several car bombings against several government buildings in the Green Zone of Baghdad in 2009 and 2010, which killed at least 376 people and injured more than 2,300. He had lived in Belgium since 2015. He was born in 1979. Authorities charged him with several murders with terrorist intent, participation in the activities of a terrorist group, war crimes, and crimes against humanity.

October 16, 2023: The *Washington Post, al-Jazeera, CNN, UPI, Le Soir, AP, TT News Agency, VRT, RTBF, AFP,* and *Reuters* reported that a gunman killed two Swedish citizens in a taxi at 7:15 p.m. near Place Sainctelette in the Brussels municipality of Schaerbeek in what the government described as a terrorist attack on Swedish soccer fans. The victims were wearing jerseys of the Swedish Red Devils national team. Authorities raised the terror alert in Brussels to 4, its highest level. The man wore a white helmet and orange fluorescent vest. He arrived at the scene on a scooter. The suspect earlier fired shots at and injured a taxi driver in a lobby, fled, but was shot by police hours later in a cafe in the Schaerbeek area of Brussels after a witness spotted him at 8 a.m. Authorities found an automatic rifle at the scene that matched the murder weapon. Belgium was hosting Sweden at the European Championships 2024 qualifier soccer game at the King Baudouin Stadium three miles from downtown Brussels; the match was postponed at halftime with the score tied 1-1. The Tunisian gunman, Abdesalem Lassoued, 45, posted a video on social media, saying he was inspired by ISIS and killed the Swedes as revenge for "the Muslims" and was targeting Swedes. He said his name was Abdesalem al-Guilani and was a "fighter for God". He had lived in Belgium illegally after his asylum application was denied in 2020. Lassoued was known to Belgian police in connection with people smuggling.

Reuters reported on February 20, 2024 that Italian police searched the homes of 18 North Africans suspected of links to ISIS gunman Abdessalem Lassoued. Carabinieri police and Bologna police said they are suspected of having been in contact online with Lassoued, who lived in Italy between 2012 and 2016.

BOSNIA-HERZEGOVINA

October 24, 2024: A 14-year-old who broke into a police station in Bosanska Krupa in northwest Bosnia at 9 p.m. killed one officer and wounded another in what authorities called an act of terrorism. The individual stabbed the officers.

CYPRUS

June 25, 2023: *Reuters* reported that Israeli Prime Minister Benjamin Netanyahu praised the thwarting of an Iranian attack against Israeli targets in Cyprus. Israeli news website *Ynet* said an attack had been planned against Israelis staying in Limassol.

December 10, 2023: *Haaretz* reported Israel announced that Mossad helped foil an Iranian-ordered attack on Israelis in Cyprus. The *Kathimerini Cyprus* newspaper and *WION* reported that authorities arrested two Iranians linked to the Iranian Revolutionary Guard and believed to be in the early stages of gathering intelligence on potential Israeli targets.

January 5, 2024: *AP* reported on January 11 that before dawn, a bomb exploded outside the office of Doros Polycarpou, leader of the Movement for Equality, Support, Anti-Racism nongovernmental organization, causing extensive damage. The migrants' rights group said it had been threatened on social media and via voicemail by far-right and extremist groups.

October 10, 2024: A court ordered eight Syrians—seven men and one woman—to remain in police detention for six days on suspicion they helped fund a "terrorist organization" in their native country. Charges included breaking of anti-terrorism laws, belonging to a criminal organization, and conspiracy. They were arrested during police raids in Limassol and Paphos.

CZECH REPUBLIC

December 21, 2023: *Al-Jazeera, Czech TV, TV Nora, CNN, NBC News, ABC News, UPI, AP,* and *Reuters* reported that at 3 p.m., a gunman killed 14 people and injured 25, nine seriously, in an attack at the philosophy building of Charles University's Faculty of Arts in Namesti Jan Palach in central Prague near the Old Town, across the Vltava River from Prague Castle and near the 14th-century Charles Bridge. Police said David Kozak, 24, was "eliminated". *UPI* reported that Kozak took his own life when cornered on the roof. Students climbed out of classroom windows and hid on the ledge of the Faculty of Arts building. Czech Police President Martin Vondrášek said the shooter had a gun permit and owned several weapons. Police said that he was a

philosophy student at the university; he was not initially formally identified due to the severity of his injuries. *CNN* reported that the police were tipped off that the suspect was traveling from his hometown of Hostouň to Prague intending to take his own life. Shortly after that, they received information that the suspect's father was found dead in Hostouň. Kozak had a lecture scheduled for 2 p.m. *CNN* added on December 22 that the Department of Musicology announced that its director Lenka Hlávková was among the victims. Czech Minister of Interior Vít Rakušan told *Czech TV* that three foreign nationals were injured. *South China Morning Post* reported that they included two UAE nationals (The *Washington Post* said they were Saudis.) and a Dutch citizen. Czech authorities were investigating whether the gunman was connected to a double homicide the previous week in Prague suburb Klanovice, where a man and a baby were found murdered in a forest. The *Washington Post* reported that Czech police head Martin Vondrášek said Kozak was inspired by a "similar case that happened in Russia" earlier in December, when a Russian teen shot and killed a fellow student before shooting herself in Bryansk.

June 19, 2024: Police arrested a man, 53, who stabbed a motorcyclist in the neck and injured two other people during an attack at a gas station in the Prague 7 district around 3 p.m. Police ruled out terrorism, saying the attack was a drunken local who had a conflict with six people.

DENMARK

December 14, 2023—Germany/Denmark/ Netherlands—*NBC News, AP, CP24, Reuters,* and *WION* reported that authorities in Germany, Denmark, and the Netherlands arrested seven Hamas members planning to conduct terrorist attacks against Jewish institutions in Europe. *NBC* said four of them were longtime members. Authorities said the network had connections with organized crime in Denmark and elsewhere, and with the Loyal To Familia gang. Germany said three people were arrested there. Denmark held two, a man in his 50s, and a woman, 19, and was searching for four others. The Netherlands arrested one suspect in Rotterdam.

January 12, 2024: The Eastern High Court in Copenhagen upheld the sentences of three members of the Iranian separatist Arab Struggle Movement for the Liberation of Ahvaz who were convicted of promoting terror in Iran and gathering information for an unnamed Saudi intelligence service. The trio were arrested in February 2020 in Ringsted. The District Court in Roskilde in February 2022 convicted them of promoting terror for their roles in the attack on a military parade in Ahvaz, Iran in September 2018 that killed 25 people and sentenced the trio to six, seven and eight years in prison, respectively, then be expelled from Denmark. They were also convicted of financing and attempting to finance terrorism by obtaining 15 million kroner ($2.2 million) and trying to obtain another 15 million kroner from Saudi Arabia for the separatist group. The appeals court ordered the revocation of the Danish citizenship of one of the men.

May 29, 2024: *AP* reported that on September 10, 2024 authorities arrested a man, 21, for arson after allegedly setting a fire to balcony furniture at a Jewish woman's home in Copenhagen on May 29. He faced preliminary terrorism charges that could lead to a life sentence, which usually means 16 years in prison. No one was injured. The man pleaded not guilty. The Danish Security and Intelligence Service said he was related to Loyal To Familia, a predominantly immigrant gang in Denmark that was banned in 2021.

June 7, 2024: The *New York Times, AP, CNN, BBC, DR, BT, UPI, TV2, Reuters, Ekstra Bladet*, and *al-Jazeera* reported that around 6 p.m., a Polish man, 39, attacked Danish Prime Minister Mette Frederiksen, 46, in Kultorvet square in central Copenhagen. She suffered a light whiplash injury after being shoved in the shoulder. Frederiksen was taken to Rigshospitalet for a medical check-up. Police arrested the man. The attack came two days before European Union parliamentary elections. Frederiksen was campaigning with the Social Democrats' EU lead candidate, Christel Schaldemose. In 2019, Frederiksen became Denmark's youngest prime minister and was reelected in 2022.

AP reported on July 3, 2024 that a Polish man was charged with assault against a civil servant or a person carrying out a public duty and faced eight years in jail. The suspect was represented by attorney Henrik Karl Nielsen, who said he would plead not guilty. The trial was scheduled for August 6-7 in Copenhagen.

On August 7, 2024, the Copenhagen District Court sentenced the Polish man to four months in jail for assaulting Frederiksen and other charges. He was to be deported and banned from returning to Denmark for the next six years. He had confessed to sexual harassment by exposing himself to passing people and groping a woman at a commuter train station, and fraud involving deposit-marked bottles and cans at two supermarkets.

October 2, 2024: *AP, TT, UPI, TV2, TV4,* and *Ekstra Bladet* reported that authorities arrested three young Swedes, aged between 15 and 20, following two 3:20 a.m. hand grenade explosions at the intersection of Strandagervej and Lundevangsvej, 100 yards from the Israeli Embassy in Copenhagen. One was arrested near the embassy while the two others were detained on a train at Copenhagen's central station. The duo on the train likely faced charges of illegal weapons possession. The nearby Carolineskolen Jewish school closed for the day. No one was injured. The embassy was apparently also hit by gunfire; a weapon and an empty shell casing were found nearby.

AP reported the next day that two Swedish teenagers were jailed in pre-trial detention to last for 27 days on preliminary charges of possessing illegal weapons and carrying five hand grenades. Danish broadcaster *DR* said the detainees, aged 16 and 19, were suspected of acting "in association and together with prior agreement with one or more perpetrators." A third suspect, 19, was released.

On November 7, 2024, *AP, Ekstra Bladet,* and Danish broadcaster *DR* reported that two teens faced preliminary charges of terror. Formal charges were pending.

FINLAND

November 21, 2014: Police detained five suspects, including a dual Finnish-Nigerian citizen born in the 1980s, in connection with separatist violence in southeastern Nigeria. Simon Ekpa, a Nigerian and a leader of the Indigenous People of Biafra separatist movement, lives in Lahti, where the Päijät-Häme District Court was to consider a request from the Finnish National Bureau of Investigation to keep the suspects in custody.

FRANCE

January 11, 2023: *CNN, UPI,* and *ABC News* reported that at 6:42 a.m., an individual injured six people, including a member of the French border police, with a homemade knife in an attack at Paris's Gare Du Nord train station. One person was critically injured. Office-duty police going home, a security agent working for rail operator SNCF, and border police fired multiple shots at 6:43 a.m., critically injuring him.

January 17, 2023: *AFP* reported that that the trial began of 11 men and two women, aged between 26 and 66, who were members of the French far-right Barjols group who allegedly conspired to assassinate President Emmanuel Macron during a WWI commemoration ceremony in November 2018. Prosecutors claimed the suspects planned to kill migrants and attack mosques. On November 6, 2018, police arrested far-right militant Jean-Pierre Bouyer, then 62, and three others suspected of far-right links in the eastern Moselle region. Police found a commando-style fighting knife and an army vest in his car, and firearms and ammunition in his home. The main charge was conspiracy to commit a terrorist act, which carries a maximum sentence of 10 years in prison. The defense team included Lucile Collot and Gabriel Dumenil. Attorney Olivia Ronen represented Bouyer.

The Barjols leader, Denis Collinet, was arrested in 2020.

News 360, Le Progrès, and *Europa* reported on February 2 that the Prosecutor's Office of France requested sentences of up to five years in prison against thirteen members of the Barjols far-right group who planned attacks against officials, migrants, and the assassination of President Macron. Prosecutors said the ringleaders were Mickael Iber and Jean-Pierre Bouyer.

Reuters reported on February 17, 2023 that a Paris criminal court convicted three members of the far-right Les Barjols group of conspiring to prepare an act of terrorism. The trio were sentenced to three to four years in jail, with one to two years suspended each. A fourth man received a suspended six months in prison for possessing a weapon. The other defendants were released.

January 24, 2023: France repatriated 32 minors and 15 adult women, ranging in age from 19 to 56, from former ISIS-controlled areas of Syria.

June 8, 2023: *CBS News, UPI,* and the *Washington Post* reported that around 10 a.m., a man with a knife and wearing a head covering seriously wounded six people, including four children and two adults, in a playground in the Jardins de l'Europe lakeside park in the Pâquier sector in the French Alpine town of Annecy. French newspaper *Le Parisien* and *BFM-TV* said police arrested a Syrian asylum seeker who was born in 1991. *CNN* reported that he was slightly injured. Local newspaper *Le Dauphiné libéré* reported that three of the children were in critical condition. The children were all about three years old and were from a kindergarten class; one was only 22 months old. One child was in a stroller. *AP* reported that one of the children is British; *UPI* said she was 15 months old. Another was either from Germany or the Netherlands. Two were cousins. A Portuguese adult was seriously injured.

One adult sustained knife wounds; a second was stabbed and hit by a shot fired by police.

An eyewitness said the man was speaking English and clearly targeted the children. *Reuters* reported that Abdalmasih, 31, a Syrian asylum seeker, carried Swedish identity documents and a Swedish driving license. He entered France legally and was not known to security agencies.

On June 10, *UPI* reported that Abdalmasih H. was indicted during a court session in Annecy on counts of attempted murder and wielding a knife in committing a criminal act. The Syrian refugee had lived in Sweden since 2013. France had recently refused him asylum because Sweden had granted him permanent residency and refugee status a decade earlier.

French media lauded Henri, 24, the "hero with a backpack", who used his backpacks to fend off H. during the attacks. The Catholic pilgrim was touring French cathedrals.

French Interior Minister Gérald Darmanin told broadcaster *BFMTV* the suspect was "obviously not someone radicalized". The attacker twice shouted "In the name of Jesus Christ" and was wearing a crucifix pendant.

June 21, 2023: The *Telegraph* reported that the French government banned Uprisings of the Earth (SLT), an activist climate group it claimed fomented eco-terrorist violence in a string of recent protests. Supporters include the Nobel Prize winner Annie Ernaux. In March 2023, circa 5,000 protesters battled more than 3,000 police officers during a demonstration against a giant irrigation reservoir near Sainte-Soline in western France.

August 12, 2023: *UPI, The Hill,* and *BFMTV* reported that police twice closed three floors and the forecourt of the Eiffel Tower to investigate bomb threats.

October 13, 2023: *Le Parisien, Reuters, CNN* affiliate *BFMTV,* and *The Telegraph* reported that at 11 a.m., a knife attack killed a French language teacher and wounded three people, two seriously, at City School Gambetta-Carnot in Arras in northern France. The injured included a sports teacher and a security guard. No students were hurt. Police arrested the attacker, 20, a former pupil of Chechen origin who cried "Allahu Akbar" during the attack. He had links to jihadis. His brother was also detained near another school but was found not to be in possession of a weapon. The attacker was known to authorities and was placed on a terror watch list. Police arrested 11 people. On October 19, French President Emmanuel Macron and his wife, Brigitte, attended the funeral for teacher Dominique Bernard, 57, at the cathedral in Arras.

On October 16, *AP* reported that French authorities evacuated the same high school in Pas-de-Calais region after police received a bomb threat via its website.

October 14, 2023: *FranceInfo, Reuters,* and *UPI* reported that the Louvre Museum, the Palace of Versailles, and Paris's Gare de Lyon train station were evacuated in the afternoon after receiving bomb threats.

October 17, 2023: *Reuters* and *CNN* reported that security alerts were issued for eight French airports (Toulouse, Biarritz, and Pau in the southwest, Nice in the southeast, Lyon in the east, Lille in the north, and Rennes and Nantes in western France); several were evacuated for checks. Lille and Toulouse airports were evacuated due to bomb threats. *BFMTV* reported that airports in Nantes and Beauvais, outside Paris, had also been evacuated for security reasons.

The Palace of Versailles was closed a third time in five days because of a security scare.

October 18, 2023: *Reuters* reported that in the early morning, Lyon-Bron airport in eastern France and the airport in Nice were evacuated due to bomb scares.

October 31, 2023: *Reuters, Actu 17, AP,* and the *Daily Beast* reported that Paris police fired one shot at and critically injured a woman wearing an abaya who threatened to blow herself up after allegedly making death threats and speaking in support of terrorism while riding the RER C suburban train heading into the Bibliothèque François-Mitterrand Metro station in the morning. She faced potential charges of making death threats, of defending terrorism, and of intimidating behavior directed at police. Paris police chief Laurent Nunez said she yelled, "You're all going to get it", "Allahu akbar", and "Boom". She was believed to have been arrested previously for threatening behavior in 2021 and then hospitalized for apparent mental health problems.

November 4, 2023: *Reuters, Le Figaro,* and the *Daily Mail* reported that at 1 p.m., a Jewish woman, 30, opened her door after hearing the doorbell, and was stabbed twice in the stomach by a masked man dressed in black who was believed responsible for leaving swastika graffiti at her home in the Montluc district in Lyon's third arrondissement.

December 2, 2023: *CNN, BFM-TV,* and *AP* reported that during the night, a man yelling "Allahu Akbar" attacked people at Bir Hakeim, near the Eiffel Tower in Paris, stabbing to death with a knife a German male tourist born in the Philippines and injuring two others with a hammer. Police arrested a French citizen previously known to intelligence services for having "serious psychiatric disorders". Police twice tased the attacker. Interior Minister Gérald Darmanin said, "After his arrest, he said he could no longer bear to see Muslims dying in both Afghanistan and Palestine." The attacker said France was an accomplice. French President Emmanuel Macron called the incident a terror attack. Emergency doctor Patrick Pelloux was told by the victim's entourage that the suspect stopped them to ask for a cigarette, then stabbed the victim, aiming at his head and back.

The suspect was born in Neuilly-Sur-Seine, France in 1997 and had been sentenced to four years in prison in 2016 for planning "violent action". *Le Parisien* reported that the suspect had a history of contacts via social networks with two men notorious for the murder of a priest during Mass in 2016 in Saint-Etienne du Rouvray and the man who killed a police couple at their home in Yvelines, west of Paris, a month earlier. French media reported that the man, who lived with his parents in the Essonne region, outside Paris, was of Iranian origin. 23120201

December 14, 2023: *Al-Jazeera* reported that led by 2018 Nobel Peace Prize winner Nadia Murad, hundreds of Yazidi Americans launched a class action lawsuit at a court in east New York accusing French cement maker Lafarge of supporting violence carried out by ISIS, which targeted the Yazidis' homeland of Sinjar in northern Iraq in 2014. Murad was kidnapped and held by ISIS for three months. She escaped and fled to Germany, where she worked with survivors of trafficking and genocide. In 2016, she sued ISIS commanders with the help of human rights lawyer Amal Clooney. The plaintiffs are represented by Clooney, former U.S. diplomat Lee Wolosky, and U.S. law firm Jenner & Block.

February 3, 2024: *Al-Jazeera* reported that Paris police arrested a man with a knife and a hammer who allegedly injured three people, one seriously, in a 7:35 a.m. attack at the Gare de Lyon railway station in Paris. The suspect carried residency papers from Italy and medicines suggesting he was undergoing treatment. Paris police chief Laurent Nunez said, "This individual appears to suffer from psychiatric troubles… There are no elements that lead us to think that this could be a terrorist act."

March 1, 2024: At 5:30 p.m., a man physically and verbally attacked another man, 62, who wore a Jewish skullcap, who was leaving a synagogue in Paris's 20th arrondissement. The attacker hit the victim, who fell on the ground and briefly lost consciousness, then fled.

The Interior Ministry and the Jewish Community Protection Service watchdog said that 1,676 antisemitic acts were reported in 2023, compared to 436 in 2022.

March 23, 2024: *CNN* reported that French Prime Minister Gabriel Attal posted on *X*, "Given the Islamic State's claim of responsibility for the attack and the threats weighing on our country, we have decided to raise the Vigipirate posture to its highest level: attack emergency."

April 9, 2024: *BBC, CNN,* and *UPI* reported that a media outlet supporting ISIS published threats against the April 9-10 Union of European Football Associations (UEFA) Champions League quarter-final games in Madrid, Paris, and London. The channel showed images of a gunman standing in front of four Champions League venues—Emirates Stadium in London, the Bernabeu and Metropolitano Stadiums in Madrid, and the Parc des Princes Stadium in Paris—with the words "kill them all." An image shared the previous week depicted the Allianz Arena in Munich. The second round of the Champions League quarterfinal matchups were held on April 16-17 in Dortmund, Germany, Barcelona, Munich, and Manchester.

April 19, 2024: *AP* and *BBC* reported that at 11 a.m., a man wearing a fake explosive vest and making threats entered the Iranian Consulate in Paris. He said he wanted to avenge his brother's death. BRI police detained him at 2:45 p.m. outside the consulate. The suspect said he was born in Iran in 1963. The Paris Criminal Court in October 2023 sentenced him to an eight-month suspended sentence for setting car tires on fire at the gate of the Iranian Embassy in Paris in September 2023. He was banned from carrying a weapon and had a two-year ban on appearing in the 16th arrondissement.

May 17, 2024: The *Washington Post, UPI, AP, AFP, al-Jazeera, Reuters, BBC, BFMTV,* and *CNEWS* reported that police shot to death a male arsonist, 29, who threw a Molotov cocktail into a synagogue in Rouen at 6:45 a.m., significantly damaging the facility but causing no injuries. Police and firefighters found him on the roof of the synagogue "brandishing an iron bar in one hand and a kitchen knife in the other". He threw a chisel at them, jumped to the ground, and ran toward an officer with the knife raised. A police officer, 25, fired five times, hitting him with four bullets. Police said he was of Algerian origin and not a French citizen. His application to stay in the country for medical reasons was denied. He was appealing an expulsion order and was placed on a police wanted list for possible return back to his country.

May 21, 2024: *BBC* and *CNews* reported that Alex G. was detained on suspicion of planning an attack on the Olympic torch relay in Bordeaux, ahead of the Paris Games, which were scheduled to begin on July 26. He had written a disturbing message that "could correspond to glorifying crime" and referred to the killing of six people in their late teens and early 20s by incel Elliot Rodger a decade earlier in Isla Vista, California. Police seized a rubber pellet revolver, several mobile phones, and a computer from his home.

May 22, 2024: *UPI* and *AP* reported that the General Directorate of Internal Security arrested a Chechen man, 18, in his home in St. Etienne on suspicion of being behind a plan to attack spectators and police attending soccer games at the Paris Olympics to be held at the Geoffroy-Guichard stadium in Saint-Etienne. He was indicted May 26 on charges of associating with a criminal group with a view to preparing crimes against a person. On May 31, French authorities raised preliminary terrorism charges against him, accusing him of planning a "violent action" on behalf of ISIS. He had been living in France since he arrived with his family in 2023.

June 3, 2024: *Al-Jazeera* reported that a man sustained serious burns following an explosion. On June 5, the Anti-Terrorism Prosecutor's Office said that the French domestic intelligence agency arrested the Russian-Ukrainian man, 26, on suspicion of planning a violent act. Authorities found at his hotel room "products and materials intended to manufacture explosive devices". On June 7, an investigating judge filed preliminary terrorism charges for participation in a terrorist group, planning criminal attacks, and for possession of explosives materials aimed at preparing an attack in connection with a terrorist group. The defendant arrived in France a few days before his arrest. French media said that he was born in Donbas and had served in the Russian army.

June 19, 2024: An individual hit a cleaning worker several times with a screwdriver and injured a police officer in the arm in the northern Paris suburb of Aubervilliers. Police shot to death the attacker.

July 5, 2024: *BBC, Le Parisien,* and *BFMTV* reported that more than 50 candidates and activists had been physically attacked in the run-up to the July 7 final round of parliamentary elections. They included government spokeswoman Prisca Thevenot, her deputy Virginie Lanlo, and a party activist, who were assaulted as they put up election posters in Meudon.

July 15, 2024: Congo-born Christian Ingondo, 40, stabbed and wounded a French soldier patrolling outside the Gare de l'Est train station in eastern Paris days before the opening ceremony of the 2024 Olympics. The attacker was taken to a psychiatric hospital. The soldier was hospitalized with a shoulder blade injury. Ingondo was under judicial investigation on murder charges in 2018. In 2020, investigating judges dropped the charges and ordered a mandatory hospitalization.

July 18, 2024: *CNN* reported that French Interior Minister Gérald Darmanin tweeted that "A police officer was attacked in the eighth arrondissement of Paris while he was responding to a call from officers securing a store" during the evening. The attacker was also injured and hospitalized.

BBC reported that arson was suspected in a morning fire that killed seven members of the same Comorian family, including three adults, a teenager, and younger children aged five, seven, and ten, in an apartment block in the Moulins area of Nice. The mayor of Nice said the fire was caused by petrol poured into a second floor stairwell by hooded people during the night. Two family members tried to escape through a window; one perished, the other was critically injured. The family had lived in Nice since 2013. Some 30 people sustained smoke inhalation.

July 20, 2024: A French alleged neo-Nazi sympathizer, 19, was sentenced to two years in prison after making threats online, sharing bomb-making instructions on social media, making posts inciting hate, making death threats, and posting personal information that put people at risk. He was suspected of wanting to target the Olympic torch relay. He was convicted after a swift trial overnight on July 19. He was arrested on July 17 in the morning at his home in the Alsace region of eastern France. He ran a group called "French Aryan division" on the social media channel *Telegram*.

July 23, 2024: *AP* and *UPI* reported that Paris prosecutors announced the arrest of a Russian man, 40, at his Paris apartment on suspicion of planning to "destabilize the Olympic Games." He was charged with "conducting intelligence work on behest of a foreign power" with an aim to "provoke hostilities in France." He faced 30 years in prison. Authorities said they had foiled several plots to disrupt the Games.

Interior Minister Gérald Darmanin told *BFMTV* that authorities arrested a man, 18, in Gironde on suspicion of "planning a violent action against the Olympic Games."

July 25, 2024: *USA Today* reported that Israel warned France of a possible Iran-backed attack against Israeli athletes at the Olympics, scheduled to open the next day.

July 26, 2024: *UPI, Reuters,* the *New York Times, CNN, France 2 TV,* and *BFMTV* reported that around 4 a.m., arsonists and cable thieves in rural areas severely disrupted the country's high-speed rail network hours before the Paris Olympics opened, affecting at least 800,000 travelers after the national rail operator SNCF was forced to cancel or divert a large number of trains on three—LGV Atlantique, Nord, and Est—of its four main 200-mph TGV lines with Paris particularly badly hit. Transit police foiled an attempt to sabotage the iconic Sud-Est line, Europe's busiest high-speed route, linking Paris with Lyon and Marseille. Sites hit included Courtalain on the Atlantic line, Croisilles in the North, and Pagny-sur-Moselle in the East—all at key junctions in the national network. The attacks coincided with the start of the "grand départ," the day millions of Parisians traditionally leave the city for their summer vacation. Trains between the UK and France were affected. The *New York Times* reported that Jean-Pierre Farandou, the head of France's SNCF national rail company said that the fires were set in pipes that carry cabling necessary for signaling, and located on key bifurcation points on the rail, meant to maximize the damage.

BBC reported on July 29 that police arrested an "ultra-left militant" male suspect, 28, in Rouen after being found behaving suspiciously near a railway site. His car contained keys to technical premises, pliers, a set of universal keys, and literature "linked to the ultra-left".

July 29, 2024: Between 1 a.m. and 3 a.m., vandals hit multiple telecommunications lines of SFR, France's second-largest telecommunications company, affecting fiber lines and fixed and mobile phone lines in at least six of the country's administrative departments, which include the region around Marseille. Olympics operations were not affected. Up to eight French and international operators, who use SFR's infrastructure, including telecom operators Bouygues and Free, were affected.

August 4, 2024: *BBC* and *Le Parisien* reported that French prosecutors were investigating death threats made against the organizers of the Paris Olympics opening ceremony, including artistic director Thomas Jolly, ceremonies director Thierry Reboul, and Alexandre Billard of events agency Ubi Bene. Religious officials and conservative politicians in France and abroad saw an offensive reference to The Last Supper. The organizers said the sequence, titled Festivity, was inspired by Greek mythology and intended to be a celebration of diversity.

August 7, 2024: *AP* reported that Israel's Olympic team said some athletes had received emailed death threats as they competed in Paris. The national cybercrime agency was investigating doxing—a leak of some Israeli athletes' personal data online. Prosecutors investigated inciting racial hated after Israeli athletes received "discriminatory gestures" during an Israel-Paraguay match. Tom Reuveny, 24, who won a gold in wind surfing, said he had received threats.

August 24, 2024: *CNN* and *Radio Franceinfo* reported that an individual set alight several cars in a parking lot across the street from Synagogue Beth Yaacov in La Grande-Motte near Montpellier before one exploded, injuring a police officer. Authorities were investigating a possible terrorist motive.

CNN and *BFMTV* later reported that police detained a suspect following a raid in Nimes. Interior Minister Gérald Darmanin said he had fired on the elite RAID police unit. The suspect was wounded. An initial investigation indicated that the perpetrator was carrying a Palestinian flag and a gun.

September 11, 2024: National counterterrorism prosecutor Olivier Christen announced that French authorities foiled three plots to attack the Olympic and Paralympic Games in Paris and other cities that hosted the summer events. Five people, including a minor, were arrested on suspicion of involvement in the three foiled plots.

October 8, 2024: French anti-terror prosecutors announced the arrests of three people, two of them Afghan nationals, regarding a suspected attack plot.

October 8, 2024: Interior Minister Bruno Retailleau announced additional steps against any effort by Omar bin Laden, one of the sons of al-Qaeda leader Osama bin Laden, to return to France. He had lived in the Orne region of Normandy since 2016 but left France in October 2023 after French authorities withdrew his residency papers and ordered him out and barred him from returning to France for two years. *Le Parisien* reported that Omar bin Laden now lives in Qatar. France had expelled him for social media posts sympathetic of terrorism.

October 12, 2024: Anti-terror prosecutors said that an Afghan national, 22, was being investigated on terrorism charges over a suspected attack plot. He was among three people who were detained in the southern Toulouse region; the others were released. The investigation began on September 27 and found a suspected "plan for violent action targeting people in a football stadium or a shopping center". Some evidence linked him to ISIS ideology.

December 15, 2024: *BBC* and *AP* reported that at 5:20 p.m., a man, 22, turned himself in to the gendarmerie brigade in Ghyvelde after allegedly shooting to death five people in northern France. At 3:15 p.m., a male owner of a company, 29, died outside his home in Wormhout. At 4 p.m., two security guards aged 33 and 37 were killed near a port in Loon-Plage, a stretch of coastline near Dunkirk. A few minutes later, two other men, aged 19 and 30, were killed near a migrant camp where they were staying. Police found several firearms in his car.

GEORGIA

December 19, 2024: *Al-Jazeera* and Abkhazia's state news agency *Apsnypress* reported that politician Vakhtang Golandzia died of wounds sustained in a shooting at the parliament building of the Russia-backed breakaway Georgian region of Abkhazia. Fellow lawmaker Kan Kvarchia was wounded. The interior ministry identified another lawmaker, Adgur Kharazia, as the suspect, and that he had fled the scene. Abkhazia broke from Georgia's control in a war after the collapse of the Soviet Union in the early

1990s, during which hundreds of thousands of ethnic Georgians fled.

GERMANY

January 7, 2023: *BBC, Bild, AP, CNN,* and *DPA* reported that North Rhine-Westphalia police raided the Castrop-Rauxel residence in the Ruhr region of an Iranian man, 32, plotting to use cyanide and ricin to commit an "Islamic-motivated" "serious act of violence". Another Iranian was arrested. The charge of a "serious act of violence endangering the state" can lead to between six months and ten years in prison.

The *Los Angeles Times* and *DPA* added on January 8 that U.S. security officials provided a tip on the plot by the brothers, aged 32 and 25, identified by prosecutors as M.J. and J.J. The defendants faced between three and 15 years in prison.

January 23, 2023: The *Washington Post* reported that prosecutors charged four men and a woman, Elisabeth R. (she was arrested in October 2022), in a plot to kidnap Health Minister Karl Lauterbach and subject him to a show trial, blow up power infrastructure, stir civil unrest, and violently overthrow the government. Prosecutors said Sven B., Thomas K., and Thomas O. had organized themselves into a "military branch", while Elisabeth R. and Michael H. were involved in an "administrative branch". The five were charged with being suspected members of a terrorist group and planning "highly treasonable" acts against the government. Two were charged with preparing a "serious act of violence that is dangerous to the state". Another was charged with terrorist financing. The group planned to have an actor imitate the country's president or chancellor in a live television broadcast and announce that the federal government had been deposed and that the constitution of 1871 was in force again, per the ideology of the extremist Reichsbürger (Citizens of the Reich) movement.

January 25, 2023: *AP, UPI, Bild, DPA,* and German public broadcaster *NDR* reported that at 3 p.m., a stateless Palestinian, 33, fatally stabbed with a knife two teenagers and injured seven on a train traveling in Schleswig-Holstein State

from Kiel to Hamburg. Passengers grabbed him before he was arrested by police. The Deutsche Bahn RE70 Hamburg Hbf regional train arrived at the Brokstedt station. Police spokesman Juergen Henningsen from Flensburg said three were severely injured and four others suffered minor injuries. The attacker was also injured and taken to the hospital. On May 15, 2024, *AP* and *DPA* reported that the state court in Itzehoe convicted Ibrahim A., 34, of murder and attempted murder and sentenced him to life in prison for the stabbing. The Palestinian grew up in the Gaza Strip and came to Germany in 2014. He had a previous criminal record.

January 30, 2023: *News 360, Der Spiegel, DPA,* and *Europa* reported that German security authorities announced that 55 suspects were accused of being part of a Reich Citizens group planning a coup in Germany that was dismantled in December 2022.

March 9, 2023: The Federal Court of Justice ordered a new sentencing hearing for Jennifer W., 31, a German Muslim convert who was sentenced to 10 years on charges that, as an ISIS member in Iraq, she and her husband, Iraqi citizen Taha al-J., allowed a 5-year-old Yazidi girl kept as a slave to die of thirst in the sun. The court quashed her appeal but partially approved a request by prosecutors. The FCJ sent the case back to the Munich state court for a new sentencing decision. She was convicted of, inter alia, two counts of crimes against humanity through enslavement, in one case resulting in death, being an accessory to attempted murder, and membership in a terrorist organization abroad. The FCJ held that the Munich judges had sentenced her for a "less severe case" of crimes against humanity and overlooked aggravating circumstances. A Frankfurt court in November 2021 convicted Taha al-J. of genocide, crimes against humanity, war crimes, and bodily harm resulting in death. He was sentenced to life imprisonment.

March 9, 2023: *NPR, Bild, RTL Germany, Reuters,* the *Jerusalem Post, DPA, CNN,* and *NBC News* reported that at 9:04 p.m., German gunman Philipp F., 35, killed six Jehovah's Witnesses and an unborn child at a JW Kingdom Hall on

Deelböge Street in the Groß Borstel district of residential Hamburg before killing himself. The mother was 28 weeks pregnant and suffered a miscarriage but survived. Four men and two women, Germans between the ages of 33 and 60, plus the baby, died. Eight people were wounded, four seriously. Six were Germans. One injured person was from Uganda and one from Ukraine. The shooter was believed to have been part of the congregation. The *Washington Post* noted that he had earlier been flagged to authorities in January as a possible threat due to his hatred of his former employer and religious groups, particularly the Jehovah's Witnesses, of which he was a member until around 18 months ago. He had legally purchased a semiautomatic handgun in December 2022 on a sports shooter license. Investigators found nine empty magazines capable of holding 15 rounds each. The gunman carried more ammunition in his backpack. One witness told German television news agency *NonstopNews* that he heard over 25 shots. He had fired nine magazines of ammunition. Police arrived at the scene at 9:08 p.m.

March 22, 2023: The *Guardian* and *NPR* reported that a German police officer was shot and wounded during raids targeting five individuals suspected of belonging to a terrorist organization in eight German states and in Switzerland in an operation related to investigations of the far-right Reichsbürger (Citizens of the Reich) movement, which is accused of plotting to overthrow the government. Police detained Markus L. on suspicion of several counts of attempted murder and grievous bodily harm after shots were fired in Reutlingen, near Stuttgart. *Spiegel Online* reported that several members of the German security services were among the suspects and witnesses whose 20 properties were searched.

April 14, 2023: *USNWR* and *Reuters* reported that thieves had set explosives that had blown up at least one ATM per day. Dutch gangs were the prime suspects. In 2021, some 392 ATM explosions were recorded, topped in 2022 by 496.

May 11, 2023: *UPI* and *CNN* reported that two men, both 44, were killed in a 7:45 a.m. workplace shooting at the Mercedes-Benz manufac-

turing plant in Sindelfingen. A man, 53, was arrested. Mercedes said the three people involved were employed by a contractor. The Sindelfingen plant is the company's longest-running factory, opening in 1915. Some 35,000 people work there, making the E-Class and S-Class.

June 21, 2023: The *Washington Post* and German broadcaster *Südwestrundfunk* reported that the Koblenz Higher Regional Court convicted ISIS member Nadine K., 37, of using weapons of war, aiding and abetting genocide and sexual violence, human trafficking, and crimes against humanity for joining her Syrian husband in enslaving a 21-year-old woman from the Yazidi religious minority group and sentenced her to nine years and three months in prison. *Sky News* identified the victim as Naveen Rasho, who was represented by human rights attorney Amal Clooney. Authorities arrested Nadine K. upon her return to Germany in March 2022.

August 5, 2023: The *Times of Israel* reported that during the evening, three men attacked an Israeli male tourist, 19, in Berlin's Kreuzberg district. Police were exploring a possible anti-Semitic motive. The youth was walking with his 18-year-old girlfriend, while speaking on the phone in Hebrew. Three men got out of a car and started talking to him in German, which he does not speak. They then beat up the man, kicking him when he was on the ground. He was hospitalized with light injuries to his arm and face.

September 19, 2023: *UPI* and *al-Jazeera* reported that Germany banned the Hammerskins Germany neo-Nazi group. More than 700 police officers raided the homes of 28 members of the organization in 10 federal German states, confiscating cash, weapons, clothing with the Hammerskins emblem, flags with swastikas, and copies of *Mein Kampf*. The Hammerskin movement grew out of the neo-confederate Hammerskins Nation in Texas in 1988 and expanded to the UK, Australia, and Germany. The group has around 130 members. The ban includes the association's regional chapters and its subgroup Crew 38.

September 27, 2023: *Al-Jazeera* reported that the government banned the "cult-like, deeply racist" far-right anti-Semitic Artgemeinschaft group, and raided 26 apartments belonging to 39 members of the network in 12 states, including Bavaria, Baden-Wuerttemberg, and Brandenburg. The Interior Ministry said the group, which has 150 members and links to several far-right groups, sought to indoctrinate children with Nazi ideology, using a "pseudo-religious Germanic belief in God to spread their worldview which violates human dignity".

October 9, 2023: *UPI* and *DPA* reported that shortly after midnight, Hamburg Airport officials suspended morning flights for 90 minutes after receiving an e-mailed threat against an Iran Air jetliner carrying 198 passengers and crew from Tehran. No bomb was found.

October 11, 2023: Authorities in Wuppertal arrested Iraqi man Abdel J.S., for membership in a foreign terrorist organization (ISIS) and participation in war crimes, including involvement in the killing of six prisoners and the amputation of a person's hand. Prosecutors said he joined ISIS by June 2014 and participated twice in ISIS's draconian public punishments. He and other ISIS terrorists allegedly took a person prisoner and beat and kicked the captive to extract information.

October 18, 2023: *Al-Jazeera, AFP, Reuters,* and *Barron's* reported that at 3:45 a.m., two masked men threw two Molotov cocktails at a synagogue belonging to the Kahal Adass Jisroel Jewish community on Brunnenstrasse in Berlin's Mitte district. The bottles, filled with flammable liquid, hit the pavement in front of the synagogue without damaging the building. No one was injured. The perpetrators fled. At 8 a.m., police arrested another man, 30, who approached the scene on an e-scooter yelling anti-Israel slogans. Police opened a probe against him on charges of incitement of racial hatred and an attempted attack on an officer.

October 23, 2023: *Al-Jazeera* reported that German police found no bomb after an e-mailed bomb threat was sent at 8:20 a.m. to broadcaster *Zweites Deutsches Fernsehen (ZDF)* in Mainz. Bomb threats were also reported in at least six schools in the Bavarian cities of Augsburg

and Regensburg, Karlsruhe and Mannheim in Baden-Wurttemberg, Solingen in North Rhine Westphalia, and the Thuringian capital Erfurt. Three schools received e-mailed bomb threats.

October 24, 2023: Authorities in Duisburg arrested a man, 29, previously convicted for membership in ISIS, on suspicion of agreeing to attack a pro-Israel demonstration.

November 2, 2023: *Al-Jazeera, USNWR,* and *Reuters* reported that Interior Minister Nancy Faeser announced a complete ban on the activities of Hamas and dissolved Samidoun Palestinian Solidarity Network, a pro-Palestine group accused of spreading anti-Israel and anti-Semitic ideas.

November 16, 2023: *UPI* and *al-Jazeera* reported that hundreds of German federal authorities raided 54 pro-Hizballah sites, including a Hamburg Islamic center and those of five affiliated groups, in a nationwide sting across seven states, including Lower Saxony, Hesse, Baden-Wurttemberg, Bavaria, Berlin, and North Rhine-Westphalia.

November 21, 2023: *AP* reported that police raided the homes of 17 people in Bavaria State who were accused of spreading anti-Semitic hate speech and threats targeting Jews online.

November 23, 2023: *AP, UPI,* and *DPA* reported that at dawn, more than 300 police officers searched 15 properties of Hamas members and sympathizers in Berlin and the states of Lower Saxony, North Rhine-Westphalia, and Schleswig-Holstein. The government banned any activity by or in support of the group.

November 28, 2023: The *Los Angeles Times* reported that German authorities in Trier arrested French woman Samra N., who allegedly committed war crimes in Syria after joining ISIS. She was suspected of having participated as a member of two foreign terrorist organizations as a teenager. She allegedly traveled to Syria in September 2013 and joined Jabhat al-Nusra. She married one of the group's fighters according to Islamic rites. In November 2013, the couple allegedly joined ISIS. While in Syria, she allegedly tried to persuade people living in Germany to come and join Jabhat al-Nusra. She also temporarily took in a woman who had been persuaded to leave the country in this way. She helped her husband obtain military equipment for ISIS. Twice, when her husband was away on combat missions, she allegedly stayed in women's houses that ISIS had occupied after driving out the original residents, which Germany considers a "war crime against property". She returned to Germany in early 2014, but remained a member of ISIS until at least February 2015, prosecutors said. It was not immediately clear why the French citizen went to Germany.

December 4, 2023: *AP* reported that arson was suspected when members of the National Council of Resistance of Iran noticed flames at their office's window in a building in Berlin's Schmargendorf district at 2:15 a.m. The oppositionists extinguished the fire before it could spread. No one was hurt. The oppositionists blamed the Iranian government. The NCRI is the political wing of the Mujahedeen-e-Khalq.

December 23, 2023: *Al-Jazeera* and *Bild* reported that German police searched Cologne Cathedral after receiving warnings of a possible car bomb attack planned for New Year's Eve. *Bild* added that authorities in Germany, Austria, and Spain received indications that an Islamist group was plotting attacks in Europe, with targets possibly including Christmas Masses in Cologne, Vienna, and Madrid. Special forces in Vienna and Germany arrested four suspects. *AP* reported that on the night of December 31, German authorities detained a German-Turkish male suspect, 41, in Bochum in North Rhine-Westphalia State. *DPA* reported that all of the detainees allegedly belong to a larger Islamic extremist network that included people across Germany and in other European countries. One was a Tajik man, 30.

February 22, 2024: *ABC News, DPA, AP,* and *Bild* reported that a man stabbed five people with a knife at the Wilhelm Dörpfeld high school in Wuppertal's Elberfeld district. Police arrested a suspect, who was injured.

February 26, 2024: *AP, Reuters,* and *Bild* reported that prosecutor Markus Heusler in Verden

announced the arrest of fugitive Red Army Faction (RAF) member Daniela Klette, 65, who had been on the run for more than three decades. *Bild* said she was arrested in Berlin the previous evening. Two weeks earlier, police asked the public for information during the cold case show *Aktenzeichen XY*, generating 250 tips. Former RAF "third generation" members Klette, Ernst-Volker Staub, and Burkhard Garweg have been linked to a dozen robberies in northern Germany between 1999 and 2016. They were also sought for attempted murder. They were put on Europol's "Europe's Most Wanted" list in 2020. The RAF disbanded in 1998.

AP reported on February 29 that police found in her apartment in Berlin's Kreuzberg district a hand grenade and two magazines and ammunition that would fit a handgun. *BBC* later added that they also found a Kalashnikov assault rifle and a replica rocket launcher.

BBC reported on June 25, 2024 that Daniela Klette had lived a quiet life on the run, walking her dog and providing math tutoring to neighbors' children.

March 3, 2024: The *New York Times* and *DPA* reported that police raided the Friedrichshain district of Berlin, arresting ten individuals believed connected to the Marxist-Leninist Red Army Faction. Police were seeking two accomplices of Daniela Klette, alias Claudia Ivone, arrested earlier, identified as Ernst-Volker Staub and Burkhard Garweg. All ten were released.

March 5, 2024: *BBC* and the *Washington Post* reported that the far-left Vulkangruppe (Volcano Group) claimed credit for a suspected early morning arson attack against an electricity pylon and high-voltage wires that caused power outages at the Tesla Gigafactory in Grünheide near Berlin and at nearby towns in Brandenburg State. Tesla sent its workers home and halted production. The Volcano Group said Tesla ate up resources and labor, contaminating groundwater and using huge amounts of drinking water. *Reuters* reported that state police were investigating the letter's authenticity. *AFP* reported that Tesla was unable to say when the plant would reopen. Tesla had hoped to double the size of the Berlin plant.

The letter noted, "We sabotaged Tesla" and the attack was a "gift" for March 8—International Women's Day. The attack on "technofascists" like Musk was a step toward "liberation from patriarchy".

March 7, 2024: In the morning, Germany's Central Office for Combating Cybercrime in Frankfurt, the Federal Criminal Police Office, and several state police agencies raided homes and interrogated 45 suspects in 11 states across Germany against people suspected of posting misogynistic hate speech on the Internet. Police had earlier interrogated 37 other suspects.

March 19, 2024: Police in Gera detained Afghan citizens Ibrahim M.G. and Ramin N. who were accused of planning to attack police near the Swedish parliament in Stockholm in response to the burning of copies of the Quran. Prosecutors said ISIS-K tasked the duo in mid-2023 with conducting an attack in Europe in response to Quran burnings in Sweden and other countries. The pair researched online the location and tried unsuccessfully to procure weapons. Prosecutors said Ibrahim M. G. joined ISIS-K in August 2023. He and Ramin N. had raised 2,000 euros ($2,170) in donations for ISIS to help a member jailed in northern Syria. The Afghans are suspected of providing support to a terrorist organization, conspiracy to commit a crime, and infringements against trade laws.

March 20, 2024: A German federal court rejected an appeal by German convert to Islam Jennifer W., now 32, of her 14-year sentence for allowing a 5-year-old Yazidi girl she and her husband kept as a slave when they were ISIS members in Iraq to die of thirst in the sun in August 2015 in Fallujah. She was convicted in October 2021 of, inter alia, two counts of crimes against humanity through enslavement — one case resulting in death — and membership in a terrorist organization abroad. The Federal Court of Justice overturned her lighter 10-year sentence on the grounds that judges had erred in sentencing the defendant for a "less severe case" of crimes against humanity and overlooked aggravating circumstances. She was resentenced in August 2023 to 14 years. Authorities took Jennifer into custody when she tried to renew her identity papers at the German Embassy in Ankara in 2016 and deported her to Germany. In November 2021, a Frankfurt court convicted her Iraqi ex-husband, Taha al-J., of genocide, crimes against humanity, war crimes, and bodily harm resulting in death. He was sentenced to life in prison.

March 27, 2024: Investigators said they had received 760 new tips on the whereabouts of Ernst-Volker Staub, 69, and Burkhard Garweg, 55, two fugitive suspected ex-members of the left-wing militant Red Army Faction following the arrest of Daniela Klette, 65, on February 26 in Berlin, where she had been living under a false identity.

April 5, 2024: No one was injured when an incendiary device was thrown at a door of a synagogue in Oldenburg in the afternoon. Minor damage was reported. *Al-Jazeera* reported that on April 11, police in northern Germany offered a 5,000-euro ($5,330) reward for providing information concerning the attack.

April 9, 2024: Authorities in Bavaria arrested a man and a woman, identified as Iraqi nationals Twana H.S. and Asia R.A., who are accused of ISIS membership and of keeping two young Yazidi girls as slaves as well as sexually and physically abusing them. They were accused of genocide, crimes against humanity, war crimes, and membership in a terrorist organization. Prosecutor said the married couple were ISIS members in Iraq and Syria between October 2015 and November 2017. They allegedly held a Yazidi girl, 5, as a slave starting in late 2015 and another girl, 12, from October 2017. Prosecutors claimed that the man raped both girls repeatedly and that the woman prepared the room and put make-up on one of the girls. The man on one occasion allegedly hit the older girl with a broomstick. Prosecutors accused the woman of scalding the younger girl's hand with hot water. Both children were often forced to stand on one leg for half an hour. Before leaving Syria in November 2017, the duo handed the girls over to other ISIS members.

April 12, 2024: *DPA, al-Jazeera,* and *AP* reported that authorities arrested two teen girls, aged 15 and 16, and a boy, 15, from the Dusseldorf region suspected of planning an "Islamist-motivated terror attack" involving "murder and manslaughter." The trio hails from various parts of North Rhine-Westphalia State. Prosecutors in Dusseldorf added that a court issued warrants over the Easter weekend. *Bild* reported that the trio were to attack worshippers in churches and on police stations using knives and Molotov cocktails in following ISIS ideology and were considering whether to obtain firearms.

April 27, 2024: *CNN, DPA, AP,* and *UPI* reported that at 5:20 p.m., two Ukrainian servicemen, aged 23 and 36, were stabbed to death at a shopping center in Murnau am Stafelsee, Bavaria, in southern Germany by a suspected Russian national, 57, who was arrested in his nearby home. The Ukrainian men resided in Garmisch-Partenkirchen district and had been in Germany undergoing medical rehabilitation. On April 28, a judge charged the Russian with murder and ordered him held in pre-trial detention.

On October 23, 2024, a Russian man, 57, who supported his country's war in Ukraine, was charged with the fatal stabbing. Prosecutors said the suspect and the two victims knew each other somewhat from previous meetings. On the day of the stabbing, the three men were drinking together and argued about the situation in Ukraine.

April 29, 2024: *Al-Jazeera, Reuters, AP, ZDF,* and *DPA* reported that the trial began in Stuttgart of nine people, aged between 42 and 60, including self-styled Heinrich XIII Prince Reuss; a retired paratrooper; and judge and former far-right lawmaker Birgit Malsack-Winkemann with the Alternative for Germany party, charged with terrorism in connection with a 2022 rightwing Reichsbuergerbewegung (Reich Citizens) plot to overthrow the German government. The group planned to install the prince as the country's provisional new leader. In December 2023, federal prosecutors filed terrorism charges against 27 people, one of whom since died. The nine defendants in Stuttgart were charged with membership in a terrorist organization and "preparation

of a high treasonous enterprise." One defendant was also charged with attempted murder for shooting at police officers during a search of Reuss's home in March 2023. Prosecutors said the group's military wing had begun forming 280 armed units.

Nine other suspects were scheduled for trial on May 21, 2024, at a Frankfurt state court. Most of them were charged with membership in a terrorist organization and "preparation of high treasonous undertaking."

The other eight were to be tried in Munich on June 18, 2024.

May 24, 2024: Authorities arrested two German men, 24 and 18 years old, suspected of plotting a knife attack on worshippers at a synagogue in Heidelberg. *DPA* reported that police arrested them in separate operations in Baden-Wuerttemberg State earlier in the month. Authorities noted that the duo talked of "the killing of one or more visitors in the attack on the synagogue followed by death as martyrs, whereby the two persons wanted to be shot to death by police". They could face charges of conspiracy to commit murder. On May 3, police searched the home of the 24-year-old, shooting him after he grabbed a knife. Police grabbed the other suspect in his apartment on May 18. The 18-year-old is a dual German-Turk.

May 31, 2024: *AP, DPA,* and *BBC* reported that during a *YouTube* livestream at 11:35 a.m., a man with a knife attacked and wounded several people, including a police officer who was critically wounded in the back, in Marktplatz square in downtown Mannheim. Police shot and wounded the attacker, who apparently targeted a rally in support of Buergerbewegung Pax Europa, a far-right, anti-hijab movement in Germany.

BBC added that the injured included anti-Islam activist Michael Stürzenberger, 58 or 59, of the Citizens' Movement Pax Europa (BPE) and PI-News, who had been preparing to hold a rally in the square. *Bild* reported that he was injured in the leg and face. Stürzenberger once led the small right-wing populist party Die Freiheit, which was dissolved in 2016. He earlier was a member of the Christian Social Union (CSU)

- the Bavarian sister party of the Christian Democratic Union (CDU) - but left before he was kicked out.

The other victims included five men aged 25, 36, 42, and 54. Three are German, one is a German-Kazakh citizen, and the fifth is an Iraqi citizen.

AP reported on June 1 that a German court ordered a man, 25, born in Afghanistan, held on suspicion of attempted murder. The suspect had lived in Germany since 2014, was married, and has two children. Police searching his apartment in Heppenheim confiscated digital devices. He had no prior police record.

AP and *UPI* reported on June 2 that the police officer was placed in an artificial coma but died of his injuries.

June 4, 2024: An individual stabbed far-right Alternative for Germany candidate Heinrich Koch with a box cutter in Mannheim.

June 16, 2024: *BBC* and the *New York Times* reported that 30 minutes after noon, a man with an axe and an incendiary device threatened police officers near a fanzone for supporters of the Dutch Euro 2024 soccer team on the Reeperbahn in Hamburg. Police fired pepper spray, then shot and seriously injured him.

June 18, 2024: The trial in Munich began of eight Germans—six men and two women—accused of involvement in a far-right plot to overthrow the German government. They were charged with preparation of high treasonous undertaking, and membership in or founding a terrorist organization. Some were charged with preparing a serious act of violence. This was the third court case regarding the plot, which involved 26 defendants. *DPA* reported that 55 trial sessions were scheduled.

The defendants included Ruth L. and Thomas T., alleged founding members of the group who prosecutors say co-led a "transcommunication" department in the group's extended leadership. The group planned to install Heinrich XIII Prince Reuss as Germany's provisional new leader. The group would storm the parliament in Berlin and arrest lawmakers, then negotiate a post-coup agreement with Russia.

June 19, 2024: Authorities in Esslingen, near Stuttgart, arrested Iraqi citizen Mahmoud A., who was accused of standing by to carry out attacks for ISIS after he arrived in Germany in October 2022. A judge ordered him held on suspicion of membership in a foreign terrorist organization pending a possible indictment. He was accused of joining ISIS in Iraq in or before May 2016 and fighting for them.

On October 22, 2024, prosecutors indicted Mahmoud A. in the state court in Stuttgart with membership in a foreign terrorist organization and preparing a serious act of violence. Prosecutors said that he fought and carried out guard duties for ISIS until October 2017. He then allegedly went to Türkiye and to Germany in October 2022. Since January 2024, he planned a bomb attack, learning to make a bomb on the Internet, and obtaining the necessary chemicals and components for an ignition device.

June 28, 2024: *DPA* reported that the Cologne state court convicted a boy, 15, of plotting an ISIS-inspired attack on a Christmas market and sentenced him to four years in prison. Charges included conspiracy to murder and disturbing the public peace by threatening crimes. Police detained him in November 2023 near Cologne. He was radicalized in the fall of 2023. Within weeks, he had agreed with an acquaintance, 16, to attack a Christmas market in Leverkusen. He would drive a rented truck into the market and kill as many visitors as possible, while his accomplice filmed the attack. The accomplice was scheduled for trial on July 17 in Neuruppin, near Berlin.

June 30, 2024: *CNN* reported that several U.S. military bases in Europe, including the U.S. Army garrison in Stuttgart, Germany went on Force Protection Condition "Charlie", the second-highest state of alert, amid concerns that terrorists could target US military personnel or facilities.

CNN reported that at 3:25 p.m., a man entered a Bochum café and poured acid on a guest sitting at an outdoor table, causing serious injuries to him, a woman sitting at the table with him, and a waitress. Four police officers and two firefighters were also injured. Authorities arrested the attacker later in the area.

July 24, 2024: The German government banned the Islamic Center Hamburg (IZH) and five suborganizations, claiming IZH was an "outpost" of Iran's theocracy, promoting the ideology of its leadership, and supporting Lebanese Hizballah. Police raided 53 properties in Berlin, Hamburg, and six other German states, including the prominent blue-tiled Imam Ali Mosque in Hamburg. Interior Minister Nancy Faeser said IZH "promotes an Islamist-extremist, totalitarian ideology in Germany," while it and its suborganizations "also support the terrorists of Hezbollah and spread aggressive antisemitism." Four Shi'ite mosques in the country will be closed and the IZH's assets will be confiscated.

August 13, 2024: *AP* and *DPA* reported the investigators suspected unauthorized entry and possible sabotage at the Wahn military barracks outside Cologne after finding a hole in a fence. Authorities suspected that the facility's water supply might have been tampered with. The barracks serves the military part of Cologne/Bonn Airport.

August 23, 2024: *CNN* reported that at 9:40 p.m., an individual fled after stabbing to death three people—two men, aged 56 and 67, and a woman, 56—and injuring eight, five severely, during the three-day Festival of Diversity in the Fronhof central square that marked the 650th anniversary of the founding of the town of Solingen. The attack took place near the stage while a musical act was performing. Police spokesman Thorsten Fleiß said the attacker specifically targeted the victims' necks.

BBC reported the next day that German police arrested a suspect, 15, who was believed to have known about the attack beforehand but did not alert the police. Two women reported to the police that they overheard the suspect talking to someone about the attack. The identity of the attacker remained unknown. Police did not rule out a "terrorist motive". Police found several knives and said the attacker targeted victims' throats and necks. The *New York Times* reported

on August 25 that the boy was being investigated for not reporting a crime, but was not a suspect in the stabbing.

CNN reported on August 24 that a Syrian man, 26, turned himself in at a refugee shelter in North Rhine Westphalia State and confessed to stabbing to death three people and injuring eight others. He was to appear before a judge in the Federal Court of Justice in Karlsruhe later that day. The Syrian had applied for asylum, but *DPA* said that his request was denied and that he was to have been deported in 2023.

AP reported on August 24 that ISIS claimed credit on *Amaq*, saying that the attacker targeted Christians and that as a "soldier of the Islamic State" he carried out the assaults "to avenge Muslims in Palestine and everywhere."

Solingen produces high-end knives and scissors and is known as the City of Blades.

August 27, 2024: At 2:45 p.m., police in Moers, near the larger cities of Duisburg and Duesseldorf, shot to death a German man, 26, who apparently threatened passersby on a street and tried to attack officers with two knives.

August 29, 2024: Six people were injured, three in life-threatening condition, in a 7:40 p.m. knife attack on a bus headed to a festival in Siegen, east of Cologne. Police arrested a German woman, 32, who had no immigrant roots. Authorities said that there was no evidence of a political or religious motive. Another 40 people were on board. The victims were aged between 16 and 30.

September 5, 2024: *Al-Jazeera, Reuters, BBC,* and *CNN* reported that an Austrian man, 18, fired an antique hunting rifle on Karolinenplatz in Munich, a square near the Israeli consulate and a Nazi documentation center, before five police officers shot him to death. The attack was on the anniversary of the Black September attack on the Israeli team at the 1972 Munich Olympics. *BBC* reported that he was previously known to security services on suspicion of supporting violent Islamist groups.

September 12, 2024: Authorities arrested a Syrian, 27, suspected of supporting jihadis, in connection with plotting an attack on German soldiers during their lunch break in Munich, killing as many of them as possible. The Munich public prosecutor's office said that he procured two machetes, each about 40 centimeters (15.75 inches) long, earlier in September, and allegedly planned to attack the soldiers with them. He appeared before a judge the following day.

October 19, 2024: *AP, al-Jazeera, Bild,* and *DPA* reported that in the evening, authorities in Bernau arrested Libyan national Omar A., 28, who had suspected ties to ISIS and was allegedly planning a firearms attack on the Israeli Embassy. *Bild* said he was believed to have entered Germany in November 2022 and to have made a request for asylum the following January, which was rejected in September 2023.

October 29, 2024: Prosecutors charged three men regarding an alleged plan to attack a Jewish target in western Germany. The main suspect, a German, 25, who was in custody, flew to Istanbul in April 2024, planning to go to Syria to join ISIS. That plan failed and he returned to Germany. He and a German-Turkish dual national, 18, allegedly planned to attack a Jewish facility in either Heidelberg or Mannheim. They discussed getting fatally shot by police after such an attack and then having a video claim of responsibility released with recriminations against German Chancellor Olaf Scholz and his policy toward Israel. The 25-year-old was accused of the attempted manslaughter of a German police officer during a raid in May 2024 related to the alleged attack plan. He was charged with preparing a serious act of violence and conspiracy to murder. The 18-year-old was charged with being an accessory to preparing a serious act of violence and conspiracy to murder. Another 25-year-old German was accused of driving the main suspect to Stuttgart Airport. He was charged with being an accessory to preparing a serious act of violence.

November 5, 2024: *Reuters, BBC,* and *AP* reported that police arrested eight suspected members of a far-right militant organization. The suspects, including minors and adolescents, were allegedly part 15-20 individuals called Sächsische Separatisten (Saxonian Separatists), which espouse racist, anti-Semitic, and partially apocalyptic ideas.

Prosecutors said they planned to seize power in Saxony and potentially other eastern German states "to establish governmental and societal structures inspired by National Socialism." Justice Minister Marco Buschmann said "Even ethnic cleansing was part of their inhuman plans." Alleged ringleader Jörg S. was apprehended in Poland. More than 450 police officers and special forces searched 20 premises in Germany, Austria, and Poland. Prosecutors identified the suspects as Kurt H., Karl K., Kevin M., Hans-Georg P., Kevin R., Jörg S., Jörn S., and Norman T. The eight were held on suspicion of being members of a domestic terrorist organization.

November 26, 2024: In the evening, authorities in Koblenz arrested a young male suspected of planning to build pipe bombs to carry out an Islamic extremist attack. Police searched his home in October, seizing two bayonets and four sections of pipe.

December 8, 2024: Police arrested two German Lebanese brothers, aged 15 and 20, who were ISIS sympathizers, in Mannheim and a German Turkish man, 22, from Hesse State for allegedly making preparations for an attack. Police found an assault rifle and ammunition at the German-Turk's home. Investigators also found a balaclava, a protective vest, several knives, and cellphones. A judge on December 9 ordered the trio kept in custody pending a possible indictment.

December 20, 2024: *CNN* and local public broadcaster *MDR* reported that at 7 p.m., a driver apparently intentionally crashed his black BMW rental car into people at a busy Christmas market in Magdeburg, killing an adult and a toddler, 9, and injuring 68, fifteen seriously, 37 moderately, and 16 slightly. *NPR* reported the next day that the death toll had reached five, with another 205 injured, 41 severely. Authorities arrested the driver, a Saudi Arabian doctor, 50, who had lived in Germany since 2006 and worked in Saxony-Anhalt. He had a permanent residency permit and currently lives in Bernburg, 25 miles south of Magdeburg. He originally lived in Mecklenburg-Western Pomerania State. *NPR* reported that he had renounced his Muslim faith, posted Islamophobic text, and showed support for the far-right Alternative for Germany (AfD) party. Police believed an explosive device could have been in the vehicle; no bomb was found.

CNN reported that Saudi officials had warned German authorities, including the German intelligence services and the foreign ministry, four times since 2007 about the suspect, Taleb al-Abdulmohsen, who had tried to "entice" Saudis, especially women, to leave Saudi Arabia and their religion, citing his "fairly radical perspective." The Saudis requested his extradition, viewing him as a fugitive.

Authorities suggested that he could face five counts of murder and 205 counts of attempted murder and dangerous bodily harm.

German media reported that the suspect was a psychiatry and psychotherapy specialist who criticized German authorities who had failed to do enough to combat the "Islamism of Europe." Atheist Refugee Relief filed a criminal complaint against him in 2019 following "the most foul slander and verbal attacks."

DPA reported that State Interior Minister Christian Pegel said the suspect completed his specialist training in Stralsund and came to the attention of authorities due to threatening criminal acts against members of the state medical association in a dispute over the recognition of examination results. A court found him guilty in 2013 of threatening an attack. *ZDF* reported that the Saudis tipped the Federal Criminal Police Office in November 2023. The Federal Office for Migration and Refugees also received a tip about the suspect in the late summer of 2023.

Police in Magdeburg said that those who died were four women aged 45, 52, 67, and 75, and André Gleissner, 9. *BBC* reported that the fire department in nearby Schöppenstedt said André was a member of the children's fire brigade in Warle, an hour's drive from Magdeburg. An online fundraiser reportedly set up to raise money for his family received more than €60,000 (£49,900) in donations as of December 22.

December 30, 2024: The federal prosecutor charged Iraqi couple Twana H.S. and Asia R.A. with enslavement, torture, and war crimes by keeping two young Yazidi girls as slaves and sexually and physically abusing them. The duo were arrested in Bavaria in April 2024. Prosecutors said they were ISIS members in Iraq and Syria between October 2015 and December 2017, the prosecutor said in a statement. They allegedly kept a Yazidi girl, 5, as a slave starting in late 2015, and a 12-year-old from October 2017. Prosecutors alleged that Asia R.A. raped both girls repeatedly and that Twana H.S. prepared the room and put makeup on one of the girls.

December 31 2024: Police in Berlin detained a Syrian man with residency in Sweden who attacked and injured two people in the Charlottenburg neighborhood. Police spokeswoman Jane Berndt announced that "Initial findings indicate that the suspect may have signs of mental illness and that there is not indication for a terrorist motivation." Police called it an "attempted murder" when the man attacked two men in a supermarket and on a sidewalk in front of a nearby hotel shortly before noon, allegedly stabbing them with a knife he had stolen from the supermarket. Several passersby pounced on the attacker and overpowered him until police arrived.

GREECE

March 28, 2023: *UPI, Times of Israel, Greek City Times,* and the *Jerusalem Post* reported that Greece's anti-terrorism police division and National Intelligence Service, acting on a Mossad tip, arrested two Pakistani men accused of planning a terrorist attack with a makeshift gas cylinder explosive against a synagogue in Athens at the direction of an Iran-based operative who promised to pay them. The Iran-based suspect remained at large. *AP* and *Fox News* reported that the two suspects entered Greece illegally from Türkiye four months earlier. Police conducted searches in Athens, southern Greece, and on the western island of Zakynthos.

February 2024: *AP* reported on February 19 that earlier in the month, a bomb exploded in central Athens outside the labor ministry, causing no injuries. Revolutionary Class Self-Defense had made a warning call.

February 12, 2024: Army bomb techs defused a parcel bomb that had been delivered to a senior judge at her Thessaloniki courthouse office. There was no immediate claim of responsibility. Leftist terrorists were suspected. *AP* reported on February 19 that the previously unknown anarchist group Armed Response claimed responsibility in an online post, naming the judge and vowing to step up attacks against the judiciary in solidarity with jailed fellow militants. "Just as easily as the parcel bomb reached her office, our bullets can find their target."

A former employee fatally shot three people in the offices of a shipping company in Glyfada near Athens before shooting himself in the head. The owner of the company was among the victims.

June 3, 2024: *Al-Jazeera* and *AFP* reported that the judicial council of the court of appeals overturned the early release granted by a board of judges on May 2 and ordered back to prison the founder of Greece's far-right Golden Dawn party Nikos Michaloliakos, 66. The *Athens News Agency* said the court found him "unrepentant", continued to praise the Nazi-style practices of Golden Dawn, and was suspected of committing new crimes. In 2020, he was sentenced to 13 and a half years in prison for heading a "criminal organization" that attacked and in some cases killed immigrants, refugees, and political opponents. The mathematician and Holocaust denier and other Golden Dawn members were believed behind the 2013 murders of an anti-fascist rapper and a Pakistani migrant, as well as the beatings of Egyptian fishermen and communist trade unionists.

June 27, 2024: A police officer guarding the house of Supreme Court President Ioanna Klapa was hospitalized with burns to his face and arms after attackers threw gasoline bombs at him. A nearby police car was severely damaged; the house was not. The attackers escaped in the pre-dawn attack in the Athens suburbs. Far-left terrorists were suspected.

October 31, 2024: An improvised bomb apparently went off early in a third-floor apartment in Ambelokipi, Athens, killing a Greek man, 36, and severely wounding a Greek woman, 33. Police seized mobile phones, two handguns, ammunition, and "digital evidence".

On November 4, Minister of Citizen Protection Michalis Chrisochoidis told *Skai TV* that the bomb would have caused extensive damage to any intended target and blamed youths who wanted to become a third generation of domestic terrorists. Municipal authorities declared the entire residential building uninhabitable due to damage from the blast. Police seized two handguns, ammunition, mobile phones, laptops, flash drives, SIM cards, hand-written notes, wigs, and full-face masks. Police believed the deceased man was putting the bomb together. Police arrested a man, 31, and the woman who was wounded in the blast, and were searching for a woman, 30, who reportedly left the country before the explosion.

November 5, 2024: Police arrested five people at five locations and seized large quantities of explosives and firearms following raids in Athens aimed at a significant criminal weapons storage and distribution network.

IRELAND

November 23, 2023: *UPI* and the *Irish Times* reported that at 1:30 p.m., a man armed with a knife injured three children, including a 5-year-old girl who sustained serious injuries, and a man and a woman at Parnell Square East in the city center of Dublin. An Garda Síochána, Ireland's national police and security service, said a woman in her 30s was seriously hurt in the attack. A 5-year-old boy and a 6-year-old girl were hospitalized. Police arrested a man in his 50s at the scene; he was hospitalized with serious injuries. Police did not believe terrorism was a motive in the attack, calling it a "stand-alone" incident. Passers-by subdued the suspect, took his knife, and began kicking him before others intervened. Brazilian delivery driver Caio Benicio, 43, from Rio de Janeiro, who lived in Dublin for a year, was hailed as a hero for using his motorcycle helmet to thwart a stabbing. An online fundraiser to "Buy Caio Benicio a pint" raised more than 350,000 euros, about $383,000, within four days.

Irish national broadcaster *RTE* quoted him as saying "I am immigrant and I was right there to protect Irish people… We are here to work. Most of the people are here to work hard and make the economy of the country better. The work we do here is good for the country. It's good for themselves. They just have hate." Violent anti-immigrant riots continued.

August 2, 2024: *AP, RTÉ,* and *BBC* reported that Gardai arrested a driver in his late 40s who around 2:40 a.m. had crashed his white transit van into the gates outside the office of Taoiseach (Prime Minister) Simon Harris and several other government buildings, including the Oireachtas Leinster House (Irish Parliament), the Irish president's official residence in Phoenix Park, and the Customs House on Custom House Quay on Upper Merrion Street in Dublin. The gate outside the attorney general's office was knocked off its hinges. Gardai arrested him on suspicion of drunk driving and said he was "known to Gardaí for drug-related and other offences". Members of the Irish Defence Force's Military Police assisted the Gardai operation.

August 15, 2024: *AP* and *BBC* reported that in the morning, a youth stabbed Irish Catholic priest/chaplain Father Paul F. Murphy in his 50s outside Renmore Barracks in County Galway, seriously injuring him. The Irish Defense Forces said shots were fired at on-duty personnel. Authorities detained a male teen.

BBC and *RTÉ* reported on October 9, 2024 that authorities at Galway District Court charged a boy, 16, with attempted murder. He was earlier charged with assault causing harm. The director of public prosecutions directed that the boy be sent forward for indictment at the Central Criminal Court. Judge Fahy said an application for bail could not be made in the District Court and remanded the accused to Oberstown Detention Centre.

August 28, 2024: *BBC* reported that Gardaí arrested a man in his 20s after suspected arson attacks on St. Baithin's Catholic Church on Chapel Road, which was built in the 1850s; an Orange hall on Main Street, which was built in the early

19th century; and a Masonic hall on Derry Road in County Donegal. He was to appear the next day before Letterkenny District Court.

ITALY

January 31, 2023: Foreign Minister Antonio Tejani announced that nearly a dozen terrorist attacks, ranging from vandalism to explosive devices, were conducted by an anarchist network in solidarity with Alfredo Cospito, 55, an imprisoned Italian militant, since late November at Italian diplomatic facilities in Argentina, Bolivia, Germany, Greece, Portugal, Spain, and Switzerland. No injuries were reported. Italy increased security at all Italian embassies and consulates and the foreign ministry. Cospito was serving ten years for shooting in the leg an energy executive for a state-controlled company and 20 years for a series of dynamite attacks in Italy. 23019902-08

October 16, 2023: *Al-Jazeera* reported that police arrested two men in Milan suspected of helping finance ISIS and spreading propaganda online. Milan's Chief Prosecutor Marcello Viola said the duo had "sworn an oath of membership and loyalty".

March 25, 2024: Italy increased security around Holy Week observances leading up to Easter following the Moscow concert hall attack by ISIS.

April 8, 2024: At noon, police arrested S.I., a Tajik national accused of being an active ISIS member after he landed at Rome's international airport on a flight from Eindhoven, the Netherlands. He used numerous aliases, birth dates, and nationalities, claiming to be from Uzbekistan, Kyrgyzstan, and Ukraine.

KOSOVO

September 24, 2023: *Al-Jazeera, Telegrafi,* and *Reuters* reported that at 3 a.m., 30 gunmen ambushed a police patrol in Banjska, killing officer Afrim Bunjaku and injuring another. Authorities surrounded the gunmen, who stormed a nearby Serbian Orthodox monastery. Prime Minister Albin Kurti claimed the attackers had the support of Serbian officials. Kosovo police claimed that two trucks without license plates had blocked a bridge at the entrance to Banjska. Three police units sent to unblock it came under fire with guns, hand grenades, and bombs. Kosovo shut its border crossings with Serbia in Brnjak and Jarinje. The siege ended that evening with the deaths of a police officer and three attackers. Four civilian suspects carrying radio equipment and weapons were also arrested. The next day, police in armored vehicles searched the village for at-large gunmen.

Al-Jazeera added on September 25 that Kosovo demanded that Serbia hand over any escaped Serb gunmen. Kosovo Interior Minister Xhelal Svecla said six gunmen had been hospitalized in Novi Pazar, near Kosovo's northern border.

Kosovo Police General Director Gazmend Hoxha said police had found weapons of various calibers, rocket launchers, explosives, detonators, a heavy armored vehicle, 24 automobiles, two 4×4 motorcycles, 150 explosives, three drones, and 30 AK47 weapons in and around the monastery, as well as six machine guns, 29 mortars, more than 100 military uniforms, pickaxes, shovels, hand saws, medicine, and food.

AP reported on October 9, 2024 that the Pristina District Court opened a trial of 45 people charged over a gunfight sparked by an incursion by Serb gunmen. Only three Serb defendants were present. They pleaded not guilty to charges of violation of constitutional and legal order, terror activities, funding terrorism, and money laundering. They faced life in prison. Among those charged in absentia was Milan Radoicic, politician and wealthy businessman with ties to Serbia's ruling populist party and President Aleksandar Vucic. Serbia had briefly detained Radoicic on suspicion of criminal conspiracy, unlawful possession of weapons and explosives, and grave acts against public safety. Radoicic denied the charges although he earlier admitted he was part of the paramilitary group involved in the gunfight. The U.S. and UK sanctioned him for financial criminal activity.

MONTENEGRO

June 20, 2024: State *RTCG* television said a bomb went off near the Cetinje town's sports hall, killing two people and seriously injuring three. The station suggested criminal drug smugglers were involved and that "some of the victims recently got out of prison."

NETHERLANDS

September 28, 2023: *Al-Jazeera, AP, ANP, UPI, Reuters,* and *CNN* reported that Dutch police said an Erasmus University student, 32, wearing combat fatigues, killed a teacher, 46, a local woman, 39, and her daughter, 14, after opening fire in a classroom at a university hospital campus in Rotterdam and a nearby house on the city's Heiman Dullaert Square. After he torched the woman's house, he went to the university hospital, Erasmus Medical Center, where he entered a classroom and shot dead a teacher. The man was arrested under the helicopter deck of the hospital, where he also set a fire. Hugo Hillenaar, Rotterdam's chief prosecutor, said "The suspect was known to law enforcement and in 2021, he was prosecuted and convicted for animal abuse."

December 12, 2023: The Dutch National Coordinator for Counterterrorism and Security raised the country's threat alert to its second-highest, saying the likelihood of attack is "substantial". It was the first time it was this high since late 2019.

January 11, 2024: South Africa brought a case of genocide against Israel at the International Court of Justice in The Hague. South Africa asked the ICJ to order an immediate suspension of Israel's military offensive in the Gaza Strip.

May 20, 2024: *BBC* reported that Karim Khan KC, chief prosecutor of the International Criminal Court (ICC), based in The Hague, applied for arrest warrants for Israeli Prime Minister Benjamin Netanyahu, Israeli defense minister Yoav Gallant, Hamas political leader Ismail Haniyeh, Yahya Sinwar, Hamas leader in Gaza, and Hamas military chief Mohammed Deif, for war crimes. Khan accused the Hamas leaders of such crimes as extermination, murder, hostage taking, rape and sexual violence, and torture. Khan said Netanyahu and Gallant were suspected of starvation of civilians as a method of warfare, murder, intentionally directing attacks against a civilian population, and extermination. A panel of 18 ICC judges was to review the request.

September 9, 2024: A three-judge panel of a Dutch court convicted two Pakistani religious and political leaders in absentia for calls to murder anti-Islam lawmaker Geert Wilders, the leader of the Party for Freedom that won the 2023 general election. The court found Muhammad Ashraf Asif Jalali guilty of attempting to provoke murder and incite Wilders's murder with a terrorist intent and of issuing threats. He was sentenced to 14 years. The court also convicted Saad Rizvi, who leads the radical Islamist Tehreek-e-Labaik Pakistan (TLP), for incitement to murder and threatening Wilders. He was sentenced to four years. The convicted men were believed to be in Pakistan, which has no extradition agreement with the Netherlands.

September 19, 2024: A man stabbed to death a man from Rotterdam, 32, and seriously injured a Swiss man, 33, in the evening near the landmark Erasmus Bridge in Rotterdam. Police arrested an injured suspect, 22, who was hospitalized. *De Telegraaf* reported that a man attacked people at random with two knives while shouting "Allahu akbar". The Rotterdam Public Prosecution Service said the attacker was suspected of murder and attempted murder with terrorist intent. Sports instructor Reniël Renato David Litecia, helped end the attack by shouting at the attacker, who was using two long knives. Police believed the assailant attacked one person in an underground parking lot and a second victim near a busy terrace near one end of the bridge that spans the New Maas River.

The Amersfoort resident had previous convictions for violent crimes and was to be arraigned on September 23 in The Hague. 24091901

November 7, 2024: On November 9, *AP* and *BBC* reported that five people were hospitalized and 62 were arrested during the night in Amsterdam following anti-Semitic attacks on Israeli soccer fans following a Europa League match. Home team Ajax FC had beaten the visiting Maccabi Tel Aviv 5-0 in the Johan Cruijff Arena.

December 7, 2024: *AP, AFP,* and *BBC* reported that an explosion went off in a three-storey apartment building in the Tarwekamp area in The Hague's northeastern Mariahoeve neighborhood, killing five people, injuring three others, and destroying several apartments around 6:15 a.m. Mayor Jan van Zanen said investigators were looking into "all possibilities." Police were searching for a car seen speeding away from the scene. Five people were taken from the rubble and hospitalized. On December 10, Dutch police arrested three suspects who might have been involved. Police also seized several vehicles.

December 11, 2024: The Hague District Court convicted Hasna A., 33, of crimes against humanity for keeping a Yazidi woman as a slave in Syria and sentenced her to 10 years in prison. Hasna traveled to Syria in 2015 to join ISIS, with her then-4-year-old son in tow. She married a fighter and was given a Yazidi woman, Z., as a domestic servant. Twelve women, including Hasna, with their 28 children, were repatriated to the Netherlands from a refugee camp in northern Syria in 2022.

NORTH MACEDONIA

December 15, 2024: Interior Minister Panche Toshkovski announced the arrests during raids on several locations in the western towns of Struga and Gostivar of four Macedonian men suspected of planning terrorist attacks. They faced eight years in prison.

NORTHERN IRELAND

February 22, 2023: *UPI* reported that before 8 p.m., Detective Chief Inspector John Caldwell, variant Cauldwell, 58, was critically injured in his torso in a fusillade of bullets as he coached U-11 soccer players at a crowded sports complex in Omagh. The next day, the Police Service of Northern Ireland arrested three male suspects aged 38, 45, and 47 under the Terrorism Act. The gunmen escaped in a small black car that was found torched at Racolpa Road outside Omagh. The New IRA splinter was suspected, but no one claimed credit.

UPI reported that later that night, detectives arrested a 22-year-old man 35 miles away near the town of Coalisland on suspicion of involvement in the shooting.

Caldwell was discharged from the hospital in April 2023.

UPI reported on May 19, 2023 that police under Section 41 of the Terrorism Act of 2000 arrested two more suspects in connection with the shooting. Police Service of Northern Ireland detectives arrested a man, 28, after a search of a house in the Omagh area and a man, 70, following the search of a property in the Dungannon area, 30 miles to the east. More than a dozen others had already been arrested, but no one had yet been charged.

March 26, 2023: MI-5 raised the terrorism threat level to "severe", the second-highest rung on the five-point scale, due to activities by dissident Irish republican paramilitary groups.

January 19, 2024: AP and NPR reported that three people wounded in IRA bombings 50 years earlier sued former Sinn Fein leader Gerry Adams. Justice Michael Soole said the IRA could not be sued because it was not a legal entity, but Adams could be sued as a private individual. The plaintiffs included:

- John Clark, a victim of the 1973 Old Bailey courthouse bombing in London
- Jonathan Ganesh, a 1996 London Docklands bombing victim
- Barry Laycock, a victim of the 1996 Arndale shopping center bombing in Manchester

They claimed Adams was an IRA leader during those events and was on its decision-making Army Council. They sought only 1 pound ($1.27) "for vindicatory purposes". Adams was represented by attorney Seamus Collins.

March 8, 2024: ABC News reported that a seven-year Operation Kenova investigation established that former Irish Republican Army double agent Freddie Scappaticci, alias Stakeknife,

was probably responsible for more lives lost than saved during the Troubles in Northern Ireland. He served as the IRA's internal security chief.

March 18, 2024: Bridget "Rose" Dugdale, 82, born on March 25, 1941, died at a nursing facility in Dublin. The Oxford-educated heiress was believed behind the April 1974 theft by the Irish Republican Army of 19 art masterpieces (including Francisco Goya's "Portrait of Doña Antonia Zárate"; Diego Velázquez's "Kitchen Maid with the Supper at Emmaus"; and Johannes Vermeer's "Lady Writing a Letter with her Maid") from the Russborough House estate south of Dublin of Alfred Beit, a former British member of Parliament and heir to a South African mining fortune. The IRA demanded that Dolours and Marian Price, two IRA car bombers, be transferred to a prison in Northern Ireland. The paintings were recovered and she was sentenced to nine years. She had also led a January 1974 attempt to bomb a police station in Strabane from a hijacked helicopter. Time Magazine called her the Renegade Debutante. She earned a doctorate in economics at Bedford College in London (now part of Royal Holloway College); the New York Times said her PhD was from the London School of Economics. She was released in 1980. She later began a relationship with IRA bomb maker Jim Monaghan.

March 19, 2024: BBC reported that convicted Garda killer Pearse McAuley was found dead at his home in Strabane. The IRA gunman was jailed for 14 years for the manslaughter of Det Garda Jerry McCabe during a failed post office raid in June 1996 in Adare in County Limerick. The four-man IRA gang fired AK47 assault rifles, killing Det Garda McCabe and wounding his partner, Det Garda Ben O'Sullivan. McAuley was jailed for stabbing Pauline Tully, his estranged wife, 13 times with a knife and breaking four of her fingers at their home in Kilnaleck, County Cavan, on December 24, 2014. He also threatened to kill her brother Tommy. In 2015, he was sentenced to 12 years for the attack, with the final four years suspended. He was freed from jail in 2021. McAuley and fellow IRA gunman Nessan Quinlivan shot their way out of Brixton prison in 1991 with a gun hidden in a shoe mailed from Ireland. McAuley was awaiting trial on charges regarding an IRA plot to assassinate the brewery chairman Charles Tidbury. McAuley fled to the Republic of Ireland. The four IRA shooters of McCabe were first charged with murder but the charge was dropped when witnesses refused to co-operate after IRA intimidation. The Special Criminal Court convicted the four of manslaughter. Sinn Féin failed to obain their release as part of the Good Friday Agreement. McAuley was granted special release in 2003 to wed then-Sinn Féin councillor Ms Tully, who was later elected to the Dáil (lower house of the Irish Parliament) for the party.

NORWAY

May 1, 2024: A man in his 30s and carrying two knives stabbed one man in the arm and charged at several others outside one of Oslo's biggest subway stations when an argument got out of control.

POLAND

May 1, 2024: *AP* and *al-Jazeera* reported that an attacker threw three firebombs at Warsaw's main Nożyk Synagogue at 1 a.m., causing minimal damage and no injuries. Poland's American-born chief rabbi, Michael Schudrich, credited "tremendous luck or miracle." Foreign Minister Radek Sikorski added that the incident fell on the 20th anniversary of Poland joining the European Union along with nine other countries. *PAP* reported that police in Warsaw arrested a 16-year-old male that evening. He had no previous police record. He faced a decade in prison.

November 5, 2024: *UPI* and the *Washington Post* reported that Polish authorities claimed that a series of parcel-borne arson attacks against logistics providers in Poland, Germany, and the UK were test runs for a campaign targeting transatlantic flights from Europe to the United States and Canada. Polish Prosecutor Katarzyna Calow-Jaszewska suggested that the Russian GRU military intelligence agency was behind the at-

tacks and noted that four people had been arrested as of the end of October amid Europe-wide investigations.

Fires broke out in July 2024 in a container being loaded onto a UK-bound DHL aircraft out of the German-based DHL's Leipzig-Halle Airport logistics hub at a transport firm near Warsaw, Poland, and at Minworth in the British midlands. The *Wall Street Journal* reported that the package contained electric massage devices that were booby-trapped with a highly flammable magnesium-based compound.

The Guardian reported that the parcel arrived by air from Lithuania, according to BfV chief Thomas Haldenwang. Polish firefighters needed two hours to extinguish a magnesium-based fire at Jablonow outside Warsaw. It was marked for delivery to a fake address in Birmingham, UK.

PORTUGAL

March 28, 2023: *USNWR* and *Reuters* reported that before 11 a.m., an individual stabbed to death two women and wounded a father of three at the Ismaili Centre in Lisbon. Police shot and arrested the attacker when he refused to surrender. The dead were Portuguese citizens who worked at the center. The *Washington Post* and *Bloomberg* added that police said several other people were injured. *SIC Television* reported that Nazim Ahmed, leader of the Ismaili community in Portugal, said the attacker was an Afghan refugee.

ROMANIA

June 3, 2024: Antiterrorism officers from the Romanian Intelligence Service detained a Syrian man, 34, after he allegedly threw a Molotov cocktail at the entrance door to the lobby of the Israeli Embassy in Bucharest, causing a small fire but no casualties. The suspect allegedly tried to set himself on fire. A police spokesperson told local news channel *Digi24* that the incident was motivated by personal grievances. Israeli Ambassador Reuven Azar called the suspect a "violent extremist".

RUSSIA

April 2, 2023: *CNN* reported that at 6 p.m., prominent pro-war Russian military blogger Vladlen Tatarsky, nee Maxim Fomin, 40, was killed and 32 other people wounded in an explosion at the Street Food Bar No. 1 café in St. Petersburg. The city's governor said 19 were hospitalized. Some 52 were injured. Tatarsky was about to address a crowd of 100 people sponsored by the pro-war Cyber Front Z when a woman identifying herself as Nastya handed him a gilded figurine of himself, which exploded in his hands five minutes later. *Baza* and *Metro* reported that the bomb was remotely detonated. The bomber had snuck the figurine past a bomb-sniffing dog. Russian state media claimed the figurine contained 200 grams of TNT. The café was owned by Wagner Group head Yevgeny Prigozhin.

Tatarsky created his *Telegram* channel, which had 500,000 followers, in 2019 and had written several books. *Vesti* reported that he had fought against Ukrainians in the Donbas in 2014. On occasion, he criticized battlefield setbacks.

CNN and *Newsweek* reported the next day that Russian authorities arrested St. Petersburg resident Daria Trepova, 26, at the apartment of a friend, who was also arrested. Her husband, Dmitry Rylov, said she had been "set up".

RIA Novosti reported that the government suggested involvement by the Ukrainian special services and associates of the Alexey Navalny-founded Anti-Corruption Foundation, which denied the accusations.

The Libertarian Party denied that Trepova had been a member or supporter of the party.

Tass reported that Trepova was born in February 1997 and lives in St. Petersburg. She was arrested on March 9, 2022 for participating in a rally when Russia invaded Ukraine on February 24, 2022, and sentenced to 10 days in prison.

The *Daily Mail* reported that Russian investigators were searching for a second female suspect, Maria Yaran, 40, who was reportedly in a hospital in St. Petersburg following the bombing.

Reuters, Rotonda, and *USNWR* reported on May 3, 2023 that Trepova said she did not know the contents of the parcel. She was held in Lefortovo Prison.

AP and the *Washington Post* reported on January 25, 2024 that a St. Petersburg court sentenced Trepova to 27 years in prison on charges of carrying out a terrorist attack, illegal trafficking of explosive devices, and forging documents in setting off a bomb in a riverside cafe that killed Tatarsky. The court also fined her about $6,700. The court convicted Trepova's acquaintance Dmitry Kasintsev of concealing a grave crime for sheltering her after the blast and sentenced him to 21 months. *Mediazona* reported that her sentence was the longest imposed on a woman in modern Russia. Russian investigators said she collaborated with a Ukrainian "sabotage and terrorism group".

April 12, 2023: *News 360, REN TV,* and *Europa* reported that during the night, the French Embassy in Moscow received a package with bones of a small animal or bird. The package was falsely sourced to Italian film producer Pietro Notarianni, who died in 2006, and marked "Mail from Russia". In June 2022, the French embassy had received another package with bones and a letter in French, and in December 2022 a package with a dead mouse and a spider. Both had the late Notarianni as sender.

May 3, 2023: The *Daily Beast, AP,* and *Tass* reported that the office of the president charged that the Kremlin was attacked by two drones at 2 a.m. in an assassination attempt against President Vladimir Putin. No injuries were reported. Ukraine denied involvement, and the U.S. rejected Russian allegations of U.S. orchestration.

May 6, 2023: The *Washington Post, UPI,* and *RTVI* reported that a car bomb injured Russian nationalist and novelist Zakhar Prilepin, 47, in the leg, and killed his friend (initially reported as his driver), Alexander Shubin, a military veteran who fought in the Luhansk region of Ukraine during Russia's invasion, in a village in the Nizhny Novgorod region. Beginning in 2014, Prilepin had fought alongside pro-Russian separatists in eastern Ukraine and had run a volunteer battalion. *Tass* reported that the bomb was placed under the car. The Investigative Committee of Russia said on *Telegram* that it had detained a man who allegedly "planted an explosive device" on Prilepin's path, observing "He fled from the scene but was detained by law enforcement officials as he was leaving the woods in another locality." The government blamed Ukrainian special services. A Crimean partisan group claimed responsibility, posting on *Telegram*, "The Atesh movement has been hunting Prilepin since the beginning of the year... Our predictions always come true, because we not only speak, but also do." Prilepin's daughter was with him but was not injured.

UPI and *TASS* reported that Alexander Permyakov appeared in court on terrorism and arms trafficking charges on May 8. Investigators claimed he testified that he was working for Ukrainian intelligence agencies.

November 11, 2023: *Bloomberg* reported that a bomb derailed a freight train in the Ryazan region southeast of Moscow, throwing 19 cars off the tracks. Fifteen cars were damaged. The state investigation committee said on *Telegram* that it had opened a criminal case into possible terrorism. Moscow Railway, a unit of the state-owned Russian Railways, blamed "illegal interference of unauthorized persons".

March 2, 2024: *AP, Interfax,* and *ABC News* reported that Russia's National Anti-Terrorism Committee (NAC) announced it had killed six ISIS members in a 7:30 p.m. shootout during a counterterrorism operation in the North Caucasus after the six men barricaded themselves in a third-floor apartment in Karabulak, Republic of Ingushetia. Three of them were on Russia's wanted list and all six had been involved in violent acts, including an attack on a traffic police unit in March 2023 that killed three officers. Security services found automatic weapons, ammunition, hand grenades, and homemade explosives inside the apartment. The Russian *Telegram* channel *Baza* set up by journalists critical of the Kremlin reported that a man walking by was killed in the shootout. The government said no civilians were harmed.

March 7, 2024: *UPI* reported that the U.S. Embassy in Moscow warned American citizens to avoid concerts and other large gatherings in the capital due to the "imminent" threat of an attack by extremists. The Federal Security Service (FSB) had claimed to have foiled an attack on a Moscow synagogue by the Wilayat Khorasan ISIS-linked cell in Kaluga, 90 miles southwest of Moscow. FSB said the group was carrying out reconnaissance when it caught the attention of security forces leading to a shootout after the terrorists resisted arrest. "During an operation to detain them, the terrorists put up armed resistance to Russian FSB agents and as a result were neutralized by return fire."

March 22, 2024: *BBC, al-Jazeera, NPR, CNN, AP, UPI, Tass, RIA Novosti, Business Insider, Yahoo! News, Reuters,* and the *Washington Post* reported that ISIS-K claimed credit on *Amaq* when at 8 p.m., four male terrorists in camouflage threw Molotov cocktails and fired machine guns at hundreds of concertgoers at a sold-out performance by the band Piknik at Crocus City Hall in Krasnogorsk during the night, killing 144, including three children, and wounding 205, many critically. The terrorists set alight the hall, causing catastrophic damage. The roof collapsed. Firefighters could not approach the 140,000 square feet that were in flames because of the ongoing shooting. People died from gunshot wounds and smoke inhalation.

The *New York Times* said that most of the identified victims appeared to be in their 40s, many traveling from other parts of the country. For example, Alexander Baklemishev, 51, had traveled from Satka, 1,000 miles away from Moscow.

UPI reported that more than 320 firefighters and 130 emergency vehicles responded; three emergency helicopters dropped water on the fire. Firefighters evacuated 100 people from the basement.

Crocus is a massive shopping and entertainment venue in the Moscow suburbs. Video of the incident showed its large sign in English proclaiming Crocus City Hall.

Russian MP Alexander Khinshtein said the terrorists escaped in a white Renault. When police tried to stop the vehicle in the Bryansk region, they arrested two people as the others fled. He said Tajikistan passports were found in the car. The Tajik minister of the interior said that in two cases, the men in question could not be responsible as they had been in Tajikistan for months and had credible alibis. Authorities later said four Tajiks were captured.

Fourteen hours after the shooting began, the FSB said it had detained 11 people, including the four directly involved in the attack.

BBC noted that unverified videos on the Internet showed a suspected attacker saying he was recruited on the Internet to carry out the attack and claims he was promised 1 million rubles (£8,600) to shoot concertgoers. Another video purported to show a leader of the attack.

It is not common for ISIS-affiliated terrorists to flee a scene or have a complex exit strategy.

The Investigative Committee of Russia said a concertgoer "neutralised one of the terrorists" while trying to protect his wife. The Committee planned to give him a departmental award for his "unparalleled courage".

Some 19 hours after the attack began, newly-reelected President Putin addressed the nation and declared March 24 a day of mourning. "The criminals in cold blood, purposefully went to kill and shoot at point-blank range our citizens and our children, as the Nazis did who committed massacres in the occupied territories. They planned to stage a demonstrative execution, a bloody act of intimidation... All perpetrators, organizers and sponsors of this crime will be fairly and unavoidably punished, whoever they are or whoever directs them." He claimed the four gunmen were trying to escape toward Ukraine through a "window" on the Ukrainian side and had accomplices helping them to do so.

BBC Verify reported that Russian *NTV* broadcast a fake video using an AI-generated composite deepfake based on two interviews of senior Ukrainian security official Oleksiy Danilov and Ukrainian military intelligence chief Kyrylo Budanov apparently saying, "It is fun in Moscow today. I think it's a lot of fun. I would like to believe that we will arrange such fun for them more often" in an attempt to blame Ukraine. The Ukrainian foreign ministry, Mykhailo Podo-

lyak, an aide to Ukrainian President Volodymyr Zelensky, and the military intelligence agency all denied involvement.

A branch of ISIS based in Syria claimed its fighters caused "major destruction" in a "big gathering for Christians in the Russian Moscow suburb". ISIS later said "the attack comes in the context of normal ongoing war between the Islamic State and [anti-Islam] countries". Its "fighters" used "machine guns, a gun, knives, and incendiary bombs". ISIS posted a photo of the four attackers.

Mourners left flowers at Russian embassies in the UK, Israel, Australia, Cyprus, and Belarus. *CNN* and *Belta* reported that Belarus Ambassador to Moscow Dmitry Krutoy claimed that his country helped prevent the terrorists' escape.

The *Washington Post* reported that Russia's Investigative Committee said 16 of the 107 hospitalized victims were in a grave condition and 44 in serious condition.

By the next day, Russia's Ministry of Health had identified 41 victims, mostly people aged between 30 and 60 years old. *Baza*, a *Telegram* channel with ties to Russian security services, reported that 28 bodies were found in one of the venue's bathrooms, including "many mothers" clasping their children. Another 14 were discovered in an emergency exit stairwell.

The U.S. on March 7 had issued a warning to Americans, also sharing it with Russian authorities per its "duty to warn" policy, regarding intelligence reporting about possible activity inside Russia from Islamic State-Khorasan, the Afghanistan and Pakistan arm of the Islamic State, to attack large venues.

The governor of Moscow region, Andrey Vorobyov, announced that the victims would receive financial compensation from the region and city governments. Relatives of each of those who died would receive three million rubles ($32,500); those injured and hospitalized would receive one million rubles ($10,840). Shaman, lead singer of the 1980s rock band Piknik, said via Russian social media network *Vkontakte* to his more than 600,000 followers that he would pay funeral expenses and treatments for the injured.

RIA Novosti reported that a shopping union vice president estimated the damage to the Crocus center at 9.5-11.4 billion rubles, or approximately $103-124 million.

NPR, CNN, Reuters, and *AP* reported that the four Tajik suspects—Saidakrami Rachabalizoda, Shamsidin Fariduni, Dalerdzhon Mirzoyev, and Muhammadsober Fayzov—were physically dragged into court and charged with committing a crime under part 3, provision "b" of article 205 of the Russian Criminal Code (terrorist act), in Basmanny District Court on March 24. *TASS* reported that three pleaded guilty. The suspects were heavily bruised, showing signs of severe beatings; Muhammadsober Fayzov was in a wheelchair, unconscious. Saidakrami Murodali Rachabalizoda had a large gauze bandage on his right ear; Russian media said his ear had been cut off during interrogation. The Basmanny District Court granted the investigators' motion for detention for all four defendants. They were remanded into pre-trial detention until May 22. They faced life in prison.

CNN and *RIA Novosti* reported that

- **Dalerdzhon Mirzoyev**, 32, had a temporary registration for three months in Novosibirsk in Siberia, but it expired.

- **Saidakrami Rachabalizoda**, 30, born in 1994, told the court via an interpreter that he had Russian registration documents but forgot where they were. Turkish officials said he checked into a hotel in Istanbul's Fatih district on January 5, and checked out on January 21.

- **Shamsidin Fariduni**, 25, born in 1998, was officially employed at a factory in Podolsk and was registered in Krasnogorsk. Turkish officials said he entered Turkey on February 20, checked into a hotel in Istanbul's Fatih district on February 21, and checked out on February 27.

- **Muhammadsober Faizov**, 19, born in 2004, was nonresponsive in a wheelchair and was accompanied by a doctor to his court appearance. *Mediazona* reported that he was brought in from intensive care. Faizov was temporarily unemployed; he earlier worked in a barber shop in Ivanovo.

Russian media broadcast videos showing a suspect who claimed he was approached by an unidentified assistant to an Islamic preacher via a messaging app and paid to take part in the raid. The *New York Times* reported on March 24 that one suspect said he had been recruited over *Telegram* to conduct the killings for money.

AP reported that Alisher Kasimov, a citizen of Kyrgyzstan, was charged for renting an apartment to the gunmen.

Billboards with a single candle and reading, "St. Petersburg Mourns 03.22.2024" sprouted throughout Russia.

UPI reported on March 24 that Hamas posted on *Telegram* "We in the Islamic Resistance Movement (Hamas) condemn in the strongest terms the terrorist attack that targeted civilians in the Russian capital, Moscow, and left dozens dead and wounded… We extend our sincere condolences to the Russian leadership and people, and to the families of the victims of this criminal attack, and we wish a speedy recovery to the injured, and we express our full solidarity with Russia, its people, and the families of the victims in this tragedy."

AP reported on March 25 that among the 80 missing was Yana Pogadaeva, wife of Igor Pogadaev. She had sent him two photos from the Crocus City Hall music venue. Her name was not among the 60 victims authorities had identified. 24032202

AP and *Tass* reported that Health Minister Mikhail Murashko said on March 26 that 22 of the injured victims, including two children, were still in serious condition.

BBC reported that President Putin on March 26 blamed radical Islamists, but still claimed Ukraine was behind the attack.

AP reported that as of March 27, 2024, the death toll had risen to 143 and 80 others remained hospitalized. Authorities were looking for another 100 people who had gone missing.

On March 28, 2024, Russia's Investigative Committee reported that another suspect was detained.

RIA Novosti noted on March 29, 2024 that Tajikistan had arrested nine residents of the Vakhdat district for contact with the attackers and ISIS-K.

A Moscow court ruled that another suspect—Lutfulloi Nazrimad—should be held in custody until at least May 22, pending investigation and trial. Russian independent news site *Mediazona* reported that Nazrimad claimed that he was born in Tajikistan.

Reuters reported on April 1, 2024 that Iran warned Russia of a likely terrorist strike.

AP reported on April 27, 2024 that Moscow's Basmanny District Court detained another suspect as an accomplice in the March 22, 2024 attack on the Crocus City Hall concert venue that killed 144 people. The judge accused Dzhumokhon Kurbonov, a citizen of Tajikistan, of providing the attackers with means of communication and financing. Kurbonov was to be kept in custody until May 22 pending investigation and trial. *RIA Novosti* said Kurbonov was detained on April 11 for 15 days on the administrative charge of petty hooliganism. Twelve defendants have been arrested in the case.

Al-Jazeera reported on May 24, 2024 that FSB chief Alexander Bortnikov told *Ria Novosti* that Russia had arrested more than 20 people in connection with the ISIS-K attack on the concert hall. It was the first time Russia attributed the attack to ISIS-K. The detention of the four Tajik suspects was extended the previous week until August 22.

April 11, 2024: The National Antiterror Committee announced that special forces killed two people suspected of plotting terror attacks on the outskirts of Nalchik, capital of the Kabardino-Balkaria republic. The duo had fired on Federal Security Service special forces.

April 28, 2024: The regional branch of Russia's Interior Ministry announced that during the night, five gunmen attacked a police checkpoint in the North Caucasus region, killing two officers and wounding four other officers. All five attackers were killed in the shootout in the Karachay-Cherkessia region.

May 3, 2024: A military court in Khabarovsk sentenced Russian activist Angel Nikolayev, 39, to 15 years in prison on terrorism charges for attempting to set fire to a military conscription office by placing two bottles containing a flammable substance in the windows of a district conscription office in the city and setting them ablaze in protest against the Russian action in Ukraine, damaging Russian flags that were put on the graves of soldiers killed in action in Ukraine at a local cemetery, removing symbols of Russian military action in Ukraine from a bus stop and several vehicles in Khabarovsk.

June 16, 2024: *RT, al-Jazeera, Interfax, Tass,* and *AP* reported that six inmates armed with a penknife, a rubber baton, and a fire ax and believed associated with ISIS took hostage two prison guards at a pretrial detention center in Rostov-on-Don before special forces freed the duo unharmed and killed the inmates. Two of the hostage-takers wore headbands that resembled the ISIS flag. The hostage-takers had demanded to be provided with a car and be allowed to leave the prison. *Tass* reported that three inmates had been found guilty on several charges, including disseminating extremist information and plotting to blow up a Russian courthouse. One of the men was sentenced to 18½ years in prison, while the other two received 18 years.

June 23, 2024: *CNN, al-Jazeera, UPI, AP, NPR, Reuters,* and *BBC* reported that apparently coordinated attacks at 5:50 p.m. at a church and the Kele-Numaz synagogue in Derbent and at a police traffic stop, a cathedral, and a second synagogue in Makhachkala killed 21 people, including 15 law enforcement officers, a church security guard, and wounded another 46 people, including a dozen police in Dagestan Province. One of the wounded police officers died later. At the Russian Orthodox Assumption Cathedral they slit the throat of Russian Orthodox priest Father Nikolay Kotelnikov, 66. The priest had worked at the church for more than 40 years. The synagogue was torched. A police officer was injured at the traffic stop. *RIA Novosti* and *Tass* reported that six "militants" were killed in a counterterrorism operation at 8:15 a.m. The Dagestan Ministry of Internal Affairs reported that Mavludin Khidirnabiev, one of the law enforcement officers killed, was the head of the "Dagestan Lights" police department. The terrorists who hit the Derbent synagogue escaped in a white Volkswagen Polo car.

Al-Azaim Media, a Russian-language channel associated with ISIS-K, credited ISIS-K. ISIS-K separately praised the attack. *AP* reported that the Washington-based Institute for the Study of War suggested that ISIS's North Caucasus branch, Vilayat Kavkaz, was responsible. Russian officials hinted at "sleeper cells" and "foreign forces" were behind "an attempt to cleave apart our unity." Dmitry Gadzhiyev, State Duma Deputy from Dagestan, unfettered by evidence, blamed "special services of Ukraine and NATO countries".

The *Washington Post* and *CNN* reported that officials arrested Magomed Omarov, head of the Sergokalinsky district of Dagestan, after a son, a nephew, and a cousin allegedly took part in the attacks. Law enforcement officials killed the duo. *AP* reported that United Russia dismissed him from its ranks. *CNN* reported that the cousin was former mixed martial arts fighter Gadzhimurad Kagirov, who had taken part in the attack on Derbent.

July 24, 2024: A bomb exploded in a car in a parking lot in the morning in Moscow, injuring a man and a woman. Turkish officials in Bodrum detained suspect Evgenii Serebriakov hours after he fled to the Turkish resort town on a direct flight from Moscow. His name was not immediately listed on an Interpol wanted persons database. *Interfax* said the wounded man is a colonel working with the military general staff.

August 23, 2024: *AP* reported that inmates seized guards at the IK-19 Surovkino prison in the Volgograd region, 535 miles east of Moscow, and declared allegiance to ISIS. The Federal Penitentiary Service (FSIN) said eight prison employees and four convicts had been taken hostage. Russian media suggested that the hostages included the prison's director and deputy director. The National Guard Service said the rebellious inmates were "neutralized" and all the hostages had been freed. *Tass* reported that four victims were taken to a local hospital and two of them were in serious condition. Russian news site *Meduza* ran a video showing men wielding knives inside and in a prison yard and several men in what appeared to be guard uniforms lying in blood on the ground. The attackers

said they supported the suspects arrested in the March terrorist attack on a Moscow concert hall that left 145 people dead. Court records showed that the hostage-takers were from former Soviet Central Asian countries; the concert hall attack suspects are from Tajikistan. *BBC* later reported that four prison employees were killed.

October 5, 2024: *UPI* and *Tass* reported that Moscow planned to remove the Taliban government from its list of designated terrorist organizations, where it had been placed in 2003.

SERBIA

May 3, 2023: *UPI, AP, NPR*, local channel *N1*, *RTS*, and the *Washington Post* reported that at 8:30 a.m., Kosta Kecmanovic, 14, a seventh-grade student, opened fire at his fellow students at Vladislav Ribnikar elementary school in Belgrade's Vracar district, killing eight children and a security guard and wounding six children and a teacher. The student was detained in the schoolyard. Police said he had drawn sketches of classrooms and drafted a hit list. He first killed a school guard, then three students in a hallway, then attacked a history classroom near the school entrance. He then phoned police. He was armed with two guns, including a handgun, belonging to his father, and four Molotov cocktails. NBA basketball player Luka Doncic announced that he would pay for the funerals of all nine victims, and for grief counselling for classmates and staff.

May 4, 2023: The *Washington Post, UPI, BBC, NPR*, and *RTS* reported that police arrested Uros R., 21, a man suspected of three drive-by shootings that killed eight people, including a police officer and his sister, and wounded 14 others—all born after 2000—during a nighttime spree in Dubona, Mali Orašje, and Sepsin in the Mladenovac area. Police confiscated four hand grenades from the home where R. was hiding. The Interior Ministry was treating the incident as an act of domestic terrorism.

Serbian President Aleksander Vucic pledged that the government will introduce tougher gun control legislation and that Serbia will hire 1,200 new police officers in the next six months. "We will carry out an almost total disarmament of

Serbia… We must make a decision to confront this evil." R.'s father is a deputy colonel in the Serbian Army.

Initial local reports indicated the suspect had two accomplices, one of whom was killed in a shootout with police. He was hiding at his grandfather's house in Kragujevac. He had opened fire on people with an automatic weapon after arguing with a police officer in a park in Dubona. He had been wearing a T-shirt with neo-Nazi symbols. The *New York Times* reported that police found in his houses an unregistered automatic rifle, a carbine with optics, a pistol, and four hand grenades.

June 29, 2024: *U.S. News and World Report*, *AP*, and *Reuters* that police killed a Serbian Islamic convert, 25, who shot a crossbow at a gendarme guarding the Israeli embassy in Belgrade. *Tanjug* reported that the policeman underwent surgery for life-threatening neck injuries. Several suspected Wahhabi accomplices were arrested. The attacker had asked the guard several times where a museum was.

July 18, 2024: Interior Minister Ivica Dačić suggested that terrorism was involved when an individual stopped by a patrol at 1 a.m. in Loznica, near the border with Bosnia, shot at police officers, killing one and wounding another. The individual stepped out of the vehicle and fired at the police, hitting one in the chest and one in the shoulder. Police found a passport issued in Kosovo and a German identification card at the scene. The Interior Minister said, "It cannot be accidental. It is an organized attack… The organized crime prosecutor will look into this case as a terrorist attack by (ethnic) Albanian people from Kosovo with certain goals." Dačić said the suspect might have taken his brother's passport. *AP* and *RTS* reported on July 19 that Serbian police near Loznica found and killed the shooter, who was from Kosovo.

SLOVAKIA

May 15, 2024: The *Washington Post*, *AP*, *BBC*, *NBC News*, *al-Jazeera*, *Reuters*, *CNN*, *CNBC*, *TA3*, Slovakia's state news agency *TASR*, and newspaper *Dennik N* reported that in the after-

noon, a gunman fired five shots and injured in the stomach and arm Slovakian Prime Minister Robert Fico, 59, after a government offsite meeting in the House of Culture in Handlova, two hours' drive northeast of the capital, Bratislava. Rescuers carried Fico to a waiting black Audi sedan. He was stabilized at a local hospital, then airlifted by helicopter to a second hospital in Banska Bystrica for five hours of surgery on life-threatening injuries from three bullets. Authorities arrested a suspect.

Fico was in his third stint as prime minister, having won the September 30 election. Fico earlier blamed "Ukrainian Nazis and fascists" for provoking President Vladimir Putin into invading Ukraine. Fico led the Smer-SSD (Direction) Party, running on a pro-Russian and anti-American populist platform.

AP, Slovakian *TV Markiza*, *UPI*, and *BBC* reported that the next day Slovak authorities charged male retiree Juraj Cintula, 71, from Levice, with premeditated murder for attempting to assassinate the Prime Minister. The lone wolf did not belong to any political groups. The amateur poet might have earlier worked as a security guard at a mall in the country's southwest. Interior Minister Matus Sutaj Estok said that the suspect had attended a recent anti-government protest. Cintula told police he did not intend to kill Fico but wanted to publicize his disagreement with government policy. Cintula co-founded a literary club in 2005 and belonged to the Slovak Writers Association. Cintula had possessed a gun legally for more than 30 years. Cintula faced 25 years in prison if convicted. The *New York Times* reported that he and his wife have two children.

AP reported on May 31 that Fico was released from the hospital in Banska Bystrica.

AP reported on July 4, 2024 that Cintula faced terrorism charges according to Prosecutor-General Maroš Žilinka.

SPAIN

January 12, 2023: The *Washington Examiner* reported that Madrid agreed to repatriate 15 people—two women and 13 children—with ISIS ties from the al-Hol camp in Syria.

January 25, 2023: *Euronews* and *TeleMadrid TV* reported that a machete-wielding man with a beard and wearing a black, white, and grey hoodie killed a church caretaker and injured four others, including a priest, in 7 p.m. attacks at two Catholic churches in Algeciras. The Moroccan, 25 (originally described as around 40), was disarmed and arrested. He entered the San Isidro church shouting and throwing icons, crosses, and candles to the floor. He attacked priest Antonio Rodriguez, 74, while he was celebrating the Eucharist, causing serious injury. Five minutes later, he assaulted Diego Valencia, the caretaker at the Nuestra Senora de La Palma church. The verger escaped outside but the attacker caught and fatally wounded him. *AFP* added that the machete-wielder was scheduled for deportation but had no prior convictions.

November 9, 2023: *CNN, EFE,* and the *Los Angeles Times* reported that around 1:30 p.m., Alejo Vidal-Quadras, 78, the former president of Spain's Popular Party in Catalonia, was shot in the face on a central street in the wealthy neighborhood of Salamanca in Madrid. Vidal-Quadras was a founder of the far-right party Vox, currently the third largest force in the lower house of the Spanish parliament. Police believed the gunman wore a black helmet and escaped on a motorcycle. The victim survived with a double jaw fracture.

Al-Jazeera added that on November 21, 2023 Spanish police arrested two Spanish men and a British woman regarding possible "terror links" to the shooting. Two suspects were arrested in the southern city of Lanjaron and the third in Fuengirola. The Paris-based Iranian opposition group Committee of the National Council of Resistance of Iran blamed Tehran. In January, the Iranian Ministry of Foreign Affairs imposed sanctions on Vidal-Quadras and others with ties to the Mujahedeen-e-Khalq, accusing them of "supporting terrorism and terrorist groups".

February 20, 2024: The *Washington Post* and *Ukrainska Pravda* reported that the previous week, police found a body at the entrance to a residential complex in Villajoyosa, in Alicante. The victim had been shot six times and run over by a car. He was later identified as Russian de-

fector Maksym Kuzminov, who flew a Russian Mi-8 military helicopter loaded with jet parts to Ukraine in August 2023. Ukrainian forces shot to death two crew members who were unaware of the plot and refused to surrender. The Ukrainian government later announced that Kuzminov had received a $500,000 reward in local currency. The *Daily Beast* added on February 22 that Russia's security chief and former president Dmitry Medvedev, the deputy chairman of the Security Council, observed, "For a dog, a dog's death." Sergei Naryshkin, Vladimir Putin's spy chief, called Kuzminov a "traitor", "criminal", and a "moral corpse". *Levante-EMV* added that the killers appeared to deliberately leave behind Russian-made shell casings.

July 18, 2024: Spain arrested three people and Germany arrested a fourth on suspicion of membership in a network that supplied Lebanese Hizballah with parts to build kamikaze drones capable of carrying explosive charges of several kilograms that would have been used in attacks in northern Israel. Investigators claimed that the Spanish companies, and others around the world, purchased items including electronic guidance components, propulsion propellers, gasoline engines, more than 200 electric motors and materials for the fuselage, wings, and other drone parts.

SWEDEN

July 6, 2023: *BBC* reported that Judge Mans Wigen of the Stockholm district court jailed a Kurdish man, 41, of Turkish origins, to 4½ years for crimes, including attempting to persuade a Kurdish businessman at gunpoint outside a bar in Stockholm to provide funds for the PKK, which the U.S. and EU consider a terrorist group. The judge said the man would be deported after serving his sentence.

August 17, 2023: Following a series of Quran burnings by anti-Islam activists, the government raised the terrorism alert level to four, "high", on its five-point scale, the first time since 2016.

January 31, 2024: *AP* and *UPI* reported that the SAPO domestic security agency was investigating "a dangerous object" that was found at the Israeli Embassy in Stockholm as terrorism. Swedish media called it a hand grenade, found near the fence of the diplomatic mission. A local bomb squad destroyed the object. No one was injured. No arrests were made as of February 2.

February 7, 2024: Swedish radio broadcaster *SR* and *AP* reported that two Iranians, a man and woman, had been suspected of planning to kill three Swedish Jews. The duo were arrested in 2021 and were expelled from Sweden in 2022 without charges. Daniel Stenling, counterespionage head at Sweden's domestic security agency, said the next day that Iran has planned attacks on the country. *SR* reported that Mahdi Ramezani and Fereshteh Sanaeifarid sought asylum in Sweden in 2015, claiming to be Afghans, and eventually got shelter in Sweden. *SR* added that they have links to Iran's Revolutionary Guard.

March 7, 2024: On the day when Sweden became the 32nd member of NATO and its Prime Minister was a guest at U.S. President Biden's State of the Union address to the U.S. Congress, Sweden's SAPO Security Service arrested four people on suspicion of preparing "terrorist offenses" with links to Islamic extremism and organized crime. Authorities searched several houses. *SVT* reported a major police operation in Tyreso, south of Stockholm, where there was a "powerful explosion in a clubhouse".

June 14, 2024: *UPI* and *CNN* reported that the U.S. Department of State designated the Nordic Resistance Movement and three of its leaders as Specially Designated Global Terrorists. Tor Fredrik Vejdeland has been in the group's national leadership for 20 years and led its national council. NRM national council member Pär Öberg heads the group's parliamentary branch. NRM national council member Leif Robert Eklund coordinates various Swedish NRM divisions. State said that NRM is Sweden's largest neo-Nazi group, with branches in Norway, Denmark, Iceland, and Finland, where it has been banned since 2020. NRM professes an openly racist, anti-immigrant, antisemitic, and anti-LGBTQI+ platform. Members and leaders have carried out violent attacks against political opponents, protestors, journalists, and other perceived adversaries. State said the group formed in 1997, initially as the Swedish Resistance movement.

September 19, 2024: Authorities charged Swedish citizen Lina Laina Ishaq, 52, who was associated with ISIS, with genocide, crimes against humanity and war crimes against Yazidi women and children from August 2014 to December 2016 in Raqqa, Syria. She was suspected of holding nine people, among them children, in her home for up to seven months, treating them as slaves and abusing several of the captives. She was accused of having molested a one-month-old baby by holding a hand over the child's mouth when he screamed to silence him. Swedish news agency *TT* reported that she was represented by attorney Mikael Westerlund.

Sweden earlier convicted her and sentenced her to three years in prison for taking her son, 2, to an ISIS-controlled area of Syria in 2014. She had claimed that she had told the child's father that she and the boy were going on a holiday to Türkiye. In 2017, she was captured by Syrian Kurdish troops. She escaped to Türkiye, where she, her son, and two other children, born in Syria to an ISIS fighter from Tunisia, were arrested. Türkiye extradited her to Sweden. She had earlier lived in Landskrona, Sweden.

On October 7, 2024, *TT* and *AP* reported that Ishaq's trial began at the Stockholm District Court.

October 2, 2024: Shots were fired during the night at the Israeli Embassy in Stockholm, causing no injuries. No one was arrested.

SWITZERLAND

February 8, 2024: In the early evening, police killed an Iranian asylum-seeker, 32, who wielded an axe and a knife to seize 15 hostages for four hours on a train stopped in Essert-sous-Champvert in the French-speaking Vaud region in western Switzerland. No passengers were injured. The man, speaking Farsi and English, demanded that the train engineer join the hostages. Police stormed the train after trying to negotiate with the man through an interpreter.

March 3, 2024: Police arrested a Swiss citizen, 15, on suspicion of stabbing and critically wounding an Orthodox Jewish man, 50, on the streets of Zurich at 9:35 p.m.

October 1, 2024: A Chinese man, 23, stabbed and injured three boys, age 5, who were heading to a day care center in Zurich's Oerlikon district. Police arrested the suspect after a center employee and another man overwhelmed and held the assailant. The children were en route to the center with a woman who works there. One child was seriously injured; two others were moderately injured.

TÜRKIYE

January 7, 2023: *News 360* and *Europa Press* reported that Turkish police arrested two suspected ISIS members of Uzbek and Tajik nationality who were planning to commit an attack in Istanbul on New Year's Eve. Police followed them after a chase in the Basaksehir district of Istanbul by shooting at the wheels of their vehicle. Tajik suspect Abu Maymuna might have collaborated with the ISIS-K and was considered to be an explosives specialist.

January 30, 2023: *Reuters* reported that the U.S. embassy warned Americans of possible terrorist attacks against churches, synagogues, and diplomatic missions in Istanbul. The embassy had released a similar notice on January 26, after Koran-burning incidents in Europe.

February 1, 2023: *News 360* and *Europa Press* reported that the German consulate in Istanbul was closed for the day "for security reasons". *AP* reported that Turkish officials complained for two days that nine countries (U.S., Netherlands, Switzerland, Sweden, UK, Germany, Belgium, France, and Italy) had not informed them of the threat information upon which their consulates' closures and travel advisories were based.

Reuters reported on February 5 that Turkish police said they had detained 15 ISIS suspects but did not find evidence of a threat to foreign diplomatic missions or non-Muslim houses of worship. *Anadolu* quoted an Istanbul police statement saying the 15 had "received instruc-

tions for acts targeting consulates of Sweden and the Netherlands, as well as Christian and Jewish places of worship".

April 25, 2023: *Anadolu* and *AP* reported that police raided homes in 21 provinces and detained 110 people for alleged links to Kurdistan Workers' Party militants.

August 1, 2023: *Al-Jazeera* and state broadcaster *TRT* reported that at 9:45 a.m., a "mentally disabled" person critically wounded a female secretary in an armed attack outside Sweden's honorary consulate in Izmir's Konak district in Izmir Province. Turkish broadcaster Habertürk reported that the incident is believed related to a dispute about the visa application process. Turkish authorities detained the assailant with the gun.

October 1, 2023: *Al-Jazeera* and *Anadolu* reported that the Kurdistan Workers' Party claimed credit for a 9:30 a.m. suicide bombing by two attackers in front of the Interior Ministry on Ataturk Boulevard in Ankara in which police officers Alim Reis Demirel and Erkan Karatas were injured. The PKK told the *Firat News Agency (ANF)*, "A sacrificial action was carried out against the Turkish Interior Ministry by a team from our Immortal Brigade." A senior Turkish official told *Reuters* that the attackers hijacked a veterinarian's vehicle and killed its driver in Kayseri. One of the injured officers suffered shrapnel injuries. The suicide bomber died in the explosion and police killed his partner in a shootout.

December 22, 2023: *Al-Jazeera* reported that Interior Minister Ali Yerlikaya said that in operations across 32 provinces, authorities arrested hundreds of people suspected of having links to ISIS. The majority of the suspects were arrested in Ankara, Istanbul, and Izmir.

December 29, 2023: *Al-Jazeera* and *Anadolu* reported that Interior Minister Ali Yerlikaya announced that police in Operation Heroes-37 and Operation Heroes-38 in 37 provinces detained 189 people, including three alleged senior ISIS terrorists, suspected of having ties to ISIS who planned attacks on churches and synagogues in Istanbul and the Iraqi Embassy in Ankara.

January 11, 2024: *AP* reported that Interior Minister Ali Yerlikaya announced that police detained 70 suspects with ties to ISIS in raids this week across the country. Police found large amounts of money, digital material, and receipts for hawala banking transactions. The next day, Yerlikaya announced police had detained 113 people suspected of ties to the PKK following raids across 32 Turkish provinces. Four people were arrested after police identified 60 social media accounts that "praised the separatist terrorist organization for provocative purposes" or had spread misleading information.

January 28, 2024: *CNN* reported that Interior Minister Ali Yerlikaya posted on *X* that two masked gunmen attacked a Sunday Mass service in Santa Maria Church in Istanbul's Sariyer District's Büyükdere neighborhood around 11:40 a.m., killing one person. Istanbul Governor Davut Gul said one person was targeted. ISIS claimed credit. Interior Minister Ali Yerlikaya said one suspect is from Tajikistan and the other from Russia. Police raided 30 locations and detained 47 people. Sukru Genc, mayor of Sariyer district told the newspaper *Birgun* that the gunmen fled when their weapons jammed after firing two rounds. People attending the Mass included Polish Consul General Witold Lesniak and his family, who were unharmed. The church is run by an Italian order of Franciscan friars.

February 1, 2024: *Bloomberg, Demiroren News Agency,* and *AFP* reported that a gunman raided the main building of a Procter & Gamble factory in Kocaeli Province around 3 p.m. and took seven staff members hostage in protest over the war in Gaza. P&G evacuated its Gebze facility. *UPI* added on February 2 that authorities "intervened and neutralized the suspect" after hour of fruitless negotiations. All hostages were reported to be in good health.

February 6, 2024: *AP, Anadolu, al-Jazeera,* and *CNN* reported that Turkish Interior Minister Ali Yerlikaya said that in the late morning, authorities shot to death a man and a woman trying to attack a security checkpoint at the Çağlayan courthouse in the Kagithane district in Istanbul. Six people were hurt, including three police offi-

cers. One person later died. Investigators found flags and banners in the woman's bag. Yerlikaya said the attackers were members of the Marxist-Leninist armed group the Revolutionary People's Liberation Party-Front. The attackers were identified as EY and PB.

February 10, 2024: *AP* and *Anadolu* reported that gunmen attacked a visit by Aziz Yeniay, a candidate for mayor in Istanbul's Kucukcemece district for the Justice and Development Party (AKP), to an association, critically wounding a woman, 32. The attackers drove away in a white car. Police arrested a suspect and found 17 spent shells at the site.

March 10, 2024: Police detained 33 suspected ISIS adherents who were allegedly preparing attacks ahead of the country's March 31 local elections. Counter-terrorism police recovered weapons, cash, and "organizational documents".

August 12, 2024: *AP* and *al-Jazeera* reported that police arrested Arka K., 18, who was wearing goggles, a helmet, and bulletproof vest, after he stabbed five people at an open-air tea garden after prayers at a mosque in Eskisehir. *HaberTurk TV* reported that he broadcast the knife attack on social media through a camera attached to his vest. *Anadolu* reported that the five victims were hospitalized; two were in serious condition. The assailant carried an ax but did not appear to have used it. *HaberTurk, Cumhuriyet,* and other media reported K. was believed to have been influenced by a video game. News sites claimed he wore a "black sun" Nazi symbol made up of several swastikas, on his chest.

August 18, 2024: *AP* and *Demiroren News Agency* reported that Israeli-Arab businessman of Palestinian origin Abdulkadir Anas was shot to death and two other Palestinian men were wounded as they sat in a car on Dilaver Street in the Kagithane district of north Istanbul. Anas's friend was critically wounded and a bodyguard was injured in the foot. The Istanbul Governor's Office said the nighttime attack was motivated by a dispute over money and that three suspects were thought to have crossed the Bulgarian border using three different cars within 2 1/2 hours of the shooting. Seven people had been involved in planning and carrying out the attack. Police arrested four people and recovered two weapons, including a silenced handgun. *AP* reported on August 20 that authorities in Romania arrested three suspects.

October 23, 2024: *AP,* the *Washington Post, Anadolu, NTV, Middle East Eye, BBC, UPI, al-Jazeera, DHA,* and *HaberTurk Television* reported that around 3:30 p.m., three terrorists arrived in a hijacked taxi then set off bombs and fired assault weapons at the entry to the state-run Turkish Aerospace Industries (TUSAS) aviation and defense company's Kahramankazan complex 25 miles outside Ankara, killing five people, including Cengiz Coskun, a quality control officer; Zahide Guclu, a mechanical engineer; security guard Atakan Sahin Erdogan; employee Huseyin Canbaz; and Murat Arslan, the taxi driver; and wounding 22, three critically. Seven special ops forces members were injured. Interior Minister Ali Yerlikaya said that a male and a female terrorist were killed. She set off a bomb after being injured. He threw grenades at responding forces, then set off a bomb in the restroom of a nearby building.

UPI, BBC, and *Anadolu* reported the next day that Turkish warplanes attacked 47 Kurdistan Workers Party (PKK) targets, including caves, shelters, depots, military facilities, ammunition depots, and energy infrastructure in northern Iraq and Syria, destroying the targets and killing 59 terrorists. The government identified the male attacker as PKK member Ali Orek.

On October 25, 2024, the PKK's military wing, the People's Defense Center, claimed credit, saying the attack was conducted by two members of Immortal Battalion in response to Turkish "massacres" and other actions in Kurdish regions. That day, Turkish police detained 176 suspected PKK members across Türkiye.

November 22, 2024: The Interior Ministry announced that two pro-Kurdish mayors were removed from office due to terrorism-related charges and were replaced with state-appointed administrators. Since October, six elected mayors had been removed. The mayor of the mainly Kurdish-populated provincial capital of Tunceli was removed because of his past conviction and

an ongoing investigation for links to the banned Kurdistan Workers' Party (PKK). The district mayor for Ovacik in Tunceli Province was fired because of his past conviction of membership in the PKK. The two mayors belong to the pro-Kurdish Peoples' Equality and Democracy Party (DEM), the third-largest party represented in Parliament. They were elected to office in local elections in March. The mayor of Esenyurt district in Istanbul, Ahmet Ozer, was sacked and arrested in October for alleged PKK connections. He was a member of the main opposition Republican People's Party (CHP).

December 29, 2024: The pro-Kurdish DEM party announced that Abdullah Ocalan, imprisoned leader of the banned Kurdistan Workers' Party (PKK), said that he is willing to contribute to peace between Turks and Kurds. He noted "I possess the necessary competence and determination to contribute positively to the new paradigm supported by Mr. Bahçeli and Mr. Erdoğan," referring to Turkish President Recep Tayyip Erdogan and his nationalist ally, Devlet Bahceli, leader of the Nationalist Movement Party (MHP). Ocalan had been serving a life term in prison on the Imrali island off Istanbul since 1999, after being convicted of treason.

UKRAINE

July 6, 2023: *Reuters* reported that after 5 p.m., a man set off a bomb at the Shevchenkivskyi court in central Kyiv after barricading himself inside part of the building. Two members of a special rapid response security forces unit were hurt during attempts to bring the man under control. He was believed to have died from the explosion. Interior Minister Ihor Klymenko said on *Telegram* that the suspect, Ihor Humenyuk, had been attending a hearing as a suspect in connection with the deaths of four Ukrainian national guardsmen in 2015. Humenyuk had first locked himself into a bathroom and tossed an explosive device at two guards, then barricaded himself in another room and refused to negotiate. He threw a device at two officers, injuring them.

August 1, 2023: The *Washington Post* reported on August 7 that the Ukrainian State Security Service (SBU) said that on August 1 security officials had arrested a Ukrainian woman "red-handed" on suspicion of helping Russian intelligence services, including preparations for an assassination attempt on President Volodymyr Zelensky during his visit to the southern Ukrainian regions of Odessa and Mykolaiv in late July. The SBU's website announced, "The security service detained an informant of the special services of the Russian Federation, who, on the eve of the recent working trip of the president of Ukraine to the Mykolaiv region, was gathering intelligence about the planned visit... The perpetrator tried to establish the time and list of locations of the approximate route of the head of state in the territory of the region." The SBU said she was "a former saleswoman in a military store on the territory of one of the military units" in Ochakiv, which Zelensky visited. After the visit, Russian intelligence services tasked her with identifying "the location of electronic warfare systems and warehouses with ammunition of the armed forces of Ukraine in the Ochakiv region... to prepare a new massive airstrike on the Mykolaiv region... To gather intelligence, she traveled around the territory of the district and photographed the locations of Ukrainian objects." She faced 12 years in prison.

November 28, 2023: Marianna Budanova, wife of Maj. Gen. Kyrylo Budanov, the head of Ukraine's GUR military intelligence agency, was hospitalized in Kyiv with heavy metals poisoning. Earlier in 2023, Budanov survived 10 assassination attempts carried out by the Russian FSB state security service. Budanov had told local media that Marianna lives with him in his office, which could suggest he was the intended target for the poisoning. Several GUR personnel were diagnosed with the same poisoning.

December 15, 2023: The *Daily Beast* and *Ukrainska Pravda* reported that a local councilor calmly detonated two or three grenades during a Keretsk village council meeting in the western Transcarpathian region, injuring 26, six seriously.

May 10, 2024: *UPI* reported that Ukrainian President Volodymyr Zelensky dismissed Serhiy Rud, chief of the State Guard Service (UDO)

as head of his security detail, after two of his colonels earlier in the week were arrested in an alleged assassination plot against Zelensky; Vasyl Maliuk, head of the SBU—the state security service; and Kyrylo Budanov, who leads the Defense Intelligence of Ukraine; for Russia's FSB security service. He was not implicated in the plot but was close friends with one of the colonels arrested, Andriy Huk. The attack would entail the kidnapping and murder of Zelensky whereas drones, rockets, or anti-tank missiles would have killed Maliuk and Budanov.

June 18, 2024: *CNN* reported that a gunman in Kyiv ran up to the car of Kazakh journalist Aydos Sadykov, head of the opposition online media *BCE* and strong critic of the government of President Kassym-Jomart Tokayev, shot him in the head, and fled. He was hospitalized in intensive care with serious injuries. The attack occurred near his house in the Shevchenkivskyi district. His wife, Natalya Sadykova, also a journalist, was also in the car, which Aydos had driven into the yard of their house. Sadykov has more than one million *YouTube* subscribers. The couple had lived in Ukraine since 2014 with refugee status. *Al-Jazeera* reported on July 2 that Sadykov died. Sadykov's wife blamed Kazakh President Kassym-Jomart Tokayev. Sadykov left behind three children.

Ukrainian prosecutors suspected a pair of assassins from Kazakhstan, one a former policeman. The Prosecutor General said the duo escaped to Moldova. Kazakhstan detained one of the suspects, Altai Zhakanbayev, but refused to hand him over to Ukraine. The second suspect was at large. 24061801

July 19, 2024: *BBC* and the *New York Times* reported that a young gunman shot in the head and killed linguistics professor and former Ukrainian nationalist MP Iryna Farion, 60, on the street in Lviv during the evening. The year before, she had argued that "true patriots" of Ukraine should not speak Russian under any circumstances, singling out the elite Azov and Third Assault Brigades units for communicating in Russian. She called Russian "the language of the enemy, who kills, discriminates, insults and rapes me... How crazy should you be to fight in the Ukrainian army and speak Russian?" Her hardline nationalist Svoboda (Freedom) political party blamed Russia directly for the killing. The award-winning linguist taught at the Lviv Polytechnic National University; she was fired in November 2023, but won on appeal. She was a member of the Communist Party when Ukraine was under Soviet rule. She joined the Freedom Party in 2005, and became an MP in 2012.

UNITED KINGDOM

January 27, 2023: *CNN* and the UK's *PA Media* news agency reported that Judge Patrick Field in a Manchester court sentenced Daniel Harris, 19, from Derbyshire in northern England, to 11 ½ years for creating and posting far-right extremist videos that "influenced" mass shooter Payton Gendron, 19, who killed 10 Black people in a Buffalo, New York, supermarket and videos linked to Anderson Lee Aldrich, who is accused of killing five people in a mass shooting at an LGBTQ nightclub in Colorado Springs, Colorado, in November 2022. Derbyshire Police said Harris tried to make a gun with a 3D printer. One video called "How to Achieve Victory" called for "total extermination of sub-humans once and for all". Harris was charged with five counts of encouraging terrorism and one count of possession of material for terrorist purposes. Harris was earlier convicted of the racially aggravated criminal damage of a memorial to George Floyd in Manchester.

May 2, 2023: *UPI, AP,* the *Washington Post,* and *BBC* reported that London's Metropolitan Police at 7 p.m. arrested a man, 59, who threw several items, including suspected shotgun cartridges, into the grounds of Buckingham Palace amid preparations for the coronation of King Charles III later in the week. Police discovered a knife on his person and held him on suspicion of possession of a knife and ammunition. Neither King Charles nor the Queen Consort, Camilla, Duchess of Cornwall, were at the palace. Police also blew up his knapsack outside the palace.

June 13, 2023: *Reuters,* the *Washington Post,* and *UPI* reported that British police in Forest Fields arrested a man, 31, on suspicion of murder after three people were found dead on the street in Nottingham. *BBC* reported that a witness saw a young man and young woman being stabbed outside his house. Three others, including a woman, were hospitalized after an attempt to run them over with a van. Two bodies were found at 4 a.m.; another man was found dead outside the city center.

July 24, 2023: *Al-Jazeera* reported that authorities charged British Muslim preacher Anjem Choudary, 56, with membership of a proscribed organization, directing an organization, and addressing meetings to encourage support for a proscribed organization after being arrested in London when he arrived on a flight at Heathrow Airport the previous week. Canadian citizen Khaled Hussein, 28, was charged with membership of a proscribed organization after being arrested on the same day as Choudary. London-born Choudary, former head of the now-banned al-Muhajiroun, was imprisoned in Britain in 2016 for encouraging support for ISIS before being released in 2018 after serving half of his five-and-a-half year sentence.

September 6, 2023: *CNN* reported that Daniel Abed Khalife, 21, a serving member of the British Army awaiting trial on terror charges, escaped from HMP Wandsworth in southwest London at 7:50 a.m. by strapping himself to the underside of a delivery van while dressed as a chef. He faced charges of terror offenses and breaches of the Official Secrets Act. *PA Media* news agency reported that the soldier was accused of planting fake bombs at a military base. He was wearing a white t-shirt, red and white checkered pants, and brown steel toe cap boots. The slim man has short brown hair and is around 6 feet 2 inches tall. *CNN* reported on September 9 that a plainclothes counterterrorism officer arrested Khalife just before 11 a.m. while riding a bike on a canal towpath in the affluent Chiswick area of west London, seven miles from the prison.

UPI reported on September 21 that Daniel Khalife pleaded not guilty at London's Old Bailey courthouse to charges of escaping custody. His next court appearance was set for October 13, with trial set for November 13. The *New York Times* reported that he was charged with leaving fake bombs at a military base to create fear of a terrorist attack, and gathering information that could benefit a foreign enemy, possibly Iran.

September 8, 2023: *Sky News* and *Reuters* reported that British police explosives experts inspected a suspicious vehicle at the Channel Tunnel terminal.

September 15, 2023: *UPI* reported that the British officially designated the Russian Wagner mercenary group as a terrorist organization, becoming the 78th group on the list. The Home Office said membership, or active support of the group, is a criminal offense punishable by a maximum prison sentence of 14 years and a fine.

October 15, 2023: *AP* reported on April 25, 2024 that on October 15, 2023, Ahmed Alid, 45, an asylum seeker from Morocco, stabbed Terence Carney, 70, six times in the center of Hartlepool minutes after he hacked at sleeping housemate and Iranian asylum-seeker Jayed Nouri while shouting "Allahu Akbar." Nouri survived. Alid was upset Nouri had converted to Christianity. On April 25, 2024, Teesside Crown Court convicted Alid of one count of murder, one count of attempted murder and two counts of assaulting two female police detectives during his post-arrest interview. Prosecutor Jonathan Sandiford said Alid told police he had done it "for the people of Gaza" and swore he would have killed more if he had a machine gun and other weapons. Alid told police the UK helped create the "Zionist entity" of Israel and Israel had "killed innocent children… They killed children and I killed an old man."

On May 17, 2024, Judge Bobbie Cheema-Grubb at Teesside Crown Court sentenced Alid to life with no chance of parole for 45 years in prison for a terrorist act.

January 4, 2024: *Insider, AP,* the *Los Angeles Times,* and the *Daily Beast* reported that neo-Nazi *Lone Wolf Radio* podcasters Christopher Gibbons, 40, and Tyrone Patten-Walsh, 36, were sentenced to eight and seven years, respectively, in prison. The two Londoners will serve three years on probation. On one episode of their show, they called for Prince Harry to be "prosecuted and judicially killed for treason" and his

son, Archie, "a creature" "should be put down". They also called on listeners to conduct acts of terrorist violence during their 21 episodes, which tended toward antisemitic, Islamophobic, racist, and homophobic views. They approved of a day of hanging for those in interracial relationships. Gibbons curated an online library of more than 500 videos of extreme right-wing speeches and propaganda documents. The duo were arrested in May 2021 and charged in August 2021 with several terrorism offenses. Their trial concluded on July 7, 2023; they were convicted of all charges by a Kingston Crown Court jury.

January 31, 2024: *CNN* and *AP* reported that following a traffic accident, a man threw a corrosive alkaline substance on a woman, 31, and her two daughters, aged 3 and 8, in south London's Clapham Common district at 7:30 p.m. Several people were injured, including three women, two in their 30s and one in her 50s, and a man in his 50s who helped the initial victims and five responding police officers who were hospitalized with minor chemical burns. A suspect, believed to have known the woman, ran away after he crashed his car into a stationary vehicle. *UPI* added on February 2 that the London Metropolitan Police released a photo of suspect Abdul Shokoor Ezedi, who sustained "significant injuries" to his right eye and face.

UPI reported on February 10 that Scotland Yard announced that Ezedi was last seen on CCTV near the Thames two hours after the attack. Scotland Yard Commander Jon Savell said, "It is our main working hypothesis that he has now gone in the water." Detective Superintendent Rick Stewart added that the "most probable outcome" was Ezedi's death, noting, "We've tracked his movements from Tower Hill … he's walked over four miles … essentially he's hugged the Thames river line. When he has got to the area of Chelsea Bridge his behavior physically appears to change, in so much as he walks up and down the bridge." After he was seen leaning over the railings he was "no longer visible on CCTV". *AP* reported on February 20, 2024 that London police said they "strongly believe" that the Met's Marine Policing Unit have pulled Ezedi's body out from the River Thames. The crew of a passing boat saw a body in the water near the Tower of London the afternoon of February 19.

Ezedi entered the UK in 2016 from Afghanistan. He was granted asylum despite being convicted of a sex offense in the UK in 2018. The *Daily Telegraph* reported that he was allowed to remain in the country after claiming he had converted to Christianity. *UPI* reported that authorities believed that Ezedi and the woman had a relationship. She remained in poor condition in the hospital as of February 9 with likely "life-changing" injuries. Three women were earlier discharged from the hospital with minor burns.

February 1, 2024: Conservative Member of Parliament Mike Freer from the London constituency of Finchley and Golders Green said he will step down when an election is called later in 2024 because of abuse and death threats he says are linked to his support for Israel. He told the *BBC* that an arson attack on his office in December 2023 was the "final straw". He had received death threats from Muslims Against Crusades and began wearing a stab-proof vest after learning his office had been staked out by Ali Harbi Ali, an ISIS supporter who stabbed Conservative lawmaker David Amess to death in 2021. A man and a woman appeared in court on February 1 for an arson attack on Freer's office.

March 20, 2024: *AP* reported that on April 26, 2024, Nick Price, head of the Crown Prosecution Service Special Crime and Counter Terrorism Division announced that British man Dylan Earl, 20, is connected to Russia's Wagner mercenary group, which the UK government has declared a banned terrorist organization. Earl, accused of plotting to torch a London business connected to Ukraine, was charged with conducting hostile activity to benefit Russia. Earl was accused of fraud, carrying out reconnaissance of targets, and recruiting others to assist Russian intelligence services in the UK, including planning of an arson attack on a Ukrainian-linked commercial property in March 2024. He allegedly planned and paid others to torch two shipping businesses at an industrial park in east

London on March 20. Court charges listed the target as "Mr. X." Earl was the first person to be charged under the National Security Act 2023.

March 25, 2024: Radical British preacher Anjem Choudary, 57, pleaded not guilty via video link in London's Central Criminal Court, known as the Old Bailey, to membership in the banned radical Muslim group al-Muhajiroun, and addressing meetings to encourage support for the group. The UK outlawed the group in 2010 as an organization involved in committing, preparing for, or promoting terrorism. Prosecutors said that the group has since operated under many numerous aliases, including the Islamic Thinkers Society, which Choudary has addressed. He faced a June 4 trial in Kingston Crown Court along with Khaled Hussein, 29, of Edmonton, Alberta, Canada, who pleaded not guilty to membership in al-Muhajiroun. Authorities arrested Choudary and Hussein on June 17, 2023 after Hussein landed at Heathrow Airport.

March 29, 2024: *AP* and *BBC* reported that in the afternoon, an attacker stabbed in the leg British citizen Pouria Zeraati, 36, a TV presenter for the Last Word program at the London-based Farsi language *Iran International* satellite news channel outside his home in London. He is a longtime critic of Iran's theocracy. On December 6, 2024, the *Washington Post* reported that Romanian authorities arrested two Romanian men accused of stabbing Zeraati. Nandito Badea, 19, and George Stana, 23, were suspected of being associates of an Eastern European crime network hired to carry out an attack directed by Iran's security services. Romania soon released a third detainee. The UK sought extradition.

April 30, 2024: *AP, BBC,* the *Washington Post,* and *UPI* reported that in a 7 a.m. attack, a sword-wielding man killed Daniel Anjorin, 14, and injured four other people, including two police officers, at a subway station in northeast London. Police chased the man wearing a yellow hoodie who was walking on the roofs of low-rise homes in the Hainault neighborhood. Police tasered and arrested the suspect, who had crashed a vehicle into a house 22 minutes earlier. The Crown Prosecution Service authorized the Metropolitan police on May 1 to charge Spanish-Brazilian dual national Marcus Aurelio Arduini Monzo, 36, with murder. He faced two counts of attempted murder, two counts of grievous bodily harm, aggravated burglary, and possession of a bladed article. He was to appear at Barkingside Magistrates' Court on May 2.

AP and *LBC Radio* added on May 1 that two London police officers remained hospitalized after suffering "horrifically serious" injuries to their arms and hands. Doctors spent hours working on the arm of a female officer.

May 1, 2024: South Yorkshire Police announced it had arrested a boy, 17, on suspicion of attempted murder after three people were assaulted with a sharp object at The Birley Academy secondary school (formerly known as Birley Community College) in Sheffield. Two adults and a child were treated for minor injuries.

The Independent Office for Police Conduct announced that West Yorkshire constable Mohammed Adil faced two counts of publishing an image in support of a proscribed organization—Hamas, which is banned and designated a terrorist group in the UK—in violation of the Terrorism Act by showing support for Hamas on *WhatsApp* in October and November 2023. The West Yorkshire force suspended him. He was scheduled to appear on May 2 at Westminster Magistrates' Court.

May 14, 2024: Westminster Magistrates' Court held without bail Walid Saadaoui, 36, and Amar Hussein, 50, who were accused of planning to use automatic weapons to kill Jews, police, and military personnel in an ISIS-inspired attack in northwest England between December 13, 2023 and May 9, 2024. Bilel Saadaoui, 35, was accused of making arrangements for the expected death of his brother Walid. He pleaded not guilty to a charge of failing to disclose information about an act of terrorism. Bilel was represented by attorney Angelo Saponiere. Greater Manchester Police had arrested them the previous week. They were to appear on May 2024 for a hearing in the Central Criminal Court.

June 4, 2024: *BBC* reported that papers filed in a New York court claimed that Standard Char-

tered, one of the UK's largest banks, conducted thousands of transactions worth more than $100 billion from 2008 to 2013 in a money laundering operation for funders of terrorist groups, including Hizballah, Hamas, al-Qaeda, and the Taliban, in breach of sanctions against Iran. The U.S. Department of Justice in 2012 had declined to continue prosecution in an earlier case in which Standard Chartered was publicly accused of falsifying transaction data on Swift.

July 9, 2024: *AP* and *UPI* reported on September 17, 2024 that the bodies of Carol Hunt, 61, and her daughters Hannah Hunt, 28, and Louise Hunt, 25, were found in the family home in Bushey, north of London. The victims were the wife and daughters of well-known horse-racing commentator for the *BBC* and *Sky Sports* John Hunt. Authorities arrested Kyle Clifford on July 10 in a cemetery in Lavender Hill in north London. On September 16, detectives from the Bedfordshire, Cambridgeshire and Hertfordshire Major Crime Unit charged Kyle Clifford, 26, with three counts of murder using a knife and crossbow at London's Westminster Magistrates' Court. Clifford was also charged with possession of offensive weapons—a crossbow and a 10-inch butcher's knife—and with false imprisonment. He had tied Louise to a chair. British media reported that Clifford served about a year in the British Army several years ago but had been working as a private security guard until a few months prior to the offenses.

July 23, 2024: A jury in Woolwich Crown Court found radical British preacher Anjem Choudary, 57, guilty of directing a terrorist group and membership in a banned organization, the radical Muslim group al-Muhajiroun (ALM), which the UK had banned in 2010 for committing, preparing for, or promoting terrorism. He was earlier convicted of supporting ISIS. Choudary was convicted with one of his followers, Khaled Hussein, 29, of Edmonton, Canada. The duo were arrested a year earlier after Hussein landed at Heathrow Airport. On July 30, 2024, Justice Mark Wall sentenced Choudary to life in prison. Choudary must serve at least 28 years behind bars.

July 23, 2024: An attacker wearing a ski mask and riding a motorcycle stabbed and seriously injured a British army officer in his 40s during the evening near Brompton Barracks, the headquarters of the British Army's 1 Royal School of Military Engineering Regiment, in Gillingham. Kent police arrested a man, 24, 30 minutes later on suspicion of attempted murder. Authorities seized several knives. Police said the assailant acted alone and the stabbing was not believed to be a terrorist act.

July 29, 2024: *AP*, the *Guardian*, the *Washington Post*, *Financial Times*, *CNN*, *Sky News*, *UPI*, and *BBC* reported that around noon, Merseyside Police in Southport, a seaside town near Liverpool, detained a UK-born man, 17, in a hooded track suit and a surgical mask and seized a knife after two girls, Bebe King, 6, and Elsie Dot Stancombe, 7, were killed and eight children were injured, five critically, in a wave of stabbings. A third girl, Alice Dasilva Aguiar, 9, died the next day of wounds received at the Hart Space community center where a Taylor Swift-themed dance and yoga event for primary school-aged children was scheduled. Two adults, including teacher and event organizer Leanne Lucas, were critically injured while trying to protect the children. Jonathan Hayes, who runs a business next door, was stabbed in the leg while trying to help the children. The slasher had arrived in a taxi and argued with the driver about the fare before his rampage.

AP reported on July 30 that police clashed with far-right English Defence League rioters outside the Southport Islamic Society Mosque in northwest England near the scene of the crime. The rioters had believed disinformation that an illegal Muslim immigrant was responsible. The *New York Times* reported that some believed he was an asylum seeker from Syria. Some 53 police officers, plus three police canines, were injured, eight seriously. The EDL was supposedly defunct. Police arrested five men, three from Southport.

Police said the suspect was born to Rwandan immigrants in Cardiff, Wales, and had lived with his family since 2013 in Banks in Lancashire, about three miles from Southport. He had lived in the UK all his life. He was charged with suspicion of murder and attempted murder.

UPI reported on July 31, 2024 that police named Axel Muganwa Rudakubana, 17, as the suspect. He was to celebrate a birthday the following week. He was charged in Liverpool Crown Court with ten counts of attempted murder.

AP and *UPI* reported on October 30, 2024 that Axel Muganwa Rudakubana, now 18, appeared in Westminster Magistrates' Court by video link from Belmarsh prison in south London. He was charged with killing three girls and wounding ten other people in a stabbing rampage at a Taylor Swift-themed dance class. He refused to speak to face new charges of production of a biological toxin (ricin), possession of information likely to be useful to a person committing or preparing to commit an act of terrorism, and possessing an al-Qaeda manual *Military Studies in the Jihad Against the Tyrants*. He was represented by attorney Stan Reiz. Rudakubana was charged in August with the stabbings in the community of Southport. He was charged with three counts of murder in the deaths of Alice Dasilva Aguiar, 9; Elsie Dot Stancombe, 7; and Bebe King, 6; and ten counts of attempted murder for the eight children and two adults who were seriously wounded. The judge ordered the new charges to be transferred to Liverpool Crown Court, where he faced a hearing on November 13. The criminal trial was set for January 20, 2025.

AP reported on December 18, 2024 that the defendant remained silent in court as not guilty pleas were entered on his behalf. He had refused to speak in each court appearance. Justice Julian Goose ordered a clerk to enter the pleas in Liverpool Crown Court.

Treasure Coast Newspapers and the *USA Today Network* reported that on December 18, 2024, Florida Attorney General Ashley Moody announced a new state charge of attempted felony murder, stemming from a vehicle crash during the police pursuit that injured a girl, 6.

August 9, 2024: Judge Adrienne Lucking of Northampton Crown Court sentenced Tyler Kay, 26, father of three, who used social media to stoke racial hatred during the far-right rioting the previous week and called for people to torch hotels housing asylum seekers, to more than three years in prison.

Earlier that day, Judge Guy Kearl in Leeds Crown Court sentenced Jordan Parlour, 28, to 20 months in prison for encouraging *Facebook* followers to attack a hotel in Leeds that housed migrants.

August 12, 2024: *AP, al-Jazeera,* the *Guardian, PA,* and *UPI* reported that at 11:30 a.m., Metropolitan Police arrested a man who stabbed a girl, 11, outside a tea shop in Leicester Square in London's theater district. Her mother, 34, was covered with blood but was not injured. Abdullah, 29, a guard, jumped on the attacker and held him down.

AP reported on August 13 that Romanian citizen Ioan Pintaru, 32, was charged with attempted murder and a knife offense. He had put the girl in a headlock and stabbed her eight times with a steak knife. She required plastic surgery for wounds to her face, shoulder, wrist, and neck. Pintaru was scheduled for a hearing on September 10, 2024 at the Central Criminal Court known as the Old Bailey.

August 14, 2024: *Al-Jazeera* reported that the Chester Crown Court sentenced Julie Sweeney, 52, from Church Lawton, Cheshire to 15 months in jail for posting on *Facebook* that mosques should not be protected and should be "blown up with the adults in it". She pleaded guilty to sending communications on a 5,100-member *Facebook* group that "threaten death or serious harm". She was represented by defense attorney John Keane.

August 25, 2024: During the first day of the Notting Hill Carnival, Europe's largest street festival, three people were stabbed. A woman, 32, who was visiting with her child, sustained "life-threatening" injuries. On August 31, *AP* reported that Cher Maximen, 32, died of her wounds. A local man, 20, who was arrested and charged with attempted murder was now likely to face a murder charge.

August 29, 2024: *Reuters* and *NPR* reported that the British government imposed a travel ban on Mustafa Ayash, whom it sanctioned in March 2024 for promoting terrorism, and suspected Hizballah financier Nazem Ahmad. The duo were previously subject to asset freezes and cannot enter the UK. Ayash was sanctioned in March for providing financial support to a media network which supported Hamas—banned in 2021—and promoted terrorism. London sanctioned Ahmad in April 2023 on suspicion of financing Hizballah. The U.S. sanctioned him in 2019. He has an extensive art collection in the UK and conducts business with several UK-based artists, art galleries, and auction houses.

September 30, 2024: A masked male on a scooter threw acid on two teens outside London's Westminster Academy. A girl, 14, may have sustained "life-changing" injuries in the afternoon attack. A boy, 16, was also hospitalized. A teacher who rushed to provide first aid was hospitalized but soon released. Two police officers who felt ill were soon released from a hospital.

November 22, 2024: *UPI* reported that a suspicious package found outside the U.S. Embassy in London's Nine Elms district was destroyed in a controlled explosion in the morning as London police closed Ponton Road near the embassy. Police suggested it was a hoax device. On November 24, UK authorities arrested Daniel Parmenter, 43, at his home and charged him the next day at Ealing Magistrates Court.

CBS News reported that London's Gatwick Airport authorities evacuated South Terminal after a prohibited item was found in a passenger's luggage around 8:20 a.m.

November 27, 2024: The Metropolitan Police said counter-terrorism officers in London arrested four men and two women, aged between 23 and 62, believed linked to the banned Kurdistan Workers Party (PKK) under the Terrorism Act of 2000. Police searched the Kurdish Community Center in the Haringey area of north London and seven other locations across London. A suspect, 31, arrested the same day was released without charge. On December 10, London's Metropolitan Police charged the six people with "membership in a terrorist organization" for belonging to the PKK.

LATIN AMERICA

ARGENTINA

July 12, 2024: President Javier Milei designated Hamas a terrorist organization and ordered a freeze on its financial assets.

August 30, 2024: *BBC* reported that police in Buenos Aires arrested Leonardo Bertulazzi, 72, sentenced to 27 years in absentia in Italy in the 1970s for the Red Brigades kidnapping of Pietro Costa, a naval engineer from a wealthy ship-owning family in Genoa. The victim was held for 81 days before a large ransom was paid. That money was used to buy a flat in Rome which was used in 1978 for the kidnap and murder of former prime minister Aldo Moro. Bertulazzi had refugee status for years in Argentina. Buenos Aires police arrested him in 2002 after reportedly entering the country from Chile on a false passport. He was freed months later and his extradition was blocked. He was given refugee status two years later. Newly-elected president Javier Milei revoked his status following his inauguration.

BOLIVIA

October 27, 2024: Gunmen fired on the car of former President Evo Morales while he was being driven in the coca leaf-growing region of Chapare. He was not injured in what he claimed was an assassination attempt. His driver was injured.

BRAZIL

January 8, 2023: *CNN*, *Reuters*, and *NPR* reported that thousands of election-denying supporters of former Brazilian President Jair Bolsonaro, an ally of former U.S. President Donald Trump, took over the Brazilian Congress building, the Supreme Court, the Planalto Presidential Palace, and areas surrounding the Plaza of the Three Powers in Brasilia. Numerous rioters clashed with police. A male protester was spotted sitting at the desk of the president of Congress. The parallels with the January 6, 2021 attack on the U.S.

Congress were striking. The Brazilian Congress building's sprinkler system flooded the main floor after rioters tried to set fire to the carpet. Rioters stole items ranging from office supplies to gifts received from international delegations, destroyed artwork, and otherwise ransacked the facilities. A dozen journalists were attacked, according to the Union of Professional Journalists in the Federal District. Police cleared the buildings and arrested 1,500 people.

President Luiz Inácio Lula da Silva called "barbaric" the work of "fascists". Da Silva, Acting President of the Senate Veneziano Vital do Rego, President of the Chamber of Deputies Arthur Lira, and President of the Supreme Court Rosa Weber denounced the riots as acts of "terrorism, vandalism, criminal and coup-like".

Bolsonaro was last seen deplaning from a flight to Orlando, Florida, on December 30, 2022, two days before Lula's inauguration. He was a guest of a friend in the Reunion gated community in suburban Orlando.

CNN reported on January 9 that former first lady Michelle Bolsonaro posted on *Instagram* that her husband was hospitalized in Orlando for abdominal "discomfort" related to injuries from a 2018 knife attack during a political rally in Juiz de Fora in the southern state of Minas Gerais.

The *Washington Post* reported on April 26, 2023 that protestors overran the presidential palace, the Supreme Court, and Congress on January 8, 2023 in the false belief that the election was stolen from Jair Bolsonaro. Anderson Torres, who was in charge of Brasília's security the day of the assault, was arrested. Bolsonaro was under criminal investigation for allegedly inspiring the uprising. His supporters claimed the leftist backers of President Luis Ignacio Lula da Silva had infiltrated the protest and sparked violence.

April 5, 2023: *UPI*, *AP*, and the *Washington Post* reported that at 9 a.m., a man, 25, with a hatchet attacked the Cantinho do Bom Pastor private daycare center in Blumenau, Santa Catarina State, killing three boys and a girl aged between 4 and 7 and injuring five others, one seriously. The suspect, who rode to a police station on a motorcycle, surrendered to police. He had no apparent connection to the center. *O Globo* reported that he worked as a delivery person for a grocery store but had skipped work in the previous fortnight.

November 8, 2023: *Al-Jazeera* reported that Brazilian police arrested two people in Sao Paulo suspected of preparing for "terrorist attacks", which Israel alleged were being planned by Hizballah. *UPI* reported that Mossad said it provided assistance to Brazilian federal police in the "arrest of a terrorist cell that was operated by Hezbollah in order to carry out an attack on Israeli and Jewish targets in Brazil". Police conducted 11 search and seizure raids in Sao Paulo, Brasilia, and the southeastern state of Minas Gerais. One of the men was arrested at Brazil's international airport in Guarulhos, São Paulo, after flying in from Lebanon. *CNN Brazil* reported that federal police believed he was there to pass on information to an alleged partner in the planned attacks focusing on Jewish community buildings. Rio's *O Globo* newspaper reported that the plan included attacking synagogues.

June 18, 2024: *BBC, UOL,* and *CNN Brazil* reported that three fellow inmates in a prison in São Paulo state murdered Janeferson Aparecido Mariano Gomes, alias Nefo, and Reginaldo Oliveira de Sousa, alias Rê, both 48, who were being held in pre-trial detention on suspicion of involvement in a plot to kidnap a famous Brazilian judge. Police in Operation Henchman arrested the duo in March 2023 when they foiled a plan to kidnap high-ranking public figures for ransom. Targets were to include former justice and security minister Senator Sergio Moro, a former public prosecutor who oversaw the Operation Car Wash corruption probe. The attackers were suspected of belonging to the First Capital Command (PCC), Brazil's most powerful criminal group.

November 8, 2024: In an afternoon drive-by, gunmen in a black car opened fire at Terminal 2 at Sao Paulo's International Airport in Guarulhos, killing Antônio Vinícius Lopes Gritzbach, who had previously received death threats from the First Command of the Capital, a powerful international criminal group, and injuring three others. He ran a cryptocurrency businesses and recently entered into a plea bargain with local prosecutors to speak about his ties to the criminal organization.

November 13, 2024: The *Washington Post, Agencia Brasil, CNN Brazil, UPI,* and *AP* reported that "political malcontent" Francisco Wanderley Luiz, 59, who unsuccessfully ran in 2020 for a municipal position in Santa Catarina on former president Jair Bolsonaro's Liberty Party platform, set off several bombs in Brasilia. At 7:30 p.m., a car exploded outside the Brazilian Congress's lower chamber near Annex 4. Twenty seconds later, more explosions hit the Supreme Court offices. Wanderley was found dead outside the Supreme Court, having apparently killed himself. He had posted on social media "Are we going to play... Federal police, you have 72 hours to disarm a bomb that's in this house of communists." No one else was injured and no buildings were damaged. Wanderley's ex-wife said he told her he planned to kill Supreme Court Justice Alexandre de Moraes. Officers found explosives and a timer attached to Wanderley's body.

CHILE

April 27, 2024: *Al-Jazeera* and *AP* reported that gunmen fired heavy-caliber weapons in an ambush, killing three national police force Carabinero officers and torched their armored patrol vehicle in the Biobio region in Arauco Province's Canete municipality near Concepcion. The police were Sergeant Carlos Cisterna, Corporal Sergio Arevalo, and Corporal Misael Vidal.

October 23, 2024: A homemade firebomb exploded inside Santiago's prestigious Barros Arana National Boarding School, injuring 34 students aged 15 to 18 and one teacher, eleven seriously. A group of students were making Molotov cocktails in a bathroom to be thrown at a protest later at a traditional farewell party for graduating seniors. Police found bottles and fuel cans likely to make the explosives.

COLOMBIA

January 16, 2023: *Reuters* reported that Colombian national police confiscated an arsenal, including 33 guns, grenades, more than 30,000 bullets, uniforms, and an M-60 machine gun in two abandoned vehicles belonging to FARC Estado Mayor Central dissidents in Narino Province. The guns were manufactured in the United States, Israel, and Russia.

March 29, 2023: *ABC News* reported that the National Liberation Army (ELN) was blamed when gunmen killed nine soldiers and wounded nine others in a morning attack using long-range weapons and improvised explosive devices on a military unit securing a northern Caño Limón-Coveñas pipeline owned by Ecopetrol in Norte de Santander State near the Venezuelan border. Seven of those killed were soldiers doing compulsory military service; two were officers.

June 9, 2023: *UPI* reported that Colombian President Gustavo Petro and ELN Commander Antonio Garcia announced a six-month cease-fire starting August 3. *France 24* reported that the two sides signed the agreement in Cuba.

August 3, 2023: The *New York Times* reported that a six-month truce began between the government and the largest remaining insurgency, the far-left ELN.

September 26, 2023: The U.N. reported that a car bomb at the National Police Academy in Bogotá killed nine and injured dozens.

October 28, 2023: *Al-Jazeera* reported on October 29 that the previous day, Luís Manuel Diaz and Cilenis Marulanda, the parents of Liverpool soccer winger Luís Diaz, 26, were kidnapped at a service station in the La Guajira area by gunmen on motorbikes. Colombian authorities rescued his mother, Cilenis Marulanda, in the Barrancas sector of La Guajira within hours that day. Diaz played 43 times for Colombia and joined Liverpool in 2022 from Porto. He signed with Liverpool in January 2022 for a reported $63 million. *Al-Jazeera* reported on November 3 that the Colombian government blamed the ELN for the attack. Police offered a $48,000 reward for information leading to Diaz's father. ELN representative Juan Carlos Cuellar shared a video with *Reuters* in which he reportedly said the group will free Diaz's father "as soon as possible". *Al-Jazeera, UPI,* the *Washington Post,* and *El Tiempo* reported that on November 9, the ELN released Luís Manuel Diaz to a humanitarian commission composed of the Colombian Ombudsman's Office, the U.N., the Catholic Church, and the Red Cross. No ransom demands were reported. He serves as an amateur soccer coach and trains young players.

January 14, 2024: The government extended to July 15 a cease-fire with the FARC-EMC splinter group that was set to expire on January 15.

February 6, 2024: *AP* and *Blu* radio reported that the government and the National Liberation Army (ELN) extended a cease-fire that began in 2023 by six months. The ELN promised to stop kidnapping civilians for ransom ("economic detentions"). The Defense Ministry said the ELN is holding at least 38 hostages.

March 17, 2024: President Gustavo Petro suspended a ceasefire with Estado Mayor Central, a group of fighters who broke away from the Revolutionary Armed Forces of Colombia (FARC), saying its fighters violated the truce by attacking an Indigenous community in Cauca the previous day, wounding three people and kidnapping a young student.

April 4-5, 2024: FARC dissidents conducted a series of attacks with explosives and firearms against the military during the evening of April 4 into the next morning, wounding a soldier who was standing guard at military headquarters in Tumaco. He was hit by shrapnel from a grenade thrown by a man on a motorcycle.

Minutes earlier, an explosive device was thrown in front of a military facility in Cali, causing no injuries.

Gunmen fired on a police station in Jamundi in the morning.

May 16, 2024: *Al-Jazeera* reported that gunmen on a motorcycle drove up next to a car and shot to death former police colonel Elmer Fernandez, the new director of Bogota's La Modelo prison as of April 4, as he was returning home from work. He died from a single shot to the head as he sat in the passenger seat. He and his family had been threatened the previous week. He had no security escort and his car was not armored. Criminal gangs were suspected.

May 17, 2024: A roadside bomb attributed to the FARC-EMC killed a child, 11.

May 20, 2024: The government blamed the breakaway FARC-EMC, led by western front commander Ivan Mordisco, for a bomb that injured six people in Jamundi and an attack on a police station in rural Morales that killed two officers. The EMC's 5,000 fighters make it Colombia's third largest armed group, behind the Gaitanista Self Defense Forces and the National Liberation Army (ELN).

June 6, 2024: *BBC* reported that Bogotá and the leftist Second Marquetalia rebels, who split off from the Revolutionary Armed Forces of Colombia, announced they will begin formal peace talks in Caracas, Venezuela, on June 24. Second's 1,000-2,000 members smuggle cocaine, conduct ransom kidnappings, and attack security forces. Former FARC commander Luciano Marin, alias Ivan Marquez, leads the group.

The Second Marquetalia's lead negotiator was Walter Mendoza; the government team was led by Armando Novoa.

June 10, 2024: *AP* and *CNN* reported that a federal Southern District of Florida jury in West Palm Beach, Florida ordered Chiquita Brands to pay $38.3 million to 16 family members of people killed during Colombia's long civil war by the violent United Self-Defense Forces of Colombia (Autodefensas Unidas de Colombia, AUC) right-wing paramilitary group funded by the company.

July 16, 2024: Bogotá announced that it would end a ceasefire with the larger faction of the FARC-EMC, led by Iván Mordisco. The ceasefire with the smaller faction, led by Marcos Calarca, would continue for three months.

July 20, 2024: On August 8, 2024, Defense Minister Iván Velásquez said that President Gustavo Petro was the target of a possible attack when he took part in the traditional military parade on July 20 to commemorate the 214th anniversary of Colombia's independence from Spain, after arriving several hours late to the public event in downtown Bogotá.

July 24, 2024: *BBC* reported that Colombia's army commander announced that a grenade fell from a drone onto a football field in El Plateado in the Cauca region, killing a boy, 10, and injuring a dozen people. The child was the first person to die in such an attack in Colombia. The Defense Ministry claimed that the attack was targeting soldiers and blamed the Carlos Patiño Front, a group of dissident FARC guerrillas. A leader of the Carlos Patiño Front, Kevin Arcos, denied responsibility.

In June, the Colombian army reported 17 drone attacks over six weeks.

August 9, 2024: *AP* and *Caracol TV* reported that on August 12, Colombia's defense ministry said that 66 soldiers who had been "kidnapped" by villagers on August 9 in the southern Guaviare area were released unharmed. The army would resume operations against rebel groups in Guaviare Province. The defense ministry said the villagers were forced to detain the troops on orders from the Jorge Suarez Briceño Front, a local rebel group. The Briceño Front is part of the FARC-EMC splinter group.

August 20, 2024: Some 80 former FARC fighters and their families abandoned the village of Miravalle, built for them seven years earlier by the government, after receiving death threats from the Iván Díaz Front, a FARC splinter battling for control of farmland and drug routes in Caqueta Province.

September 17, 2024: *Al-Jazeera* and *AP* reported that military leaders blamed the National Liberation Army (ELN) for an attack on a military base in eastern Colombia that killed two soldiers and injured 26. Terrorists fired homemade rockets from a cargo truck that had been parked near a base in Puerto Jordan in Arauca Province. President Gustavo Petro said, "This is an attack that practically closes a peace process, with blood." The next day, the government suspended peace talks. The government offered a reward of up to

$23,700 for information leading to the capture of those responsible for the attack, along with a reward of up to $948,000 for the main leaders of the ELN.

December 7, 2024: A motorcycle carrying explosives detonated at a police checkpoint in the community of Las Penas in the Jamundi municipality in southwestern Colombia, killing the rider and injuring seven civilians and seven police officers.

December 22, 2024: The National Liberation Army (ELN) posted on *X* that it would unilaterally halt attacks on the military through January 3, 2025. A previous ceasefire broke down in August.

Costa Rica

January 10, 2024: The Judicial Investigation department said that Joao Maldonado, 34, an exiled member of the Nicaraguan opposition, was shot seven times and seriously wounded by two attackers aboard a motorcycle while he was driving with his Nicaraguan partner near Costa Rica University on the east side of the capital. It was the second attempt on Maldonado's life. The previous attack, also in Costa Rica, came in 2021, months after his father, retired military officer Tomás Maldonado, died in a Nicaraguan prison. Joao fled to asylum in Costa Rica in 2018 and had police protection. Maldonado had recently been moved to a new safe house. He had studied computer science. 24011022

Cuba

December 9, 2023: *Reuters* reported that Cuban authorities announced that they had thwarted a terrorist plot hatched in south Florida, after a Cuban man residing in Florida allegedly arrived on the island by jetski with a Florida registration to commit acts of violence. He abandoned the jetski in a mangrove swamp on the north coast, then traveled overland to Cienfuegos, in south-central Cuba. He tried to recruit others to assist in committing acts of violence, arson, and vandalism before he was arrested. State-run media said the plot involved Nueva Nacion Cubana and La Nueva Nacion Cubana en Armas, which Cuba has labeled as terrorist entities. One of the detained men was armed with several handguns, ammunition clips, and ammo.

May 15, 2024: *Military.com* and the *Miami Herald* reported that the Biden administration removed Cuba from the Department of State's list of countries "not cooperating fully" with anti-terrorist efforts. North Korea, Iran, Syria, and Venezuela remained on the list. Cuba remained on the separate list of state sponsors of terrorism.

Ecuador

February 2023: *UPI* reported that Omar Menendez, a candidate for the mayor of Puerto Lopez, was assassinated.

May 2023: The *Washington Post* reported that gunmen shot at the motorcade of the mayor of Durán, a town outside Guayaquil, in an apparent assassination attempt. The mayor survived, but several others died or were wounded.

July 2023: *CNN* reported that Agustin Intriago, mayor of the port city of Manta, was shot dead alongside Ariana Chancay, a young athlete he was talking with on the street.

August 9, 2023: *CNN* and *AP* reported that presidential candidate Fernando Villavicencio, 59, was assassinated at a Movimiento Construye (Build Ecuador Movement) political rally on a school north of Quito, 11 days before the first round of the presidential election was set to take place on August 20. Twelve gunshots were heard on a video of the attack. Local TV network *Ecuavisa* reported that Villavicencio was shot in the head three times. A gunman threw a grenade to cover his tracks, but it did not explode. The attorney general's office announced injuries to nine others, including a candidate for the National Assembly and two police officers. *The Hill* added that a suspect eventually died from injuries sustained during an exchange of gunfire. The candidate had received three death threats, including from associates of Mexico's Sinaloa cartel. President Guillermo Alberto Santiago Lasso Mendoza blamed organized crime.

Villavicencio was a legislator in the National Assembly before it was dissolved by President Lasso in May, leading to early elections. The *Washington Post* reported that he was a former investigative journalist.

UPI and the *New York Times* reported that on August 10 Interior Minister Juan Zapata announced that six suspects, all Colombian nationals who were members of gangs, had been arrested in Quito shortly after the assassination. Four were earlier charged with crimes, two with drug trafficking and violent crimes. *AP* noted that police seized four shotguns, a 5.56 mm rifle, ammunition, three grenades, a vehicle, and a motorcycle. The six were charged with murder.

Eight candidates were vying for president. Candidates Yaku Perez Guartambel, Bolivar Armijos, and Jan Topic suspended their campaign activities. Presidential candidate Daniel Noboa Azin posted on *X (Twitter)*, "This is an attack against the country, democracy and peace of all Ecuadorians." *Al-Jazeera* reported on August 13 that the Contruye party named Andrea González, 36, an environmental activist who had not held public office before becoming Villavicencio's running mate, to stand in his place in the August 20 elections. However, *al-Jazeera* reported on August 14 that the Movimiento Construye party announced that journalist Christian Zurita, 53, would replace Villavicencio. The party had worried that election authorities might void González's candidacy because she was registered as the vice presidential candidate.

Lasso, who had been facing impeachment and opted not to seek reelection, declared a 60-day national state of emergency, barring large gatherings, but said the elections for president and National Assembly would proceed as scheduled.

Ecuadoran police Cmdr. Fausto Salinas told reporters that the shooter had used a 9 mm pistol. He was arrested in June on an arms offense but was released by a judge. The suspect had a tattoo associated with the Latin Kings, a gang founded by Puerto Ricans in the United States in the 1950s.

Officials in the Ministry of Interior and national police said that 20 collaborators infiltrated the political rally in preparation for the assassination, wearing Villavicencio T-shirts and hiding in the crowd of about 100 people.

Villavicencio, who campaigned against corruption, was survived by his wife and five children.

Authorities on August 13 transferred Adolfo Macias, alias Fito, the leader of Los Choneros prison gang, accused of threatening Villavicencio before he was assassinated, to a 150-person maximum security prison in Guayaquil. He was serving a 34-year sentence for drug trafficking, organized crime, and homicide.

CNN reported on August 20 that Luisa González, of the Movimiento Revolución Ciudadana party, finished first in the first round of Ecuador's presidential and legislative elections, and would face the surprise second-place finisher Daniel Noboa in a run-off election on October 15. González was a protégé of former leftist President Rafael Correa, who was sentenced in absentia in 2020 to eight years in prison for aggravated bribery.

Days after Villavicencio was killed, leftwing local party official Pedro Briones was shot dead in Esmeraldas Province.

Authorities reported cyberattacks from Russia, Ukraine, China, and Bangladesh on the country's telematic voting platform.

Al-Jazeera reported that on September 28, U.S. Secretary of State Antony Blinken said the FBI was collaborating with Ecuadoran police to probe the murder and was offering $5 million for insight into the assassination. Six Colombian suspects remained in police custody.

The *Guardian* and *Reuters* reported on October 7, 2023 that six Colombians who had been arrested on the day anti-corruption candidate Fernando Villavicencio was assassinated were killed in Litoral Penitentiary in Guayaquil.

UPI reported that on October 15, the National Electoral Council of Ecuador announced that Daniel Noboa, 35, of the National Democratic Action Alliance party, secured 52.08% of the vote compared to the 47.92% of his rival, leftist politician Luisa González of the Citizen Revolution Movement party. Noboa, a center-right politician, is heir of Ecuador's wealthiest man, who ran a banana empire.

On July 14, 2024, *AP* and *BBC* reported that a court sentenced the two instigators of the assassination to 34 years and eight months in prison and fined them $460,000 and ordered a compensation payment of $100,000 by each to the politician's family. Three accomplices were sentenced to 12 years in prison, fined $156,400, and ordered to pay $33,000 to the family. Prosecutors said Carlos Angulo, alias "Invisible," alleged leader of the Los Lobos gang, coordinated the murder from a prison. Fellow instigator Laura Castillo was in charge of providing the gunmen with logistical elements including motorcycles and money. Erick Ramírez, Víctor Flores, and Alexandra Chimbo alerted the actual killers of the victim's movements. Some 13 people, including six Colombians, were accused in the case.

August 30, 2023: *Al-Jazeera* and *Reuters* reported that a car loaded with two petrol tanks exploded when suspects set it on fire in a commercial area of Quito. No casualties were reported in the evening incident. Another vehicle containing two cylinders of petrol and a slow fuse exploded nearby at an office of Ecuador's prisons agency. Hours later, police arrested six people, including a Colombian, several kilometers away from the scene. The six had rap sheets that included extortion, robbery, and murder. 23083001

September 7, 2023: *Al-Jazeera* reported that Duran municipal councilor Bolivar Vera was kidnapped. His body was found the next day in a vacant lot near a rural road, his hands bound and his clothes bloodied. *El Universo* reported that the right-wing Social Christian Party member had been shot in the chest and face eight times.

December 16, 2023: *UPI* reported that gunmen kidnapped British businessman Colin Armstrong, OBE, former UK honorary consul in Guayaquil and president of Agripac, a large agricultural products company in Ecuador, along with his Colombian partner, Katherine Paola Santos, from his home in Baba. The gunmen drove Armstrong away in his BMW, which was found abandoned. Ecuadoran police on December 20 rescued him in Los Rios on the road to Manabi, arresting nine suspects. He stepped down as honorary consul in 2016. 23121606

January 8, 2024: Los Choneros gang leader Adolfo "Fito" Macias escaped from the La Regional prison in Guayaquil. President Daniel Noboa ordered a 60-day state of emergency. Some 3,000 police officers and members of the armed forces were deployed to find him. The Insight Crime research center reported that Los Choneros has been linked to maritime drug trafficking to Mexico and the United States, working with Mexico's Sinaloa cartel and the Oliver Sinisterra Front in Colombia. Macias was serving a 34-year sentence.

January 9, 2024: *CNN* reported Ecuador's President Daniel Noboa, 36, declared an "internal armed conflict" in the country, ordering security forces to "neutralize" several criminal groups after hooded and armed men interrupted a live state-owned *TC Television* broadcast from Guayaquil and took hostages. One person was shot and another injured. Police soon arrested 13 gunmen and confiscated four firearms, two grenades, and explosives. Authorities attributed the violence to armed criminal gangs. In violence that began the previous day, eight people were killed in Guayaquil and two police officers died in Nobol. Authorities freed three police officers in Machala and arrested ten suspects. At least seven police officers were kidnapped in three cities since the state of emergency was announced. In one of the incidents, gunmen set off a bomb in a vehicle carrying police officers, three of whom were kidnapped. By January 10, authorities had arrested 70 people and seized eight bombs, 15 Molotov cocktails, nine firearms, 308 firearm cartridges, six motorcycles, and six vehicles. In Esmeraldas, two vehicles were set on fire; one caused a blaze at a gas station. In Guayaquil, hospital security guards stopped armed individuals from entering the facility. In Quito, police found a burned vehicle with traces of gas cylinders inside. Witnesses reported an explosion at a pedestrian bridge outside Quito.

Another alleged gang leader, Fabricio Colon Pico, escaped with 38 other inmates from a prison in Riobamba. He had been captured on January 5 after being publicly identified by Attorney General Diana Salazar as being part of a plan to attack her.

A local *al-Jazeera* correspondent reported on January 10 that "Authorities say there have been at least 23 different violent incidents in eight provinces, including a number of car bombs going off… A number of police cars were incinerated and at least seven police officers were kidnapped by gang members." Five bombs went off in Quito, targeting two vehicles, a pedestrian bridge, and a prison, causing minor damage but no deaths or injuries.

By January 18, some 13 suspects were in custody.

January 11, 2024: A nightclub arson in Coca killed two people and injured nine. The blaze damaged 11 nearby stores.

Quito Police evacuated people from the area surrounding the Playón de la Marín bus station when they were alerted about a backpack with an alleged explosive placed in a garbage can. No explosives were found.

January 17, 2024: Gunmen shot to death Prosecutor César Suárez, who was investigating the earlier January attack on the state-owned *TC Television* broadcast from Guayaquil, as he was driving a vehicle in Guayaquil. Suárez was also in charge of the Metastasis case involving an Ecuadorian drug lord who had corrupted judges, prosecutors, police officers, and senior officials.

March 24, 2024: *BBC* reported that the bodies of Brigitte García, 27, the country's youngest mayor, and communications director Jairo Loor, were found in the early morning in a car along in the town of San Vicente in Manabí Province, where she had won the mayoral election in 2023. Police said the shots which killed them had been fired from inside their rental car. García, a nurse, won the election at age 26 running for the opposition Citizens' Revolution party.

March 30, 2024: At 7 p.m., gunmen in a grey Chevrolet Spark fired on a group of people playing sports, killing nine and injuring ten in Guayaquil's Guasmo neighborhood. No group claimed credit.

EL SALVADOR

May 31, 2024: The National Police foiled a plot by former leftist guerillas in the country's 1980-1992 civil war to plant bombs around the country to coincide with President Nayib Bukele's inauguration on June 1. Police seized small cylinders of explosives with fuses and sacks of ammonium nitrate that were to target gasoline stations, supermarkets, and government buildings. Police blamed the Salvadoran Insurrection Brigade for the plot, and detained eight people, including former congressman José Santos Melara of the leftist FMLN party—formed by former guerrillas—for financing the plot. Melara leads the national association of FMLN Veterans of the war.

GUANTÁNAMO BAY

February 2, 2023: The *Washington Post* and *UPI* reported that the Biden administration released former al-Qaeda courier and Gitmo prisoner Majid Khan to Belize after he spent more than 15 years at the facility. He was captured in Pakistan in 2003. He was accused of involvement in a plot to assassinate former Pakistani president Pervez Musharraf and of acting as a courier for funds used in the 2003 JW Marriott Hotel bombing in Jakarta, Indonesia. The former Baltimore-area resident, a "high value" prisoner, cut a plea deal with U.S. prosecutors in February 2012, admitting to taking part in al-Qaeda plots and later providing testimony in other terrorism cases. His ten-year sentence concluded in March 2022.

Khan was born in Saudi Arabia and later moved with his family to Maryland.

February 24, 2023: U.S. authorities freed Pakistani brothers Abdul and Mohammed Rabbani from Gitmo and sent them to Islamabad. Pakistan had arrested the duo in Karachi on suspicion of links to al-Qaeda in 2002. They were to go to Karachi to live with their families. The U.S. had accused the duo of helping al-Qaeda with housing and logistical support.

March 8, 2023: *UPI* and *CNN* reported that the Defense Department announced it transferred alleged al-Qaeda bombmaker Ghassan al-Sharbi, 48, from Guantánamo Bay to Saudi Arabia. The Saudi had been held in detention at Guantánamo Bay for 20 years. He had studied at Embry-Riddle Aeronautical University in the U.S. from 1999 to 2000, associating with two of the 9/11 hijackers. He traveled to Afghanistan and began training with al-Qaeda. In Pakistan, he learned to manufacture remote-controlled bombs, planning to teach others. He was captured on March 28, 2002 at a senior al-Qaeda facilitator's Pakistan safe house and handed over to the U.S. He arrived at Gitmo in June 2002.

April 20, 2023: *The Hill* reported that the Defense Department announced the transfer to Algeria of Guantánamo Bay prisoner and Algerian citizen Said bin Brahim bin Umran Bakush, 52, who was captured in Pakistan in 2002. He had been accused of serving as an instructor for extremist groups and of ties to al-Qaeda.

July 25, 2023: *Lawfare* reported that the D.C. Circuit ruled that Guantánamo Bay detainee Ali Hamza Ahmad Suliman al-Bahlul will continue serving the life sentence imposed by a military commission and affirmed multiple times by the U.S. Court of Military Commission Review (CMCR). Circuit Judges Gregory Katsas and Florence Pan and Senior Circuit Judge David Sentelle denied the petitions of al-Bahlul to vacate the conspiracy conviction and life sentence against him. The Yemeni had joined al-Qaeda in the late 1990s. The court sentenced him to life in 2006 based on three convictions. The U.S. Court of Appeals for the District of Columbia Circuit vacated two of the three convictions (providing material support for terrorism and soliciting others to commit war crimes) but it upheld the conspiracy conviction. The *New York Times* reported that al-Bahlul is the only convict serving a life sentence at Guantánamo Bay. Lawyers had appealed his case six times.

May 20, 2024: *NBC News* reported that the Biden administration scuttled a plan to transfer 11 detainees from Gitmo to Oman following the October 7, 2023 Hamas attack. Officials said the 11 were either Yemeni citizens or have ties to Yemen. On May 22, the *Washington Post* reported that Omani officials planned to expel 28 Yemeni Gitmo alumni in July. The Yemenis had arrived between 2015 and 2017. Oman recently allowed two Afghan Gitmo alumni to return to Afghanistan.

June 20, 2024: The *New York Times* reported that military judge Col. Charles L. Pritchard, Jr. of a military commission announced that a military jury ordered Abd al-Hadi al-Iraqi, 63, to spend eight more years in prison under a plea agreement regarding war crimes committed in Afghanistan in 2003 and 2004. The former al-Qaeda battlefield commander admitted that his insurgents killed 17 U.S. and allied forces. He had been in U.S. custody since 2006, when he was captured in Türkiye. He is disabled by a paralyzing spine disease. He claimed his true name is Nashwan al-Tamir. He was represented by a defense team led by civilian attorney Susan Hensler.

December 30, 2024: *Al-Jazeera* and *BBC* reported that the Pentagon repatriated Tunisian detainee Ridah bin Saleh al-Yazidi, 59, held in Gitmo since the first day it opened, on January 11, 2002. He was never charged. He was approved for release a decade earlier. The *New York Times* reported that Pakistani soldiers seized him near the border with Afghanistan in December 2001 on suspicion of being an al-Qaeda fighter.

GUATEMALA

June 6, 2024: Gunmen ambushed and killed attorney José Domingo, who was with two members of the United Farmworkers Committee, who were wounded. He was helping to legalize a land title involving Indigenous peoples and farmworkers in the area. The Council of the Wuxhtaj Peoples condemned the attack and said he was of the Popti or Jakalteko people and a "defender of Mother Earth."

HAITI

January 26, 2023: The *Washington Post* and *Reuters* reported that in the morning, Haitian National Police officers raided Prime Minister Ariel Henry's official residence in Port-au-Prince and the country's main airport to protest the gang killings of 15 police officers in the previous 15 days. They smashed car windows and shot weapons into the courtyard. They did not attack Henry's living quarters. Protestors in police uniforms broke a window at Toussaint Louverture International Airport and trashed an entryway.

December 12, 2023: *Al-Jazeera* reported that Doctors Without Borders indefinitely suspended work at an emergency medical facility in Port-au-Prince, after an armed group pulled a critically ill patient from an ambulance and shot him dead in the street. An MSF ambulance convoy was leaving the medical center in the area of Turgeau, in central Port-au-Prince, for patient transfers.

January 19, 2024: Gunmen kidnapped six Congregation of the Sisters of St. Anne nuns and other people as they traveled on a bus through Port-Au-Prince, according to the Haitian Conference of the Religious. *AP* reported on January 25 that the six nuns and two other hostages were freed, according to Archbishop Max Leroy Mésidor. He declined to say whether a ransom was paid.

January 23, 2024: A gunman killed Claude Joazard, a doctor, former senatorial candidate, and former Haitian vice-consul to Dajabon in the Dominican Republic, near an international airport in Cap-Haitien.

February 23, 2024: Gunmen kidnapped a teacher and six male members of the Congregation of Brothers of Sacred Heart while gathered in front of a school in Port-au-Prince. The school temporarily closed.

March 6, 2024: *BBC* reported that gang leader Jimmy "Barbecue" Chérizier warned if "Ariel Henry does not resign {as Haitian Prime Minister} ... we'll be heading straight for a civil war that will lead to genocide". On March 2, Haitian gangs freed 4,000 prisoners from two Haitian jails, and had attempted to take over the Port-au-Prince airport to stop Henry from returning from Kenya, where he was arranging for Kenya to lead a multinational police operation to stem the violence.

On March 7, the government extended into April 3 its previously-announced three-day state of emergency after dozens of gunmen, backed by hundreds of onlookers, broke into Port-au-Prince's Caribbean Port Services (CPS) terminal's gated warehouse area.

AP and *ABC News* reported on March 8 that during the evening, several gangs simultaneously assaulted several government buildings, including the Presidential Palace, the Interior Ministry, and a police headquarters for Haiti's western district in or near downtown Port-au-Prince. A dozen gang members were killed.

On March 9, gangs attacked three police stations in Port-au-Prince. The U.S. military evacuated some U.S. Embassy staffers.

Prime Minister Ariel Henry announced on March 11 that he would resign after a transitional council was named.

June 24, 2024: A federal court in Washington, D.C. sentenced Germine Joly, 31, alias Yonyon, self-described "king" of the 400 Mawozo (400 Simpletons) gang in Haiti, to 35 years in prison. He was linked to the kidnapping of 16 U.S. citizens in October 2021. He pleaded guilty in late January 2024 to weapons smuggling and the laundering of ransoms related to the kidnappings. The gang is led by Joseph Wilson, alias Lanmò San Jou (Death has no date), and is allied with the G-Pep gang federation.

Joly's former girlfriend, Eliande Tunis, 46, of Pompano Beach, Florida, had been sentenced in June 2024 to 12 1/2 years in prison after she pleaded guilty in late January 2024 to the same charges Joly faced.

November 12, 2024: *UPI* reported that the U.S. Federal Aviation Administration banned flights to and from Haiti for at least 30 days after a JetBlue Airways plane and Spirit Airlines flight 951 were hit by gunfire by suspected gangs on November 11, 2024 near Toussaint Louverture International Airport in Port-au-Prince. FAA also temporarily prohibited most U.S. flights from traveling under 10,000 feet in Haitian territory or airspace. The Spirit flight departed from Fort Lauderdale, Florida. JetBlue was en route to New York's JFK Airport. A Spirit Airlines flight crew member sustained minor injuries. The plane was diverted to Santiago, Dominican Republican about 11:30 a.m.

December 9, 2024: *Al-Jazeera* reported that Wharf Jeremie gang leader Jean Monel Felix, alias King Micanor, ordered the weekend massacre of 184 people, including 130 over the age of 60, in the Cite Soleil slum of Port-au-Prince after his child became sick. He believed a Vodou priest who claimed they were witches who had the child killed on December 7. Gang members killed at least 60 people on December 6 and 50 on December 7 using machetes and knives. Felix is allied to the Viv Ansanm (Living Together) gang coalition, led by a former policeman, Jimmy "Barbecue" Cherizier.

Mexico

November 13, 2023: *UPI* reported that prominent LGBTQ+ activist Jesus Ociel Baena Saucedo, 39, the first non-binary electoral magistrate in Latin America, died from a morning knife attack in his home in Aguascalientes State. A person thought to be Baena's partner was also stabbed to death in the home. Baena was an appointed judge with the Electoral Tribunal of the State of Aguascalientes, a division of the Mexican justice system that specializes in election-related matters. Born in Saltillo, Coahuila, he had lived in Aguascalientes for 11 years. He earned a law degree from the Faculty of Jurisprudence of the Autonomous University of Coahuila, and also received a master's degree in constitutional law and government policies. He received a reissued birth certificate with a box added for "non-binary", and later obtained Mexico's first non-binary passport from the Civil Registry of Coahuila in honor of the International Day Against Homophobia.

November 16, 2023: *Al-Jazeera* reported that photojournalist Ismael Villagomez was shot dead in Ciudad Juarez. Three people were arrested for the killing.

November 19, 2023: *Al-Jazeera* reported that on November 25 three kidnapped Mexican journalists were released unharmed days after being abducted in Guerrero Province. Gunmen kidnapped Marco Antonio Toledo, editor of the weekly newspaper *El Espectador*, on November 19 in the tourist town of Taxco. Silvia Nayssa Arce and Alberto Sanchez, reporters for digital media site *RedSiete*, were abducted from their offices on November 22 in Taxco. Toledo's wife, Guadalupe Denova, was also released, but their son, who was kidnapped with his parents, remained missing.

January 10, 2024: Authorities in the northern Mexico border state of Sonora found the dead body of local Cucapah Indigenous leader Aronia Wilson. The Cucapahs, members of the Cocopah Indian Tribe, also live across the border near Yuma, Arizona. Prosecutors questioned a person of interest in the death of Wilson.

May 31, 2024: *Al-Jazeera, AFP,* and *NPR* reported that local candidate Jorge Huerta Cabrera was shot dead at a political rally in Izucar de Matamoros in Puebla State two days before the elections. His wife and a colleague were wounded. He was the 37th assassinated candidate.

June 3, 2024: *BBC* reported that gunmen killed Mayor Yolanda Sánchez in central Cotija, Michoacán, which she had governed since September 2021. She was ambushed and shot 19 times. Her bodyguard also died. Organized crime was suspected. She had received death threats since assuming office. She was kidnapped and held at gunpoint for three days during a visit to neighboring Jalisco State in 2023. The kidnappers demanded that she hand over town security to state police officers on the take from criminal groups. Newspapers speculated that the Jalisco New Generation cartel (CJNG) was responsible. The group traffics in drugs, kidnaps for ransom and extortion, and assassinates public officials.

June 17, 2024: *UPI, El Sur de Guerrero, and El Universal* reported that retired Navy captain Salvador Villalba Flores, mayor-elect of Copala, near Acapulco, was assassinated while traveling around 3 a.m. on a bus near San Pedro las Playas on a highway in Guerrero State. He was to take office in October. Although he was usually protected by National Guard escorts, he was traveling alone, pulled off the bus, and shot. He ran for mayor after a candidate, a friend, was murdered in June 2023.

October 20, 2024: *Al-Jazeera* and *AP* reported that two gunmen on a motorcycle shot to death Catholic priest Marcelo Pérez, a Tzotzil Indigenous activist for Indigenous peoples and farm laborers in southern Mexico in San Cristóbal de las Casas in Chiapas state, while he was in a van. He had finished saying Mass. He served the community for two decades. He had recently received death threats.

November 8, 2024: Gunmen killed Navy Rear Admiral Fernando Guerrero Alcántar as he was driving his private vehicle near Manzanillo.

December 8, 2024: A passenger on a domestic Volaris Airlines flight tried to divert an aircraft to the United States by force. The crew detained him after the flight was diverted to Guadalajara. No one was injured. The passengers continued on to their destination in Tijuana. 24120801

PANAMA

June 7, 2024: At 11 a.m., two gunmen arrived in a car and shot at six first-year agricultural sciences students on a rural campus of the University of Panama in Veraguas, killing Álvaro Leones, 27, and wounding Anel Terreros in the gluteus before escaping.

PERU

September 4, 2023: *Al-Jazeera* reported that in a morning ambush of soldiers by Shining Path rebels in Putis in Huanta Province in the Ayacucho region, four soldiers and two rebels were killed and three soldiers were wounded. The attack occurred in the Valley of the Apurímac, Ene, and Mantaro rivers, known in Spanish as VRAEM, a cocaine production center.

March 7, 2024: Police Chief Gen. Óscar Arriola announced the arrest of two Peruvian citizens and Majid Azizi, 56, an Iranian citizen who was purportedly a member of Iran's Quds Force and allegedly planned to kill an Israeli citizen in Peru.

Police were searching for a third Peruvian. Azizi entered Lima on March 3. Foreign intelligence services alerted the Peruvians. Police detained Azizi after he withdrew money from an ATM. He is married to a Peruvian woman. He and the Peruvians were to remain in prison for an initial 15 days under terrorism charges.

MIDDLE EAST

February 13, 2023: The *Washington Post* and *Reuters* reported that a report to the U.N. Security Council indicated that many countries suggested that former Egyptian army special forces lieutenant colonel Mohammed Salahuddin Zeidan, alias Saif al-Adel (sword of justice), believed to be hiding in Iran, was the new "de facto and uncontested" leader of al-Qaeda. The U.S. State Department's Rewards for Justice Program earlier offered a $10 million reward for information leading directly to his "apprehension or conviction". He established AQ training camps in Sudan, Pakistan, and Afghanistan in the 1990s. AQ had not publicly named a new leader.

May 17, 2024: The *Washington Post* reported that ISIS had created an artificial intelligence-generated news anchor in a helmet and fatigues as part of a new AI-generated media program called *News Harvest*, which resembles *al-Jazeera*.

June 9, 2024: *BBC* ran a two-hour Iraqi prison interview of Umm Hudaifa, the first wife of deceased ISIS emir Ibrahim Awad al-Badri, popularly known as Abu Bakr al-Baghdadi. She was born in 1976 into a conservative Iraqi family and married al-Baghdadi in 1999.

June 14, 2024: *UPI* reported that the U.S. Department of the Treasury and Türkiye imposed sanctions on four people—Olimkhon Makhmudjon Ugli Ismailov, Muhammad Ibrohimjon Niyazov, Muhammadyusuf Alisher Ogli Mirzoev, and Adam Khamirzaev—believed involved in an ISIS-linked Eurasian human smuggling network.

Treasury said Mirzoev was involved in establishing an ISIS militant training camp in mid-2023.

The State Department called Khamirzaev the ISIS Georgia Province emir, accused of helping guide smuggling network activities to support ISIS.

Treasury said Ismailov is involved in an ISIS-linked human smuggling network while Niyazov supports the network by providing administrative and logistic work for ISIS members in Turkey.

AFGHANISTAN

January 1, 2023: *NPR, AP, CBS News,* and *PBS* reported that in the morning, a bomb exploded near a checkpoint on Airport Road at Kabul's military airport, killing and wounding "several" people, according to Interior Ministry spokesman Abdul Nafi Takor. ISIS-K was suspected.

On January 4, *al-Jazeera* reported that the Taliban killed eight ISIS-K terrorists, including foreigners, and arrested several others in raids in Kabul and western Nimroz Province. They were searching for individuals involved in recent attacks on Kabul's Longan Hotel, Pakistan's embassy, and the military airport. Seven ISIS-K members were arrested in Kabul; another seven were picked up in Nimroz. ISIS-K said the airport and hotel attacker was Abdul Jabbar. The Taliban seized light weapons, hand grenades, mines, vests, and explosives in a raid on an ISIS-K hideout in the Shahdai Salehin neighbourhood of Kabul.

January 11, 2023: The *Washington Post* reported that a bomb went off outside the Ministry of Foreign Affairs in Kabul, killing five civilians and wounding many more. No one claimed credit.

January 15, 2023: *CNN* and *NPR* reported that around 3 a.m., gunmen shot to death former Afghan member of Parliament Mursal Nabizada and her security guard and wounded her brother in her home in Kabul. She represented Kabul in the parliament from 2019 until the Taliban takeover in August 2021. *Reuters* reported on February 17, 2023 that Afghan police arrested her former bodyguard, who confessed.

March 9, 2023: The *Washington Post* and *Reuters* reported that a bomb near the office of Balkh Province governor Mullah Muhammad Dawood Muzamil killed him and a civilian and wounded two members of the Taliban's security forces. No one claimed credit.

April 3, 2023: *Al-Jazeera* reported that Taliban forces killed six ISIS-K members during an overnight raid on a hideout in Nahri Shahi district in Balkh Province.

June 3-4, 2023: The *Washington Post* reported that more than 80 Afghan students and teachers—most of them girls but including 18 boys—were apparently poisoned over the past two days in two separate incidents. No critical injuries or deaths were reported. The victims fell unconscious after entering their classrooms, suggesting that a gas was used. Shafiullah Rahimi, spokesman for the Ministry of Disaster Management, added that "in one school, three teachers and 60 students were affected. In the second school, four teachers and 22 students were affected."

June 6, 2023: A car bomb killed Nisar Ahmad Ahmadi, the deputy governor of Badakhshan, and his driver and wounded 10 other people. ISIS-K claimed credit.

June 8, 2023: A suicide bomber attacked a memorial service for Nisar Ahmad Ahmadi, the deputy governor of Badakhshan who was killed in a car bombing two days earlier, near Nabawi Mosque in Faizabad in Badkhshan Province, killing 13, including Safiullah Samim, a former Taliban police chief in Baghlan, and injuring 30.

August 14, 2023: *Al-Jazeera* reported that an explosion at a Khost Province hotel frequented by Afghan people and people originally from Pakistan's North Waziristan Province killed three people and injured seven.

October 27, 2023: *Al-Jazeera* and *AFP* reported that ISIS-K claimed credit for the parcel bombing in the evening of a boxing sports club in a commercial center in the Dasht-e-Barchi neighborhood of Kabul, a Hazara enclave, killing four and injuring seven. ISIS-K said on *Telegram* it was "placed in a room where [Shia Muslims] gather".

November 7, 2023: A minibus exploded in the mostly Shi'ite Muslim Dashti Barchi neighborhood of Kabul, killing seven civilians and wounding 20. *Al-Jazeera* added that ISIS-K claimed credit the next day, saying it was targeting Shi'a Hazaras.

ISIS-K also claimed credit for bombing a sports club in the same neighborhood that killed four people and critically wounded seven in late October.

December 31, 2023: Defense Minister Mohammad Yaqoob Mujahid announced that security forces during 2023 killed dozens of Tajiks and more than 20 Pakistanis and arrested scores of Tajiks and hundreds of Pakistanis involved in attacks against religious clerics, the public, and mosques.

January 6-7, 2024: ISIS-K claimed responsibility for a minibus explosion in western Kabul that killed five people.

January 9, 2024: ISIS-K claimed credit for setting off a bomb belonging to a minivan of employees of Kabul's main prison, killing three people and wounding ten. Police spokesman Khalid Zadran said three civilians were killed and four injured in the Alokhail area of the city. Police detained a suspect.

January 14, 2024: ISIS-K was suspected when a suicide bomber hit the provincial governor's compound in Zaranj, capital of Nimroz Province, and wounded three security guards. He detonated his suicide vest as he was shot by security guards while trying to enter the compound.

March 21, 2024: *AP* and *BBC* reported that at 8 a.m., a suicide bomber hit a private bank in Kandahar city, killing 21 people and injuring 50 others who had gathered at the branch of New Kabul Bank to collect their monthly salaries. Most of the victims were government employees. ISIS-K claimed credit the next day. The government claimed that three people died and 12 were wounded.

April 20, 2024: A sticky bomb attached to a car exploded in the mostly Shi'ite Kot-e-Sangi Kabul during the night, killing the driver and wounding three others. ISIS-K was suspected.

April 29, 2024: The state-run *Bakhtar News Agency, Tolo, AP* and *al-Jazeera* reported that at 9 p.m., a gunman ran into the Shi'ite Imam Zaman Mosque in Andisheh in the Guzara district of Herat Province, killing six people, including the imam, who were praying, and wounding seven people, including a child, before fleeing. ISIS-K claimed responsibility.

May 8, 2024: ISIS-K claimed credit for setting off a booby-trapped motorcycle that hit a Taliban patrol in Faizabad in Badakhshan Province, killing and wounding 12 members of the patrol and destroying a four-wheel drive vehicle. Interior Ministry spokesman Abdul Mateen Qani said the officers were on their way to eradicate poppy crops in the area.

May 17, 2024: *Reuters, AP,* the *New York Times,* and the *Jerusalem Post* reported that at 5:30 p.m., gunmen killed three Spanish tourists and three Afghan citizens and injured four foreigners from Spain, Norway, Australia, and Latvia, and three Afghans on a bus carrying tourists and their guides in Bamiyan Province. The *New York Times* said that the tourists were leaving a bazaar when the gunmen fired. Authorities arrested seven people. ISIS-K claimed credit on *Aamaq* on May 19, explaining "The attack was in response to the IS leaders' directions to target citizens of the European Union wherever they are found."

May 20, 2024: A hand grenade went off near the road toward Kandahar airport, killing a civilian and wounding three. No group claimed credit.

August 11, 2024: ISIS-K claimed credit for setting off a bomb in a minivan carrying Shi'ites in the Dushti Barachi neighborhood in western Kabul, killing a civilian and wounding 13.

September 2, 2024: *AP* and *UPI* reported that a suicide bomber hit the Qala-e-Bakhtiar neighborhood in Kabul, killing six people, including one woman, and injuring 13 civilians. *Al Jazeera* added that ISIS-K claimed credit, claiming it was targeting the Taliban government's prosecution service. ISIS-K said the bomber waited until government employees finished their shifts and then set off the explosive in the middle of a crowd. ISIS-K claimed to have caused more than 45 casualties.

September 12, 2024: ISIS-K gunmen fired a machine gun on Hazaras traveling between Ghor and Daikundki Provinces, killing 14 and wounding six. *IRNA* reported that the terrorists attacked people welcoming Afghan Shi'ites returning home from visiting Iraqi shrines.

October 24, 2024: An explosion in a crowded second-hand clothes market in the Pamir Cinema district of Kabul injured 11 people, including a girl, 3, and a boy, 4. A man was in critical condition.

December 10, 2024: The lower house of Russia's State Duma (parliament) gave initial approval to a long-discussed bill that would set the stage for Moscow to remove the designation of the Taliban in Afghanistan as a terrorist group. Under the bill passed by the State Duma in the first of three required readings, a court could temporarily suspend the terrorism designation. The legislation would become law if approved by the upper house and signed by President Vladimir Putin. The Taliban was designated in 2003.

December 11, 2024: *Al-Jazeera, BBC, Reuters, AFP,* the *Washington Post,* and *AP* reported that a suicide bomber walked into the Ministry of Refugees in Kabul and killed acting Taliban refugee minister Khalil ur-Rahman Haqqani and six others, injuring four. Khalil Haqqani is the uncle of acting interior minister Sirajuddin Haqqani. There was no immediate claim of responsibility. Taliban spokesman Zabihullah Mujahid blamed ISIS-K, which later claimed credit. Reports differed as to how many were killed, ranging from three to seven. The U.S. had designated Khalil Haqqani, a senior member of the Haqqani Network, a global terrorist.

ARABIAN SEA

December 14, 2023: Gunmen boarded the Malta-flagged bulk carrier *MV Ruen*, managed by Navigation Maritime Bulgare (Navibulgar), off the Yemeni island of Socotra. Bulgarian authorities said the ship's 18 crew members were from Angola, Bulgaria, and Myanmar. Somali pirates were suspected. The Spanish frigate *Victoria* was on its way to intercept the ship.

The *Ruen* had sent a Mayday message on the United Kingdom Maritime Trade Operations portal indicating that six unknown people had boarded the vessel. The Indian Navy sent its anti-piracy patrol warship and maritime patrol aircraft to locate and assist the vessel. *AP* added on December 16 that the Indian Navy said that it was shadowing a bulk carrier that was boarded by unknown attackers in the Arabian Sea and may have been taken by Somali pirates who were sailing to the Somali coast.

No group immediately claimed credit.

December 15, 2023: Hijackers believed to be from Somalia seized a Bulgarian ship. 23121504

January 27, 2024: A "Somali-style" small craft carrying people armed with assault rifles and a rocket-propelled grenade came within 300 meters of a vessel. The United Kingdom Trade Operations agency said, "The onboard security team fired warning shots and post an exchange of fire, the small craft then retreated." All on board were reported safe.

April 26, 2024: A Houthi drone attacked the Portuguese-flagged *MSC Orion* container ship 375 miles off the coast of Yemen and bound for Salalah, Oman, causing minor damage and no injuries. The *MSC Orion* was operating on behalf of the Mediterranean Shipping Co., a Naples, Italy-based firm, and has been associated with London-based Zodiac Maritime, part of Israeli billionaire Eyal Ofer's Zodiac Group.

June 22, 2024: *Al-Jazeera* reported that Houthis claimed they fired ballistic missiles that hit the Liberia-flagged commercial bulk carrier *Transworld Navigator* after it used an Israeli port.

Houthis also claimed they fired ballistic and cruise missiles at the *USS Eisenhower* aircraft carrier after it was ordered home after months of responding to Houthi attacks.

EGYPT

October 8, 2023: *NPR* and *al-Jazeera* reported that an Egyptian police officer shot to death two Israeli tourists and an Egyptian in Pompey's Pillar site in Alexandria. *Extra News* television channel added that another Israeli was moderately wounded. The suspect was detained.

December 16, 2023: Egypt's state-run media reported that Egyptian air defense had shot down a "flying object" off the resort town of Dahab on the Red Sea.

GAZA STRIP

January 27, 2023: The *New York Post*, Israel's *Channel 12*, and *Reuters* reported that Palestinians fired rockets; one landed in an open area, one was intercepted, and another fell inside Gaza. No one claimed responsibility. No injuries were reported. The IDF conducted airstrikes on rocket manufacturing sites in Gaza.

February 2, 2023: *CNN* and *AFP* reported that the IDF conducted pre-dawn airstrikes in Gaza after intercepting a rocket fired from the coastal enclave. Israeli fighter jets hit a chemical production site and a weapons manufacturing facility owned by Hamas.

February 23, 2023: *UPI* reported that IDF sorties hit several Palestinian targets after Hamas fired six rockets into Israel. Five rockets were intercepted, the sixth fell into an open area. The IDF claimed it hit a weapons manufacturing site and a Hamas military compound adjacent to a mosque, medical clinic, hotel, police station, and school.

March 8, 2023: *UPI* reported that the Israel Defense Forces struck a Hamas military post in Gaza after claiming Hamas exploded a remote device near personnel and a bulldozer on the Gaza border.

April 5, 2023: *CNN* reported that nine rockets were fired from the Gaza Strip toward Israel. Four of them were intercepted by the IDF aerial defense array, another four landed in open areas. Later that day IDF fighters struck Hamas weapons manufacturing and storage sites in the Gaza Strip.

April 27, 2023: *Reuters* reported that the Izz el-Deen al-Qassam Brigades, the armed wing of Hamas, said it would stop receiving funds via Bitcoin.

May 2, 2023: The *Times of Israel* and *UPI* reported that Palestinian terrorists fired 104 projectiles from the Gaza Strip in retaliation for PIJ leader Khader Adnan's death. A man, 25, was seriously wounded and two others were moderately wounded at a construction site in Sderot. All three were foreigners of undisclosed nationalities. The Iron Dome knocked down 24 rockets, stopping 90% of the projectiles aimed at populated areas. IDF spokesman Rear Admiral Daniel Hagari said terrorists fired rockets, mortars, and shoulder-launched missiles at Israeli aircraft over Gaza. The Joint Operations Room claimed credit.

May 8, 2023: *CNN* and *AP* reported that 5 a.m., Israeli airstrikes on Iran-backed Islamic Jihad targets in the Gaza Strip killed 13 people, including three IJ commanders, two of their wives, several of their children, and other bystanders, and injured 20. Four men and four children were among the dead. The strikes by 40 planes hit the top floor of an apartment building, a house in Gaza City, a house in Rafah, and gunmen carrying anti-tank guided missiles in Khan Younis. The targeted men included

- Khalil Bahtini, variant Khalil Salah al-Bahtini, variant Bahitini, 44, IJO commander of the Northern Region in the al Quds Brigades

- Tareq Izzeldeen, variant Tariq Muhammad Ezzedine, 49, IJO intermediary between its Gaza and West Bank members and one of the leaders of the military wing of the al Quds Brigades in the West Bank

- Jehad Ghanam, variant Jihad Shaker al-Ghannam, 63, secretary of the Military Council in the al Quds Brigades

The Russian diplomatic delegation in Ramallah in the West Bank said that dentist Jamal

Khaswan, who was killed, was a Russian national. His wife and son were also killed. Khaswan lived downstairs from Izzeldeen in Gaza City.

May 9, 2023: *UPI* and the *Telegraph* reported that the Israeli Defense Forces announced that it killed Ali Ghali, the leader of the Islamic Jihad Organization's rocket launching force, in a nighttime attack. IDF said it also killed two other senior Islamic Jihad commanders, believed to be his brother Mahmoud Hassan Muhammed Ghali, and Mahmud Walid Abdul Jawad, on May 10 in a strike on a residential building in Khan Yunis where Ghali had been hiding.

The IDF claimed that four Palestinian civilians, including a girl, 10, died from misfired PIJ rockets in the Gaza Strip.

May 10, 2023: *UPI, AP,* and the *Washington Post* reported that the IDF tweeted that 289 rockets were fired from Gaza toward Israel. The Iron Dome defense system intercepted 60; another 56 rocket launches failed. Some 212 hit 108 targets in Israel. Some rockets were aimed at Tel Aviv. One house in Sderot was reported aflame. For the first time, the David's Sling mid-range air defence system intercepted a rocket. The military later revised the number of rockets fired to 547.

The *Times of Israel* reported that an IDF airstrike killed PIJ commander Ahmed Abu Daqqa, variant Ahmad Abu Deka, who was meant to replace Ali Ghali, in the southern Gaza town of Bani Suheila, near Khan Younis. Another four were wounded.

July 5, 2023: *Reuters* reported that terrorists fired five rockets toward Sderot in Israel after Israeli forces withdrew from the Palestinian city of Jenin. The Iron Dome intercepted the rockets and no casualties were reported. The *Times of Israel* reported that in retaliation, at 5 a.m., IDF airstrikes hit an underground weapons manufacturing facility used by the chemical unit of Hamas and a site for processing rocket components. The sites were in al-Baydar, west of Gaza City, and Beit Lahiyeh, in the northern Strip.

August 21, 2023: *Al-Jazeera* reported that the IDF announced that the Iron Dome missile defense system shot down two rockets coming

from Gaza. The previous day, IDF shot down a Gaza-originated drone over the area of the settlements of Alumim.

October 17, 2023: *CNN* and *NPR* reported that more than 500 people were dead in an explosion at the al-Ahli Baptist Hospital. Hamas blamed Israel. The IDF attributed the explosion to a failed Palestinian Islamic Jihad rocket. Scores of injured people were taken to al-Shifa Hospital. President Biden suggested the "other team" was responsible. *CNN* reported on October 21 that forensic analysis indicated that a rocket was the only viable theory regarding the size of the crater found; airstrikes and bombs did not produce that specific type of damage. The analysis suggested that the rocket set off gasoline in nearby parked cars, which enhanced the explosive effect.

An Israeli air strike on the Bureij refugee camp killed senior Hamas military commander Ayman Nofal, the most high-profile terrorist killed so far in the war. He had been the intelligence chief of the group's armed wing. He was in charge of Hamas activities in the central Gaza Strip, including coordinating activities with other groups.

Israeli airstrikes hit the Gaza City house of Ismail Haniyeh, Hamas's top political official, killing 14 people. He operates in Doha, Qatar.

December 2, 2023: *CNN* reported that the al-Qassam Brigades military wing of Hamas said it fired rockets from the Gaza Strip at Tel Aviv in response to "Zionist massacres against civilians".

January 4, 2024: *UPI* reported that Gaza's Ministry of Health posted on *Facebook* that 22,438 Palestinians had died and another 57,614 were wounded since the October 7, 2023 Hamas attack.

The IDF announced it killed Palestinian Islamic Jihad leader Mamdoh Lulu in an airstrike, adding on *X* that he "served as an assistant to the heads of the northern region of the Gaza Strip in the Palestinian Islamic organization, and was in contact with senior officials of the organization's headquarters abroad… Lulu was killed in an attack by an IDF aircraft, led by the Fire and

Intelligence Center in the Southern Command and directed by the Shin Bet and the Intelligence Division."

January 8, 2024: *CNN* reported that Israel's Iron Dome system intercepted half a dozen rockets fired from the Gaza Strip during the evening. Hamas's al-Qassam Brigades said on *Telegram*: "We hit 'Tel Aviv' with a rocket barrage in response to the massacres against civilians." No casualties were reported.

January 16, 2024: *CNN* reported that Hamas's al-Qassam Brigades took credit on *Telegram* for firing 25 rockets toward Netivot in Israel in the morning. The Iron Dome air defense system knocked down most of them. No injuries were reported.

January 17, 2024: *AP* and *NPR* reported that France and Qatar mediated a deal between Hamas and Israel in which medicine could be shipped to dozens of hostages via Egypt. A senior Hamas official confirmed that for every box provided for the hostages, 1,000 boxes of medicine would be sent in for Palestinians. The International Committee of the Red Cross would deliver the medicines. Some 45 hostages have chronic illnesses. *NPR* added that Gaza's health ministry claimed that 24,448 Palestinians had died and more than 60,000 were wounded.

February 19, 2024: The Gaza Health Ministry said 29,000 Palestinians had been killed in the war.

March 9, 2024: On March 18, 2024, *CNN* reported that the White House announced that during an operation on March 9, an Israeli airstrike killed Hamas's number three, Marwan Issa. IDF spokesman Rear Admiral Daniel Hagari said that Israeli forces had attacked an underground compound used by Issa and other senior Hamas officials in the Nazirat area of central Gaza. The IDF was not able to verify whether Issa was killed. Issa was the deputy of Mohammed Deif, the head of Hamas's military division. Issa was one of the planners of the October 7 attack.

March 26, 2024: *Al-Jazeera* reported that Israeli military spokesman Rear Admiral Daniel Hagari claimed that in an attack on March 9-10, the IDF killed Hamas deputy military commander Marwan Issa, a deputy to Mohammed Deif, the longtime leader of Hamas's military wing the Qassam Brigades.

March 27, 2024: The U.S. and UK imposed sanctions on two individuals and three entities that are key financial facilitators of fundraising for Hamas. Senior Hamas official Sami Abu Zuhri said "These institutions have no connection with the Hamas movement." Sanctioned was the Gaza Now organization, which started raising funds after October 7, 2023.

March 28, 2024: *UPI* reported that Israeli troops of Shayetet 13 killed Hamas leader Ra'ad Thabet in the maternity ward of Al-Shifa Hospital as he was attempting to escape into the courtyard with two other militants. He was one of the group's ten senior commanders, responsible for research and development, strengthening systems, and headed the group's production unit.

April 10, 2024: *AP, Shehab,* Hamas's *al-Aqsa TV,* and *al-Jazeera* reported that Israeli airstrikes killed three sons (Hazem, Amir, and Mohammed Haniyeh) and three grandsons and a granddaughter of Hamas leader Ismail Haniyeh in the Shati refugee camp in Gaza City, where Ismail Haniyeh is originally from. The brothers were traveling with family members in a single vehicle targeted by an Israeli drone. The IDF said Mohammed and Hazem were Hamas military operatives and that Amir was a cell commander.

April 12, 2024: *UPI* reported that the U.S. Department of the Treasury's Office of Foreign Assets Control imposed sanctions against four members of Hamas based in Gaza and Lebanon involved in cyber and unmanned aerial vehicle operations. They included:

- Hudhayfa Samir 'Abdallah al-Kahlut, alias Abu Ubaida, spokesman of the military wing of Hamas in Gaza since at least 2007. He publicly threatened to execute civilian hostages held by Hamas following the October 7, 2023 attacks.

- William Abu Shanab, commander of Hamas's Construction Bureau in Lebanon

- Bara'a Hasan Farhat, Shanab's assistant

- Khalil Muhammad 'Azzam, a Hamas intelligence officer

April 21, 2024: *USA Today* and the *Florida Times-Union* reported that the UN Secretary General accepted an independent review that indicated that there was no evidence to back Israel's accusation that 12 UNRWA employees were directly involved in the Hamas attack on Israel on October 7, 2023 and that another 30 supported the attack in some way. The U.S. and a dozen other nations had altered funding for the UN Relief and Works Agency for Palestine Refugees when Israel's accusation became public. Israel had also claimed 12 percent of UNRWA staff belonged to Hamas.

AP reported on April 27, 2024 that U.N. Office of Internal Oversight Services investigators were exploring allegations against 14 of the 19 staffers from the UNWRA who Israel claims were involved in the attack.

April 22, 2024: The Gaza Health Ministry said 34,151 Palestinians had been killed and 77,084 have been injured during the Israeli ground offensive.

April 24, 2024: *Politico* reported Gaza-based militants fired mortar rounds at Israeli forces preparing for the U.S.-led effort to establish a new maritime aid route for Gaza. No American equipment was damaged.

May 26, 2024: *NPR, AP,* and *CNN* reported that Hamas claimed credit for a rocket barrage into Israel. Air raid sirens went off in Tel Aviv for the first time in months.

June 14, 2024: *UPI* reported that the U.S. Department of State designated the Israeli Tzav 9 a violent extremist group for its efforts to stop humanitarian aid from entering Gaza by blocking roads and violently preventing aid trucks from reaching besieged Palestinians.

August 6, 2024: *CNN* and *NPR* reported that Hamas named Yahya Sinwar as the new chief of its political bureau, to succeed the assassinated Ismail Haniyeh. Sinwar was the group's leader in Gaza and allegedly planned the October 7, 2023 attack on Israel. He was elected to the Hamas Politburo in 2017. The U.S. Department of State declared him a global terrorist in 2015. France and the UK imposed sanctions on him.

September 16, 2024: *Al-Jazeera* reported that an IDF air raid killed Ahmed Aish Salame al-Hashash, head of Palestinian Islamic Jihad's rocket unit in Rafah.

October 17, 2024: Between 2-3 p.m., an IDF Bislach Brigade patrol killed three militants during operations in Rafah, Gaza and later confirmed that one of them was Hamas leader Yahya Sinwar, 61, who oversaw the October 7, 2023 massacre. *CNN* reported that Israel's chief pathologist said he was killed by a bullet to the head. He died seated in a damaged armchair in his Tal as-Sultan home after it was bombed and he was shot after throwing a stick at an Israeli drone. *Al-Jazeera* and the *New York Times* said a group of Israeli trainee soldiers came upon him by chance. Sinwar and his two bodyguards died on Sukkot, known as the Jewish Thanksgiving for the renewal of life. He was wearing a bulletproof vest and had grenades and $11,000 in cash on him. He spent years in an Israeli prison for killing IDF soldiers and alleged Palestinian collaborators. The IDF identified him by DNA, dental, and fingerprint records.

October 23, 2024: *CNN* reported that the IDF and the Israeli Security Agency claimed that United Nations Relief and Works Agency worker Mohammad Abu Etewi, who was killed in an air strike was a Hamas commander "involved in the murder and abduction of Israeli civilians on October 7" and who led an attack on a bomb shelter in Re'im, southern Israel that day. IDF spokesperson Daniel Hagari said that a bomb shelter that Abu Etewi allegedly attacked was where the hostages Hersh Goldberg-Polin, Alon Ohel, Or Levi, and Eliya Cohen were taken captive.

November 1, 2024: An IDF airstrike killed Hamas politburo member Izz al-Din Kassab in Khan Younis.

November 3, 2024: An IDF airstrike killed Ahmed al-Dalu, a member of the Islamic Jihad's Military Intelligence Unit who participated in a massacre of the kibbutz community of Kfar Aza during the October 7 attacks. The IDF killed an unnamed second terrorist next to al-Dalu.

GOLAN HEIGHTS

July 27, 2024: *CNN* reported that Hizballah denied responsibility when 30 rockets were fired from an area north of Chebaa in southern Lebanon at the Majdal Shams village, a Druze community in the Golan Heights, killing 12 children and wounding 29. One of the targets was a soccer field where children and teens were playing.

CNN reported on July 30 that Israel retaliated with an airstrike in Beirut against Fu'ad Shukr, 62, variant Fouad Shukur, Hizballah's seniormost military commander, whom it blamed for the Golan Heights attack and various attacks after October 8, 2023. The IDF said the airstrike killed him and two others and wounded 74. A senior Lebanese government official said he survived. *AP* reported on July 31 that the U.S. had accused him of orchestrating the October 23, 1983 truck bombing of a Marine Corps barracks in Beirut that killed 241 U.S. servicemen. The U.S. Department of the Treasury had offered $5 million for information about him and had named him a "specially designated national" on July 21, 2015. He was a member of the group's military Jihadi Council.

GULF OF ADEN

November 26, 2023: *AP* reported that attackers seized the Liberian-flagged *Central Park*, a tanker linked to Israel and managed by London-based Zodiac Maritime, which said, "Our priority is the safety of our 22 crew onboard... The Turkish-captained vessel has a multinational crew consisting of a crew of Russian, Vietnamese, Bulgarian, Indian, Georgian, and Filipino nationals. The vessel is carrying a full cargo of phosphoric acid." The ship is owned by Clumvez Shipping Inc., though other records directly

linked Zodiac as the owner. Zodiac Maritime is part of Israeli billionaire Eyal Ofer's Zodiac Group. Houthis were suspected.

AP added that the hijackers released the vessel on November 26 before being apprehended by the United States Navy. U.S. Central Command said that its forces and allies, including the Arleigh Burke-class destroyer *USS Mason*, responded to the seizure and demanded the armed assailants release the tanker. Five gunmen left the *Central Park* and tried to flee in a small boat, but soon surrendered.

Al-Jazeera reported on November 28 that Pentagon spokesman Brigadier General Patrick Ryder said that the attackers were probably Somali pirates rather than Houthi fighters.

January 12, 2024: *CNN* reported that Houthis fired an anti-ship ballistic missile toward the *M/T Khalissa*, a commercial vessel, but missed.

January 17, 2024: *USNWR, AP,* and *Reuters* reported that the Indian Navy rescued the 22 crew, including nine Indian nationals, of the Marshall Islands-flagged, U.S.-owned and -operated *M/V Genco Picardy* bulk carrier after a Houthi explosive drone attack. No injuries were reported and a fire was extinguished. The ship had a cargo of phosphate rock bound for India. The New York City-based Genco Shipping and Trading Ltd., trades on the New York Stock Exchange.

January 18, 2024: *UPI* reported that at 9 p.m., Houthis fired two anti-ship missiles at the Marshall Islands-flagged, U.S.-owned, and Greek-operated *M/V Chem Ranger* tanker, but hit waters nearby. There were no reports of injuries or damage. Houthi spokesman Mohammed al-Bukhaiti claimed to have achieved "direct hits".

January 24, 2024: *UPI* reported that at 2 p.m., an explosion struck 100 meters near a ship traveling through the Bab el-Mandeb Strait off Yemen. *Military Times* reported that the *USS Gravely* guided missile destroyer shot down two other missiles. No damage or injuries were reported. *USA Today* reported that Houthis fired three anti-ship ballistic missiles at the U.S.-flagged, -owned, and –operated *M/V Maersk Detroit*. The *Maersk Detroit* container vessel is operated by

Maersk Line, a U.S. subsidiary of Danish shipping giant A.P. Moller-Maersk. *CNN* reported that the Houthis claimed credit.

January 26, 2024: The *USS Carney*, an Arleigh-Burke class destroyer, shot down a Houthi projectile aimed at it southwest of Yemen's port city of Aden. No damage or injuries were reported.

CNN, UPI, and *AP* reported that a Houthi missile hit the Marshall Islands-flagged *Marlin Luanda* oil tanker, which is managed by a UK firm, owned by the UK-based Oceonix Services, and operated by the Singapore-based Trafigura commodities trading group, causing an hours-long fire in a starboard tank. The Indian navy guided-missile destroyer *INS Visakhapatnam* assisted in extinguishing the fire. The tanker carried Russian-produced naphtha, a flammable oil. The ship had a crew of 25 Indians and two Sri Lankans.

Earlier that day, the *Marlin Luanda* reported an explosion in the air above the *Achilles* oil tanker under contract to an Indian shipper.

January 31, 2024: *The Hill* reported that the *USS Carney* shot down an anti-ship ballistic missile launched from Houthi-controlled areas of Yemen at 8:30 a.m. Forty minutes later, the *Carney* shot down three Iranian drones. No injuries or damage was reported.

February 15, 2024: *UPI* reported that Houthi rebels claimed to have attacked with "appropriate naval missiles" the Barbados-flagged British supermax bulk carrier *Lycavitos* transiting the Gulf of Aden. The *Lycavitos* is operated by Helikon Shipping, which was established in London in 1961, and also has offices in Athens, and Dalian, China. The Lycavitos was built in 2007 and has a deadweight tonnage of 58,786.

February 18, 2024: *AP* and *UPI* reported that one of two missiles fired by Yemen's Houthi rebels badly damaged the engine room of a 32,000 ton Belize-flagged, UK-registered, Lebanese-owned ship traveling through the Bab el-Mandeb Strait that connects the Red Sea and the Gulf of Aden. The crew abandoned ship. *Rubymar* had been en route to Bulgaria after leaving Khorfakkan, United Arab Emirates on February 11.

CNN added on February 24 that the *Rubymar* had left an 18-mile long oil slick in the Red Sea while continuing to take on water. It was carrying 41,000 tons of fertilizer.

AP reported on March 2 that the *Rubymar* became the first Houthi-attacked vessel to sink. U.S. CENTCOM warned that the cargo of fertilizer and fuel leaking from the ship could cause ecological damage to the Red Sea.

February 22, 2024: *AP* and *ABC News* reported that Houthis were suspected of firing two missiles, one of which set the Palau-flagged, Liberian-owned cargo ship *Islander* ablaze and wounded a crew member. It came from Thailand bound for Egypt, and had sent out messages "SYRIAN CREW ON BOARD".

March 4, 2024: *CNN* reported that Houthis fired two anti-ship ballistic missiles, damaging the Swiss-owned *M/V MSC Sky II* container ship. One of the missiles hit the ship. U.S. CENTCOM added that there were no injuries and the ship continued on its way. The Indian navy released images of it fighting a fire aboard the container ship. The Swiss-based Mediterranean Shipping Company said the missile struck the ship as it was traveling from Singapore to Djibouti.

CENTCOM noted that several hours later, the U.S. "conducted self-defense strikes against two anti-ship cruise missiles that presented an imminent threat to merchant vessels and U.S. Navy ships in the region."

March 6, 2024: *AP* and *UPI* reported that Houthis were suspected when at 11:30 a.m., a missile damaged the Barbados-flagged, Liberian-owned bulk carrier *M/V True Confidence* in the Gulf of Aden. *NPR, AP,* and *CNN* reported that three crew—one Vietnamese and two Filipino—were killed—the first time a Houthi anti-ship attack was deadly—and four wounded, three critically. *AP* reported that the crew of 20 included one Indian, 15 Filipinos, and four Vietnamese, plus three armed guards, two from Sri Lanka and one from Nepal. The ship had been carrying steel from China to Jeddah, Saudi Arabia. The crew abandoned ship. The ship had previously been owned by Oaktree Capital Management, a Los Angeles-based fund that finances vessels on installments.

The U.S. destroyer *USS Carney* separately shot down bomb-carrying drones and an anti-ship ballistic missile launched by the Houthis.

Another U.S. airstrike destroyed four anti-ship missiles, three aerial drones, and three bomb-carrying drone boats.

March 8, 2024: Houthis conducted a drone attack against the Singapore-flagged, British bulk carrier *Propel Fortune*, causing no injuries or damage. Two explosions went off in front of the ship.

U.S. airstrikes destroyed two Houthi truck-mounted anti-ship missiles in Yemen.

April 23, 2024: The master of a merchant vessel near the Bab el-Mandeb Strait reported seeing an explosion in the distance, some 80 miles southeast of Djibouti in the Gulf of Aden. Houthis were suspected.

April 24, 2024: *Al-Jazeera* reported that Houthi military spokesman Yahya Saree said that his group launched an anti-ship ballistic missile which hit the *Maersk Yorktown* cargo ship, a U.S.-flagged, owned, and operated vessel with 18 U.S. and four Greek crew members in the Gulf of Aden. U.S. CENTCOM reported that there were no injuries or damaged to U.S. coalition, or commercial ships.

April 25, 2024: Houthis attacked a ship traveling in the Gulf of Aden after U.S. CENTCOM said that in the early morning, an allied warship shot down a Houthi missile targeting a vessel the day before near the same area. The British military's United Kingdom Maritime Trade Operations center said the ship was targeted 15 miles southwest of Aden.

April 26, 2024: *UPI* and *AP* reported that CENTCOM said that an anti-ship ballistic missile was launched in the morning from an area controlled by Houthi rebels in Yemen but fell into the Gulf of Aden without making contact with a ship. No injuries or damage was reported to military or commercial ships.

May 7, 2024: *AP* and *al-Jazeera* reported that Houthis claimed credit for two early morning missile and drone attacks in the Gulf of Aden on the *MSC Diego* and *MSC Gina*, two Panama-flagged container ships, which caused no damage. Both vessels were operating for Geneva-based Mediterranean Shipping Co.

June 8, 2024: Houthis were suspected when a missile struck the forward station and started a fire on an Antigua and Barbuda-flagged cargo ship during the night. Another missile missed. People on small boats opened fire on the ship. No one was hurt onboard.

June 9, 2024: Houthi missiles hit two ships. Two anti-ship ballistic cruise missiles hit the Antigua and Barbuda-flagged cargo ship *Norderney* forward station late, starting a fire.

A Houthi ballistic missile hit the Liberian-flagged, Swiss-owned-and-operated container ship *Tavvishi*, which reported damage but continued. A coalition warship intercepted a second Houthi ballistic missile fired at the ship.

Houthi spokesman Saree also claimed an unreported attack on a warship, without providing any evidence.

June 13, 2024: *AP, al-Jazeera,* and *BBC* reported that Houthis launched two anti-ship cruise missiles that set ablaze the Palauan-flagged, Ukrainian-owned, and Polish-operated bulk cargo carrier *M/V Verbena*, severely wounding a civilian mariner. The *Verbena* had docked in Malaysia and was on its way to Italy carrying wood.

June 21, 2024: *AP* reported that a commercial ship saw explosions near the vessel. Houthis were suspected.

June 24, 2024: Houthis were believed responsible for targeting a ship 280 miles southeast of Nishtun, Yemen, off Socotra Island, further away from nearly all of their previous assaults in the Gulf of Aden. The next evening, Houthi military spokesperson Brig. Gen. Yahya Saree claimed the group attacked the Liberian-flagged, Greek-managed container ship *MSC Sarah V* with a ballistic missile.

June 26, 2024: Houthis were suspected of an early morning attack on a ship off the coast of Aden. A missile hit the water near the ship.

July 9, 2024: An explosion went off near a vessel in the Gulf of Aden off the coast of Nishtun, Yemen, close to the country's border with Oman. The Houthis said they launched missiles at the *Maersk Sentosa*, a U.S.-flagged container ship in the Gulf of Aden. No injuries to the crew or damage to the ship were reported.

August 4, 2024: A Houthi missile hit the Liberian-flagged *Groton* container ship just about its waterline as it was traveling through the Gulf of Aden en route from Fujairah in the United Arab Emirates bound for Jeddah, Saudi Arabia. The crew reported minor damage. An earlier missile attack missed.

The rebels claimed to have shot down another $30 million U.S. MQ-9 (Reaper) military spy drone over Saada Province.

August 30, 2024: Houthis were suspected of firing two missiles at the Liberian-flagged container ship *Groton* in the Gulf of Aden some 150 miles east of Aden in the evening, hitting water nearby without causing injuries or damage.

November 18, 2024: A missile splashed down close to a commercial vessel 70 miles southeast of Aden in the Gulf of Aden.

December 9-10, 2024: The U.S. Navy Institute, *AP*, and *al-Jazeera* reported that the Arleigh Burke-class guided-missile destroyer *USS Stockdale* (DDG-106) and *USS O'Kane* (DDG-77) shot down a Houthi antiship cruise missile and four drones while escorting three U.S.-owned, -operated, and -flagged merchant vessels in the Gulf of Aden sailing for Djibouti. None of the ships were damaged and no one was injured. A U.S. Navy helicopter and French Air Force aircraft also helped repel the attack.

GULF OF OMAN

January 11, 2024: *CNN* and *Al-Jazeera* reported that at 7:30 a.m., four gunmen wearing military-style uniforms and black masks boarded the Marshall Islands-flagged crude oil tanker *St*

Nikolas, formerly known as the *Suez Rajan*, east of Sohar in Oman and diverted it toward Bandar-e-Jask in Iranian territorial waters. The U.S. government seized the *Suez Rajan* in 2023 after a court found that it was used to "covertly sell and transport Iranian oil to a customer abroad". The *St Nikolas*, which is operated by the Greek shipping company Empire Navigation, was sailing from Basra, Iraq, to Türkiye. The company said the vessel was carrying 145,000 tonnes of oil from Basra to Aliaga in Türkiye and that a crew of 18 Filipinos and a Greek national were on board.

IRAN

January 27, 2023: *UPI* reported that at 8:30 a.m. Azerbaijan time, a gunman attacked the Azerbaijan embassy in Iran, killing First Lieutenant Orkhan Rizvan oglu Asgarov, the head of the security service, and injuring two guards. The Azerbaijani government said "The attacker destroyed the guard post with a Kalashnikov automatic weapon and killed the head of the security service… Two security guards of the embassy were also injured while preventing the attack. Their condition is satisfactory." The *BBC* reported that local police arrested an Azeri citizen who claimed his wife had been held at the embassy for nine months. He had been waiting outside the embassy before using his car to hit a diplomatic vehicle and then started firing with an AK-47 rifle. *Eurasia Diary* reported on January 29 that Azerbaijan announced that it will evacuate embassy staff and family members from Iran.

January 28, 2023: The *Business Standard, Iran State TV*, and *IRNA* reported that Iran's Defence Ministry said a drone struck at 11:30 p.m. at a military ammunition factory near Isfahan, causing minor damage and no casualties. No one claimed credit.

February 28, 2023: *Reuters* reported that Health Minister Bahram Einollahi said that hundreds of Iranian girls in 30 schools in four cities, including Qom, had suffered "mild poison" attacks since November 2022. *IRNA* reported that some politicians, including Alirez Monadi and Azar Mansoori, blamed religious groups opposed to girls' education. State media reported that a boys' school in Boroujerd was also targeted. *NPR* reported on March 1 that 900 girls had been affected. *AP* and *IRNA* reported that Supreme Leader Ayatollah Ali Khamenei said on March 5 that the culprits should be sentenced to death for an "unforgivable crime". By March 5, more than 60 schools had reported incidents in 21 of Iran's 30 provinces. *UPI* added that on March 7 Deputy Interior Minister Majid Mirahmadi said Iranian officials arrested suspects in five provinces. State-run media said 1,200 schoolgirls were affected; one lawmaker said the number was 5,000.

April 26, 2023: The *Washington Post* reported that Iranian officials reported another apparent gas attack at a girls' elementary school in the Kurdish region of western Iran. Amnesty International reported that in recent months, some 300 suspected gas attacks had hit more than 100 schools for girls. The *Shargh* daily newspaper quoted Deputy Health Minister Saeed Karimi as indicating in March that 13,000 students had been treated for symptoms of suspected poisoning. No deaths were reported. The attacks began in November 2022 in Qom. In March, more than 100 suspects in 11 provinces were arrested, according to *Hamshahri*.

April 26, 2023: *UPI* and the official *Islamic Republic News Agency* reported that a security guard shot to death high-ranking Iranian cleric Ayatollah Abbasali Soleimani, in his mid-to-late 70s, who was sitting in a chair at a Babolsar city bank in northern Mazandaran Province. Two men wrestled the gun away from the guard, who was arrested.

May 21, 2023: *AP* and Iranian state television reported that gunmen trying to enter Iran near the Pakistani border killed five Iranian border guards and wounded two in Saravan in Sistan and Baluchistan Province. The gunmen fled, having taken casualties. No group claimed credit.

June 1, 2023: *UPI* reported that the U.S. Department of the Treasury imposed sanctions against Iranian operatives and affiliates accused of attempting to assassinate former Trump administration officials and Iranian dissidents around the world. Those sanctioned included three Islamic Revolutionary Guard Corps members and two members of the IRGC's Intelligence Organization as well as an associated airline that is believed to have assisted with covert operations. Among them were:

- Shahram Poursafi, 46, an Iranian charged by the Justice Department in August 2022 with plotting to assassinate former national security adviser John Bolton. Prosecutors said he tried to hire a hitman to kill Bolton in retaliation over the U.S. airstrike that killed Gen. Qassem Soleimani of Iran's elite Quds Force in January 2020.

- Mohammad Reza Ansari, 47, a longtime IRGC Quds Force official and a member of its external operations unit that conducts international covert operations, including assassinations of Iranian dissidents and others in the United States, the Middle East, Europe, and Africa. Treasury said he and Poursafi planned to assassinate two former U.S. government officials, including Bolton.

- Hossein Hafez Amini, 53, a dual Turkish and Iranian national based in Türkiye, used his aviation industry connections and his Türkiye-based Rey Airlines to assist the IRGC Quds Force with kidnapping and assassination plots targeting dissidents in Türkiye. Rey Airlines was also sanctioned.

- Rouhallah Bazghandi, former IRGC-IO chief, and Reza Seraj, the group's foreign intelligence head, were accused of being behind failed operations in Asia and intelligence operations targeting U.S. citizens. The IRGC-IO and Bazghandi were designated in April over taking U.S. nationals hostage in Iran.

July 8, 2023: *USNWR*, Iranian state television, and *Reuters* reported that gunmen and suicide bombers stormed a police station in Zahedan, capital of Sistan-Baluchistan Province. Two police officers and four terrorists were killed in the ensuing gun battle.

August 13, 2023: *UPI, al-Jazeera,* and the state-run *Islamic Republic News Agency (IRNA)* reported that at 7 p.m., gunman Rahmatollah

Nowruzof from Tajikistan, fired 11 shots inside the Shah Cheragh shrine in downtown Shiraz in Fars Province, killing one person and injuring seven. Authorities arrested the suspect. The shooter carried an assault rifle and eight magazines with 240 bullets. *Al-Jazeera* and the *Tasnim News Agency* reported on August 14 that Iran blamed ISIS and arrested ten foreign nationals on suspicion of being involved in the assault. The governor of Fars Province said "The motivation of this Daeshi [ISIS-affliated] individual was to take revenge for the executions of the two terrorists of the previous incident."

September 24, 2023: *Al-Jazeera, Reuters,* and *Tasnim* reported that the Ministry of Intelligence claimed it thwarted terrorists who planned to set off 30 bombs in a crowded center in Tehran, arresting 28 ISIS-linked individuals during raids in Tehran, Alborz, and West Azerbaijan Provinces. The Ministry announced, "The explosions were planned with the aim of breaking the country's security authority, creating an unstable image of the country, sowing despair and fear in the society, and instigating chaos and protests exactly during the anniversary of last year's riots." The Intelligence Ministry said some of the detainees had a history of cooperating with "takfiris in Syria, Afghanistan, Pakistan and the Kurdistan region in Iraq". Two intelligence agents were wounded in the raids, which netted large quantities of explosives, electronic detonators, 17 U.S.-made pistols and ammunition, communication devices, military-grade clothing, suicide vests, and foreign currencies.

January 3, 2024: *AP, CNN, IRNA,* the *Los Angeles Times,* and the *Washington Post* reported that Iranian state media claimed that two suicide bombers hit a memorial ceremony in Kerman near the tomb of General Qassem Soleimani (the head of the Revolutionary Guards' Quds Force who was killed in a U.S. airstrike in Iraq on January 3, 2020) killed 103, including 30 children, and injured 141 (*Al-Jazeera* said 211 were wounded. *IRNA* said 84 were killed and 284 injured; the official number ratcheted up to 94.). Iran said 14 of the dead were Afghans. The blasts occurred 15 minutes apart. *Al-Jazeera* reported that Melika Hosseini, a member of the Iranian Red Cres-

cent Society, was among those killed. *NBC News* reported that the Iranians said that the bombs, hidden in bags, were remotely detonated. *NBC* added that ISIS claimed credit.

CNN, IRNA, Press TV, and the *Jerusalem Post* reported on January 5 that ISIS-K claimed on *al-Furqan* and *Telegram* that two suicide bombers, who are brothers, set off their suicide vests and explosive belts amongst the Shi'ite "polytheist" mourners. The statement was titled "And Kill Them Wherever You Find Them". *IRINN* said the first explosion was caused by a bomb placed in a suitcase inside a car and detonated remotely rather than being caused by a suicide bomber. *Reuters* and the *Washington Post* reported that Iran arrested 11 suspects in six provinces. Iranian authorities said one of the two suicide bombers was a Tajik citizen.

The *New York Times* on January 7, 2024 ran a long discussion of Iran's unacknowledged domestic terrorism problem. Iranian President Ibrahim Raisi blamed Israel and the United States for the attack. *Tasnim News Agency,* the media arm of the Revolutionary Guards, claimed that "Israel ordered ISIS to take responsibility for the attack."

AP and *IRNA* reported on January 11 that Iranian military intelligence named the top suspect as a Tajik bombmaker known by his alias Abdollah Tajiki, who entered Iran in mid-December 2022 via Iran's southeast border, and left on January 1, after making the bombs. Iran said one of the bombers was named Bozrov, 24, and had Tajik and Israeli nationality. It said he arrived in Iran via the southeastern border after months of training by ISIS in Afghanistan. ISIS-K named the two bombers as Omar al-Mowahed and Seif-Allah al-Mujahed. In a follow-up statement, ISIS-K said the attack was "the beginning of our war" with Iran.

AP and the *New York Times* reported that Iranian authorities arrested 35 people in at least six provinces. Authorities arrested two people in Kerman where the attackers had stayed and discovered two suicide vests, remote control devices for detonating explosives, grenades, thousands of pieces of shrapnel, wires, and explosive devices, suggesting that more attacks were planned.

The *Wall Street Journal*, *CNN,* and *NPR* reported on January 25 that the United States quietly warned Iran that ISIS was planning a potential terrorist attack inside Iran before the January 3 attack. The intelligence information was shared based on the U.S. government's "duty to warn" policy, which applies even to U.S. adversaries. The Office of the Director of National Intelligence noted that any Intelligence Community entity that collects or acquires "credible and specific information indicating an impending threat of intentional killing, serious bodily injury, or kidnapping directed at a person or group of people…shall have a duty to warn the intended victim or those responsible for protecting the intended victim, as appropriate."

January 17, 2024: Jaish al-Adl claimed responsibility for an attack on an Islamic Revolutionary Guard Corps (IRGC) vehicle in Sistan and Baluchistan Province that Iranian state media claimed killed an Iranian colonel.

January 21, 2024: An Iranian soldier shot to death five resting soldiers in a barracks dormitory in Kerman.

January 27, 2024: *AP* and *Mehr* reported that gunmen shot to death nine Pakistanis and wounded three other people in a home near Saravan in Sistan and Baluchestan Province on the Pakistani border. The victims worked at an auto repair shop.

February 13, 2024: *Al-Jazeera* reported that oil minister Javad Owji told state TV that "terrorism and sabotage" was involved in two 1 a.m. explosions on gas pipelines. One explosion went off on the mainline gas route running from Iran's central Chaharmahal and Bakhtiari Province north to major gas fields in the Caspian Sea. The other explosion went off in Fars Province.

ABC News reported on February 21 that Iran's Oil Minister Javad Owji blamed Israel for a sabotage attack on a 790 mile-long Iranian natural gas pipeline running from Iran's western Chaharmahal and Bakhtiari Province up north to cities on the Caspian Sea that caused multiple explosions on the line. He told *IRNA* the "explosion of the gas pipeline was an Israeli plot… The enemy intended to disturb gas service in the provinces and put people's gas distribution at risk… The evil action and plot by the enemy was properly managed."

April 3, 2024: *Al-Jazeera* reported that 11 Iranian security force members were killed and ten injured in an attack on an Islamic Revolutionary Guard Corps (IRGC) headquarters in Sistan-Baluchestan Province. Sixteen members of Jaish al-Adl (Army of Justice), a Sunni group, died, according to Iranian state television. The overnight clashes occurred in Chabahar and Rask in Sistan-Baluchestan which borders Afghanistan and Pakistan. The gunmen wore suicide vests.

April 6, 2024: *Al-Jazeera* reported that Iran announced the arrests of three ISIS members, including "senior" ISIS member Mohammad "Ramesh" Zaker, who were planning a suicide attack at the end of Ramadan in Mahdasht in Alborz Province. Another eight people were accompanying the terrorists.

April 9, 2024: *AP* and *yjc.ir* reported that gunmen ambushed a police convoy in Sistan and Baluchistan Province, killing six policemen and wounding two policemen. The website said Jaish al-Adl claimed credit.

July 31, 2024: *CNN* and *USA Today* reported that a suspected Israeli airstrike or bombing killed Hamas political chief Ismail Haniyeh in his residence in Tehran following his participation in the inauguration of Iran's new president, Masoud Pezeshkian. He had run Hamas political operations from exile in Qatar, and was the lead negotiator for a possible ceasefire in Gaza. His bodyguard also died. The *New York Times* reported on August 4, 2024 that Iran had arrested more than two dozen suspects, including senior intelligence officers, military officials, and staff workers at a military-run guesthouse in Tehran, in the case.

October 2024: On October 31, 2024, the Afghan Taliban government claimed that two Afghan citizens died earlier in the month in Iran from explosions and gunfire in the Kalgan Valley near Saravan in Sistan and Baluchistan Province. The Taliban said some of the 34 eyewitnesses were injured.

October 1, 2024: Gunmen killed six people, including a local chief of the paramilitary Revolutionary Guard, town council head Parviz Kadkhodaei, and two volunteer members of the Guard, in two attacks in Sistan and Baluchistan Province. The victims had participated in a school ceremony in Nikshahar. Two police officers died in the second attack in Khash. No one claimed credit.

October 26, 2024: *AP* and *IRNA* reported that gunmen attacked two vehicles in a police convoy in Goha Kuh in Sistan and Baluchestan Province, killing ten officers. No one claimed credit.

November 10, 2024: *AP* and *IRNA* reported that Revolutionary Guard forces killed three terrorists and arrested nine others.

Later that day, gunmen attacked ethnic Baluch members of the paramilitary Revolutionary Guard's volunteer Basij force, killing five in Saravan in Sistan and Baluchistan Province near the Pakistani border. No group claimed credit.

December 28, 2024: *AP* and the *Javan Daily* reported that a suicide bomber stopped Police Captain Mojtaba Shahid's car during the evening in Bandar Lengeh in Hormozgan Province then set off his explosive vest. Shahid's deputy, who was in the car, was critically injured. Local news services blamed Ansar al-Furqan, an al-Qaeda-linked Sunni militant group.

IRAQ

February 1, 2023: *Al-Jazeera* reported that the Islamic Resistance Ahrar al-Iraq Brigade, part of Iraq's Iran-backed paramilitary Popular Mobilization Forces, claimed credit for firing eight rockets at Türkiye's Zilkan military base in Nineveh Province in northern Iraq. No damage or injuries were reported.

March 2023: *UPI* and *NPR* reported on July 5, 2023 that dual Israeli-Russian citizen Elizabeth Tsurkov, 36, was kidnapped in March 2023 in Baghdad's Karrada neighborhood by the Iranian-backed Kataib Hezbollah (Brigades of the Party of God) Shi'ite militia while conducting research for her post-doctoral dissertation in

comparative politics at Princeton University. She was traveling on her Russian passport. She contributes to the Newlines Institute for Strategy and Policy, a think tank based in Washington, D.C. *BBC* added that the group's demands were unknown. Her page at the Middle East Institute's website noted that the Levant expert worked as a consultant with the Atlantic Council and International Crisis Group. She had also worked at the Israeli NGO Gisha. New Lines noted that she had been an outspoken critic of Israel, Iran, and Russia. The *Washington Post* reported on July 6, 2023 that the Israeli Prime Minister's office said that "Elizabeth Tsurkov is still alive… and we hold Iraq responsible for her safety and well-being." Her family had asked the news media not to publicize the March abduction. She had undergone back surgery in an Iraqi hospital days before the kidnapping.

June 8, 2023: *UPI* reported that U.S. Secretary of State Antony Blinken announced while in Riyadh for the Global Coalition to Defeat ISIS ministerial opening session the blacklisting of two ISIS regional leaders. The State Department said the two leaders were being labeled Specially Designated Global Terrorists as the ISIS Core had relied upon its regional offices for operational guidance and funding. They were Abdallah Makki Muslih al-Rufay'i, the Iraq-based ISIS GDP Bilad al-Rafidayn Office emir; and Abu Bakr ibn Muhammad ibn 'Ali al-Mainuki, a Sahel-based ISIS GDP al-Furqan Office senior leader. The al-Furqan office serves ISIS in Nigeria and the neighboring countries.

August 9-10, 2023: *Al-Jazeera* reported that six Turkish soldiers died in clashes with Kurdistan Workers Party (PKK) fighters in Zap in northern Iraq during the Turkish military's cross-border Operation Claw-Lock. Turkish air raids killed four PKK fighters.

August 28, 2023: French Sgt. Nicolas Mazier of parachute commando No. 10, serving alongside Iraqi forces, was killed in combat on a reconnaissance mission during a counterterrorism operation in the al-Aith area of Salahaddin Province, 60 miles north of Baghdad. Two Iraqi soldiers and four French troops were wounded in an ISIS ambush. Mazier had been deployed since July in France's Operation Chammal, designed to help train Iraqi anti-terrorism forces.

October 17, 2023: *Reuters* and the *Jerusalem Post* reported that the U.S. military intercepted two one-way attack drones before they could strike Iraq's al-Asad air base, which hosts American troops. *Military Times* added that another drone targeting a base in the north was shot down, but caused injuries to coalition forces. Tashkil al-Waritheen, an Iranian-backed militia, claimed responsibility for the drone against the al-Harir airbase in northern Iraq. Ahmad "Abu Hussein" al-Hamidawi, head of the Kataib Hezbollah militia, said "Our missiles, drones, and special forces are ready to direct qualitative strikes at the American enemy in its bases and disrupt its interests if it intervenes in this battle." He also threatened to fire missiles at Israeli targets.

October 18, 2023—Iraq/Syria—U.S. Central Command said 24 military personnel sustained minor injuries in drone attacks at al-Tanf and al-Asad. *Task and Purpose* and *Politico* added on October 26 that 19 U.S. troops were diagnosed with Traumatic Brain Injury (TBI). Fifteen of those troops were injured in the attack on the al-Tanf garrison in Syria; the other four were diagnosed with TBI following the attack on al-Asad Air Base in Iraq. CENTCOM officials said they all quickly returned to duty. An attack destroyed an aircraft hangar and small airplane in Syria. The *Washington Post* added that one incident injured 20 personnel at al-Tanf Garrison in southeastern Syria.

October 19, 2023—Iraq/Syria—The *Washington Post* reported that rockets were fired at three coalition installations: Mission Support Site Euphrates in Syria, Ain al-Asad Air Base and the Baghdad Diplomatic Support Center in Iraq, causing no casualties.

During the next three days, one-way drones hit unoccupied areas in Bashur, Iraq, and targeting Ain al-Asad and al-Tanf again.

October 20, 2023: *AP* reported that a U.S. official said two rockets were fired in the early morning on U.S. and coalition forces at a diplomatic sup-

port center near the Baghdad International Airport. One was intercepted by a counter-rocket system and the other struck an empty storage facility. No casualties were reported.

October 24, 2023: *Reuters* reported that two rockets landed inside Ain al-Asad air base in Anbar Province, which hosts U.S. and other international forces west of Baghdad. The rocket launcher was found about 50 kilometers southeast of the base.

NBC News and the *Jerusalem Post* reported that during the previous week, 13 drone attacks on American bases in Syria and Iraq caused minor injuries to two dozen American military personnel. 23102402-13

Stars and Stripes added that U.S. forces recently experienced attacks by Iran-supported groups at the al-Tanf garrison in southeastern Syria and the Ain al-Asad and al-Harir air bases in Iraq. The attacks resulted in four minor injuries. The Defense Department said troops at the bases were repeatedly being targeted. Air Force Brig. Gen. Pat Ryder, the Pentagon's top spokesman, said that "Between Oct. 17 and [today] U.S. and coalition forces have been attacked at least 10 separate times in Iraq and three separate times in Syria via a mix of one-way attack drones and rockets." *Military.com* added that Army units brought Patriot missile batteries and a Terminal High Altitude Area Defense (THAAD) battery to the region after the drone attacks.

October 25, 2023: The *Wall Street Journal* reported on November 2 that a drone believed launched by an Iranian-based militia and loaded with explosives crashed into a U.S. barracks but failed to detonate. There were no reports of injuries.

November 17, 2023: *Military Times* reported the U.S. imposed sanctions on six people affiliated with the Iranian-backed Iraqi militia Kataib Hezbollah, which was believed behind recent attacks against U.S. forces in Iraq and Syria. The list included KH's foreign affairs chief, a member of its governing council, its military commander, and a media spokesman.

Meanwhile, terrorists conducted three attacks on U.S. military facilities in Iraq and Syria, including a one-way drone targeted al-Harir air base in Erbil, with no casualties reported—an infrastructure damage assessment was ongoing; an attack by multiple one-way drones at al-Asad air base in Iraq that resulted in no injuries or infrastructure damage; and a multiple one-way drone attack at Tal Baydar, Syria, that resulted in minor injuries to one service member who was able to return to duty.

November 22, 2023: *CNN* reported that in the afternoon, a one-way attack drone was launched against Erbil Airbase. There were no casualties or infrastructure damage reported.

November 23, 2023: *CNN* reported U.S. and coalition forces in Iraq and Syria came under attack four times on Thanksgiving Day.

In the morning, multiple one-way attack drones were launched against troops at al-Asad Airbase. There were no casualties or infrastructure damage.

A one one-way attack drone targeted Erbil Airbase in Iraq. There were no casualties or infrastructure damage.

November 30, 2023: *Al-Jazeera* reported that during the night, ISIS gunmen using bombs and firearms killed 11 civilians and wounded 12 others in Muqdadiyah in Diyala Province. *AP* reported that after a roadside bomb exploded, gunmen shot at rescuers and bystanders. *Reuters* and *AFP* reported that the terrorists targeted relatives of a local MP and two bombs destroyed a minibus in which several people were travelling.

December 3, 2023: *Air and Space Forces Magazine* and *CNN* reported that a U.S. drone strike against Iranian-aligned militias in Kirkuk killed five Harakat Hezbollah al-Nujaba terrorists preparing to attack U.S. troops. Akram al-Kabbi founded HHN, which the U.S. Department of State earlier designated as a terrorist organization.

December 8, 2023: *The Hill* and *AP* reported that at 4:15 a.m., 14 Katyusha rockets were fired at the U.S. Embassy complex and the Union III base, which houses offices of the U.S.-led coalition in Baghdad, causing minor damage but no casualties. No group claimed credit, but Iran-aided militias were suspected.

The Islamic Resistance in Iraq, an umbrella group of Iran-backed militias, claimed separate attacks on the al-Asad airbase and on a base located at the Conoco gas field in eastern Syria.

December 20, 2023: *Al-Arabiya* reported that a rocket attack targeted U.S. troops at Iraq's al-Asad Airbase, the 102nd attack on American forces in Iraq and Syria since October 17.

December 22, 2023: *Bloomberg* reported that six Turkish soldiers died in an attack.

December 23, 2023: *Bloomberg* reported that six Turkish soldiers died and one was wounded in a second attack on an outpost in northern Iraq in two days. Authorities claimed 13 terrorists were "neutralized".

December 25, 2023: *CNN* reported that at 8:45 p.m., U.S. Central Command conducted airstrikes on three facilities used by the Iraq-based Kataib Hezbollah and "affiliated groups" during the night after an attack injured three U.S. troops. Army 82nd Airborne Division pilot Chief Warrant Officer 4 Garrett Illerbrunn was critically injured with shrapnel. *Task and Purpose* reported that the pilot, stationed at Fort Liberty, North Carolina, was transported to a hospital in Germany for treatment for a severe head injury. As of January 4, 2024, he remained in intensive care. The Iranian-backed KH claimed credit for using a one-way attack drone to target the U.S. forces on al-Harir Airbase in Erbil that morning. The airstrikes likely killed several KH members.

January 4, 2024: *Reuters* and the *Times of Israel* reported that an air strike on Palestine Street in Baghdad against a vehicle carrying Mushtaq Talib al-Saidi, variant Abu Taqwa al-Saidi, the deputy commander of operations for Baghdad of the Iraqi militia Harakat al-Nujaba, which the U.S. blames for attacks against U.S. forces in the country, killed him and another person and wounded seven others near Popular Mobilization Forces headquarters. *Newsweek* added that the group threatened retaliation against the U.S.

January 12, 2024: The Turkish Defense Ministry blamed the Kurdish Workers' Party (PKK) for attacking a military base during the night in northern Iraq's semi-autonomous Kurdish region that killed nine Turkish soldiers and wounded seven, two seriously. The Ministry said 15 gunmen were "neutralized".

Türkiye carried out airstrikes against Kurdish militants in Metina, Hakurk, Gara, and Qandil in northern Iraq and in unspecified locations in Syria on January 13.

Türkiye's state-run *Anadolu* news agency reported that senior PKK militant Faik Aydin was "neutralized" in Iraq in an operation run by the Turkish intelligence agency MIT.

January 20, 2024: *Reuters* reported that rockets hit the Ain al-Asad Air base, injuring four U.S. personnel and seriously wounding a member of Iraq's security forces. *USA Today* reported that U.S. airstrikes on January 23 hit three facilities used by the Iran-backed Kataib Hizballah militia, hitting headquarters, storage, and training locations for rocket, missile, and one-way attack drones.

January 30, 2024: *Military Times* and *Reuters* reported that the Iran-backed Kataib Hezbollah directed its fighters to halt attacks on U.S. troops in Iraq and Syria. There had been more than 160 attacks on U.S. forces in Iraq and Syria since the October 7, 2023 Hamas massacre of Israelis.

February 7, 2024: *CNN* reported that a 9:30 p.m. a U.S. military drone strike on an SUV in al-Mashtal, a predominantly Shia neighborhood in eastern Baghdad, killed two people, including Wisam Mohammed Saber al-Saedi, a Kataib Hizballah commander who was responsible for attacks on American forces in the region.

February 23, 2024: Prime Minister Mohammed Shia al-Sudani announced the reopening of the Beiji refinery, Iraq's largest, which had been shut down since 2014 after being damaged by ISIS.

February 24, 2024: The Iraqi National Intelligence Service announced it had captured two ISIS members in an operation outside the country and brought them home, where they confessed to committing crimes. Issam Abed

Ali Sueidan, alias Abu Zeid, was a main propagandist for the group in Fallujah. In a video, he talked about how he beheaded an Iraqi soldier in Fallujah in addition to doing propaganda videos for the group. Bashir Abed Ali Sueidan, alias Abu Ahmad, was in charge of telecommunications in Fallujah. He said he was once held in the U.S.-run prison of Camp Bucca. He fled to Qaim near the Syrian border, where he stayed until 2017. He then fled Iraq.

March 19, 2024: Turkish airstrikes targeted suspected Kurdish PKK militants in the Metina, Zap, Hakurk, Gara, and Qandil areas in northern Iraq's semi-autonomous Kurdish region hours after a Turkish soldier was killed and four others were wounded in an attack in the region. The jets reportedly destroyed 27 PKK targets, including caves, bunkers, and shelters.

April 21, 2024: *Task and Purpose, AP,* and *France24* reported that at 9:50 p.m., Iraqi militants fired five rockets from Zummar, northwest of Mosul, at U.S. forces in a U.S. Kharab al-Jir base at Rumalyn inside northeastern Syria. No Americans were injured. A coalition fighter destroyed the launcher. *Reuters* reported that Iraqi forces burned the vehicle used to launch the rockets. Khataib Hezbollah was suspected.

U.S. forces shot down two drones near al-Asad Air Base in Iraq.

April 26, 2024: A drone attack on the Khor Mor gas field in Sulaymaniyah in the semi-autonomous Kurdish region of northern Iraq killed four Yemeni workers and wounded three others. No group claimed responsibility.

CNN, al-Jazeera, AFP, and *BBC* reported that during the night, a motorcyclist shot to death Iraqi social media star Ghufran Sawadi, better known as Umm Fahad, variant Om Fahad, in her black SUV outside her home in the Zayouna, variant Zayne, area east of Baghdad. The attacker appeared to have been pretending to be making a food delivery. The U.S.-owned *al-Hurra* news agency reported that another woman was injured. Fahad was popular on *TikTok* for sharing videos of herself dancing to pop music in form-hugging clothes. She was sentenced to six months in prison in 2023 for sharing videos that the court ruled undermined "modesty and public morality".

June 16, 2024: The *Washington Post* reported that an elite Iraqi counterterrorism force began protecting U.S. and American-style food chains in Baghdad following several incidents of vandalism in protest of the war in Gaza. Masked men had hit branches of the Jordanian-owned Chili House, an American-style burger chain, KFC, and Lee's Famous Recipe Chicken. Individuals had also thrown sound bombs at a language institute and an office of Caterpillar Inc., a U.S. construction equipment manufacturer that supplies the Israeli military with armored bulldozers. Protests were held outside the Baghdad offices of PepsiCo and Procter & Gamble. Kataib Hizballah claimed involvement.

June 18, 2024: *UPI* reported that the U.S. Department of State declared as a Specially Designated Global Terrorist organization the Iraq-based and Iran-backed Harakat Ansar Allah al-Awfiya along with its secretary general, Muzhir Ma'lak al-Sa'idi, 46. Harakat Ansar Allah al-Awfiya is part of the Islamic Resistance in Iraq.

June 29, 2024: *Al-Jazeera* reported that UNESCO announced the discovery of five large ISIS-era bombs hidden in the southern wall of the Prayer Hall of the historic al-Nuri Mosque in Mosul.

July 10, 2024: *AP, AFP, Reuters,* and *al-Jazeera* reported that the Karkh Criminal Court sentenced to death by hanging Asma Mohamed, a widow of late ISIS caliph Abu Bakr al-Baghdadi, for her role in ISIS and using her Mosul home to hold Yazidi women ISIS terrorists kidnapped in Sinjar in northern Iraq. The ruling must be ratified by an Iraqi appeals court. Al-Baghdadi had four wives. She was arrested in Turkey in 2018 and handed over to Iraqi authorities in 2023.

July 16, 2024: Two Iraqi militia officials claimed they used two drones in an attack on the Ain al-Asad air base in Iraq. Pentagon Spokesperson Sabrina Singh said U.S. forces shot one down, and the other one hit the base, with "minimal damage."

July 17, 2024: U.S. Central Command said Wednesday that ISIS had claimed 153 attacks in Iraq and Syria during the first six months of 2024. It was responsible for 121 attacks in those countries in 2023.

July 25, 2024: *Fox News* reported that four rockets struck near Ain al-Asad airbase, which houses U.S. troops. No injuries or damage were reported.

July 30, 2024: *ABC News* reported that U.S. Central Command conducted a defensive air strike in Musayib in Babil Province, targeting combatants attempting to launch one-way attack uncrewed aerial systems (OWAUAS, popularly known as drones). The *Washington Post* reported on August 6, 2024 that the U.S. airstrike in Musayib killed four Kataib Hizballah militia members and Hussein Abdullah Mastoor al-Shabal, a Yemeni drone specialist who had traveled to Iraq to train other Iranian-backed fighters.

August 5, 2024: *NBC News, Reuters, al-Jazeera, Defense News,* and *CNN* reported that at 9 p.m., two Katyusha rockets believed fired by an Iran-backed militia landed in al-Asad Airbase, which houses Americans, injuring five U.S. troops and two U.S. civilian contractors, one seriously. *Stars and Stripes* reported on August 8 that authorities arrested five individuals.

The Iraqi military intercepted a vehicle carrying rockets after the attack. Two rockets were launched from the vehicle in the Haditha district. Eight more rockets were being prepared for launch.

August 29, 2024: *CNN* and the *Washington Post* reported that CENTCOM and Iraqi security forces in four coordinated morning raids in the al-Hazeemi area east of Wadi al-Ghadaf, a river bed that runs through the Anbar desert, killed 15 ISIS operatives armed with numerous weapons, grenades, and explosive suicide belts. *AP* added that five American troops were wounded; two others suffered injuries from falls during the operation. The raids killed four senior ISIS leaders, among them:

- Ahmad Hamid Husayn Abd-al-Jalil al-Ithawi, in charge of all ISIS operations in Iraq

- Abu Hammam, who oversaw all operations in western Iraq

- Abu Ali al-Tunisi, in charge of technical development

- Shakir Abud Ahmad al-Issawi, who ran military operations in western Iraq

September 9, 2024: *Reuters* reported that a Turkish soldier died in a gun battle with the Kurdistan Workers Party (PKK) in the Gara region in northern Iraq.

September 10, 2024: Iraqi security officials said an explosion targeted a logistics support site used by the U.S. military next to Baghdad airport at 11 p.m., one day before an expected visit by Iranian president Masoud Pezeshkian to Baghdad. No one claimed credit.

September 22, 2024: *Reuters* reported that the Islamic Resistance in Iraq claimed that they fired cruise missiles and explosive drones at Israel at dawn.

October 1, 2024: *Reuters* reported that three Katyusha rockets were fired near Baghdad International Airport. U.S. officials said U.S. military forces were not a target. One missile landed near buildings used by Iraqi counter-terrorism forces, causing damage and fire to vehicles but no casualties.

October 2, 2024: ISIS ambushed Iraqi troops from the 42nd Brigade's Intelligence Unit that were on a reconnaissance mission near Kirkuk, killing four and wounding three others.

October 22, 2024: Prime Minister Mohammed Shia al-Sudani announced that counterterrorism forces and the national security service under the Joint Operations Command killed ISIS leader Jassim al-Mazroui Abu Abdul Qader (the Wali of Iraq) and eight other senior ISIS leaders in an operation in the Hamrin Mountains in Salahuddin Province. Authorities seized large quantities of weapons, ammunition, and equipment. *Military.com* reported that two U.S. troops were injured.

ISRAEL

January 2023: The *Jerusalem Post* reported on March 17, 2023 that two Tel Aviv teenagers, aged 16 and 19, were indicted for firebombing the Sidna Ali Mosque in Herzliya in January for nationalistic reasons. Shin Bet found that the duo originally planned to jump an Arab citizen. The Tel Aviv District Attorney's Office charged them with conspiracy to commit acts of terrorism, a terrorist act of arson in a team, and acting with weapons for the purpose of terrorism in a team.

January 27, 2023: *CNN, Bloomberg,* and the *New York Times* reported that authorities "neutralized" a gunman who killed eight people and critically injured three others, including a woman, 70, in an 8:15 p.m. shooting at a synagogue in East Jerusalem's Neve Yaakov neighborhood on International Holocaust Remembrance Day. The attacker fled in a car, but police intercepted and killed him. Israeli media said the 21-year-old was from East Jerusalem and had no history of political violence. Israel arrested 42 suspects—family members and neighbors—in the At-Tur neighborhood. No one claimed credit, but in the Gaza Strip, Hamas members fired into the air. *Reuters* reported on January 29 that Israeli police sealed off the shooter's home in Jerusalem. The *Washington Post* reported that victims included Rafael Ben-Eliyahu, 56; Eli Mizrahi, 48; and his wife, Natalie Mizrahi, 45.

The Palestinian health ministry reported that during the night, an Israeli car approached the West Bank village of Bita, near Nablus, and its occupants shot and injured three Palestinians, one seriously.

January 28, 2023: *Al-Jazeera, AP,* the *New York Times, UPI,* the *Times of Israel, Deutsche Welle,* and *Israeli Army Radio* reported that in a 10:42 a.m. shooting, a father and son, aged 47 and 23, were seriously injured on Ma'alot Ir David Street in the neighborhood of Silwan in Neve Yaacov outside the Old City in occupied East Jerusalem. A police spokesman said the teen attacker "was neutralised". *UPI* added that the attacker was a 13-year-old Palestinian boy, clad only in underwear, who was shot and wounded by armed civilians, taken into custody, and brought to a hospital. He had fired on a group of five civilian Jews wearing skullcaps and tzitzit (knotted ritual tassels).

February 10, 2023: The *Washington Post* reported that a car crashed into a crowd at a Jerusalem bus stop, killing two people, including a 6-year-old, and injuring five, two critically. An off-duty police officer shot to death the Palestinian driver at the scene.

March 9, 2023: *AFP* reported that a Hamas gunman wounded three people, including David Friedmann, who fired three rounds at him, outside a café in Tel Aviv's Dizengoff Avenue before being shot dead by police. A fellow officer also fired three rounds. The next day, one of the wounded remained in critical condition in a local hospital. Israeli Defence Minister Yoav Gallant ordered the immediate destruction of the gunman's house in Nilin, near the West Bank city of Ramallah.

April 7, 2023: *AFP, Times of Israel, Corriere Della Sera, Reuters,* and *CNN* reported that in the evening, Italian tourist and Rome-based attorney Alessandro Parini, 35, was killed and seven other tourists wounded when a car rammed into people walking on a bike path of the Tel Aviv boardwalk. The car then overturned on a lawn. Responding police "noticed the driver trying to reach for what looked like a rifle-like object that was with him" before killing him. Police said that the driver was a 45-year-old resident of Kfar Kasem, an Arab-Israeli city east of Tel Aviv.

April 17, 2023: The *Jerusalem Post* reported that the Jerusalem Municipality and Israel Police announced that police and security forces had recently thwarted eight terrorist attacks.

April 24, 2023: *UPI* reported that a Palestinian man, Hatem Najma, 39, drove his vehicle into a busy market in Jerusalem, injuring seven people before an armed civilian killed him. A man in his 70s was in serious condition; a woman in her 30s was in moderate condition, while three men, one in his 50s and two 25-year-olds, suffered minor injuries. Najma, married with five children, had a history of mental illness but was not known to security authorities.

May 2, 2023: *AP* and *Washington Post* reported that Palestinian Islamic Jihad leader Khader Adnan, 45, imprisoned in an Israeli jail, died after an 87-day hunger strike. During his earlier incarcerations, the father of nine had held other hunger strikes lasting 66, 56, and 58 days. *UPI* added that he was arrested on February 5, 2023 on terrorism charges. He weighed less than 125 pounds. He was represented by attorney Jamil Khatib.

June 3, 2023: *Reuters* reported that three Israeli soldiers and a gunman were killed near the border with Egypt after a group had infiltrated the frontier leading to a firefight. The *Washington Post, New York Times, AFP,* and the *Times of Israel* added that the gunman was an Egyptian policeman who had chased drug smugglers across the border, shot two soldiers—a man and a woman, Sgt. Lia Ben Nun, 19, of Rishon Lezion, who served as a combat soldier in the Bardelas Battalion—at a border guard post near the Nitzana border crossing between Mount Sagi and Mount Harif in the Negev desert, then was caught in a manhunt, during which he killed another male Israeli soldier. A non-commissioned Israeli officer was lightly wounded. Around 2:30 a.m., hours before the shooting, Israeli soldiers had seized contraband goods estimated at 1.5 million shekels ($399,777).

July 4, 2023: *CNN* and *BBC* reported that a driver crashed a pickup truck into pedestrians on Pinchas Rosen Street at a bus stop near a shopping center in northern Tel Aviv, then got out of his vehicle to stab two civilians, injuring eight before an armed civilian killed him. One woman, 46, was seriously injured. The *Times of Israel* reported that a pregnant woman lost her baby. Hamas spokesman Abdel Latif al-Kanoa praised the "heroic operation", as did Palestinian Islamic Jihad (PIJ) leading member Khaled al-Batsh. The *Washington Post* reported that Hamas later said the attacker, Hamas member Abdel Wahhab Issa Hussein Khalayleh, came from a village near Hebron in the southern West Bank. The group initially misidentified his brother, Hussein, as the attacker. The *Los Angeles Times* reported that Israeli media initially identified the attacker as Hasin Halila, 23, a Palestinian man from a village near Hebron. *AP* reported that Shin Bet said the attacker had no prior security record. Several colleagues were arrested.

August 5, 2023: The *Inquirer* and *ABC News* reported that a Palestinian gunman, Kamel Abu Bakr, 27, killed Chen Amir, 42, a Tel Aviv municipal patrol officer, on a street in central Tel Aviv. Another municipal patrol inspector shot the attacker, who resided in Jenin on the West Bank, to death. Hamas and Islamic Jihad praised the attack but did not claim credit. Amir was married and had three daughters. Bakr had been wanted for the past six months.

August 30, 2023: *Al-Jazeera, AFP,* and *Wafa* reported that a border police officer killed Palestinian Khaled Samer al-Zaanin, 15, in East Jerusalem after he carried out a stabbing attack against a settler at a light rail station near Damascus Gate in the Old City. The settler was lightly injured. Police raided the al-Zaanin family home in Beit Hanina, north of East Jerusalem.

October 7, 2023: *CNN* reported that in the morning, Hamas fired 3,000 rockets from Gaza into Israeli territory, killing 1,200 (initial reports said 1,400) and injuring 985 in Operation al-Aqsa Storm. Hamas military commander Muhammad al-Deif claimed that 5,000 rockets had been launched so that "the enemy will understand that the time of their rampaging without accountability has ended". Gunmen from the Nukhba brigade entered southern Israel by land, sea, and air, using paragliders, shooting and kidnapping civilians and several Israeli soldiers. Palestinian gunmen had used heavy equipment, including bulldozers, to breach the border fence, according to the *New York Times*.

Pundits filled the media with questions about how such a massive intelligence failure could have happened regarding a complex operation that must have taken months to plan. Many called it "Israel's 9/11", with proportionally more killed, given Israel's much smaller population, than on 9/11. *CNN* ran overhead and ground video of six Hamas training camps, one just hundreds of yards from the Israeli border. A document dated October 2022 showed extensive planning of the attack.

The Palestinian Health Ministry in Gaza said 198 Palestinians were killed and 1,610 were injured in the first day of fighting.

Israel Prime Minister Benjamin Netanyahu said "We are at war."

The next day, the Palestinian Health Ministry said 370 Palestinians were killed and 2,200 injured. The Zaka emergency service estimated that 500 Israelis, including 44 servicemen and servicewomen and 30 security service members, were killed and 2,156 were wounded in the first two days of fighting. By October 10, at least 900 Israelis had been killed. As of October 15, the *New York Times* reported that 1,300 were killed in the attack; nearly half of Gaza's population of 2 million were displaced. *CNN* added that three Americans were killed; others were missing. The figure later reached 32 dead Americans. The tally soon totaled 4,500 Palestinians injured. By October 26, reported *al-Jazeera*, 7,000 Gaza residents, including 3,000 children, had been killed in Israeli bombing.

The Israel Defense Forces (IDF) battled terrorists at 22 locations, including Erez Crossing, Nahal Oz, Magen, Kibbutz Beeri, Rehim Army Base, Ziikim Army base, Kfar Azz, several villages, and border crossings.

The *New York Times* reported that Ofir Libstein, head of a local council in southern Israel, died in a gun battle against Hamas.

Residents of two Israeli communities, including Kibbutz Nir Oz, told *Channel 12* television that assailants from Gaza were trying to break into their homes.

The surprise attack came on the 50th anniversary of the 1973 Yom Kippur War.

Israeli Emergency Services Magen David Alom said one of its staffers was killed and another four were wounded. One of their vehicles was taken into the Gaza Strip.

Lebanese Hizballah on its *al-Manar TV* praised the attacks. The next day, it fired mortars at Israel.

Within three days, Israel had flushed the terrorists from its territory, although sporadic gun fire was heard.

By October 12, Israel had called up 360,000 reservists for a likely ground operation into Gaza.

CNN ran video of hostages being taken from their homes and cars and moved to Gaza. The al-Qassam Brigades said they grabbed dozens of soldiers. Hamas claimed on October 8 to have 100 Israeli hostages. Islamic Jihad said it was holding at least 30 hostages in Gaza. Israel said on October 16 that Hamas had 199 hostages. The number increased to 240 by October 31, according to *NPR*.

Hamas's military wing al-Qassam Brigades spokesman Abu Obaida claimed that 22 hostages in Gaza were killed in Israeli airstrikes, including an Israeli artist who died on October 14. Palestinian sources said 2,800 had died in Gaza and 12,500 were wounded.

CNN reported that attendees at the Israeli Nova trance music festival in a rural farmland area two miles near the Gaza-Israel border had come under fire at 6:30 a.m. Some 260 bodies were found; numerous others were taken hostage. The revelers were celebrating the Jewish holiday of Sukkot. An Israeli woman and her boyfriend—Noa Argamani and Avinatan Or, who had attended the festival—were kidnapped. She was placed on the back of a motorcycle while he was made to walk with his hands held behind his back.

CNN reported that more than 100 bodies were found in the Israeli kibbutz Be'eri, with civilian hostages having been shot to death.

President Biden said in his speech to the American public on October 10 that Hamas was holding an unspecified number of Americans hostage.

By October 10, reporting by *CNN*, the *Washington Post*, *AP*, *UPI*, and *al-Jazeera* established the following litany of foreign dead, injured, missing, and abducted. They came from 36 nations. The *Washington Post* updated the list on October 16. *CNN* reported on October 25 that Israel claimed that Hamas was holding 135 people from 25 countries with foreign passports, including 12 Americans.

Argentina: eight dead; 15 missing; 625 citizens requested evacuation. Among the dead was Matías Burstein, 41, who attended the music festival and had two daughters, ages 9 and 12.

Australia: Australian citizen Galit Carbone was killed.

Austria: The media initially reported that three Austrian-Israeli dual citizens who recently stayed in southern Israel independently of each other were missing. Austria's Foreign Ministry said on October 11 that an Austrian-Israeli dual national was killed and two more remained missing.

Azerbaijan: eight Azerbaijanis were killed, including two dual Azerbaijani-Israeli nationals.

Belarus: *AFP* reported that the Belarusian Embassy in Tel Aviv said that three Belarusian nationals were killed and one was missing.

Brazil: *Globo* and *BBC Portuguese* reported that the Foreign Ministry said that Ranani Nidejelski Glazer, 23; Bruna Valeanu, 24; and Karla Stelzer Mendes, 42, were killed. Three dual Brazilian-Israeli nationals were initially reported missing after attending the music festival; 1,700 citizens, mostly tourists in Tel Aviv and Jerusalem, expressed interest in being repatriated

Cambodia: The *Phnom Penh Post* quoted Cambodian Prime Minister Hun Manet as saying that a Cambodian studying in Israel was killed.

Canada: *CTV News* reported that Julie Sunday, Assistant Deputy Minister for Consular Security and Emergency Management, said a week later that five Canadians were killed and three were missing.

Chile: two missing, including Loren Garcovich. She and her husband, Ivan Illarramendi, a Spaniard, were reportedly kidnapped by Hamas. Comunidad Judia de Chile tweeted that the couple lived in a kibbutz near the Gaza border and that their home was destroyed. The Chilean Foreign Ministry was organizing repatriation flights.

China: China's special envoy for Middle Eastern issues, Zhai Jun, said four Chinese nationals were killed, six were injured, and two were missing.

Colombia: Ivonne Rubio and Antonio Macías Motano were missing since attending the Supernova music festival. Colombia's Foreign Ministry confirmed the death of Colombian Israeli woman Ivonne Rubio, who had been missing along with her boyfriend, Antonio Macías. Her identity was confirmed through a DNA test. Local authorities informed the victim's father. Macías remained missing.

Estonia: a man with dual Estonian-Israeli citizenship was killed.

France: 30 dead; 17, including a 12-year-old child, believed to have been kidnapped. The French Foreign Ministry said 15 were missing, down to seven on October 19. Some were hostages.

Germany: several people with dual German-Israeli nationality were believed to have been kidnapped. *Bild* reported that the husband of a hostage from the festival said that his wife, Shani Nicole Louk, 22, was a German-Israeli dual national. German Foreign Minister Annalena Baerbock said a week later that at least eight German citizens—most of them dual nationals—were among the hostages. The Foreign Ministry said a "single-digit number" of Germans were killed. *CNN* reported that the Israeli Ministry of Foreign Affairs announced on October 30 that Louk's body had been found after being "tortured and paraded around Gaza by Hamas terrorists," having "experienced unfathomable horrors". Israeli President Isaac Herzog told *Bild* that she was likely beheaded. Authorities believed that she had been killed at the music festival and was not kidnapped.

Honduras: Arik Kraunick, a Honduran, and his wife (of undisclosed citizenship) were killed.

Ireland: Irish Prime Minister Leo Varadkar said that Kim Damti, a "vibrant young Irish-Israeli woman", was killed.

Italy: two Israeli-Italians were missing. *ANSA* reported that Italian Foreign Minister Antonio Tajani added that three of the hostages are Italian nationals.

Mexico: Foreign Minister Alicia Bárcena tweeted that a man and woman were believed to have been kidnapped. A third Mexican initially thought to have been taken hostage was found safe. Mexico sent two planes to evacuate its citizens. Some 500 Mexican citizens in Israel registered with the federal department for emergency assistance.

Nepal: 10 Nepalese agricultural trainees were killed by Hamas at Alumim Kibbutz in southern Israel. Four Nepalis were hospitalized. One Nepali remained missing. *Al-Jazeera* reported on October 13 that the dead included

- Prabesh Bhandari, 24, who wanted to save money to build a house for his family in Nepal's Salyan district. He arrived in Israel on September 12 as a pomelo harvester.

- Rajan Phulara, 24, from western Doti district, an only son.

- Rajesh Kumar Swarnakar, 25, from Nepal's southern Sunsari district that borders India. The agriculture student planned to join Nepal's civil service.

Panama: Daryelis Denises Saez Batista was missing

Paraguay: two Paraguayans who had been living in Israel were missing

Peru: four citizens missing. Seven Peruvians left Israel aboard commercial flights, with 73 more to follow them in the next two days. More evacuations were planned. Peru's Foreign Ministry announced that Peruvian nationals Brando David Flores García and Daniel Levi were killed. The ministry said that two missing Peruvians were found, adding that it was "redoubling its efforts" to look for one other missing person.

Philippines: seven Filipinos missing; another 22 were rescued by Israeli forces, one of whom was being treated for injuries sustained in the rescue. Of the 137 Filipinos in Gaza, 25 indicated that they wanted to leave. More than 30,000 Filipinos live in Israel; most work in health care. The Philippine Embassy in Tel Aviv later announced that four Filipinos were killed, two Philippine nationals remained missing, but 26 had been found or rescued. One was treated for moderate injuries.

Portugal: Portuguese Foreign Affairs Minister João Gomes Cravinho said that one Portuguese national was killed. The Israeli Embassy in Portugal told *CNN Portugal* that Hamas had kidnapped four dual Portuguese-Israeli nationals: Moshe Sadyaan, 26, Gilad Bem Yehuda, 28, Idan Shtivi, 28, and Orin Bira, 53. Another Portuguese national, Menachem Hillel Ben Kalifa, 22, was injured.

Romania: The Romanian Foreign Ministry announced that four dual Israeli-Romanian nationals were killed. One was serving in the IDF.

Russia: Marina Ryazanova, press secretary for the Russian Embassy in Israel, told *Tass* that 19 Russians were killed and seven were missing. At least two were being held hostage in Gaza.

Serbia: Alon Ohle, 22, a dual Israeli-Serbian national, was kidnapped from the music festival and as of October 19 remained missing.

South Africa: two South African nationals were killed and one was missing.

Spain: The Spanish Foreign Affairs Ministry that Spanish-Israeli national Maya Villalobo Sinvany was killed. Spanish newspaper *El Pais* reported that she was doing her military service in Israel.

Sri Lanka: *Ceylon Today* reported that Sri Lanka's ambassador to Israel, Nimal Bandara, said that Sri Lankan nationals Anula Ratnayake, 49, and Bandara Yatawara, 48, were missing.

Switzerland: Swiss Foreign Minister Ignazio Cassis said that a 70-year-old Swiss-Israeli dual national was killed.

Tanzania: Tanzania's Ambassador to Israel told *AFP* that two Tanzanians were missing.

Thailand: 18 initially reported dead; nine injured; 11 workers taken hostage; hundreds in high-risk areas near Gaza were evacuated. More than 3,000 requested evacuation. Some 30,000 Thais work in Israel; about 3,000 requested to be returned to Thailand. Among the hostages, according to *al-Jazeera*, were Khomkrit Chombua; Natthaporn On-kaew, 26; and Owat Suriyasri, 40. Hometowns listed by families on the "Thai laborers in Israel" *Facebook* site included impov-

erished Kalasin, Surin, and Sisaket. *AFP* and *Nikkei Asia* reported that Thai Prime Minister Srettha Thavisin said a week later that 29 Thai nationals were killed, 16 were injured, and 18 were taken hostage.

Türkiye: a Turkish-Israeli dual national was killed.

Ukraine: 18 dead, including two Ukrainian women who had lived in Israel for years. Foreign Ministry spokesman Oleg Nikolenko said on October 11 that seven Ukrainians were dead, nine injured, and nine others were missing. A Ukrainian boy was injured in Sderot. On October 19, Ukrainian Ambassador to Israel Yevhen Korniychuk said 18 were killed.

United Kingdom: 12 Britons, including Bernard Cowan, were killed. Nathaniel Young, 20, a Briton serving in the Israeli Army, died while fighting Hamas. Nine others, including Jake Marlowe, 26, who was working as a security guard at the music festival, were initially missing. Prime Minister Rishi Sunak reported on October 24 that five remained missing.

United States: President Joe Biden said that at least 11 Americans were killed and an unspecified number of Americans were unaccounted for. Several were believed taken hostage. By the evening of October 10, *PBS News Hour* reported that 14 Americans were killed. *CNN* put the death toll at 1,200 Israelis, among them 189 soldiers, and 900 Gazans. On October 12, *NPR* said 14 were missing. On October 19, *CNN* said 32 Americans were killed. Among the dead were

- Hayim Katsman, 32, an Israeli-American dual citizen, was hiding in a closet with his neighbor, Avital Alajem, when he was fatally shot in Kibbutz Holit, founded in 1978. Katsman's body absorbed all of the bullets, saving Alajem. Katsman's sibling said he was "very pro-peace". The musician, car mechanic, and landscaper DJd and played bass. He volunteered at the community garden in Rahat. His parents moved to Israel from the United States in 1990. He earned his PhD from the University of Washington's Henry M. Jackson School of International Studies in 2021. His dissertation was dedicated to "all life forms that exist between the Jordan River and the Mediterranean Sea". He had served a mandatory stint with the IDF.

- Deborah Matias, 50, a dual Israeli-American citizen who lived in Israel and attended the Rimon School of Music in the Tel Aviv area, was shot and killed by Hamas gunmen while shielding her son Rotem, 16, from their bullets. Ilan Troen, a professor emeritus of Israel studies from Brandeis University, was on the phone with his daughter when she was killed. Deborah's husband, Shlomi Matias, 49, was also killed. Rotem was shot in the stomach, but was expected to survive. The terrorists used explosives to blow up the front door of the house, then blew up the door to their safe room. Rotem hid for 12 hours after being shot, texting with people who told him how to manage the blood flowing from his abdomen. The family had moved to Israel in 1975. Deborah was born in Missouri. She and Shlomi were musicians.

- Jonathan Rom, 23, was born in South Carolina and moved to suburban Jerusalem with his family in 2003. He loved playing soccer and video games. He had recently returned to Israel after months-long travels in South America; he had worked as a bartender for months to pay for the trip to Ecuador, Brazil, Peru, and Colombia. He finished his military service two years ago. Rom was living with his parents and deciding where to apply to college, perhaps to study communications. He died at the Nova festival. He helped a friend try to flee, first by car and then, after being caught in the gunfire and the crowd of frantic concertgoers, on foot. The phone of the woman he tried to aid was tracked to Gaza, but it was not clear if she was with it or alive. Hundreds of neighbors attended his funeral.

- Danielle Ben-Senyor, 34, who grew up in Los Angeles. During the pandemic, she served as an intensive-care nurse at a Tel Aviv hospital, then changed careers. She hoped to organize and promote concerts like the Tribe of Nova trance music festival where she was killed. While she enjoyed California, she wanted both of her ailing parents to be around family members in Israel.

- Igal and Amit Wachs, 53 and 49, were the two eldest brothers in a family of four sons. Their mother grew up in the United States, then raised her children in a small village, Netiv HaAsara, near northern Gaza. Igal was a project manager for a large agricultural company. Amit volunteered as head of the village's self-defense unit. Amit's family survived the attack. Igal was survived by his son, who lives in Massachusetts with his ex-wife.

- Roey Weiser, 21, an Israeli-American sergeant in the 13th Battalion of the Golani Brigade stationed at the Kerem Shalom border crossing, was killed while diverting Hamas's attention, allowing 12 others to escape. He was a volunteer firefighter.

- Aryeh Ziering, 27, served as a captain in an Israel Defense Forces canine unit for six years. He died while trying to help a wounded fellow soldier. His parents moved to Israel three decades earlier. One of four siblings, he loved sports, especially the Boston Red Sox. He recently ran the San Francisco marathon and spent childhood summers in Maine, where his grandfather is a former state senator. He lived in a mixed Hebrew- and English-speaking neighborhood.

Others who were missing and suspected of being taken hostage by Hamas, included:

- U.S. citizen Cindy Flash, 67, originally from St. Paul, Minnesota and her Israeli husband, Igal Flash, 66, who vanished from Kfar Aza kibbutz. (The couple married in 1983 and raised three daughters.) She texted her daughter Keren, 34, a Pilates instructor who was a few houses away, that "they are breaking down the safe room door. We need someone to come by the house right now." Cindy worked as an administrator in a local college and loved to sing, travel, and bake. The family had planned an afternoon picnic with kite-flying as part of an annual community event. The Israeli security services rescued Keren's family.

- U.S. citizens Judith Tai Raanan, 59, and daughter Natalie Raanan, 18, who live in Evanston, Illinois, were visiting relatives in the Nahal Oz kibbutz. The duo arrived in Israel on September 2. Natalie had recently graduated from Deerfield High School, where she was viewed as a talented artist. They were the first hostages to be freed.

- Abbey Onn, a U.S. citizen who lived in Israel for eight years, said her family members in that area taken over by Hamas included her cousin, Carmela Dan, 80, who held triple French-U.S.-Israeli citizenship; Dan's son-in-law Ofer Kalderon, 50; and Dan's grandchildren, Sahar Kalderon, 16; Erez Kalderon, 12; and Noya Dan, 13. The bodies of Carmela and Noya Dan were found on October 19.

Relatives of missing U.S. citizens attended a news conference in Tel Aviv on October 10, saying they had received "zero communication" regarding the status of their loved ones. They included Jonathan Dekel-Chen, father of Sagui Dekel-Chen; Ruby Chen, father of Itay Chen, 19; Ayala and Nahal Neta, daughter and son of Adrienne Neta, 66; Rachel Goldberg and Jonathan Polin, mother and father of Hersh Goldberg-Polin, 23.

- Sagui Dekel-Chen, 35, went missing from Kibbutz Nir Oz, where he lived with his wife and two daughters. The *Sarasota Herald-Tribune* and *USA Today Network* reported that he holds dual U.S.-Israeli citizenship. He sent his wife and daughters to their house's bomb shelters while he confronted the Hamas attackers. He since vanished and Hamas destroyed their home. The novice inventor repurposed an old bus into a mobile grocery store. He served as a project manager for the Jewish National Fund.

Three other Americans from Dekel-Chen's Nir Oz kibbutz were missing; two other Americans were killed.

- Hersh Goldberg-Polin, 23, from Jerusalem, was born in California. He attended the Tribe of Nova music festival. He left his parents two text messages at 8:11 a.m., then went silent. Witnesses told his parents, who grew up in Chicago, that he left the festival in a car and entered a public bomb shelter with 30 other people. The terrorists threw grenades and fired weapons, then told survivors to walk outside. He helped throw grenades out of the bunker until he was injured. Goldberg-Polin walked out, missing his arm from his elbow down and wearing a tourniquet. He was forced onto a pickup truck with three other young men and two women.

CNN reported on October 20 that two U.S. hostages, Judith Tai Raanan and Natali Raanan, a mother and a daughter, were turned over to the Red Cross because of the mother's ill health.

CNN reported on October 11 that the IDF said it found children "butchered" in an Israeli kibbutz. Bodies of residents and terrorists were found in kibbutz Kfar Aza. The IDF said that women, children, toddlers, and elderly were "brutally butchered in an ISIS way of action". Some observers said that children were beheaded. Other kibbutzim that were targeted included Be'eri, Ofakim, Sderot, Yad Mordechai, Yated, Kissufim, and Urim.

Israeli airstrikes on October 10 hit the home of Hamas military leader Mohammed Deif, killing his father, brother, and two other relatives in Khan Younis. An IDF airstrike also killed Zakaria Abu Ma'amr, a senior member of the Hamas Political Bureau and the head of the Ministry of National Relations. The IDF said he was involved in planning terrorist attacks. The IDF also killed Hamas Minister of Economy Jawad Abu Shamala, who funneled money to finance and direct terrorism inside and outside Gaza. By October 13, the death toll in Gaza had reached 1,799.

The Biden Administration said there was no indication of advance knowledge by Iranian authorities.

Hamas military spokesman Abu Obeida threatened to kill one Israeli hostage each time Israel targets Gaza civilians without warning.

The *Washington Post* and *AP* reported on October 12 and 13 and *Haaretz* and *New York Times* added on October 22 that the Israeli hostages included:

- Yaffa Adar, 85, of Nir Oz, was kidnapped from her home

- Limor Aharonovitch

- Danielle Aloni, 44, and her daughter Emilia Aloni, 5, were kidnapped from Kibbutz Nir Oz in Yavneh. Danielle appeared in a hostage video released by Hamas on October 30, calling for Prime Minister Netanyahu to obtain their release immediately.

- Ofir Angel, 18, from Ramat Rachel, was kidnapped from Kibbutz Be'eri

- Noa Argamani, 26, of Be'er Sheva, was at the outdoor rave near Re'im

- Karina Ariev, 19, from Jerusalem, served as an IDF Observer in the 414th Regiment, Combat Intelligence Collection Corps

- Doron Katz Asher, 34; Raz Katz Asher, 4; and Aviv Katz Asher, 2 were kidnapped from their home in Nir Oz

- Liraz Assulin, 38, of Kiryat Malakhi, was at the outdoor rave near Re'im

- Sharon Avigdori, 52; and daughter Noam Avigdori, 12, were kidnapped from Kibbutz Be'eri near Hod Hasharon

- Or Avinathan, 30, from Tel Aviv, was at the outdoor rave near Re'im

- Elma Avraham, 84, was kidnapped from her home in Nahal Oz

- Idan Barzilai

- Nick Beiser, 19, from Be'er Sheva, was kidnapped from Kibbutz Nir Oz

- Ohad Ben-Ami, 55, and his wife Raz Ben Ami, 57, were kidnapped from their home in Be'eri

- Agam Berger, 19, from Holon, was an IDF Observer in the 414th Regiment, Combat Intelligence Collection Corps

- Shiri Bibas, 32, of Nir Oz, was kidnapped with her two children Ariel Bibas, 4; and Kfir Bibas, 9 months

- Irad Bilton

- Elkana Bohbot, 24, from Mevasseret Zion, was at the outdoor rave near Re'im

- Hagar Brodetz, 40, from Kfar Azza, was kidnapped with her children Ofri Brodetz, 10; Yuval Brodetz, 8; and Oriya Brodetz, 4.5. Their father was Avichai Brodutch.

- Meir Carmeli

- Elia Cohen, 26, from Tzur Hadassah, was at the outdoor rave near Re'im

- Mor Cohen

- Alexander Dancyg, 75, was kidnapped from his home in Nir Oz

- Evyatar David, 26, from Kfar Saba, was at the outdoor rave near Re'im

- Liri Elbag, 18, of Moshav Yeruhav, served as an IDF Observer in the 414th Regiment, Combat Intelligence Collection Corps. She was seen in the back seat of an Israeli military truck that Hamas had commandeered.

- Eden Yizhaki Elbaz and Adi Vaknin-Elbaz

- Itzhk Elgarat, 68, was kidnapped from his home in Nir Oz

- Ella Elyakim, 8; and Dafna Elyakim, 14; were kidnapped from their home in Nahal Oz

- Ronen Engel, 54, wife Carina Engel-Bert, 51, and family members Mika, 18, and Yuval, 11, kidnapped from their home in Nir Oz

- Tom Farage

- Carmel Gat, 39, of Be'eri, was kidnapped from her home

- Yarden Roman Gat, 36, kidnapped from her home in Be'eri

- Daniella Gilboa, 19, from Petah Tikvah, served as an IDF Observer in the 414th Regiment, Combat Intelligence Collection Corps

- Guy Gilboa-Dalal, 22, was at the outdoor rave near Re'im

- Chen Almog-Goldstein, 48; Agam Goldstein, 17; Gal Golstein, 11; and Tal Goldstein, 9, were kidnapped from their home in Kfar Azza

- Barmargalit.gridish

- Ilana Gritzewsky, 30, was kidnapped from her home in Nir Oz

- Tamar Gutman, 27, was at the outdoor rave near Re'im. He lives in Beit Hashmonai.

- Mazzi Habut

- Ditza Haiman, 84, of Nir Oz, was kidnapped from her home

- Inbar Haiman, 27, from Haifa, was at the outdoor rave near Re'im

- Louis Har, 70, kidnapped from his home in Urim

- Shoshan Haran, 67, kidnapped from her home in Be'eri

- Avigail Idan, 3, kidnapped from her home in Kfar Azza; her parents were killed

- Tsachi Idan, 51, was kidnapped from his home in Nahal Oz

- Osnat Itshak

- Almog Meir Jan, 21, of Or Yehuda, was at the outdoor rave near Re'im

- Ofer Kalderon, 53, and Sahar Kalderon, 16, from Nir Oz, were kidnapped from their home

- Michal Karten-Lahav

- Doron Asher Katz, 34, a German-Israeli; Raz, 5; Aviv, 2; lived in the Nir Oz kibbutz. They locked down in their security room after Hamas entered their house. Doron's partner left the safe room to talk to the terrorists, but the terrorists took him. Doron's cellphone pinged inside Gaza. Still missing from the family home were Efrat Kat, 70, and her partner, Gadi Moses, 79.

- Efrat Katz, 68, kidnapped from her home in Nir Oz

- Elad Katzir, 47, kidnapped from his home in Nir Oz

- Hanna Katzir, 77, kidnapped from her home in Nir Oz

- Rimon Kirsht, 36, one of three women who appeared in a hostage video released by Hamas on October 30. Her husband, Yegev, was also kidnapped from the Nirim kibbutz.

- Mor_Kobi

- Sharon Aloni Konio, 34; David Konio, 33; Yuly Konio, 3; Ema Konio, also 3; were kidnapped from their home in Nir Oz

- Roni Krivoi, 25, from Carmiel, was at the outdoor rave near Re'im

- Bar Kuperstein, 21, from Holon, was at the outdoor rave near Re'im

- Gabriela Leimberg, 59, and Maya Leimberg, 17, from Jerusalem, were kidnapped from Kibbutz Nir Yitzhak

- Eden Levi

- Naama Levy, 19, from Ra'anana, served as an IDF Observer in the 414th Regiment, Combat Intelligence Collection Corps

- Or Levy, 33, of Givatayim, was at the outdoor rave near Re'im

- Yocheved Lifschitz, 85, and Nurit Cooper, 79, Israeli women who are friends and neighbors of kibbutz Nir Oz, were released on October 23 thanks to mediation by Egypt and Qatar. Lifschitz said she was taken underground into Hamas's underground tunnel network. She said she was beaten with sticks and thrown onto the back of a motorcycle. Their husbands, Oded Lifschitz, 83, and Amiram Cooper, 84, were still being held in Gaza as of October 24.

- Bat-el Mangisto

- Noa Marciano, 19, of Modi'in, was an Observer in the 414th Regiment, Combat Intelligence Collection Corps of the IDF

- Fernando Marman, 60, and Clara Marman, 63, from Nir Yitzhak, were kidnapped from their home

- Tamar Metzger, 78, was kidnapped from her home in Nir Oz

- Yoram Metzger, 80, was kidnapped from his home in Nir Oz

- Omri Miran, 46, kidnapped from his home in Nahal Oz

- Gadi Moshe Mosez, 79, was kidnapped from his home in Nir Oz

- Adina Moshe, 72, was kidnapped from her home in Nir Oz

- Nofar Muchtar

- Ohad Munder, who marked his late October 9th birthday in captivity, according to *NBC News*.

- Natalia (last name undisclosed)

- Alon Ohel, 22, from Lavon, was at the outdoor rave near Re'im

- Rut Hodaya Perez, 17, who suffers from myotonic dystrophy, cannot walk, and uses a wheelchair. Hamas grabbed her at the concert.

- Chaim Peri, 79, and Channa Peri, 79, kidnapped from their home in Nir Oz

- Olga Pilnik

- Nadav Popplewell, 51, kidnapped from his home in Nirim

- Yelizaveta Prudnikova

- Hofit Rahamim

- Maya Regev, 21; and Itai Regev, 18, from Herzliya, were at the outdoor rave near Re'im

- Tali Rutherford

- Mia Schem, variant Shem, 21, of Shoham, a French-Israeli woman tattoo artist, kidnapped at the Nova festival. She had texted her parents at 7 a.m., "They are shooting at us, come save us." *CNN*, the *Jerusalem Post*, and the *Washington Post* reported that Hamas released a video on October 16 of her lying on a bed, her right arm being bandaged by someone out of the frame. A long, fresh scar was visible. The video released was the first footage of any of the 250 hostages the al-Qassam Brigades claimed were being held in the enclave. She said she was injured and taken to Gaza, then pleaded to be returned to her family.

- Ori Shabat

- Tomer Shallom

- Alon Lulu Shamriz, 26, kidnapped from his home in Kfar Azza

- Eli Sharabi, 55; Yossi Sharabi, 53; and Noa Sharabi, 16, of Be'eri, were kidnapped from their home

- Omer Shem-Tov, 21, a DJ from Herzliya, tried to escape the music festival by car. A Hamas video showed him and a friend being held hostage.

- Ron Sherman, 19, of Lehavim, was kidnapped from a military base near Gaza

- Tal Shoham, 38; his wife Adi Shoham, also 38; their son Nave Shoham, 8; and daughter Yahel Gani Shoham, 3; were kidnapped from Kibbutz Be'eri in Ma'ale Tzviya

- Keith Samuel Siegel, 64; and Adrienne "Aviva" Siegel, 62, from Kfar Azza, were kidnapped from her home

- Elena Trupanov, who appeared in a hostage video released by Hamas on October 30

- Omer Wenkert, 22, of Gedera, attended the music festival. Video on *Telegram* showed him on the back of a white pickup truck, stripped to his underwear, with his hands tied behind his back. The video was recorded inside Gaza. Wenkert and his family lived in Gedera, where he was a restaurant manager. He needed medication for a stomach condition.

- Dolev Vanunu

- Ohad Yahalomi, 49; and Eitan Yahalomi, 12, were kidnapped from their home in Nir Oz

- Moran Yanai, 40, of Be'er Sheva, was at the outdoor rave near Re'im

- Hanita Yudovski

- Shlomi Ziv, 40, who lives in Elkosh, was at the outdoor rave near Re'im

- Dead Israelis included:

- Osher Barzilian, killed while serving with her IDF team in the Nahal Oz station

- Ohad Cohen, 43, his 10-month-old daughter Mila, and mother Yona, 73, were buried on October 22, according to *UPI*. Cohen's wife, Sandra, was hit by four bullets and their 9-year-old son grazed by shrapnel.

- Eden Guez, killed at the music festival. Her funeral was held in Ashkelon.

- Five members of the Kotz family who lived in Kibbutz Kfar Azza

- Shani Kupervaser, a recent Ben-Gurion University economics graduate who had begun a job at a top accounting firm. Her boyfriend was Ohad Malul. The *New York Times* reported on October 15 that Ben-Gurion had lost 46 people.

- Amit Man, a medic who rushed to help when Hamas gunmen stormed the Be'eri kibbutz

- Soldier Shilo Rauchberger, who was buried at the Mount Herzl cemetery in Jerusalem

- Yahav Winner, 37, husband of Shaylee Atary, 34, and father of 1-month-old daughter Shaya, who lived in Kfar Aza. He told his family to run. The IDF found his body later.

Hamas demanded the release of 5,200 prisoners in Israeli jails in exchange for the 200+ hostages, the bodies of two Israeli soldiers killed in the 2014 war, plus two Israeli civilians who entered Hamas territory years earlier.

On October 30, *CNN, UPI,* and the *New York Times* reported that the IDF and Shin Bet rescued a kidnapped female soldier, Cpl. Ori Magidish, 19, during ground operations in Gaza. She had been taken from a military base in Nahal Oz.

ABC News reported that on October 11 in a campaign speech at Palm Beach County Convention Center in West Palm Beach, Florida, former President Donald Trump called Israeli Defense Minister Yoav Gallant a "jerk" and deemed Lebanese Hizballah "very smart".

Al-Jazeera reported on October 13 that Israel ordered 1.1 million Gazans to leave northern Gaza, probably in preparation for a ground offensive.

Gaza's health ministry announced on October 16 that 2,750 Palestinians have been killed and 9,700 wounded in Israeli airstrikes on the Gaza Strip.

Catholic News Service reported on October 16 that Cardinal Pierbattista Pizzaballa, the Latin patriarch of Jerusalem, the Catholic Church's highest ranking prelate in the Holy Land, offered his "absolute availability" to be exchanged for Israeli children taken hostage by Hamas.

AP reported on October 20 that it was likely that Hamas fired North Korean weapons, including the F-7 RPG, Type 58 self-loading rifle, and possibly the Bulsae guided anti-tank missile, during the attack.

UPI reported on October 27 that IDF air raids and a second consecutive overnight ground incursion into Gaza killed Hamas's deputy chief of intelligence, Shadi Barud, who Israel said planned Hamas's October 7 attacks, plus Rifaat Abbas, Ibrahim Jadba, and Tarek Maarouf—the three seniormost commanders of Hamas's key Daraj Tuffah Battalion.

By October 30, *NPR* reported that 8,300 Gazans had been killed.

CNN reported on October 30 that Hamas released a short video showing three women—Elena Trupanov, Danielle Aloni, and Rimon Kirsht—held captive. Aloni addressed Israeli Prime Minister Benjamin Netanyahu with pointed criticism. "You promised to release us all," she says, suggesting she was aware of hostage negotiations. She finished with a demand to "Free, free us now! Free their civilians, free their prisoners, free us, free us all, let us return to our families now. Now! Now! Now!"

On October 31, *UPI* reported that an IDF airstrike on the Jabalya refugee camp in northern Gaza killed Ebrahim Biari, the head of the Jabalya battalion of Hamas and one of the leaders of the October 7 massacre. The *Jerusalem Post* reported Biari used the stronghold to train for terrorist attacks.

The *Washington Post* added to the list of dead Americans Danielle Waldman, 24, born in Palo Alto, California, the same year her father founded a technology company in Silicon Valley. When she was young, the family moved back to Israel. She became a talented dancer and amateur photographer. A wildlife photo she took won an award in an international competition. She served in the IDF, meeting fellow recruit Noam Shay. They moved to Tel Aviv, where she was studying interior design and he was pursuing a degree in project management. Days before the attack, the she told her father they were thinking of getting married. The couple was at the music festival. They tried to escape in their car, but Hamas riddled it with bullets. Four people in the car were killed; a fifth was believed to be a hostage in Gaza.

Business Insider reported on November 10 that that IDF was hunting for Yahya Ibrahim Hassan Sinwar, 61, believed to be the Hamas leader behind the attacks, in the ruins of Gaza City. Israeli officials called him a "dead man walking". The IDF reported that its 7th Brigade had raided the office of Sinwar's brother, Muhammad, capturing military documents and killing 30 "terrorists". Yahya was freed in a prisoner swap for the Israeli soldier Gilad Shalit in 2011. In Gaza, he worked closely with Mohammed Deif, the commander of the Izz-al-Din al-Qassam Brigades, the Hamas military wing. The Jewish Virtual Library reported that Yahya was born in Khan Younis, a Palestinian refugee camp, in southern Gaza in 1962. His parents fled Ashkelon in Israel. He studied Arabic at the Islamic University of Gaza. *The Economist* reported that in the 1980s, Sinwar killed Gazans who collaborated with Israel. He was jailed for 24 years on various charges, including murdering two Israeli soldiers and four Palestinian men he had accused of collaborating. Israeli doctors saved his life in 2006 after operating on a brain tumor. He became fluent in Hebrew while in prison.

CNN reported that on November 9, Palestinian Islamic Jihad (PIJ) released a video of an Israeli child and a senior woman being held hostage. Abu Hamza, a leader of al-Quds Brigades, the military wing of PIJ, texted that PIJ was prepared to release a woman, 77, "for medical reasons" and a second, a boy, 13, "for humanitarian reasons and for his young age".

CNN added on November 10 that Israel had lowered the death toll from the attacks to 1,200.

VOA and *Reuters* reported that on November 13 the IDF shared video and photographs showing what it said were weapons including grenades, suicide vests, and other explosives stored by Hamas in the basement of Rantissi Hospital, a pediatric hospital in Gaza where it also said hostages appear to have been held. Soldiers found a motorcycle with gunshot marks which appeared to have been used to bring hostages to Gaza.

Reuters and *CNN* reported on November 14, 2023 that Israel confirmed the death of captive IDF Corporal Noa Marciano, 19, who was shown alive in a Hamas video that also showed her body after she was killed in an Israeli strike. In the video, she had called on Israel to stop its bombing campaign. *CNN* reported that Marciano's body was retrieved from a structure near the al-Shifa Hospital in Gaza City.

On November 15, 2023, *NBC News* reported that a hostage gave birth.

CNN reported that on November 16, 2023, Israeli soldiers found the body of hostage Yehudit Weiss, 65, an Israeli grandmother who lived in kibbutz Be'eri, in a structure near Gaza's al-Shifa Hospital, where the IDF had determined that Hamas had held hostages and maintained a command center. IDF spokesman Daniel Hagari said in a televised news briefing that Hamas had killed Weiss. Weiss's husband, Shmuel, was among those killed in the October 7 Hamas attack.

AP, the *Daily Beast,* and the *Times of Israel* reported on November 17 that dual Irish-Israeli citizen Emily Tony Korenberg Hand, of Kibbutz Be'eri, marked her 9th birthday as a hostage. Her father, Thomas Hand, 63, was initially told by Be'eri leaders that she was among the dead after she had spent the night at a friend's house on the kibbutz. Emily's friend's mother, Raya Rotem, was also taken hostage. *Reuters* reported that Thomas Hand had moved to Be'eri in 1992. Emily's mother, Liat, died when Emily was 2 ½ years old. Tom's first wife, Narkis, also lived there, but was killed in the October 7 attack. Emily has a half-sister Natalie, 26. Thomas Hand unveiled a billboard of Emily in Times Square.

CNN reported on November 19, 2023 that the IDF released CCTV videos and still images it claimed showed Hamas fighters bringing hostages—one Nepali, one Thai—into the al-Shifa Hospital on October 7. One hostage was brought into the hospital through the main entrance. A second hostage had a bandaged hand and was clearly bleeding. That hostage was pushed on a gurney down a hallway and into a room.

AP and *CNN* reported on November 21, 2023 that the Israeli government and Hamas had apparently agreed on the release of 50 of the 240 hostages and 150 Palestinian prisoners, plus a four-day break in the fighting which would entail six hours during which Israeli drones would not overfly Gaza. The first hostages to be released were to be women and children. The U.S. and Qatar brokered the truce. The Israeli government said the truce would be extended an extra day for every additional 10 hostages released by Hamas. Officials said three Americans could be part of the deal to release 50 women and children.

Fox News and the *Jerusalem Post* reported on November 22, 2023 that the body of Israeli woman Shani Gabay, 26, who vanished following the October 7 attack, was found. She worked at the music festival in Kibbutz Re'im. The *Times of Israel* reported that Gabay had been presumed to be a hostage.

AP reported on November 23, 2023 updated biographic information on several hostages:

- Itay Chen, 19, an Israeli-American, is a 5-foot-9 basketball player with a big outside shot. He was taken captive while on military duty. He grew up in New York City, idolizing Kobe Bryant and the Los Angeles Lakers. He earlier was a Boy Scout.

- Liat Beinin, 49, an Israeli-American teacher who volunteered to give tours at Yad Vashem, and Aviv Atzili, 49, an artist and mechanic who kept the farm machinery at Kibbutz Nir Oz in excellent shape and used old equipment as a canvas for his paintings, recently traveled as a couple to Oregon and New York. They met as youth counselors. After completing their military service, they travelled for three years, visiting India and Australia, where they wed. They settled at Kibbutz Nir Oz, where they raised three children. They had adopted a special needs dog with three legs. Hamas killed the dog.

- Luis Har, 70, is a grandfather to ten grandchildren and has a daughter, Rinat Sheleg. He was visiting a kibbutz near the Gaza border with his longtime partner, Clara Marman, for a child's birthday party. The couple were taken hostage in the attack, along with Marman's brother Fernando Marman, her sister Gabriela Leimberg, and her niece Mia Leimberg, 17. Har spent his childhood in Argentina. He enjoys dancing and cooking.

- Alex Dancyg, 75, a retired Yad Vashem historian and the son of Holocaust survivors, left Poland at age 9, sailing by ship to Israel in 1957. He was abducted from the Nir Oz kibbutz, where he carried out academic work and contributed to the communal sowing and harvesting of potatoes, peanuts, and other produce, according to his son Yuval Danzig. He was the only known Polish-Israeli among the hostages still held, according to the Israeli Embassy in Warsaw.

- Gong Sae Lao, 26, a Thai, traveled a year earlier to Israel's Kibbutz Be'eri to work as a farmhand, delivering fruits and vegetables to market. His family was in debt; his father was long dead and a brother was in prison. Gong was the main provider. Three Thai workers in his group also were taken hostage. Their living quarters were burned to the ground. Gong's Hmong family is from the village of Mae Fah Luang, in northern Chiang Rai Province.

- Oded Lifshitz, 83, spent his life fighting for Arab rights during a long career in journalism. In retirement, he drove to the Erez border crossing on the northern edge of the Gaza Strip once a week to ferry Palestinians to medical appointments in Israel as part of a group called On the Way to Recovery. Oded and his wife, Yocheved, helped found Kibbutz Nir Oz, where they were abducted. Yocheved Lifshitz and another elderly woman, Nurit Cooper, were freed October 23. Oded Lifshitz remained in captivity.

- Joshua Loitu Mollel, 21, a Tanzanian agriculture intern from the Manyara region, was working on a cow farm and living in Kibbutz Nahal Oz not far from the Gaza Strip when he was abducted. He is the eldest of five children. He recently graduated from an agriculture college.

- Bibas family members Yarden Bibas, his wife, Shiri, and their sons, 4-year-old Ariel and 9-month-old Kfir, were kidnapped from their home in the Nir-Oz Kibbutz.

- Omer Neutra, an American-Israeli soldier, turned 22 seven days after the attack during which his unit was taken hostage. Omer was born in Manhattan a month after 9/11 to Israeli-born parents. He attended a conservative Jewish school and loved the New York Knicks. He captained the basketball, soccer, and volleyball teams at the Schechter School of Long Island, and served as a regional president of United Synagogue Youth. He was offered admission to the State University of New York at Binghamton, but took a gap year and then moved to Israel to join the army to patrol the Gaza border.

- Ten members of the Haran family, including Shaked Haran's parents, sister, little niece and nephew, two aunts, an uncle, and a cousin, spanning three generations. Her parents' house at Kibbutz Be'eri was burned but the shelter was intact and there were no bodies found in it. Haran's brother-in-law had been seen being put into a Hamas car. The body of her father, Avshalom Haran, was identified. Her uncle, Eviatar Kipnis, also died. Her mother, Shoshan, a longtime social activist, founded the nonprofit Fair Planet, which works to fight food insecurity in the developing world by helping farmers. Also among the missing were Haran's sister, Adi, a psychologist; her husband, Tal; and their children Naveh, 8, "a bright, open-hearted boy that makes friends in an instant"; and Yahel, 3, "creative and full of life". Also believed abducted were Haran's aunt Sharon, her daughter, Noam, 12, and another aunt, Lilach Kipnis.

- Hamas dragged 3-year-old Geffen, her father, Alon Gat, and Alon's wife and Geffen's mother, Yarden Roman, 36, into a car at Kibbutz Be'eri. The family fled under fire. Alon emerged with their daughter from a small forest when he thought it was safe. The two made it back to Be'eri, where Israeli soldiers had arrived. Alon last saw his wife hiding behind a tree as he ran with their child. Yarden's sister-in-law is also missing and her mother-in-law was murdered at the kibbutz. Yarden works as a physical therapist specializing in elder care and is a rock climber and hiker.

- Or and Eynav Levy recently took a family trip to Thailand and drove to the Tribe of Nova festival, arriving minutes before the attack. Eynav Elkayam Levy, 32, was confirmed dead inside a shelter. Or, 33, is missing. They left behind two-year-old son Almog Levy with his grandparents. Or taught himself computer programming and was part of a successful startup.

- Sagui Dekel-Chen, 35, managed community development projects for the U.K. branch of the Jewish National Fund, organizing the construction of schools and youth centers in the underdeveloped Negev Desert. The Israeli-American was tinkering with an engine in the machine shop at Nir Oz, when he saw intruders, sounded the alarm, rigged the door of a safe room so it could not be opened from the outside, kissed his pregnant wife, and told her to lock herself and their two daughters inside. He then borrowed a gun and tried to protect his community. His family believed that he was abducted.

- Romi Gonen, 23, daughter of Meirav Leshem Gonen, was at the music festival. Romi phoned her mother to say, "Mommy I was shot, the car was shot, everybody was shot… I am wounded and bleeding. Mommy, I think I'm going to die."

- Judith Weinstein, 70, and her husband, Gad Haggai, 72, were on their morning walk in Kibbutz Nir Oz and took cover in a field. A daughter, Iris Weinstein Haggai, 38, lives in Singapore. Weinstein had called for medical help saying they were shot by terrorists on a motorcycle. Irish said "Paramedics tried to send her an ambulance. The ambulance got hit by a rocket" and lost contact with Weinstein. Haggai is a retired chef and jazz musician. Weinstein, a New York native, is a retired teacher. They raised their children at the kibbutz.

- Yaffa Adar, 85, lived in Nir Oz and loved reading, writing, and keeping connected on *WhatsApp* and *Facebook*. Video surfaced showing her being driven in a golf cart in Gaza, wrapped in a pink flowered blanket. She left behind three children, eight grandchildren, and seven great-grandchildren. She did not have her medication for blood pressure and chronic pain. She was freed on November 24, 2023.

- Roni Eshel, 19, an IDF soldier, was stationed in a communications unit at a military base near Nahal Oz near the Gaza border. She grew up in a small village north of Tel Aviv. She reported for military service two weeks after finishing school. She had returned to the base from a brief vacation three days before the attack. She was proud to be a third generation of her family to join the Israeli military, following her father, uncle, and grandfather. She planned to travel and enroll in a university.

- Maya, 21, and brother Itay Regev, 18, were on their way to the Tribe of Nova music festival. She had bought her ticket for an extended trip to South America in December. She phoned her father, Ilan Regev, saying, "Dad, they shot me, they shot me! He is killing us, Dad, he is killing us." Ilan Regev jumped in his car from his home in Herzliya, near Tel Aviv, and drove south to the festival, but was barred from entering. Hamas released a video that showed Itay in captivity in Gaza. Maya was not pictured. Following her November 26, 2023 release, she was taken to Soroka Hospital for treatment of a moderate injury.

- Hersh Goldberg-Polin, 23, of Jerusalem, had finished his military service. He planned to go to a university, wanted to see the world, and loved psychedelic trance music. Hamas loaded him into the back of a pickup with other hostages abducted from the Tribe of Nova music festival. Born in Berkeley, California, he moved to Israel with his family when he was seven years old. He once took a nine-week trek through six European countries so he could attend a series of raves. He lost part of an arm when attackers threw grenades into a temporary shelter where he and others had taken refuge. He tied a tourniquet around it and walked out before being hustled into the truck.

- Ada Sagi, 74, born in Tel Aviv in 1948, daughter of Holocaust survivors from Poland, mother of three, grandmother of six, was getting ready to travel to London to celebrate her birthday with family. Her husband of 54 years died of cancer in 2022. She had struggled with allergies and was recovering from hip replacement surgery. She moved to a kibbutz at age 18. She taught Arabic to other Israelis as a way to improve communication with Palestinians who live near Kibbutz Nir Oz.

- Hamas shot and killed Iraq-born David Moshe, 75, as he and wife Adina, 72, huddled in their bomb shelter in Nir Oz kibbutz. Terrorists burned the couple's house. Two gunmen drove her away on a motorbike. She had heart surgery in 2022, and was without her medication. The two met at the pool. Adina worked as a minder of small children. Adina was freed on November 24, 2023.

- Moran Stela Yanai, 40, a jewelry designer, disappeared at the music festival. She was seen on a video on *TikTok*, sitting on the ground, looking terrified, amid derogatory Arabic text about Jews.

Televised news services ran video, apparently taken by Hamas body cameras, of gunmen shooting into occupied Port-a-Potties.

CNN and *USA Today* reported on November 24, 2023, that the Israeli Prime Minister's office released the names of 13 freed Israeli hostages:

- Margalit Moses, 77, mother of three and grandmother of ten, is a retired biology teacher who is a cancer survivor. She has diabetes and fibromyalgia. *CNN* reported on November 26, 2023 that the nature lover planned on traveling to Mozambique in the winter of 2023.

- Adina Moshe, 72, retired educator, Nir Oz resident, mother of four, and grandmother of 12. Her husband David (Sa'id) Moshe was killed in their home on October 7.

- Danielle Aloni, variant Alony, 45, abducted from Kibbutz Nir Oz. She was among three women who appeared in a hostage video released by Hamas in late October. She came to Nir Oz to visit family and was abducted alongside her daughter Emilia. Her sister Sharon Aloni-Cunio and other family members remained captives.

- Emilia Aloni, variant Amelia Alony, 5, Danielle's daughter, abducted from Kibbutz Nir Oz

- Yafa Adar, 85, was taken from Kibbutz Nir Oz. The mother of three, grandmother of eight, and great-grandmother of seven was driven away by Hamas in a golf cart. Adar is a founder of Nir Oz and was the oldest person to be taken hostage. Her eldest grandson, Tamir Adar, 38, a father of two, remained in captivity. She lost weight during captivity.

- Ohad Munder, 9, Ruthy's sole grandson and Keren's sole son, abducted from Kibbutz Nir Oz

- Keren Munder, 54, abducted from Kibbutz Nir Oz, lives in Kfar Saba. She is a special education teacher and a volleyball coach. She was born and raised in Nir Oz. She and her mother lost between six and eight kilograms, subsisting on a diet principally of rice and pita bread.

- Ruthy Munder, variant Ruth, 78; abducted from Kibbutz Nir Oz, a retired librarian, hairdresser, and seamstress who knits, paints, and sews. Avraham Munder, 78, Ruthy's husband and Ohad's grandfather, was not released in the initial tranche. Her son, Roee, was killed on October 7.

- Doron Katz Asher, 34, an accountant from Ganot Hadar, and her children were in Kibbutz Nir Oz visiting relatives when they were taken hostage with other members of their family. Her cousin, Dori Roberts, said that he received a video posted to social media showing two women and the girls being taken hostage from Nir Oz. Her cousin, Dori Roberts, said his aunt's 79-year-old partner and another relative remained captives.

- Aviv Katz Asher, 2, daughter of Doron

- Raz Katz Asher, 4, daughter of Doron

- Hana Katzir, variant Chana, 76, a member of Kibbutz Nir Oz and the wife of the late Rami Katzir, 79, who was killed in their home. She is the mother of three and grandmother of six. Her son, Elad, 47, remained a hostage. She had been feared dead before she was spotted in the back seat of a Red Cross vehicle heading into Egypt. The *New York Times* reported that Palestinian Islamic Jihad announced on November 21 that she had died, but did not offer proof. She was the daughter of Holocaust survivors.

- Channa Peri, 79, who immigrated to Israel from South Africa in the 1960s and lives in Kibbutz Nirim, where she works in a grocery store. The mother of three (one of whom was murdered and another kidnapped) has diabetes and severe vision loss in one eye. She enjoys gardening and going to exercise classes with her friends. One of her grandchildren, Tamir Adar, 38, was also taken and remained captive.

Qatar's Foreign Ministry confirmed that 11 foreign nationals (10 Thais and a Filipino) were also released. Some 39 Palestinian prisoners—24 women and 15 minors—were freed. Ninety aid trucks entered Gaza. Meanwhile, Hamas health authorities said that 14,800 people had been killed in Israeli bombings.

CNN reported that Philippine President Ferdinand "Bongbong" Marcos confirmed the release of Philippine national Gelienor "Jimmy" Pacheco in the first tranche of hostages.

The released foreigners included Gelienor "Jimmy" Pacheco, and Thai nationals Kanthawri Mulkan, Santi Bunphrom, Bunthom Pankhong, Mongkol Phajuabbun, Withun Phumi, Vichai Kalapat, Bancha Kongmani, Buddi Sengbun, Uthai Thunsri, and Uthai Sengnual. By the next day, the freed Thais (with variant spellings) included Nattawaree Munkan, Santi Boonprom, Boonthom Pankhong, Mongkol Phachuabboon, Vetoon Phoome, Vichai Kalapat, Bancha Kongmanee, Buddhee Saengboon, Uthai Toonsri, Uthai Saengnuan, Natthaporn Onkaew, Komkrit Chombua, Anucha Angkaew, and Manee Jirachart.

Reuters and the *Jerusalem Post* reported on November 25 that Thai farm worker and freed hostage Vetoon Phoome, 33, assured his family "I'm not dead." He had lived in Israel for five years. He and other Thais were kidnapped from Kibbutz Kissufim. He told his family he had yelled, "Thailand, Thailand!" when the terrorists attacked. Among those released was the only Thai woman known to be held by Hamas, a factory worker and mother from an impoverished rural area. The Thai Foreign Ministry thanked the governments of Egypt, Iran, Israel, Malaysia, and Qatar, and the International Committee of the Red Cross, as well as others involved in the "immense efforts" that led to the release. Thai farm worker Natthaporn Onkaew, 26, was not among those released in the first tranche.

The *Times of Israel* reported on November 25, 2023 that newly-freed Israeli hostages included:

- Hila Rotem, 12 or 13, kidnapped by Hamas from Kibbutz Be'eri with her mother Raya, variant Raaya, Rotem, 54, who was not released. An Israeli government official said that mothers and children were not supposed to be separated under the agreement with Hamas.

- Emily Hand, 9, initially thought by Emily's father Thomas (a single parent whose wife died of cancer) to have been among those killed in the attack on Kibbutz Be'eri. She was at a sleepover at a friend's house on the kibbutz when she was abducted without any family.

- Noam Or, 17, and Alma Or, 13, were kidnapped from their home in Kibbutz Be'eri, with their father Dror Or, 48, and their cousin, Liam Or, 18. Mother Yonat Or was killed in the attack. Dror and Liam were not released.

- Noam Avigdori, 12, and her mother Sharon Avigdori, 52, and 10 members of their extended family, were kidnapped from Kibbutz Be'eri. Several family members were killed that day.

Hamas said that imprisoned Palestinian bomber Israa Jaabis was released from an Israeli prison. At age 31 in 2015, she detonated a gas canister in her car after being pulled over by police near the Ma'ale Adumim settlement outside Jerusalem. Israeli authorities said she was heading into Israel, where she intended to carry out a suicide bombing. The fire burned police officer Moshe Chen's face and chest and seriously injured Jaabis. In 2022, Jaabis asked the Israel Prisons Service for a nose job to repair the damage to her face, but was turned down.

NBC News reported on November 25, 2023 that a second group of 13 Israelis and four Thai nationals were released from the Gaza Strip after an hourslong delay. They included

- Sharon Hertzman Avigdori, 52

- Noam Avigdori, 12, Sharon's daughter

- Emily Hand, who marked her 9th birthday the day before.

- Mia Regev Jarbi, variant Maya Regev 21

- Siblings Noam Or, 17, and Alma Or, 13, who along with their father, Dror, were taken from their home in Kibbutz Be'eri. Their mother Yonat was murdered. Their older brother Yahli survived while at his post in northern Israel where he was doing a year of national service.

- Shoshan Haran, 67

- Adi Shoham, 38, Shoshan Haran's daughter; Shoshan Haran's grandchildren Neve Shoham, 8, and Yahal Shoham, 3
- Hila Rotem Shoshani, 12
- Shiri Weiss, 53, taken hostage from Be'eri kibbutz
- Noga Weiss, 18, taken hostage from Be'eri kibbutz

CNN reported on November 26, 2023 that Poland indicated that a Polish woman was released.

Al-Jazeera and *Forbes* reported on November 24 that of the 39 Palestinians released by Israel, 17 were minors, including

- Yousef Mohammad Mustafa Ata from Ramallah
- Qusai Hani Ali Ahmad from Bethlehem
- Jibreel Ghassan Ismail Jibreel from Qalqilya
- Mohammad Ahmad Suleiman Abu Rajab from al-Khalil
- Ahmad Nu'man Ahmad Abu Na'im from Ramallah
- Baraa Bilal Mahmoud Rabee from al-Khalil
- Aban Iyad Mohammad Said Hammad from Qalqilya
- Moataz Hatem Moussa Abu Aram from al-Khalil
- Iyad Abdul Qader Mohammad Khateeb from Jerusalem. *AP* added that Iyas Khatib, 17, son of a U.N. aid worker who was put in "administrative detention" in 2022 based on secret evidence without being publicly charged of a crime or put on trial.
- Hazma Laith Khalil Othman Othman from Ramallah
- Mohammad Mahmoud Ayoub Dar Darwish from Ramallah
- Jamal Khalil Jamal Barahmeh from Areeha
- Jamal Yousef Jamal Abu Hamdan from Nablus
- Mohammad Anis Saleem Tarabi from Nablus

- Abdul Rahman Abdul Rahman Suleiman Rizq from Jerusalem
- Zeina Raed Abdou from Jerusalem
- Noor Mohammad Hafez al-Tahir from Nablus

Zeina and Noor are girls, the others are boys.

The remaining 22 Palestinians released in the initial tranche were women. They are:

- Rawan Nafez Mohammad Abu Matar from Ramallah
- Marah Joudat Moussa Bakeer from Jerusalem. *Al-Jazeera* added that Marah Bakeer, 24, was a 16-year-old high school student at al-Maimouna School in occupied East Jerusalem's Sheikh Jarrah neighborhood when on October 12, 2015, Israeli forces shot at and arrested her for allegedly trying to stab an Israeli officer, which she denies. *Al-Jazeera* reported on November 25 that she walked from the family home in Beit Hanina en route to school, crossing an expressway that runs between East and West Jerusalem. Bakeer sustained 12 gunshot wounds to her arm and hand, leaving her with permanent damage. She was sentenced to eight years and six months in prison. Bakeer became a political figure, representing all female prisoners before the administration at Damon prison in northern Israel, where female Palestinian prisoners and minors are detained. After the October 7 attack, she and other prison leaders were moved to another prison in Jalame and placed in solitary confinement.
- Malak Mohammad Yousef Suleiman from Jerusalem
- Amani Khaled Nu'man Hasheem from Jerusalem
- Nihaya Khader Hussein Sawan from Jerusalem
- Fayrouz Fayez Mahmoud al-Baw from Jerusalem
- Tahreer Adnan Mohammad Abu Suriya from Nablus

- Falasteen Fareed Abdul Latif Najm from Nablus
- Walaa Khaled Fawzi Tanja from Tulkarem
- Maryam Khaled Abdul Majid Arafat from Nablus
- Asil Muneer Ibrahim al-Tayti from Nablus. The *Washington Post* reported on November 25 that Aseel al-Titi, 23, had lived in the Balata camp in Nablus. She had been in prison for 15 months. She was arrested while visiting her brother Sabea in prison. Her family said a guard had asked her to undergo a humiliating physical search. Israeli media reported that she attempted to stab the guard with a pair of scissors. Her family said she pushed the guard. Her uncle, a member of one of Nablus's armed groups, had been killed in fighting in Gaza.
- Azhar Thaer Bakr Assaf from Jerusalem
- Raghd Nashat Salah al-Fanni from Tulkarem
- Fatima Nu'man Ali Badr from Jerusalem
- Rawda Moussa Abdul Qader Abu Ujaima from Bethlehem
- Sara Ayman Abdul Aziz Abdullah al-Suweisa from Nablus
- Fatima Ismail Abdul Rahman Shahin from Bethlehem
- Samira Abdul Harbawi from Jerusalem
- Samah Bilal Abdul Rahman Souf from Qalqilya
- Fatima Bakr Moussa Abu Shalal from Nablus
- Hanan Saleh Abdullah al-Barghouthi from Ramallah
- Fatima Nasr Mohammad Amarnah from Jenin

They were transferred from Israeli prisons to the Israel-controlled Ofer prison in the occupied West Bank, then put on International Committee of the Red Cross buses.

USNWR and *Reuters* reported on November 26, 2023 that Hamas said it had released a hostage from Gaza who held Russian citizenship.

CNN added on November 27 that Russian-Israeli hostage Roni Kriboy, 25, escaped from a Hamas-controlled building in Gaza that collapsed during an Israeli airstrike, but after hiding out for four days, was recaptured and returned to the terrorists. Kriboy was abducted from the Nova music festival. He suffered a head injury when the building collapsed. He was the first adult male captured on October 7 to be released by Hamas. His release was not officially part of the swap between Israel and Hamas.

CNBC reported on November 26 that the Israeli Prime Minister's office announced that Hamas released another 17 hostages. They included 14 Israeli citizens, and three foreign nationals. The 14 Israelis were:

- Abigail Mor Edan, 4, an Israeli-American who was orphaned in the attack. *CNN* reported on November 26 that she was the youngest American hostage. She has a 6-year-old sister and 10-year-old brother, who saw their parents being murdered. They hid in a closet for 14 hours.
- Alma Avraham, variant Elma, 84
- Aviva Adrian Siegel, variant Adrienne, 62
- Ron Cariboy, 25
- Hagar Brodetz, variant Brodutch, 40
- Ofri Brodetz, variant Ofry Brodutch, 10
- Yuval Brodetz, variant Brodutch, 8
- Uriah Brodetz, variant Oria Brodutch, 4
- Chen Goldstein Almog, 48 or 49
- Agam Goldstein Almog, 17
- Gal Goldstein Almog, 11
- Tal Goldstein Almog, 8
- Dafna Elikim, 15, variant Dafna Elyakim, 14
- Ella Elikim, variant Ela Elyakim, 8

Haaretz and *Reuters* reported on November 27 that the fourth tranche of freed hostages included 11 dual nationals: three French citizens, two Germans, and six Argentinians. *CNN* identified them as:

- Eitan Yahalomi, 12, a French dual national

- Sharon Kunio, 34, Emma Kunio, 3, and Yuli Kunio, 3, members of an Argentine-Israeli family
- Karina Engel, Mika Engel, 18, and Yuval Engel, 11, members of an Argentine-Israeli family
- Sahar Kalderon, 16, and Erez Kalderon, 12, members of a French-Israeli family
- Or Yaakov, 16, and Yagil Yaakov 13

On November 27, *UPI* reported that Qatari Foreign Ministry spokesman Majed al-Ansari announced via *X* that the pause in fighting between Israel and Hamas was extended for two more days. Qatari Prime Minister Sheikh Mohammed bin Abdulrahman al-Thani noted that some 40 women and children hostages had been abducted by several different groups, and Hamas did not know where they were. *CNN* noted that Palestinian Islamic Jihad had taken 40 to 50 hostages.

CNN reported on November 28 that the IDF confirmed the death of hostage Ravid Katz in Gaza. He was kidnapped from Kibbutz Nir Oz. He was the brother of Doron Katz Asher, who was freed on November 24.

Haaretz reported on November 28 that the Israeli army released the names of three soldiers who were killed on October 7 and whose bodies were dragged to Gaza by Hamas terrorists:

- Staff Sgt. Tomer Yaakov Ahimas, 20, from Lehavim
- Sgt. Kiril Brodski, 19, from Ramat Gan
- Sgt. Shaked Dahan, 19, from Afula

Haaretz also reported that the hostages freed on November 28 included two Thais and ten Israelis. The latter included:

- Ditza Haiman, 84, from Nir Oz
- Tamar Metzger, 78, from Nir Oz
- Ofelia Roitman, 77, from Nir Oz
- Meirav Tal, 53, from Rishon Letzion, abducted from Nir Oz
- Gabriela and Maya Leimberg, 59 and 17, from Jerusalem, abducted from Nir Yitzhak

- Clara Marman, 63, from Nir Yizhak, kidnapped from Nir Oz
- Ada Sagi, 75, from Nir Oz
- Rimon Kirsht Buchshtab, 36, from Nirim
- Noralin Babadilla Agojo, 60, from Yehud, abducted from Nirim

Some of their family members remained in captivity. Israel freed 30 Palestinian prisoners.

Reuters and *CNN* reported on November 29 that Hamas made an unconfirmed claim that 10-month old Israeli hostage Kfir Bibas, his four-year-old brother Ariel, and their mother Shiri had been killed in an earlier Israeli bombing. Their father Yarden had also been held. Discussions continued for extending the pause in fighting.

On November 29, the *Times of Israel* reported that Russian-Israeli hostages Yelena Trupanov, 50, and her mother Irena Tati, 73, were freed. *ToI* added that four Thais were freed and ten freed Israelis were

- Raz Ben Ami, 58
- Yarden Roman Gat, 36, a German-Israeli citizen, was kidnapped with her husband and young child by Hamas from Kibbutz Be'eri. She, her husband Alon, and three-year-old Gefen escaped when the car briefly stopped, but Yarden became separated from the others.
- Liat Atzili, variant Liat Beinin, an Israeli-American dual citizen who teaches high school civics and history and serves as a tour guide at the World Holocaust Remembrance Center in Jerusalem
- Moran Stela Yanai, 40
- Liam Or, 18, whose brother and sister, Noam and Alma, were released on November 25.
- Itay Regev, 18, who was seized from the Supernova festival with his sister Maya Regev, 21, who was released on November 25. The family had spotted Itay in handcuffs in the back of a vehicle in a video released by Hamas.

- Ofir Engel, 18, an Israeli-Dutch national, who was visiting his girlfriend, Yuval, at Be'eri. He was abducted along with Yuval's father, Yosi Sharabi, 51, and her uncle, Eli Sharabi, 55. Eli's wife and two daughters were murdered in the attack.

- Amit Shani, 16, the only member of his family taken when he was ordered into a car by Hamas gunmen after they broke into the family's safe room in Kibbutz Be'eri

- Gali Tarshansky, 13, was kidnapped from Be'eri. Her brother, Lior, was killed in the attack.

- Raaya Rotem, 54, variant Raya. Her daughter, Hila Rotem Shoshani, 13, was released on November 25. They were taken from Kibbutz Be'eri.

CNN reported on November 30 the IDF confirmed the deaths of two Israeli men—Ofir Tzarfati, 27, and Aviv Atzili, 49, husband of Israeli-American woman Liat Beinin—who were missing after Hamas's attack.

The *Express Tribune* reported on November 30 that Hamas freed two Israeli hostages:

- Mia Schem, 21, a French-Israeli who was seized at the rave party and who appeared in the first hostage video released by Hamas saying that she had been abducted from the Supernova festival

- Amit Sosna, variant Soussana, 40, a French-Israeli dual national lawyer taken from her home in Kibbutz Kfar Aza while hiding in a safe room and suffering from a fever.

BBC, the *Times of Israel*, and the *New York Post* added Hamas released other Israeli hostages later that day:

- Aisha al-Ziadna, 17, and her brother Bilal, 18, residents of Rahat, a predominantly Arab Bedouin city just north of Beersheba, who were kidnapped from a Bedouin village in southern Israel. They were kidnapped alongside their father Yosef, 49, a father of 18 and grandfather to 20, and their brother Hamza, 21, while working at Kibbutz Holit's cowshed.

- Ilana Gritzewsky, 30

- Nili Margalit, 41

- Sapir Cohen, 29

- Shani Goren, 29

NPR reported that after a breakdown in talks to extend the pause in fighting, Israel resumed its military operations in Gaza on December 1, 2023.

USNWR, Kan radio, and *Reuters* reported on December 3, 2023 that a three-person Israeli medical committee, including Health Ministry official Hagar Mizrahi, a forensic pathologist, and a physical trauma clinician—had declared some of the missing as dead in captivity, giving relatives closure. The Health Ministry group viewed videos of the Hamas attack for signs of lethal injuries among those abducted, cross-referencing them with the testimony of freed hostages. Hamas had freed 108 hostages. Since the truce expired, Israeli authorities declared six civilians and an army colonel dead in captivity. This has not been confirmed by Hamas. In late November, the IDF declared dead Shaked Gal, 19, a conscript missing since October 7. The IDF recovered the bodies of a captive soldier and two civilian hostages, and freed a soldier in a rescue operation.

CNN added on December 3, 2023 that the IDF said that an airstrike killed Haitham Khuwajari, the Commander of Hamas's Shati Battalion who was responsible for carrying out raids into Israeli territory in the October 7 attack.

USA Today reported that on December 4, 2023, thousands of people attended the funeral of Colonel Asaf Hamami, 41, the Israeli commander of the Gaza Division's Southern Brigade, although Hamas held his remains in Gaza.

The Israeli Health Ministry reported on December 4, 2023 that Hamas had drugged, possibly with Clonazepam, the to-be-freed hostages to make them appear calm and happy. Hostages told Israeli authorities of beatings and rapes. Family members said their loved ones had returned malnourished, wounded, ill, infested with lice, and/or traumatized.

Reuters and *India Times* reported on December 8, 2023 that Hamas's al-Qassam Brigades said on *Telegram* that it had repelled an attempted hostage rescue by Israeli special forces in the Gaza Strip, inflicting several military casualties, and that captive Israeli soldier Sa'ar Baruch, variant Sahar Baruch, 25, died in the incident. Israel said Sahar Baruch, then 24, was a civilian student when he was kidnapped.

On December 8, 2023, the U.S. vetoed a U.N. Security Council resolution that called for a ceasefire but did not condemn the Hamas attack. The UK abstained. The U.S. abstained on December 22 on a second resolution that called for a pause in fighting to get more aid into Gaza.

CNN reported on December 13, 2023 that the Israeli prime minister's office announced the death of Israeli hostage in Gaza Tal Chimi, 41. He was the grandson of the founders of kibbutz Nir Yitzhak, where he lived. He left behind his wife, three children—9-year-old twins and a 6-year-old son—his father, Zohar, and his sister, Or.

On December 15, 2023, *Reuters* and the *Voice of America* reported that the IDF said that its soldiers had recovered the bodies of two soldiers and one civilian hostage: Cpl. Nik Beiser, 19; Sgt. Ron Sherman, 19; and Elia Toledano, 28.

CNN reported on December 15 and 16, 2023 that the IDF mistakenly killed three hostages, including Yotam Haim (a drummer set to perform at a heavy-metal festival in Tel Aviv) and Alon Shamriz (about to start college computer courses), both abducted from Kibbutz Kfar Aza, and Samer Talalka (a Bedouin working at a chicken hatchery who was abducted from Kibbutz Nir Am), during military operations in Shejaiya in northern Gaza. It was not clear whether they had escaped or were abandoned by Hamas. The shirtless hostages had been holding a makeshift white flag. *NPR* reported that an IDF soldier believed the trio posed a threat and shot and killed two of them. A third hostage, wounded, ran to a building, from which emitted cries for help in Hebrew. The soldier then finished off the hostage, in violation of the rules of engagement, according to the *New York Times*. *NDTV* reported on December 18 that Hebrew-language cloth signs written in red, likely with leftover food, reading "SOS" and "help, three hostages" were found on the walls of the building where the three Israeli hostages were hiding, 200 meters from where they were shot.

USA Today reported on December 16, 2023 that Israel believes that 21 of the hostages had died. *CNN* reported that Israeli Prime Minister Benjamin Netanyahu's office and the Hostages and Missing Persons Families Forum announced that female hostage Inbar Haiman, 27, from Haifa, had died. She was kidnapped from the Re'im nature festival.

Al-Jazeera reported that on December 18, the al-Qassam Brigades posted a video, titled Don't Let Us Grow Old Here, on its *Telegram* account of three elderly Israeli captives pleading for their immediate release. Israeli officials said Chaim Peri, 79, Yoram Metzger, 80, and Amiram Cooper, 84, were taken from the Nir Oz kibbutz to Gaza on October 7. Peri said in Hebrew that he was being held along with other elderly hostages with chronic illnesses and that their conditions were harsh. "We are the generation who built the foundation for the creation of Israel. We are the ones who started the IDF military. We don't understand why we have been abandoned here. You have to release us from here. It does not matter at what cost. We don't want to be casualties as a direct result of the IDF military air strikes. Release us with no conditions." The trio then said, "Don't let us grow old here."

CNN reported on December 19 that the Quds Brigades, the armed wing of Palestinian Islamic Jihad, released a video showing hostages Gadi Moses, 79, and Gadi Katzir, 47, speaking in front of a camera, asking the Israeli government to arrange their release. Moses called on Israeli Prime Minister Benjamin Netanyahu, Defense Minister Yoav Gallant, war cabinet member Benny Gantz, and IDF Chief of Staff Herzi Halevi to make every effort to return them to their families. Katzir said, "We do not want to die in Gaza. Our lives here are extremely dangerous. And we want everything necessary to be done, in order to bring us back home." Moses was taken alongside his ex-wife Margalit Moses, who was released on November 24. Katzir's father, Rami, was killed on October 7, and his mother, Hanna, was abducted and then released.

By December 20, Palestinian health officials said 20,000 people had died in Gaza.

CNN reported on December 22, 2023 that Israeli-American dual national and hostage Gadi

Haggai, 73, died in Gaza. The flutist played in the IDF Orchestra. Israeli officials said he and his wife, Judi, were out for a walk on the morning of October 7. He was critically injured by a gunshot. Both were taken captive by Hamas; she remained in Hamas's hands.

Reuters reported on December 24, 2023 that the IDF found five hostages dead in a tunnel. *CNN* identified them as Ziv Dado, Eden Zecharya, Ron Sherman, Nik Beizer, and Elia Toledano.

On December 26, 2023, *al-Jazeera* reported that Chief Cabinet Secretary Hayashi Yoshimasa announced that Japan imposed sanctions against three senior Hamas members, freezing assets belonging to the three individuals and imposing sanctions on payments and capital transactions on the trio believed to have been involved in Hamas's October 7 attacks on Israel and be in a position to use funds to carry out similar attacks in future. Tokyo in October had imposed sanctions on nine people and a company over their alleged links to Hamas.

CNN reported on December 28, 2023, that Kibbutz Nir Oz announced that Judi Weinstein, 70, who held Canadian, Israeli, and U.S. citizenship and who was abducted by Hamas, died of her injuries while being kidnapped on October 7. Hamas still held her body. Her husband, Gadi Haggai, 73, was pronounced dead on December 22.

The *New York Times*, in a long article on Hamas's sexual violence, on December 31, 2023 noted that "the woman in the black dress"—a rape victim burned beyond recognition, was believed to be Gal Abdush, 34, mother of two sons, Eliav, 10, and Rafael, 7, from the working-class Kiryat Ekron in central Israel, who was killed at the rave. Her husband, Nagi, 35, was also murdered and his body burned. Sapir, 24, an accountant who had been shot in the back, said she saw five women raped.

NBC News, i24News, and *Israel Hayom* reported on January 3, 2024 that during a failed nighttime hostage rescue effort by the IDF on December 8, 2023, hostage Sahar Baruch, 25, was killed. He was abducted from Kibbutz Be'eri. His brother, Idan, was killed in the October 7 attack by Hamas. Hamas had thrown grenades into

their safe room. The brothers escaped through a window, but Sahar went back to get Idan's inhaler. He was captured, and Idan was shot.

On January 4, 2024, *CNN* ran a long interview with Doron Katz Asher, 34, who, along with her mother and daughters Raz, 5, and Aviv, 2, were thrown into the back of a tractor with other hostages from their Nir Oz kibbutz, before gunmen opened fire. Asher was shot in her back; Aviv was shot in the leg; her mother was killed. The family was taken to a Gaza apartment home, then a hospital in Khan Younis where she said Hamas hid hostages, then were released in November. Her daughters' grandfather, Gadi Moses, was not released and was believed to be held by Palestinian Islamic Jihad. Doron said she was subjected to "psychological warfare". She added that Hamas tried to give the impression of compassion to Red Cross staff, but "It's one big show… Before I was released, my girls and I were barefoot for 50 days. We were cold because they were wearing short sleeves in November… We didn't see daylight that entire time."

CNN reported on January 5, 2024 that the Hostages and Missing Persons Families Forum in Israel announced the death of hostage Tamir Adar, 38, a third-generation member of kibbutz Nir Oz, husband of Hadas, and father of two young children. His grandmother, Yafa, 85, who was also abducted on October 7, became one of the most known hostages when she was pictured being driven on a golf cart by her Hamas captors. She was among the first group of hostages to be released in November 2023.

That day, the Health Ministry in Gaza said 22,722 Palestinians were killed and 58,166 were wounded since the start of the war.

CNN reported on January 8, 2024 that the Palestinian Islamic Jihad's Quds Brigade released a video showing Israeli hostage Elad Katzir, 47, held in Gaza. It was the second time he appeared in a PIJ video; he earlier appeared in mid-December 2023. He spoke in English and Hebrew for 3 ½ minutes, standing in front of a PIJ banner. He mentioned the late fellow hostage Tamir Adar, 38, also from Kibbutz Nir Oz, saying, "Tamir Adar, my dear friend, may you rest in peace, may your memory be blessed, I share your family's grief… It's a miracle I'm still alive.…

I'd like to tell my family that I love them very, very much, and I miss them very, very much… I want them [the government] to get me back, as well as all other hostages, and end this damn war… With each day of the war, more soldiers and more hostages are being killed. Stop the war and bring us hostages home in peace. Make a deal to exchange prisoners of war, together with the Hamas, and bring us home." Katzir's mother, Hana, was in the first group of hostages to be released in November.

AP reported on January 10, 2024 that the IDF said it found evidence that hostages were present in an underground tunnel in the Gaza Strip city of Khan Younis.

CNN and *Time Magazine* reported that on January 14, 2024, the 100th day of the war, Hamas released a 30-second video showing Israeli hostages Noa Argamani, 26, Yossi Sharabi, 53, and Itai Svirsky, 38, saying their name, age, and place of residence, and asking Israeli Prime Minister Benjamin Netanyahu to "stop the war" and "bring us home." Two title cards in Hebrew, Arabic, and English at the end of the video read, "Tomorrow we will inform you of their fate." And "Your Government is Lying." *CNN* and *Time* reported on January 16 that Hamas released three videos of the three hostages within 24 hours. The second video, released on January 15, echoed themes of the first video. The third video apparently showed that two of the hostages, Svirsky and Sharabi, had died. It also showed Noa Argamani saying both men had been killed by Israeli bombing. IDF chief spokesperson Daniel Hagari said Itai Svirsky had not been hit by Israeli forces and that the IDF had not struck the building where the three were being held, but had hit nearby.

Time added that Hamas claimed it lost contact with some hostages and warned that they might have been killed amid Israel's ongoing military campaign in Gaza.

CNN reported on January 15, 2024 that a senior Hungarian official said that some Israeli hostages have been granted Hungarian citizenship and issued Hungarian passports while in Gaza to add an extra layer of protection to the hostages.

CNN reported on January 17, 2024 that Israel announced that the official number of hostages taken was 253.

UPI reported that on January 16, 2024 the European Council sanctioned Yahya Sinwar, political leader of Hamas, over the threat Hamas poses to the EU's member states and its October 7 attack on Israel, freezing all of his funds and financial assets held in the union's 27-member states. The U.S. sanctioned him in 2015. Sinwar has been the subject of U.S. sanctions since 2015. The EU blacklisted Mohammed Deif, commander general of Hamas military wing and Marwan Issa, his deputy commander, in December 2023.

On January 17, 2024, *CNN* reported that released hostage Sharon Aloni Cunio, 34, who was freed in November 2023 with her twin three-year-old daughters, Yuli and Emma, told the media that she was held in Gaza's Nasser Hospital with dozens of other hostages. Her husband David remained captive. She said three rooms at Nasser hospital each held 10-12 captives and that they were tended to by a male nurse every other day. The terrorists had set fire to the Cunio's home in kibbutz Nir Oz.

CNN reported on January 22, 2024 that Gaza's Health Ministry said 25,105 Palestinians had been killed and 62,681 were wounded in the war.

The IDF announced the death of hostage Sgt. Shay Levinson, 19. His date of death was given as October 7; his body was still in Gaza.

The IDF released footage of a tunnel under a residential neighborhood in Khan Younis where the army said at least 20 hostages were kept at different times.

CNN and *NPR* reported on January 26, 2024 that International Court of Justice granted emergency measures against Israel in a genocide case brought against it by South Africa, saying Israel must "ensure with immediate effect that its military does not commit any acts" which could breach the Genocide Convention. The ICJ did not call for a ceasefire.

CNN added on January 26, 2024 that the United Nations Relief and Works Agency (UNWRA) Commissioner-General Philippe Lazzarini said Israeli authorities provided the agency "with information" alleging 12 of its employees participated in the October 7 attack. He said the contracts of those accused would be "immediately" terminated.

Hamas's Ministry of Health claimed that 26,083 people had died in the war.

CNN reported on January 31 that Israel Police announced the death of Sgt. 1st Class Ran Gvili, who was killed during the Hamas attack before his body was taken to Gaza. Police said that 29 hostages were believed to have died.

NBC News reported on January 31, 2024 that 67 U.S. citizens filed a federal lawsuit in U.S. District Court for the District of Columbia, brought by attorney Alex Spiro of the law firm Quinn, Emanuel, Urquhart and Sullivan LLP, charging that the Hamas-led massacre was "masterminded and funded by the Islamic Republic of Iran". The plaintiffs included people who were injured or taken hostage, plus family members of those who were murdered.

Israel's chief military spokesperson Rear Admiral Daniel Hagari said on February 6, 2024 that 31 of the remaining hostages had died.

Al-Jazeera quoted Palestinian health sources as saying that 28,000 Gazans had died by February 9, 2024.

Reuters reported on February 11, 2024 that Hamas claimed via *Telegram* that Israeli airstrikes in the previous 96 hours killed two Israeli hostages and seriously injured eight others. The IDF also claimed that it had found a tunnel beneath UNWRA headquarters in Gaza.

CNN reported on February 12, 2024 that the IDF, the Israeli Security Agency, and Israel Police rescued two dual Israeli-Argentine hostages during a special operation conducted at 1:49 a.m. in Rafah. Hamas kidnapped Fernando Simon Marman, 60, and Louis Har, 70, from the Nir Yitzhak kibbutz 128 days earlier. The duo were in good medical condition and sent to Sheba Medical Center at Tel HaShomer.

The *Times of Israel* reported on February 23, 2024 that several dual Israeli-U.S. nationals and Americans who attended the Supernova music festival at Kibbutz Re'im on October 7 filed a federal lawsuit in the Southern District of Florida against the *Associated Press*, accusing the news agency of being complicit in the Hamas killing

spree over four months ago by working with freelance photojournalists they believe were embedded with the thousands of terrorists who overran southern communities. The lawsuit named four freelance photographers—Hassan Eslaiah, Yousef Masoud, Ali Mahmud, and Hatem Ali—claiming they are "known Hamas associates who were gleefully embedded with the Hamas terrorists during the October 7th attacks". *Honest Reporting* said Eslaiah crossed the border into Israel and took pictures of a burning IDF tank, then photographed attackers entering Kibbutz Kfar Aza. Mahmud and Ali both photographed people being abducted from Israel into Gaza. Eslaiah appeared in a 2020 photo being kissed by Hamas's Gaza leader Yahya Sinwar.

AP reported on February 29, 2024 that more than 30,000 Palestinians had died in the fighting.

The *BBC* and *al-Jazeera* reported on March 1, 2024 that the al-Qassam Brigades of Hamas announced on *Telegram* that seven hostages had died during an Israeli bombardment and suggesting that the number of hostages killed could exceed 70.

CNN reported on March 4, 2024 that Pramila Patten, UN special envoy on sexual violence and women, told reporters that there is "clear and convincing information" that some hostages were taken to Gaza and subjected to sexual violence and "reasonable grounds" to believe the sexual violence is ongoing.

CNN, Haaretz, and *USA Today* reported on March 12, 2024 that the IDF announced that U.S.-Israeli dual citizen Itay Chen, 19, was killed on October 7; the terrorists took his remains into Gaza. Chen was serving on the Gaza border in the Israeli Army's 75th Battalion. His father said Itay was the middle child of three brothers. Itay was a former Boy Scout and a basketball player.

Al-Jazeera reported that on March 25, 2024, the UN Security Council passed by a vote of 14-0-1 a resolution demanding an immediate ceasefire in Gaza. The U.S. abstained because the resolution did not condemn the Hamas attack.

CNN and the *New York Times* reported on March 26, 2024 that attorney Amit Soussana became the first Israeli woman to speak publicly about a sexual assault and other forms of violence during her 55 days in captivity. She was taken from her home by ten men who destroyed her house at the Kibbutz Kfar Aza, beaten, dragged into Gaza, was locked alone in a child's bedroom, chained by her ankle, and forced into performing sexual acts at gunpoint. She was released in late November 2023.

Al-Jazeera reported on April 5, 2024 that an Israeli Army investigation determined that Efrat Katz, 68, an Israeli woman who was seized from the Nir Oz settlement during the Hamas attack, was "most likely" killed when an Israeli combat helicopter fired on her kidnappers' vehicle. She and most of the terrorists in the vehicle were killed when the aircraft fired on them. Her daughter, Doron Katz-Asher, and her two children were also kidnapped, but were released on November 24, 2023. Katz's partner Gadi Moses and his ex-wife Margalit Moses were seized, too. Moses was later released but Gadi was believed as of early April 2024 to remain in captivity in Gaza and still alive.

Reuters, BBC, NBC News, AP, the *Times of Israel, The Hill,* and *NPR* reported on April 6, 2024 that the previous night, Israeli commandos unearthed the body of Elad Katzir, 47, an Israeli farmer from Kibbutz Nir Oz who was killed by his Palestinian Islamic Jihad captors and buried in Khan Younis in mid-January 2024. Katzir was abducted with his mother, Hanna, 77, who was freed with 104 other hostages during a six-day ceasefire in late November 2023. His father, Avraham, was murdered in the kibbutz. In January 2024, Palestinian Islamic Jihad published a video purporting to show Katzir speaking from captivity in Gaza.

The Hamas Health Ministry reported on April 6, 2024 that 33,137 people had been killed in Gaza.

BBC reported on April 22, 2024 that the IDF announced that military intelligence chief Major General Aharon Haliva said he would retire once his successor was selected.

CNN reported on April 24, 2024 that Hamas released a video of Israeli-American hostage Hersh Goldberg-Polin, the first proof-of-life after the then-23-year-old was kidnapped at the Nova music festival. Part of his left arm was missing several inches above the hand, an injury

from when he was helping to throw grenades out of a bomb shelter that was protecting 29 people before Hamas began lobbing grenades.

UPI, BBC, Bloomberg, and *al-Jazeera* reported that on April 27, 2024, Hamas's military wing released a video of Israeli hostages Keith Siegel, 64, and Omri Miran, 47, pleading for the Israeli government to reach a deal with Hamas. They said the video was filmed two days earlier, during April 22-30 Passover. Siegel, a dual U.S.-Israeli citizen, was abducted from his home in Kibbutz Kfar Aza with his wife, Aviva Adrienne Siegel, who was released 53 days later in November 2023. Miran was abducted in front of his wife and two young daughters in Nahal Oz.

UPI reported on May 3, 2024 that the Israeli government announced the death of Hamas hostage Dror Or, 49, whose body was being held by Hamas in Gaza. Or, 49, and two of his three children, Alma, 13, and Noam, 17, were among the 253 Israelis and foreign citizens who were abducted. His wife, Yonat, was killed. Alma and Noam were released in November 2023 during a brief cease-fire.

BBC reported on May 3, 2024 that the body of Elyakim Libman, a hostage thought to have been abducted by Hamas, was found in Israel. He was working as a security guard at the Nova festival. He was last seen trying to help two badly-injured women.

ABC News reported that on May 7, 2024, the Israeli government declared hostage Lior Rudaeff, 61, dead. The volunteer ambulance driver was married to his wife, Yaffa, for 38 years. They had four children: Noam, Nadav, Bar, and Ben.

BBC and *al-Jazeera* reported that on May 11, 2024 Hamas claimed that British-Israeli hostage Nadav Popplewell, 51, died of wounds sustained in an Israeli airstrike more than a month ago. He was seized from the Nirim kibbutz with his mother Channah Peri, who was released in November 2023; the terrorists killed his brother Roi. The al-Qassam Brigades released an 11-second video showing Popplewell with a bruised eye.

The *Jerusalem Post* and *CNN* reported on May 17, 2024 that the IDF recovered from a tunnel in Gaza the bodies of three hostages who were killed at the Nova Music Festival. Hamas took their bodies into Gaza.

- Fashion stylist Amit Buskila, 28, was kidnapped while she was on the phone with her Uncle Shimon. She tried to hide between cars. Her uncle heard her pleading with her attackers: "No, no, no," before she uttered, "I love you" as the line went dead. She had her birthday in captivity.

- Shani Louk, 23, a German-Israeli woman who was declared dead by the Israeli Ministry of Foreign Affairs in late October after forensic examiners found a bone fragment from her skull. Her dead body was seen on video on the back of a Hamas truck.

- Itshak Gelernter, 57

CNN reported on May 18, 2024 that the IDF received the body of hostage Ron Benjamin, who was killed on October 7 at the Mefalsim intersection during the Hamas attack. Hamas had abducted his body and took it to Gaza.

The *Washington Post* reported that on May 22, 2024, that the families of five female Israeli soldiers taken hostage by Hamas at the Nahal Oz outpost released three minutes of Hamas body-cam footage of the hostages' first minutes of captivity, surrounded by gunmen in military fatigues shoving them into the vehicles that took them to Gaza. Among those injured, their legs streaked with blood, in the video clips were:

- Naama Levy, 19, who had participated in an Israeli-Palestinian peace project

- Liri Albag

- Agam Berger

Among the seven female soldiers were abducted alive from Nahal Oz was Ori Megadish, whom the IDF rescued on October 30, 2024, and Noa Marciano, whose body was retrieved in November from Gaza City's al-Shifa Hospital.

CNN and *NBC News* reported on May 24, 2024 that the IDF and the Israel Security Agency announced that they had identified the bodies of three other hostages: Hanan Yablonka, 42, Brazilian-Israeli Michel Nisenbaum, 59, and French-Mexican national Orion Hernan-

dez-Radoux, 30, in Jabalya. The three died at the Mefalsim intersection near the border with Gaza. Hamas had taken their bodies into Gaza. Hernandez-Radoux, 30, was the partner of Shani Louk, 23, whose body was recovered from Gaza earlier in May. He had resided in Mexico and left behind a young daughter. Nisenbaum was the father of two daughters from Sderot. He was taken hostage as he tried to rescue his 4-year-old granddaughter who was with her father in the area of Re'im. Yablonka was the father of two children from Tel Aviv. He was taken hostage from the Nova music festival, which he had attended with friends.

The *Washington Post* ran a long feature on June 1, 2024 regarding the experiences of former hostage Moran Stella Yanai, 40, a designer and an artist, who kept the hostages' plight in the public eye by meeting with activists, diplomats and the U.N. secretary general. She was captured three times on October 7. She was selling her handmade jewelry at the Nova music festival. She fled from the initial Hamas terrorist wave for five hours, running through potato fields and stretches of desert. She was caught, and the captors live-streamed a video showing Moran begging for her life in a ditch. "This is one of the Jewish dogs," a man narrates. She convinced them that she was Arab, using her limited Arabic vocabulary and pointing to her necklace, which had her middle name, Stella, in Arabic font — a gift from an Egyptian friend. They released her. A second group captured and freed her after she told the same tale. She tried to hide in a tree, but fell and fractured her ankle in two places. Thirteen other terrorists captured her. She was taken to a Gaza hospital, then was moved from house to house for seven weeks. On her second day in Gaza, an IDF bomb shattered a window of her room. She is half Egyptian and half Moroccan. She was released to Israel on November 29, 2023. She had lost 17 pounds, 12 percent of her body weight, and lost most of her hearing. She was diagnosed with complex regional pain syndrome, a rare chronic condition. She attended funerals for other hostages, including Itay Svirsky, 38, who was with her in the last place she was held and whom Israeli authorities declared dead in January 2024.

UPI reported on June 3, 2024 that medical officials from Israel's National Institute of Forensic Medicine and Shura military base identified the body of Dolev Yehud, 35, who was presumed to have been taken hostage by Hamas in Kibbutz Nir Oz along with his sister, Arbel Yehud, 28, who remains in Hamas custody in Gaza. Bring Our People Home added that Dolev Yehud, father of four, was a volunteer with Israel's national emergency services Magen David Adom and United Hatzalah.

CNN reported on June 3, 2024 that the IDF told the families of Chaim Peri, Yoram Metzger, Amiram Cooper, and Nadav Popplewell "who were brutally abducted to the Gaza Strip on October 7, that they are no longer alive and that their bodies are held by the Hamas terrorist organization."

Chief spokesperson for the IDF, Rear Admiral Daniel Hagari, said they "were killed a few months ago during Hamas captivity in Gaza … while together in the area of Khan Younis during an operation there against Hamas." In May, Hamas said Popplewell, an Israeli-British citizen, had died from an Israeli airstrike.

Al-Jazeera, the *Washington Post*, and the *New York Times* reported on June 8, 2024 that the IDF rescued Nova music festival hostages Chinese-born Noa Argamani, 25 or 26; Almog Meir Jan, 21 or 22; Andrey Kozlov, 27; and Shlomi Ziv, 40 or 41, from Nuseirat in central Gaza while killing 274 Palestinians. (The Hamas-run Gaza government media office said they included 64 children and 57 women.) They were rescued in two separate locations then flown to safety in two helicopters. Israeli police special forces Chief Inspector Arnon Zamora was killed in the 11 a.m. rescue mission. The *Washington Post, Axios,* and the *New York Times* reported that U.S. special operations and intelligence officers had provided drone imagery to the IDF. *BBC* and *Kan* reported on June 10, 2024 that freed hostage Almog Meir Jan's father Yossi died of an apparent heart attack a day before he could be reunited with his son.

CNN reported on July 1, 2024 that the Anti-Defamation League and the Crowell & Moring law firm, representing more than 100 U.S. victims and their families, filed a lawsuit in the U.S. District Court in Washington, D.C., accusing Iran, Syria, and North Korea of providing material support to Hamas. The lawsuit cited training, weapons and financial support from Iran; training and financing from Syria; and weapons and tunnel-digging know-how from North Korea.

CNN and the *Washington Post* reported on July 12, 2024 that rescued hostage and Russian-Israeli citizen Andrey Kozlov, 27, who was kidnapped while serving as a security guard at the Nova music festival, was psychologically and physically abused by Hamas while in captivity. He was kept with two other hostages, Almog Meir Jan and Shlomi Ziv. He was tied with rope and later held in chains.

CNN reported on July 13, 2024 that Israel conducted an air strike in southern Gaza targeting Mohammed Diab Ibrahim al-Masri, alias el Deif (the Guest), alias Mohammed Deif, leader of Hamas's military wing, the Qassam Brigades, and the head of the Khan Younis brigade, Rafe Salama, in the al-Mawasi displacement camp west of Khan Younis. Some 90 Palestinians were killed and 300 wounded. *BBC* reported that Hamas claimed 141 were killed. *Politico* reported on July 14 that Hamas said Deif was in good health. *CNN* reported on July 15, 2024 that the IDF claimed that Rafe Salama was killed. The *New York Times* reported that he was born in 1965 and grew up in Khan Younis. He may be missing an eye and some limbs; Israel bombed his home in 2014, killing his wife and infant son. He commanded the Shadow Brigade, which guards Israeli captives.

Al-Jazeera reported on July 22, 2024 that the IDF confirmed that captives Alex Dancyg, 75, and Yagev Buchstav, 35, who were taken by Hamas fighters from their homes near the Gaza fence, were dead. They might have been killed by Israeli fire in southern Khan Younis several months earlier. Their bodies were not recovered. Hamas announced their death in March 2024, saying Buchstav died due to lack of food and medicine, and Dancyg was killed by Israeli military attacks. Buchshtav's wife, Rimon Kirsht Buchshtav, was kidnapped, then released on November 28, 2023.

The *Times of Israel* reported that on July 24, 2024, the IDF recovered the bodies of Ravid Katz, 51, Oren Goldin, 33, Maya Goren, 56, Sgt.

Kiril Brodski, 19, and Staff Sgt. Tomer Yaakov Ahimas, 20, who were all previously declared dead. They were found in a tunnel in Khan Younis by troops, including special forces under the IDF's 98th Division and Shin Bet agents. Brodski and Ahimas were killed while serving in the forward command team of Col. Asaf Hamami, the commander of the Gaza Division's Southern Brigade, who was also killed as they tried to fight off dozens of Hamas terrorists invading kibbutz Nirim. Goldin ran Kibbutz Nir Yitzhak's mechanic shop. Goren, 56, from Nir Oz, was setting up the kibbutz's kindergarten. Her husband, Avner, 56, was murdered inside the couple's home during the attack. Katz was a member of the Kibbutz Nir Oz security team.

USA Today reported on July 29, 2024 that former hostage Maya Regev, who was released in November, said Gazan doctors purposely caused pain, and would "take chlorine, alcohol, and sometimes even something like apple cider vinegar and would pour it in (the wound) and apply pressure."

Israel announced on August 1, 2024 that it was responsible for the July 13, 2024 airstrike that killed Mohammed Diab Ibrahim al-Masri, alias el Deif (the Guest), alias Mohammed Deif, leader of Hamas's military wing, the Qassam Brigades, who was believed to be the mastermind of the October 7 massacre. *USA Today* reported that he had survived seven previous assassination attempts.

AP reported on August 5, 2024 that the U.N. Secretary General's office announced that it fired nine staff members from its UNRWA agency for Palestinian refugees after an internal investigation found they may have been involved in the October 7 attack. The nine included seven staffers who were fired previously over the claims.

Meanwhile, on the same day, *AP* reported that hundreds of Israelis celebrated the fifth birthday of Ariel Bibas, who with his brother Kfir, 1, were held captive by Hamas. The boys and their parents Shiri and Yarden Bibas were kidnapped from Kibbutz Nir Oz. Photos suggested that Yarden, who was taken separately, was wounded. Orange has come to represent the Bibas family across Israel.

Al-Jazeera reported that on August 12, 2024 Abu Obeida, a spokesman for the al-Qassam Brigades, the armed wing of Hamas, announced that an Israeli captive was killed in Gaza and two female captives were seriously injured in a separate incident. He said on *Telegram* that guards killed the Israeli hostage. Meanwhile, Gaza's Ministry of Health claimed that 39,897 people have been killed and 92,152 wounded since October. The Ministry reported on August 15, 2024 that the death toll had passed 40,000.

The *New York Times* on August 14, 2024 ran "Portraits of Survival: The Israeli Hostages Who Made It Home."

CNN reported on August 20, 2024 that the IDF announced the retrieval from Khan Younis tunnels of the bodies of hostages Yoram Metzger, 80; Alexander Dancyg, Avraham Munder, 79, Chaim Peri, 80; Nadav Popplewell, 51; and Yagev Buchshtab, 35. All but Munder had been pronounced dead earlier. Munder, Metzger, and Periwere residents of Kibbutz Nir Oz.

Munder was taken along with his wife, daughter, and grandson, who were later freed in November 2023. Munder's son, Roee, was killed during the attack. Metzger's wife Tami was kidnapped and later released in the November truce. Popplewell and Buchshtab were taken from Kibbutz Nirim. In May 2024, the al-Qassam Brigades claimed dual British-Israeli citizen Popplewell had died more than a month earlier of wounds he sustained after an Israeli airstrike. The IDF said he was believed to have been held in Khan Younis and died several months ago. *AP* reported on August 23, 2024 that the IDF confirmed that gunshot wounds were found on the bodies of the six Israeli hostages. Hamas had used a false wall to hide the bodies. Four bodies, possibly of Hamas members, were found next to the hostages with no signs of gunfire. *Ynet* had earlier reported that the IDF was investigating the possibility that the hostages suffocated to death as a result of a fire started during an IDF airstrike in the area.

On August 21, 2024, Jon Polin and Rachel Goldberg, parents of American-Israeli hostage Hersh Goldberg-Polin, addressed the Democratic National Convention's third evening.

On August 27, 2024, *AP,* Israel's *Channel 12, BBC,* and *CNN* reported that the IDF and Shin Bet rescued hostage Kaid Farhan al-Qadi, 52, a Bedouin father of 11 and husband of two wives, in a "complex operation" in southern Gaza. The first-time grandfather was working as a guard at a packing factory in Kibbutz Magen.

UPI reported on August 28, 2024 that the IDF announced that it had recovered the body of an Israeli soldier who had been taken into Gaza during the attack.

NPR reported on September 1, 2024 that the IDF recovered the bodies of six hostages from a tunnel in Rafah, Gaza. The IDF said they were "brutally" murdered an hour before they were found. CNN identified them as:

- Hersh Goldberg-Polin, 23, an Israeli-American, and his friends from the Nova festival were hiding inside a small bomb shelter. Hamas threw grenades into it; he threw several out before one blew off his arm from the elbow down. His parents, Jon Polin and Rachel Goldberg-Polin, addressed the Democratic National Convention in August 2024. Hersh was born in Oakland, California. The family immigrated to Israel when he was 7.

- Alexander Lobanov, 32, father of a two-year-old and a five-month-old, hailed from Ashkelon and was working as a bar manager at the Nova festival. He helped evacuate people at the festival and ran with five others into the Be'eri forest; he was captured by Hamas. His younger child was born while he was in captivity.

- Carmel Gat, 40, from Tel Aviv, was staying at her parents' home in Be'eri when Hamas broke in at 10 a.m. and forcibly took her away. After 50 days, released hostages told her family that the occupational therapist taught them meditation and yoga to help them endure.

- Almog Sarusi, 27, and his girlfriend of five years were at the Nova festival. While trying to escape by car with friends, she was shot and severely injured. He stayed by her side, but she died.

- Eden Yerushalmi, 24, from Tel Aviv, was working as a bartender at the Nova festival. She sent a video of rocket fire to her family group chat. She was studying to become a Pilates instructor.

- Ori Danino, 25, a Jerusalem native and eldest of five siblings, planned to study electrical engineering. She was kidnapped at the Nova festival while driving back to assist others.

Hersh Goldberg-Polin, Eden Yerushalmi, and Carmel Gat were slated to be released as part of the "humanitarian category" based on the framework Israel and Hamas agreed to in early July 2024.

CNN reported on September 3, 2024 that the U.S. Department of Justice unsealed an indictment that charged several Hamas leaders over the October 7 attack.

CNN later added that the U.S. Department of Justice charged Hamas leaders Ismail Haniyeh, Yahya Sinwar, Mohammad al-Masri alias Mohammed Deif, Marwan Issa, Khaled Meshaal, and Ali Baraka on seven counts for the October 7 massacre, including terrorism, conspiracy to murder U.S. nationals, and conspiracy to use weapons of mass destruction resulting in death. The charges were originally filed on February 1, 2024, but kept under seal. Three of the Hamas leaders (Haniyeh, Deif, and Issa) charged are deceased.

The same day, *CNN* reported that Hamas had given the terrorists guarding the Israeli hostages in buildings and tunnels "new instructions" to kill them if the IDF closed in. Hamas released a comic-book style image of a kneeling figure threatened with a gun, followed by a video of Eden Yerushalmi. It released a second video of another murdered hostage, Ori Danino.

Al-Jazeera reported on September 15, 2024 that the IDF announced that there is a "high probability" its November 10, 2023 air strike killed three Israeli captives in a tunnel in Gaza. The bodies of Corporal Nik Beizer, Sergeant Ron Sherman, and French-Israeli national Elia Toledano were recovered on December 14, 2023. The air strike also killed Hamas Northern Brigade commander Ahmed Ghandour.

UPI and the *Times of Israel* reported on October 7, 2024 that the Hostages and Missing families Forum announced that Hamas hostage Idan Shativ, 28, one of the dozens of Israelis kidnapped by Hamas during the assault on the Nova music festival, was killed during the attack. Hamas took his body into Gaza. Shativ left behind his parents, Eli and Dali, three brothers, and partner, Stav.

AP reported that on October 7, 2024, vandals in Milan, Italy, defaced the mural "October 7th, Escape" by AleXsandro Palombo, depicting Vlada Patapov escaping the Hamas attacks. Vandals erased the figure's head and legs from the mural near Milan's state university.

The *Times of Israel* and *NPR* reported on November 14, 2024 that the Palestinian Islamic Jihad released its third proof of life video of Russian hostage Sasha Trufanov. In the clip, he said he was 28, although the video was released two days after his 29th birthday. He was taken hostage from Kibbutz Nir Oz with three members of his family—grandmother Irena Tati, mother Yelena (Lena) Trufanova, and girlfriend Sapir Cohen. Trufanova and Tati were released by Hamas on November 29, 2023 at the request of Russian President Vladimir Putin. Cohen was released on November 30, 2023 during a temporary ceasefire between Israel and Hamas. Sasha Trufanov is an engineer employed at Annapurna Labs, an Israeli microelectronics company purchased by Amazon.

CNN reported that on November 19, 2024 that Israeli Prime Minister Benjamin Netanyahu offered $5 million and safe passage out of Gaza to anyone returning a hostage.

Al-Jazeera reported on November 23, 2024, that al-Qassam Brigades spokesman Abu Obeida said a female captive was killed in an Israeli strike in northern Gaza. He did not specify when/where she was killed nor give her name. *NBC News* reported on November 24 that Hamas released video purporting to show her body.

Al-Jazeera reported on November 28, 2024 that Fursan al-Aqsa: The Knights of the Al-Aqsa Mosque, released in 2022, a computer game that allows users to recreate aspects of the October 7 attack was removed from the popular gaming platform *Steam* in the United Kingdom at the request of Metropolitan Police counter-terrorism police. Gamers are the first-person fictional character Ahmad al-Falastini, a young Palestinian student who takes revenge on Israeli soldiers who tortured him and killed his family. An updated version of the game called Operation al-Aqsa Flood, the name Hamas uses for its October 7, 2023 attack, was released on *Steam* in November 2024. In one scene, the main character enters Israel's Re'im military base via a motorized hang glider. Fighters attack Israeli soldiers and vehicles and execute a line of unarmed soldiers with shots to the back of the head. Operation al-Aqsa Flood has age restrictions in Germany and Australia.

CNN reported on November 30, 2024 that Hamas released a video of Israeli-American hostage Edan Alexander begging the Israeli Prime Minister Benjamin Netanyahu leader and U.S. President-elect Donald Trump for his release.

CNN added on November 30, 2024 that an Israeli airstrike on a car in the Gaza Strip killed five people, including employees of World Central Kitchen, in a strike the IDF said targeted WCK worker Ahed Azmi Qdeih, alias Hazmi Kadih, who was part of the Hamas attack on kibbutz Nir Oz.

On December 2, 2024, *UPI*, the *Washington Post,* and *AP* reported that IDF officials now believed that armored corps tank platoon commander Captain Omer Neutra, 21, originally from Long Island, New York was killed during the attack on Nir Oz. He was earlier thought held hostage. His grandparents were Holocaust survivors.

Al-Jazeera reported on December 2, 2024 that Hamas said that 33 captives held by the group in Gaza have been killed since the start of the war.

USA Today reported that on December 2, 2024, President-elect Donald Trump warned in a social media post that "there will be ALL HELL TO PAY in the Middle East, and for those in charge who perpetrated these atrocities against Humanity" if the hostages were not released prior to his January 20, 2025 inauguration.

BBC reported on December 3, 2024 that Mandy Damari, mother of Emily Damari, 28, the only British-Israeli hostage, feared for her child's life. Hamas gunmen shot Emily and killed her dog when they attacked Kibbutz Kfar Aza.

UPI reported on December 5, 2024 that the IDF and Shin Bet recovered the body of Itay Svirsky, 38, an Israeli hostage held by Hamas in Gaza for more than a year. He had been visiting his parents in Kibbutz Be'eri. In January 2024, Hamas claimed in a video that an Israeli strike on Gaza had killed Svirsky and hostage Yossi Sharabi, 53.

UPI reported on December 6, 2024 that the IDF announced that an airstrike killed Majdi Aqilan, commander of the Hamas Shatti Battalion, who led the attack on Kibbutz Nahal Oz in which 66 soldiers defending a base there, along with 15 civilians, were killed. Aqilan later participated in attacks targeting IDF forces in north and central Gaza. The IDF also killed Mehdoh Mahana, who served as a senior member of the Hamas's Gaza Brigade tunneling unit, during the week-long operation. He was part of the raid on Nahal Oz. Also killed was Ahmed Suidan, a Shatti Battalion company commander who was involved in the kidnapping of Israeli citizens and their transfer into Gaza.

AP reported that Hannah Katzir, 78, a former hostage who was freed in November 2023, died on December 23, 2024. Her husband, Rami, was killed during the attack on their home in Kibbutz Nir Oz. Her son Elad was also kidnapped and his body was recovered in April by the IDF, who said he had been killed in captivity.

BBC reported on December 25, 2024 that an IDF investigation found that IDF "ground activities in the area, although gradual and cautious, had a circumstantial influence on the terrorists' decision to murder the six hostages" in August 2024 in Rafah in Gaza. The soldiers were unaware of the presence in an underground shaft in the Tal al-Sultan area of Alex Lobanov, Eden Yerushalmi, Almog Sarusi, Master Sgt Ori Danino, Hersh Goldberg-Polin, and Carmel Gat.

CNN reported on December 25, 2024 that dual Israeli-American citizen Yona Brief lost both legs in the attack, was put into medically induced comas, and ultimately died of liver failure at age 23 in late November 2024 after 417 days of fighting to survive. He was shot 13 times while defending fellow soldiers in Kibbutz Kfar Aza. He became a symbol of the sacrifice of 800 fallen IDF soldiers in the Gaza/Lebanon conflict. Thousands of others were wounded, many seriously. He had earlier been seriously wounded in his legs by a pipe bomb during a commando raid in the West Bank. The October 7 weekend was his first on duty after his recovery. He underwent more than 20 surgeries and received more than 200 units of blood. Some 45,000 Palestinians died in Gaza; another 3,500 in Lebanon.

October 12, 2023: *Al-Jazeera* and *AFP* reported that two Israeli police officers were wounded, one seriously, when a gunman, 20, from East Jerusalem fired on them in front of Shalem police station near the Old City. The gunman was killed in a crossfire.

October 15, 2023: *Reuters* reported that Lebanese Hizballah launched a missile at Shtula, a farming community that abuts the border fence opposite the Lebanese community of Ayta a-Shab, killing one person and wounding three others.

October 30, 2023: *UPI* reported that a Palestinian stabbed and seriously wounded an Israeli border patrol officer near the Shivtei Israel light rail station in Jerusalem's Old City. Police opened fire and killed the suspect. The officer was transported by ambulance to Shaare Zedek Medical Center, where doctors treated him for a wound to his upper body.

November 13, 2023: *NBC News* reported that a terrorist critically injured a police officer outside the Shalem police station on Salah al-Din Street near the Herod's Gate entrance to Jerusalem's Old City. The *Times of Israel* reported that Israeli-American Sergeant Rose Elisheva Lubin, 20, died from her stab wounds. Other Border Police shot the Palestinian attacker, 16, dead; he lived in East Jerusalem's Issawiya neighborhood. Lubin lived in Kibbutz Sa'ad in southern Israel. She had moved to Israel from the United States in August 2021, and was drafted to police as a "lone soldier" in March 2022. A second officer was moderately wounded. A second suspect was detained.

November 26, 2023: *UPI* and *Haaretz* reported that the Tel Aviv-based software company Wix created a website to spread anti-Hamas propaganda during the war in Gaza. The Palestinian group's actual website, Hamas.ps, was offline. Indian Cyber Force hackers posted to *X* in October 2023 that they had taken down Hamas.ps. GoDaddy reported that Wix registered Hamas.com, which had been parked by cybersquatters since about 2000, after its creation in December 1999. Hamas.shop and hamas.life remained available to purchase. The new website, oct7map.com, included an interactive online map of where Israelis were killed or kidnapped. Hamas-massacre.net showed graphic videos and images to "document the horrors of that day".

November 30, 2023: *CNN, AP, Army Radio,* and *Reuters* reported that at 7:40 a.m., two brothers fired on cars, buses, and people at a Jerusalem bus stop, killing three, including a 24-year-old woman, and injuring seven. Hamas said they were members of its military wing, the al-Qassam Brigades. Jerusalem District Commander Doron Turgeman said two soldiers and a civilian killed the attackers. Hamas called the attack "a direct response to the unprecedented crimes committed by the occupying forces, including brutal massacres in the Gaza Strip, the killing of children in Jenin, and widespread violations against Palestinian prisoners. Moreover, the continued violations in the Al-Aqsa Mosque and the prevention of worshippers' access to it." Police said that the two gunmen drove toward the bus stop armed with a handgun and an M16 rifle and opened fire. In 2022, a bomb exploded at the same bus stop, killing a boy, 16, and wounding 18.

December 3, 2023: *CNN* reported that an anti-tank missile was fired toward an IDF vehicle in Beit Hillel, lightly injuring several Israeli soldiers. The IDF identified several missile launches in the Har Dov area, also known as Shebaa Farms, some of which fell inside Lebanese territory. Hizballah claimed that it targeted several

sites, including the Shebaa Farms, in "support of our steadfast Palestinian people in the Gaza Strip".

December 16, 2023: *CNN* reported that an IDF soldier was killed and two others injured in a drone attack by Hizballah that hit Israeli troops in the Margaliot area near the Lebanese border. One drone was intercepted, but the other hit IDF soldiers.

December 26, 2023: *Al-Jazeera* reported that Houthi military spokesman Yahya Sarea claimed his group conducted drone attacks targeting the Israeli port city of Eilat and launched missiles at the *MSC United VIII* vessel in the Red Sea.

January 14, 2024: *Reuters* reported that the IDF fired artillery and mortars, killing four Palestinians attempting to cross from Lebanon into Israel. *AP* reported that the Islamic Glory Brigades claimed credit. Hamas and Palestinian Islamic Jihad said they were not affiliated.

January 15, 2024: *Fox News, AP,* and *NPR* reported that Israel woman Mira Ayalon, in her 70s, and her son Barak, in his 40s, were killed when their home in Kfar Yuval was hit by anti-tank missile near the Lebanon border.

January 15, 2024: *Fox, CNN,* and the *Jerusalem Post* reported that a terrorist stabbed a woman, carjacked her white sedan, and crashed into pedestrians in Ra'anana, north of Tel Aviv, injuring 16 people, three seriously. One woman in her 70s later died of her injuries. Central District commander Avi Biton announced that police arrested two individuals from the same family in the Hebron area of the West Bank, who worked nearby. Police said they entered Israel illegally. Hamas claimed credit.

January 21, 2024: Hizballah said that it had launched an attack against Avivim in northern Israel in retaliation for the Kafra, Lebanon strike. The IDF said that an anti-tank missile had hit a house in Avivim; no injuries were reported.

February 1, 2024: *CNN* reported that the U.S. Department of state imposed financial and travel sanctions against four Israelis—David Chai Chasdai, Einan Tanjil, Shalom Zicherman, and

Yinon Levi—for violence against and intimidation of residents of the West Bank, such as initiating and leading a riot; setting buildings, fields and vehicles on fire; assaulting civilians; and damaging property.

February 14, 2024: *CNN* and *Israel Channel 12* reported that rockets fired from Lebanon on Safed killed one person and injured eight. Hizballah was suspected.

February 16, 2024: *UPI* reported that a gunman fired on a bus stop on Highway 40 near Bnei Re'em, killing two people and wounding six, one critically, three seriously, two moderately, before a passing civilian motorist shot and killed the attacker. The killer was from east Jerusalem with Israeli residency.

February 22, 2024: *AP* and *ABC News* reported that the IDF's Arrow missile defense system intercepted a suspected Houthi missile attack near Eilat.

March 4, 2024: *CNN* reported that in the morning, an anti-tank missile landed in northern Israel, killing a foreign worker and injuring seven others, two seriously, in the Margaliot area on the border with Lebanon. Two of the victims were Thai workers. All of the injured were men in their 30s.

March 13, 2024: *CNN* reported that IDF troops shot to death two Palestinians and wounded three others at the al-Jib checkpoint in the northern outskirts of Jerusalem. The IDF said the Palestinians had thrown Molotov cocktails over a security barrier fence onto Route 436, which runs from the Ramot neighborhood in occupied east Jerusalem to the Israeli settlement Givat Ze'ev. The IDF said they apprehended the Palestinians and transferred them for medical treatment. The dead Palestinians were Zaid Ward Shukri Khalifa, 23, and Abdullah Mamoun Hassan Assaf, 16.

March 31, 2024: *UPI* reported that during the night, a terrorist with two knives seriously injured three men, aged 25, 20 and 17, at the Friendly Shopping Mall in Gan Yanve, six miles east of Ashdod. A policeman and an inspector

of the Gan Yavne municipal police department shot and killed the terrorist, who had tackled a police officer.

In dawn raids, police arrested Bedouin suspects believed to have driven the attacker to the mall. Police said the terrorist was a Palestinian male, 19, from Dura in the West Bank, residing in Israel without residence permits.

Earlier that day, authorities shot to death a terrorist, 28, of the Bedouin city of Rahat, at Beersheba central bus station who had stabbed an off-duty Israel Defense Forces officer.

April 1, 2024: *UPI* reported that police detained Sabah Haniyeh, 57, resident of Tel Sheva and sister of Hamas leader Ismail Haniyeh. Police also arrested two of her children but released them that day. *Haaretz* and *al-Jazeera* reported that on April 21, 2024, Israel's Justice Ministry charged her with incitement and identification with a terrorist group. She was accused of sending messages to her brother and other contacts that allegedly included words of praise and encouragement following the October 7, 2023 massacre.

April 17, 2024: *CNN* reported that Hizballah fired a drone from Lebanon at the northern Israeli city of Nahariya, injuring 18 people, one critically, two seriously, and four moderately. The other eleven people injured sustained minor injuries.

April 19, 2024: U.S. Department of the Treasury imposed sanctions on two entities—the Mount Hebron Fund and Shlom Asiraich—accused of fundraising for extremist Israel settlers Yinon Levi and David Chai Chasdai already sanctioned, plus the founder of an organization whose members often assault Palestinians. Treasury said the Mount Hebron Fund for Levi and by Shlom Asiraich for Chasdai generated the equivalent of $140,000 and $31,000, respectively.

Meanwhile, the U.S. Department of State designated Ben-Zion Gopstein, the founder and leader of Lehava, an organization whose members have assaulted Palestinian civilians.

April 22, 2024: A car crashed into three ultra-Orthodox pedestrians in Jerusalem's Rome-ma neighborhood, wounding them; two flew over the dashboard. Police arrested two suspects who fled and hid near a closed business.

April 25, 2024: Shortly before midnight, Lebanese Hizballah fired anti-tank missiles and artillery shells at an Israeli military convoy in a disputed area known in Lebanon as the Kfar Chouba hills and in Israel as Har Dov along the border, killing an Israeli civilian doing infrastructure work and destroying two vehicles.

April 28, 2024: *Al-Jazeera* reported that Hizballah fired dozens of rockets from Lebanon into northern Israel's Meron farming collective. Several rockets appeared to breach Israel's Iron Dome air defense system.

May 5, 2024: The *New York Times* reported that Hamas fired 14 rockets and mortars near the Rafah crossing between Gaza and Egypt toward the Kerem Shalom border crossing between Gaza and Israel, a conduit for aid into Gaza, killing three soldiers and critically wounding three soldiers. A home in the kibbutz was hit. Israeli military planes destroyed the launcher that had fired the projectiles.

May 9, 2024: *CNN* reported that the UNRWA agency for Palestinian refugees announced it would close its East Jerusalem headquarters after the compound was set on fire by "Israeli extremists" while staff were inside. No casualties were reported but extensive damage to outdoor areas was noted.

May 17, 2024: The *Jerusalem Post* reported that the brother of a terrorist who carried out an attack in 2022 was arrested on suspicion of publishing incitement and support for terrorism online.

June 6, 2024: *Al-Jazeera* reported that Houthis and the Islamic Resistance in Iraq claimed to have conducted two joint military operations with drones against ships at Israel's Haifa port. The IDF denied the claim.

June 26, 2024: Islamic Resistance in Iraq rebels allied with Houthis claimed to have fired a drone that fell off the coast of the port of Eilat.

July 3, 2024: *Al-Jazeera* reported that two men in their 20s were wounded, one severely, in a stabbing attack on the second floor of the Hutzot Karmiel Mall in Karmiel. Israeli police suspected that a Palestinian Israeli was responsible. *UPI* reported that Sgt. Aleksandr Iakiminskyi, 19, from Nahariya, a driver in the 71st Battalion, 188th Brigade, died of his wounds. The wounded soldier also served in the 71st Battalion, 188th Brigade. He disarmed and shot the terrorist, identified as Jawwad Omar Rubia, 21, an Israeli citizen from the Arab town of Nahf. Several members of Rubia's family, some who worked at the mall, were detained for questioning. Hamas said the incident was a "natural response" to ongoing events and called Rubia "one of the heroes of our people".

July 7, 2024: *CNN* reported that Hizballah fired two anti-tank missiles into northern Israel, injuring a soldier and two civilians, including an American man, 31, who was hospitalized in serious condition.

July 11, 2024: *CNN* reported that the U.S. Department of State imposed sanctions on the Israeli violent extremist organization Lehava, three Israeli individuals, and four "outposts" connected to violence in the West Bank. The State Department earlier sanctioned Lehava's founder and leader, Ben-Zion Gopstein. The Biden administration sanctioned

- Isaschar Manne and his farm outpost in the South Hebron Hills.
- Meitarim Farm
- Neriya's Farm
- Hamahoch Farm
- Reut Ben Haim and Aviad Shlomo Sarid, leaders of Tsav 9, which was sanctioned in June.

July 14, 2024: A Palestinian resident of east Jerusalem carried out a car-ramming attack at two bus stops along a busy road in central Israel, injuring four IDF members, two of them seriously. Israeli border police shot dead the attacker.

July 19, 2024: *CNN* and *AP* reported that Houthis claimed credit for an Iranian-made Samad-3 drone explosion at 3:10 a.m. at an apartment on Shalom Aleichem Street in an area of Tel Aviv's central district that houses several diplomatic missions, including a U.S. Embassy branch office 100 meters away. A man, 50, was killed and ten others were injured, four with shrapnel wounds. Houthis said the drone was a Yafa, undetectable by radar.

July 21, 2024: *CNN* and *AP* reported that the IDF said that its air defense system had intercepted a surface-to-surface missile that approached from Yemen. Houthis claimed they had launched "a number of ballistic missiles" towards Israel against "important targets" in the Umm al-Rashrash area, also called Eilat, on the coast of the Gulf of Aqaba in the Red Sea.

July 26, 2024: *AP* reported that the IDF claimed it had downed one of three rockets fired from northern Gaza into Israel.

August 4, 2024: *CNN* and *al-Jazeera* reported that a male resident, 34, of Salfit in the West Bank stabbed to death a man, 68, and a woman, 66; the latter's 80-year-old male partner was injured in Holon. Two others, including Yaakov Levertov, 26, who was walking his dog when the attacker stabbed him in the shoulder, were injured. *Al-Jazeera* reported that the attack occurred during morning rush hour near a gas station and a park. The *Washington Post* said the injured were Rina Danib, 66, who was on a morning run with her husband, Shimon, 69, who was badly wounded. The Popular Resistance Committees, an umbrella organization of armed groups, and the al-Qassam Brigades posted messages of support on their social media channels. Hamas called the attacker a "martyred hero... Hamas views this act as a natural response to ongoing Israeli occupation crimes against the Palestinian people, including brutal acts in Gaza, escalating violations in the West Bank, and the assassination of movement leader Ismail Haniych."

The *Washington Post* reported that the IDF said five rockets were launched from Gaza, sparking air raid sirens around Lachish, Ashdod, and Gan Yavne, in central Israel. One projectile fell near the Hof Ashkelon Regional Council in Nitzanim, causing no injuries.

August 18, 2024: *AP, Jerusalem Post, BBC,* and the *Washington Post* reported that Hamas and Palestinian Islamic Jihad claimed responsibility for a failed nighttime "martyrdom operation" on Lehi Street in southern Tel Aviv that killed the middle-aged Palestinian man carrying the bomb and moderately wounded in the limbs and chest a bystander, 33. The suicide bomber was seen on video walking down the street wearing a large backpack, perhaps en route to a nearby synagogue where dozens of people were praying. The two groups threatened more attacks "as long as the occupation's massacres, displacement of civilians, and the continuation of the assassination policy continues."

September 15, 2024: *NPR* and *CNN* reported that at 6 a.m., Houthis fired a "new hypersonic ballistic missile" from Yemen into an open field. A fragment landed on an escalator of a train station in Modi'in, a city between Tel Aviv and Jerusalem. The IDF said the missile "most likely fragmented in mid-air", causing no injuries. An interceptor fragment fell in the Shfela area, aka the Judean Foothills.

September 17, 2024: The *New York Times* reported that Israel accused Hizballah of attempting to assassinate Moshe Yaalon, a retired military chief of staff and defense minister, with a bomb that could be remotely detonated from Lebanon.

September 19, 2024: *UPI* and the *Times of Israel* reported that Jewish Israeli businessman Moti Maman, 73, appeared in court in southern Israel in connection with an alleged Iranian plot to assassinate senior Israeli leaders, including Prime Minister Benjamin Netanyahu, former Prime Minister and Defense Minister Naftali Bennett, Defense Minister Yoav Gallant, and domestic security chief Ronen Bar. He allegedly was twice smuggled across the Iranian border from Türkiye. Shin Bet and Israeli police said that Iranians suggested Maman recruit Americans or Russians to kill Iranian critics of the regime living in Europe and the United States and also to try to recruit a Mossad operative to work as a double agent. Mamen allegedly requested a $1 million advance but received only a one-off $5,580 payment for attending the meetings. He was represented by attorney Eyel Besserglick.

October 1, 2024: *AP, Times of Israel, Channel 11, CNN, Express,* and *UPI* reported on a day when Iran and Hizballah were raining missiles down on Israeli targets (Iran alone fired 200 missiles), *CNN* reported that two terrorists armed with an M16, cartridges and a knife killed seven and wounded 16, some critically, in a 7 p.m. spree near a light rail station in Tel Aviv's Jaffa neighborhood. The attack began in a rail carriage and continued on the platform. Images posted on social media showed the gunman shooting at bystanders in the Jaffa area. Members of the public "neutralized" the terrorists, who were from Hebron. *UPI* claimed police shot the duo when they exited the train.

CNN reported on October 2 that Lev Kreitman, a former October 7 hostage, was hailed as a "hero" after firing a handgun at the shooters near his home. He was attacked by Hamas at the Nova music festival. He had served for six months in Gaza as a reservist with the IDF.

The *Washington Post* reported on October 2 that Hamas claimed responsibility for its armed wing, the Izzedine al-Qassam Brigades. Police identified the terrorists as Muhammad Masek, 19, who was killed at the scene, and Ahmed Himoni, 25, who was seriously injured. The duo were armed with an M16 weapon, cartridges, and a knife.

Eyewitnesses told Magen David paramedics Omri Gorga and Noam Eliyof that a railcar was hit by gunfire as it traveled along Jerusalem Boulevard before stopping at Makhrozet Street.

October 6, 2024: *CNN* and *BBC* reported that police killed a gunman who killed border police sergeant Shira Chaya Suslik, 19, and injured ten people at a bus station in Be'er Sheva. Transport Minister Miri Regev called for the families of "terrorists" to be deported.

October 6, 2024: *UPI, New York Times,* and the *Times of Israel* reported that five people were injured by shrapnel in a nighttime barrage of five rockets from Lebanon aimed at Haifa that hit a restaurant, a house, and a main road. A fifth

person hurt in a separate rocket strike on Tiberias. Hizballah said it fired Fadi 1 missiles at a military base south of Haifa, Kfar Vradim, and Karmiel, northeast of Haifa. Karmiel took two direct hits, damaging more than 60 apartments, 20 cars, and five EV buses.

Hamas fired ten rockets from the Gaza Strip. Five of them hit Tel Aviv, slightly injuring two women.

October 9, 2024: *CNN* reported that in the afternoon, Hizballah fired 90 rockets into the Upper Galilee, Western Galilee, and southern Golan Heights, killing a couple who were walking their dogs in Kiryat Shmona. Another rocket damaged an ambulance. Six people were injured after rockets hit Krayot near Haifa.

October 13, 2024: The *Times of Israel* reported that two Hizballah Mirsad (known in Iran as the Ababil-T) drone strikes in the Binyamina area injured 67 people, four critically, five seriously, 14 moderately. Israeli radar picked up the two drones; the IDF shot down one off the coast north of Haifa. The second dropped off the radar, flying close to the ground. *CNN* and *NPR* reported that four IDF soldiers were killed and seven others wounded in a Hizballah drone attack on an army base in central Israel. Hizballah said it targeted the IDF's Golani Brigade.

October 19, 2024: *AP* and *UPI* reported that the government said Hizballah launched three drones from Lebanon in the morning at the residence of Prime Minister Benjamin Netanyahu in Caesarea in an apparent assassination attempt. Two were knocked down, the third hit the house. No casualties were reported. Neither he nor his wife were at home.

Hizballah fired another 180 projectiles in two separate morning barrages at northern Israel from Lebanon. A man, 50, was killed after being hit by shrapnel while sitting in his car in northern Israel.

October 23, 2024: *AP, Sky News,* and *USA Today* reported that Hizballah fired two projectiles at the Tel Aviv hotel in which U.S. Secretary of State Antony Blinken was staying. Israeli air defenses downed the missiles while hotel guests, including Blinken, sheltered downstairs.

October 27, 2024: *NPR, Reuters, Ynet, BBC,* and *AP* reported that at 10 a.m., a truck driven by Arab Israeli citizen Rami Natur from Qalansawe in central Israel crashed into the Glilot Junction bus stop in Ramat Hasharon, northeast of Tel Aviv, outside a military base and near the headquarters of Mossad, killing a man and wounding more than 30 people, six seriously, who were returning to work after a weeklong holiday. Eight people were stuck under the truck. Many of the injured were retirees on a day trip to a nearby museum. A civilian shot the driver to death. Hamas and Islamic Jihad praised the apparent attack but did not claim credit.

AP reported that a drone and a projectile fired from Lebanon wounded five people. 24102701

November 17, 2024: During the night, two flares were fired at Prime Minister Benjamin Netanyahu's private residence in the coastal city of Caesarea, causing no injuries. The family was not at the residence. Police arrested three suspects.

December 9, 2024: *Al-Jazeera* reported that Yemeni Houthis claimed to have conducted a drone attack in Tel Aviv area in "a specific military operation". The IDF said a drone hit a building in Yavne after air defence systems failed to detect it and an investigation into the failure is under way. No injuries were reported although several apartments were damaged.

December 19, 2024: *CNN* reported that the IDF conducted airstrikes against Houthi targets at a port and oil facility near Sanaa, Yemen hours after the group fired missiles and drones at Israeli targets. An Israeli school was damaged but no one was injured.

December 21, 2024: Houthis fired a rocket from Yemen that hit Tel Aviv at 4 a.m., slightly injuring 16 people with flying glass. Another 14 were slightly injured as they rushed to shelters. Houthis claimed on *Telegram* that the hypersonic ballistic missile was aimed at a military target; it landed in a playground.

December 24, 2024: The IDF's air defense system intercepted a projectile launched from Ye-

men at Israel during the night. A woman, 60, was seriously wounded after being hurt on her way to a protected space.

December 30, 2024: The IDF shot down a missile fired toward the country by Yemen's Houthi rebels.

JORDAN

January 28, 2024: *CNN* reported that a nighttime drone attack on Tower 22, a small U.S. outpost near the border with Syria, killed three U.S. troops and injured 47 service members, some with traumatic brain injuries. The drone apparently followed a U.S. drone back to the base. *NPR* and the *Washington Post* reported that the Islamic Resistance in Iraq, an umbrella group that includes Kataib Hizballah, Harakat Hizballah al-Nujaba and other Iranian-backed terrorists, claimed credit. Iran denied involvement. *CNN* reported on January 29 that the Pentagon identified the dead U.S. soldiers as interior electrician Sgt. William Jerome Rivers, 46, of Carrollton, Georgia and Willingboro, New Jersey; Specialist Kennedy Ladon Sanders, 24, of Waycross, Georgia; and Specialist Breonna Alexsondria Moffett, 23, of Savannah, Georgia. Pentagon Deputy Press Secretary Sabrina Singh said that they were all assigned to the 718th Engineer Company, a U.S. Army Reserve unit based out of Fort Moore, Georgia. U.S. authorities cast doubt on Kataib Hizballah's announcement of a ceasefire against U.S. forces.

Military.com reported on January 31 that the Army Reserve posthumously promoted Sanders and Moffett to the rank of sergeant.

- Sanders enlisted in the Army Reserve in 2019 as a horizontal construction engineer. She deployed in 2021 for an eight-month rotation to Djibouti in support of Operation Enduring Freedom. Awards included an Army Service Ribbon, an Overseas Service Ribbon, and the Armed Forces Reserve Medal with "M" device.

- Moffett enlisted in the Army Reserve in 2019 as a horizontal construction engineer. Awards included the National Defense Service Medal and the Army Service Ribbon.

- Rivers enlisted in the Army Reserve in 2011 as an interior electrician. He deployed to Iraq for nine months in support of Operation Inherent Resolve in 2018. Awards included an Army Achievement Medal, an Army Service Ribbon, several Overseas Service Ribbons, an Armed Forces Reserve Medal with "M" device, and the Inherent Resolve Campaign Medal with Campaign Star. Rivers was posthumously promoted to Staff Sergeant.

AP, UPI, USA Today, Florida Times-Union, al-Jazeera, and the *Washington Post* reported on December 16, 2024 that Mahdi Mohammad Sadeghi, a naturalized U.S. citizen who prosecutors said worked at Massachusetts-based semiconductor company Analog Devices and lived in Natick, Massachusetts, and Mohammad Abedininajafabadi, 38, alias Mohammad Abedini, a dual citizen of Switzerland and Iran, who was arrested in Milan, Italy, were charged with one count of conspiracy to violate the International Emergency Economic Powers Act by conspiring to export sensitive technology to Iran that was used in a Shahed drone attack in Jordan on January 28, 2024. The three troops were part of the 926th Engineer Brigade, an Army Reserve combat engineer brigade at Fort Moore, Georgia. FBI specialists who analyzed the drone traced its navigation system to the Tehran-based San'at Danesh Rahpooyan Aflak Co. (SDRA, a navigational modules manufacturer that almost exclusively works for Iran's Islamic Revolutionary Guard Corps) founded and operated by Abedini. The duo conspired to circumvent American export control laws and procure sensitive technology into Iran. Abedini separately faced charges of conspiring to provide material support to Iran. U.S. officials blamed the attack on the Islamic Resistance in Iraq, an umbrella group of Iran-backed militias that includes Kataib Hizballah. The prosecution was coordinated through the U.S. government's Disruptive Technology Strike Force. Prosecutors said the duo conspired to illegally export technology from Sadeghi's em-ployer to SDRA via Switzerland-based front company Illumove, which Abedini established to evade sanctions and export controls. SDRA's proprietary Sepher Navigation System is used in Iran's one-way attack drones, cruise missiles, and ballistic missiles. The men each faced 20 years in prison for the IEEPA violation charge. Abedini's two additional charges of providing material support to a foreign terrorist organization resulting in death each carry a penalty of up to life in prison.

November 24, 2024: Police shot and killed a man who opened fire near the Israeli Embassy in Amman's Rabiah neighborhood, wounding three police officers.

LEBANON

January 24, 2023: *UPI* reported the U.S. Department of the Treasury's Office of Foreign Assets Control imposed new sanctions on several people and financial entities supporting Hizballah, including Lebanese money lender Hassan Moukalled, his business, CTEX Exchange, and his sons Rayyan Moukalled and Rani Moukalled.

April 6, 2023: *UPI* reported that the Israel Defense Forces said 34 rockets were fired at Israel. The IDF Aerial Defense array intercepted 25, five landed in Israel, and another four were "under review". *AP* reported that a male, 19, was hit by shrapnel and a woman, 60, was injured after falling while running to a bomb shelter. Islamic Jihad praised the attack.

July 6, 2023: *AFP* reported the Israeli army conducted strikes in southern Lebanon after a mortar launched from there exploded near the border town of Ghajar. Lebanon's *National News Agency* said Israel had fired "more than 15 artillery shells" which hit around Kfar Chouba and Halta. *BBC* reported that no group claimed credit immediately. UNIFIL peacekeepers detected explosions near al-Majidiya shortly after 8 a.m. *Reuters* quoted Lebanese security sources who said that two rockets were fired towards Israel; one landed in Lebanese territory, the other near Ghajar.

July 29, 2023: *Reuters* and *AP* reported that a failed assassination attempt on Mahmoud Khalil, a leader of a group sympathetic to hardline Islamists, killed his companion instead. Militants then attacked Fatah headquarters.

July 30, 2023: *Reuters* reported that a Fatah commander was killed in an ambush that injured several of his aides in the Ain el-Hilweh camp near Sidon. A mortar fell inside a military headquarters, wounding a soldier. *New Indian Express* and Lebanon's state-run *National News Agency* reported that six people, including two children, were wounded in the clashes.

August 10, 2023: *Al-Jazeera* reported that two bullets hit a window of the car of caretaker Defence Minister Maurice Slim as he was travelling in the Jisr el-Bashra neighborhood of Beirut. No injuries were reported.

August 16, 2023: *UPI* reported that the U.S. Department of the Treasury imposed economic sanctions on the Lebanon-based Green Without Borders and its leader Zuhair Subhi Nahla for allegedly supporting and covering Hizballah's activities in southern Lebanon near Israel.

October 11, 2023: *Reuters* reported that Hizballah fired rockets into Israel, sparking retaliatory Israeli shelling against southern Lebanese towns.

October 15, 2023: *UPI* reported that Hizballah claimed credit when it fired anti-tank missiles into Israel from Lebanon, hitting military posts, hospitalizing three, and forcing the evacuation of 28 Israeli border communities, including Metula and Hanita. The group later said it had targeted five Israeli posts. *USA Today* said they were concentrating on destroying surveillance cameras placed on Israeli border posts.

October 17, 2023: *UPI* reported that the IDF announced that a drone strike killed four terrorists attempting to place a bomb at a gate at the Lebanon border in the small town of Metula. The bomb would have opened a hole in a border fence, allowing terrorists to enter Israel.

October 20, 2023: The *Washington Post* reported that Omer Balva, 22, an American-Israeli who grew up in Rockville, Maryland, was killed by a Hizballah antitank missile fired from Lebanon. His IDF reserve infantry unit had recalled him. Before his return, Balva and Ethan Missner, who knew Balva since they were 7-year-old students at Charles E. Smith Jewish Day School in Rockville, bought knee pads, elbow pads, earmuffs, and other supplies for the 9203rd Battalion of the Alexandroni Brigade. He finished high school in 2019, moved to Israel with his parents, enlisted, and enrolled in Reichman University. He left behind three siblings. His father's family resided in the Israeli city of Tiberias since the 1400s. His father, Eyal Balva, came to the United States in 1996 to join his brothers and start his own business. Eyal serves as chief executive of Floranation, a company based in Landover, Maryland, that imports flowers.

November 12, 2023: Hizballah fired antitank missiles at a rural Israel community in Dovev across the border, badly wounding six Israel Electric Corporation utility workers. The workers were repairing lines damaged in a previous attack. One worker was critically injured. Hizballah said it attacked a "logistical force belonging to the occupation army that was about to install transmission poles and eavesdropping and spying devices near the Dovev barracks". It added that it hit an Israeli military bulldozer in a separate strike.

November 23, 2023: *AP* reported that Hizballah fired more than 50 rockets at military posts in northern Israel, a day after an Israeli airstrike on a home in Beit Yahoun in southern Lebanon killed five of the group's senior fighters. Some 48 Katyusha rockets were directed at an Israeli army base in Beit Zeitem, and struck tanks and locations where Israeli troops were taking positions. The Israeli airstrike killed five senior fighters, including Abbas Raad, the son of the head of Hizballah's 13-member parliamentary bloc in Lebanon, Mohammed Raad.

December 10, 2023: *Reuters* reported that at 10 a.m., Lebanese Hizballah claimed to have sent explosive drones at an Israeli command position near Ya'ara. The IDF said two "suspicious aerial targets" had been intercepted. Two Israeli soldiers were moderately wounded and others lightly injured from shrapnel and smoke inhalation.

January 2, 2024: *CNN,* the *Jerusalem Post, al-Jazeera, NPR, USA Today,* and *al-Aqsa TV* reported that during a nighttime Israeli airstrike in Beirut, Saleh al-Arouri, 57, Deputy Head of the Political Bureau of Hamas, and a founder of its Izz ad-Din al-Qassam Brigades military wing, was killed. He was in a meeting when the drone blast killed seven people, including al-Arouri, and injured 11 in an office belonging to Hamas in Mushrifiiyah in the southern suburb of Dahiyeb. The IDF said he was in charge of the Hamas's activities in Judea and Samaria. He also was involved in liaison with Lebanese Hizballah. The IDF demolished his house in the occupied West Bank town of Aroura near Ramallah on October 31, 2023. He had spent 15 years in Israeli prisons before he was released in a 2010 swap. The U.S. had designated him as a Global Terrorist in 2015 and issued a $5 million reward for information leading to his identification or location.

Al-Jazeera added that the other dead included:

- Azzam al-Aqra, alias Abu Abdullah, 54, a leading commander of the Qassam Brigades' military operations outside Gaza. He was arrested twice for short periods. In 1992, he was exiled to Marj al-Zuhur in Lebanon along with 415 other members of Hamas and other Palestinian armed groups. He settled in Lebanon and married there.

- Samir Fendi, alias Abu Amer, a senior leader of the Qassam Brigades and its top commander in southern Lebanon.

Also killed were Hamas members Mahmoud Zaki Shaheen, Mohammed al-Rayes, Mohammed Bashasha, and Ahmed Hamoud.

January 6, 2024: *Reuters,* the *New York Times,* and *AP* reported that Hizballah claimed it fired between 40 and 62 rockets at an Israeli air surveillance base on Mount Meron, five miles from the border. Rockets also hit two army posts near the border. Israel reported no casualties. 24010601

January 8, 2024: An Israeli airstrike on an SUV in southern Lebanon killed Wissam al-Tawil, a Hizballah commander in the secretive Radwan Force that operates along the border.

January 9, 2024: Hizballah sent several drones against the IDF's northern headquarters in Safed. No damage or injuries were reported. An Israeli drone strike on a car in Ghandouriyeh killed three Hizballah members. Hizballah claimed it attacked at least six Israeli posts along the border.

CNN reported that an Israeli drone strike on Khirbet Selm killed Ali Hussein Barji, variant Burji, who was in charge of Hizballah's drones in southern Lebanon. The IDF said he commanded the Southern Lebanon Region of Hizballah's Aerial Unit and "led dozens of terror activities against Israel using explosive UAVs and surveillance UAVs against Israel and IDF soldiers." The IDF claimed he was responsible for the attack on an Israeli command center earlier that day.

January 16, 2024: *CNN* and *NNA* reported that the IDF announced that it had struck dozens of Hizballah posts, military structures, and weapons infrastructure in the area of Wadi Saluki and Ayta ash Shab in Lebanon via aerial and artillery strikes. *NNA* tallied "more than 15 raids, strikes the outskirts of Houla, Wadi al-Saluki, Wadi al-Hujair, and the Rab Thalateen al-Taybeh road". The IDF added that overnight, one of its aircraft struck a Hizballah anti-tank missile launcher in KafarKila in southern Lebanon.

January 20, 2024: An IDF airstrike near Tyre killed two people in a car—one of them Hizballah commander Ali Hudruj, the other tech sector businessman Mohammad Baqir Diab—and two people in a nearby orchard.

January 21, 2024: An IDF airstrike hit two vehicles near a Lebanese army checkpoint near Kafra in south Lebanon, killing Hizballah member Fadel Shaar in one car and a woman, Samar al-Sayyed Mohammed, in the other and wounding several other people.

January 31, 2024: *UPI* reported that the U.S. Department of the Treasury imposed sanctions against three entities and one individual in Lebanon and Turkey for supporting Hizballah and the Iranian Islamic Revolutionary Guards Corps Quds Force, generating hundreds of millions of dollars worth of revenue from selling Iranian commodities while supporting the IRGC-QF financial network.

- Türkiye-based Mira Ihracat Ithalat Petrol was accused of buying, transporting, and selling Iranian commodities.

- Lebanon-based Hydro Company for Drilling Equipment Rental allegedly facilitates Iranian commodities shipments worth hundreds of millions of dollars operating under IRGC-QF senior officers' directions.

- Lebanon-based Yara Offshore SAL was sanctioned for large sales to Syria and conducting transactions on behalf of Hizballah and IRGC-QF front company Concepto.

The sanctioned individual was Ibrahim Talal al-Uwayr, alias Ibrahim Agaoglu, the alleged CEO owner or person controlling Mira. Treasury said he works with Hizballah finance officials Muhammad Qasir, who allegedly oversees Mira, and Muhammad Amir Alchwiki.

February 15, 2024: *Al-Jazeera* reported that Hizballah claimed it fired dozens of Katyusha-type rockets at Kiryat Shmona, an Israeli town on the border, following airstrikes on Nabatieh and as-Sawana. Israel said it killed Ali Muhammad Aldbas, a senior commander of Hizballah's elite Radwan Force, his deputy Ibrahim Issa, and a third fighter in an air raid on Nabatieh. Aldbas was believed involved in a roadside bombing in northern Israel in March 2023, and had been involved in cross-border fighting since October 2023.

March 10, 2024: *Al-Jazeera* reported that Lebanese Hizballah claimed to have fired dozens of rockets in the morning into Meron in northern Israel. Meron is home to a major air control base.

March 13, 2024: Hizballah fired 100 Katyusha rockets at several Israeli military positions, including two bases in northern Israel. 24031301

In retaliation, an Israeli drone strike targeted a car near the coastal city of Tyre, Lebanon, killing Hadi Mustafa, a member of the Qassam Brigades, the Hamas military wing, and a civilian. Lebanese state media said Mustafa was from the Rashidieh refugee camp near Tyre. The IDF said Mustafa was directing cells to attack "Israeli and Jewish targets" in different parts of the world.

Lebanon's state-run *National News Agency* said the dead Syrian citizen was on a motorcycle near the targeted car. Two people were wounded.

March 27, 2024: *Reuters* reported that Hizballah said it launched dozens of rockets at Kiryat Shmona, Israel, in response to Israeli strikes on Hebbariyeh, Lebanon that killed seven people the previous day. Israeli emergency services said a rocket strike killed a factory worker. 24032701

March 31, 2024: *Reuters* and *al-Jazeera* reported that an IDF airstrike on a vehicle in Kounine killed Ismail al-Zin, a commander in the anti-tank missile unit of Hizballah's Radwan Forces.

April 7, 2024: *Al-Jazeera* reported that an overnight IDF air strike killed four Hizballah fighters, including Ali Ahmad Hussein, a commander of Hizballah's elite Radwan Force, in the area of as-Sultaniyah in southern Lebanon.

Dozens of rockets were launched from Lebanon into the Israeli-occupied Golan Heights. Hizballah said they were targeting an army base and air defence posts in the area.

April 10, 2024: Lebanese man Mohammad Srour, 57, who was sanctioned by the U.S. Department of the Treasury in August 2019 for giving "financial, material, technological support, financial or other services" to Hamas and his affiliation with Hizballah, was found dead after he went missing for a week. He was accused of laundering tens of millions of dollars annually from Iran's Islamic Revolutionary Guard Corps to Hamas's military wing, the al-Qassam Brigades. Lebanon's state-run *National News Agency* said his body had three bullet wounds.

April 12, 2024: *CNN* reported that Hizballah fired 40 Katuysha rockets from Lebanon at locations in Israel during the evening, causing no injuries. Some were intercepted and others fell in open areas. IDF air defenses also intercepted two explosive drones, which the IDF said were sent by Hizballah.

April 15, 2024: *Al-Jazeera, AFP,* and *Reuters* reported that Hizballah claimed credit for setting off explosive devices in the Tel Ismail area, injuring four Israeli soldiers who had crossed a few hundred meters across the border.

April 23, 2024: *Al-Jazeera* reported that Hizballah launched dozens of Katyusha rocket and drone attacks against two Israeli bases between Acre and Nahariyya. The IDF said it had no knowledge of any of its facilities being hit, but had said earlier that it intercepted two "aerial targets" off Israel's northern coast.

April 26, 2024: *AP* and Lebanon's state-run *National News Agency* reported that an Israeli drone strike on a car in the village of Maydoun in eastern Lebanon killed two people. The IDF said it targeted Musab Khalaf, an official with Lebanon's al-Jamaa al-Islamiya (Islamic Group), which is allied with Hizballah. The IDF claimed that Khalaf was behind attacks on Israeli troops in the disputed Chebaa Farms that Israel captured from Syria during the 1967 Mideast war.

May 2, 2024: *UPI* reported that the United States Departments of Treasury and State blacklisted five people and two companies accused of aiding a U.S.-designated financier of Hizballah with sanctions evasion. Hassan Moukalled, 57, was blacklisted in January 2023 along with his money service business, CTEX Exchange, and two of his sons, Rayyan Moukalled, 30, and Rani Moukalled, 25. Also sanctioned were Andriyah Samir Mushantaf, 58; Bashir Ibrahim Mansur, 44, who founded CTEX with Moukalled; Moukalled's son, Firas Hasan Moukalled, 33; and the younger Moukalled's company, Teleport Company SAL. Firas Hasan Moukalled jointly owns Teleport with Mushantaf and Rayyan Hassan Moukalled. The U.S. sanctioned Mazen Hassan al-Zein, 49, a United Arab Emirates-based business consultant for Moukalled, and his The Crystal Group. The U.S. also sanctioned Adnan Mahmoud Youssef, 67, a CTEX Exchange employee, on accusations of attempting to court investors to set up companies in the UAE for Moukalled.

May 17, 2024: The *Jerusalem Post* and *CNN* reported that Hizballah claimed credit for firing 50 Katyusha rockets toward an Israeli military

base in the Golan Heights, slightly injuring two Israelis, according to the Marom HaGilil Regional Council.

May 17, 2024: The al-Qassam Brigades of Hamas said an IDF airstrike in Lebanon's West Bekaa area near the Syrian border killed Sharhabil Ali al-Sayyid, alias Abu Amr. The IDF said he was "a senior commander of the Jamaa Islamiya" in Lebanon "who cooperated with Hamas against Israel".

June 1, 2024: Hizballah claimed it shot down an Israeli Hermes 900 Kochav drone over southern Lebanon hours after Israeli drone strikes killed at least one person and wounded others.

June 5, 2024: *AP, UPI, Today, NBC News, Reuters,* the *Washington Post,* and *al-Jazeera* reported that at 8:34 a.m., a gunman in a black vest with ammunition pouches and jeans and carrying an assault rifle attacked the entrance of the U.S. Embassy in the Christian suburb of Aukar, north of Beirut, injuring an embassy security guard. Following a 30-minute gun battle, Lebanese soldiers shot him thrice in the stomach and leg and captured the shooter. The attacker wore a black vest with the words "Islamic State" written in Arabic and the English initials "I" and "S." A Lebanese security official and two judicial officials said he lived in the eastern Lebanese border town of Majdal Anjar near Syria. The Lebanese military said he was a Syrian. No group claimed credit. The military raided Majdal Anjar and nearby Suweiri, arresting three relatives of the suspect, including his brother, and two other people believed to be associated with him. On July 2, 2024, a judge at Lebanon's military court charged Kaiss Farraj, a Syrian, with ISIS affiliation. Government Commissioner to the Military Court Judge Fadi Akiki charged two others who sold weapons to Farraj with selling unlicensed firearms.

June 10, 2024: The *Long War Journal* reported that Hizballah conducted drone and rocket attacks across Israel's northern Galilee from the Mediterranean Sea to the Golan Heights toward the areas of Manara, Yir'on, Avivim, Margaliot, and Yiftach. The group downed an Israeli Hermes 900 drone, which is larger than the U.S.-made Predator but smaller than the Reaper.

June 11, 2024: Senior Lebanese Hizballah official Hachem Saffieddine threatened more cross-border attacks after an IDF airstrike in the nighttime killed senior commander Taleb Sami Abdullah, 55, alias Abu Taleb, and destroyed a house where he and three other officials were meeting. Abdullah was the commander of the Nasr Unit that is in charge of parts of south Lebanon close to the Israeli border.

June 12, 2024: Hizballah fired 215 rockets into northern Israel. *Defense News* reported that Hizballah fired two missiles that hit the Israeli Plasan defense factory in Sasa in the morning. The firm makes vehicle-protection products and components. It has factories in France and the United States. Plasan partnered with Oshkosh Corporation for the production of the mine-resistant, ambush-protected M-ATV vehicle chosen to replace the Humvee.

June 18, 2024: *CNN* reported that Hizballah released a nine-minute video, apparently taken by a drone, showing Israeli military and civilian locations in several Israeli cities, including Krayot, north of Haifa. Israeli Foreign Minister Israel Katz said on *X* that "We are getting very close to the moment of deciding to change the rules of the game against Hezbollah and Lebanon… In an all-out war, Hezbollah will be destroyed, and Lebanon severely beaten."

June 19, 2024: Lebanese state media reported Israeli strikes north of Tyre in southern Lebanon killed three Hizballah fighters. The IDF said it was responding to two Hizballah rocket launches that damaged several vehicles in northern Israel.

July 3, 2024: An IDF airstrike in Tyre killed senior Hezbollah commander Mohammad Naameh Nasser, alias Abu Naameh, who headed the group's Aziz Unit, one of three regional divisions in southern Lebanon.

Hizballah fired more than 200 Katyusha and Falaq rockets and more than 20 drones at several military bases in Israel and the occupied Syrian Golan Heights in retaliation. It fired more rockets the next day.

July 9, 2024: *CNN* reported that Hizballah fired dozens of projectiles into the Israeli-controlled Golan Heights during the evening, killing a woman and a man when a missile hit their vehicle. Firefighters reported battling eight resultant fires.

July 12, 2024: An Israeli sergeant, 33, was killed in cross-border fire with Hizballah.

July 17, 2024: *Al-Jazeera* reported that Hizballah leader Hassan Nasrallah warned that the group would find new rocket attack targets should Israeli attacks continue to "target" civilians in Lebanon.

July 20, 2024: Hizballah said it fired dozens of Katyusha rockets into northern Israel, targeting Dafna kibbutz for the first time in nine months in retaliation for an Israeli drone strike that wounded several Syrian citizens, including children, in Burj al-Muluk.

Hamas said it fired rockets from Lebanon toward an Israeli army post in the northern Israeli village of Shomera in retaliation for the "Zionists massacres" in the Gaza Strip.

NNA reported that during the night, an Israeli airstrike on Adloun hit an arms depot. The state-run *National News Agency* said that three people in Kharayeb were slightly wounded and hospitalized.

The IDF said that about 45 projectiles were detected crossing from Lebanon into northern Israel in three separate barrages. It said that some were intercepted.

July 24, 2024: *Al-Jazeera* reported that Hizballah released eight minutes of drone video showing Israeli air defense facilities, planes, and fuel storage units at the Ramat David air base. It was the third such video from Hizballah; the first showed Haifa and the second the Israeli-occupied Golan Heights.

August 4, 2024: *CNN* reported that Hizballah fired 30 rockets into Israel. *AP* reported that the Iron Dome air defense system downed the rockets over the Galilee region.

August 5, 2024: Hizballah claimed it fired a drone against a military base in northern Israel, wounding two Israeli soldiers.

August 6, 2024: Hizballah launched drones into northern Israel, wounding 19 people, including six soldiers. Many were hurt by an Israeli interceptor rocket that missed and crashed.

August 11, 2024: *CNN* reported that during the night, Hizballah fired 30 rockets at northern Israel. No injuries were reported.

August 19, 2024: *Al-Jazeera* reported that during the previous week, Hizballah released a video, titled *Our Mountains, Our Treasures*, of fighters driving motorbikes and large trucks carrying missiles through well-lit tunnels.

August 21, 2024: *AP* and the *National News Agency* reported that an Israeli airstrike on a vehicle in Sidon killed Khalil al-Maqdah, the brother of Fatah Gen. Mounir al-Maqdah. Israeli officials had accused Mounir al-Maqdah of facilitating the smuggling of weapons into the West Bank.

Hizballah fired more than 50 rockets, hitting private homes in the Israeli-annexed Golan Heights. First responders treated a man, 30, who was moderately wounded by shrapnel.

August 25, 2024: The *Washington Post* reported that Hizballah said it fired more than 320 rockets against Israeli military targets.

September 10, 2024: *CNN* reported that an IDF airstrike on Qaraoun village in western Beqaa district killed Mohammed Qassem al-Shaer, a commander of Hizballah's elite Radwan Force, who had "advanced numerous terrorist activities against the state of Israel". In retaliation, Hizballah launched dozens of Katyusha rockets and several drones toward two locations in northern Israel. No casualties were reported.

September 15, 2024: In the morning, Hizballah fired 40 projectiles into northern Israel, causing no injuries.

September 17, 2024: *CNN, BBC, Reuters, NNA, al-Manar TV,* and *al-Jazeera* reported that at 3:30 p.m., hundreds of members of Hizballah were injured when their apparently hacked pagers exploded in Beirut's Dahiyeh suburb, Sidon, Tyre, Ali al-Nahri, and Riyaq in the Beqaa valley. *Fars* and *IRNA* reported that Iran's Ambassador to Lebanon Mojtaba Amini and two of his bodyguards were hurt in the incident. Lebanese Minister of Health Firass Abiad said 12 people, including two children, among them Fatima Abdullah, 9, and a boy, Bilal Kanj, 11 or 12, were killed and nearly 3,000 were injured, including 200 critically. Fatima had picked up her father's beeping pager to take it to him. Hizballah said two of its members, including Mohammad Mahdi Ammar, son of a Hizballah lawmaker, were killed. Abbas Fadel Yassin also died. Fatima was buried in Saraain, the day after her first day of fourth grade.

The *New York Times* added that Hizballah blamed Israel. Israel declined public comment, but two American officials said that Israel tipped the U.S. that something—unspecified—was afoot.

Witnesses said that they heard beeping for several seconds from pagers, and saw smoke coming from victims' pockets before the explosions. Many people were injured in their hands, stomachs, and faces. So many people were injured in their eyes that medical staffs were reporting a shortage of eye surgeons.

Hizballah had moved to pagers after believing that Israel had hacked into the cell phone network.

The pagers, manufactured in Hungary, were booby-trapped before delivery. The *New York Times* reported that Israel had included a switch to permit remote detonation. A senior Taiwanese official said there was no record of Taiwan-based Gold Apollo pagers being shipped to the Middle East; images of the damaged pagers with the Gold Apollo trademark ran in news accounts of the blasts. *CNN* reported that Gold Apollo claimed that the AR-924 model pagers were designed and made by Budapest-based BAC Consulting KFT, which had licensed the Gold Apollo brand. The company's website noted that the waterproof AR924 uses a rechargeable lithium battery that can last for 85 days on a single charge. Zoltan Kovacs, Hungary's secretary for international communication, posted that the firm was just an intermediary and has no manufacturing or operational site in the country. *UPI* reported on September 20 that Taiwan's government and Bulgarian authorities both denied making the exploding pagers. Bulgaria's National Security State Agency said that the Nortal Global company did not carry out transactions under Bulgarian jurisdiction with respect to the devices. *Reuters* reported that Romania and Norway also opened investigations into possible counterfeiting of pagers and supply chain compromise.

AP reported on September 20 that Cristiana Bársony-Arcidiacono, 49, CEO of Budapest-based BAC Consulting that was linked to the pagers, had received unspecified "threats" and was advised by the Hungarian secret services "not to talk to media". Her mother, Beatrix Bársony-Arcidiacono from Sicily, claimed that her daughter "is currently in a safe place protected by the Hungarian secret services". Hungary's Special Service for National Security disputed the claim.

AP and *NTB* reported on September 26 that Norway's National Criminal Investigation Service issued an international wanted notice for a man, 39, working for the Norway-based DN Group who was linked to a Bulgaria-based company that may have been involved in the dissemination of the exploding electronic devices. *NTB* and *VG* reported that he had traveled to the U.S. the previous week, but his whereabouts are unknown. The Norwegian passport-holder lived in Norway for 12 years but was born elsewhere.

The *Times of Israel* reported on November 11, 2024 that during a November 10 Cabinet meeting, Israeli Prime Minister Benjamin Netanyahu confirmed that Israel conducted the pager and walkie-talkie attacks.

September 18, 2024: *BBC, CNN, UPI, NNA, Washington Post, Reuters,* and *AFP* reported that handheld two-way radios, known as walkie-talkies, used by Hizballah exploded throughout the country, including Sohmar in the Bekaa Valley, killing 20 and injuring 450 people, many in the stomach and hands. The *New York Times*

reported fires in homes, cars, and shops in several parts of Lebanon. Hizballah bought the radios five months earlier, at the same time when they purchased the deadly pagers. One detonation occurred near a funeral organized by Hizballah for pager explosion victims. Osaka, Japan's Icom, Inc. said it had not made the IC-V82 model walkie-talkies that exploded, observing "It was discontinued about 10 years ago, and since then, it has not been shipped from our company."

September 19, 2024: The IDF said it hit 100 Hizballah rocket launchers, 1,000 rocket launcher barrels, and other infrastructure.

September 20, 2024: The *Washington Post, Reuters, CNN*, Israeli Army radio, and *al-Jazeera* reported that 45, including seven women, 16 Hizballah members, and three children, were killed and 68 injured in an IDF airstrike in Beirut's southern Jamous suburb that killed Ibrahim Aqil, variant Akil, who sits on Hizballah's military Jihad Council and was part of its Radwan Force. Lebanon's *National News Agency* said four missiles collapsed two residential buildings. The U.S. Department of State's Rewards for Justice Program had offered a $7 million reward for information leading to his arrest for abducting Americans in Lebanon in the 1980s, the 1983 Islamic Jihad strike on the U.S. Embassy in Beirut that killed 63 people, and the PIJ bombing of the Beirut Marine barracks that killed 241 U.S. personnel that year. Lebanese state media reported that IDF warplanes also hit the towns of Mays al-Jabal, Kfarkela, Adaisseh-Kfarkela, Taybeh, and Aitroun.

The IDF said that more than 140 projectiles were fired from Lebanon toward northern Israel.

AP added the next day that the airstrikes also killed Ahmed Wahbi, another senior commander in Hizballah's military wing.

September 22, 2024: *CNN* reported that Hizballah fired numerous rockets into Israel after Israel conducted 300 air strikes overnight, killing two people in al-Khiyyam and Aitaroun. The IDF intercepted most of the rockets, but reported impacts in Kiryat Bialik, Tsur Shalom, and Moreshet near Haifa. Hizballah said it fired the previously-unknown Fadi-1 and Fadi-2 missiles at the Ramat David airbase southeast of Haifa. Hizballah usually fires short-range Katyusha and Burkan rockets. Israeli emergency services reported that three people were wounded.

September 23-24, 2024: *UPI* and *AP* reported that IDF air strikes hit 1,600 Hizballah targets in Beirut, killed 564 people, and injured 1,800. Among the dead was Ibrahim Kobeisi, who was responsible for rocket launches against Israel. The IDF said that Hizballah fired 55 rockets into Israel, setting fires and damaging buildings.

September 25, 2024: *CNN* and *NPR* reported that the IDF intercepted a Hizballah missile fired at Tel Aviv. Hizballah claimed it had targeted Mossad's headquarters.

September 26, 2024: *UPI* reported that the IDF announced that an airstrike in Lebanon had killed Hizballah Aerial Command chief Muhammad Hussein Srour.

September 27, 2024: *CNN, NPR,* and *AP* reported that an IDF airstrike hit Hizballah headquarters in Beirut, killing Hizballah leader Hassan Nasrullah, 64, and several other Hizballah leaders, along with Iranian Islamic Revolutionary Guard Corps General Abbas Nilforushan, 58, deputy commander for operations, and another senior Hizballah leader, Ali Karaki. Nasrullah headed Hizballah since 1992.

September 29, 2024: *CNN* reported that an IDF airstrike in Beirut's Chyah suburb killed Sheikh Nabil Qaouk, head of Hizballah's Preventive Security Unit and member of Hizballah's central council. The U.S. had named him a Specially Designated Global Terrorist in October 2020.

Hizballah fired ten rockets across the border into Israel.

An IDF airstrike killed senior Hamas commander Fatah Sharif, his wife, son, and daughter in al-Buss refugee camp. He was also an employee of the UNRWA teachers association in Lebanon, and had been placed on administrative leave.

October 1, 2024: *CNN* reported that Hizballah claimed that during the morning, it fired Fadi-4 long-range surface-to-surface rockets at Mossad headquarters in Tel Aviv, along with a base housing an Israeli intelligence unit. The IDF said two people were injured when their vehicles were hit on a highway north of Kfar Qassim in central Israel. A bus driver, 54, sustained moderate head and back injuries from shrapnel when his bus carrying ten passengers was hit. A man, 31, was lightly injured when his car was hit.

October 3, 2024: On October 23, 2024, *CNN, Cipher Brief, Financial Times, Reuters,* the *Guardian,* and the *New York Times* reported that the IDF announced that an October 3, 2024 air strike in Dahiyeh, Lebanon killed possible Hizballah successor Hashem Safieddine and Ali Hussein Hazima, the head of Hizballah's intelligence branch.

October 4, 2024: *CNN* reported that Hizballah lost contact with Hashem Safieddine, a possible successor to its late leader Hassan Nasrallah, following an Israeli strike in Beirut's southern suburbs which targeted him. Safieddine served as head of the group's executive council and is a maternal cousin of Nasrallah. They studied together in Iran in the 1980s. In 2017, the U.S. designated Safieddine a foreign terrorist.

October 5, 2024: *CNN* reported that Hizballah fired rockets at the Karmiel and Deir al-Assad area of northern Israel, causing minor injuries to three people. Twelve other people received medical assistance to cope with the shock and anxiety of the incident.

NPR and *CNN* reported that an IDF air strike on the Beddawi refugee camp near Tripoli killed Saeed Atallah Ali, a senior commander of the Hamas military wing, his wife, and two daughters.

October 8, 2024: *AP* and *UPI* reported that an IDF airstrike in Beirut killed Suhail Hussein Husseini, military commander of Hizballah's headquarters in Beirut, who oversaw logistics, budget, and management for Hizballah. He was a member of the Jihad Council, in charge of military operations. Husseini coordinated the flow of arms from Iran and internal weapons research and development.

Sheikh Naim Kassem, acting leader of Hizballah, warned of new attacks against Israeli troops in southern Lebanon and rocket fire into Israel. *CNN* noted that he was one of the founding members of the Shi'ite group. The U.S. earlier sanctioned him. He was born in Kfar Fila in southern Lebanon and studied chemistry at the Lebanese University, then taught chemistry for several years. He pursued religious studies and participated in founding the Lebanese Union for Muslim Students, an organization that aimed to promote religious adherence among students. In the 1970s, he joined the Movement of the Dispossessed, a political organization founded by Imam Moussa Sadr that pushed for greater representation for Lebanese Shi'ites. The group became the Amal movement. From 1991, he served as Hizballah's deputy secretary-general, initially under Nasrallah's predecessor, Abbas Mousawi, who was killed by an Israeli helicopter attack in 1992.

October 10, 2024: *UPI* reported that the IDF said airstrikes killed Ahmad Moustafa al-Haj Ali, commander of Hizballah's Houla Front, whom the Israeli military held as responsible for hundreds of missile and anti-tank attacks targeting the Kiryat Shmona area in northern Israel; and Mohammad Ali Hamdan, commander of Hizballah's anti-tank unit in the Meiss El Jabal area in southern Lebanon, "responsible for extensive anti-tank missile attacks toward communities in northern Israel."

October 16, 2024: *UPI* reported that the U.S. Department of the Treasury imposed sanctions against Silvana Atwi, Haidar Houssam al-Din Abdul Ghaffar, and Houssam Hamadi and companies G.M. Farm, Global Tradeline SARL, and United Sons that provided millions of dollars to Hizballah via Captagon smuggling. Alleged Lebanon-based drug trafficker Khaldoun Hamieh was sanctioned for "controlling Captagon labs in the Syrian city of Sayyida Zainab, in an area that is largely under the control of Iran's Islamic Revolutionary Guard Corps and Hezbollah."

October 19, 2024: The IDF killed Nasser Rashid, Hizballah's deputy commander in Bint Jbeil.

October 29, 2024: *AP, BBC,* and the *Washington Post* reported that Hizballah announced that its Shura Council elected cleric Sheikh Naim Kassem, 71, as its new Secretary General.

October 30, 2024: *AP, Reuters,* Israel's *Channel 12, Haaretz,* and *BBC* reported that two Hizballah rocket attacks hit northern Israel within hours of each other, killing seven people. In one attack, rockets landed near Metula, killing an Israeli farmer and four foreign agricultural workers. In the second attack near Haifa, a woman in her 60s and a man around 30 died near Kubbutz Afek.

November 2, 2024: Hizballah rockets hit a building before dawn in Tira, a predominantly Israeli Arab town in central Israel, injuring 11 people, three moderately.

Hizballah claimed it fired missiles at the Israeli military's Unit 8200 base in Glilot, on the edge of Tel Aviv, rockets toward military facilities in Zvulun, and drones at Palmachim Air Base. It claimed it fired rockets into the northern Israeli towns of Dalton, Yesud HaMa'ala, and Bar Yohai.

Israeli special forces snatched Hizballah naval commander Ihad Amhaz in an amphibious raid on Batroun, 30 miles north of Beirut.

November 4, 2024: An Israeli airstrike killed Abu Ali Rida, Hizballah's commander for the Baraachit area of southern Lebanon. The IDF said he planned and executed rocket and anti-tank missile attacks against IDF troops.

The IDF also killed Ali Barakat, a senior member of Hizballah's Aerial Unit who spent more than a decade planning and carrying out attacks on Israel using unmanned aerial vehicles. He developed cruise missiles and UAVs for Hizballah.

November 16, 2024: Hizballah fired rockets into Haifa, Israel, wounding two civilians and damaging a synagogue.

November 17, 2024: *AP, CNN, UPI,* and *al-Jazeera* reported that an Israeli airstrike on a building housing the Arab socialist Baath party's office in central Beirut's Ras al-Nabaa district killed Hizballah spokesman Mohammad Afif and injured three other people. Afif managed Hizballah's *al-Manar* television station for several years, then became Hizballah's lead media relations officer.

November 21, 2024: Gunmen fired several rockets into northern Israel, killing one man and causing damage.

November 24, 2024: Hizballah fired 185 rockets and other projectiles into Israel, wounding 11 people, including a 60-year old man in severe condition from rocket fire on northern Israel, a 23-year-old man who was lightly wounded in Petah Tikva, and a 70-year-old woman who suffered smoke inhalation from a car that caught fire. In Haifa, a rocket hit a residential building that police said was in danger of collapsing. *Al-Jazeera* reported that Hizballah claimed it targeted the Ashdod naval base in southern Israel and a "military target" in Tel Aviv using advanced missiles and strike drones.

November 27, 2024: *BBC* reported that at 4 a.m., a ceasefire between Israel and Hizballah began.

LIBYA

January 1, 2023: *Al-Jazeera* reported that Libyan authorities discovered 18 bodies buried in a mass grave in the Sabaa area of Sirte, a former ISIS stronghold.

May 29, 2023: *Reuters* reported that a Misrata court sentenced 23 people to death and another 14 to life in prison for their role in a deadly Islamic State campaign that included a 2015 attack on the luxury Corinthia Hotel in Tripoli in which nine people were killed, beheading a group of Egyptian Christians, and seizing the city of Sirte in 2015. One other person was sentenced to 12 years in prison, six to 10 years, one to five years, and six defendants to three years. Five were acquitted and three others died before their case came to trial.

August 9, 2024: Hours-long fighting involving heavy weapons in Tripoli's eastern Tajoura neighborhood pitting the Rahba al-Duruae militia, led by warlord Bashir Khalfallah, alias al-Baqrah, against the al-Shahida Sabriya militia killed a dozen people and wounded 16.

August 18, 2024: *UPI* reported that Musab Msallem, director of the Tripoli-based Central Bank of Libya's Information Technology Department, was kidnapped from his home at 9 a.m. The bank suspended all operations. A week earlier, gunmen sieged the Tripoli financial institution to force the resignation of its governor, Seddik al-Kabir.

OMAN

July 16, 2024: *AP, AFP,* and *BBC* reported that a nighttime shooting in the Shi'ite Imam Bargah Ali bin Abu Talib mosque in the Wadi Kabir neighborhood of Muscat killed six people, including four Pakistanis, an Indian citizen, and a police officer, and wounded others, including 30 Pakistanis and one Indian national. The Pakistani embassy said its dead were Ghulam Abbas, Hasan Abbas, Sayyed Qaisar Abbas, and Sulaiman Nawaz. Security forces killed the three ISIS terrorists on the eve of the Shi'ite holy day of Ashura.

RED SEA

October 19, 2023: *USNI News* and *CNN* reported that the guided-missile destroyer *USS Carney* (DDG-64) took out three land attack missiles fired from the shore in Houthi-controlled territory in western Yemen in a nine-hour battle. No U.S. casualties were reported. The *Carney* fired Standard Missile-2s to down the land attack missiles over the Red Sea and eight drones launched from Western Yemen. A Pentagon spokesman told reporters that the missiles were headed north, "potentially toward targets in Israel". The *USA Today Network* reported that the *Carney* is based in Mayport, Jacksonville, Florida.

November 15, 2023: *Navy Times* reported that Arleigh Burke-class guided missile U.S. Navy destroyer *USS Thomas Hudner* (DDG 116), transiting international waters, shot down an air drone in the Red Sea that originated from Yemen.

Navy Times and the *Florida Times-Union* reported that on November 23 the Naval Station Mayport, Florida-based *Thomas Hudner,* while operating in the Red Sea, shot down "multiple one-way attack drones" launched by Iran-backed Houthi rebels in Yemen. U.S. Central Command said there was no damage to the ship or injuries to the crew.

November 19, 2023: *CNN* reported that a Yemeni Houthi helicopter was used to hijack the *Galaxy Leader* cargo ship carrying 25 crew members in the Red Sea. The ship is owned by a British company and operated by the Japanese firm Nippon Yusen, also known as NYK Line. It is owned by Ray Car Carriers, a company linked to Israeli national Abraham Ungar. The crew included 17 Filipinos, two Bulgarians, three Ukrainians, two Mexicans, and a Romanian. The ship departed Türkiye en route to India.

CNN reported on March 14, 2024 that Eduardo de Vega, the Filipino foreign affairs official overseeing millions of Filipino migrant workers, said he did not expect a release until the war in Gaza is over. Houthi spokesman Nasr al-Din Amer announced that "The ship and its crew are in the hands of the brothers in the Hamas resistance movement and the al-Qassam Brigades... We have no claims of our own regarding this vessel." An "honorary consul," a Yemeni national given special status to represent the Philippines, visited the hostages in January 2024.

November 19, 2023: *CNN* reported that Yemeni Houthi rebels hijacked a cargo ship carrying 25 crew members in the Red Sea. The ship is owned by a British company and operated by a Japanese firm. The ship departed Türkiye en route to India.

November 29, 2023: The U.S. Navy destroyer *USS Carney,* sailing near the Bab-el-Mandeb Strait, shot down an Iranian-made KAS-04 drone launched from Yemen.

December 3, 2023: *USNWR* and *Reuters* reported that the UK's Maritime Trade Operations agency (UKMTO) received reports of drone activity originating from Yemen and a possible explosion in the Red Sea's Bab al-Mandab strait.

First Coast News TV in Jacksonville, Florida and *AP* reported that the Mayport-based Arleigh Burke-class guided-missile destroyer *USS Carney,* during a six-hour battle, shot down in self-defense three attack drones fired by Houthi rebels in Yemen.

AP, Military Times, and *CNN* reported that at 9:15 a.m., ballistic missiles fired from Houthi-controlled Sanaa struck three commercial ships in the Red Sea, including Bahamas-flagged bulk carrier *Unity Explorer,* which sustained minor damage, and the bulk carriers Panamanian-flagged *Number 9* and Romanian-flagged M/V *Sophie II.* U.S. Central Command said the *Number 9* reported some damage but no casualties, and the *Sophie II* reported no significant damage. Houthi military spokesman Brig. Gen. Yahya Saree claimed two of the attacks, observing, "The Yemeni armed forces continue to prevent Israeli ships from navigating the Red Sea (and Gulf of Aden) until the Israeli aggression against our steadfast brothers in the Gaza Strip stops... The Yemeni armed forces renew their warning to all Israeli ships or those associated with Israelis that they will become a legitimate target if they violate what is stated in this statement." Saree said one vessel was the *Unity Explorer,* which is owned by a British firm that includes Dan David Ungar, who lives in Israel, as one of its officers. Israeli media said Ungar is the son of Israeli shipping billionaire Abraham "Rami" Ungar. The *Number 9* is linked to Bernhard Schulte Ship Management. Kyowa Kisen of Imabari, Japan owns the *Sophie II.*

December 6, 2023: *Navy Times* reported that at 10:30 a.m., the U.S. Navy destroyer *USS Mason* shot down an air drone attributed to Houthis.

December 9, 2023: France's Armies Ministry announced that the Navy frigate *Languedoc* was targeted during the night by drones from direction of Yemen. Both were intercepted and shot down two hours apart about 110 kilometers (70 miles) off the Red Sea port of al-Hudaydah on the Yemeni coast.

December 9, 2023: The U.S. Naval Institute reported that French Minister of Armed Forces Sébastien Lecornu told the French Senate that two lethal drones were fired from Yemen at the French guided-missile frigate *FS Languedoc*

(653) while it was operating in the Red Sea. The ship downed the two drones with Aster 15 guided missiles.

December 12, 2023: Houthis fired a missile that hit the Norwegian-flagged oil and chemical tanker *M/T Strinda* close to the Bab el-Mandeb Strait. Houthi military spokesperson Brig. Gen. Yahya Saree said the rebels fired on the vessel when it "rejected all warning calls." The *USS Mason* responded and rendered assistance. Geir Belsnes, CEO of the *Strinda*'s operator, J. Ludwig Mowinckels Rederi, said, "All crew members are unhurt and safe… The vessel is now proceeding to a safe port." The *Strinda* was coming from Malaysia en route for the Suez Canal and then on to Italy with a cargo of palm oil. On July 11, 2024, *AP* reported that the U.S. Defense Intelligence Agency released its assessment that Houthis fired an Iranian-made Noor anti-ship cruise missile at the *Strinda*. DIA said it found an Iranian Tolu-4 turbojet engine, used in the Noor. Iran reverse engineered the Noor from the Chinese C-802 anti-ship missile.

December 13, 2023: Houthis in Yemen fired two missiles that missed the Marshall Islands-flagged commercial tanker *Ardmore Encounter* loaded with Indian-manufactured jet fuel near the Bab el-Mandeb Strait en route from Mangalore, India. It was the first time missiles were fired at an energy shipment heading to the Suez Canal. An armed security crew opened fire to drive off skiffs loaded with men trying to board the vessel. The *USS Mason* shot down a suspected Houthi drone flying in its direction during the incident. No one was hurt.

The ship was carrying jet fuel from Shell MRPL Aviation Fuels and Services Ltd., a joint operation of Shell and India's national oil company. The fuel was heading to either Rotterdam, Netherlands or Gavle, Sweden.

December 13, 2023: The British military's United Kingdom Maritime Trade Operations reported a separate incident off the coast of Oman during which a vessel had been followed by smaller boats carrying machine guns and men in gray uniforms before escaping unharmed.

December 15, 2023: *AP, AFP,* and *al-Jazeera* reported that Yemeni Houthis fired a missile that hit the Liberia-flagged *al-Jasrah* cargo ship's port side. A container fell overboard and the projectile caused a fire on the 1,200-foot container ship built in 2016, which is operated by German-based shipper Hapag-Lloyd. No crew were hurt. The ship was en route from Piraeus, Greece, to Singapore.

Hours later, another Houthi missile hit the Liberian-flagged *MSC Palatium III* cargo ship near the strategic Bab el-Mandeb Strait. The ship caught fire. Authorities believed the missile was fired at the *al-Jasrah*.

The Switzerland-based Mediterranean Shipping Company reported that Houthis threatened the *MSC Alanya* in the Bab el-Mandeb.

December 16, 2023: The Royal Navy's *HMS Diamond* destroyer fired a Sea Viper missile to shoot down an aerial drone that was "targeting merchant shipping" over the Red Sea.

U.S. Central Command announced that the *USS Carney* "successfully engaged 14 unmanned aerial systems" launched from Houthi-controlled areas of Yemen.

Houthi rebels said they fired a barrage of drones toward the port city of Eilat in southern Israel.

Many commercial shipping firms paused their operations in the Red Sea.

December 18, 2023: At 9 a.m., Houthis fired drones at the merchant vessel *Swan Atlantic*. The *USS Carney* responded. Houthi spokesperson Yahya Sarea claimed they had attacked the Norwegian-owned *Swan Atlantic* and the Panama-flagged *MSC Clara* using naval drones to show solidarity with Palestinians in Gaza. *Swan Atlantic*'s owner, Norway's Inventor Chemical Tankers, said the vessel had no link to Israel and was managed by a Singaporean firm. He added that none of the crew were hurt. The *Swan*'s water tank was damaged. The ship, carrying vegetable oils, continued to Reunion.

December 18, 2023: *Al-Jazeera* reported that U.S. Secretary of Defense Lloyd Austin announced that the UK, Bahrain, Canada, France, Italy, and the Seychelles were forming a 10-nation multi-national security initiative to protect trade in the Red Sea after a dozen shipping lines, including UK oil giant BP, the Italian-Swiss giant Mediterranean Shipping Company, France's CMA CGM and Denmark's AP Moller-Maersk, suspended operations. The coalition might also include Egypt and Jordan. *Reuters* reported on December 22 that 20 countries had joined the coalition; eight declined to be publicly named.

December 23, 2023: *CNN* reported that the Norwegian-flagged, -owned, and -operated chemical tanker *M/V Blaamanen* operating in the southern Red Sea reported a "near miss" from a one-way drone. No injuries or damage was reported.

The *USS Laboon* (DDG 58), a Navy destroyer, shot down four drones that were heading toward it. *Navy Times* reported that U.S. Central Command said the drones originated from Iran-allied Houthi rebels in Yemen. No injuries or damage was reported.

The Gabon-owned, Indian-flagged *M/V Saibaba* crude oil tanker reported that it was hit by a one-way attack drone with no injuries reported. The *USS Laboon* responded to the distress calls.

December 26, 2023: *UPI* reported that Houthi rebels in Yemen launched a missile strike against the container ship *MSC United VIII*, which is owned by Swiss shipping giant MSC, en route from Saudi Arabia to Pakistan. No crew were hurt.

December 26, 2023: *Reuters* reported that two unmanned aircraft were observed before two explosions occurred five nautical miles from a vessel located 50 nautical miles west of Hodeidah on Yemen's west coast. *NDTV* added that two other explosions occurred nearer a vessel.

Navy Times reported that U.S. Central Command announced that the Navy destroyer *USS Laboon* and F/A-18 Super Hornets from the *USS Eisenhower* Carrier Strike Group "shot down twelve one-way attack drones, three anti-ship ballistic missiles, and two land attack cruise missiles in the Southern Red Sea that were fired by the Houthis over a 10 hour period. There was no damage to ships in the area or reported injuries."

December 28, 2023: *ABC News* reported that the *USS Mason* shot down one drone and an anti-ship ballistic missile fired by the Houthis during the night. CENTCOM said there was no damage to any of the 18 vessels, mostly cargo ships, in the area at the time.

December 30, 2023: *CNN* reported that a missile struck the Singapore-flagged and Denmark-owned and -operated container ship *Maersk Hangzhou* while transiting the Southern Red Sea during the night.

CNN and *AP* reported that U.S. Central Command (CENTCOM) announced that the U.S. Navy warship *USS Gravely* shot down two anti-ship ballistic missiles fired toward a container ship from Houthi-controlled areas in Yemen during the night.

December 31, 2023: *AP* and *ABC News* reported that U.S. Central Command announced that U.S. forces fired on four Houthi boats attempting to attack the Singapore-flagged *Maersk Hanzghou*, which had earlier been hit by a missile. When U.S. helicopters from the *USS Dwight D. Eisenhower* aircraft carrier and *USS Gravely* responded to a 6:30 a.m. distress call, the small boat crews opened fire on the helicopters using crew-served weapons and small arms. *Reuters* reported that ten rebels died and three of the four boats sank. The fourth fled. No one was injured on the Maersk ship.

January 2, 2024: *Reuters* reported that a Malta-flagged container ship reported seeing three explosions towards its port quarter off Yemen, 15 miles southwest of Mocha. The three missiles had been fired from the direction of Taiz Governorate. Houthis said they had "targeted" a container ship bound for Israel with two anti-ship ballistic missiles.

January 4, 2024: *Reuters* reported that a Houthi drone boat packed with explosives detonated in the Red Sea, causing no damage or casualties. The previous day, 12 countries including the U.S., UK, and Japan cautioned the Houthis of unspecified "consequences" unless it halts its attacks.

January 6, 2024: The *U.S. Naval Institute News* reported that in the morning, the *USS Laboon* (DDG-58) shot down a Houthi-launched drone over the Red Sea. On December 23, 2003 *Laboon* shot down four drones. No casualties or damage to ships were reported.

January 10, 2024: *AP* and *CNN* reported that at 9:15 p.m., F-18s from the *USS Dwight D. Eisenhower*, American Arleigh Burke-class destroyers *USS Gravely, USS Laboon,* and *USS Mason,* as well as the UK's *HMS Diamond,* shot down 18 drones, two cruise missiles, and an anti-ship missile off the Yemeni port cities of Hodeida and Mokha. No damage to the ships was reported. The Houthis claimed credit.

The U.N. Security Council was considering a resolution drafted by the U.S. and Japanese delegations that noted that the Houthi attacks impede global commerce "and undermine navigational rights and freedoms as well as regional peace and security." The resolution demands the immediate release of the first ship the Houthis attacked, the Japanese-operated *Galaxy Leader* cargo ship with links to an Israeli company that the rebels seized in November 2023 along with its crew. The resolution affirms that the navigational rights and freedoms of merchant and commercial vessels must be respected, and takes note "of the right of member states, in accordance with international law, to defend their vessels from attacks, including those that undermine navigational rights and freedoms." The resolution passed 11-0-4 (Russia, China, Algeria, Mozambique abstaining).

January 12, 2024: *Newsweek* and *Reuters* reported that the Houthis mistakenly targeted a tanker carrying Russian oil in a missile attack off Yemen. Hawkish Russian politician Aleksey Zhuravlyov, chairman of the Rodina (Motherland) political party, had told *60 Minutes* on the *Russia 1* channel how Houthi attacks in the Red Sea were "totally beneficial for us" because "everybody is forgetting about Ukraine". The missile landed within 1,500 feet of the vessel, 90 nautical miles southeast of Aden.

Director of the Joint Staff Lt. Gen. Douglas Sims II said that the Houthis had fired at least one anti-ship ballistic missile toward a commercial vessel.

January 14, 2024: *CNN, al-Jazeera,* the *Los Angeles Times,* and *AP* reported that U.S. fighter aircraft shot down an anti-ship cruise missile fired from near Hodeida, a Red Sea port city in a Houthi-controlled area of Yemen, at the *USS Laboon,* a U.S. Navy Arleigh Burke-class destroyer. No injuries or damage were reported.

January 15, 2024: *Reuters* reported that the port side of a vessel was hit from above by a missile 95 nautical miles southeast of Aden. *CNN* added that U.S. CENTCOM said the *M/V Gibraltar Eagle,* a Marshall Islands-flagged bulk carrier owned and operated by U.S.-based Eagle Bulk, sustained minor damage and did not report any injuries on board.

January 16, 2024: *CNN* reported that Houthis claimed credit for attacking the Malta-flagged, Greek-owned *M/V Zogravia* bulk carrier headed toward Israel with a "number of suitable naval missiles", 76 nautical miles northwest of Yemen's port city of Saleef.

January 28, 2024: *Al-Jazeera* reported that the UK's Ministry of Defence announced on *X* that the *HMS Diamond* shot down a Houthi drone. No injuries or damage were reported.

January 30, 2024: *CNN* and *Military Times* reported that the *USS Gravely,* an Arleigh Burke-class guided-missile destroyer, intercepted a Houthi-fired anti-ship cruise missile shortly before midnight. U.S. CENTCOM reported that there were no injuries or damage. *Military Times* reported that the missile came within a nautical mile of the ship.

February 1, 2024: Houthis fired two ballistic missiles at a Liberian-flagged *Koi* container ship in the Red Sea west of Hodeida.

February 6, 2024: *AP* and *UPI* reported that Houthi rebels attacked two ships. One attack by a small boat occurred in the southern part of the Red Sea, west of the Yemeni port of Hodeida, with the projectile causing "slight damage" to windows on the bridge of the Barbados-flagged, United Kingdom-owned cargo ship *Morning*

Tide. The ship's owner, British firm Furadino Shipping, said no one was hurt and the ship was continuing onward to Singapore.

Houthis also attacked a Marshall Islands-flagged, Greek-owned vessel coming from the U.S. heading to India off Yemen's southern port city of Aden. The Houthis claimed it was a U.S. ship *Star Nasia.*

February 12, 2024: *Al-Jazeera* and *AP* reported that Houthi rebels fired two missiles at the Marshall Islands-flagged, Greek-operated bulk carrier *Star Iris,* a ship heading from Brazil through the Bab el-Mandeb Strait to Bandar Khomeini port in Iran, causing minor damage to its starboard side but no injuries. Star Bulk Carriers Corp. of Athens, Greece, is traded on the Nasdaq Stock Market in New York. The Houthis claimed the ship was U.S.-owned.

February 16, 2024: *AP* and *al-Jazeera* reported that at 13:31 GMT, a missile struck the port side of the *Pollux,* a Panama-flagged British oil tanker in the Red Sea off al-Mukha, variant Mocha, Yemen. All crew were reported safe and the ship was not damaged. Houthis claimed credit. The tanker was carrying crude oil to India.

February 19, 2024: A Greek-flagged, U.S.-owned bulk carrier *M/V Sea Champion* bound for Aden, Yemen, and carrying grain from Argentina was attacked twice by Houthis between 12:30 p.m. and 1:50 p.m.

The Houthis claimed they shot down an American MQ-9 Reaper drone near Yemen's port city of Hodeida.

UPI reported that a Houthi drone damaged the Marshall Islands-flagged, U.S.-owned bulk carrier *M/V Navis Fortuna* at about 7:20 p.m.

February 20, 2024: The *USS Laboon* shot down an anti-ship cruise missile fired toward it from Houthi-controlled areas of Yemen.

February 22, 2024: Zaydi Shi'ite Houthi spokesman Brig. Gen. Yahya Saree claimed a drone attack on a U.S. warship in the region. U.S. Central Command said it and an allied warship shot down six Houthi drones in the Red Sea. France's military announced it hit two Houthi drones.

February 27, 2024: A rocket exploded during the night several miles off the bow of a ship traveling through the Red Sea. No one was injured. The vessel targeted appeared to be a Marshall Islands-flagged, Greek-owned bulk carrier in the area at the time. Another ship, a Panama-flagged, Emirati-owned chemical tanker was nearby.

U.S. CENTCOM announced that a U.S. and an allied warship shot down five Houthi bomb-carrying drones in the Red Sea during the night.

March 4, 2024: *CNN* reported that Hong Kong telecoms company HGC Global Communications announced that undersea cables in the Red Sea belonging to four major telecoms networks had been "cut" causing "significant" disruption to global telecommunications networks and forcing Internet providers to reroute 25% of traffic between Asia, Europe, and the Middle East. Houthis were suspected. Damaged systems included the Asia-Africa-Europe 1 and the Europe India Gateway (EIG).

March 9, 2024: *Al-Jazeera* reported that CENTCOM announced that U.S. Navy ships and aircraft shot down 15 drones fired by Houthis between 4 a.m. and 6:30 a.m. The UAVs presented "an imminent threat to merchant vessels, U.S. Navy and coalition ships in the region". Houthi military spokesperson Yahya Saree, said the group targeted U.S. bulk carrier Propel Fortune in the Gulf of Aden and later the Houthis targeted "37 drones" against several U.S. military destroyers in the Red Sea and the Gulf of Aden. A French warship and fighter jets also shot down four combat drones that were flying toward naval vessels belonging to the European Aspides mission in the region. The French army said "This defensive action directly contributed to the protection of the cargo ship *True Confidence*, under the Barbados flag, which was struck on March 6 and is being towed, as well as other commercial vessels transiting in the area."

Task and Purpose reported on March 11 that U.S., UK, and French forces shot down 28 Houthi attack drones in a four-hour period overnight and into the morning. Houthis said the drones targeted the Singapore-owned and flagged merchant vessel *Propel Fortune.*

March 11, 2024: Houthis were suspected when an explosion went off near a ship in the Red Sea. No damage was reported and no one was hurt.

March 11, 2024: *UPI* and *Mehr* reported that Houthis fired two anti-ship missiles at the Singaporean-owned Liberian-flagged *Pinocchio* 63,000-ton container vessel as it transited the Red Sea in the morning. The missiles missed, causing no injuries or damage.

Six CENTCOM strikes against Houthi military assets destroyed an unmanned underwater drone and 18 anti-ship missiles in Yemen.

March 12, 2024: *CNN* reported that Houthis fired a close-range ballistic missile at the *USS Laboon* but missed. No injuries or damage was reported.

CENTCOM reported that U.S. forces and a coalition ship destroyed two drones launched from Houthi-controlled areas of Yemen.

March 15, 2024: Houthis attacked a tanker off Hodeida in the morning. No damage was reported. The Panama-flagged, Vietnamese-owned *Pacific 01* had reported a near miss the previous day. The private security firm Ambrey said the ship had been owned by Singapore-based Eastern Pacific Shipping, which is ultimately controlled by Israeli billionaire Idan Ofer. The ship changed owners in February 2024.

March 16, 2024: *CNN* reported that in the early morning, the master of a merchant vessel 85 nautical miles east of Aden reported an explosion in close proximity to the vessel. No damage was reported and the crew was unharmed.

March 22, 2024: *AP* and *NPR* reported that Houthis fired four anti-ship ballistic missiles toward the Red Sea, causing no injuries or damage.

March 23, 2024: The *US Naval Institute News* reported that Houthis launched five anti-ship ballistic missiles at the Chinese-owned and operated oil tanker MV *Huang Pu*, which sails under a Panamanian flag of convenience. One of the missiles hit the ship, causing a small onboard fire and minimal damage. No casualties were re-

ported. The *South China Morning Post* reported that the ship's registered owner changed in February 2024.

The *USS Carney* (DDG-64) tracked six Houthi drones over the Red Sea. Five crashed into the Red Sea; one flew inland into Yemen.

March 28, 2024: *UPI* reported that U.S. Central Command destroyed four Houthi drones fired between 6 p.m. and 10:56 p.m. at a U.S. warship and a coalition vessel in the Red Sea.

April 3, 2024: *Military Times* reported that U.S. Navy destroyer *Gravely* and U.S. forces destroyed an inbound anti-ship ballistic missile and two aerial drones launched by Houthis in Yemen. U.S. forces also destroyed a mobile surface-to-air missile system in Houthi-controlled territory.

April 8, 2024: *Business Insider* reported that during the night an Israeli warship downed a drone near Eilat via a first-time use of its new C-Dome air-defense system outfitted on the Sa'ar 6-class corvette. The C-Dome is the naval version of the Iron Dome and uses the same Tamir interceptor missiles manufactured by Rafael Advanced Defense Systems.

April 24, 2024: *BBC* and *al-Jazeera* reported that the UK said the Royal Navy warship *HMS Diamond* shot down a missile fired by Houthis from Yemen targeting a merchant vessel. The Ministry of Defence said the ship used its Sea Viper missile system.

April 25, 2024: *Al-Jazeera* reported that the Greek Ministry of National Defence said that in the morning, one of its military frigates serving in the European Union's naval mission Aspides (Greek for shields) intercepted two drones Houthis had launched from Yemen toward a commercial ship.

A Houthi missile targeted the *MV Yorktown*, a U.S.-flagged, -owned, and -operated vessel with 18 U.S. and four Greek crew members.

A second missile targeted the *MSC Darwin*.

April 26, 2024: *UPI, Reuters, al-Jazeera*, and *AP* reported that one of three missiles caused minor damage to a Panama-flagged, Seychelles-registered *Andromeda Star* British oil tanker traveling some 14 nautical miles southwest of al-Mukha (Mocha) in Yemen from Primorsk, Russia, to Vadinar, India. No injuries were reported.

The U.S. said the Antiqua-Barbados-flagged, Liberia-operated *MV Maisha* was attacked off Mocha, Yemen, near the Bab el-Mandeb Strait, which connects the Red Sea to the Gulf of Aden. No damage was reported.

April 29, 2024: Houthis were suspected when three missiles targeted a Malta-flagged Marseille, France-based CMA CGM *Manta Ray* container ship traveling from Djibouti onward to Jeddah, Saudi Arabia off the coast of Mokha, Yemen. CMA CGM said its vessel was at harbor in Djibouti and could not have been targeted.

A Houthi Samad-style bomb-carrying drone attacked the Malta-flagged, Greece-owned *Cyclades* bulk carrier. The Houthis called it a "Shihab" drone, a new name for their drone fleet.

May 1, 2024: U.S. CENTCOM announced it had downed a Houthi drone boat.

May 13, 2024: *AP* reported that on May 15, Yemen's Houthi rebels claimed to have targeted a U.S. Navy Arleigh Burke-class guided-missile destroyer and the commercial ship *Destiny* in the Red Sea on May 13. The *USS Mason* intercepted the missile during the night.

May 18, 2024: *NPR* quoted Kurdish sources who said that a missile was fired at a ship off the coast of Yemen. *AP* reported that the Panama-flagged, Greek-owned vessel *M/T Wind* sustained damage in the 1 a.m. attack. Houthis were suspected. *Wind* had recently docked in Russia and was en route to China. U.S. CENTCOM reported that the attack "caused flooding which resulted in the loss of propulsion and steering… The crew of *M/T Wind* was able to restore propulsion and steering, and no casualties were reported. *M/T Wind* resumed its course under its own power."

May 23, 2024: A missile attributed to Houthis landed in the Red Sea near the Bab el-Mandeb Strait.

May 28, 2024: A missile damaged the cargo hold of the Marshall Islands-flagged bulk carrier *M/V Laax* off the port city of Hodeida near the Bab el-Mandeb Strait. The ship was heading to Fujairah in the United Arab Emirates. Grehel Ship Management of Piraeus, Greece, manages the *Laax*. Houthi military spokesman Brig. Gen. Yahya Saree claimed credit for the attack on May 29.

May 31, 2024: *Al-Jazeera* reported that Houthi spokesman Yahya Saree claimed that Houthis launched a missile attack on the aircraft carrier *USS Eisenhower*.

June 5, 2024: *Reuters* reported that Houthis said they attacked three ships, including *Roza* and *Vantage Dream*, in the Red Sea and the Arabian Sea using missiles and drones. Shipping giant Maersk challenged the militants' claim that the targets included *Maersk Seletar*.

June 12, 2024: *AP* and *BBC* reported that Houthis near Hodeida launched a white drone boat loaded with explosives. After traveling 66 miles, the drone hit the Liberian-flagged, Greek-owned bulk carrier *M/V Tutor*, a commercial ship, causing extensive damage to the ship's stern and engine room. Crew reported severe flooding. An airborne projectile later hit the *Tutor*, which recently docked in Russia. *Reuters* reported on June 16, 2024 that U.S. Naval Forces Central Command announced that it had rescued the crew from the *Tutor* the previous day. NAVCENT reported that a Filipino civilian sailor remained missing and was believed dead. *UPI* reported that the 44,000-ton *Tutor* was unable to maneuver and sank on June 19.

June 12, 2024: The U.S. military destroyed a Houthi drone. Houthis launched two anti-ship ballistic missiles over the Red Sea, causing no damage.

June 23, 2024: Houthis were suspected when an aerial drone damaged a Liberia-flagged container ship bound for Qingdao, China at dawn off the coast of Hodeida, Yemen.

June 27, 2024: Houthis were suspected when a ship off the coast of Hodeida reported being hit.

The Malta-flagged bulk carrier *Seajoy* reported being hit in an attack. Houthis said they used a drone boat.

June 28, 2024: Five missiles landed near the Liberian-flagged *Delinox* tanker off the coast of Hodeida, causing no damage. Houthi military spokesperson Brig. Gen. Yahya Saree said the group was responsible for two attacks on ships in the Red Sea.

June 30, 2024: *Stars and Stripes* reported that U.S. Central Command destroyed three Houthi unmanned surface vehicles that "presented an imminent threat to U.S. and coalition forces, and merchant vessels in the region."

July 7, 2024: *Stars and Stripes* reported American forces and their partners destroyed four aerial drones launched by Houthi militants in Yemen over the weekend. CENTCOM said two of the drones were destroyed in Houthi-controlled areas of Yemen. The other two drones were shot down by unspecified partner forces over the Gulf of Aden.

July 10, 2024: Houthis were suspected of targeting the *Mount Fuji*, a Liberian-flagged tanker, south of Mocha in the Bab el-Mandeb Strait. The captain reported explosions off the ship's side.

July 15, 2024: *AP* and *UPI* reported that three small blue and white Houthi vessels, two crewed and one uncrewed, attacked the Panama-flagged and Israeli-owned *MT Bently I* off the coast of Al Hudaydah, Yemen. The captain reported three separate waves of missile attacks that exploded in close proximity to the vessel around 8 a.m.

A Houthi drone crashed into the Liberian-flagged and Marshall Islands-owned *MT Chios Lion* oil tanker, causing some damage. *BBC* reported that the Houthis released a video of the attack. The ship had left Tuapse, Russia on July 2 and entered the Red Sea on July 11.

Later that day, the Houthis claimed responsibility for the attacks.

U.S. Central Command said U.S. forces destroyed five uncrewed Houthi aerial vehicles, three over the Red Sea and two in Houthi-controlled areas of Yemen.

July 21, 2024: Houthis claimed responsibility for targeting the *Pumba*, a Liberia-flagged container vessel transiting the Red Sea. The captain of the ship reported attacks from three small Houthi vessels, an uncrewed Houthi aerial vehicle, and missile fire off the coast of Mocha, Yemen, causing "minor damage" to the ship.

August 8, 2024: Houthis were suspected of four attacks on the Liberian-flagged oil tanker *Delta Blue* in the Bab el-Mandeb Strait linking the Gulf of Aden to the Red Sea. In one attack, a rocket-propelled grenade exploded close to the ship. Two smaller craft, with men aboard wearing white and yellow raincoats, launched the RPG. On August 9, a missile exploded near the ship, causing no injuries or damage. Private security guards shot and destroyed a bomb-laden drone boat. In a fourth attack, suspected Houthi missiles splashed in water near the ship.

August 13, 2024: A ship was attacked three times, including by a bomb-carrying drone boat. Houthis were suspected. Initially, an explosive went off near it, then a small vessel "acting suspiciously" flashed a light near the ship and came close, followed by a second blast. Hours later, the drone boat attacked but was "successfully disabled".

August 21, 2024: *AP* reported that numerous 3 a.m. attacks, including by gunmen on small boats, against the Greek-flagged *Sounion* oil tanker left the ship "not under command" and drifting ablaze. Four projectiles hit the ship, which was traveling from Iraq to Cyprus. No injuries were reported among the 29 mariners, who were rescued by a French destroyer. The vessel was staffed by a crew of 25 Filipinos and Russians, as well as four private security personnel, who were taken to nearby Djibouti. Houthis claimed credit. *Sounion* is associated with the Greek firm Delta Tankers. *Reuters* reported that by August 23, the ship was at anchor and no longer drifting. The European Union mission in the Red Sea said that the ship carried 150,000 tons of crude oil and represented a "navigational and environmental hazard". By August 28, the ship, still on fire, was leaking oil.

CNN reported that the French ship was part of Eunavfor Aspides, a European Union defensive maritime security operation aimed at protecting merchant and commercial vessels in the Red Sea, the Indian Ocean, and the Gulf. 24082101

AP reported on August 30 that Houthis released a video showing them boarding the ship and placing explosives on it while chanting, "God is the greatest; death to America; death to Israel; curse the Jews; victory to Islam."

September 2, 2024: *UPI* and *AP* reported that two projectiles believed fired by Houthis hit the Panama-flagged oil tanker *Blue Lagoon I* some 70 nautical miles from Saleef, Yemen; a third explosion was reported nearby. No casualties were reported. The ship, which is operated by a Greece-based firm, was coming from Russia's port of Ust-Luga on the Baltic Sea and had been broadcasting that it had Russian-origin cargo on board. It had traveled in recent months to India, which gets more than 40% of its oil imports from Russia.

In a separate attack a few miles away, an aerial drone hit a merchant ship off Hodeida, Yemen, causing no damage or injuries.

September 27, 2024: *Stars and Stripes* reported that the Pentagon announced that it had shot down missiles and bomber drones as Navy destroyers transited the Bab al-Mandeb Strait. Houthis claimed their 23 missiles and bomber drones damaged three U.S. Navy warships. Destroyers in the region include the *USS Spruance, USS Stockdale,* and *USS O'Kane.*

October 1, 2024: An explosives-loaded drone boat crashed into a ship while a missile exploded against another. Houthis were suspected. Houthi military spokesman Brigadier General Yahya Saree claimed the two attacks in a prerecorded message, although he incorrectly identified the second ship.

The first attack occurred 70 miles off Hodeida, Yemen, targeting the Panama-flagged oil tanker *Cordelia Moon,* a ship heading north to the Suez Canal with armed private security guards aboard. The drone punctured one of the ship's ballast tanks. The Indian managers of the ship also manage the *Andromeda Star,* which the Houthis attacked in April 2024.

In the second attack, a missile targeted the Liberian-flagged bulk carrier *Minoan Courage.*

October 10, 2024: Houthis were suspected when a projectile damaged the Liberian-flagged chemical tanker *Olympic Spirit.* No injuries were reported. Two other projectiles fell into nearby waters.

October 28, 2024: *Military.com* reported that Houthis fired on the Liberian-flagged bulk carrier *Motaro* traveling through the narrow Bab el-Mandeb Strait off the Red Sea, causing no damage or injuries. The ship's captain reported two explosions near the ship.

November 11, 2024: *Military Times* and *al-Jazeera* reported that Houthis fired missiles at U.S. Navy destroyers *USS Stockdale* and *USS Spruance* as the warships transited the Bab al-Mandeb strait that links the Red Sea and Gulf of Aden. Pentagon spokesman Air Force Maj. Gen. Pat Ryder told reporters that the ships shot down "at least eight attack drones, five anti-ship ballistic missiles, and three anti-ship cruise missiles... The vessels were not damaged, no personnel were hurt." Houthi military spokesman Yahya Sarea claimed they attacked the U.S. aircraft carrier *USS Abraham Lincoln* and the two destroyers.

November 12, 2024: Houthis were suspected when multiple explosions struck near a vessel traveling through the Red Sea. No damage was reported.

November 17, 2024: Houthis were suspected of attacking a commercial ship traveling during the night through the Red Sea and Gulf of Aden near the Bab el-Mandeb Strait, causing no damage or injuries.

December 1, 2024: U.S. Navy destroyers *USS Stockdale* and *USS O'Kane* shot down three anti-ship ballistic missiles, three drones, and one anti-ship cruise missile fired by Yemen's Houthi rebels at the warships and three American merchant vessels they were escorting through the Gulf of Aden. No damage or injuries were reported.

SAUDI ARABIA

June 28, 2023: *CBS News, Saudi Press Agency,* and *CNN* reported that a gunman was killed by the Makkah al-Mukarramah Police after he killed a Nepalese security guard outside the U.S. Consulate General in Jeddah. No Americans were harmed. The gunman stopped his car near the consulate during the evening.

September 25, 2023: *Al-Jazeera* and the official *Bahrain News Agency* reported that Bahrain claimed that a drone attack by Houthis killed two Bahraini soldiers and wounded several other Bahraini troops on the Saudi border with Yemen. *Al-Jazeera* reported on September 28 that a third Bahraini soldier, First Warrant Officer Adam Salem Naseeb, died. *AP* and the state-run *Bahrain News Agency* added that a fourth Bahraini soldier, 1st Lt. Hamad Khalifa al-Kubaisi, died on September 29 from his wounds.

SYRIA

January 2023: *UPI* reported that U.S. Central Command (CENTCOM) and coalition forces, including the Syrian Democratic Forces and Iraqi Security Forces, killed 11 ISIS operatives and apprehended 227 in 43 operations targeting ISIS operatives in Iraq and Syria in January.

January 4, 2023: *News 360* and *Europa Press* reported that at 9 a.m., two shells hit the Conoco support base of the U.S.-led international coalition in Deir Ezzor Province, causing no casualties. The Syrian Democratic Forces (SDF) found a third unused shell. The London-based Syrian Observatory for Human Rights indicated that the shots were allegedly fired by pro-Iranian militiamen.

January 8, 2023: *AP* and the *News Movement* reported that Hoda Muthana, 28, who left her Alabama home in 2014 at age 20 to join ISIS and had a son with one of its fighters, said that she wanted to return to the U.S., serve prison time if necessary, and advocate against the extremists. Kurdish forces held her in the Roj detention camp in Syria. In 2015, she tweeted that Americans should join ISIS and carry out

attacks in the U.S., such as drive-by shootings or vehicle rammings on national holidays. Her first two husbands were killed in battle; she divorced a third. She said she was brainwashed online and claimed that the tweets were from ISIS fighters who took her phone. She fled from an ISIS enclave in early 2019.

She was born in New Jersey to Yemeni immigrants and once had a U.S. passport. She grew up in a conservative Muslim household in Hoover, Alabama. In 2014, she told her family she was going on a school trip but flew to Türkiye and crossed into Syria instead. She used tuition checks to fund the trip. The Obama administration cancelled her citizenship in 2016, saying her father was an accredited Yemeni diplomat at the time she was born. The Trump administration refused to allow her to return.

January 18, 2023: *Fox* reported that a U.S. CENTCOM and SDF coalition forces helicopter assault captured an ISIS extremist involved in global recruiting.

January 19, 2023: *UPI* reported that in the early morning, three attack drones were launched at the U.S. military's At-Tanf Garrison, injuring two Syrian Free Army militia fighters but no Americans. Two of the drones were shot down.

January 21, 2023: *Reuters* and *Task and Purpose* reported that U.S. CENTCOM forces captured ISIS facilitator Abdallah Hamid Muslih al-Maddad, alias Abu Hamza al-Suri; ISIS logistician Husam Hamid al-Muslih al-Maddad al-Khayr; and a third associate during a joint helicopter and ground assault in eastern Syria. One male civilian sustained minor injuries.

February 10, 2023: *Task and Purpose* reported that U.S. CENTCOM said its troops and the Syrian Democratic Forces killed "ISIS official" Ibrahim al-Qahtani, who was associated with planning ISIS detention center attacks. U.S. troops captured weapons, ammunition, and a suicide belt.

February 12, 2023: *News 360, SANA,* and *Europa* reported ISIS terrorists firing machine guns attacked people picking truffles near Palmyra, killing four, including a woman, injuring ten, and abducting 75, including several women.

February 13, 2023: *AP* and the *Florida Times-Union* reported that during the night gunmen attacked a hospital in Afrin where a baby girl was receiving care after being born under the rubble of her family's home following the February 6 7.8-magnitude earthquake. Aya ("sign from God") lost her mother (Afraa Abu Hadiya), father (Abdullah Turki Mleihan), and four siblings. The attackers beat the clinic's director. A hospital administrator denied reports that the gunmen planned to kidnap the infant; his wife had been breastfeeding the child. The gunmen told local police that they were going after the director for firing their friend, a nurse who was believed to be taking pictures of the child.

February 16, 2023: *CNN* and *Military Times* noted that four U.S. troops and a working dog were wounded in a helicopter raid that killed senior ISIS leader Hamza al-Homsi.

February 17, 2023: *Al-Jazeera*, *AP*, the *Jerusalem Post*, and *NDTV* reported that 53 people died in an ISIS raid against an army checkpoint and people collecting truffles near Sukhna.

February 23, 2023: The *Daily Beast* reported that Ahmet, 13, and Hamid, 14, told SDF officers at the newly-opened Orkesh rehab center in camp al-Hol that ISIS women were forcing ten teen boys to impregnate them to increase the ISIS population. Similar reports came from the al-Roj camp.

March 23, 2023: The *Washington Post* and *AP* reported that an Iranian self-detonating drone hit a U.S. military position in Tanf on the Iraqi border, killing an American contractor and wounding five U.S. troops, two Free Syrian Army members, and a second U.S. contractor. Coalition forces downed two other drones. The Pentagon launched retaliatory F-15 airstrikes from al-Udeid Air Base in Qatar against an Iranian Islamic Revolutionary Guard Corps maintenance facility within a military base near Hasakah. The Deir Ezzor 24 activist group said that four members of Iranian-linked militias were killed in the American strikes around Deir el-Zour, variant Ezzor, variant ez-Zor, variant al-Zor, and that others, including Iraqi citizens, were wounded. The Syrian Observatory for Human Rights reported that the next day, three rockets were fired at al-Omar oil field in Deir el-Zour, which houses U.S. troops.

March 24, 2023: *AFP* reported that ISIS killed 15 people, including seven civilians and eight pro-regime fighters, foraging for desert truffles in central Syria, by cutting their throats. Another 40 were missing in Hamas Province. Since February, ISIS had killed 150 truffle hunters directly or via land mines.

March 31, 2023: *News 360* and *Europa* reported that the SDF killed two ISIS suicide bombers in Hasaka Province.

April 2, 2023: The *Telegraph* reported a car bomb exploded close to a crowded roundabout by a busy restaurant in an upmarket suburb of Damascus near Mezzah military airport, causing no injuries. The area houses senior government and security officials and a United Nations headquarters.

April 3, 2023: *CNN*, *Newsweek*, and *UPI* reported that a unilateral U.S. strike killed senior ISIS leader Khalid 'Aydd Ahmad al-Jabouri, who planned attacks into Europe. The London-based Syrian Observatory for Human Rights said al-Jabouri had moved to Idlib ten days before the attack.

April 8, 2023: *SANA* reported that an ISIS anti-tank mine killed six truffle hunters near Homs.

The *Hill* reported that U.S. forces captured ISIS attack facilitator Hudayfah al-Yemeni and two of his associates in a late-night raid in eastern Syria.

April 9, 2023: *DW* and *SANA* reported that nine workers foraging for truffles were killed when their vehicle hit an ISIS land mine in Deir Ez-Zor Province.

April 10, 2023: *UPI*, *The Hill*, and *AP* reported that two rockets were fired at 9 a.m. against coalition forces at Mission Support Site Conoco in Deir el-Zour Province. No one was injured and no damage was reported. The SDF found a third unfired rocket. No one claimed credit. Iran-backed fighters based in eastern Syria were suspected.

April 11, 2023: *UPI* reported that the U.S. State Department designated Jordanian citizen Sami Mahmud Mohammed al-Uraydi, leader of Hurras al-Din, an al-Qaeda-affiliated jihadist group in Syria, as a Specially Designated Global Terrorist. The group, which was formed in February 2018 after the merger of seven Syrian rebel factions with ten other AQ affiliates, was designated in September 2019. State's Rewards for Justice Program offered $5 million for information on him. State said he was a senior sharia official of Hurras al-Din and a member of its shura senior decision-making body.

April 16, 2023: *AFP, UPI, BBC,* and *The Week* reported that ISIS was suspected of killing 36 truffle hunters in the Badia desert east of Hama.

ISIS gunmen on motorbikes and firing rifles were suspected of killing five shepherds in Deir El-Zour. The gunmen stole sheep.

April 17, 2023: *CNN* reported that U.S. CENTCOM announced that a morning helicopter raid killed a senior ISIS leader and planner and two other gunmen in northeast Syria.

April 29, 2023: *CNN, UPI, CBS News,* the *Jerusalem Post,* and *AFP* reported that Turkish President Recep Tayyip Erdogan announced that Türkiye's National Intelligence Organization (MIT) had killed the suspected leader of ISIS, Abu Hussein al-Husseini al-Qurashi, at an abandoned farm that was being used as an Islamic school in Jindires (variant Jandaris), in the northwest region of Afrin in Syria, on April 29.

Business Day and *Reuters* reported that al-Qurashi detonated a suicide vest during a four-hour Turkish special forces raid after refusing to surrender in his hideout in a two-storey building. Qurashi never made a public address.

May 2, 2023: *UPI* reported that the United States and Türkiye announced economic sanctions against Syrian Abu Ahmed Zakour, alias Omar al-Sheak, 44, a leader of Hay'at Tahrir al-Sham, and Turk Kubilay Sari, 31, who were accused of being financial facilitators for U.S. and U.N. designated al-Qaeda-linked terrorist groups in Syria.

Zakour is a member of the HTS Shura council and an emir of the Aleppo army. He supervised the group's international economic portfolio.

Istanbul-based Sari is affiliated with Katibat al-Tawhid wal-Jihad, a predominantly Uzbek jihadist group that operates out of Syria's Idlib Province. The group was blamed for the Saint Petersburg Metro bombing of April 2017 that killed 14 people and the suicide car bombing of China's Kyrgyzstan embassy in August 2016. The U.S. designed KTJ as a Specially Designated Global Terrorist Organization in March 2022; the U.N. Security Council also sanctioned the group. Sari allegedly received funds in Türkiye from donors for KTJ fundraisers who used the money to purchase weapons systems, including firearms and mortars.

July 7, 2023: *CNN* reported that a U.S. CENTCOM MQ-9 Reaper drone killed ISIS leader Usama al-Muhajir in eastern Syria. Russian aircraft had harassed the drones earlier that day.

July 25, 2023: *Al-Jazeera* reported that two civilians were wounded after a bomb on a motorcycle was detonated in the Sayeda Zeinab neighbourhood.

July 27, 2023: *Al-Jazeera* and *al-Ikhbariya* state TV reported that a bomb on a motorcycle exploded near a taxi near a Shi'a shrine south of Damascus, a day before the Ashura day of mourning, killing six and wounding more than 20. The bomb went off near the mausoleum of Sayeda Zeinab, granddaughter of the Prophet Muhammad and the daughter of Imam Ali.

August 3, 2023: *Reuters, al-Jazeera,* and *AP* reported that ISIS spokesman Abu Huthaifa al-Ansari confirmed on *Telegram* that on August 3, 2023 the death of its emir Abu Hussein al-Husseini al-Quraishi and named Abu Hafs al-Hashimi al-Quraishi as his replacement. Turkish President Tayyip Erdogan said in April 2023 that Turkish intelligence forces had killed him in Syria. ISIS claimed al-Quraishi was killed during a gun battle with Hayat Tahrir al-Sham (HTS) in Idlib Province, Syria. The ISIS spokesman said HTS was acting on behalf of Turkish intelligence and handed al-Quraishi's body to

Türkiye. "The Sheikh (Quraishi), may God have mercy on him, was killed after they (HTS) tried to take him captive. He clashed with them with his arms until he died of his wounds." Al-Ansari added that HTS detained some ISIS members, including spokesman Abu Omar al-Muhajir, and that they were still being held.

August 9, 2023: *Al-Jazeera* and *SANA* reported a roadside bomb killed Firas al-Ahmad, a reporter for the Damascus-based outlet *Sama TV*, and three Syrian government soldiers on a road in the area of al-Shayyiah in Deraa Governorate. A cameraman in the car was rescued by local villagers.

August 11, 2023: *Al-Jazeera* and *AFP* reported that suspected ISIS gunmen ambushed a bus carrying Syrian soldiers near Mayadeen in Deir el-Zour Province that borders Iraq, killing 23 and injuring ten.

August 21, 2023: *Al-Jazeera* reported that a bomb exploded near an Israeli military vehicle near Lake Tiberias in the southern occupied Golan Heights, injuring an Israeli soldier.

September 23, 2023: *AP* and *UPI* reported that in the morning, U.S. CENTCOM captured ISIS operative Abu Halil al-Fad'ani during a helicopter raid in northern Syria.

October 5, 2023: *UPI* and *AP* reported that a multiple drone attack on cadets and their families attending a graduation ceremony at a military school in Homs killed 89 people, including 31 women and six children, and injured 277. Defense Minister Ali Mahmoud Abbas left the academy minutes before the attack. Many of the wounded were in serious condition.

November 8, 2023: *Al-Jazeera* reported that in the morning, ISIS conducted machine gun attacks in the regions of Raqqa, Homs, and Deir el-Zour, killing 26 Syrian pro-government National Defence Forces militia and four soldiers and wounding several others, some critically, stationed in the desert.

November 11, 2013: *CNN* reported that in the morning, a one-way attack drone targeted U.S.

forces at al-Tanf Garrison, but was shot down before reaching its target. There were no casualties or infrastructure damage reported.

November 12, 2023: *CNN* reported that in the evening, Iran-backed groups fired several rockets at troops at Mission Support Site Euphrates and two one-way drone attacks were launched on troops at Mission Support Site Green Village and al-Shaddadi, Syria. Both drones were shot down.

November 13, 2023: *CNN* reported that in the morning, several one-way attack drones were launched against U.S. forces at Rumalyn Landing Zone. One drone was shot down, another drone hit the landing zone and caused minor damage to four tents. No casualties were reported.

As of November 13, there had been 52 attacks by Iranian-backed groups against U.S. and coalition forces since October 17, including 24 attacks in Iraq, and 28 attacks in Syria. Some 56 troops were injured, including 25 traumatic brain injuries.

November 23, 2023: *CNN* reported that a multi-rocket attack was launched against forces at Mission Support Site Euphrates in Syria. There were no casualties or infrastructure damage.

In the afternoon, a one-way attack drone was launched against forces at Mission Support Site Green Village in Syria. There were no casualties or infrastructure damage. 23112304

November 29, 2023: *CNN* reported that a rocket was fired at U.S. and coalition forces at Mission Support Site Euphrates. The rocket did not hit the base, causing no injuries or infrastructure damage.

January 8, 2024: *CNN* reported that the IDF said it killed Hamas militant Hassan Hakashah in Beit Jinn, Syria. The IDF noted that he was a central figure in firing rockets from Syria toward Israel in recent weeks.

January 29, 2024: *CNN* reported that several rockets were fired at U.S. Patrol Base Shaddadi in the morning.

January 30, 2024: *UPI* reported that the U.S. Departments of State and Treasury sanctioned alleged ISIS supporters Egyptian nationals Mu'min al-Mawji Mahmud Salim, 32, and Sarah Jamal Muhammad al-Sayyid, 38, and Turkish citizen Faruk Guzel, 55. Two were accused of providing ISIS with cybersecurity expertise. State and Treasury said they facilitated ISIS "use of virtual currency, recruitment and promotion of its terrorist ideology—as well as ISIS's transfers of funds to its supporters". The FBI said Mahmud Salim created the ISIS-affiliated Electronic Horizons Foundation platform with the support of al-Sayyid, his fiancée. Both are on its Most Wanted Terrorists List. The FBI offers $20,000 for their locations.

February 4, 2024: A nighttime drone attack on al-Omar base housing U.S. troops in Deir el-Zour Province in eastern Syria killed six or seven allied Kurdish SDF fighters and wounded 18, some critically. No casualties were reported among U.S. troops. The Islamic Resistance in Iraq released a video claiming responsibility.

March 6, 2024: ISIS attacked villagers collecting truffles in eastern Syria, killing 18 people, including four members of the pro-government National Defense Forces. Sixteen were injured and 50 went missing in a desert area near Kobajeb, in Deir el-Zour Province that borders Iraq. ISIS set alight a dozen vehicles. The pro-government *Dama Post* said 44 died.

March 8, 2024: Abu Mohammed al-Golani, leader of the al-Qaeda-linked Hayat Tahrir al-Sham group, released one of its Iraqi founders, Maysara al-Jubouri, alias Abu Maria al-Qahtani, who had been jailed since August 2023 on suspicion of having links with forces outside the country and for misuse of social media. An investigation proved him innocent. Hundreds of members of the public had been protesting in Idlib, demanding al-Golani leave and asking for the release of detainees. Earlier in the week, the group released 420 detainees.

March 31, 2024: *BBC* reported that seven people, including two children, were killed and several others injured when a car bomb exploded at a busy market in Azaz in Aleppo Province, near the Turkish border. Pro-Turkish militias fighting Syrian President Bashar al-Assad run Azaz. Shoppers were buying new clothes for their children ahead of Eid al-Fitr, which marks the end of Ramadan. No group claimed credit.

April 4, 2024: A suicide bomber killed Iraqi citizen Maysara al-Jubouri, alias Abu Maria al-Qahtani, co-founder of the Nusra Front in Syria, a militant group that later renamed itself Hayat Tahrir al-Sham and claimed it had ended ties with al-Qaeda. Between two and nine guests at al-Qahtani's house were wounded. The UK-based Observatory for Human Rights reported that the bomber entered al-Qahtani's guesthouse in Sarmada in Idlib Province in the evening and set off his explosives. Other reports said the bomb was remotely detonated.

April 6, 2024: *AP* and *SANA* reported that a roadside bomb in Daraa killed seven or eight children and injured two other people.

April 18, 2024: Gunmen attacked a bus carrying members of the Quds Brigade, a government and Russian-backed faction of mostly Palestinian fighters in Syria, near Sukhna during the night, killing 22. The UK-based Syrian Observatory for Human Rights and the pro-government radio station *Sham FM* blamed ISIS.

April 25, 2024: Kurdish-led authorities in northeastern Syria repatriated 17 women and 33 children—family members of ISIS militants—to a delegation from Tajikistan headed by the Tajik ambassador to Kuwait, Zubaydullo Zubaydzoda.

May 3, 2024: ISIS was suspected when gunmen attacked three posts for Syrian government forces and pro-government gunmen in the morning, killing between 13 and 15 people and wounding two others near Sukhna in Homs Province.

May 7, 2024: *NPR* and *AP* reported that a family of ten U.S. citizens—Brandy J. Salman, 50, and her nine children, ranging in age from seven to 26—returned to the U.S. after years in a Syrian refugee camp and detention center for relatives of ISIS terrorists. The U.S. arrested one of her adult daughters on May 7, 2024. Initially, at least, she will live with her mother in New Hampshire.

Salman was born in western Massachusetts and also lived in Michigan, New Hampshire, and New York City. She married a Turkish-American man, who took the family into ISIS-controlled territory around 2016 and was later killed.

Also returning were the 7-year-old son and 9-year-old stepson of Abelhamid al-Madioum, 27, a Minnesota man who pleaded guilty to supporting ISIS. They were to live with their grandparents in Minnesota. The 9-year-old is not a U.S. citizen.

During the week, Canada, Finland, and the Netherlands repatriated 11 of their citizens, mostly children, held in the camps. Six minors went to Canada, an adult in his 20s to Finland, and two women and two minors to the Netherlands.

May 10, 2024: The U.S.-backed Kurdish-led Syrian Democratic Forces handed over to Baghdad two ISIS terrorists suspected of involvement in the killing of 1,700 Iraqi soldiers trying to flee from Camp Speicher after ISIS had seized Saddam Hussein's home town of Tikrit in 2014.

May 22, 2024: Syrian Kurdish-led authorities handed over to a U.K. delegation a British woman and three children linked to ISIS who had been held at the Roj camp.

May 25, 2024: A sticky bomb attacked to a car exploded in the early morning in the Mazze neighborhood of Damascus, near several diplomatic missions, including the Iranian Consulate which was destroyed in April in a strike blamed on Israel. *SANA* reported that one person died and two cars were burned. The Syrian Observatory for Human Rights said the man killed was a Mazze resident who carried a card identifying him as a Syrian army officer; he had close ties to the Iranians.

June 16, 2024: *The Hill* reported that a CENTCOM airstrike killed senior ISIS official Usamah Jamal Muhammad Ibrahim al-Janabi.

August 9, 2024: *CNN* reported that a drone attack on the Rumalyn Landing Zone injured several United States and coalition personnel and damaged a facility. *Military.com* reported on August 13 that eight U.S. service members were treated for smoke inhalation and traumatic brain injury. By then, three service members had returned for duty.

August 23, 2024: A CENTCOM drone strike in the Jabal al-Zawiya area of Idlib Province killed Abu Abdul Rahman Makki, a senior Saudi leader in the al-Qaeda-linked Horas al-Din (Guardians of Religion) as he was riding on a motorcycle. CENTCOM said he was "responsible for overseeing terrorist operations from Syria." The group includes AQ members who broke away from Hayat Tahrir al-Sham, which had imprisoned Makki. Makki was a former leader of the now-defunct extremist Jund al-Aqsa.

September 1, 2024: In a morning raid, CENTCOM and Syrian Democratic Forces captured Khaled Ahmed al-Dandal, an ISIS facilitator who helped five ISIS foreign terrorist fighter detainees—two Russians, two Afghans and one Libyan—escape from Raqqah detention facility on August 29. The SDF recaptured escapees Imam Abdulwahed Akhwan of Russia, and Muhammad Noh Muhammad of Libya. Three remained at large: Timor Talbrken Abdash of Russia, and Shuab Muhammad al-Abdli and Atal Khaled Zar of Afghanistan.

September 16, 2024: A CENTCOM air strike on an ISIS training camp in central Syria killed 28 terrorists, including four senior Syrian leaders.

September 17, 2024: The *New York Times* reported that 14 people were injured by pager explosions similar to those in Lebanon. *Saberin News*, an outlet affiliated with Iran's Revolutionary Guards, claimed that seven people were killed in the Seyedah Zeinab area.

September 24, 2024: A U.S. CENTCOM airstrike killed nine militants, including a senior leader of the al-Qaeda-linked al-Hurras al-Deen group who oversaw military operations.

September 26, 2024: *Stars and Stripes* reported that in the early morning, a rocket hit U.S. Mission Support Site Euphrates in eastern Syria. No personnel were injured.

October 28, 2024: *UPI* reported that CENT-COM announced that airstrikes on ISIS camps killed 35 terrorists.

November 10, 2024: *Military Times* reported that Iran-backed militants fired drones and rockets at U.S. forces at Mission Support Sight Green Village, causing no injuries. *UPI* reported that CENTCOM hit nine targets across two storage facilities and logistics headquarters "associated with Iranian groups" in retaliation for the attack at Patrol Base Shaddadi.

November 25, 2024: *Stars and Stripes* reported that CENTCOM conducted an airstrike on November 25 against an Iran-backed militant weapons storage facility in Syria. The strike came in response to an Iranian-backed militant attack on November 25 against U.S. forces in Syria which caused no injuries to U.S. personnel or damage to base facilities.

The Pentagon said U.S. forces had been attacked 125 times in Syria and 79 times in Iraq since the Hamas attack of October 7, 2023 in Israel.

December 8, 2024: Islamist Hayat Tahrir al-Sham rebels, led by Abu Mohammed al-Golani, toppled the regime of Bashar al-Assad, who had supported terrorist groups and fled to Moscow. Many HTS members had links to ISIS and HTS had been an al-Qaeda affiliate.

December 8, 2024: *Defense News* reported that dozens of CENTCOM airstrikes by B-52 bombers, F-15 fighters, and A-10 Warthogs using 140 munitions hit more than 75 ISIS sites, targeting leaders, operatives, and camps.

December 19, 2024: *Stars and Stripes* reported that a U.S. CENTCOM airstrike killed ISIS leader Abu Yusif and another operative in a region previously controlled by the government of former President Bashar Assad and Russian forces.

December 20, 2024: *CNN* reported that Assistant Secretary of State for Near Eastern Affairs Barbara Leaf announced that the U.S. had dropped the $10 million Rewards for Justice bounty it had offered regarding Ahmad al-

Sharaa, alias Abu Mohammad al-Jolani, head of Hayat Tahrir al-Sham (HTS) and de facto leader of Syria who met with a senior U.S. delegation that included Leaf, Special Presidential Envoy for Hostage Affairs Roger Carstens, and NEA Senior Adviser Daniel Rubinstein.

TUNISIA

May 9, 2023: *The Guardian*, the *Washington Post*, *TAP, UPI, AP*, and *Reuters* reported that a member of the national guard at a naval installation in Aghir turned his gun on a colleague, seized his ammunition, then killed a security officer and two visitors and injured five security officers and four visitors in an attack near the 2,500-year-old Ghriba synagogue on Djerba. Security forces shot him dead. Former tourism minister René Trabelsi, a prominent member of the Tunisian Jewish community who was at the synagogue at the time of the attack, said among the dead was French Tunisian bakery owner Benjamin Haddad, 42, who had traveled from Marseille, France. Another was Tunisian-Israeli jeweler Aviel Haddad, 30, his cousin. More than 5,000 Jews, mostly from overseas, participated in this year's Lag B'Omer pilgrimage to Ghriba, Africa's oldest synagogue.

In April 2002, an al-Qaeda truck bomber killed 21 people, mostly German tourists, at the synagogue.

February 25, 2024: *AP* reported on March 2 that authorities arrested a public official in his late 40s believed to have started a fire in a garden at a synagogue in Sfax on February 25. No casualties were reported.

UNITED ARAB EMIRATES

November 21, 2024: Israeli security authorities suggested that Israeli-Moldovan rabbi Zvi Kogan, 28, who had gone missing at noon, may have been kidnapped. *CNN, BBC*, the *Washington Post*, and *AP* reported on November 24 that Israeli authorities said he was found dead, victim of an antisemitic terrorist attack. His abandoned car was found an hour's drive from his home. Kogan was a representative of Chabad

Lubavitch, a movement of ultra-Orthodox Hasidic Jews based in Brooklyn's Crown Heights neighborhood. Chabad's website said he was abducted from Dubai, where he ran the Rimon Market, a Kosher grocery store, on al-Wasl Road. Kogan's wife Rivky is a U.S. citizen. Her uncle, Rabbi Gavriel Holtzberg, died in the 2008 terrorist attacks in Mumbai, India.

NBC News reported on November 24 that UAE authorities arrested three suspects. *AP* and the state-run *WAM* news agency on November 25 identified the male Uzbek suspects as Olimboy Tohirovich, 28, Makhmudjon Abdurakhim, 28, and Azizbek Kamilovich, 33. *AP*, *Hürriyet*, and *Sabah* reported on November 26 that Istanbul police and Turkey's National Intelligence Organization arrested the three Uzbek suspects as they left an airport in a taxi in Istanbul. The trio were immediately extradited.

WEST BANK

January 14, 2023: *Reuters* and *UPI* reported that two Palestinians, aged 23 and 24, fired on Israeli troops from a car in Jenin. The soldiers shot back, killing the duo. The *Jerusalem Post* reported that the Palestinian Health Ministry identified them as Izz al-Din Basem Hamamra, 24, and Amjad Adnan Khaliliya, 23, members of the Palestinian Islamic Jihad.

January 26, 2023: *AP* and *CNN* reported that the IDF raided Jenin in a "counterterrorism operation" against Islamic Jihad, killing nine people in a lengthy shootout that left extensive destruction. Seven gunmen, a civilian man, and a woman in her 60s were killed in the urban refugee camp and 20 others were wounded, four seriously. Islamic Jihad said two of its fighters were killed; Hamas said four of its members were dead. Another slain fighter was a member of the al-Aqsa Brigades. The IDF said another individual surrendered.

January 31, 2023: The *Jerusalem Post* reported that two IDF reservist soldiers were moderately and lightly injured, respectively, in a car ramming at the Tapuah junction in the West Bank in the evening. The reservists were evacuated to Beilinson Medical Center. The driver turned himself in, claiming the incident was a car accident.

February 9, 2023: The *Washington Post* reported that Israeli forces shot dead a Palestinian in Hebron after he charged a checkpoint with a knife.

February 26, 2023: The *Times of Israel* and *CNN* reported that during a traffic jam, a Palestinian gunman fired on a nearby Israeli-owned car at the Einbus junction in Huwara on the Route 60 highway, killing Israeli brothers Hillel Menachem Yaniv, 21 (or 22), and Yagel Yaakov Yaniv, 16 (or 20), residents of the West Bank settlement of Har Bracha. The IDF said the terrorist apparently fled on foot. Troops found 12 nine-millimeter shell casings from a handgun or makeshift submachine gun. The gunman reportedly was wearing a Lions' Den shirt.

The *Washington Post* reported that dozens of Israeli settlers retaliated by attacking Palestinian towns, especially Huwara, torching cars and homes and shot in the abdomen Sameh al-Aqtash, 37, who died of his wounds in Zatara village. He left behind five children. Palestinian officials said 100 people, including Ammar Demandi, were injured in the nighttime raids.

February 27, 2023: *BBC* and *CNN* reported that during an evening attack on vehicles on Route 90, north of the Beit Ha'Arava Junction near Jericho, Israeli-American Elan Ganeles, 27, was shot and killed. No one claimed credit, although a Hamas spokesman observed, "The crimes conducted by the occupation and the herds of settlers will not be met but with stabbing, shooting, and car ramming". Ganeles, who lived in the U.S., was in Israel for a friend's wedding. He had attended the five-month course at Kibbutz Sde Eliyahu in 2015 before joining the Israeli army and later studied at Columbia University. *Reuters* reported on March 1 that Israeli security forces in a daylight raid in the Aqabat Jabr refugee camp killed one Palestinian and arrested three others suspected of involvement in the shooting.

March 4, 2023: The *Times of Israel* reported that during the night, Palestinian gunmen in a car fired on Israeli soldiers near the village of Shuweika, close to the Palestinian city of Tulkarem. Authorities detained seven terror suspects. No troops were hurt.

Gunmen fired on motorists on the Route 60 highway near the Beit Hagai settlement, causing no injuries. The previous evening, Palestinian gunmen in the same area lightly hurt an Israeli man.

March 10, 2023: *AFP* reported that a settler killed a Palestinian attacker armed with knives and explosive devices at the Dorot Illit settlement in the northern West Bank. The Palestinian health ministry identified him as Abd al-Karim al-Sheikh, 21.

March 12, 2023: *Middle East Eye* and *AP* reported that Israeli forces shot to death three Palestinians who had fired on troops near Nablus. The al-Aqsa Martyrs Brigade claimed credit. The Palestinian Health Ministry identified the gunmen as Jihad Mohammed al-Shami, 24; Uday Othman al-Shami, 22; and Mohammed Raed Dabeek, 18. The IDF confiscated three M16 rifles. Another gunman surrendered.

April 7, 2023: *Reuters, AP, AFP,* the *Washington Post,* and *UPI* reported that gunmen killed two British-Israeli sisters, aged 16 and 20, whose car came under fire near the Jewish settlement of Hamra. Hamas praised the shooting, but did not claim credit for the shooting on Route 57 Highway in the northern Jordan Valley near Hamra Junction, which left the sisters' mother, 45, in critical condition; she later died of her injuries. The family lived in Efrat. Their father was driving a second vehicle, arriving after rescue crews reached the women's vehicle, which appeared to have been pushed off the road. The attack occurred hours after Israel conducted airstrikes in Lebanon and the Gaza Strip in retaliation for rocket barrages from southern Lebanon and Gaza.

NPR and the *Evening Standard* reported on May 4, 2023 that Israeli troops in Nablus killed three Palestinian militants wanted in connection with a shooting that killed three British-Israeli women on April 7. Rabbi Leo Dee lost his daughters Rina, 15, and Maia, 20, and wife Lucy, 48, in the terrorist attack. He told *Sky News:* "We were tremendously comforted by the thought they were apprehended and eliminated and that everybody in the western world can effectively

sleep safer in their beds tonight… Therefore the Israeli army has done a tremendous kindness to the world by taking out two people who could theoretically go and bomb New York, London, Paris, Tel Aviv, and kill many more innocent civilians." The family of seven had moved from the UK to Israel in 2014. Hamas identified the killers as Hamas members Hassan Qatnani, Moaz al-Masri, and Ibrahim Jabr.

May 2, 2023: An Israeli man was lightly wounded in a suspected Palestinian shooting attack.

May 28, 2023: *The Times of Israel* reported that Palestinian terrorists shot at a settlement in the northern West Bank and a town in Israel bordering the security barrier, causing slight damage.

May 29, 2023: *The Times of Israel* reported that during the night, gunmen fired on a military ambulance in the south.

May 30, 2023: *The Times of Israel* reported that Israeli man Meir Tamari, 32, was shot and killed in a drive-by shooting on a road near the Hermesh settlement west of Jenin in the northern West Bank. The Al Aqsa Martyrs Brigades claimed credit. The victim moved to Hermesh four years earlier after marrying Tal, a Hermesh resident. He left behind his wife and two children, aged one and three.

June 9, 2023: Israeli forces shot and killed a Palestinian man who attacked a soldier at a checkpoint near Ramallah in a stolen vehicle. The attacker went after the soldier who was inspecting his papers and tried to steal his weapon. Another soldier shot the terrorist, who had slightly wounded the first soldier. The Palestinian Health Ministry said the individual was Mahdi Biadsa, 29.

June 19, 2023: The *Times of Israel* reported that two Israeli soldiers were wounded during a car-ramming attack during the evening. The IDF said that a suspicious Palestinian-owned car accelerated toward troops carrying out a patrol at a checkpoint near the Palestinian village of Nazlet Zeid. Soldiers fired on the car, injuring the suspects. One soldier was treated for a sprained leg at the scene. The second, aged 38, was treated for a shrapnel wound at the Hillel Yaffe hospital in Hadera.

A roadside bomb exploded near an army vehicle in Jenin. Five Palestinians died and 100 were wounded in the ensuing gun battle. Eight IDF soldiers were wounded.

June 19, 2023: The *Washington Post* reported that the IDF conducted a raid in Jenin to arrest two suspected militants, including the son of an imprisoned senior Hamas official and a member of the Palestinian Islamic Jihad, killing six Palestinians. The Palestinians had set off a 40-kilogram bomb, damaging armored vehicles. The Jenin Brigade and PIJ claimed that several of their members were killed. The Palestinian Health Ministry said fatalities included Ahmad Yousef Ahmad Saqer, 15, and that 91 other Palestinians were injured.

June 20, 2023: *CNN, BBC, Fox News,* and the *Washington Post* reported that four Israelis were killed and another four were wounded in shootings near the settlement of Eli in the Binyamin region. Terrorists fired near a gas station; a civilian shot a Palestinian gunman to death. *Fox* reported that officials said the car arrived from the village of Urif. Two Hamas-affiliated terrorists shot into a restaurant near Eli, killing three civilians. They later fired at a gas station near the restaurant, killing another civilian. A civilian killed a terrorist; the other terrorist fled in a stolen Toyota. Shin Bet and the IDF gave chase. The terrorist tried to escape, but was shot and killed. Police found in the car the weapon used in the attack.

Israeli authorities said Muhannad Faleh Shehadeh, 24, and Khaled Mustafa Sabah, 25, opened fire at a gas station, killing Harel Masood, 21; Elisha Anteman, 17; and Ofer Fayerman, 64; and Shmuel Mordoff, 17. The IDF scheduled the homes of the terrorists for demolition.

June 20, 2023: *Reuters* and *UPI* reported that 400 Israeli settlers from Shilo injured 37 Palestinian villagers during overnight attacks in the northern West Bank from Turmus'ayya, east of Ramallah, to Deir Sharaf, west of Nablus. Fire or stones damaged 147 vehicles, including an ambulance.

Settlers damaged 23 homes and 16 shops and set fire to crops. The *Washington Post* later reported that a Palestinian was killed.

July 5, 2023: The *Times of Israel* reported that Palestinian gunmen fired from a passing vehicle at a police cruiser and a nearby store in a tiny Samaritan community close to Nablus, causing no injuries.

On July 7, 2023, *Reuters* reported that Israeli security forces killed two Palestinians in Nablus who carried out a shooting attack against police earlier in the week. The armed wing of the Popular Front for the Liberation of Palestine said the duo were members of its group.

July 6, 2023: The *Times of Israel, Reuters,* and *al-Jazeera* reported that a Palestinian gunman shot to death an Israeli man near the Kedumim settlement in the afternoon. Another person was seriously injured. A civilian security officer and IDF troops had stopped a suspicious car driving around the settlement, but the driver fired a handgun at them. The authorities chased and killed the assailant. The Izz ad-Din al-Qassam Brigades, the military wing of Hamas, claimed credit, saying the gunman was Ahmed Yassin Ghaidan of Qibya. *Wafa* identified the shooter as Ahmad Yasin Hillal Gheithan. The group warned Finance Minister Bezalel Smotrich, who lives in Kedumim, that "the al-Qassam Brigades almost knocked on your door." Ghaidan had no prior security offenses.

The *Times of Israel* reported the next day that that Staff Sgt. Shilo Yosef Amir, 22, of the IDF's Givati Brigade, was the victim. He lived in the northern town of Meirav.

July 10, 2023: *UPI* reported that the IDF's Kfir Brigade's 94th Duchifat Battalion shot and killed Palestinian Bilal Qadah, 33, who opened fire on soldiers after his small white sedan was ordered to stop on Route 450, near the Palestinian village of Deir Nidham and the Israeli village of Neve Tzuf. He exited his car with a homemade Carlo submachine gun and a hand grenade, which he hurled toward the guard. No Israeli troops were injured. *Al-Jazeera* and *Wafa* reported that Qadah lived in the village of Shuqba near Ramallah and was married with three children. The Popular Front for the Liberation of Palestine praised the "heroic martyr".

July 16, 2023: *Al-Jazeera* reported that a Palestinian gunman fired on a car near the Tekoa checkpoint near Bethlehem, seriously injuring an Israeli man, 35, and lightly injuring his daughters, 9 and 14. The family lives in the Nokdim settlement. Authorities arrested the gunman and two others in a raid in Bethlehem. They seized the gunman's car and confiscated an M16 assault rifle. Some 15 Palestinians were injured in the raid.

July 21, 2023: *AFP* and *al-Jazeera* reported that soldiers killed a Palestinian in a car-ramming attempt in Sebastia near Nablus.

July 25, 2023: *Al-Jazeera* reported that the IDF said three armed Palestinian terrorists fired on its soldiers from a vehicle in a Nablus neighborhood. The soldiers returned fire, killing the terrorists. Hamas said the trio were members. The IDF confiscated three M16 rifles and other equipment from the car.

August 1, 2023: *AFP* reported that a Palestinian gunman wearing a yellow vest fired a pistol at Israelis near a shopping mall in Maaleh Adumim settlement, wounding six people, including a teenager, before being shot dead by an off-duty border police officer. The off-duty officer was in a barbershop when he heard shots and raced to the scene. The Palestinian health ministry identified the gunman as Muhannad Mohammad al-Mazaraah, 20. Two people were in serious condition.

Later in the southern West Bank, soldiers questioned a suspicious Palestinian at a bus stop. The Army said the "suspect attempted to stab them. One of the soldiers neutralised the assailant." The Palestinian health ministry identified the assailant as Mohammad Farid al-Zaarir, 15.

August 4, 2023: The *Inquirer* and *ABC News* reported that Israeli civilians killed a Palestinian, Qusai Matan, 19, during an attack on Burqa, a Palestinian herding village. Israeli police arrested two Israeli settlers.

August 6, 2023: *AFP, BBC,* and *Reuters* reported that the Army killed three Palestinians near Arraba in "a vehicle carrying a squad of terrorists from the Jenin refugee camp... while on its way to carry out an attack". The IDF noted that suspected squad leader Nayef Abu Swiess, 26, was a "leading military operative" from the Jenin refugee camp. Palestinian Islamic Jihad announced that "The enemy will soon see that its foolish actions and terror will be met with a strong response by the resistance." Hamas added, "Our Palestinian people and their courageous resistance will not let the occupation's aggression pass without a price." *BBC* added that an automatic rifle was found in the car.

August 10, 2023: *Al-Jazeera* reported that the IDF raided the village of Zawata, west of Nablus, and shot in the head and back Palestinian armed fighter Amir Ahmad Khalifa, 27, a resident of the Ein Beit al-Ma' refugee camp, who had fired on them, killing him. The al-Aqsa Martyrs Brigades said he was a member. *AFP* said a family member said he was "wanted by Israeli forces for two years and had refused to surrender".

August 19, 2023: *UPI, Wafa, al-Jazeera,* and *Ynet* reported that gunmen killed two Israeli citizens—father and son Silas Nigerker, 60, and Aviad Nir, 28—in an attack on a car wash near Huwara. Hamas spokesperson Abdul Latif al-Qanoua praised the "heroic shooting", the "result of the resistance's continuous promise to defend our people and respond to the crimes of the occupation".

August 21, 2023: *NPR* and *al-Jazeera* reported that an Israeli woman, 40, was shot to death and her driver, 39, seriously wounded in a shooting attack on a car on Route 60 near Hebron. The woman's young daughter was unharmed. *Israeli Army Radio* reported that the attackers fired 25 bullets, 22 of which hit the settlers' car directly. Palestinian Islamic Jihad said the shooting is "a natural and legitimate response to the crimes of the occupation and its settlers' aggression against our people". Hamas spokesman Hazem Qassem said the attack "comes within its natural context in confronting the religious war against our sanctities. The [Palestinian] resistance can strike anywhere and at any time, despite the state of security alert imposed by the occupation."

Al-Jazeera reported on August 22 that joint forces from the army, the Shin Bet security service, and commandos of the Border Guard, known as Yamam, captured two Palestinian suspects, who are related, near Hebron. The IDF said the suspects confessed. The IDF confiscated the rifle used in the shooting. Palestinian media identified the duo as Saqer and Mohammed al-Shantir.

August 30, 2023: *Al-Jazeera* and *Reuters* reported that during the night, a bomb exploded, injuring four Israeli soldiers who were escorting Jewish settlers to Joseph's Tomb in Nablus.

August 31, 2023: *Al-Jazeera* and *Reuters* reported that a Palestinian truck driver, 41, crashed his vehicle into Israeli soldiers at the Maccabim checkpoint, known to Palestinians as Beit Sira, killing a soldier and injuring two others, then hitting several pedestrians. He was later killed by Israeli police at a checkpoint four miles away, according to *Haaretz*. The driver had a permit to work in Israel.

October 5, 2023: *Al-Jazeera* reported that IDF soldiers confronted two men in a "suspicious vehicle" near Shufa village in the Talkarem area. The passengers fired on a settler on a motorcycle, then engaged in a gunfight with troops, who shot them to death. Local news site *WAFA* identified the duo as Abd al-Rahman Atta and Hudhayfah Fares.

October 28, 2023: A Jewish settler shot in the chest and killed Bilal Saleh, a Palestinian man harvesting olives with his wife and their four children in Sawiya near Nablus, bringing to seven the number of Palestinians reported killed by settlers since Hamas's incursion into Israel. Settler leader Yossi Dagan posted on *Facebook* that the shooter was accompanied by family members and fired in self-defense after they were "attacked with rocks by dozens of rioting Hamas supporters".

November 2, 2023: *Al-Jazeera* and *Haaretz* reported that in the morning, gunmen killed El-hanan Klein, an Israeli reservist who was wearing a military uniform, when they fired at a vehicle that overturned as a result of the shooting near the settlement of Einav. In retaliation, dozens of Israeli settlers descended on the nearby Palestinian town of Deir Sharaf, east of Nablus, torching three cars, throwing rocks at Palestinian homes, and attacking shops.

November 16, 2023: *Al-Jazeera* reported that gunmen injured six members of the security forces, one critically, at a checkpoint near Bethlehem before Israeli forces killed three Palestinian terrorists who had arrived by car. Shin Bet said at least two of the attackers belonged to Hamas. Police found two automatic rifles, two handguns, hundreds of rounds of ammunition, 10 fully loaded magazines, and two axes on the suspects and in their vehicle. Authorities arrested the families of the three Palestinians.

January 7, 2024: A roadside bomb killed an Israeli paramilitary policewoman and injured three others during overnight clashes in the Jenin refugee camp.

Seven Palestinians throwing explosives and a member of Israel's paramilitary border police were killed in a helicopter airstrike. At a funeral for those killed in Jenin, four of the men were wrapped in the green flags of Hamas. Another was covered by the Palestinian flag and a second by the Fatah flag.

A Palestinian resident of Jerusalem driving his car with Israeli license plates was fatally shot at a busy intersection in the West Bank. The attackers fired through the victim's front windshield. Security forces found an abandoned car that was likely used to carry out the attack; the suspect fled on foot.

CNN reported that Israeli forces fired at a vehicle that attacked the Ras Bidu military checkpoint. Police shot and killed the man and woman in the vehicle, but also killed a three-year-old Palestinian girl in another vehicle. Two other people, including a 20-year-old woman hit in the limbs, were injured.

January 9, 2024: *Al-Jazeera* and *Wafa* reported that Israeli forces near the Ein Sinya checkpoint north of Ramallah shot dead a Palestinian youth accused of attempting a stabbing attack against them.

January 12, 2024: Israel's *Army Radio* reported that the IDF killed three Palestinian men who infiltrated a West Bank settlement and fired upon soldiers patrolling the settlement of Adora in the southern West Bank. A Palestinian male attacker, 34, sustained a gunshot wound to the leg.

January 17, 2024: *CNN* reported that the IDF and Israel Security Agency (Shin Bet) announced that "during joint IDF and ISA activity in the Balata camp in the city of Nablus, a terrorist cell headed by Amed Abdullah Abu-Shalal was eliminated during a precise airstrike" Three people were killed. *WAFA* claimed that the occupation forces "abducted" the bodies of two young men from the vehicle before withdrawing from the area. The Palestine Red Crescent Society said the IDF fired on Red Crescent teams who were present at the scene.

January 30, 2024: *AP* and *UPI* reported that at 5:30 a.m., dozen members of the IDF, Shin Bet, and Yamam police in a counter-terrorism operation disguised as civilian women and medics went to the third floor of the Ibn Sina Hospital in Jenin, killing three Palestinian militants in an apparent targeted killing. The IDF noted that one Palestinian had transferred weapons and ammunition to others for a planned attack. The IDF said Hamas member Mohammed Jalamneh, 27, was planning an imminent attack and that brothers Basel and Mohammed Ghazawi, PIJ members, were hiding inside the hospital and were involved in attacks. Jalamneh was armed with a pistol and was a spokesperson for Hamas's military wing in the Jenin refugee camp. Hospital spokesperson Tawfiq al-Shobaki said Basel Ghazawi had been a patient since October 2023, with partial paralysis. Jalamneh allegedly communicated with Hamas officials in other countries and had been injured in preparing a car bomb attack. He was also said to have provided weapons to other militants to carry out shootings. The IDF said that Muhammad Ghazawi had shot at Israeli troops in the West Bank.

February 13, 2024: *UPI* reported that the UK government sanctioned four "extremist" Israeli for conducting violent attacks against Palestinians in the West Bank. *Al-Jazeera* added that France sanctioned 28 Israeli settlers.

February 22, 2024: *NPR, ABC News,* and *UPI* reported that three gunmen opened fire on cars lined up at a checkpoint on Highway 1 between the West Bank town of Ma'ale Adumim and Jerusalem during morning rush hour, killing an Israeli in his 20s and hospitalizing five others, including a woman, 23, in critical condition. Another five were treated for minor injuries. Israeli Police said it shot dead two gunmen at the scene and tracked down and "neutralized" a third trying to escape (*ABC News* said he was detained.). Police added that "The gunmen arrived by car, exited the vehicle and started shooting using automatic weapons, towards vehicles standing in a traffic jam on the road towards Jerusalem." Police found assault rifles, makeshift submachine guns, and a grenade. Hamas said the attack was "a natural response... to the Occupation's massacres and crimes in the Gaza Strip and the West Bank".

March 13, 2024: *CNN* reported that two security personnel, a man, 25, and a woman, 19, were wounded in a stabbing near a tunnel checkpoint between Jerusalem and the West Bank. A 15-year-old arrived on his bicycle at the checkpoint at about 8:15 a.m. and pulled a knife on security forces as they tried to check him. An IDF soldier and security guard fatally shot the attacker.

March 14, 2024: *AP* reported that the U.S. Departments of State and Treasury imposed sanctions on three extremist Israeli settlers in the West Bank who are accused of harassing and attacking Palestinians to pressure them to leave their land. The U.S. also sanctioned two farms that the settlers run. Those sanctioned include:

- Zvi Bar Yosef and his Zvis Farm outpost. He is accused of violence against Palestinians in the West Bank. Bar Yosef founded his now-sanctioned outpost northwest of the Palestinian city of Ramallah in 2018. In August 2023, Israeli media reported that Bar Yosef kicked a Palestinian man in his mouth, knocking out four of his teeth while Israeli soldiers looked on.

- Moshe Sharvit, who founded a settlement in the north Jordan Valley. Sharvit allegedly attacked Palestinians and Israeli human rights activists in the vicinity of his outpost, known as Moshe's Farm. British officials in February 2024 noted that Sharvit and another settler threatened Palestinian families at gunpoint and destroyed property.

- Neriya Ben Pazi, who U.S. officials say attacked and expelled Palestinian shepherds from hundreds of acres of land in August 2023. Ben Paz grew up in an Israeli settlement in Gaza. He founded the outpost Rimonim in 2019. The outpost is not included on the sanctions list.

April 12, 2024: *Al-Jazeera* reported that Israeli settlers attacked Palestinians and their homes in al-Mughayir, northeast of Ramallah. Settlers shot and killed Jihad Afif.

April 13, 2024: The body of Binyamin Achimair, 14, was found in the West Bank, dead of a "terrorist attack," according to the IDF. His disappearance had sparked a large attack by Israeli settlers on the Palestinian village of Mughayyir that killed a Palestinian man, 26, and injured 25 other people. There was no immediate claim of responsibility for the killing of the Israeli shepherd. *BBC* and *AP* reported on April 22 that Shin Bet arrested Palestinian man Ahmed Dawabsha, 21, from Duma.

April 20, 2024: *CNN* reported that the IDF said it killed ten "terrorists" in a refugee camp.

April 21, 2024: *AP* and *Wafa* reported that a gunman fired at Israeli troops at a junction near Hebron while another attempted to stab them. Soldiers shot to death the two Palestinian attackers, aged 18 and 19.

A woman at a checkpoint further north tried to stab soldiers, who shot her to death.

April 24, 2024: *CNN* reported that Israeli troops shot dead Palestinian woman Maimunah Abdel

al-Hamid Harahsha, 20, after she tried to stab an Israeli soldier with a knife at the Okfim Junction checkpoint in Hebron. No one else was injured.

May 17, 2024: *CNN* reported that an IDF airstrike on an operations center in Jenin killed a "significant wanted" militant, Islam Khamaysa, a senior operative in the Jenin Camp, responsible for numerous attacks in the area. The al-Quds Brigade, the military wing of Islamic Jihad, said he was a leader of the Jenin Brigade. The Palestinian Ministry of Health said eight people were injured.

July 15, 2024: *UPI* reported that the European Union imposed sanctions on five violent Israeli settlers, including right-wing Jewish supremacist group Lehava leader Ben-Zion "Bentzi" Gopstein, and three associated organizations, including Tzav 9, on accusations of systematically abusing the human rights of Palestinians in the West Bank. The EU sanctioned Moshe Sharvit and his Moshe's Farm in the Jordan Valley for having "engaged in settler violence and threats toward Palestinian residents in shepherding communities" close to his West Bank outpost. Zvi Bar Yosef and his illegal Zvi's Farm outpost were named as he "repeatedly attacked and committed acts of violence against Palestinians from the villages of Jibya, Kaubar and Umm Safa, causing severe injuries to some of them." Baruch Marzel and Isaschar Manne were also named.

August 3, 2024: *Al-Jazeera* reported that two Israeli airstrikes near Tulkarem killed nine people, including Haitham Balidi, leader of the Qassam Brigades in the Nablus area, and one of the leaders of al-Quds Brigades, the armed wing of the Palestinian Islamic Jihad. *Wafa* reported that the second air attack hit a vehicle in Bal'a, east of Tulkarem, killing four.

August 16, 2024: *UPI, BBC,* and *Wafa* reported that dozens of Israeli settlers, some masked rioted in Jit village during the night, throwing stones and Molotov cocktails, torched six vehicles and four buildings, shot to death Rashid Mahmoud Sedda, 22, variant Mahmoud Abdel Qader Sadda, 23, and critically injured by gunshot another Palestinian in the chest. Israel police arrested a settler. *Al-Jazeera* said several people were injured. The settlers also attacked the town of Huwara. The UN had recorded 1,250 attacks by Israeli settlers against West Bank Palestinians since the October 7 massacre.

August 18, 2024: *BBC* reported that a Palestinian laborer wielding a hammer killed Israeli security guard Gideon Perry, 38, father of three, at an industrial area near the Kedumim settlement. The attacker stole Perry's firearm and drove away.

August 28, 2024: The IDF said it killed five Palestinian militants, including Islamic Jihad commander Muhamad Jabber, alias Abu Shujaa, within and near a mosque in Tulkarem. The IDF said he was behind numerous terror attacks, including a shooting attack in the West Bank city of Qalqilya in June, when an Israeli civilian was killed. PIJ said he was the commander of the Tulkarem Battallion of the al-Quds Brigades, the PIJ armed wing.

August 30, 2024: *UPI* reported that the IDF announced that Wassem Hazem, variant Hazam, head of Hamas in Jenin, was killed during a West Bank counterterrorism airstrike. Maysara Masharqa and Arafat Amer, who operated under Hazem's command and "took part in shooting attacks against Israeli communities" died in an airstrike as they attempted to flee from a vehicle they were in with Hazem.

September 1, 2024: The Khalil al-Rahman Brigade fired on a vehicle on a road in the south, killing three Israeli police officers before escaping. Among the dead was Roni Shakuri, 61, from Sderot near the Gaza border. His daughter, Mor, also a police officer, was killed in a battle with Hamas during an attack on the Sderot police station during the October 7 attack. *AP* reported that the IDF released a video of a military raid in the West Bank during which they killed a suspected Palestinian gunman who had barricaded himself in a building in Hebron. He was believed to have killed the three policemen.

September 8, 2024: The *Washington Post, Wafa, UPI,* and *Reuters* reported that a Jordanian gunman killed three Israeli civilians in a commercial cargo area under Israeli control where Jordanian trucks offload cargo at the Allenby Bridge (aka

King Hussein Bridge) border crossing between Jordan and the West Bank before Israeli security forces shot him to death. Jordanian truck driver Maher Thiyab Hussein al-Jazi, variant Maher Dhiab Hussein al-Jazi, 39, got out of the truck during an inspection at the terminal and began firing. The resident of Udhruh, east of Petra, was from the Huwaitat tribe in southern Jordan. Victims Yuri Birnbaum, Yohanan Shchori, and Adrian Marcelo Podsmesser, all men in their 50s, worked for a subcontracting company for the cargo terminal. Yohanan Shchori, 61, was a father of six from the West Bank settlement of Ma'ale Efraim; Yuri Birnbaum, 65, was from the settlement of Na'ama; and Adrian Marcelo Podzamczer, hailed from the settlement city of Ariel. Hamas praised the attack that was "executed by a fearless Jordanian individual".

October 3, 2024: *AP, Reuters, AFP,* and *Wafa* reported that an Israeli air strike on Tulkarm killed 18 people including several Hamas fighters, among them commander Zahi Yaser Abd al-Razeq Oufi, who was in a cafe. The IDF said he attempted a car bombing in September and supplied weapons. Hamas's al-Qassam Brigades armed wing said on *Telegram* that seven of its fighters were killed.

October 9, 2024: *CNN* reported that Israeli special forces shot at a car in Nablus, killing five Palestinians, including the head of the al-Aqsa Martyrs Brigades. The IDF said they were "wanted for terrorist activities" and were "involved in exporting and planning terrorist activities against civilians and IDF forces." The Palestinian Ministry of Health identified them as Abdul Halim Muhammad Nasser, Salim Izz al-Din Mahmoud Abu Saada, Naeem Muhammad Raji Abdul Hadi, and Issam Muhammad Suleiman Salah.

BBC added that in a separate raid, the IDF killed Ibrahim al-Nabulsi, 26, head of the al-Aqsa Martyrs Brigades, and two other people and injured 40 at a house in Nablus.

November 29, 2024: *UPI* reported that a Hamas gunman fired at a bus in Ariel, injuring four people, three seriously. Four others sustained injuries from broken glass. The driver was the most seriously injured. Four of the victims were IDF soldiers. The gunman was killed. Hamas's al-Qassam Brigades claimed responsibility and identified the gunman as Samir Muhammad Ahmad Hussein, 46. The IDF raided Hussein's home in the village of Einabus, located in the northern part of the Palestinian enclave and seven miles from Nablus.

December 4, 2024: *CNN* reported that 20 IDF soldiers dressed in civilian clothes raided a hospital in Nablus during the night and detained Ayman Ghanam, who had taken part in an August 2024 shooting near an Israeli settlement that killed an Israeli civilian and injured another and who had on December 3 been injured in an Israeli airstrike on a car near Aqaba that killed two Hamas members. Ghanam was in the ICU after undergoing surgeries to treat abdominal and leg injuries.

December 12, 2024: *BBC* reported that a Palestinian fired on a bus in the al-Khader Junction as it travelled from the settlement of Beitar Illit to Jerusalem, killing Israeli boy Yehoshua Aharon Tuvia Simha, 12, and wounding a woman and two men. Ezzedine Malluh from Beit Awwa fled the scene but later turned himself in to Israeli security forces. A Hamas official called the attack "heroic" but did not claim credit.

December 20, 2024: *Al-Jazeera* ran video of reported Israeli settlers defacing a mosque in Marda, spraying "death to Arabs" and "Revenge", and setting it on fire.

WESTERN SAHARA

October 28, 2023: *Reuters* reported that in the late evening, four bombs exploded in Smara in Morocco-controlled Western Sahara, killing a man, injuring three others, and damaging two houses.

YEMEN

March 1, 2023: The *Jerusalem Post* and *AFP* reported that a U.S. airstrike killed Hamad bin Hamoud al-Tamimi, alias Abdel Aziz al-Adani,

a senior AQAP figure, and his bodyguard at al-Tamimi's house in the Marib Governorate. The Saudi served as president of the consultative council and judge.

March 25, 2023: *Europa, News 360, Arab News,* and the Yemeni news portal *South24* reported that a drone attack on a convoy from Mocha of Governor of Taiz Nabil Shamsan, Minister of Defense Mohsen al Daari, and Chief of Army Staff Sagheer bin Aziz in Taiz Governorate killed one and wounded two bodyguards. Houthis were blamed.

July 21, 2023: *Al-Jazeera, Saba,* and *DPA* reported that a gunman on a motorbike killed a U.N. World Food Programme staff member while he was lunching at a restaurant in Turbah in Taiz Province. Others were injured.

August 2023: *Al-Jazeera* reported on August 10 that in early August, security officials told *AP* that AQAP killed five troops from the Southern Armed Forces, a large force loyal to the Southern Transitional Council.

August 1, 2023: *Al-Jazeera* reported that AQAP was suspected when gunmen armed with mortars and rocket-propelled grenades ambushed members of the secessionist Southern Transitional Council, killing five, in Wadi Omran in Abyan Province. Four fighters from the Southern Armed Forces were wounded.

August 10, 2023: *Al-Jazeera* reported that AQAP was suspected when an attack on a convoy in Abyan Governorate killed Commander Abd al-Latif al-Sayyid and the three fighters from the Security Belt Forces, an armed group loyal to Yemen's secessionist Southern Transitional Council.

October 31, 2023: *Al-Jazeera* reported that Yahya Saree, a spokesperson for Houthi rebels, claimed they launched a "large number" of ballistic missiles and drones towards Israel and warned of further attacks. Israel said it destroyed an unidentified "aerial target" over the Red Sea that morning. Abdelaziz bin Habtour, prime minister of the Houthi regime, told *AFP* that the group had sent drones towards southern Israel.

November 9, 2023: A U.S. Central Command (CENTCOM) official told *CNN* that Houthis shot down an unmanned US military MQ-9 Reaper drone operating in international airspace and over international waters off the coast of Yemen.

November 27, 2023: U.S. CENTCOM said Houthis launched a missile into the Gulf of Aden, 10 miles from the *USS Mason*.

December 7, 2023: The U.S. Department of the Treasury imposed sanctions against 13 people and firms alleged to be providing tens of millions of dollars from the sale and shipment of Iranian commodities to the Houthis in Yemen. Among them was previously-sanctioned Houthi and Iranian financial facilitator Sa'id al-Jamal, who uses a network of exchange houses and firms to help Iranian money reach the country's militant partners in Yemen. The list included money lenders in Lebanon, Türkiye, and Dubai for assisting al-Jamal, along with shipping firms from Russia to St. Kitts and Nevis, which allegedly move al-Jamal's Iranian commodity shipments. The sanctions block access to U.S. property and bank accounts and prevent the targeted people and companies from doing business with Americans.

December 9, 2023: *Al-Jazeera* reported that Yemen's Houthi movement announced, "If Gaza does not receive the food and medicines it needs, all ships in the Red Sea bound for Israeli ports, regardless of their nationality, will become a target for our armed forces."

January 11, 2024: *CNN* and *USA Today* reported that at 2:30 a.m., U.S. warplanes, ships, and submarines and four British Typhoon fighter jets struck 60 targets in 16 locations in Houthi-controlled areas. Targets included command-and-control nodes, munitions depots, launching systems, production facilities, and air defense radar systems.

President Biden announced, "Today, at my direction, U.S. military forces—together with the United Kingdom and with support from Australia, Bahrain, Canada, and the Netherlands—successfully conducted strikes against a number of targets in Yemen used by Houthi rebels to endanger freedom of navigation in one of the world's most vital waterways." He added that he will "not hesitate to direct further measures to protect our people and the free flow of international commerce as necessary".

The *Washington Post* reported on January 13 that the coalition struck 12 other locations not initially disclosed. Lt. Gen. Douglas Sims said that more than 150 munitions were used to destroy dozens of sites. Houthi spokesman Saree said 73 strikes hit Sana'a and four other regions, killing five of the group's fighters and wounding six.

January 12, 2024: *CNN* reported that a nighttime airstrike by the U.S. targeted a radar facility used by the Houthis.

January 15, 2024: *CNN* reported that U.S. CENTCOM announced that Houthis attempted to launch an anti-ship ballistic missile that failed in flight and crashed in Yemen.

January 16, 2024: *CNN* reported that U.S. forces destroyed four Houthi anti-ship ballistic missiles.

January 17, 2024: *CNN* reported that the U.S. re-designated the Houthis as a specially designated global terrorist (SDGT) entity. The administration removed the SDGT designation and de-listed it as a foreign terrorist organization (FTO) in February 2021, after it was designated by former President Donald Trump's administration in its final weeks.

January 18, 2024: *USNWR, AP,* and *Reuters* reported that U.S. CENTCOM hit 14 Houthi missiles that "presented an imminent threat to merchant vessels and U.S. Navy ships in the region".

January 20, 2024: *Reuters* and *AP* reported that U.S. CENTCOM hit a Houthi anti-ship missile that was aimed into the Gulf of Aden, hours after the United States struck three other Houthi anti-ship missiles as part of Operation Prosperity Guardian.

January 25, 2024: *CNN* reported that the U.S. and UK governments imposed sanctions against the Houthis' self-described Minister of Defense, Mohamed al-Atifi, and leaders of the Houthi naval forces.

January 27, 2024: In the morning, a U.S. airstrike hit a Houthi anti-ship missile that was aimed at the Red Sea and prepared to launch.

January 31, 2024: *Al-Jazeera* reported that the Houthis announced that they planned more attacks against U.S. and UK warships.

Business Insider reported that at 3:30 p.m., U.S. CENTCOM forces hit and destroyed a surface-to-air missile that the Houthis were preparing to launch from Yemen against American aircraft.

February 1, 2024: *Al-Jazeera* reported that CENTCOM announced airstrikes that targeted a "Houthi UAV ground control station and 10 Houthi one-way UAVs" that "presented an imminent threat to merchant vessels and the US Navy ships in the region".

February 4, 2024: U.S. CENTCOM airstrikes hit four anti-ship missiles being prepared to be fired at vessels in the Red Sea from Houthi rebel-controlled areas in Yemen.

The previous day, U.S. and UK airstrikes hit 36 Houthi targets.

February 7, 2024: *CNN* reported the U.S. CENTCOM conducted airstrikes against two Houthi anti-ship cruise missiles preparing to launch against ships in the Red Sea and against a Houthi mobile land attack cruise missile that was prepared to launch.

February 16, 2024: The *New York Times* reported that the U.S. Department of State redesignated the Houthis as a terrorist organization.

February 17, 2024: *CNN* reported that U.S. Central Command conducted five airstrikes against three Houthi anti-ship cruise missiles, one unmanned underwater vessel (the Houthis' first) and one unmanned surface vessel between 3 and 8 p.m.

February 27, 2024: The U.S. announced sanctions against Houthi member Ibrahim al-Nashiri.

March 10, 2024: *AP, BBC,* and *al-Jazeera* reported that al-Qaeda in the Arabian Peninsula (AQAP) official Abu Khubaib al-Sudani announced the death of its leader, Khalid al-Batarfi. In 2018, the U.S. Department of State named him a Specially Designated Global Terrorist with a $5 million bounty on his head. He was believed to be in his early 40s. AQAP's shura council said he would be succeeded by Saad bin Atef al-Awlaki; the U.S. has a $6 million bounty on him. Al-Batarfi took over in February 2020, succeeding Qassim al-Rimi, who was killed by a U.S. drone strike. Al-Batarfi had close ties to al-Qaeda leader Saif al-Adel. Al-Batarfi was born in Riyadh, Saudi Arabia. He traveled to Afghanistan in 1999 and fought alongside the Taliban during the U.S.-led invasion. He joined AQAP in 2010 and led forces in taking over Yemen's Abyan province. He was freed from prison in 2015. In 2021, he said in a video that the January 6 Capitol insurrection was "only the tip of the iceberg of what will come to them, God willing".

March 14, 2024: *AP* and *RIA Novosti* that Yemen's Houthi rebels claimed to have a new, hypersonic, March 8 missile in their arsenal.

March 19, 2024: In the early morning, Houthis set off booby traps at the house of Ibrahim al-Zalei, killing nine people—two parents and their seven children in the Radea district of Bayda Province. On March 18, two Houthis died in an ambush believed set up by the owner. Neighboring buildings were severely damaged.

March 22, 2024: *AP* reported that fighter jets from the *USS Dwight D. Eisenhower* aircraft carrier struck three underground storage facilities in Houthi-controlled areas around Sana'a during the night. U.S. Central Command said its forces also destroyed four unmanned aerial vehicles.

March 24, 2024: AQAP claimed credit on *Telegram* for killing two troops loyal to a secessionist group in the mountainous Wadi Omran area of Abyan Province. During the late night ambush on a security patrol, AQAP also wounded four troops from the UAE-backed Southern Armed Forces, which is loyal to the secessionist Southern Transitional Council. The gunmen burned a military vehicle during an hours-long gun battle.

March 30, 2024: *AP* reported that in the morning, CENTCOM destroyed one unmanned aerial vehicle while it was prepared to launch in a Houthi rebel-held area of Yemen and another over a shipping route in the Red Sea.

April 24, 2024: *Al-Jazeera* reported that the U.S. military said within two hours of the *Yorktown* attack, its forces "successfully engaged and destroyed" four drones over Yemen.

April 25, 2024: *Al-Jazeera* reported that the U.S. military said within two hours of the *Yorktown* attack, its forces "successfully engaged and destroyed" four drones over Yemen.

    UPI reported that CENTCOM said it had destroyed an unmanned vessel and an airborne drone in the afternoon in Houthi-controlled areas of Yemen.

April 26, 2024: *Al-Jazeera* reported that the Houthis downed another U.S. MQ-9 Reaper drone in the airspace of the Saada governorate. *CBS News* confirmed that an MQ-9, which costs about $30 million, "crashed" inside Yemen in the morning.

April 29, 2024: AQAP was suspected when a bomb hit a military vehicle carrying troops loyal to the Southern Armed Forces, the military arm of the United Arab Emirates-backed secessionist Southern Transitional Council, killing six soldiers and wounding 11 troops in a mountainous area in the Modiyah district of southern Abyan Province.

May 2, 2024: *UPI* reported that at 2 p.m., U.S. military forces destroyed three uncrewed aerial systems in a Houthi-controlled area of Yemen.

May 3, 2024: *The Hill* and *Reuters* reported that the Houthi-run Sanaa University offered slots to students suspended at U.S. universities during campus demonstrations against the Israel-Gaza war.

May 16, 2024: Houthi military spokesman Brig. Gen. Yahya Saree claimed to have shot down a $30 million American MQ-9 Reaper drone with a surface-to-air missile over Yemen's Marib Province.

May 21, 2024: Houthi military spokesman Brigadier General Yahya Saree claimed one of its missiles downed another U.S. MQ-9 Reaper drone over Bayda Province.

May 26, 2024: Houthis released 113 war prisoners in Sana'a.

May 29, 2024: *Military Times* and *AP* reported that another U.S. MQ-9 Reaper drone went down in a desert region of Yemen's central Marib Province. It was not immediately clear why the drone crashed.

May 30, 2024: *CNN* reported that the U.S. and UK conducted airstrikes against 13 Houthi targets for the first time since February 24. The U.S. separately destroyed eight aerial attack drones over Yemen and the Red Sea. *AP* reported the next day that the Houthis claimed that the strikes killed at least 16 people and wounded 42 others.

June 7, 2024: *Al-Jazeera* and Houthi-run *al-Masirah TV* reported that the United States and United Kingdom conducted six air strikes. Four attacks targeted the Hodeidah airport and the seaport of Salif north of it. Two air raids hit the al-Thawra region north of Sanaa.

June 7, 2024: *AP, Reuters,* and *BBC* reported that Houthi intelligence officers detained 11 United Nations Yemeni aid workers and 18 employees of other international organizations in Amran, Hudaydah, Saada, and Sana'a. The UN said that of its 11 Yemeni staffers, six worked for the U.N.'s human rights agency, and one each at its special envoy's office, its development arm, UNICEF, the World Food Program, and UNESCO. The UN said the staffers included two women and nine men. *Reuters* reported that several members of the U.S.-backed National Democratic Institute (NDI) were targeted. Save the Children and CARE International said one each of their staffers were missing.

June 10, 2024: Maj. Gen. Abdulhakim al-Khayewani, head of the Houthis' intelligence agency, announced that they had arrested members of an "American-Israeli spy network" which had first operated out of the U.S. Embassy in Sanaa, which was closed in 2015. He claimed they continued "their subversive agenda under the cover of international and UN organizations." He did not say how many people were arrested. Houthi authorities issued what they purported to be videotaped confessions by 10 Yemenis, several of whom said they were recruited by the U.S. Embassy.

June 12, 2024: The U.S. military destroyed three anti-ship cruise missile launchers in Houthi-held Yemen.

June 13, 2024: The Washington-based National Democratic Institute said that Houthis had detained three of its staff earlier in the month. 24069901

June 14, 2024: *UPI* reported that USCENTCOM air raids destroyed seven Houthi radar sites plus several of their sea and aerial drones.

June 15, 2024: CENTCOM destroyed seven Houthi radar sites, two bomb-laden drone boats in the Red Sea, and a drone launched by the Houthis over the waterway.

June 17, 2024: *UPI* reported that the U.S. Department of the Treasury imposed financial sanctions on Houthi procurement and revenue-generating networks, including two people and five companies, and an additional one person, one company, and one shipping vessel for facilitating the shipment of commodities, the sales from which officials said are an important funding stream for the group. Many of those designated were based in China.

June 26, 2024: Exiled Yemeni government minister of the Hajj Mohamed Shabiba charged that Houthis at Sanaa International Airport seized four Yemenia commercial aircraft, including two Airbus A320s, that were scheduled to bring back pilgrims from the Hajj in Saudi Arabia.

July 20, 2024: *CNN* reported that the IDF conducted retaliatory airstrikes on Yemen's Hodeidah Port, killing three people and injuring 87, following the Houthi drone attack on Tel Aviv. The Houthi-run *al-Masirah TV* said the F-15 and F-35 strikes targeted oil facilities. Spokesman Mohammed Abdulsalam said the strikes hit civilian targets, storage facilities for oil and diesel, and a power station.

August 3, 2024: U.S. CENTCOM announced it had destroyed a Houthi missile and launcher.

August 13, 2024: Houthis stormed the headquarters of the United Nations Human Rights Office in Sanaa, seizing documents, furniture, and vehicles.

August 16, 2024: *Al-Jazeera* reported that al-Qaeda in the Arabian Peninsula (AQAP) claimed credit when a suicide car bomber hit a military post in the Mudiyah district of Abyan Province, killing 16 Yemeni pro-government soldiers and wounding 18 others.

September 8, 2024: Houthis claimed to have shot down an American-made General Atomics MQ-9 drone flying over Marib Province.

September 16, 2024: Houthis claimed to have shot down with a surface-to-air missile another American-made MQ-9 Reaper drone over Dhamar Province.

September 30, 2024: Houthis claimed on *al-Masirah* to have shot down an MQ-9 Reaper drone.

October 17, 2024: *BBC* reported that U.S. CENTCOM B-2 Spirit stealth bombers conducted precision strikes against five underground weapons storage locations housing missiles and other munitions in Houthi-controlled areas around Sanaa and Saada.

November 8, 2024: Houthis claimed to have downed a U.S. MQ-9 Reaper drone in al-Jawf Province.

AP and the state-run *Saudi Press Agency* reported that a soldier for Yemen's exiled government opened fire on Saudi troops as they exercised at a Saudi-led base in Seiyun in eastern Hadramawt Province, killing a Saudi officer and a noncommissioned Saudi officer and wounding a Saudi soldier. Aidarous al-Zubaidi, leader of Yemen's Southern Transitional Council, said the attacker belonged to the First Military Region, based out of Seiyun. Police offered a 30-million Yemeni rial reward ($15,000 on the black market) for his arrest.

November 9, 2024: *ABC News* reported that U.S. CENTCOM airstrikes hit Houthi weapons storage facilities in Yemen during the night.

December 16, 2024: *Al-Jazeera* reported that Houthi military spokesman Yahya Saree claimed in a TV address that the group fired a Palestine 2 hypersonic ballistic missile at central Israel. The IDF said it had intercepted the missile before it reached Israel.

December 19, 2024: *Al-Jazeera* reported that the U.S. Department of the Treasury announced sanctions on Hashem al-Madani, the governor of the central bank in Houthi-controlled Sana'a, Yemen, and several Houthi officials and associated companies, accusing them of helping the group acquire "dual-use and weapons components". Treasury called al-Madani the "primary overseer of funds sent to the Houthis" by the Quds Force of Iran's Islamic Revolutionary Guard Corps.

North America

Canada

January 20, 2023: *UPI* and *AP* reported that Canada's Federal Court ruled that Ottawa must repatriate four of its male citizens being held in detention centers in northeastern Syria run by the Kurdish-led Syrian Democratic Forces. The court held that "There is no evidence any of them have been tried or convicted, let alone tried in a manner that recognized or sanctioned by international law." Among them was UK-born Jack Letts, alias Jihadi Jack, a dual UK-Canadian national who had admitted to having joined ISIS at age 18 in 2014 during a 2019 interview. The SDF captured him in 2017. The UK revoked his citizenship in 2019. A UK court convicted Letts's Canadian father, John Letts, and British mother,

Sally Lane, in June 2022 of funding terrorism by sending money to their son to help him escape from Syria.

The previous day, the Canadian government agreed to repatriate six Canadian women and 13 children from Syria.

June 28, 2023: *UPI* reported that an individual stabbed a professor and two students during an ongoing philosophy class on gender studies at the Hagey Hall of the Humanities on the main campus of the University of Waterloo. Police arrested the suspect after the 3:30 p.m. attack by the member of the university.

July 5, 2023: *Al-Jazeera* reported that the Royal Canadian Mounted Police arrested two men in connection with their involvement with a "terrorist group... linked to neo-Nazi ideology". Patrick Gordon Macdonald, 26, allegedly helped produce propaganda for the Atomwaffen Division, an accelerationist neo-Nazi group originally formed in the United States. Authorities also detained a second person in Kingsey Falls, Quebec.

Macdonald was charged with participating in the activity of a terrorist group, facilitating terrorist activity, and the willful promotion of hatred. He allegedly produced three "terrorist propaganda videos... intended to promote the group and recruit members, and encourages the commission of terrorist activities". *Vice News* earlier reported in 2021 that Macdonald in 2021 was a prolific neo-Nazi propagandist using the Internet alias "Dark Foreigner" and had lived in suburban Ottawa with his parents.

November 6, 2023: *CNN* reported that during the night, a Molotov cocktail was thrown at Beth Tikvah Synagogue.

November 7, 2023: *CNN* reported that a shot was fired at Montreal's Talmud Torah Elementary School. No one was injured. As of November 15, no arrests had been made.

November 9, 2023: *The Guardian* reported that shots were fired at two Jewish schools, including Yeshiva Gedolah, in Montreal's Côte-des-Neiges neighborhood.

Earlier that week, two Molotov cocktails were found outside a synagogue and Jewish community center in Montreal.

In Surrey, British Columbia, a man egged a rabbi's house and drew a swastika on it.

In Ottawa, someone smeared feces on the doors of a mosque.

November 12, 2023: *CNN* reported that gunshots were fired at Montreal's Yeshiva Gedola. Police found a bullet hole on the front façade of the building, along with shell casings. Police spokeswoman Constable Caroline Chèvrefils said that "a suspicious vehicle was seen fleeing the scene quickly". An unarmed guard was unhurt.

December 15, 2023: The Royal Canadian Mounted Police arrested a youth in Ottawa and charged him with terrorism-related offenses that included communicating instructional material related to an explosive substance and knowingly instructing a person to carry out terrorist activity against "Jewish persons."

March 3, 2024: *Al-Jazeera* reported that police arrested a Toronto man, 27, on assault and weapons charges for attacking with a nail gun pro-Palestinian protesters who were demonstrating against an Israeli real estate company event at a Toronto synagogue which only seemed open to Jews. He yelled "Every **** Palestinian will die. Every **** Palestinian." *Al-Jazeera* said the Keller-Williams realty was believed to be selling property in Israeli settlements. No serious injuries were reported.

May 30, 2024: The Jewish Federation of Greater Vancouver said an "incendiary device" was thrown at the front doors of the Schara Tzedeck synagogue at around 9:30 p.m., causing minor damage and no injuries.

Bullet holes were found recently at two Jewish schools in Montreal and Toronto.

June 20, 2024: *Al-Jazeera* and *BBC* reported that Canada listed Iran's Islamic Revolutionary Guard Corps (IRGC) as a "terrorist" entity and urged its citizens in Iran to leave. Ottawa said the move was aimed at combating the group's ter-rorist activity and countering terrorist financing. The United States made the same designation in 2019.

August 7, 2024: The Royal Canadian Mounted Police, with the assistance of the York Regional Police in Ontario, arrested Dawid Zalewski, 33, of no fixed address, on two counts of making violent threats against Prime Minister Justin Trudeau online.

In July, the RCMP said that two Alberta men were charged after allegedly posting threats to kill Trudeau and other politicians on *X* and *YouTube*.

August 21, 2024: The Royal Canadian Mounted Police announced that more than 100 synagogues, Jewish organizations, hospitals, and doctors in several cities received the same threatening email. Authorities swept the Toronto office of B'nai Brith for explosives.

September 11, 2024: Authorities announced the arrest in Quebec the previous week of Pakistani Muhammad Shahzeb Khan, 20, who was accused of plotting to attack a Jewish center in Brooklyn. He arrived in Canada in June 2023 on a student visa that was granted in May 2023. U.S. authorities said that he planned to use guns and knives to carry out a mass shooting in support of ISIS on the one-year anniversary of the October 7 Hamas attack in Israel.

October 30, 2024: *UPI* reported that the Canadian government accused Indian Home Minister Amit Shah of being involved in plots targeting Sikh separatists within Canada.

December 18, 2024: Police believed arson was involved in 3 a.m. attacks on the Congregation Beth Tikvah synagogue on the island suburb of Dollard-des-Ormeaux and the West Island office of the Federation CJA, a building frequented by the Jewish community in Montreal. No injuries were reported. The same synagogue and the CJA building were attacked by arsonists in November 2023.

UNITED STATES

2023: *NBC News* reported on January 31, 2024 that reports to the Federal Aviation Administration in 2023 of lasers illegally pointed at aircraft in flight rose to a new high of more than 13,000 for the year, compared to 9,457 reports in 2022. Half the reported strikes occurred at altitudes of less than 6,000 feet, and nearly 5% of strikes were at altitudes less than 1,000 feet. Green laser pointers are the most commonly used.

January 4, 2023: Czech officials arrested Polad Omarov on January 4, 2023 in connection with an Iranian plot to kill an exiled oppositionist. *AP* and *UPI* reported on February 21, 2024 that Polad Omarov, 39, a Georgian suspect charged in a murder-for-hire plot to kill New York-based Iranian American author, journalist, and human rights and opposition activist Masih Alinejad, was extradited from the Czech Republic to face charges in the U.S. Rafat Amirov, 45, of Iran and Khalid Mahdiyev, 25, of Yonkers, New York, were also charged with money laundering and murder-for-hire in federal court in New York. Both men pleaded not guilty in 2023. Charges against Zialat Mamedov were added in a revised indictment in May 2023. Department of Justice officials said that Mamedov was also in the custody of Czech authorities.

On January 27, 2023, *CNN* reported that Attorney General Merrick Garland announced the arrests of three more people believed involved in a plot to kill Alinejad. The trio were believed associated with an Eastern European criminal organization with ties to Iran. They faced murder-for-hire and money laundering charges.

Alinejad was targeted in another alleged kidnapping plot by Iranian nationals in 2021 organized by an Iranian intelligence official.

Voice of America reported on October 22, 2024 that federal prosecutors in New York charged Ruhollah Bazghandi, a Brigadier General in Iran's Islamic Revolutionary Guard Corps, and three other men linked to Tehran, with participating in a failed attempt to assassinate *VOA* Persian service journalist Masih Alinejad in Brooklyn in 2022.

January 4, 2023: *The Hill* reported that on February 1, 2023, Las Vegas Judge Cristy Craig determined that Mohammed Mesmarian, 34, who was facing terror-related charges connected to a fire at the Mega Solar Array solar energy facility in southern Nevada, was not competent to stand trial and was not competent to understand the charges against him. Mesmarian allegedly rammed a car through a fence at the facility and set the car on fire next to a transformer. No one was hurt in the fire. Police found him at a campground in Boulder Beach at Lake Mead on January 5. Mesmarian was escorted from the court after becoming disruptive during his initial appearance in early January. His attorney requested a mental health evaluation. *KLAS* reported that Mesmarian's car was registered in Idaho. Police found two laptops and an iPhone with an account registered to him in the burned car.

The facility is run by Invenergy and provided energy to MGM properties. *AP* reported that MGM properties have since switched to the statewide electrical grid.

January 5, 2023: *Al-Jazeera* reported that the United States Departments of the Treasury and State and Türkiye announced sanctions against a network providing financial support to ISIS. Treasury sanctioned four individuals and two firms.

Treasury sanctioned Abd al-Hamid Salim Ibrahim Ismail Brukan al-Khatuni, an Iraqi national living in Türkiye, plus his two sons and the Turkish money service business where they worked. State said they "facilitated money transfers to ISIS through their [Türkiye]-based financial entities" with the help of Lu'ay Jasim Hammadi al-Juburi, a Türkiye-based ISIS financial facilitator. Al-Juburi was also accused of using Sham Express, founded by al-Khatuni in 2020, to transfer funds to ISIS. That business and al-Khatuni enterprise Wadi Alrrafidayn for Foodstuffs were also sanctioned.

January 5, 2023: *CBS News* and *KRQE* reported that Albuquerque detectives and "federal partners" were investigating several incidents of gunfire targeted at the homes or offices of local elected Democratic leaders.

On the afternoon of December 4, 2022, eight rounds were fired at the home of Bernalillo County Commissioner Adriann Barboa in Southeast Albuquerque.

Shots were fired on December 8, 2022 at the home of state House Speaker Javier Martinez.

Police found more than a dozen gunshot impacts following an incident on December 11, 2022 at the home of then-Bernalillo Commissioner Debbie O'Malley in the North Valley.

On January 3, 2023, eight shots were fired after midnight at the Southwest Albuquerque residence of state Senator Linda Lopez. Some bullets entered her 10-year-old daughter's bedroom.

On the morning of January 5, 2023, shots were heard at the law office of state Senator Moe Maesta, although no damage was reported. Albuquerque Police Commander Kyle Hartsock said, "[Republican Solomon] Peña himself went on this shooting and actually pulled the trigger on at least one of the firearms that was used." But an AR handgun he tried to use malfunctioned. Another shooter fired more than a dozen rounds from a separate handgun.

Later that night, shots were fired at the former campaign office of New Mexico Attorney General Raúl Torrez. Shots were also detected in the area in the early morning of December 10. Torrez was not occupying the office at the time, having moved out following the election in November. Shots were also fired at the law office of a state senator. Police later decoupled these shootings from the others.

CNN reported on January 17 that an Albuquerque SWAT team arrested Republican Solomon Peña, who lost his 2022 run for the New Mexico House of Representatives District 14A seat, on charges of paying and conspiring with four men to shoot at the homes of two state legislators and two county commissioners. Peña, an ex-felon, was held on suspicion of "helping orchestrate and participate in these four shootings, either at his request or he conducted them personally, himself". Albuquerque Mayor Tim Keller said Peña is an election denier. *KOAT* reported that Peña served nearly seven years in prison after a 2008 conviction for stealing a large volume of goods in a "smash and grab scheme".

January 12, 2023: *Stars and Stripes* reported that Kevin Iman McCormick, 29, of Hamden, Connecticut, pleaded guilty in Bridgeport federal court to attempting to provide material support to a terrorist group by trying to join ISIS. Court documents indicated that between August and October 2019, he made several statements to others about wanting to travel to Syria and to fight for ISIS. In October 2019, he observed, "I gotta fight bro, because those people, Abu Masa and ISIL, they fought for me bro, I know it, I can feel it, in my heart. So it's my time to fight... It just is what it is bro, it's just my – it's just my time to go bro... I don't know, I don't know bro – it's gotta be like Syria. Where ISIL is at...whichever place is easiest, whatever place I can get there the fastest, the quickest, the easiest, and where I can have a rifle and I can have some people bro. That's what I need, I need a rifle and I need some people, I need Islamic law, I need, that's what I need, because if I have these things, it's gonna to be very hard to kill me."

On October 12, 2019, the Department of Homeland Security stopped McCormick from boarding a flight from Connecticut to Jamaica. The next week, he made a video pledging allegiance to ISIS emir Abu Bakr al-Baghdadi. The same day, he bought a plane ticket from Toronto to Amman, Jordan. He was arrested the next day.

U.S. District Judge Kari A. Dooley scheduled sentencing for April 6. McCormick faced 20 years.

January 18, 2023: The *Daily Mail* reported that alleged "Antifa terrorist" Sarah Wasilewski, 35, and six other activists were arrested at the future $90 million Atlanta Public Safety Training Center in a raid that left a protester dead and a Georgia State Trooper seriously injured. She is a "brand ambassador" who worked for fitness guru Les Mills, where she was a Group Fitness Instructor for Les Mills US for two years before the pandemic. She travelled with her boyfriend and fellow extremist Spencer Liberto, 29, from Pittsburgh, Pennsylvania, who was arrested on domestic terrorism charges, as were another native Pennsylvanian, Matt Macar, 30; Geoffrey Parson, 20, of Baltimore; Timothy Murphy, 25, of Maine; Christopher Reynolds, 31, of Ohio; and Terese Yue Shen, 31, of New York.

Wasilewski was charged with domestic terrorism and aggravated assault of an officer. The *Daily Mail* reported that extremists called for murdering police. She was a University of Pittsburgh graduate in Communication and Rhetoric who had worked as an Income Maintenance County Caseworker for the Commonwealth of Pennsylvania. She studied abroad at the University of New South Wales.

Manuel Esteban Paez Teran, 26, was shot dead after allegedly shooting at a Georgia State Patrol trooper during a "clearing operation". Scenes from the Atlanta Forest tweeted "A call for retaliation. Consider this a call for reciprocal violence to be done to the police and their allies. On Friday, January 20th, wherever you are, you are invited to participate in a night of rage to honor the memory of our fallen comrade. Defend the Atlanta Forest Night of Rage Friday Jaunary (sic) 20th Make Them Pay".

January 21, 2023: *AP,* the *Los Angeles Times, NBC News,* and *CNN* reported that at 10:22 p.m. a lone gunman killed 10 people—five men and five women—and wounded 10 others at Star Ballroom Dance Studio on the 100 block of West Garvey Avenue in Monterey Park following a Lunar New Year celebration. He escaped. His motives were unknown and it was initially unclear whether it was an anti-Asian hate crime. Twenty minutes later, an armed Asian man, believed between 30 and 50, walked into the Lai Lai Ballroom and Studio in Alhambra. Brandon Tsay, whose family had owned Lai Lai for three generations, grabbed the attacker's gun and wrested the Cobray M11 9 mm semi-automatic weapon from him. The attacker fled. Police vehicles surrounded a white cargo van in Torrance, and after a standoff, discovered the body of the suspect inside, dead from a self-inflicted gunshot. Police also found a handgun. Police identified the individual as Chinese immigrant Huu Can Tran, 72, a regular and informal instructor at the Star studio, where he had met his ex-wife (they divorced in 2006).

The dead included two women: My Nhan, 65, and Lilan Li, 63. Nine of the 10 victims were in their 60s or 70s, and all were over 50. Another woman died in the hospital on January 23.

CNN added on January 23 that Tran went with complaints on January 7 and 9 to a police station in Hemet in Riverside County. He lived in a mobile home in a senior community in Hemet, 86 miles from Monterey Park. Police said he alleged "past fraud, theft, and poisoning" involving his family in the Los Angeles area 10 to 20 years earlier. He failed to return with promised documentation.

CNN reported on January 25 that the female victims included:

- Xiujuan Yu, 57
- Hongying Jian, 62
- Lilian Li, 63
- Mymy Nhan, 65, aunt of the husband of Tiffany Liou, a reporter for *CNN* affiliate *WFAA* in Dallas, Texas. The family started a GoFundMe to help with funeral costs.
- Muoi Dai Ung, 67
- Diana Man Ling Tom, 70

The male victims included:

- Wen-Tau Yu, 64
- Valentino Marcos Alvero, 68, a hospitality worker, planned to retire in a year with hopes of returning to his native Philippines.
- Ming Wei Ma, 72, an employee of the Star Ballroom Dance studio, was known by the nickname Little Ma Brother.
- Yu-Lun Kao, 72
- Chia Ling Yau, 76

January 24, 2023: *CNN* reported that the Forest City Police Department in North Carolina issued a community service advisory regarding "multiple instances of razor blades being placed in gas pump handles in Forest City and surrounding areas". The police said there were three confirmed instances during the past month.

January 26, 2023: *CNN* and *Fox News* reported that Ali Shukri Amin, of Dumfries, Virginia, who pleaded guilty at age 17 in 2015 to providing support to ISIS, was accused of violating his release conditions after allegedly meeting several times with "American Taliban" John Walker

Lindh, who served 17 years in prison for aiding the group. The FBI photographed Amin having three conversations with Lindh in 2021. Lindh was released in 2019 on supervised release and subject to the same condition as Amin at the time of the alleged meetings. Amin was also in contact with another known extremist who lives in the United Kingdom for more than a year; UK authorities arrested that individual in February 2022. Amin was arrested in January 2023. Amin admitted helping classmate Reza Niknejad, 18, to travel to Syria to join ISIS.

January 28, 2023: *UPI* reported that members of a church in Monmouth County, New Jersey were attacked.

January 29, 2023: *UPI* reported that at 3:19 a.m., a white man wearing a ski mask threw a Molotov cocktail at the front doors of the Temple Ner Tamid in Bloomfield, New Jersey, then ran off. The bottle broke, but did not cause any damage. *CNN* added on February 1 that Nicholas Malindretos, 26, of Clifton, New Jersey, was arrested and charged with one count of attempted use of fire to damage a building. He was to appear in federal court in Newark on February 2 for an initial appearance. A license plate reader nearby recorded the car that Malindretos allegedly used in the attack. Officials found in the car a hooded sweatshirt, items made of a white cloth material similar to the gloves the suspect was wearing during the incident, and bottle of unidentified liquids. He faced 20 years in prison and a $250,000 fine.

January 30, 2023: *USA Today* reported that a federal jury, following a nine-day trial, convicted Ibraheem Izzy Musaibli, alias Abu Shifa Musaibli, alias Abu 'Abd al-Rahman al-Yemeni, 32, of Dearborn, Michigan, of three of four counts relating to his supporting ISIS. He faced 50 years in prison. Prosecutors said he traveled in October 2015 to Syria and participated in an ISIS religious training camp. He also learned how to shoot a machine gun in a military training camp. The Syrian Democratic Forces captured him in 2018 and turned him over to the FBI. The *New York Times* noted that he was flown to the U.S. on the same flight as Samantha Marie Elhassani,

an American woman who in 2020 was convicted of financing ISIS. She was married to an ISIS fighter. He was convicted of:

- Count one: Attempting to provide material support to a designated terrorist organization and providing material support to a designated terrorist organization.

- Count two: Conspiracy to provide support to a foreign terrorist organization.

- Count four: Receiving military-type training from a foreign terrorist organization.

February 1, 2023: *ABC News* and *Fox Business* reported that Victoria Jacobs, alias Bakhrom Talipov, 43, of Manhattan's Upper East Side in New York City, was charged with 11 counts of providing support for an act of terrorism, conspiracy in the fourth degree as a crime of terrorism, money laundering in support of terrorism, and six counts of criminal possession of a weapon for allegedly purchasing combat knives and throwing-stars. Prosecutors said she used cryptocurrency to provide financial support to terrorist groups in Syria. Prosecutors said she provided material support to Hay'at Tahrir al-Sham, which the U.S. State Department had designated as a foreign terrorist organization, and provided more than $5,000 to the terrorist training group Malhama Tactical, which fought with and provided special tactical and military training to Hay'at Tahrir al-Sham. She allegedly laundered $10,661 on behalf of Malhama Tactical by receiving cryptocurrency and Western Union and MoneyGram wires from supporters around the globe and sending the funds to Bitcoin wallets controlled by Malhama Tactical. She also allegedly purchased Google Play gift cards for the organization. Prosecutors said that in December 2019, she provided a comprehensive U.S. Army Improvised Munitions Handbook to an online group which she believed was associated with both Hay'at Tahrir al-Sham and al-Qaeda affiliated Hurras al-Din. Prosecutors added that she purchased military-style combat knives, metal knuckles, and throwing stars in August 2021 that were found in her Upper East Side apartment. Assistant District Attorney Edward Burns said in a court filing that "defendant posted a 15-second video clip of an unknown person ominously moving around with a firearm... The timing of this post and the defendant's acquisition of the weapons supports the conclusion that she intended to use the weapons in an unlawful manner." She was remanded.

February 6, 2023: *CNN* reported that the U.S. Department of Justice charged Sarah Beth Clendaniel, alias Nythra88 and Kali1889, of Catonsville, Maryland, and neo-Nazi leader and founder of Atomwaffen Division (AWD) Brandon Clint Russell, alias Homunculus, of Orlando, Florida with conspiracy to damage energy facilities due to ethnically or racially motivated extremist beliefs. U.S. Attorney of Maryland Erek Barron said the duo "conspired and took steps to shoot multiple electrical substations" in the Baltimore area. The duo planned to "completely destroy" Baltimore. Tom Sobocinski, Special Agent in Charge of the FBI's field office in Baltimore, added that they "conspired to inflict maximum harm on the power grid. The accused were not just talking, but taking steps to fulfill their threats and further their extremist goals." Charging documents said that Russell started his own local National Socialist Group and had plotted with his roommates in Florida to attack energy facilities there. Russell had been in contact with an FBI source since June 2022. The FBI had offered two $25,000 rewards for information leading to the conviction of those behind damage to two substations in Moore County, North Carolina, on December 2022 and for shooting a substation in Randolph County North Carolina, on January 17, 2023.

February 7, 2023: *Business Insider, AP,* and *ABC News* reported that a New York federal court convicted Kazakhstan-born naturalized U.S. citizen Ruslan Maratovich Asainov of five counts, including providing material support to ISIS in Syria resulting in death by training 100 fighters on weapons use. He had worked as a stockbroker in Brooklyn before he dropped out of Borough of Manhattan Community College and abandoned his wife and daughter to go to Syria in December 2013. He fought for ISIS until March 2019. The Department of Justice said that he received military-type training on machine guns, automatic rifles, and rocket-propelled grenades and later

volunteered to become a lethal sniper for ISIS. The former resident of Bay Ridge converted to Islam in 2009. He tried to recruit another U.S. individual to travel Syria to fight for ISIS. He sent a photograph to his ex-wife of three dead fighters. He was captured near the Syria-Iraq border in July 2019. He faced a life sentence.

February 23, 2023: *AP* and the *Florida Times-Union* reported that Muhammed Momtaz al-Azhari, 25, pleaded guilty to attempting to provide material support to ISIS, seeking to spot targets in the Tampa Bay area, seeking to acquire weapons, and pledging an oath of allegiance to ISIS. He agreed to an 18-year prison sentence. He was accused in 2020 of plotting terrorist attacks in the U.S.

March 1, 2023: The FBI arrested and charged Michigan resident Jack E. Carpenter, III, 41, for a February 17 tweet from Texas threatening "to carry out the punishment of death to anyone" who is Jewish in the Michigan government. The *Washington Post* reported that Michigan Attorney General Dana Nessel said that list included her. He was arrested in Texas on February 21, appeared in federal court in Texas, and was transported to Detroit. He appeared in federal court in Detroit on March 1 on one count of using interstate communications to make threats. He faced a five-year sentence. Carpenter was represented by the public defender's office. His mother told authorities that her son owned three handguns, a shotgun, and two rifles, including a military-style weapon. Carpenter was employed at the University of Michigan from June 2011 to December 2021. He served as a systems administrator in the College of Literature, Science, and the Arts.

March 3, 2023: *Task and Purpose* and *NBC News* reported that former Army soldier Ethan Melzer, alias Etil Reggad, 24, from Kentucky, was sentenced to 45 years in prison for an attempted plot to ambush and kill his comrades in a "jihadi attack" while deployed abroad. In June 2022, he pleaded guilty to attempted murder of U.S. Army soldiers, illegally sharing national security information, and providing and attempting to provide terrorists with material support. Melzer was a private while in the Army. He had joined the Order of Nine Angles, a Neo-Nazi and Satanic organization which has praised both Adolf Hitler and al-Qaeda. The Department of Justice noted that he planned to ambush soldiers at a base in Türkiye to "cripple" the base's fire teams and cause a mass casualty attack.

He joined the Army in 2018, which U.S. Attorney for the Southern District of New York Damian Williams deemed "an infiltration". Melzer was assigned to the 173rd Airborne Brigade Combat Team, which was deployed to Italy. In 2020 he was told he would move to a "sensitive" base in Türkiye; he allegedly began plotting the attack. He transmitted location, schedule, and security information to the O9A subgroup known as RapeWaffen Division and to a purported al-Qaeda member. He was arrested in May 2020 in Italy.

He was represented by defense attorney Jonathan Marvinny and two other attorneys.

March 6, 2023: *UPI* and *AP* reported that the Atlanta Police Department announced domestic terrorism charges by the Georgia Bureau of Investigation against 23 of 35 people arrested over the weekend for attacking the 85-acre construction site of the $90 million Atlanta Public Safety Training Center (familiarly known as Cop City), a planned Atlanta police and firefighter training facility in the Weelaunee Forest in DeKalb County. The 35 allegedly broke away from a nearby peaceful protest to conduct a "coordinated attack" on construction equipment and police officers. The "violent agitators", dressed in black, destroyed several pieces of construction equipment by fire and vandalism. Officers said the suspects threw rocks, bricks, Molotov cocktails, and fireworks at them. The Georgia Department of Public Safety said the demonstrators shined green lasers into their officers' eyes. Only two of the 23 people charged with domestic terrorism were from the state of Georgia. One person was from France; another from Canada. Among those charged with domestic terrorism was Thomas Jurgens, a Southern Poverty Law Center lawyer who was acting as a legal observer on behalf of the National Lawyers Guild. Supporters of the

demonstrators said that the arrests occurred at a concert a mile away. The felony charges carry a 35-year prison term.

March 23, 2023: *CNN* reported that a Manhattan court sentenced Abdullah el-Faisal, the first person tried under New York terror laws passed in the wake of 9/11, to 18 years in prison on five terrorism-related charges, including soliciting or providing support of an act of terrorism and conspiracy as a crime of terrorism. Assistant District Attorney Gary Galperin said the defendant was "one of the most influential English-speaking terrorists of our time", who thought images of the coffins of U.S. service members were laughable. The Jamaican-born Muslim convert radicalized in the UK in the late 1990s. The UK deported him after he served less than half of a nine-year sentence on charges of inciting hatred and soliciting the murder of Jews, Americans, and Hindus. Prosecutors said el-Faisal had influenced several convicted terrorists, including:

- Jermaine Lindsay, who blew himself up on a London Underground train in 2005.
- Richard Reid, the "shoe bomber" of 2001.
- Umar Farouk AbdulMutallab, the "underwear bomber" of Christmas 2009.
- Faisal Shahzad, built and drove a truck bomb into Times Square in 2010.

Authorities believed a 9/11 hijacker was inspired by el-Faisal.

He was also connected an undercover FBI officer with an ISIS fighter in Raqqa, Syria.

March 24, 2023: *CNN* reported that a large portion of a public park near Atlanta on the proposed site of the "Cop City" South River Forest Public Safety Training Center for police and fire fighters was temporarily closed after county officials located "life threatening" hidden "booby traps, boards with nails that were hidden by leaves and underbrush," according to DeKalb County CEO Michael Thurmond.

April 4, 2023: *AP* reported that a Miami federal court sentenced Emraan Ali, 55, a U.S. citizen born in Trinidad and Tobago, to 20 years in prison after he moved his family to Syria to join ISIS.

He pleaded guilty in November 2022 to conspiring to provide material support to a foreign terrorist organization. He had moved his family to Brazil, then to Türkiye, then to Syria in March 2015, telling his children that they were going on vacation. In Syria, ISIS trained him on the AK-47 assault rifle and PKC machine gun. He worked in residential construction in Raqqa, became a merchant, and bought and sold livestock, cars, weapons, weapons accessories, and telephones. He provided money remittance services to other Trinidadian ISIS fighters in Syria and donated money to ISIS. He and his son, Jihad Ali, 22, surrendered to the Syrian Democratic Forces in Baghuz in March 2019. The son was born in New York and began ISIS military and religious training at age 15. He was sentenced to five years in prison.

April 13, 2023: The *Irish Star* reported on May 4, 2023 that on April 13, Harvard University's police department received six calls regarding bombs and demand for payment in Bitcoin. On May 2, police arrested William Giordani, of Nashua, New Hampshire, on charges of conspiracy and aiding and abetting extortionate threats. The caller gave a location and a description of a device, which police found and destroyed. The device had a metal locking safe, a package of wire, fireworks inside the safe, and a small rectangular box with wires attached to it. It also had a yellow Home Depot sticker and another man's name. Giordani was seen on video picking up those items from Home Depot.

April 23, 2023: *CNN* reported on May 1, 2023 that on April 29, 2023, the Blue Earth County Sheriff's Office arrested and charged with arson Jackie Rahm Little, 36, alias Joel Arthur Tueting, for setting fires at two Minneapolis mosques. He was turned over to agents from the FBI and the Bureau of Alcohol, Tobacco and Firearms. He had a history of arson and suspected arson, including one in 2022. An affidavit indicated that he allegedly started a fire the evening of April 23 in a restroom at the Masjid Omar Islamic Center, commonly known within the community as Somali Mall. The next day, he was seen in surveillance footage going into the Masjid al-Rahma Mosque, also known as the Mercy Islamic

Center, where a fire erupted on the third floor soon after, prompting an evacuation, including about 40 children. The damage totaled tens of thousands of dollars. No one was hurt in either incident. In December 2022, he allegedly harassed a member of the U.S. House of Representatives, entering the representative's district office and spray-painting "500" on the front door. Little spray-painted the same "500" on the side of a patrol vehicle belonging to a Somali officer for the Minneapolis Police Department and in an entryway to Somali Mall. Its meaning is unknown. In cases where no one is hurt, a conviction on a federal arson charge carries a minimum sentence of five years up to 20 years.

May 6, 2023: *CNN* and *NBC News* reported on May 7 that the Texas Department of Public Safety announced that Mauricio Garcia, 33, had opened fire at the Allen Premium Outlets mall in Allen, Texas, killing eight people and wounding seven others. An Allen Police Department officer who was at the mall on an unrelated call shot to death the suspected neo-Nazi sympathizer, whose social media showed a fondness for white supremacist views. His clothing included an insignia for RWDS, possibly meaning Right Wing Death Squad. He was wearing body armor and had eight weapons (six in his grey 2014 Dodge Charger parked at the scene), all obtained legally, including an AR-15-style assault weapon, and several extra magazines. He had taken firearms proficiency training for his work as a commissioned security officer in Texas from April 2016 until April 2020. He had worked for three security companies. *Military Times* reported that he had been a soldier in the U.S. Army, dismissed from infantry training at Fort Benning, Georgia after three months due to a mental health issue.

Victims included Christian LaCour, 20, a mall security guard. *KTVT* reported that a child survived after his mother shielded him from the bullets, but she was struck and killed. The *Dallas Morning News* and *Yonhap* reported that a Korean-American husband Cho Kyu Song, 37, and wife, Kang Shin Young, 35, and their son, James, 3, were killed. Another son, William, 6, was hospitalized. *CNN* reported on May 8 that Daniela and Sofia Mendoza were elementary school students in the Wylie Independent

School District. Daniela was a 4th-grader; sister Sofia was a 2nd-grader. Their mother was critically injured. *WFAA* reported that India-born Telugu engineer Aishwarya Thatikonda, a few days away from turning 28, was killed while visiting the mall with a friend. She had moved to the U.S. five years earlier to pursue her Master of Science degree in construction management, which she obtained from Eastern Michigan University in December 2020. Elio Cumana-Rivas, 32, was also killed.

May 7, 2023: *CNN* reported that around 8:30 a.m., a driver crashed his Land Rover into 20-25 Venezuelan immigrants at a bus stop across the street from the Bishop Enrique San Pedro Ozanam Center, a non-profit homeless shelter that has been helping house immigrants in Brownsville, Texas, killing eight immigrants and injuring a dozen immigrants. Witnesses detained the driver until police arrested him on a reckless driving charge. The Hispanic man was "uncooperative" with authorities, giving them multiple names. The driver ignored a red light, jumped a curb, and ran into people, all of them men.

Al-Jazeera added that George Alvarez, who attempted to flee, was charged with eight counts of manslaughter and ten counts of aggravated assault with a deadly weapon. He had an extensive criminal history. He was held on a $3.6 million bail.

Luis Herrera, 36, a Venezuelan, was injured in his arm.

May 22, 2023: *The Hill, Reuters, NBC, New York Post,* and *AP* reported that at 10 p.m., Sai Varshith Kandula, 19, of Chesterfield, Missouri, crashed a rented 26-foot U-Haul box truck into security barriers on the north side of Lafayette Square near the White House. Uniformed Secret Service officers arrested the driver. The U.S. Park Police said he faced charges of threatening to kill, kidnap, or inflict harm on the president, vice president, or a family member; assault with a dangerous weapon; reckless driving; destruction of federal property; and trespassing. No one was injured. *WUSA9* reported that investigators found a Nazi flag in the truck. Authorities said he lauded Hitler. *CNN* added that the Park Police also found a backpack and a roll of duct

tape in the truck. The Secret Service requested that the Hay-Adams Hotel, next to Lafayette Square, be evacuated. The *Washington Post* added that that the D.C. fire and police departments also responded to the scene. Bomb techs found no explosives or incendiary devices.

CNN reported on May 24 that Kandula said that he aimed to "kill the President" if necessary to overthrow the government and install himself in power. He was charged in federal court with one count of depredation of property of the United States in excess of $1,000. D.C. Superior Court ordered him held in custody without bail.

June 10, 2023: *CNN* reported that Theodore "Ted" Kaczynski, 81, alias The Unabomber, was found at 12:25 a.m. dead in his cell at the Federal Medical Center in Butner, North Carolina. His mail bombs had killed three people and wounded 23 others from 1978 to 1995. He had been held at Supermax in Florence, Colorado, before he was transferred to the FMC on December 14, 2021. *NBC News* reported that he was suffering from cancer, and committed suicide.

June 14, 2023: *Military Times* reported that Army Pfc. Cole Bridges, 22, alias Cole Gonzales, pleaded guilty to plotting the murder of U.S. service members with an FBI employee he believed to be an ISIS supporter living in New York. The Ohio native was arrested in January 2021. He joined the Army in September 2019, and served as a cavalry scout in the 3rd Infantry Division based at Fort Stewart, Georgia. In August 2020, weeks before a scheduled three-month rotation to Germany, he began posting jihadist propaganda on his social media accounts under the name "Cole Gonzales". His *Facebook* page included quotations from Salafist preachers exalting "war between Islam and Kufr [infidels]" and photos of his M4 rifle captioned with verses and emojis popular with ISIS. An undercover FBI agent approached Bridges online in September 2020. The next month, Bridges began advising the phony fighter and his crew on how to stage an attack, citing his training and combat expertise. He soon sent illustrations of battlefield maneuvers from the U.S. Army Field Manual accompanied with detailed explanations over encrypted messaging apps. In November, he allegedly outlined potential attack targets in New York City, including the 9/11 memorial. In December, he walked the undercover agents through a potential attack on American troops stationed in the Middle East, offering color-coded unit schematics and tactical formations. Bridges faced 40 years in prison. Sentencing was set for November 2, 2023.

June 20, 2023: *CNN* reported that Kansas lawmakers, including Republican state Representative Stephen Owens, Representative Tory Marie Blew (R), and House Speaker Daniel Hawkins (R) and public officials received 100 letters containing a white powder. The Kansas Bureau of Investigation indicated that preliminary tests indicated that "the substance is presumptively negative for common biological agents of concern". No injuries were reported. The letter to Hawkins read:

> "SalUTatioNS
>
> To hOnor your rEcenT ACcOmplishMeNtS
>
> I SEnD TO yoU a Gift fROm the exclusive aSTruC bAruCH collection
>
> It Is iMpOrtaNt nOT to cHokE oN YoUR aMbitIoN
>
> yOuR SEcreT deSpirER"

Following the broken English entry were several passages in what appeared to be at least five Asian languages. A return address on an envelope included the name of a transgender woman who died. Another return address was for a church in Owens's district.

July 14, 2023: The *Washington Post* reported that former Germany-based Tunisian professional soccer player Nizar Trabelsi, 53, was acquitted of plotting to kill Americans at Kleine Brogel Air Base in Belgium with an ammonium nitrate bomb, conspiring to murder Americans abroad, attempting to use a weapon of mass destruction, and supporting a terrorist group. Richard Reid, the failed "shoe bomber", testified during his trial. Trabelsi was arrested two days after 9/11. He was indicted in a Washington, D.C. federal court 17 years earlier, and had been in custody await-

ing trial for a decade. The Department of Justice announced that Trabelsi would be placed in U.S. Immigration and Customs Enforcement custody for removal proceedings. The Tunisian citizen was convicted in absentia in Tunisia on terrorism charges; the extradition agreement between the United States and Belgium bars sending him to a third country without Belgian approval. In 2022, a Belgian court ordered the government to request Trabelsi's return to Belgium, which had extradited him in 2013.

Trabelsi had told Belgian authorities that he planned an attack at the Air Base. He also claimed that he and Osama bin Laden flew by helicopter to take part in the Taliban's destruction of ancient Buddhist statues carved into a cliff in Afghanistan. He served a 10-year sentence in Belgium.

Saajid Badat, another wannabe shoe bomber who served 11 years in a UK prison, testified that he was to help with the plot but failed to make contact before Trabelsi's arrest.

In his trial, Trabelsi argued that his earlier confessions and the incriminating testimony were false and improbable.

Reid testified that he knew Badat but had never seen or heard of Trabelsi. He also said the terrorist group would not have recruited a married father like Trabelsi to become a suicide bomber and that an al-Qaeda operative's wife would not know details Trabelsi's ex-wife testified about or have gotten weapons training as she claimed. "As the Americans say, loose lips sink ships… Nothing was done in writing." He added "men and women don't mix".

Trabelsi was represented by attorneys Marc Eisenstein and Sabrina Shroff.

Trabelsi also claimed that he met bin Laden through "best friend" Abu Zubaida and knew French AQ recruiter Djamel Beghal.

July 27, 2023: *Reuters* reported that U.S. District Judge Colleen McMahon ordered the release after 90 days of three of the "Newburgh Four" who were convicted in 2011 and sentenced to 25 years for plotting to blow up New York City synagogues, a Jewish community center, and shoot down military planes. She said "hapless" petty criminals Onta Williams, David Williams, and Laguerra Payen had been manipulated in an FBI sting in 2009. James Cromitie, called the ringleader by the government, did not seek compassionate release and was expected to serve his prison time until 2030.

July 30, 2023: *CNN, AP*, and *Report for America* reported that at 1 p.m., an older white male drove an older model mid-size black SUV with a luggage rack into a group of migrant workers, injuring six, at a Lincolnton, North Carolina Walmart in an apparent "intentional assault". *UPI* reported that driver Daniel González, 68, of Hickory, turned himself in around 6 p.m. on July 31, claiming he accidentally pressed the gas pedal while trying to park and that he fled the scene in a panic. He was arrested, held on a $50,000 bond, and charged with felony hit-and-run. Jeff Crotts of Knob Greek Farm in Lawndale told *NBC News* that the migrants were legally in the United States as seasonal farm workers with agricultural-related visas. Police identified the victims as Jorge A. Lopez, Zalapa M. Hermosillo, Jose L. Calderon, Luis D. Alcantar, Rodrigo M. Gutierrez-Tapia, and Santiago Baltazar.

July 31, 2023: *CNN* reported on August 3, 2023 that Joel Alejandro Bowman, 33, fired a handgun outside the Margolin Hebrew Academy-Feinstone Yeshiva of the South in Memphis, Tennessee, after failing to enter. No one was injured. He drove away in his truck, but was stopped by Memphis police officers. He exited with a gun with his hand and was shot by an officer. He was arrested and faced multiple charges, including criminal attempted second-degree murder; carrying weapons on school property; reckless endangerment; possessing a firearm during the commission or attempt to commit a dangerous felony; and assault against a first responder. U.S. Representative Steve Cohen said Bowman was Jewish and a former student of the school.

August 26, 2023: Local tv news and radio, *CNN*, and *al-Jazeera* reported that a white male neo-Nazi in his 20s living in Clay County, Florida, drove his grey Honda Element to Jacksonville, Florida, was denied entrance in the area of the Centennial Library at Edward Waters University (an HBCU) after he refused to iden-

tify himself, put on a tactical vest, then drove to a Dollar General at 2161 Kings Road in New Town where shortly after 1 p.m., he shot to death three African Americans, two men and a woman. He ran into the Dollar General, then turned the gun on himself. He had an AR-15-style rifle and a Glock handgun, both of which he legally purchased. At least one of the guns had swastikas drawn in white paint. He left behind a will, a suicide note, and three anti-Black manifestos at his parents' home, where he lived.

CNN reported that shooter Ryan Christopher Parmeter, variant Palmeter, was born on November 28, 2001.

He wore a facial covering, ball cap, and blue latex gloves, according to Jacksonville Sheriff T.K. Waters. The Sheriff observed, "This shooting was racially motivated and he hated Black people." The manifestos outlined a "disgusting ideology of hate" and his motive in the attack.

Parmeter was the subject of a 2017 law enforcement call under the Baker Act, which allows people to be involuntarily detained and subject to an examination for up to 72 hours during a mental health crisis. He had also been involved in a 2016 domestic violence incident. At age 15, he left his parents a suicide note and rode his bike toward downtown to jump off the Bank of America tower. He was found on 103rd Street and Baker Acted.

Jacksonville Mayor Donna Deegan said the Parmeter's writings indicated he was aware of a mass shooting at a Madden video gaming tournament at the erstwhile Jacksonville Landing where two people were killed exactly five years earlier. The attack also coincided with the commemoration of the 60th anniversary of the March on Washington, D.C. It was one day before the 63rd anniversary of Ax Handle Saturday in Jacksonville.

Parmeter bought a handgun in April and an AR-15-style rifle in June.

The victims were Angela Michelle Carr, 52; Anolt Joseph "AJ" Laguerre, Jr., 19; and Jerrald De'Shawn Gallion, 29. At 1:08 p.m., the gunman shot into a black Kia at the Dollar General parking lot, and killed Carr. He then entered the store and fatally shot Laguerre. He walked out of the store, but returned to fatally shoot Gallion, who had just walked into the store. He chased after and shot at Gallion's fleeing girlfriend, but missed.

The *Florida Times-Union* provided background on the victims.

Gallion left behind a daughter, Je Asia, 4. He and his girlfriend had walked into the store ahead of Parmeter. Gallion sometimes worked two or three jobs, including as a restaurant manager. He attended St. Paul Missionary Baptist Church. He was a fan of the Jacksonville Jaguars and the Florida State Seminoles football team.

Uber driver Angela Michelle Carr, 52, was dropping someone off at the store when Parmeter fired into her Kia sedan. She left behind an adult daughter, Ashley, along with two other children and 14 grandchildren. She attended Saint Stephen A.M.E. Church. She had left Key West years earlier. Her mother gave birth to her as a teen.

AJ Laguerre, Jr., lost his mother on January 10, 2009 when he was five years old. He was the youngest of five siblings, all raised by their grandmother. He graduated from Raines High School in 2022. He worked at the Dollar General store for several months to help his grandmother pay the bills. His brother Quantavious Laguerre set up a GoFundMe page because AJ died without life insurance. He had aspirations of becoming a professional streamer and was looking to study cybersecurity in college. He was adept at Fortnite, using the tag galaxysoul. He never had a police record, never had a referral in school, and never fought.

The *Florida Times-Union* and *USA Today Network* reported on August 30 that Parmeter had worked at a Dollar Tree in the Oakleaf area from October 2021 to July 2022. He had stopped at the Family Dollar store at Myrtle Avenue and Kings Road at 12:23 p.m., shortly before the Dollar General attack.

His parents said he had flunked out of Flagler College and lost his job at Home Depot.

Dollar General announced on September 1, 2023 that it would donate $2.5 million to employee resources and Jacksonville nonprofits supporting those affected by the shooting. The donation included $50,000 to local area food banks, $500,000 to the First Coast Relief Fund,

and $1 million to nonprofits or community organizations. Another $1 million went to DG's Employee Assistance Foundation.

The Reverend Al Sharpton and civil rights attorney Ben Crump participated in the September 8 funeral service for Angela Michelle Carr.

Attorney Michael Haggard and famed civil rights attorney Ben Crump, representing the victims' families, filed on December 4, 2023 in Duval County Circuit Court a $50,000+ lawsuit against COLGENCORP LLC and DC Strategic LLC, which operate/manage the Dollar General store, Corso General II LLC—owners of the land it stands on, the Missouri-based Interface Security Systems, LLC contracted for store security, and Parmeter's family, charging the firms of negligence and responsibility under Florida's wrongful death law.

The *Florida Times-Union* reported that the New Town Dollar General reopened on January 12, 2024, five months after a gunman killed three people at the store.

USA Today and the *Florida Times-Union* reported on January 21, 2024 that Jacksonville Sheriff T.K. Waters released a 27-page diatribe from shooter Ryan Christopher Palmeter that focused on his hatred for Black people. Palmeter left behind copies for his parents, the media, and federal agents. He used the N word 183 times and added his hate for the LGBTQ community.

The *Florida Times-Union* and *USA Today* reported that the Players Championship and PGA Tour along with Florida State College at Jacksonville announced the A.J. Laguerre Jr., Endowed Scholarship during an assembly at Raines High School, where he graduated in 2023. He was the youngest victim of the Dollar General shooting. He had planned to major in Cybersecurity at FSCJ. FSCJ President John Avendano gave his family his honorary Associate in Science degree in Cybersecurity.

August 29, 2023: *CNN* reported that the FBI was investigating more than a dozen Uzbek nationals allowed into the U.S. after they sought asylum at the southern border with Mexico after U.S. intelligence officials discovered that the migrants traveled with the help of a smuggler—arrested by Türkiye—with ties to ISIS.

September 1, 2023: *CNN, Canton Repository, COIO, and WKYC* reported on December 14, 2023 that authorities arrested a 13-year-old in Ohio on criminal misdemeanor counts of inducing panic and disorderly conduct after allegedly crafting "a detailed plan" for a mass shooting at Temple Israel synagogue in Canton in September. The defendant posted the plans on the social media platform *Discord*, on which he conspired with a person in Washington State. *ABC News* reported that *Discord* alerted the FBI. He was booked into the Multi-County Juvenile Detention Center in Canton Township. He was to appear in mid-December 2023 in Stark County Family Court.

September 24, 2023: *CNN, NBC News,* and *al-Jazeera* reported that two Molotov cocktails were thrown at the Cuban Embassy in Washington, D.C. after 8 p.m., causing no injuries and minor damage. Foreign Minister Bruno Rodrìguez Parilla posted on *X* that an individual "launched 2 Molotov cocktails" from the sidewalk over the perimeter fence, hitting the front wall but failing to ignite. No one claimed credit. Havana blamed Cuban exiles. No arrests were made.

September 28, 2023: *CNN* reported on November 2, 2023 that on October 30, special agents from the U.S. Capitol Police and FBI arrested Alaska man Arthur Charles Graham, 46, after allegedly sending a threatening message to U.S. Senator Lisa Murkowski (R-Alaska), writing that he planned to hunt down and physically harm her. The Department of Justice charged him with making interstate threats to kidnap and injure a current U.S. Senator. Graham wrote on a Congressional e-form that he was facing eviction and that he had "nowhere else to live". He confessed to the FBI. He was to appear before a U.S. magistrate judge on November 3. He faced five years in prison.

October 10, 2023: *Al-Jazeera* reported that a car crashed into the lobby of the visa section of the Chinese consulate in San Francisco. Police shot to death the driver.

October 14, 2023: *CNN, AP,* and *al-Jazeera* reported that the Will County, Illinois, Sheriff's Office announced that Chicago-area landlord Joseph M. Czuba, 71, was charged with first-degree murder, attempted first-degree murder, two counts of a hate crime, and aggravated battery with a deadly weapon after he stabbed and killed Wadea al-Fayoume, 6, and seriously wounded his mother, Hanaan Shahin, 32, allegedly because the tenants are Muslim. The U.S. Department of Justice opened a federal hate crime investigation into the attack. The family is Palestinian. The boy was stabbed 26 times with a large military-style knife and died. His mother sustained more than a dozen stab wounds and was expected to survive. The family had lived on the house's ground floor in unincorporated Plainfield Township for two years. Wadea's mother and father had moved from a village in the West Bank to the United States 12 and nine years ago, respectively, and their son was born in the U.S. *AP* reported on October 30 that Czuba was due to appear in court following his indictment by an Illinois grand jury the previous week on eight counts. He pleaded not guilty. Czuba was represented by attorney George Lenard.

October 17, 2023: *UPI* reported on October 25 that Fraser Michael Bohm, 22, of Malibu, California, was arrested on murder charges for the October 17, 2023 car crash on the Pacific Coast Highway that killed four Pepperdine University seniors and sorority sisters Niamh Rolston, Peyton Stewart, Asha Weir, and Deslyn Williams. He was held on $8 million bond. He initially was held on a charge of gross vehicular manslaughter and released as detectives gathered more evidence. Pepperdine posted on its *Facebook* site:

Niamh was a senior business administration major. She planned to continue her post-graduate studies at Pepperdine, where she hoped to pursue an MBA. She was a member of the Alpha Phi sorority and served on the Red Dress Gala committee for their philanthropy event.

Peyton was a senior international business major. She served as vice president for finance of the Alpha Phi sorority and worked part-time in the Seaver College Career Center. In her sophomore year, Peyton studied abroad at Pepperdine's London campus.

Asha was a senior English writing and rhetoric major. She served as an orientation leader, a member of the Indian Student Association, and an active sister in Alpha Phi. Asha participated in Pepperdine's London Program as well as the London Internship program.

Deslyn was a senior pre-med biology major. She served as vice president of the pre-veterinary club, recruitment chair for Alpha Phi, and as a Panhellenic recruitment counselor.

They were to receive posthumous degrees alongside their graduating class of 2024.

October 21, 2023: *CNN* reported that in the morning, Samantha Woll, 40, president of the board of the Isaac Agree Downtown Synagogue in Detroit, was found dead with multiple stab wounds outside her home in Lafayette Park, hours after returning from a wedding. Police said they found a "trail of blood" leading from her to her home, where police believed she was killed. *CNN* reported on November 8 that Detroit Police Chief James E. White announced the arrest of a suspect in Kalamazoo, but soon released the person without charges. *CNN* reported on December 10 that the Detroit Police Department took into custody a person of interest. The *Los Angeles Times* reported on December 14 that Michael Jackson-Bolanos, 28, of Detroit, was charged with murder, home invasion, and lying to police. He pleaded not guilty during his appearance in 36th District Court and was remanded without bond. He was represented by attorney Brian Brown.

Woll had worked for Democratic U.S. Representative Elissa Slotkin and on the political campaign of state Attorney General Dana Nessel.

CNN, *WDIV*, and *WXYZ* reported on July 18, 2024 that jurors in the trial of Michael Jackson-Bolanos, 29, accused of killing Samantha Woll, deadlocked on the charges of felony first-degree premeditated murder and home invasion, found him not guilty of premeditated murder, and found him guilty of lying to a police officer.

On August 10, 2024, Judge Margaret Van Houten dismissed the remaining felony murder charge against Michael Jackson-Bolanos. The judge held that putting him on trial against for murder would be unconstitutional "double jeopardy." The jury was not unanimous on the separate charge of felony murder committed during

another crime—a home invasion. The judge sentenced Jackson-Bolanos to 18 months in prison for lying to police during the investigation. Defense attorney Brian Brown requested probation.

October 24, 2023: *CNN* reported on November 2, 2023 that Jordanian man Sohaib Abuayyash, 20, who was arrested on October 24 in Houston on a federal charge of illegal possession of a firearm by a prohibited person, had spoken of "martyrdom". A federal judge said in a court order that he was "plotting to attack a Jewish gathering". Abuayyash was in the United States on an expired nonimmigrant visa. The FBI began investigating Abuayyash in August after video of him firing multiple firearms, including AR-style rifles, was posted on social media, according to a probable cause affidavit filed on October 19 in the U.S. District Court for the Southern District of Texas. He had applied for asylum after his nonimmigrant visa expired in 2019. He was authorized to work in the U.S. until August 2025, but is not allowed to "possess or use firearms or ammunition". The affidavit noted that he "has been in direct contact with others who share a radical mindset, has been conducting physical training, and has trained with weapons to possibly commit an attack". U.S. Magistrate Judge Christina A. Bryan wrote that Abuayyash "has viewed specific and detailed content posted by radical organizations on the internet including lessons on how to construct bombs or explosive devices; and that Defendant has made statements to others that support the killing of individuals of particular religious faiths… In his communications with another individual about martyrdom, the Defendant referenced an event in Houston for members of a particular religious group".

October 25, 2023: *NPR* and *AP* reported that Maine Governor Janet Mills announced that in two shooting attacks around 6:56 p.m., a lone shooter with an AR-15-style rifle killed 18 people and wounded 13, including Schemengees Bar and Grille restaurant on Lincoln Street during industry night and Just-in-Time Recreation (also reported as Sparetime) bowling alley on Mollison Way during youth night, in Lewiston in Androscoggin County, Maine. Initial reports during the fog of war said 22 people were killed and 60 wounded. Preliminary reports of a shooting at the Walmart Distribution Center on Alfred A. Plourde Parkway were incorrect.

The FBI identified Robert R. Card, II, 40 (born April 4, 1983), as a person of interest. Authorities issued an arrest warrant on eight counts of murder. Card's white Subaru was found in Lisbon, near an Androscoggin River boat ramp. He owned a 15-foot boat. Residents were urged to shelter in place.

A police bulletin said Card was a firearms instructor believed to be in the U.S. Army Reserve and assigned to a training facility in Saco, Maine. He had been committed to a mental health facility for two weeks in the summer of 2023 after he reported "hearing voices and threats to shoot up" a military base while at New York's Camp Smith.

WMTW-TV reported that Zoey Levesque, 10, who was at the bowling alley with her mother, was grazed by a bullet. "It's scary… I had never thought I'd grow up and get a bullet in my leg. And it's just like, why? Why do people do this?"

Seven bodies were found at the bowling alley; eight at Schemengees; three others died at the hospital.

Among the dead were:

- Tricia Asselin, 53, who worked part-time at Just-In-Time Recreation and was there bowling. She ran to the counter and was trying to call 911 when she was shot. Her sister, Bobbi Nichols, was also at the bowling alley and escaped.

- William Frank Brackett, 48

- Peyton Brewer-Ross, 39, who was playing in a cornhole tournament at Schemengees. He also enjoyed comics and playing games. His daughter Elle, celebrated her second birthday two weeks ago. In the past five years, he worked his way through an iron pipefitter apprenticeship program and graduated in 2022.

- Tommy Conrad, 34, manager at the bowling alley, was survived by his 9-year-old daughter.

- Michael Deslauriers, II, 51, killed while attempting to charge at Card at the bowling alley. Deslauriers Sr., who is the chairman of the Sabattus Historical Society, announced on the organization's *Facebook* page that his son and his friend died trying to stop Card. "They made sure their wives and several young children were under cover then they charged the shooter," Deslauriers Sr. said.

- Maxx Hathaway, 35, a full-time, stay-at-home dad of two daughters, with a third child on the way in a month, was at Schemengees playing pool. His wife, Brenda Hathaway, left the bar early when their toddler, Lilian, got fussy.

- Bryan MacFarlane, 40, who was participating in a cornhole tournament at Schemengees, was part of the local Deaf community, which usually plays cornhole on Wednesdays. MacFarlane was one of the first Deaf people in the state of Vermont to get his commercial trucking driver's license. He loved riding his motorcycle and hanging out with his dog, M&M.

- Keith Macneir, 64

- Ronald Morin, 55, died at Schemengees

- Joshua Seal, 36, an American Sign Language interpreter and director of interpreting services for the Pine Tree Society, had been competing in the cornhole tournament. He was the father of four.

- Arthur "Artie" Strout, 42, father of five, was also at Schemengees. His father, Arthur Bernard, had just left Schemengees when he received the call that there was an active shooter.

- Robert "Bob" Violette, 76, was teaching a youth bowling league at Just-In-Time Recreation. He died protecting his students by standing between them and Card, according to the *Portland Press Herald*. He died days before his 77th birthday.

- Lucille Violette, 73, wife of Bob Violette

- Stephen "Steve" Vozzella, 45, an active member of the New England Deaf Cornhole community and a member of the National Association of Letter Carriers.

NORTH AMERICA 238

- Joseph Walker, 57, manager of the bar at Schemengees, was killed after picking up a knife and trying to stop the gunman. He was the son of Leroy Walker, a city councilor in Auburn, Maine.
- William "Bill" Young, an auto mechanic, and his son, Aaron, 14, a high school sophomore honor student, were bowling together.

FBI SWAT teams on October 26 searched Card's last known address in Bowdoin, Maine.

CNN reported late on October 27 that Card's body was found near Lisbon, eight miles from Lewiston, in an unlocked trailer in the parking lot of the recycling center from which he had been recently fired. He was killed by an apparent self-inflicted gunshot to the head.

CNN reported on October 28 that a note left by Card indicated he did not expect to be found alive. The note was found at his residence, and was addressed to a loved one. It noted the passcode to his phone and his bank account numbers.

On July 24, 2024, a U.S. Army investigation into Card found that his unit missed several warning signs. Three officers in his chain of command were disciplined for dereliction of duty.

October 26, 2023: *CNN* reported on October 30 that police on October 26 arrested Las Vegas man John Anthony Miller, 43, for leaving anti-Semitic voicemail threats to kill U.S. Senator Jacky Rosen (D-Nevada), the third Jewish woman to serve in the Senate. He made his first court appearance on October 27, facing one count of threatening a federal official. The federal complaint noted that between October 11 and October 19, Rosen received numerous anti-Semitic voicemail messages calling her slurs and threatening "to finish what Hitler started". The caller said, "You done picked your side b*tch and you done chose evil." Miller left his name in one of his voicemails; law enforcement officials linked the number to the previous calls. The complaint added that on October 18, Miller tried to get into the Las Vegas courthouse to see the senator but was refused entry. He walked down Las Vegas Boulevard vowing, "To kill every last Is-

raeli terror-f***king-rist." The case was scheduled for November 13 before U.S. Magistrate Judge Elayna Youchah.

October 28, 2023: *CNN, Today,* and *NBC News* reported that in the morning, the body of Diego Barajas Medina, 20, of Carbondale, Colorado, armed with a semi-automatic rifle, a semi-automatic handgun, multiple loaded magazines for both weapons, and explosive devices, was found dead of an apparent self-inflicted gunshot wound at Glenwood Caverns Adventure Park in Glenwood, Colorado. Police said his death averted "an attack of devastating proportions" against the amusement park. The Garfield County Sheriff's Office said he apparently entered the park illegally after it had closed. He was wearing body armor and a ballistic helmet. Authorities found a note on the wall of the women's restroom where Medina was found that read, "I am not a killer. I just wanted to get into the caves." Medina lived with his mother and brother. Two weapons were ghost guns, which have no serial numbers, do not require background checks, and provide no transfer records for easy traceability. Investigators found a "very well-put-together" fake hand grenade in Medina's car, plus a real pipe bomb. The sheriff said patches affiliated with law enforcement groups were in the car.

October 29, 2023: *CNN,* the *Washington Post,* and *AP* reported that several anti-Semitic threats were made against Cornell University's Jewish community in online posts over the weekend. President Martha E. Pollack indicated that the threats named 104 West—the home of the Center for Jewish Living. The *Cornell Daily Sun* reported that the posts threatened to shoot Jewish students at the 104 West building, which houses their kosher dining hall, and called on others to harm Jews. New York Governor Kathy Hochul called those who made the threats "terrorists". Some of the usernames from those making the threats included the word Hamas. The student-run *Cornell Review* reported that in previous days, several sidewalks on campus were vandalized with anti-Israel graffiti. The *Washington Post* added that one posting called Jewish students "rats" and said, "If you see a Jewish 'person' on campus follow them home and slit their throats." Another post was titled "gonna shoot up 104 west".

CNN reported on October 31 that police arrested as a person of interest Patrick Dai, 21, a junior. He appeared in federal court in Syracuse on November 1 on federal charges of "posting threats to kill or injure another using interstate communications". He faced up to five years in prison. Dai attended Pittsford Mendon High School. His parents told the *New York Post* that he has severe depression dating to 2021 and had no history of violence.

November 1, 2023: *AP* reported that LAPD police shot to death a knife-wielding man in his 50s on the patio of the popular Southern California Sagebrush Cantina restaurant in the Woodland Hills area of Los Angeles during the night after pursuing him from the scene of a nearby machete attack. The victim was not seriously injured. Initial reports said someone with a machete was outside a McDonald's. The victim had taken away the machete, but the attacker also had a knife. He ran from the McDonald's to the Cantina's parking lot, holding a knife and a glass bottle. Officers fired two Tasers, but the assailant ran into the restaurant's patio. He turned and faced the officers while still armed, then was shot.

November 3, 2023: The *Florida Times-Union* reported that around 8:05 p.m., a driver tried to crash his car with Arkansas plates through the exit gates of the Oconee Nuclear Station near Seneca, South Carolina, an hour after a Duke Energy security guard asked him to leave when he tried to enter. A pop-up security barrier stopped the silver 2002 Toyota Camry. The driver tried to hit a security truck with a guard in it, then drove through a fence and off the property. No one was injured. *AP* and *ABC News* reported that the next day, person of interest Doyle Wayne Whisenhunt, 66, of Lockesburg, Arkansas, was charged with attempted murder, malicious injury to personal property, and unlawful entry into an enclosed place. He was wanted on drugs and weapons charges out of Arkansas. Whisenhunt was taken into custody at an abandoned home in neighboring Pickens County, South Carolina.

He had driven into Pickens County and pulled onto residential property on Jones Mill Road. The homeowner fired warning shots and the suspect drove away. He was charged in a separate incident with one count of hit and run for being involved in a motor vehicle accident and failing to remain on the scene on November 2 on Rochester Highway.

November 3, 2023: *CNN* reported that an email sent to the rabbi of a Scottsdale, Arizona synagogue threatened to "execute" him and other Jewish people. The email noted "I have come to the realization that YOU people are to blame for everything evil in this world," and that Jews ran the court system. He told the rabbi to convince a Utah district court judge to drop charges filed against him. "If you do not use your influence to right this wrong, I will execute you and every other JEW I can find tonight at midnight of your Sabbath." Jeffrey Mindock, 50, faced a federal charge of transmitting a threat in interstate commerce. The U.S. Attorney's Office for the District of Arizona added that among his other emailed threats was one to "hang" a judge. Mindock was held without bond and was represented by a public defender.

November 5, 2023: *CNN* reported that around 2:15 a.m., U.S. Capitol Police noticed a car sitting at a green light several blocks from the Capitol building. When officers attempted to make a traffic stop, the stolen car sped away and crashed blocks from the Capitol near several Senate office buildings. After a foot chase, police arrested Ricardo L. Glass and Onosetale Okojie, both 20. Police searching the car found two pistols, one of which had a "Giggle Switch" device, which converts a semi-automatic Glock pistol into an illegal machine-gun pistol capable of firing multiple rounds with one pull of the trigger. The duo were charged with carrying a pistol without a license, fleeing from police, unlawful possession of a machine gun, and illegally possessing a large capacity magazine. A preliminary hearing was scheduled for November 8, 2023 in the D.C. Superior Court.

November 6, 2023: *CNN* reported that suspicious mail was delivered to four Seattle Jewish centers in the previous several days. *KIRO* reported that a hazmat response team was called to a synagogue during the night of November 6.

November 7, 2023: *CNN* reported U.S. Capitol Police tased and apprehended an individual that appeared to have a gun around the upper Senate park near the Russell Senate Office Building across from Union Station.

November 7, 2023: The *Pensacola News Journal, USA Today Network-Florida,* and the *Florida Times-Union* reported that Florida representative Michelle Salzman (R-Pensacola), when asked by Representative Angie Nixon (D-Jacksonville), "We are at 10,000 dead Palestinians. How many will be enough?" answered "All of them." Salzman and her family immediately received death threats. Salzman soon clarified on *X* "On Tuesday I was proud to stand with my colleagues in absolute solidarity with Israel's right to defend itself. I also commented that every single terrorist that attacked Israel and triggered this war should be eliminated—ALL OF THEM. Hamas are the ones responsible for all the death on both sides of this conflict. I will continue to call out the brutal attack and continue to fight against the rise in anti-semitism in our state... I never said Palestine... the heartbreaking loss of Palestinian lives is never a desire of mine."

November 8, 2023: *CNN* reported that Sean Patrick Cirillo, 34, of Macon, Georgia, was charged with using communications devices to make threats by phoning House of Representatives member Marjorie Taylor Greene (R-Georgia), and threatening to shoot and kill her, her family, and her staff. Her staff released an audio of the call, which said in part, "I'm going to murder her; I'm going to shoot her in the (expletive) head and kill her, OK... Tell the FBI... You're going to die. Your family is going to die."

November 9, 2023: *CNN* reported that the FBI and U.S. Postal Inspection Service were investigating reports of more than a dozen suspicious letters sent to public officials, mostly election officers at ballot counting centers, in California, Georgia, Nevada, Oregon, Texas, and Washington State. One envelope received by Fulton County was suspected of containing deadly fen-

tanyl. Election offices in several Washington state counties, including King County, had received the letters that contained powdery substances on November 8. Another letter received during the summer also contained fentanyl. A similar piece of mail was received in Lane County in Oregon. Another letter was mailed to Texas state Attorney General Ken Paxton's office.

November 13, 2023: *CNN* reported that Michigan man Seann Pietila, 19, pleaded guilty to a single federal charge of transmitting threatening communications in interstate commerce by threatening to commit a mass shooting of Jewish people in a series of *Instagram* messages with another user in June 2023. Pietila specifically said he wanted to inspire others to "take arms against the Jewish controlled state". The FBI searched his home, finding firearms, tactical vests, scopes, a Nazi flag, and black skull masks. His phone included the name of an East Lansing, Michigan, synagogue, a date, and a list of weapons, including bombs, Molotov cocktails, and guns. He faced up to five years in prison, a $250,000 fine, and three years of supervised release. Sentencing was scheduled for March 2024. He will no longer be allowed to possess any firearms.

November 22, 2023: *ABC News* and *CNN* reported that authorities closed the Rainbow Bridge connecting the U.S. and Canada at Niagara Falls, New York, after a 2022 Bentley crossing into the U.S. from Canada exploded at 11:30 a.m. at a security checkpoint, killing the two occupants, initially reported as two men, later reported as husband and wife Kurt P. Villani and Monica Villani, both 53, from Grand Island, New York. The vehicle had sped up, hit a low median, bounced high into the air in a U.S. Customs and Border Protection area just east of the main vehicle checkpoint, flew for yards, twisted, and then crashed into a line of booths in the secondary screening area. Authorities were initially treating the incident as a terrorist attempt, but later ruled out terrorism. *AP* reported that a Customs and Border Protection worker in a checkpoint booth was treated at a hospital for minor injuries. The driver had resided in western New York. The FBI Buffalo field office said no explosives were found. All four Canada-U.S. bridges over the Niagara River, including the Peace Bridge and Lewiston-Queenstown Bridge, were closed.

CNN reported that authorities determined that the driver had plans to attend a KISS concert in Canada, but when it was canceled he went to a casino in the U.S.

November 22, 2023: *Al-Jazeera, Reuters,* and the *Financial Times* reported that U.S. authorities thwarted a plot to kill Sikh separatist/attorney and U.S. citizen Gurpatwant Singh Pannun in the U.S. and warned India regarding concerns the government in New Delhi was involved. *CNN* reported on November 29 that U.S. federal prosecutors charged with murder-for-hire and conspiracy to commit murder-for-hire Indian national Nikhil Gupta, 52, who paid an undercover officer he believed to be a hitman $100,000 to target Pannum, who runs the New York-based Sikhs for Justice, which has held referenda for a separate Khalistan state. The organization is unlawful in India, where its website is not accessible. Czech officials arrested Gupta in June 2023, holding him pursuant to a bilateral extradition treaty. Authorities alleged that he worked with a senior Indian field intelligence officer, who "directed the assassination plot from India". The *New York Times* reported on December 3, 2023 that the case was cracked in a sting operation in which a Drug Enforcement Administration agent posed as a hit man and agreed to $100,000 for the hit. The *Times* noted that Pannum was a lawyer for Hardeep Singh Nijjar, a Sikh activist who was assassinated in Vancouver, British Columbia, Canada on June 18, 2022. The *Times* added that U.S. law enforcement officials had suspected Gupta of involvement in weapons, heroin, and cocaine trafficking.

November 25, 2023: *CNN* reported that at 6:25 p.m., three Palestinian college students, all 20, were shot by a white man with a handgun while walking on Prospect Street while visiting a relative in Burlington, Vermont, for the Thanksgiving holiday near the University of Vermont campus. Two were shot in the torso and one in the "lower extremities", according to police. One was seriously injured. All were hospitalized. Police said of the attacker, "Without speaking, he dis-

charged at least four rounds from the pistol and is believed to have fled on foot." Police said that two of the victims are American citizens and one is a legal resident. Two were wearing keffiyehs, traditional Palestinian scarves. The Institute for Middle East Understanding identified the students as Hisham Awartani, a student at Brown University in Rhode Island; Kinnan Abdalhamid, a junior at Haverford College in Pennsylvania; and Tahseen Ahmad, a student at Trinity College in Connecticut. Marwan Awartani, a former Palestinian minister of education and the great uncle of Hisham Awartani, said the students were visiting Hisham's grandmother. The three students had graduated from Ramallah Friends School, a Quaker-run private nonprofit school in Ramallah, in the occupied West Bank. They had participated together in Model United Nations. The American-Arab Anti-Discrimination Committee said that they "have reason to believe this shooting occurred because the victims are Arab". The Council on American-Islamic Relations offered a $10,000 reward for "information leading to the arrest and conviction of the perpetrator or perpetrators".

NPR reported that on November 26 at 3:38 p.m., agents from the Bureau of Alcohol, Tobacco, Firearms and Explosives arrested Jason J. Eaton, 48, while searching the shooting area in Burlington. He was scheduled to be arraigned on November 27. Eaton pleaded not guilty to three counts of attempted murder. Police said they found in Eaton's apartment, which is next to the scene of the shooting, a pistol and ammunition that were connected to bullet casings found at the scene.

CNN reported on December 3, 2023 that Hisham Awartani was paralyzed from the chest down after a bullet became lodged in his spine. Awartani's family launched a GoFundMe campaign to help him to receive rehabilitation care. Awartani sustained an "incomplete spinal injury" (he can feel his legs but cannot move them), a broken clavicle, and a fractured thumb. He has difficulty regulating his body temperature.

AP reported on November 13, 2024 that Jason Eaton, 49, who was charged with the shooting and wounding, was declared fit to stand trial. Eaton pleaded not guilty to three counts of attempted murder. He was represented by attorney Peggy Jansch. Judge John Pacht set a May 31, 2025 deadline to conduct depositions. A status hearing was scheduled for early March 2025.

December 1, 2023: *Al-Jazeera* reported on December 5, 2023 that the FBI arrested a U.S. citizen, 58, near Heber-Overgaard, Arizona on December 1, 2023 on charges of posting online comments that allegedly incited a "religiously motivated terrorist attack" in Wieambilla, Queensland, Australia on December 12, 2022 in which six people died. On that date, two police officers and a bystander were fatally shot by Gareth Train, his brother Nathaniel, and Nathaniel's wife Stacey in an ambush at the Trains' property. Four officers were investigating reports of a missing person. Two officers escaped and raised the alarm. The Trains engaged in an hours-long gun battle before police shot them dead. Queensland police assistant commissioner Cheryl Scanlon said, "We know the offenders executed a religiously motivated terrorist attack in Queensland. They were motivated by a Christian extremist ideology." Gareth Train began following the suspect on *YouTube* in May 2020. By 2021, they were communicating directly, as "The man repeatedly sent messages containing Christian end-of-days ideology to Gareth and then later to Stacey."

December 4, 2023: *CNN* reported that the Las Vegas Metropolitan Police Department arrested a 16-year-old who allegedly threatened a lone wolf terrorist attack in support of ISIS. Investigators found a handmade ISIS flag, al-Qaeda and ISIS propaganda, and components and instructions to build an explosive device during a search of his home. The previous week, authorities were tipped to an online post threatening "lone wolf operations in Las Vegas against the enemies of Allah". The poster cited their support for the Islamic State. The suspect faced multiple felony charges, including making terroristic threats, attempting to further an act of terrorism, providing material support to a terrorist organization, and five counts of possession of explosive components.

December 6, 2023: *Navy Times* reported that authorities received a bomb threat at 9:35 a.m. at Naval Air Station Pensacola, which was temporarily shut down. The base was reopened at 11:46 a.m.

December 7, 2023: *ABC News* and the *Daily Mail* reported that at 5:45 p.m., Atlanta Police arrested a woman, 26, who poured gasoline on the birth home of Martin Luther King, Jr. She was held on charges of criminal attempted arson in the second degree and interference with government property. The National Park Service owns the house, so federal charges could be forthcoming. Several citizens, including two off-duty NYPD officers and two tourists from Utah, held her until police arrived. King's birth home was built in 1895 at 501 Auburn Avenue NE, near the MLK, Jr. National Historical Park and the King Center. King's maternal grandfather bought the home in the Sweet Auburn District in 1909 for $3,500. The *New York Times* reported that the suspect is a veteran.

December 7, 2023: *CNN* and *AP* reported that police arrested local resident Mufid Fawaz Alkhader, 28, after he yelled "Free Palestine" and fired a shotgun twice into the air outside Temple Israel synagogue in Albany around 2 p.m., hours before the observance of Hanukkah would begin. No injuries were reported. Alkhader was charged with possession of a firearm by a prohibited person. New York State Police and the federal Bureau of Alcohol, Tobacco, Firearms and Explosives were looking at the possibility of firearms charges.

December 8, 2023: *AP* reported on August 7, 2024 that Andrew Buchanan, 38, allegedly threatened via cell phone to conduct a "mass casualty event" at the Army-Navy college football game at Gillette Stadium in Foxboro, Massachusetts on December 8, 2023. As of August 7, 2024, he was in federal custody in Arizona, awaiting extradition to Rhode Island. He was also accused of making threats to shoot up the campus of Bryant University in Smithfield, Rhode Island, a few days after the football game. He faced one felony count of interstate threatening communications, which carries a maximum penalty of five years in prison and $250,000 in fines. Authorities arrested the former resident of Burrillville, Rhode Island on July 31, 2024 in Tucson, Arizona, where authorities said he was homeless. He was represented by a public defender.

December 11, 2023: *CNBC* reported that federal prosecutors charged Dover, New Hampshire man Tyler Anderson, 30, with threatening to kill Republican presidential candidate Vivek Ramaswamy and his supporters during a campaign stop in Portsmouth. Anderson was charged with transmitting in interstate commerce a threat to injure another person. He faced five years in prison and a fine of up to $250,000.

December 12, 2023: The *Palm Beach Post, Florida Times-Union,* and *USA Today Network* reported that a vandal destroyed a sand-sculpted menorah on Juno Beach Pier, Florida and defaced it with a large swastika. Members of the Jewish Community Synagogue in North Palm Beach traditionally finance the sculpture and paid the artist to restore it.

December 21, 2023: *Fox News* reported that the Phoenix Police Department arrested Arizona man William Hill, 35, for aiming a laser pointer at commercial aircraft that were about to land at Phoenix Sky Harbor Airport around 5:30 p.m. Police said he "continued to shoot the laser pointer at the Phoenix police helicopter as patrol officers arrived in the area". He was booked into the Maricopa County jail on two felony counts of aiming a laser pointer at an occupied aircraft. The FAA announced, "The flight crew of Southwest Airlines Flight 2418 reported being illuminated by a green laser near Phoenix, Arizona, around 8:30 p.m. local time."

Pilots reported 9,500 laser strikes to the FAA in 2022. The FAA noted that "278 pilots have reported an injury from a laser strike to the FAA since 2010. People who shine lasers at aircraft face FAA fines of up to $11,000 per violation and up to $30,800 for multiple laser incidents. The FAA issued $120,000 in fines for laser strikes in 2021."

December 28, 2023: *NBC News, KNBC-TV,* and *UPI* reported that the FBI arrested Karrem

Nasr, 23, alias Ghareeb al-Muhajir, of New Jersey, for allegedly attempting to provide material support to al-Shabaab. He allegedly told an FBI confidential source that "evil America" is the No. 1 enemy and threatened "jihad on your home turf. Coming soon to a US location near you" in a post on *X*, followed by plane, bomb, and fire emojis. Charging documents indicated that Nasr flew from Egypt to Kenya on December 14 to join the terrorist organization. He was arrested in Nairobi on December 14 and flown to the U.S. The U.S. Attorney's Office for the Southern District of New York said Nasr "expressed his intent to join al Shabaab to receive military training and engage in jihad, that he was prepared to kill and be killed, and that he specifically aspired to be a martyr for the jihadist cause". He was motivated by the October 7 Hamas attack on Israel. He was originally from Lawrenceville, New Jersey. He faced 20 years in prison.

January 1, 2024: *CNN* and *WHAM* reported that at 12:50 a.m., Michael Avery, 35, from Syracuse, New York, crashed his rental car outside a New Year's concert by moe., a Grateful Dead tribute band in Rochester, New York, killing two people and injuring five others. He allegedly left a suicide note and journal in his hotel room. The incident was being investigated as domestic terrorism. The FBI's Joint Terrorism Task Force noted that a black Ford Expedition SUV carrying gas canisters slammed into a rideshare Mitsubishi Outlander that was leaving a nearby parking lot, then plowed into pedestrians outside a New Year's concert at the Kodak Center. Two passengers in the Mitsubishi, Justina Hughes, 28, and Joshua Orr, 29, were killed and the driver was hospitalized with non-life-threatening injuries. Avery was hospitalized with life-threatening injuries and later died. Nine pedestrians who were struck were taken to a hospital, one with life-threatening injuries. A resulting fire took an hour to extinguish. First responders then discovered a dozen gasoline canisters in and around the Ford. *CNN* reported that police believed Avery "intentionally" sped toward the pedestrians. Avery's family suggested that he may have had undiagnosed mental health issues.

Investigators said Avery drove to Rochester in his personal vehicle circa December 27 and checked into a suburban hotel. On December 29, he rented a Ford Expedition from a rental agency at the Rochester. Much of December 30 was devoted to making at least six purchases of gasoline and gas containers from various locations.

CNN reported that on January 10, 2024, Dawn Revette, 54, of Rochester, died from injuries sustained. As of January 14, one victim remained in an in-patient treatment facility with injuries that are not life-threatening.

January 2, 2024: *CNN* reported that at 1:15 a.m., a man fled a two-car accident scene, shot out a window of the Ralph L. Carr Colorado Judicial Center, broke into the Colorado Supreme Court, forcibly took keys from an unarmed security guard, opened fire inside the building, and set a fire in a stairwell. He surrendered to police two hours later. No injuries were reported. Two weeks earlier, the court had ruled 4-3 to bar former President Donald Trump from the state's 2024 ballot, determining that he was not eligible to hold office under the 14th Amendment's insurrectionist ban. Several violent threats were made against the Court justices. Brandon Olsen, 44, was scheduled to appear before a judge at 10:30 a.m. on January 3. He was held without bail on felony charges of first-degree arson, aggravated robbery, and second-degree burglary.

January 3, 2024: *NBC News* and *CNN* reported that at 6 a.m., a gunman shot to death New Jersey imam Hassan Sharif, who was in his car near the Masjid-Muhammad Mosque in Newark. Police said they found no evidence that an anti-Muslim bias played a part in the shooting. He had been resident imam for five years and was a leader in the interfaith community that worked to keep the city safe. Sharif was hit in the abdomen and arm. He worked as a TSA officer and was active in protesting gun violence. Police offered a $25,000 reward for information leading to his killer.

January 3, 2024: *CNN* reported that police arrested Florida man Michael Shapiro, 72, for threatening to kill Representative Eric Swalwell (D-California) and his children in several voicemail messages allegedly left at the lawmaker's office in Washington, D.C. He called Swal-

well's office the evening of December 19 from his home in Greenacres, leaving five threatening voicemail messages. "I'm gonna come after you and kill you." "I'm gonna kill your children." Some of the messages called Swalwell "a Chinese spy" and a "greaseball". The U.S. Capitol Police Investigations Division, Threat Assessment Section, told the court that phone records matched the phone that called Swalwell's office with a phone owned by Shapiro. Shapiro made his initial appearance in court in the Southern District of Florida and was "found to be indigent". A public defender was appointed. The Department of Justice noted that "the complaint further alleges that Shapiro pleaded guilty in federal court in 2019 for making threatening communications to another victim."

January 3, 2024: *CNN* reported that Capitol buildings in 23 states, including Connecticut, Georgia, Kentucky, Michigan, Minnesota, and Mississippi, were temporarily shut down and evacuated because of threats sent via mass e-mails to Secretaries of State and other state officials. The sender claimed to have placed explosives inside "your state Capitol". No bombs were found.

January 5, 2024: *Military Times* and *AP* reported that military veteran Aubrey Wayne Rose Jr., 43, of Hartford, Connecticut, was charged with making threats against members of Congress, the Department of Veterans Affairs Medical Center in West Haven, and other government employees over the course of several months in 2023. No one was injured. He sent emails to government officials in March and May 2023 threatening to exercise his Second Amendment right to bear arms. He allegedly showed up at an unnamed Congress member's office in June 2023 wearing a tactical vest with knives. Rose returned later that day and made threats over the building's intercom. Rose was arrested two days later on a state misdemeanor charge of breach of peace, but the charges were dropped. Rose was referred for mental health treatment. Rose on December 20, 2023, entered the West Haven VA facility wearing a tactical vest and carrying a bullhorn. He threatened to come back armed if the VA did not help.

He was assigned a public defender. Rose told federal agents he has post-traumatic stress disorder and suffered a traumatic brain injury from deployments to Iraq and Afghanistan. He claimed that the Defense Finance Accounting Service was not calculating his benefits correctly.

January 8, 2024: *Fox News* reported that the Department of Justice announced that Murat Kurashev, 36, a Russian national who resided in Sacramento, pleaded guilty to attempting to provide material support to a designated foreign terrorist organization, Hayat Tahrir al-Sham (HTS, Organization for the Liberation of the Levant). The FBI arrested him after a federal grand jury handed down a single-count indictment on February 18, 2021. He was accused of using money transfer services between July 2020 and February 2021 to send circa $13,000 in increments of $1,000 to two couriers in Türkiye for an HTS fundraiser. U.S. District Judge Kimberly J. Mueller scheduled sentencing for March 18, 2024. Kurashev faced a maximum statutory penalty of 20 years in prison and a $250,000 fine. The Department of State designated the Salafist HTS as a Foreign Terrorist Organization in May 2018.

January 24, 2024: *Fox News* reported that Logan Timothy James, 23, from Stokesdale, North Carolina, stole a Cessna 172 from the Dallas-area ATP Flight School in Addison and crashed it 80 miles away at 8:30 p.m. in a rural area nine miles northeast of Telephone, Texas, near the Red River in Fannin County in northeast Texas. He was pronounced dead at the scene. He was the only person in the plane. No other injuries were reported.

January 30, 2024: *Yahoo* reported that on February 15, 2024, the Bucks County, Pennsylvania District Attorney's Office charged Pennsylvania man Justin Daniel Mohn, 32, with three counts of terrorism for fatally shooting and beheading his father in Levittown on January 30, 2024 and showing his decapitated head on *YouTube*. The prosecutors also charged Mohn with two counts of possession of an instrument of crime; and one count each of robbery, carrying firearms without a license, theft, receiving stolen prop-

erty, criminal use of a communication facility, terroristic threats, and defiant trespassing. He was earlier charged with first-degree murder in the death of Michael Mohn, 68, who worked for the U.S. Army Corps of Engineers. On the night of the murder, Mohn posted a 14½-minute video to social media urging "patriots around the country" to take up arms against federal employees. He was arrested at a military base and held without bail. A preliminary hearing was scheduled for April 2, 2024. Prosecutors said he used a machete. In the video, he claimed his father was a "traitor to his country" and called on members of "Mohn's militia" to take up arms against other federal employees, including a federal judge whose address he disclosed. The video had been viewed 5,000 times before it was taken down. *NBC News* reported that Mohn reportedly targeted the federal government in several self-published books. In *The Revolution Leader's Survival Guide,* he included "the transcript of a letter to then-President Donald Trump warning of 'a peaceful revolution helped by the author if positive change does not come to America and the world soon.'" Police found a flash drive in his pocket that contained "several pictures of federal buildings along with instructions that appeared to show the steps needed to make an explosive device".

February 11, 2024: *CNN* affiliate *KPRC* reported that 30 rounds were fired just after 2 p.m., as parishioners were getting ready for the 3 p.m. Hispanic service at pastor Joel Osteen's Lakewood Church at 3700 Southwest Freeway, six miles from Houston. Harris County Sheriff Ed Gonzalez posted, "It is believed that a possible shooter is down, shot by one of our deputy's [sic] on-scene." Later reports indicated that the shooter was Genesse Ivonne Moreno, 36, wearing a trench coat and backpack, armed with a long rifle, and accompanied by her son, 7. Two off-duty law enforcement officers, including a Houston police officer, 28, and a Texas Alcoholic Beverage Commission agent, 28, shot to death the woman, who had pointed her weapon at them. Both officers had less than five years of service. The single mother was pronounced dead at 2:07 p.m. Osteen's five-year-old son was hospitalized in critical condition with a gunshot wound to the head. Tom George Thomas, 57, was hit in the leg and hospitalized. Despite her threat that she had a bomb, no explosives were found in her vehicle nor backpack. She also sprayed a substance on the ground. *NPR* said she had left behind anti-Semitic writings.

Moreno fired a legally purchased AR-15 with a "Palestine" sticker on it, and had a .22 caliber weapon in her bag which was not used in the attack.

Moreno had a history of mental health challenges while trying to turn her life around and launch a business. Houston Homicide Commander Christopher Hassig said the shooter used multiple aliases, including both male and female names. Moreno was put under an order for emotional detention in 2016. Records from the Texas Department of Public Safety listed arrests for minor offenses over the last two decades, including possession of marijuana, an assault, illegal possession of a weapon, resisting arrest, and forgery. She said on social media that she had founded a real-estate and financial services firm, coverting condos to shopping malls. She had made a donation to Lakewood in March 2020. In 2022, when she had her divorce proceeding transferred to county court, she was arrested on a weapons charge, a misdemeanor, which was cleared with two days' time served in the Fort Bend County Jail. Attorney William Capasso, who represented Moreno in 2021-2022 said she went by the name Jeffrey Moreno Carranza at the time. He later withdrew as her attorney; she represented herself in divorce proceedings. She lived in Conroe, Texas, 50 minutes north of Lakewood Church.

February 14, 2024: *CNN* reported that police took two people into custody who were believed to have fired on the Kansas City Chiefs Super Bowl Victory Parade, killing *KKFI* 90.1 FM radio DJ Lisa Lopez-Galvan, and injuring 29, three critically, five seriously, including 9-11 children. A third person was soon detained. One million people were at the parade. *CNN* reported on February 16 that two teens are charged with gun-related and resisting arrest offenses.

February 16, 2024: The U.S. Attorney's Office in New York in federal court in Manhattan charged naturalized U.S. citizen Harafa Hussein Abdi, 41, of Minneapolis, who rapped about flying to "shoot New York up" after training with ISIS in his native Somalia, with supporting a terrorist organization. He was earlier arrested in East Africa and taken to the U.S. earlier in the week. He moved from Minnesota to Somalia in 2015 and joined a group of ISIS fighters at a training camp. For two years, he trained in weapons and worked in the group's media wing, making and appearing in a recruiting video distributed by a pro-ISIS outlet. In a 2017 audio clip he allegedly raps about inflicting violence in New York City while automatic gunfire and an explosion are heard in the background: "We going to carry on jihad; fly through America on our way to shoot New York up. They trying to shut this thing. We ain't going. We going to come blow New York up." Abdi left the camp, was jailed by the ISIS leadership, escaped, and traveled to Hargeisa, Somalia, where he was arrested.

Abdi was born in Somalia in 1982, entered the United States in 1999, and became a naturalized U.S. citizen in 2006.

Prosecutors charged him with conspiring to provide and providing material support to a designated foreign terrorist organization and conspiring to receive and receiving military-type training from a terrorist organization. He faced 20 years in prison.

February 21, 2024: The *Washington Post* reported that U.S. prosecutors indicted Japanese yakuza boss Takeshi Ebisawa, 60, who sought to sell uranium and plutonium for $6.85 million on behalf of the leader of an insurgent group in Myanmar to an undercover U.S. law enforcement agent who was posing as an associate of an Iranian general. Starting in early 2020, he also tried to obtain surface-to-air missiles, M60 machine guns, and AK-47 rifles on behalf of the insurgent leader. Ebisawa and Thai co-defendant Somphop Singhasiri faced eight criminal counts that could result in life sentences. Authorities arrested the duo in Manhattan in April 2022.

February 24, 2024: *CNN* reported that a small bomb exploded outside the office of Alabama Attorney General Steve Marshall in the early morning, causing no injuries.

February 25, 2024: *CNN* and *AP* reported that at 1 p.m., an active-duty member of the U.S. Air Force died after he set himself on fire outside the Israeli Embassy on the 3500 block of International Drive, NW, in Washington, D.C. Aaron Bushnell, 25, of San Antonio, Texas, said on a video, "I will no longer be complicit in genocide" and yelled "Free Palestine" while pouring an unknown liquid over himself and igniting it.

March 1, 2024: *BBC* reported on March 6 that the FBI warned an Iranian spy allegedly was plotting to kill U.S. officials in retaliation for the U.S. killing of Iranian Quds force General Qassam Suleimani during the Trump administration in a U.S. drone attack in Iraq on January 3, 2020. Majid Dastjani Farahani, born July 26, 1982, speaks Farsi, English, Spanish, and French. The Bureau said he traveled between Iran and Venezuela and recruited individuals for "surveillance activities focused on religious sites, businesses, and other facilities" in the U.S. The U.S. Department of the Treasury imposed sanctions against him in December 2023. The U.S. government provided security details for former Secretary of State Mike Pompeo and then-President Trump's special envoy for Iran, Brian Hook.

March 9, 2024: *CNN* reported on March 20, 2024 that on March 9, the U.S. Border Patrol at the El Paso Border Patrol Sector apprehended Lebanese national Basel Bassel Ebbadi, who threatened border personnel and told a tactical terrorist response team that he was a member of a foreign terrorist organization and had come to the United States in order to build a bomb.

March 20, 2024: Aryan Knights white supremacist Idaho prison inmate Skylar Meade, 31, and accomplice Nicholas Umphenour fled after Umphenour shot and wounded two Idaho Department of Correction officers during a 2:15 a.m. ambush in an ambulance bay as they were transporting Meade from Saint Alphonsus Regional Medical Center in Boise. Author-

ities issued a warrant with a $2 million bond for Umphenour's arrest on two charges of aggravated battery against law enforcement and one charge of aiding and abetting an escape. The duo drove off in the morning in a gray 2020 Honda Civic with Idaho plates. Meade was sentenced in 2017 to 20 years for shooting at a sheriff's sergeant during a high-speed chase.

Umphenour is 5-foot-11 and weighs 160 pounds. He has brown hair and hazel eyes. Meade is 5-foot-6 and weighs 150 pounds. He sports face tattoos with the numbers 1 and 11 — for A and K, the first and 11th letters of the alphabet, representing the Aryan Knights gang he is affiliated with. He also has A and K tattooed on his abdomen.

AP reported that on March 21 police arrested the duo after a car chase in Twin Falls, 130 miles from the hospital. Investigators were looking into whether they killed two men in Clearwater County and Nez Perce County, which borders Washington State. Both victims were men. Police found shackles at the scene of one of the murders.

March 23, 2024: *Today* and *NBC News* reported a Lancaster Pride-sponsored drag queen story hour event at The Lancaster Public Library in Pennsylvania was canceled after a suspicious package was found amid bomb threats. Police said they received "additional bomb threats via email" warning of "explosive devices" in two more locations, as well as outside of Lancaster city's jurisdiction. No bombs were found.

March 30, 2024: *BBC* reported on April 16 that Kansas women Veronica Butler, 27, and Jillian Kelley, 39, vanished on March 30. Their car was later found along with evidence suggesting foul play. Their bodies were found on April 14 in Texas County, Oklahoma. Police arrested four members of the anti-government God's Misfits group on kidnapping and murder charges stemming from a custody dispute. Butler and Kelley had arranged with the grandmother of Butler's children to meet at a highway intersection in Oklahoma to pick up the two children—aged six and eight—and take them to a birthday party. The four people arrested are the children's grandmother, Tifany Adams, 54; her boyfriend Tad Callum, 43; Cole Twombly, 50; and his wife Cora, 44.

April 5, 2024: *Salon* reported that police suspected arson when a "small blaze" was found around 10:45 a.m. in front of the third floor Church Street office in Burlington, Vermont of Senator Bernie Sanders (I-Vermont). An unknown male fled the scene after spraying a possible accelerant. No injuries were reported.

CNN reported on April 7 that authorities arrested Shant Soghomonian, alias Michael, 35, previously of Northridge, California, on charges of using fire to damage the building that is also used for interstate commerce. He faced 20 years in prison and a $250,000 fine. *ABC News* added that federal charges were filed. He was to appear before U.S. Magistrate Judge Kevin J. Doyle.

April 6, 2024: *BBC* reported that authorities arrested Alexander Scott Mercurio, 18. U.S. Attorney General Merrick Garland said "The defendant swore an oath of loyalty to ISIS and planned to wage an attack in its name on churches in Coeur d'Alene, Idaho." Prosecutors said that he planned the next day to attack churches with "flame-covered" weapons, explosives, knives, and a pipe, moving from church to church until he was killed. He faced 20 years in prison on charges of attempting to provide material support or resources to a foreign terrorist organization. Prosecutors said he planned the beating and handcuffing of his father in order to obtain guns from a locked closet in the family home. He had revealed his plans to an FBI source. The FBI had known of his online alias since July 2022. In an April 7 raid on his family home, the Bureau seized a pipe, butane, hand sanitizer, a machete, and the firearms locked in his father's closet.

CNN added on April 10 that Mercurio pleaded not guilty to attempting to provide material support or resources to a designated foreign terrorist organization during a court appearance. A jury trial was scheduled for May 28; a pretrial conference was set for May 14.

April 12, 2024: *NBC News* reported that Afghan migrant Mohammad Kharwin, 48, who was on the terrorist watchlist, spent nearly a year inside

the U.S. after he was apprehended and released by Border Patrol agents in 2023. Authorities arrested him in San Antonio on February 28, 2024, but he was released on bond following a hearing on March 28, 2024 by an immigration judge in Pearsall, Texas, who was not told he was a national security threat. He paid a $12,000 bond and ICE released him on March 30. His immigration hearing in Texas was scheduled for 2025. The court placed no restrictions on his movements inside the U.S. The Department of Homeland Security announced that Immigration and Customs Enforcement agents took him into custody again on April 11, 2024. He had crossed the Mexico-U.S. border illegally and was apprehended on March 10, 2023, near San Ysidro, California. The national terrorist watchlist, maintained by the FBI, indicates he is a member of Hezb-e-Islami (HIG), a virulently anti-Western political and paramilitary organization that the U.S. has designated a terrorist organization. HIG attacks killed nine U.S. soldiers and civilians from 2013 to 2015.

April 17, 2024: *NBC News* reported on May 1, 2024 that Immigration and Customs Enforcement arrested in Baltimore Uzbek man Jovokhir Attoev, 33, who has alleged ISIS ties, after he had been living inside the United States for more than two years. The Border Patrol arrested him in February 2022 when he crossed the border into Arizona. Neither Customs and Border Protection nor ICE found any derogatory information, so they released him inside the U.S. on bond. In May 2023, Uzbekistan put out an international notice that Attoev was wanted for his alleged ISIS affiliation. ICE arrested him on April 17, 2024. He was held in custody in Pennsylvania, awaiting trial in immigration court in early May in New Jersey.

April 25, 2024: *NBC News* reported that Afghan national Mohamad Kharwin, 48, was arrested on April 25, 2024. He was on the FBI terrorist watchlist for membership in Hezb-e-Islami, or HIG, an Afghanistan-based political and paramilitary group that the U.S. has designated a terrorist organization. He had spent 10 months in the U.S., enrolled in the Immigration and Customs Enforcement's Alternatives to Detention program on March 12, 2023 that tracked his location via ankle monitor, mobile app, or telephone. His participation in AtD lasted a little over a fortnight; ICE dropped him from the program on March 28, 2023. Customs and Border Protection agents initially arrested Kharwin on March 10, 2023, near San Ysidro, California, after he crossed the Mexico-U.S. border illegally, but they did not have complete information about Kharwin and could not confirm that he was on the terrorist watchlist. In February 2024, ICE arrested him after receiving information from the FBI indicating that Kharwin had potential terrorist ties. But in court, ICE prosecutors did not share some classified information with the immigration judge regarding Kharwin's ties to a terrorist group. Prosecutors said he was a flight risk, but did not add that he was a national security risk. The judge ordered Kharwin released on $12,000 bond. Kharwin was arrested on April 25, 2024 in San Antonio and taken into ICE custody.

May 2024: *USA Today* reported on July 15, 2024 that in May, a woman pleaded guilty to plotting to destroy the Baltimore power grid as part of her white supremacist ideology that calls for the collapse of government.

May 2, 2024: U.S. District Judge Ann Montgomery was scheduled to announce the sentence for naturalized U.S. citizen and St. Louis Park, Minnesota man Abelhamid al-Madioum, 27, who once fought for ISIS in Syria but now expresses remorse for joining a "death cult" and has been cooperating with federal authorities. Federal prosecutors recommended 12 years; his attorney countered with seven years. The statutory maximum is 20 years. ISIS recruited al-Madioum, then 18, in 2014 while in college. He slipped away from his family on a visit to their native Morocco in 2015, going to Syria. He lost his right arm below the elbow and suffered two broken legs and other severe injuries in an explosion in Iraq, but used his computer skills to help the group. He surrendered to U.S.-backed Kurdish led Syrian Democratic Forces rebels in 2019. He returned to the U.S. in 2020 and pleaded guilty in 2021 to providing material support to a designated terrorist organization. He has four

children with ISIS widows Fatima, whom he met in 2016, and Fozia, whom he met in 2018. Both wives are dead—Fatima was shot in front of him in 2019. *CBS News* reported that the May 2 sentencing was postponed. His two sons were returned to the U.S. later in the month.

On June 13, 2024, U.S. District Judge Ann Montgomery sentenced the naturalized U.S. citizen to 10 years in federal prison. Prosecutors had requested 12 years. He was represented by attorney Manvir Atwal.

May 3, 2024: *CNN* reported that Stanford University officials sent the FBI a photo of a masked individual at a campus encampment location on White Plaza who appeared to be wearing a green headband similar to those worn by Hamas al-Qassam Brigades members.

May 3, 2024: *Marine Corps Times* reported on May 15 that on May 3, two people drove a box truck up to the Fuller Road Gate of Marine Corps Base Quantico, Virginia, where military sentries stopped them. The duo claimed they worked for an Amazon subcontractor and were making a delivery to the USPS in Quantico. The duo had no affiliation with the base and no credentials to enter it, and were directed to go to a holding area. The driver instead attempted to get onto the base, but was stopped by vehicle denial barriers. No one was injured. The Criminal Investigations Division turned the duo over to U.S. Immigration and Customs Enforcement's Enforcement and Removal Operations. *Potomac Local News* reported that one of the truck's occupants was a Jordanian national who had recently crossed the southern border into the United States and another was on the U.S. government's terrorist watch list. *Marine Corps Times* reported on May 17 that U.S. Immigration and Customs Enforcement announced that both were Jordanians.

May 4, 2024: *AP* and *ABC News* reported that at 10:30 p.m., a male driver died after crashing his vehicle "at a high rate of speed" into a security barrier at the intersection of 15th Street and Pennsylvania Avenue, NW at an outer perimeter gate of the White House complex.

May 7, 2024: *AP* reported on May 9 that New York real estate developer Reuven Kahane, 57, was arrested in the morning after driving his car into volunteer safety marshal Maryellen Novak, 55, during a pro-Palestinian demonstration led by students connected to the Columbia University protest movement. She was treated for minor injuries. The Manhattan district attorney dropped charges of criminal mischief against her and another 63-year-old safety volunteer. On May 9, he was charged with felony assault and released from custody. Reuven Kahane is related to Rabbi Meir Kahane, the Brooklyn-born founder of the Jewish Defense League, which the U.S. classified as a terrorist group.

May 13, 2024: *Marine Corps Times* reported on May 16 that former Pfc. Joshua Cobb, 23, of Trenton, New Jersey, who was discharged from the Marine Corps on May 10 after serving for less than a year was arrested on May 13 for making online threats to kill white people. He was charged with one count of transmitting a threat in interstate and foreign commerce. In December 2022, a social media user with an IP address linked to Cobb's New Jersey residence declared he was planning to "erase" white people in a shooting. "I want to cause mayhem on the white community. The reason i specifically want to target white people is because as a black male, they will NEVER understand my struggles." On another platform, in spring 2023 1dayUsuffer said he wanted to become a serial killer. "I'd probably (overdose) on my own adrenaline after the 10th body goes down." In another post, he said he had killed his cat with a crossbow. "Very bloody scene and I loved it." He faced five years in prison and a $250,000 fine. He was represented by Saverio Viggiano, a federal public defender with the District of New Jersey.

May 29, 2024: *CNN* reported that New York City officials instituted safety precautions after ISIS-K in April "globally" threatened the upcoming ICC Men's T20 Cricket World Cup on Long Island, New York. The group later made more specific threats on the India versus Pakistan game, scheduled for June 9, and issued a video calling for "that lone wolf to act out." The

games were to start the first weekend of June at Nassau County International Cricket Stadium in Eisenhower Park.

May 30, 2024: *CNN* ran video showing a man, 58, driving near a Brooklyn, New York City yeshiva, yelling "I'm going to kill all you Jews", apparently trying to run over pedestrians on the sidewalk. Police arrested him.

June 7, 2024: A federal appeals court upheld the conviction of British national El Shafee Elsheikh, one of the ISIS Beatles, for his role in taking 26 Westerners captive a decade earlier. He was convicted and sentenced to life in 2022 in federal court in Alexandria, Virginia, regarding the deaths of American hostages James Foley, Steven Sotloff, Peter Kassig, and Kayla Mueller.

June 11, 2024: Authorities in New York, Philadelphia, and Los Angeles arrested eight people from Tajikistan with suspected ties to ISIS. The suspects entered the U.S. through the southern border last spring. They were held on immigration violations in the custody of U.S. Immigration and Customs Enforcement.

June 17, 2024: The *Washington Post, CNN, Reuters, New York Times,* and *UPI* reported that Nikhil Gupta, 52, an Indian citizen accused of attempting to kill Sikh separatist Gurpatwant Singh Pannun, a dual U.S.-Canadian citizen who advocates for an independent Sikh state, in New York, pleaded not guilty to murder for hire in federal court in Manhattan. Gupta was charged with trying to hire a hitman, who turned out to be an undercover Drug Enforcement Administration agent. Gupta was held at the Metropolitan Detention Center in Brooklyn, a federal administrative detention facility. He was represented by Jeffrey Chabrowe, a criminal defense lawyer, in the U.S. and by Rohini Musa in India. Gupta, was detained in the Czech Republic in June 2023, and extradited to the U.S. on June 14, 2024. Prosecutors said he reported to an Indian government official. Gupta faced 20 years in prison.

June 24, 2024: *Stars and Stripes* reported Jordan Duncan, 29, a Marine veteran who was previously stationed at Camp Lejeune in North Carolina and final defendant in a group of five former military members with ties to white-supremacist organizations, pleaded guilty in a federal court in Wilmington, N.C., to weapons charges stemming from a plot to attack the power grid in the northwestern United States. He also admitted to aiding and abetting the manufacture of firearms. He faced ten years in prison. Co-defendants Paul James Kryscuk, 38; Liam Collins, 25; Justin Wade Hermanson, 25; and Joseph Maurino, 25 had already pled out. Authorities arrested Duncan in Boise, Idaho in October 2020, finding secret Defense Department documents on his hard drive, along with documents detailing how to craft homemade explosives. He and Collins were previously stationed at Camp Lejeune.

July 10, 2024: Authorities at Newark Liberty International Airport arrested New Jersey man Andrew Takhistov, 18, who authorities say was en route to Ukraine via Paris to join the Russian Volunteer Corps, a pro-Ukrainian group fighting Russian forces. He was held in an alleged plot to attack a U.S. electrical substation to advance his white supremacist views. He had talked in January with an undercover agent about his plan. The duo drove to two electrical substations in North Brunswick and New Brunswick, New Jersey. Takhistov provided information on how to construct Molotov cocktails. Law enforcement authorities added that he outlined "strategies for terrorist attacks, including rocket and explosives attacks against synagogues," and wanted to bring back illegal supplies from Ukraine in order to carry out attacks that would threaten the U.S. government. New Jersey U.S. Attorney Philip Sellinger noted that Takhistov espoused white supremacist views in his conversations with the undercover agent, and in posts "encouraged violence against Black and Jewish communities, praised mass shooters, and discussed causing death and destruction on a large scale." His "three-step plan for white domination" entailed ending the war in Ukraine, invading Russia, and starting "political activism in Europe and America, supporting National Socialist political parties." His "ultimate dream was to attack a synagogue with a Hamas-style rocket." *USA Today* reported that he faced ten years in prison and a $125,000 fine.

July 13, 2024: At 6:15 p.m., Thomas Matthew Crooks, 20, firing an AR-style rifle from a nearby warehouse's rooftop, attempted to assassinate former President and presumptive Republican Presidential nominee Donald J. Trump, 78, at a campaign rally a few hundred feet away in Butler, Pennsylvania. A bullet grazed Trump's right ear. Trump, blood on his ear and face, defiantly pumped his fist into the air while the Secret Service rushed him to an armored limousine. Secret Service snipers killed Crooks after his bullets had killed volunteer firefighter Corey Comperatore, 50, father of two, of Sarver in Butler County, Pennsylvania, and critically wounded two other adult men, identified by the *New York Times* as former Marine David Dutch, 57, of New Kensington, Pennsylvania, and James Copenhaver, 74, of Moon Township, Pennsylvania.

Comperatore died protecting his family from the gunfire. They included daughters Allyson, 27, and Kaylee, 24. He worked at JSP, a plastic manufacturing company, and had served as a fire chief in Buffalo Township, Pennsylvania. He was selected as a future trustee of Cabot Church in 2021.

The attack at the Butler Farm Show Grounds came two days before the opening of the Republican National Convention in Milwaukee that was set to nominate Trump.

Crooks's rifle, plus DNA and biometric information helped identify him; he was not carrying ID. He lived with his parents in Bethel Park, Pennsylvania, 40 miles away.

BBC reported that he graduated in 2022 from Bethel Park High School, was a registered Republican, and donated $15 to the Progressive Turnout Project, a liberal voter turnout group, through the Democratic donation platform ActBlue on President Biden's inauguration day in 2021. His mother was a Democrat and his father a Libertarian. Law enforcement officials believe his father purchased the AR-style 556 rifle six months earlier. *NPR* reported that Crooks was a member of the Clairton Sportsmen's (gun) Club. *CNN* and the *New York Times* reported that police found two explosive devices in Crooks's car and a possible third at his residence. A schoolmate said Crooks "had a target on his back" and did not fit in. The *New York Times* reported on

July 14, 2024 that in May, Crooks graduated with an associate degree in engineering science from the Community College of Allegheny County. He played chess and video games and was learning computer coding. He worked as a dietary aide at Bethel Park Skilled Nursing and Rehabilitation. He lived in the affluent Pittsburgh suburb of South Hills.

Trump campaign national finance director Meredith O'Rourke set up a GoFundMe page for the families of the injured. Within hours, it had raised more than $1 million.

Representative Ronny Jackson (R-Texas) told *Fox News* that his nephew "was grazed in the neck, a bullet crossed his neck, cut his neck and he was bleeding."

Some conspiracy theorists suggested that the shooting was staged, others said that Democratic rhetoric spurred the shooting. The administration quickly denied claims that protection had been denied to former President Trump, or that the Secret Service was negligent, and noted on July 16 that it had been increased in light of reports of Iranian plans for an assassination attempt. *CNN, New York Times,* and *Washington Post* reported on July 21 that the Secret Service said it had denied some requests for the former President's security team during the previous two years.

Video showed civilians pointing out Crooks to police immediately before the shooting. A police officer had climbed a ladder to the roof, but was not in a position to fire at Crooks, who pointed his rifle at him before he climbed down.

CNN reported on July 18 that Crooks posted on the popular gaming platform *Steam* that "July 13 will be my premiere, watch as it unfolds." Authorities deemed it a fake soon after. He visited the Trump rally location twice, had images of Trump and Biden on his cell phone, and his search history included FBI Director Christopher Wray, Attorney General Merrick Garland, a member of the British royal family, dates of the Democratic National Convention and future Trump events, and major depression disorder. He had also researched mass shooter Ethan Crumbley and his family. He visited websites on how to build explosives.

CNN, the *New York Times,* and *BBC* added that investigators recovered a bullet-proof vest, four ammunition magazines of the type he used in the attack, and a drone in his Hyundai Sonata. *BBC, CNN, CBS,* and *NPR* reported on July 21 that investigators believed that he had flown the drone over the rally area hours or days before the assassination attempt. Federal authorities found a ladder and backpack belonging to Crooks at the scene. A search of his family home yielded 14 firearms, additional explosives, a second cellphone, a laptop, and a hard drive.

BBC reported on July 23, 2024 that FBI Director Christopher Wray told the House Judiciary Committee that Crooks researched the Kennedy assassination on July 6, searching "how far away was Oswald from Kennedy". Crooks used a firearm with a "collapsible stock", making it easier to conceal. Crooks fired eight shots. Meanwhile, Secret Service Director Kimberly Cheatle resigned after testifying before a different congressional committee.

NPR reported on July 29 that Crooks had made 25 gun-related purchases under various aliases. *USA Today* reported that date that a sniper had spotted Crooks 90 minutes before the attack.

FBI Deputy Director Paul Abate testified to two Senate committees that Crooks visited the site on July 7. The Bureau also found 700 online comments, apparently by Crooks, that included anti-Semitic and anti-immigrant language.

July 16, 2024: *CNN* reported that the U.S. Department of Justice indicted Michail Chkhikvishvili, 21, alias Commander Butcher, alleged Georgian head of the Maniac Murder Cult neo-Nazi extremist group based in eastern Europe, on charges of plotting to have an associate dress up as Santa Claus and hand out poisoned candy to Jewish children in Brooklyn. Chkhikvishvili tried to recruit an undercover law enforcement officer to join his group and commit violent crimes such as bombings and arsons. Prosecutors said since September 2021, Chkhikvishvili has distributed the "Hater's Handbook" in which he states that he has "murdered for the white race". He traveled to New York City twice in 2022, staying with his paternal grandmother in Brooklyn. Prosecutors said that in November

2023, Chkhikvishvili began planning a "mass casualty event" for New York City on New Year's Eve. He faced 20 years in prison for solicitation of violent felonies, five years for conspiring to solicit violent felonies, 20 years for distributing information pertaining to the making and use of explosive devices, and five years for transmitting threatening communication.

July 25, 2024: *Marine Corps Times* and *USA Today* reported that a judge sentenced former Marines Liam Collins, 25, of Johnston, Rhode Island, to 10 years in prison and Justin Wade Hermanson, 25, of Swansboro, North Carolina, to one year, nine months for their participation in a plot to attack the U.S. power grid. Collins and Hermanson both pleaded guilty to federal firearms charges. The duo were part of a neo-Nazi group that sought to destroy transformers, substations, and other components of the power grid at about a dozen locations across Idaho and its surrounding states. Attorney General Merrick B. Garland said, "As part a self-described 'modern day SS,' these defendants conspired, prepared, and trained to attack America's power grid in order to advance their violent white supremacist ideology... These sentences reflect both the depravity of their plot and the Justice Department's commitment to holding accountable those who seek to use violence to undermine our democracy." Paul James Kryscuk, 38, of Boise, Idaho, was sentenced to six years, six months after pleading guilty to one charge of conspiracy to destroy an energy facility. Two other men, who had pleaded guilty to weapons charges regarding the 2017-2020 plot—Joseph Maurino, a member of the New Jersey Army National Guard, and Jordan Duncan, a Marine veteran—awaited sentencing. The group communicated via the now-defunct Iron March web forum. Collins was accused by federal authorities of threatening to shoot Black Lives Matter protestors and conspiring to destroy government-owned energy facilities. He asked group members to purchase thermite, a powdered mixture used in incendiary bombs, to burn through transformers.

August 5, 2024: *BBC* and *CNN* reported that federal prosecutors charged Frank Carillo, 66, of

Winchester, Virginia with making violent threats on GETTR, a conservative microblogging website against Vice President Kamala Harris on July 27, shortly after she began her campaign for president. He also threatened President Joe Biden, FBI Director Christopher Wray, and several Arizona officials, inter alia. One message said she "needs to be put on fire alive", another that she would "regret ever trying to become president". The Bureau arrested him on August 2 and seized an AR15-style rifle, a handgun, and thousands of rounds of ammunition at his home. Prosecutors said investigators found 4,359 messages threatening various people or groups, including 19 directed at Ms. Harris. Other messages included "AR15 locked and loaded" and threats to "go out with your guns and kill all Muslims" and shoot "illegals... in the head". I vowed to "cut your eyes out", referred to Harris, who was a "b*tch" whom he hoped would "suffer a slow agonizing death." GETTR was founded by Jason Miller, former President Trump's chief spokesperson.

August 6, 2024: *NPR* and *CNN* reported that the Department of Justice charged Asif Merchant, 46, a Pakistani man with alleged ties to the Iranian government, with seeking to conduct political assassinations. FBI investigators believed that former President Donald Trump and other current and former U.S. government officials were the intended targets. Authorities arrested Merchant on July 12 while preparing to leave the United States, after he met with purported hit men who were actually undercover law enforcement officers. He was accused of traveling to New York City and working with a hit man in a murder-for-hire plan to carry out the assassinations in late August or early September. Investigators found no evidence of a connection with would-be Trump assassin Crooks. Merchant has family in Iran. Prosecutors said he wanted to find New Yorkers to steal documents or USB drives from one victim's home, plan protests at political rallies, and carry out assassinations. Merchant allegedly offered to pay the hit men a $5,000 advance. He created codes, such as "the word 'tee-shirt' would mean a 'protest' (because it was the 'lightest' job), the phrase 'flannel shirt' would mean 'stealing,' because it was 'heavier work,' and the phrase 'fleece jacket,' would mean 'the third task … commit the act of the game.'"

August 10, 2024: *CNN* reported on August 12 that at 2 a.m., police officers responded to Kingston Avenue in Crown Heights, around the corner from the headquarters of the Chabad-Lubavitch movement on Eastern Parkway in Brooklyn, New York, and arrested Vincent Sumpter, 22, who had slashed a Jewish man, 33, with long-standing ties to the community, in the torso. They charged Sumpter with 14 counts, including attempted murder, assault with intent to cause serious injury with a weapon, menacing, aggravated harassment based on race or religion, and hate crimes. Bail was set at $100,000. The next court hearing was scheduled for August 15. Sumpter said "Free Palestine" and asked the victim, "Do you want to die?" before stabbing him.

August 17, 2024: *Air Force Times, AP,* and the *San Antonio Express-News* reported that the driver of a passing vehicle shot at U.S. Air Force security guards at an entrance to Joint Base San Antonio-Lackland at 4:30 a.m. No injuries were reported. Joint Base San Antonio includes Randolph Air Force Base, Fort Sam Houston, and the Camp Bullis training camp. Lackland is home to more than 24,000 active duty members and 10,000 Department of Defense civilians. It includes the 37th Training Wing; 149th Fighter Wing; 59th Medical Wing; the Air Force Intelligence, Surveillance and Reconnaissance Agency; 24th Air Force Wing, 67th Network Warfare Wing; the Cryptologic Systems Group; the National Security Agency; and 70 associated units.

August 19, 2024: The U.S. Attorney's Office for the Eastern District of North Carolina indicted active-duty soldier Kai Liam Nix, alias Kai Brazelton, 20, who is stationed at Fort Liberty, North Carolina on charges of lying in 2022 to military authorities regarding his association with a group that advocated overthrowing the U.S. government and of trafficking firearms. A federal grand jury indicted him on August 14, authorities arrested him on August 15, and he made his first federal court appearance on the four criminal counts on August 19. He was held pending a detention hearing in Raleigh. The indictment also accuses him of one count of dealing in firearms without a license and two counts of selling a stolen firearm. He faced 30 years in prison.

August 21, 2024: Marine Corps veteran Russell Richardson Vane IV, 42, of Vienna, Virginia, who was jailed in April and who authorities said tried to fake his own death after a falling out with the Virginia-based Kekoas militia, pleaded guilty in federal court in Alexandria, Virginia, to illegal possession of ricin. Vane admitted that he used castor beans to create ricin at his home. The Kekoas expelled him after becoming alarmed by his loose talk about homemade explosives, worrying that he might be a government informant. Vane tried to legally change his name in Fairfax County court and posted a fake online obituary of himself. U.S. District Judge Anthony Trenga agreed that Vane could be released until a sentencing hearing set for November. He faced five years in prison.

August 30, 2024: *CNN* reported that University of Pittsburgh police arrested a person suspected of attacking a group of Jewish students with a bottle near the Cathedral of Learning during the night. Two students were treated at the scene. The suspect has no known affiliation with the school.

September 6, 2024: *Al-Jazeera* reported that authorities arrested white supremacists Dallas Erin Humber, 34, of Elk Grove, California, and Matthew Robert Allison, 37, of Boise, Idaho, for using *Telegram* to encourage acts of violence against minorities, government officials, and critical infrastructure in the United States. They faced 15 federal counts in California, including soliciting hate crimes and the murder of federal officials, including a federal judge, a senator, and a former US attorney, distributing bomb-making instructions, and conspiring to provide material support to terrorists. The indictment accused of leading a "transnational terrorist group" known as Terrorgram Collective which operates on *Telegram* and espouses white supremacist ideology.

September 15, 2024: The *New York Times* and *CNN* reported that former President Donald Trump was safe after an apparent assassination attempt around 1:30 p.m. while he was walking from the fifth hole with donor Steve Witkoff at the Trump International Golf Club in West Palm Beach. *NPR* reported that a Secret Service officer at the sixth hole noticed an SKS-style rifle barrel sticking through a fence 300-500 yards away and fired at the gunman, who escaped in a black Nissan. A witness spotted the vehicle, photographing it and its (stolen) license plate. Forty-five minutes later, two Martin County, Florida Sheriff's deputies detained Ryan Wesley Routh, 58, the driver of a vehicle wanted by the Palm Beach County Sheriff's Office as he was driving northbound on Interstate 95 and crossed from Palm Beach County to Martin County. Authorities found the weapon loaded with 12 rounds, with scope, two backpacks with ceramic tiles, some food, and a GoPro from the bush where Routh hid. The backpacks were hanging on a fence. *CNN* and *USA Today* reported that Routh was driving his daughter's black Nissan Xterra. The FBI said Routh had not fired any shots. The license plates were from a Ford truck earlier reported stolen.

The game was a last-minute addition to Trump's schedule. However, *NPR* reported that Routh's phone GPS location system indicated that he had been lurking along the fence line for 12 hours.

CNN reported that the former construction worker/roofing contractor from Greensboro, North Carolina, posted on *LinkedIn* that he started a small construction company in 2018 called Camp Box Honolulu in Hawaii, which builds storage units and tiny houses. The *Honolulu Star-Advertiser* said the resident of Kaaawa donated a structure for homeless people.

BBC said he was originally from North Carolina, spending most of his life there. On *X*, he posted, "I am coming to Ukraine from Hawaii to fight for your kids and families and democracy.. I will come and die for you." He had no military experience. *BBC* found pro-Palestinian, pro-Taiwan, and anti-China messages—he had self-published a book on Taiwan, Afghanistan, and North Korea—on his profile, including allegations about Chinese "biological warfare" and references to the Covid-19 virus as an "attack". *CBS News* reported that Routh supported President Trump in 2016, but later said that Trump was "getting worse and devolving" and "I will be glad when you [are] gone." Routh told the *New York Times* in a 2023 telephone interview that he wanted to assist the war effort in Ukraine, and wanted to recruit Afghan soldiers who had fled the Taliban. "We can probably purchase some passports through Pakistan, since it's such a corrupt country." Routh had visited Ukraine more than two years ago. *AFP* interviewed him in Kyiv in April 2022, when he called Putin a "terrorist" and observed "he needs to be ended."

The North Carolina State Board of Elections said Routh voted Democratic in person during the party's 2024 primary although he registered in 2012 as an unaffiliated voter. At different points in his life, he had supported presidential candidates Bernie Sanders, Tulsi Gabbard, Nikki Haley, and Trump.

CBS News reported that his legal issues began in the 1990s, including writing bad checks. He was charged and convicted of numerous felony offences in Guilford County, North Carolina between 2002 and 2010. *CNN* and *Greensboro News & Record* reported that he was arrested and charged with possession of a weapon of mass destruction after being pulled over by police and allegedly putting his hand on a fully automatic machine gun before barricading himself in a business. He later was ordered to pay tens of thousands to plaintiffs in civil suits. He was repeatedly accused by state and federal authorities of failing to pay his taxes on time. He was charged with misdemeanors such as hit-and-run with a motor vehicle, resisting arrest, and a concealed weapons violation. Other brushes with the law entailed driving with a revoked license and possession of stolen property. A former neighbor noted that federal agents had once raided Routh's property.

The *New York Times* reported that Routh appeared before a judge on September 16, 2024 at the Palm Beach County courthouse near Mar-a-Lago, charged with possessing a firearm as a felon and possessing a firearm with an obliterated serial number. The felony possession charge carries a 15 year sentence; the serial number charge five years. *USA Today* reported that a detention hearing was scheduled for September 23 and an arraignment for September 30.

Trump and vice presidential candidate J.D. Vance blamed the Biden administration and Vice President Kamala Harris. Trump told *Fox News Digital*, "Their rhetoric is causing me to be shot at."

The *Washington Post* reported on September 16 that Routh traveled to Ukraine in 2022 to help recruit foreigners, principally Afghan nationals, for its defense, but a representative of the International Legion of the Main Directorate of Intelligence of the Ministry of Defense of Ukraine at the time said it did not find him useful, being too old and without military experience.

AP added on September 16 that in his self-published *Ukraine's Unwinnable War* 2023 book, Routh called on Iran to kill Trump.

CNN reported on September 23, 2024 that federal prosecutors announced that a witness claimed that Routh had dropped off a box at his home months before, which "contained ammunition, a metal pipe, miscellaneous building materials, tools, four phones, and various letters." One letter was addressed to The World, and said "This was an assassination attempt on Donald Trump but I failed you. I tried my best and gave it all the gumption I could muster. It is up to you now to finish the job; and I will offer $150,000 to whomever can complete the job."

Reuters reported on September 24, 2024 that the FBI found a fingerprint resembling Routh's on tape attached to the SKS rifle.

That day, a grand jury in Miami returned a five-count indictment, including attempted assassination of a presidential candidate, possessing a firearm in furtherance of a violent crime, assault on a federal officer, being a felon in possession of a firearm, and possessing a firearm with an obliterated serial number. On September 30, 2024, Ryan Routh pleaded not guilty to all five charges in federal court in West Palm Beach presided over by U.S. Magistrate Judge Brue Reinhart. He was represented by attorney Kristy Militello. Routh faced life in prison.

On October 30, 2024, Judge Aileen Cannon refused to recuse herself in the case.

September 16, 2024: Secretaries of state and state election offices in Iowa, Kansas, Nebraska, Tennessee, Wyoming, and Oklahoma received suspicious packages containing powder. None of them contained hazardous material. The material sent to Oklahoma contained flour.

BBC reported on October 24, 2024 that Jeffrey Michael Kelly, 60, suspected of carrying out three nighttime shootings targeting a Democratic campaign office in Arizona was arrested and charged with terrorism offences among others. Kelly allegedly had more than 120 guns, scopes, body armor, noise suppressors, and more than 250,000 rounds of ammunition in his home, including a machine gun that was in his car. Prosecutors suggested that he was planning a mass casualty event. No one was hurt in the shootings at the campaign building in Tempe. The first shooting was on September 16, using either BB gun pellets or real bullets. Kelly was also accused of using razor blades to line campaign signs in a nearby village, and hanging these signs with suspicious white powder. His lawyer said that Kelly had no criminal record and was licensed to own firearms. Bond was set at $500,000 (£385,000).

September 17, 2024: *BBC* reported that the U.S. Department of Justice announced the arrest of Alaska resident Panos Anastasiou, 76, for allegedly sending hundreds of messages threatening to hang and shoot six U.S. Supreme Court justices and two of their family members. DOJ charged him with 22 counts of making threats. He appeared in court in Anchorage the next day, represented by a public defender. The complaint noted that the messages "contained violent, racist, and homophobic rhetoric coupled with threats of assassination via torture, hanging, and firearms, and encouraged others to participate in the acts of violence". He faced nine counts of making threats against a federal judge, which carries a maximum sentence of 10 years in prison, and 13 counts of making threats in interstate commerce, which carries a maximum of five years. Threats included vows to "hang" justices "from an Oak tree", along with "lynching", "putting a bullet" in the head of a justice, and sending "fellow veterans" to "spray" homes of the justices with bullets, "hopefully killing" them.

September 18, 2024: *CNN* and *AP* reported that the Philadelphia district attorney announced that Muhyyee-Ud-din Abdul-Rahman, 17 at the time of his arrest and now 18, would be tried as an adult on charges of wanting to travel overseas and make bombs for terrorist organizations Katibat al Tawhid wal Jihad (KTJ) and Hay'at Tahrir al Sham (HTS). Prosecutors say he conducted at least 12 tests on homemade bombs near his family's home. Potential targets included the Philadelphia Pride parade and critical infrastructure sites such as power plants and domestic military bases. Bail was set at $5 million. He faced charges of possessing weapons of mass destruction, conspiracy, arson, and causing or risking a catastrophe.

September 25, 2024: *CNN* reported that a bomb exploded in the morning at the Santa Barbara County Superior Courthouse in Santa Maria, California, injuring five people. Police arrested a suspect.

September 27, 2024: *AP* and the *New York Times* reported that the U.S. Department of Justice indicted three Iranian Islamic Revolutionary Guard Corps hackers—Masoud Jalili, Seyyed Ali Aghamiri, and Yasar Balaghi, on charges of conspiracy related to getting information from a protected computer, supporting terrorism, wire fraud, identity theft, and other cybercrimes. The trio, who apparently live in Tehran, were believed to have hacked the Trump campaign and tried to leak "final prep" for the presidential debate to journalists and the presidential campaign of Joe Biden, which refused to reply to their offer. The *New York Times* reported that the filing indicated that from 2020 to May 2024, the trio targeted dozens of current and former officials of the White House, National Security Council, DOD, CIA, and a former U.S. ambassador to Israel, apparently without success. Susie Wiles, a senior adviser to Trump, was among the targets. Iran infiltrated the Trump campaign via email accounts of Roger J. Stone. The U.S. Department of State offered a $10 million reward for information on the hackers. The Department of the Treasury issued sanctions against the trio.

October 5, 2024: Minneapolis Police Chief Brian O'Hara announced the arrest of a Minnesota man who allegedly threatened to "shoot up" a Minneapolis synagogue, Temple Israel, which had received several threatening phone calls on September 11. On October 3, staff reported a man outside with a firearm. He fled, but officers arrested a man, 21, on October 4. He had used a phone app to mask his voice. He was held on charges of making "terroristic threats".

October 7, 2024: *AP* and *CBS News* reported that the FBI arrested Afghan national Nasir Ahmad Tawhedi, 27, in Oklahoma City after he purchased two AK-47 rifles and ammunition from an undercover law enforcement officer. DOJ said Tawhedi was allegedly plotting a terrorist attack in support of ISIS on Election Day in the United States. Charges included conspiring and attempting to provide material support to ISIS. Court documents indicated that Tawhedi and an unnamed juvenile intended to liquidate his assets, repatriate his family to Afghanistan, purchase assault rifles, and "stage a violent attack" in the U.S. The juvenile—Tawhedi's brother-in-law—was also arrested. Tawhedi entered the United States in September 2021 on a Special Immigrant Visa and was on parole status pending the adjudication of his immigration proceedings. He lives in Oklahoma City with his wife and child. During the summer, he allegedly conducted searches for "How to access Washington dc cameras," "which US state does not require relations to get a firearm," and "Which US States Have Passed Permitless Carry Gun Laws." Tawhedi visited the web cams for the White House and the Washington Monument in July 2024. Tawhedi began discussing firearms with an ISIS recruiter on *Telegram* in August 2024. DOJ found ISIS propaganda on Tawhedi's phone. He donated $540 in cryptocurrency to a charity in Syria known to funnel money to ISIS. A video found on the phone showed him telling his child about the rewards a martyr receives in the afterlife. Tawhedi said his father-in-law's house had sold for $185,000. He asked for help in resettling his mother-in-law, wife, their young daughter, and five of his wife's siblings, in Afghanistan. Tawhedi purchased one-way plane tickets for the family to travel to Kabul on October 17.

On October 18, U.S. Magistrate Judge Suzanne Mitchell in Oklahoma City ordered Tawhedi to remain in custody after officials disclosed that he had previously worked as a security guard for a U.S. military installation in Afghanistan. FBI agent Derek Wiley linked him to an investigation in France that led to the October 12 arrests of three people, including two of Tawhedi's brothers, who were plotting a terrorist attack there. Tawhedi was represented by attorney Craig Hoehns, who said his client had worked as a rideshare driver in Dallas and at several oil change locations in Oklahoma City. The court provided a Dari language interpreter.

October 11, 2024: *Reuters* reported that the Department of Justice announced that U.S. Army PFC Cole Bridges, aka Cole Gonzales, 24, was sentenced to 14 years in prison for attempting to help ISIS ambush U.S. troops. He will undergo supervised release for ten years following his release from prison. He was charged in 2021 with giving "military advice and guidance on how to kill fellow soldiers to individuals he thought were part of ISIS." Bridges, who joined the Army in 2019, pleaded guilty to terrorism charges in June 2023.

October 12, 2024: *NPR, USA Today, CBS News,* and *BBC* reported that at 5 p.m., police detained at a checkpoint Las Vegas man Vem Miller, 49, whose black SUV carried a loaded Glock handgun, a shotgun, and a high-capacity magazine, several passports with different names, and multiple driving licenses near a Trump rally in Coachella, California. His unregistered vehicle had a homemade license plate. He reportedly was involved in a Sovereign Citizens anti-government group. He was charged with two misdemeanor weapons offenses. He was later released on $5,000 bail and told the news media that he was a Trump supporter. Miller posted footage of himself at the Republican National Convention in July 2024, and regularly attended pro-Trump rallies. He posted numerous conspiracy theories regarding Covid, vaccines, 9/11, and the weather, promoting violence against Democrats for "treason" over the Hurricane Helene response. He claimed he ran for office in Nevada in 2022 as a Republican. *USA Today* reported that he filed

a lawsuit on October 15, 2024 against Sheriff Chad Blanco, Riverside County, Deputy Coronado, and ten unnamed staff members of the sheriff's department.

October 14, 2024: The *Baltimore Sun* reported on October 17 that authorities charged a Hanover, Maryland man, 21, with trying to aid a foreign terrorist organization by providing material support after he allegedly attempted to join ISIS. In December 2019, his social media account expressed "extremist Islamist ideology". Soon after, he began conversing with an undercover FBI officer. Between March and April 2023, he told the officer that he wanted to travel to Africa to fight for ISIS. Failing that, he would conduct an attack in the United States against people who support Israel. Thrice in May and June, he purchased ammunition and range time at a shooting range in Severn to train. In July, he tried to purchase a Kalashnikov 9 mm rifle, but he was denied because of his probation status. He planned to fly first to Turkey and then to Ethiopia, and cross the border into Somalia. He received an Ethiopian E-Visa from an ISIS fighter. On October 4, 2024, he told the undercover officer that he had received airline tickets from the ISIS fighter and sent screenshots of his travel itinerary. He planned to leave Baltimore Marshall Airport on October 14 and flying to Istanbul with a layover in London. A week later, he shared a photo of himself wearing a black mask and holding a large machete, captioned "Abdullah the islamophobe slayer". The FBI arrested him while he was checking in for his flight. The Maryland U.S. Attorney's Office reported that he told the arresting agents: "You will never stop me. Jihad will never stop… I'll be like 40 when I get out, then I'll just do it. I don't care. You will never stop me. Jihad will never stop. I'll come, and I'll kill your soldiers." The suspect has a history of mental illness.

October 17, 2024: The U.S. Department of Justice charged former Indian government employee Vikash Yadav, 39, who specialized in intelligence, with murder-for-hire in connection with a planned killing of Sikh separatist leader Gurpatwant Singh Pannun, who was living in New York City. The plot was disclosed in 2023 when

DOJ charged Nikhil Gupta, who was recruited in May 2023 by a then-unidentified Indian government employee (Yadav) to orchestrate the assassination. It was to precede a string of other politically motivated murders in the United States and Canada. Yadav was at large. Canada had announced on October 14 that India's senior diplomat was a person of interest and expelled him and five other diplomats. India png'd Canada's acting high commissioner and five other diplomats in retaliation. The Czech Republic extradited Gupta to the U.S. in June 2024, following his 2023 arrest.

Hardeep Singh Nijjar, a Sikh activist who had been exiled from India, was shot and killed outside a cultural center in Surrey, British Columbia, on June 18, 2023, days before the scheduled Pannun hit. Prosecutors say the gunmen were to kill at least four people in Canada and the U.S. by June 29, 2023, with more after that.

October 26, 2024: *CBS* and *CNN* reported on October 31 that Chicago Police Supt. Larry Snelling announced that Sidi Mohamed Abdallahi, 22, was charged with one felony count of terrorism, one felony count of a hate crime, six counts of attempted first-degree murder, seven counts of aggravated discharge of a firearm, and one count of aggravated battery involving a firearm in the October 26 shooting of an Orthodox Jewish man, 39, who was wearing a kippah while walking to his synagogue in the 2600 block of West Farwell Avenue in the West Ridge, or West Rogers Park, North Side neighborhood around 9:30 a.m. and opening fire on responding police and paramedics. No officers or paramedics were hit. Police returned fire, hitting Abdallahi multiple times. He was hospitalized in critical condition. Police found evidence on his phone indicating he was specifically targeting people of Jewish faith. His next court date was set for November 7.

Abdallahi was a citizen of Mauritania. He encountered the U.S. Border Patrol in San Ysidro, California, on March 31, 2023. Following his arrest, Immigration and Customs Enforcement lodged an immigration detainer with Cook County Jail.

October 28, 2024: *Military.com* reported that former Marine Jordan Duncan, 29, previously assigned to Camp Lejeune, North Carolina, was sentenced to seven years in prison for manufacturing a short barrel rifle as part of his participation in a neo-Nazi plot to attack energy facilities in and around Idaho. He was the final member of a five-man group sentenced in connection with the scheme. Three of those members sentenced to prison are former Marines. The five were part of the online neo-Nazi forum Iron March, where white supremacists gathered until it closed in 2017. For the next three years, members of the group stole military gear, manufactured firearms and gathered information on nerve toxins and explosives as they plotted their targets. The group trained near Boise, Idaho, flashed Heil Hitler signs under a Nazi flag, and wore masks used by members of the white supremacist Atomwaffen Division.

The other Marine veterans were infantrymen Liam Collins and Justin Wade Hermanson, both 25, of the 1st Battalion, 2nd Marine Regiment. Collins was discharged by the Corps after three years as a lance corporal, having tried to recruit veterans into the neo-Nazi group. *Stars and Stripes* reported that Duncan served in the Marine Corps between 2013 and 2018. After a plea deal, Collins and Hermanson were sentenced in July 2024 to 10 years and more than one year in prison, respectively. Paul James Kryscuk, 38, was sentenced to six years and six months in prison for conspiracy to destroy an energy facility. *Fox 8* reported that former National Guardsman Joseph Maurino, 25, was sentenced to prison in late October 2024.

October 28, 2024: *AP, USA Today, ABC News, Florida Times-Union,* and *New York Times* reported that authorities reported that between 3:30 and 4 a.m., incendiary devices damaged ballot drop boxes in Portland, Oregon, and 15 miles away in Vancouver, Washington. The fires destroyed or damaged 488 ballots in Vancouver; three ballots were damaged in Portland. Portland Police Bureau spokesperson Mike Benner said the suspect, a balding white man aged 30 to 40, was believed to be experienced in metal fabrication and welding and could strike again. Surveillance video showed him driving a black or dark-colored 2001 to 2004 Volvo S-60 lacking a front license plate. The incendiary devices were marked with the message "Free Gaza." A third device placed at a different drop box in Vancouver on October 8 carried the words "Free Palestine" and "Free Gaza." No ballots were damaged in that incident.

November 2, 2024: *AP* and *CNN* reported that the Department of Justice announced that federal agents arrested Tennessee man Skyler Philippi, 24, believed to have ties to white nationalist groups, including the National Alliance, which calls for eradicating the Jewish people and other races. Unsealed court records indicated the he attempted to use what he believed to be a drone carrying three pounds of C-4 explosives to destroy a Nashville electric substation. A confidential FBI source introduced him to an undercover FBI employee. Philippi was scheduled for a court hearing on November 13 on charges of attempted use of a weapon of mass destruction and attempted destruction of an energy facility. He initially had told a confidential source in June 2024 that he wanted to commit a mass shooting at a YMCA facility in Columbia, Tennessee.

November 5, 2024: Hoax bomb threats, attributed to Russian email domains, were reported at polling places in Arizona, Georgia, Michigan, Pennsylvania, and Wisconsin. Polling locations in three metro Atlanta counties reported threats. In Georgia's Fulton County, 32 of 177 polling places received bomb threats; five were briefly evacuated. Bomb threats targeted polling locations in Cochise, Navajo, and Yavapai counties in Arizona.

November 8, 2024: The Department of Justice in Manhattan announced an indictment regarding an Iranian murder-for-hire plot to kill Donald Trump, charging a man who said he had been tasked by an Iranian government official with planning the assassination. Farhad Shakeri, 51, an accused Iranian government asset, told investigators that a contact in Iran's Revolutionary Guard instructed him in September 2024 to develop a plan within seven days to surveil and ultimately kill Trump. Shakeri is at large in Iran.

He came to the U.S. as a child, and was deported around 2008 after serving 14 years in prison for robbery.

Authorities arrested two other male suspects, Carlisle Rivera, 49, and Jonathon Loadholt, 36, of New York, who were recruited to participate in other assassinations, including of a prominent Iranian American journalist. Shakeri said he was offered $500,000 for the murder of two Jewish American citizens living in New York City. All three were charged with murder-for-hire, which carries a ten-year maximum sentence; conspiracy to commit murder, with a ten-year sentence; and money-laundering conspiracy, which entails a twenty-year sentence.

November 14, 2024: *CNN* reported that on November 14, 2024, the FBI announced the arrest outside an apartment in Houston, Texas, the previous week of Anas Said, who allegedly created and disseminated ISIS propaganda and wanted to commit a "9/11-style" attack in the United States. He was arraigned before a federal judge on November 14 for attempting to provide material support to a terrorist organization. He told agents that "he tried several times to travel to join ISIS and stated he would readily move back to Lebanon if he were released." The FBI/Houston field office added that he admitted to offering his home as a "safe sanctuary" to ISIS operatives. The FBI had been aware of Said's support of ISIS since 2017, when he ordered stickers related to ISIS. Said told agents that he started believing in ISIS's ideology in 2015, following his returning to the U.S. from Lebanon. Said was born in Houston in 1996 but traveled "shortly thereafter" to Lebanon where he and his family lived until 2014. In late 2023 and into 2024, Said used several *Facebook* accounts "to support ISIS and the violent attacks carried out in its name". Investigators said he told them that he researched locations, layouts, and security measures at synagogues and the Israel Consulate in Houston and intended to confront the head of an unnamed Jewish organization to stop funding Israel.

November 15, 2024: The *New York Post* reported on November 28, 2024 that Border Patrol agents caught Jordanian migrant Mohammad Hasan

Abdellatif Albana, 41, at the northern border in Lynden, Washington. Federal officials believe he is a terrorist. He was expelled from the U.S.

November 19, 2024: *UPI* reported that the Biden administration sanctioned six Hamas leaders on accusations they aided it in raising funds and smuggling weapons into Gaza. They included Türkiye-based Hamas leaders.

- Abd al-Rahman Ismail abd al-Rahman Ghanimat, in his early 50s, is a longtime member of the Izz al-Din al-Qassam Brigades. He is accused of founding a group supporting Hamas efforts in the West Bank, and was involved in multiple attempted successful terrorist attacks, including the 1997 bombing of a cafe in Tel Aviv that killed three people and injured 48 others. He had received five life sentences but was among the more than 1,000 Palestinian prisoners released in 2011 in exchange for the freedom of Israeli soldier Gilad Shalit.

- Musa Daud Muhammad Akari, in his early 50s, was convicted and imprisoned for kidnapping and murdering an Israeli border police officer. He received three life sentences and was freed in the Shalit swap.

- Salama Mari, in his early 50s, was convicted and imprisoned for his involvement in a 1993 West Bank attack that resulted in the death of an Israeli soldier.

- Ghazi Hamad, believed to be in his mid to late 50s, is a Hamas spokesman in Gaza who had overseen border crossing into Gaza.

- Mohammad Nazzal, a Gaza-based senior leader on the Hamas Council on International Relations

- Basem Naim, Gaza-based senior leader involved in Hamas engagements with Russia, et al.

November 25, 2024: *CNN* reported that authorities arrested Manuel Tamayo-Torres of Arizona after allegedly threatening to kill President-elect Donald Trump and his family in a series of *Facebook* videos, including one in which he appears to hold up an AR-15-style rifle. Court documents indicated that on November 21, Tamayo-Torres

said in a video posted on *Facebook* (Individual 1 is Donald Trump), "[Individual 1] you're gonna die, [Individual 1], your son's gonna die. Your whole family is going to die, [Individual 1]. This is reality now for you. This is the only reality you have in your future, [Individual 1], dying." Tamayo-Torres was also charged with several counts of making false statements on federal forms while trying to purchase a gun in 2023 in Phoenix, Arizona.

November 27, 2024: *CNN, CBS News,* and *BBC* reported several of President-elect Donald Trump's Cabinet choices and senior administration appointees and their families received bomb threats and were targeted by swatting. None of them were U.S. Secret Service protectees. Among the targets were:

- Pam Bondi, Attorney General-designate

- Lori Chavez-DeRemer, Labor Secretary-designate

- Matt Gaetz, who withdrew as Attorney General-designate

- Pete Hegseth, Defense Secretary-designate

- Howard Lutnick, Commerce Secretary-designate

- John Ratcliffe, Director-designate of CIA

- Brooke Rollins, Agriculture Secretary-designate

- New York Representative Elise Stefanik, chair of the House GOP conference and Ambassador-designate to the United Nations

- Scott Turner, Secretary-designate of Housing and Urban Development

- Susie Wiles, incoming White House Chief of Staff

- Lee Zeldin, designated to lead the Environmental Protection Agency

December 4, 2024: *CNN* reported that at 6:44 a.m., a gunman shot to death UnitedHealthcare CEO Brian Thompson, 50, outside the New York Hilton Midtown hotel in Manhattan where he was to address his company's annual investors' conference at 8 a.m. Police Commissioner Jessica Tisch said it was a premeditated, preplanned, targeted attack. Forensic investigators found three 9mm rounds. Surveillance video showed the shooter, who arrived on foot, waiting for Thompson for five minutes at 1335 Avenue of the Americas between West 53rd Street and West 54th Street. Thompson sustained gunshot wounds to his back and leg. The shooter got onto an electric e-Citi bike and rode north on Avenue of the Americas toward Central Park. UnitedHealthcare is part of UnitedHealth Group, America's largest insurance company and one of the country's biggest companies. *Fortune* indicated that UnitedHealth Group is the fourth-largest company in America as ranked by revenue.

NYPD Chief of Detectives Joseph Kenny said "The shooter appears to be a light-skinned male. He's wearing a light brown or cream colored jacket, a black face mask, black-and-white sneakers, and a very distinctive gray backpack." NYPD Crime Stoppers offered a $10,000 reward for information leading to the arrest and conviction of the suspected shooter. The FBI on December 7 offered a $50,000 reward.

An official said the gun apparently had a noise suppressor.

BBC, ABC News, and *CBS News* reported on December 5 that the words "deny," "defend," and "depose" were written on the shell casings recovered at the scene of the attack, possibly a reference to an insurance company's handling of claims. Police later recovered a backpack filled with Monopoly money.

USA Today and *NBC News* reported that Thompson's wife Paulette said Brian had received threats. They lived in Maple Grove, Minnesota, a Minneapolis suburb.

By December 7, the NYPD suggested that the shooter hopped an interstate bus; he had arrived from Atlanta on one on November 24. Authorities went to Georgia during the chase.

Police at a McDonald's in Altoona, Pennsylvania arrested Luigi Nicholas Mangione, 26, on December 9 after an employee recognized him at 9:15 a.m. from the police photos. He was carrying a 3D-printed "ghost" gun and suppressor like those used in the murder. He also had several fake IDs—including for Mark Rosario of New Jersey—and a three-page handwritten manifesto showing "ill will toward corporate

America", according to NYPD Detective Chief Kenny. He was initially charged with possession of an unlicensed firearm, forgery, and providing false identification to police. Pennsylvania prosecutor Peter Weeks said in court that Mangione was found with a passport and $10,000 in cash, $2,000 of it in foreign currency. New York authorities charged Mangione with murder on December 10.

CNN noted that Mangione was raised in a prominent Baltimore family, was valedictorian at the elite all-boys prep Gilman School in Maryland in 2016, and spent a summer at Stanford from May-September 2019. He obtained, cum laude, a BA and MA in engineering and applied sciences with a minor in mathematics in 2020 at the University of Pennsylvania, where he was a member of the Phi Kappa Psi fraternity. He started a video game development club. His last known address was Honolulu, Hawaii. From January to June 2022, Mangione lived at Surfbreak, a "co-living" space at the edge of Waikiki. He worked as a software engineer for the online car sales company TrueCar, leaving in 2023. He is the grandson of Nicholas Mangione, a prominent Baltimore real estate developer, and his wife, Mary C. Mangione, a philanthropist who died in 2023. The Mangione family owns Lorien Health Systems, a nursing home chain in Maryland, where Luigi volunteered in 2014, according to his *LinkedIn* page. Mangione is registered to vote at his family's address in Cockeysville, Maryland, listing himself as unaffiliated with a political party. His cousin is Maryland State Delegate Nino Mangione, a Republican.

Mangione's manifesto stated "these parasites had it coming," and "I do apologize for any strife and trauma, but it had to be done." It said that he acted alone and that the attack was self-funded.

On February 2, 2024, he gave a 4 of 5 star review to the 1995 manifesto of Ted Kaczynski, alias the Unabomber, on a *Goodreads* website. "It's easy to quickly and thoughtless[ly] write this off as the manifesto of a lunatic, in order to avoid facing some of the uncomfortable problems it identifies. But it's simply impossible to ignore how prescient many of his predictions about modern society turned out... He was a violent individual - rightfully imprisoned - who maimed innocent people. While these actions tend to be characterized as those of a crazy luddite, however, they are more accurately seen as those of an extreme political revolutionary." He quoted a *Reddit* thread in which a commenter described Kaczynski's acts as "war and revolution," saying that he "had the balls to recognize that peaceful protest has gotten us absolutely nowhere" and that "'Violence never solved anything' is a statement uttered by cowards and predators." Mangione's *Goodreads* profile listed him as reading or wanting to read nearly 300 books, including a book about mental illness, a biography of the creator of the atomic bomb, and Michael Pollan's book on the science of psychedelics.

His *Goodreads* profile also listed several books about coping with back pain. A roommate said he injured his back during a surfing lesson, and was bedridden for a week. On *X*, he posted an x-ray of an individual who had four long screws in his spine.

CNN reported on December 10, 2024 that UnitedHealth Group lost $45 billion in value since the murder. Meanwhile, Mangione yelled as he entered a Pennsylvania courtroom, was denied bail, and was fighting extradition to New York, where he faced charges of

- Murder in the Second Degree
- Criminal Possession of a Weapon in the Second Degree
- Criminal Possession of a Weapon in the Second Degree
- Criminal Possession of a Forged Instrument in the Second Degree
- Criminal Possession of a Weapon in the Third Degree

He faced 15 years to life on the charges.

A Pennsylvania court gave him 14 days to file for writ of habeas corpus. He was held at Huntingdon State Correctional Institution in Pennsylvania. He was represented in Pennsylvania by Thomas Dickey.

He was represented in New York by attorney Karen Friedman Agnifilo.

AP reported on December 17, 2024 that Manhattan District Attorney Alvin Bragg charged Mangione with murder as an act of terrorism.

"Wanted" posters with other health care executives' names and faces appeared on New York streets.

Mangione was extradited on December 19, 2024 to New York, where he was indicted on 11 charges, including first-degree murder as an act of terrorism. He still faced charges in Pennsylvania in connection to the 3D-printed firearm and false ID allegedly in his possession when he was arrested. He also faced four federal charges, including two counts of stalking, a count of murder through the use of a firearm and a firearms offense. He pleaded not guilty on December 23, 2024 to 11 state charges in New York.

December 9, 2024: The terrorism trial presided over by U.S. District Judge David Novak in U.S. District Court in Alexandria began of Mohammed Chhipa, 35, a naturalized U.S. citizen living in Springfield, Virginia, who was accused of funneling tens of thousands of dollars to ISIS. Defense lawyer Zachary Deubler claimed his client was a lonely man looking for a wife and relentlessly targeted by FBI sting operations, including by an undercover operative who pretended to be a willing bride. Prosecutors argued that Chhipa met several times with an undercover FBI operative who gave him hundreds of dollars in numerous instances in 2021 and 2022, earmarked for Syrian female ISIS member Umm Dujanah. Prosecutor Andrew Dixon said Chhipa converted more than $74,000 from donors into Bitcoin and sent it to accounts in Türkiye en route to ISIS. The Bureau searched his home in 2019 and found ISIS propaganda.

After he was arrested, Chhipa said in 2023 that he considered himself to be married to Allison Fluke-Ekren, an American from Kansas who was serving a 20-year prison sentence. She pleaded guilty in 2023 to organizing and leading the Khatiba Nusaybah, an ISIS battalion in which roughly 100 women and girls learned how to use automatic weapons and detonate grenades and suicide belts. Prosecutors said that the marriage was apparently conducted online and had no legal status in the U.S. They said Chhipa, originally from India, had been trying to adopt Fluke-Ekren's children.

AP reported that on December 13, 2024, a jury deliberated for three hours before it convicted Chhipa of all five terrorism charges against him, including providing material support to a terrorist organization, after a weeklong trial. He was represented by defense attorney Jessica Carmichael. Sentencing was scheduled for May 2025.

December 9, 2024: *CNN* reported that the home of Michigan attorney Jordan Acker, a Jewish member of the University of Michigan's Board of Regents, was vandalized at 2 a.m. The university called it "a clear act of antisemitic intimidation." It was the third time Acker had been targeted since the start of the Israel-Hamas war. His front windows were smashed and his wife's car vandalized with "messages about Palestine with a Hamas upside-down triangle", "Divest", and "Free Palestine."

December 16, 2024: *CNN* reported that the FBI arrested Egyptian national Abdullah Ezzeldin Taha Mohamed Hassan, a freshman majoring in information technology at George Mason University in Virginia and living in Falls Church, Virginia, for allegedly plotting a mass casualty attack on the Israeli consulate in New York. He faced federal charges filed on December 16, 2024 in U.S. District Court in Virginia regarding distributing information related to explosives, destructive devices, and weapons of mass destruction and the intent to murder internationally protected persons. He was in the process of being deported. A tipster noted his "radical and terrorist-leaning behavior" on *X*, in which he made posts "revering Osama bin Laden and Ayman Al Zawahiri" and operated "several pro-ISIS and al Qaeda accounts that promoted violence against Jews." The FBI traced the posts to his phone and a university campus IP address. An undercover FBI informant posed as an extremist to communicate with Hassan, who believed he had "recruited" the informant "to conduct a mass casualty attack", sending him the address of the Consulate General of Israel in New York, bomb-making

instructions, and links to purchase cartridges and a rifle to carry out the attack. George Mason University president Gregory Washington announced that Hassan had since been banned from entering campus property.

The *Washington Post* reported that earlier in December, George Mason University banned two sisters who are the current and past presidents of the university's chapter of Students for Justice in Palestine from campus for four years, after authorities searched their family home in November and found "relatives' guns, ammunition and insignia calling for death to Jews".

December 17, 2024: *BBC* reported on December 31, 2024 that the FBI discovered more than 150 bombs during a raid on a farm in Isle of Wight County, Virginia and arrested Brad Spafford after a tip-off that he was stockpiling weapons and homemade ammunition on the 20-acre farm he shares with his wife and two young children. Some of the devices were found in a bedroom in an unsecured backpack that was labelled "#nolivesmatter". Other pipe bombs were stored in a garage. Some bombs were stored in an explosives vest. Investigators also found a jar of HMTD, which is so unstable it can be exploded merely by a temperature change and does not require a detonator to explode; it was stored in a freezer next to food accessible to the children. Spafford was initially charged with possessing an unregistered short-barreled rifle. More charges were likely. Spafford had allegedly used photos of President Joe Biden for target practice and expressed hope that Vice-President Kamala Harris would be assassinated. A neighbor who used to work in law enforcement said Spafford lost three fingers on his right hand in 2021 "while working with a homemade explosive device". The neighbor added that Spafford had discussed fortifying the property with a turret for a 50-caliber firearm on the roof.

The New Jersey Office of Homeland Security and Preparedness noted that the right-wing extremist Nolivesmatter movement promotes extremist ideology, targeted attacks, mass killings, and criminal activity, encouraging members to engage in self-harm and animal abuse.

Spafford's lawyer noted that his client had no criminal record. A federal judge ordered that

Spafford be released with electronic monitoring. The government continued to keep the suspect in pre-trial detention.

December 18, 2024: *CNN* reported on January 1, 2025 that Colorado man Patrick Thomas Egan, 39, of Grand Junction, Colorado was arrested for possible bias-motivated charges for allegedly attacking KKCO/KJCT television reporter Ja'Ronn Alex after demanding to know whether he was a citizen, saying "Are you even a US citizen? This is Trump's America now! I'm a Marine and I took an oath to protect this country from people like you!" Police said he followed Alex's news vehicle in a taxi for around 40 miles from the Delta area to a stoplight in Grand Junction. Alex is a Pacific Islander and Detroit native. Egan tackled Alex, put him in a headlock, and began to strangle him. Egan was arrested on suspicion of bias-motivated crimes, second degree assault, and harassment. He was represented by attorney Ruth Swift.

UPDATES OF PRE-2023 INCIDENTS

AFRICA

BURKINA FASO

January 2016: *UPI* reported on May 19, 2023 that Australian doctor Kenneth Elliott, 88, was freed after being held hostage since January 2016 by al-Qaeda in the Islamic Maghreb. Australian Foreign Minister Penny Wong said Elliott was reunited with his wife Jocelyn and their children. The couple, who were both kidnapped by AQIM, had run a 120-bed clinic in Djibo since 1972. He was the clinic's sole surgeon. The group released Jocelyn after three weeks.

KENYA

2002: *AP, UPI,* and *al-Jazeera* reported on December 17, 2024 that the U.S. repatriated Kenyan man Mohammed Abdul Malik Bajabu after 17 years at Guantánamo Bay without charge. Kenyan authorities arrested him in Mombasa in 2007 for the 2002 bombing of an Israeli-owned hotel in that city that killed 13 and injured 80. They transferred him to Gitmo weeks later for alleged involvement with al-Qaeda's branch in East Africa. The Periodic Review Board determined in 2021 that he "was no longer necessary to protect against a continuing significant threat to the national security of the United States".

April 2019: On February 15, 2024, U.S. Africa Command carried out an airstrike against al-Shabaab at a house near Jilib, Somalia. *CNN* reported on February 19, 2024 that the U.S. was assessing whether Cuban doctors Assel Herrera and Landy Rodriguez were killed. Al-Shabaab had kidnapped them from a government vehicle on their way to a hospital where they worked in April 2019 in Kenya near the Somali border. A police officer who was escorting the doctors was killed. Cuba's Ministry of Health identified them as Assel Herrera Correa, a specialist in general medicine, and surgeon Landy Rodriguez Hernandez. It was the first time al-Shabaab acknowledged holding the hostages. The U.S. said there was no evidence of civilian casualties.

MALI

February 22, 2019: *Al-Jazeera* reported on January 26, 2023 that Bamako's criminal court sentenced a man to death for a 2019 attack that killed three United Nations peacekeepers from Guinea who were travelling through the rural commune of Siby. He was convicted of acts of criminal association, murder, robbery, and illegal possession of firearms.

May 2022: *BBC* reported on February 27, 2024 that Italian Jehovah's Witnesses couple Rocco Langone and Maria Donata Caivano, and their son, Giovanni Langone, who were kidnapped by

Group to Support Islam and Muslims (JNIM) gunmen from their home outside Koutiala in May 2022, were released in good health. The couple are in their 60s and their son in his 40s. The jihadis also kidnapped their Togolese domestic worker, whose fate is unclear.

NIGER

October 14, 2016: *AP* reported on March 20, 2023 that American aid worker Jeffery Woodke, who was kidnapped from his home in Abalak in October 2016 by men who ambushed and killed his guards and forced him at gunpoint into their truck, was released from custody. He had done humanitarian aid work in Niger for more than 30 years. A senior Biden administration official said no ransom was paid and no concession was made to his captors. Els Woodke, Jeffery's wife, said at a November 2021 news conference in Washington that the captors had made a multi-million-dollar ransom demand for his release. She believed he was held by JNIM. Officials believed he was moved during captivity into Mali and Burkina Faso.

French journalist Olivier Dubois was also freed from JNIM kidnappers.

NIGERIA

April 14, 2014: *AP* reported on April 18, 2024 that Nigerian soldiers rescued Lydia Simon, who is five months pregnant, whom Boko Haram kidnapped on April 14, 2014 while she was a schoolgirl in Chibok. The army also rescued her three children. The troops found her in Ngoshe in the Gwoza council area of Borno State. Her children appeared to be between two and four.

March 2018: The *New York Times* reported on November 24, 2024 that the Islamic State West Africa Province in March 2018 kidnapped Alice Loksha Ngaddah, a nurse and mother of two, who worked for UNICEF at a clinic in Rann, Nigeria. She was earning money to care for her mother's dementia. Gunmen killed some of the aid workers and kidnapped Loksha and two midwives. The group kept the trio in Kangaruwa camp, while demanding a ransom from the aid

organizations. On September 16, 2018, the terrorists killed midwife Saifura Khorsa. Midwife Kauwa Mohammed Liman was killed in October 2018. The group said the Muslim midwives deserved to die because they worked for the Red Cross.

Loksha tended to injuries of her captors and delivered babies. She was given to Abu Umar, a senior commander, as a sex slave. After a year, she offered to convert to Islam and took the Muslim name Halima. She prayed to Jesus in private. She gave birth to Umar's son, Mohammed, making her a wife. Umar was stoned to death in 2021 for sleeping with a Muslim abductee. Loksha was married off to another senior commander, Abu Simak. She counseled four other enslaved Christian women to fake conversion.

On October 24, 2024, Loksha, now 42, and her 3-year-old son, and a fellow abductee, Fayina Ali Akilawus (whom she met in October 2023), escaped from the terrorists' camp at dusk, then traveled by donkey, ox cart, boat, and car for more than three days to a military outpost near Geidam. They had paid off a Fulani family $90 to help them escape. Akilawus was captured by Boko Haram in 2020 while traveling in her car. She had tried to escape three times before succeeding with Loksha.

SOMALIA

January 2012: *UPI* and *The Hill* reported that on November 12, 2024, the U.S. Attorney's Office for the Southern District of New York announced that U.S. District Judge Allyne R. Ross sentenced Somali pirates Abdi Yusuf Hassan, 56, a naturalized U.S. citizen residing in Minneapolis, Minnesota and who served as Somalia's Minister of the Interior, and Mohamed Tahlil Mohamed, 43, a former army officer from Mogadishu, to 30 years in prison for kidnapping of American journalist Michael Scott Moore, who was held in captivity for 977 days in Galmudug Province, along with terrorism and firearms offenses. Both were also sentenced to one day of supervised release. Attorney Damian Williams of the Southern District of New York said Moore was "beaten, chained to the floor, and threatened with assault rifles and machine guns."

A New York jury convicted the two of the related offenses in February 2023. Moore, 45 at the time of his capture while driving in the Galkayo area, is a U.S.-German dual citizen. He was grabbed while conducting research on piracy for a book on a grant from the Pulitzer Center for Crisis Reporting. He is the author of *Sweetness and Blood*, a 2010 book about the history of surfing, and *The Desert and the Sea*, a 2018 book about his captivity in Somalia. The group tried to obtain a ransom from Moore's elderly mother. The group released "proof of life" videos of Moore. He was held with two Seychellois fishermen abducted in October 2011 off the Somali coast. The pirates released Moore in September 2014 after a ransom payment. Moore was held with 26 Asian sailors later freed and returned home to Vietnam, Taiwan, Cambodia, Indonesia, China, and the Philippines. Mohamed was represented by attorney Susan Kellman.

2022: *Military Times* and the *Long War Journal* reported on January 9, 2023 that U.S. Africa Command announced that it had conducted 15 airstrikes in Somalia in 2022 against al-Shabaab, killing 107 terrorists.

SOUTH AFRICA

April 10, 1993: *AP* reported on December 6, 2024 that Janusz Walus, 71, the convicted killer of South Africa's anti-apartheid leader Chris Hani, was to be deported to his home country of Poland after his parole came to an end during the week. Hani led the African National Congress's military wing, Umkhonto we Sizwe, and served as general secretary of the South African Communist Party. Hani was shot outside his Boksburg home, east of Johannesburg, on April 10, 1993. Walus served 28 years in jail after being sentenced to life for the murder. He was released on parole following a ruling of the Constitutional Court in 2022.

December 2022: On January 7, 2023, *USNWR, EE Business Intelligence,* and *Reuters* reported that South African power utility Eskom said police were investigating whether an attempt was made in December 2022 to poison its outgoing Chief Executive Officer Andre de Ruyter, who

resigned on December 14 after failing to solve a crisis in the company that led to record levels of power cuts. He took office in January 2020 and planned to leave on March 31, 2023.

ASIA

HONG KONG

December 8, 2019: *AP* reported on November 14, 2024 that Judge Judianna Barnes in a Hong Kong court sentenced Ng Chi-hung, who had previously pleaded guilty to conspiring to commit the bombing of prescribed objects under the anti-terror law and possession of arms or ammunition with intent to endanger life, during anti-government protests in Hong Kong on December 8, 2019, to 23 years and 10 months in the city's first case brought under an anti-terrorism law. He was among seven convicted defendants regarding a plot to plant two bombs and shoot officers along a rally route. The defendants were members of two groups—one led by Ng and another called "Dragon-Slaying Brigade," which planned to lure police officers onto an area where bombs would be detonated and a sniper would fire on them. Wong Chun-keung, leader of the brigade, was sentenced to more than 13 years. Five other defendants received prison terms ranging from nearly six to 12 years. In August 2024, six other defendants, who had pleaded not guilty, were acquitted by a jury.

INDIA

November 26-28, 2008: *Al-Jazeera* reported on December 29, 2023 that India's Ministry of External Affairs formally asked Pakistan to extradite Mumbai attack suspect Hafiz Saeed. The attacks killed 166 people. A Pakistani court on April 9, 2002 sentenced the Lashkar-e-Taiba (LeT) co-founder to 31 years for terrorism financing.

INDONESIA

October 12, 2002: *Al-Jazeera and Benar News* reported that on January 16, 2024 that Malaysians Mohammed Nazir Bin Lep, 47, and Mohammed Farik Bin Amin, 48, pleaded guilty in front of a military court at the U.S. naval base in Guantánamo Bay to five of the nine charges against them, including conspiring in the October 12, 2002 Bali bombings that killed 202 people, including seven Americans. The *New York Times* reported that charges related to the August 5, 2003 attack on the Marriott Hotel in Jakarta that killed 11 people were dropped as part of a plea deal in which the men agreed to give evidence against alleged Indonesian mastermind Encep Nurjaman, alias Hambali. They were brought to Gitmo 17 years ago. Bin Lep and Bin Amin were accused of being Hambali's accomplices. Sentencing was scheduled for the next week, after which they are expected to be returned home.

The Diplomat reported that on January 26, 2024, the war court sentenced the duo to 23 years each, without any reductions for time served, on charges of murder, conspiracy, accessory after the fact, intentionally causing serious bodily injury, and destruction of property. A plea deal drafted under the Trump administration and then adjusted over the summer, which superseded the judge and jury sentences, capped the men's sentences to a maximum of six years of detention. The judge dropped the sentences to five years.

AP, UPI, and *al-Jazeera* reported that on December 18, 2024, the U.S. transferred two Malaysian detainees at Gitmo—Mohammed Farik bin Amin and Mohammed Nazir bin Lep—to their home country, after they pleaded guilty to charges related to the October 12, 2002 bombings in Bali and agreed to testify against Encep Nurjaman, alias Hambali, Indonesian leader of al-Qaeda affiliate Jemaah Islamiya, the alleged ringleader of that and other attacks. Prosecutors said the two worked for years with him, inter alia, helping Nurjaman escape capture. They were handed over to the Malaysian government to serve the remainder of the five-year prison sentences they received after pleading guilty in a Military Commission court to multiple breaches of the laws of war including murder, causing bodily harm, conspiracy, and destruction of property. They provided deposition testimony available for use against Hambali regarding the al-Qaeda-affiliated attacks on nightclubs in Bali, Indonesia in 2002, and the attack on the J.W. Marriott Hotel in Jakarta, Indonesia in 2003. They were arrested in Thailand in 2003.

JAPAN

1975: On February 2, 2024, *AP, NHK, and Kyodo News* reported that man who died at a hospital near Tokyo on January 30, 2024 told police that he was one of the country's most wanted fugitives and had been on the run for nearly 50 years for being part of a radical group that carried out bombings in the 1970s. He said he was Satoshi Kirishima, 70, was dying of cancer, and offered previously unknown details about several bombings. He died four days after questioning. He was born in 1954, attended college in Tokyo, and joined the East Asia Anti-Japan Armed Front, which bombed major Japanese companies in the 1970s. Eight people died and more than 160 were injured in the 1975 bombing of a Mitsubishi Heavy Industries building. He was wanted for setting off a time bomb in a building in Tokyo's Ginza district in April 1975 in which no one was injured. He was the only one of the group's 10 members who was never caught. He kept under the radar using the alias Hiroshi Uchida for about 40 years by not having a cellphone or health insurance and had his salary paid in cash to avoid detection. Police raided a construction company where he had lived and worked.

Two EAAJAF members were sentenced to death, including founder Masashi Daidoji, who died on death row in 2017. Two of the eight members of the group who were indicted in the bombings as of 2014 were at large after their release in 1977 as part of a deal negotiated by the Japanese Red Army, when it hijacked a Japan Airlines plane in Bangladesh.

July 18, 2019: *UPI* reported on September 5, 2023 that Shinji Aoba of Saitama Prefecture admitted in Kyoto District Court to setting the July 18, 2019 fire at Kyoto Animation studio that killed 36 people and injured 34. He was charged with homicide and arson and faced the death penalty. He observed, "I now think that I went overboard." He did not apologize to the victims. Defense lawyers said he was not guilty due to mental incapacity.

On January 25, 2024, the *Washington Post, AP, CNN, UPI, al-Jazeera, and NHK TV* reported that Judge Keisuke Masuda of the Kyoto District Court sentenced defendant Shinji Aoba, 45, to death after finding him guilty of murder and other crimes in an arson attack on Kyoto Animation's No. 1 anime studio. The court found him mentally capable of facing punishment for the attack. Aoba had plotted a separate attack on a train station north of Tokyo a month before the Kyoto attack after studying past criminal cases involving arson. Aoba was hospitalized for 10 months with severe burns over 90% of his body before being arrested in May 2020. *Mainichi Shimbun* reported that among the dead was Naomi Ishida, 49.

July 8, 2022: *UPI* reported on January 13, 2023 that Japanese prosecutors formally indicted Tetsuya Yamagami for the July 8 assassination of former Prime Minister Shinzo Abe. On December 24, 2022, prosecutors had determined that Yamagami was mentally fit to stand trial.

Malaysia

April 2000: *AP* reported on October 30, 2024 that the Regional Trial Court in Taguig, a Manila suburb, on October 21, 2024, convicted and sentenced to life 17 Abu Sayyaf members for kidnapping for ransom 21 people, including European tourists and Asian workers, from the Sipadan Island dive resort in Malaysia in April 2000. Among those convicted were Abu Sayyaf leaders Hilarion Santos and Redendo Dellosa, who had been included in a United Nations terrorism blacklist. The convicts could be pardoned after 30 years. The hostages included a German family of three, two tourists from Finland, a South African couple, a Lebanese woman, two French citizens, and Malaysians and Filipinos who worked in the resort. Police commandoes killed Ghalib Andang, who led the kidnapping,

during an attempted jailbreak and siege in a high-security detention center in 2005 in metropolitan Manila.

Philippines

July 2019: *AP* reported on October 30, 2024 that Assistant U.S. Attorney Jon Bodansky told a federal jury in Manhattan that Kenyan citizen Cholo Abdi Abdullah plotted for four years a 9/11-style attack on a U.S. building on behalf of al-Shabaab. He was in a two-year commercial pilot training program in the Philippines when he was arrested in July 2019. After he was transferred in December 2020 to the U.S. authorities charged him with terrorism related crimes. He faced a mandatory minimum 20 years in prison.

On November 4, 2024, a federal jury in Manhattan found Abdullah guilty on all six counts. Sentencing was scheduled for March 2025. Abdullah represented himself during the trial.

Thailand

August 17, 2015: On November 7, 2024, *AP* reported that the Bangkok Southern Criminal Court acquitted Thai woman Wanna Suansan, 36, who had been charged with involvement in the August 17, 2015 bombing at the Erawan Shrine in Bangkok that killed 20 people and injured 120. The court held that there was not enough evidence to link her to the bombing. Wanna was accused of leasing accommodation for the bombers. Police found gunpowder, fertilizer, and other bomb-making materials in a suburban Bangkok apartment that was leased under her name. Her Turkish husband, not in custody, is also a suspect in the case.

The two other suspects, Yusufu Mieraili and Bilal Mohammad, alias Adem Karadag, being tried separately are ethnic Uyghurs, who were arrested in 2015 as the main bombers. The three were charged with murder, attempted murder, and illegal possession of explosive materials. Wanna was arrested when she voluntarily returned to Thailand from Turkey in 2017 to turn herself in when she was named as a suspect.

Thai authorities have said the bombing was revenge by human traffickers whose activities had been disrupted by the police. Some analysts attributed the bombing to Uyghur separatists angry that Thailand had forcibly repatriated scores of Uyghurs to China in July 2015.

AUSTRALIA/OCEANIA

AUSTRALIA

December 12, 2022: On July 29, 2024, Queensland State Coroner Terry Ryan began hearing an inquiry regarding evidence that three Christian extremists—brothers Gareth and Nathaniel Train and Gareth's wife Stacey Train—who killed two police officers—Rachel McCow and Matthew Arnold—and neighbor Alan Dare and wounded police officer Randall Kirk in an ambush in the sparsely populated Wieambilla region west of Brisbane on December 12, 2022 committed an act of terrorism aimed at intimidating state authorities. Stacey had been married to Nathaniel and had two children with him before marrying his older brother.

EUROPE

BALTIC SEA

September 26, 2022: On August 14, 2024, German prosecutors issued the first arrest warrant in their investigation into the undersea explosions of September 26, 2022 that damaged the Nord Stream 1 and 2 natural gas pipelines between Russia and Germany. Polish prosecutors said that they received a warrant for a Ukrainian man, but that he left the country before he could be arrested. German public broadcaster *ARD*, the daily *Sueddeutsche Zeitung*, and the weekly *Die Zeit* reported jointly that federal prosecutors obtained an arrest warrant in June against Ukrainian man Wolodymyr Z., believed to have lived until recently in Poland. He crossed the border from Poland into Ukraine in early July.

BELGIUM

March 22, 2016: *CNN, al-Jazeera, HLN,* the *Washington Post,* and *RTBF* reported that on July 25, 2023, a Brussels court convicted six (Mohamed Abrini, Oussama Atar, Osama Krayem, Salah Abdeslam, Ali El Haddad Asufi, and Bilal El Makhoukhi) out of ten suspects guilty of "terrorist murder" in the March 22, 2016 ISIS suicide attacks at Brussels Zaventem Airport and the Maelbeek metro station that killed 36 and injured more than 300. The six, plus Hervé Bayingana Muhirwa and Sofien Ayari, were found guilty of participating in the activities of a terrorist organization.

Abdeslam was found guilty in 2022 of carrying out deadly gun and bomb attacks in Paris in November 2015 that killed 130 people at the Bataclan theater, the national stadium, and cafes.

Brothers Smail Farisi and Ibrahim Farisi were both acquitted of the charge of participation in activities of a terrorist group.

Reuters reported that the trial included testimony from more than 370 witnesses and experts.

AP, Le Soir, and the *New York Times* reported that on September 15, 2023 presiding judge Laurence Massart announced that a Belgian court sentenced five men to 20 years to life in prison on charges of terrorist murder in connection with the March 22, 2016 suicide bombings that killed 32 people and wounded 340 at Brussels airport and a subway station. Chief suspect Salah Abdeslam, 34, a French citizen, had earlier been sentenced to 20 years for involvement in a shootout on March 18, 2016 and received no further jail time. Abdeslam was serving a life sentence without parole in France for his part in ISIS attacks that hit Paris cafes, the Bataclan theater, and France's national stadium in November 2015.

Also convicted of terrorist murder was Mohamed Abrini, a childhood friend of Abdeslam and a Brussels native who walked away from Zaventem Airport after his explosives failed to detonate. He was sentenced to life in prison.

Osama Krayem and Bilal El Makhoukhi were sentenced to life in prison, while Ali El Haddad Asufi received a 20-year term.

Oussama Atar, a possible organizer of the attacks in Paris and Brussels, was convicted of terrorist murder in absentia. He was believed to have died in ISIS's final months of fighting in Iraq and Syria, but was also sentenced to life in prison.

Belgium's largest trial included testimony from nearly 1,000 registered survivors, witnesses, and experts.

FRANCE

1982: On November 15, 2024, *al-Jazeera* reported that a French court ordered the release of Lebanese citizen Ibrahim Abdallah, 73, a former head of the Lebanese Armed Revolutionary Brigade, first detained in 1984 and convicted in 1987 over the murders of U.S. and Israeli diplomats in France in the early 1980s. Prosecutors said he would be released on December 6, 2024 on the condition that he leaves France. France's antiterrorism prosecutor's office said it would appeal the decision. Abdallah was sentenced to life in 1987 for his involvement in the murders of U.S. diplomat Charles Ray in Paris and Israeli diplomat Yacov Barsimantov in 1982, and in the attempted murder of U.S. Consul General Robert Homme in Strasbourg in 1984. Requests for Abdallah's release were rejected and annulled in 2003, 2012, and 2014. This was his 11th bid for release. *AFP* reported that he was represented by attorney Jean-Louis Chalanset. Abdallah never expressed remorse. After being wounded in 1978 during Israel's invasion of Lebanon, he joined the Popular Front for the Liberation of Palestine (PFLP). The Christian soon founded the pro-Syrian and anti-Israeli Marxist Lebanese Armed Revolutionary Factions (LARF), which had contact with Italy's Red Brigades and the German Red Army Faction (RAF). He was arrested in 1984 after entering a police station in Lyon and claiming that assassins from the Israeli intelligence agency Mossad were stalking him.

December 11, 2018: *BBC* and *AFP* reported that on April 5, 2024, Audrey Mondjehi, 42, was convicted of obtaining a gun used by Cherif Chekatt, who shot and stabbed his victims in a Strasbourg Christmas market on December 11, 2018, killing five and wounding 11. Mondjehi was sentenced to 30 years. Mondjehi and Chekatt were former prison cell mates. Two other men received shorter sentences for helping Chekatt. A fourth man was acquitted. Their trial had begun on February 29, 2024 at the Court of Assize in Paris. The court did not convict Mondjehi of a terrorism offence because he did not know how Chekatt planned to use the weapon in an ISIS-claimed attack that killed:

- Antonio Megalizzi, 29, an Italian journalist
- Kamal Naghchband, a garage mechanic who was originally from Afghanistan
- Barto Pedro Orent-Niedzielski, 36, a Strasbourg musician of Polish origin
- Anupong Suebsamarn, 45, a Thai national on holiday with his wife
- Pascal Verdenne, 61, a retired bank worker from Strasbourg

October 16, 2020: *Reuters, AP,* and *Yahoo News* reported on November 27, 2023 that the trial began of six teenagers for the beheading of French history teacher Samuel Paty, 47, on October 16, 2020. He had shown his students caricatures of the Prophet Mohammad in a class on freedom of expression, angering some Muslim parents. Paty was killed outside his school in a Paris suburb by an 18-year-old assailant of Chechen origin, who was shot dead by police soon after the attack. Five minors on trial for premeditated criminal conspiracy were aged between 14 and 15 at the time of the attack and were suspected of pointing out Paty to the killer or helping monitor his exit from the school. The sixth, a girl who was 13 at the time, allegedly told her parents that Paty had shown caricatures of the prophet in her class. She faced false accusation charges; she was not in the class when it happened. The teens were referred to children's court and faced 30 months in prison. Eight accused adults were to appear before a special criminal court.

CNN reported that on December 8, 2023, a French court convicted six teenagers for the beheading. A teenage girl who had allegedly told her parents that Paty had asked Muslim pupils to leave the room before showing the caricatures was convicted of making false accusation charges and slanderous comments. The others were found guilty of charges related to taking part in a pre-meditated criminal conspiracy and helping to prepare an ambush. The court found them guilty of having pointed out Paty to the murderer. The heaviest sentence was a six-month prison sentence; the defendant might serve this at home while under electronic surveillance. The girl who was found guilty of making false accusations and slanderous comments was given an 18-month suspended sentence and put on probation measures for two years. All six suspended sentences are tied to the perpetrators following a strict set of probation measures for two to three years.

AP, AFP, and *al-Jazeera* reported that on November 4, 2024, the trial began in Paris of seven men and one woman on terrorism charges regarding Paty's killing by a Russian of Chechen origin—the Islamic extremist Abdoullakh Anzorov, 18. Defendants included Anzorov's friends who allegedly helped purchase weapons for the attack, plus people accused of spreading false information online about Paty and his class.

Among the defendants was Brahim Chnina, 52, Moroccan Muslim father of a teenager who claimed that she had been excluded from Paty's class when he showed the caricatures on October 5, 2020. Chnina doxed Paty's school in the Paris suburb of Conflans Saint-Honorine. Chnina's daughter had lied to him and had never attended the lesson. Chnina was charged with alleged association with a terrorist enterprise for targeting Paty through false information.

Also on trial was Abdelhakim Sefrioui, 65, self-described spokesperson for Imams of France, although he had been dismissed from that role. He founded the pro-Hamas Cheikh Yassine Collective in 2004, which was dissolved a few days after Paty's killing. Sefrioui and Chnina faced 30 years in prison. Sefrioui was represented by attorney Ouadie Elhamamouchi.

Naim Boudaoud, 22, and Azim Epsirkhanov, 23, a Russian of Chechen origin, were accused of helping Anzorov buy a knife and a pellet gun. They faced life imprisonment if convicted on charges of complicity in murder in connection with a terrorist enterprise. Boudaoud also drove Anzorov to Paty's school. They turned themselves in at a police station. Boudaoud was represented by attorneys Adel Fares and Hiba Rizkallah.

The other four were charged with criminal terrorist conspiracy for communicating with the killer on pro-jihad *Snapchat* groups.

- Yusuf Cinar, 22, a Turk, shared an armed group's *Snapchat* account with the killer that later published images of Paty's killing.

- Ismail Gamaev, 22, a Russian of Chechen origin with refugee status, and Louqmane Ingar, 22, exchanged content on a *Snapchat* group with Anzorov. Gamaev posted an image of Paty's head with smiley faces after the killing.

- Priscilla Mangel, 36, conversed with Anzorov on *X*, describing the teacher's class as "an example of the war waged by [France's] Republican institutions against Muslims".

CBS News and *BBC* reported on December 20, 2024 that France's anti-terrorism Special Assize Court convicted eight people of involvement in the beheading.

- Naïm Boudaoud, 22, and Azim Epsirkhanov, 23, friends of Anzorov, were convicted of complicity in murder and sentenced to 16 years in prison each. Neither can be paroled for two thirds of their term. Boudaoud was accused of driving Anzorov to the school, while Epsirkhanov helped him obtain weapons.

- Brahim Chnina, 52, was sentenced to 13 years for association with a terrorist enterprise.

- Abdelhakim Sefrioui, a Muslim preacher, was sentenced to 15 years for organizing a hate campaign online against Paty.

GERMANY

October 9, 2019: On February 27, 2024, *AP* and *DPA* reported that German far-right extremist Stephan Balliet, 32, already serving a 2020 life sentence following an attempt to attack a synagogue in Halle on Yom Kippur 2019 during which he killed a passer-by and a man inside a nearby fast-food restaurant, was convicted of hostage-taking for his actions in a December 2022 jailbreak attempt in Burg. He was sentenced to seven years in prison and ordered to make payments to several people.

IRELAND

March 7, 2021: *BBC* reported on March 19, 2024 that on March 7, 2021, Michael Murray, 54, while in prison serving a sentence in Midlands Prison, Portlaoise for rape, harassment, and making death threats, phoned a false bomb threat to the Samaritans claiming to be the Irish National Liberation Army (INLA) and that explosives had been planted at the home of Minister for Justice Helen McEntee, a Fine Gael politician. Two years were added to his current term. Murray, formerly of Seafield Road, Killiney, Dublin, was found guilty of knowingly making a false report giving rise to an apprehension for the safety of someone else.

October 7, 2022: *BBC* reported on May 27, 2024 that the Gardaí (Irish police) arrested a man and woman, both aged in their 40s, as part of an investigation into an explosion at a petrol station in County Donegal which killed 10 people, including four men, three women, two teenagers, and a girl, 5, in Creeslough on October 7, 2022. They were detained in separate police stations in County Donegal over alleged offences contrary to the Non-Fatal Offences Against the Person Act 1997.

Kosovo

January 2018: On June 28, 2024, a Pristina court sentenced four ethnic Serbs to four to 10 years in jail for the shooting death of moderate Serb leader Oliver Ivanovic, 64, in front of his party office headquarters in the Serb-dominated northern part of the Kosovo town of Mitrovica in January 2018. The court said the accused were part of an organized crime ring. Five other defendants remained at large. A Kosovo court

had convicted Ivanovic of war crimes during the 1998-99 war, but the verdict was overturned and a retrial had begun.

NETHERLANDS

2018: *Al-Jazeera* reported on September 11, 2023 that a Dutch court at the Schiphol Judicial Complex, Badhoevedorp, sentenced Pakistani ex-cricketer Khalid Latif, 37, to 12 years for urging people to murder Dutch far-right leader Geert Wilders. In a 2018 video, he offered a three million rupee (21,000 euro) reward for Wilders's death. Latif lives in Pakistan and was tried in absentia. In 2017, he was banned from cricket for five years over a sports-fixing scandal during a Pakistan Super League match in Dubai.

NORTHERN IRELAND

January 30, 1972: *AP* reported on December 6, 2024 that a former British soldier, identified only as Soldier F, was charged at Belfast Crown Court with two counts of murder and five counts of attempted murder stemming from a civil rights march and the rioting that followed it on January 30, 1972. British Army gunfire killed 13 people on Bloody Sunday disturbances in Londonderry. Soldier F pleaded not guilty. Justice Stephen Fowler scheduled the next hearing in the case for January 24, 2025.

August 15, 1998: *UPI* reported that on February 2, 2023, Chris Heaton-Harris, the secretary of state for Northern Ireland, told Parliament that the British government would launch an independent investigation into the Omagh car bombing that killed 29 people and injured 220 in Northern Ireland in August 1998 in response to a High Court judgement in 2021 that found plausible arguments that the Real IRA's attack could have been prevented. The investigation was to examine the handling and sharing of intelligence, the use of cell phone analysis, whether there was advanced knowledge or reasonable means of knowledge of the bomb, and whether disruption operations could or should have been mounted. On July 30, 2024, *UPI* reported that a public inquiry began at Omagh's Strule Arts Center regarding the car bombing.

NORWAY

July 22, 2011: *Al-Jazeera, Aftenposten,* and *Reuters* reported that on August 18, 2023, neo-Nazi mass killer Anders Behring Breivik, 44, sued the government for allegedly violating his human rights due to being held in "extreme" isolation, and filed another application for parole. He was represented by attorney Oeystein Storrvik, variant Øystein Storrvik.

Reuters, AP, and *CNN* reported on January 8, 2024 that Anders Behring Breivik, 44, who has changed his name to Fjotolf Hansen, the far-right fanatic who killed 77 people in a bombing and shooting rampage in Norway on July 22, 2011, launched a legal bid to end his 12 years in isolation. His spacious area includes a training room, a kitchen, a TV room, and a bathroom. *NTB* reported that he is allowed to keep three budgerigars as pets who fly freely in the area. Attorney Oeystein Storrvik, variant Øystein Storrvik, had earlier argued the isolation in a dedicated section of Ringerike prison on the shore of the Tyrifjorden Lake had left her client suicidal and dependent on Prozac. Breivik also asked the court to lift restrictions on his correspondence with the outside world. His attorneys included Marte Lindholm.

Al-Jazeera reported that on February 15, 2024, the Oslo District Court concluded that Breivik's sentencing conditions are not a violation of human rights, and he was to remain in isolation to serve a 21-year sentence in prison. *Aftenposten* reported that Breivik immediately appealed the ruling.

AP and NTB reported on November 19, 2024 that Breivik, 45, requested parole for a second time. Under Norwegian law, he is eligible for a parole hearing after a decade in prison. He had the letter Z shaved on the side of his head—a symbol seen on Russian military vehicles in Ukraine.

June 25, 2022: On March 12, 2024, *AP* reported that the trial began in Oslo District Court of Zaniar Matapour, 44, a Norwegian citizen originally from Iran, accused of aggravated terrorism for shooting to death two people and seriously wounding nine at three locations, chiefly outside the London Pub, a popular gay bar, at an LGBTQ+ festival in Oslo's nightlife district on June 25, 2022. Prosecutor Sturla Henriksbø said Matapour fired 10 rounds with a machine gun and eight shots with a handgun into a crowd. Matapour had sworn allegiance to ISIS. He faced 30 years in prison. He complained that the trial was held during Ramadan. He was represented by defense attorney Marius Dietrichson. Matapour was born in Iran of parents of Kurdish background. The family fled to Norway when he was 12.

AP reported on May 3, 2024 that Pakistan expelled radical Norwegian Islamist Arfan Bhatti, 46, to Oslo, where he was suspected of complicity in the deadly shooting. Bhatti knew Zaniar Matapour, who faced 30 years in prison.

Bhatti was a Norwegian citizen born in Oslo to Pakistan immigrants. He was involved in criminal gangs, and was a leading figure in radical Islamic circles, including an ISIS-affiliated group, in Norway for years. He was represented by attorney John Christian Elden.

AP and NTB reported on July 4, 2024 that the Oslo District Court found Zaniar Matapour guilty of terrorism in the June 25, 2022 attack. Among the victims was Espen Evjenth, who was hit by a bullet in the forehead at the London Pub.

SPAIN

November 24-December 1, 2022: On January 22, 2023, the online *New York Times* reported that U.S. and European officials believe that Russian military intelligence officers working for the Main Directorate (GRU) 161st Special Purpose Specialist Training Center, whose headquarters in eastern Moscow house Unit 29155, directed associates of the Russia-based Russian Imperial Movement white supremacist group to send six letter bombs in Spain in November-December 2022 that targeted the prime minister, the defense minister, and foreign diplomats.

The *Daily Beast, Fox News, El Pais, Reuters, BBC, ABC, La Sexta,* and *AP* reported on January 25, 2023 that Spain's interior ministry announced the arrest of a "lonely" and "strange" Spanish man, 74, in Miranda de Ebro in Castile and León Province on suspicion of sending six letter bombs. The retired civil servant worked for the town hall at Vitoria-Gasteiz, the nearby Basque capital, and had no previous criminal record. He was active on social media, espousing pro-Russian views. Investigators believed he was working alone. The suspected him of the letter bombs, but not the packages containing animal eyeballs sent to Ukrainian embassies throughout Europe. He faced one charge of terrorism before a judge at the Audiencia Nacional, the country's top criminal court. *AFP* reported on January 27, 2023 that the pensioner was placed in pre-trial detention on grounds he could flee to "Russian territory". He faced 20 years in jail. Investigators searching his home discovered a workshop containing soldering equipment, tools, metal parts and screws compatible with the letter bombs sent, and indications of preparatory work to construct more.

On July 23, 2024, the National Court sentenced Pompeyo González Pascual, 76, to 18 years—ten years for committing acts of terrorism and eight years for the manufacturing and use of illegal explosives for terrorist purposes—after finding him guilty of sending six parcels containing explosives to Spain's prime minister and other government, military, and diplomatic targets, including the U.S. and Ukrainian embassies, in November-December 2022. The Court said he acted "with the goal of ... pressuring the Spanish and American governments ... into giving up their support of Ukraine in its prolonged war with Russia." Authorities arrested the resident of Miranda de Ebro in January 2023 for sending the letter to Spain's Prime Minister Pedro Sánchez and to the U.S. and Ukrainian embassies in Madrid in 2022. A Ukrainian Embassy employee was slightly injured. Letters bombs also arrived at Spain's Defense Ministry, a European Union satellite center located at the Torrejón de Ardoz air base outside Madrid, and an arms factory in northeastern Spain that makes grenades sent to Ukraine.

TÜRKIYE

November 13, 2022: *AP* and *Anadolu* reported on April 26, 2024 that a court sentenced Syrian woman Alham Albashir to seven consecutive life sentences for a bombing of a busy shopping district on Istiklal Avenue in Istanbul on November 13, 2022 that killed six people, including two children, and wounded 99. The indictment said that she and Bilal el-Hacmaus were intelligence operatives of the YPG, a Syrian Kurdish militia group and the Syrian arm of the outlawed Kurdistan Workers Party (PKK), and its political branch, the PYD. The prosecution said the YPG and PYD specially trained the duo and sent them with explosives to Türkiye. El-Hacmaus fled the country.

UNITED KINGDOM

December 21, 1988: *CNN* reported on February 8, 2023 that Libyan man Abu Agila Mohammad Mas'ud Kheir al-Marimi pleaded not guilty to three federal charges brought against him in Washington, D.C. regarding making the bomb that destroyed Pan Am Flight 103 over Lockerbie, Scotland, on December 21, 1988. He faced two charges of destruction of an aircraft resulting in death and one charge of destruction of a vehicle used in foreign commerce by an explosive, resulting in death. He faced life in prison. A detention hearing was scheduled for February 23.

2013: *AP* reported on April 18, 2024 that Woolwich Crown Court in east London sentenced British man Gary Preston, 64, who targeted schools and businesses with threatening letters in a six-week terror campaign in 2013 to more than four years in prison and an additional five years over a sexual assault in 1988. He sent 42 envelopes containing white powder, which was later found to be talcum powder, and threatening messages that caused concern at the targeted venues. Some of the envelopes had small texts in Arabic on white paper, such as "Think fast, you have seconds Inshallah." Venues included Westfield shopping centers in east and west London, schools and colleges in Essex, and the Premier Inn hotel at London's Stansted Airport. Police arrested him in September 2020; he pleaded guilty to 21 charges in August 2023. He was also sentenced to a further five years and three months in prison for a separate charge of serious indecent assault involving a knife in January 1988 at a women's public toilet in Rainham in Essex.

2015: *CNN* and *PA Media* reported on February 22, 2023 that Judge Robert Jay upheld the Home Office's February 19, 2019 revocation of the UK citizenship of Shamima Begum, 23, who left the UK to join ISIS at age 15. Her newborn son Jarrah died in a hospital near Syria's al-Hawl refugee camp in March 2019. She was represented by attorneys Gareth Pierce and Daniel Furner, of Birnberg Pierce Solicitors.

February 2015: *CNN* and the *New York Times* reported on February 23, 2024 that Shamima Begum, now 24, then-15, who flew to Syria in February 2015 with two school friends—Kadiza Sultana and Amira Abase, to join ISIS, lost her Court of Appeal challenge over the decision to remove her British citizenship. She married an ISIS fighter and spent several years living in Raqqa. Her friends also married ISIS fighters; their parents believed they were killed in air strikes.

May 22, 2017: *UPI* reported on March 2, 2023 that Judge John Saunders said that the third and final report on the 2017 ISIS attack on the Ariana Grande concert in Manchester concluded that the attack could have been prevented by MI5 and North West Counter Terrorism Police who were watching attacker Salman Abedi, 22, but did not act quickly enough to stop his attack. The inquiry compiled more than 172,000 documents and evidence from nearly 300 witnesses.

AP reported on April 15, 2024 that lawyers from three law firms representing more than 250 survivors of the bombing that killed 22 people at the May 22, 2027 Ariana Grande concert in Manchester sued Britain's domestic intelligence agency, MI5.

On October 23, 2024, *AP* reported that British citizen Martin Hibbert and his daughter, Eve, who were seriously wounded by suicide bomber Salman Abedi who killed 22 people and

injured 260 after an Ariana Grande concert in Manchester on May 22, 2017 won a harassment lawsuit against former television producer Richard Hall, who claimed in videos, a film and a book that the tragedy was staged using actors and no one was injured or killed. Hibbert was paralyzed from the waist down and Eve, who was 14 at the time, nearly died and sustained severe brain damage.

On November 8, 2024, *AP* reported that Martin Hibbert and his daughter, Eve, crippled by suicide bomber Salman Abedi who killed 22 people and wounded 260, were awarded 45,000 pounds ($58,000) by Justice Karen Steyn in the High Court in London in a case against former television producer Richard Hall. The Hibberts also won an injunction preventing Hall from further harassment, and Hall was ordered to pay 90% of their legal costs that were estimated at 260,000 pounds ($335,000).

On November 22, 2024, the U.K.'s Investigatory Powers Tribunal rejected a legal claim against MI5 by more than 300 survivors of the bombing, holding that the claimants waited too long to bring their case. A 2023 official inquiry charged that MI5 did not act swiftly enough on key information and missed a significant opportunity to prevent the bombing. Bomber Salman Abedi was a "subject of interest" to MI5 officials in 2014, but his case was closed shortly after because he was deemed to be low risk.

December 25, 2021: *UPI* reported on February 4, 2023 that Jaswant Chail, 21, pleaded guilty in the Old Bailey to making threats to kill, possession of an offensive weapon, and an offense under the 1842 Treason Act. On Christmas 2021 at 8 a.m., police arrested him at Windsor Castle, saying the hooded man was armed with a loaded crossbow and had broken into the grounds in order to kill the Queen. The Crown Prosecution Service said he was the first person to be convicted of treason in the UK in more than 40 years. The court ordered medical reports be prepared for Chail. Sentencing was scheduled for March 31, 2023. He had threatened to kill the Queen in a video he recorded four days earlier which was posted online and sent to his contacts list 10 minutes before his arrest. Police found crossbow bolts and a metal file in his hotel room. He said in the video that he wanted to avenge a 1919 incident when British troops opened fire on 400 Sikh protestors in India, and for those killed, humiliated, or discriminated against due to their race. In February 2023, he pleaded guilty to three charges, including treason and possession of an offensive weapon.

CNN and the *PA Media* news agency reported on October 5, 2023 that Sentencing Judge Justice Hilliard in London's Old Bailey court sentenced British citizen Jaswant Singh Chail, 21, to nine years in jail with a further five years on extended licence. He was arrested on Christmas Day 2021 after he broke into Windsor Castle with a loaded crossbow and plans to assassinate Queen Elizabeth II, who was staying at the castle during the pandemic. He apparently scaled the castle's perimeter with a nylon rope ladder while wearing black clothes and a metal mask. He told a police protection officer, "I am here to kill the Queen."

Chail was sentenced under a "hybrid order" under the Mental Health Act to serve his term at Broadmoor high-security psychiatric hospital until he is well enough to be transferred to prison. He referred to himself as a Star Wars Sith who had been pushed to break into the castle by his AI chatbot "girlfriend".

LATIN AMERICA

ARGENTINA

July 18, 1994: The *Washington Post* and *al-Jazeera* reported that on December 20, 2023, U.S. federal prosecutors in New York indicted alleged Hizballah member Samuel Salman El Reda, 58, a dual Colombian-Lebanese citizen, for helping to orchestrate the July 18, 1994 bombing of the Asociación Mutual Israelita Argentina (AMIA) Jewish community center in Buenos Aires that killed 85 people and injured 300. He allegedly played a leading role in the group for decades, and helped recruit and train operatives, deploying them to Thailand, Panama, and Peru so that they could help plan attacks and stockpile explosives and chemicals such as ammonium nitrate. He remained at large in Lebanon. El Reda was charged

with conspiring to provide and providing material support to Hizballah, aiding and abetting the receipt of military-type training from Hizballah, and conspiring to receive military training from the terrorist organization. *Al-Jazeera* added that U.S. authorities said he helped coordinate the activities of Hizballah's Islamic Jihad Organization in South America, Asia, and Lebanon since at least 1993. The U.S. Department of State sanctioned him in 2019 and offered $7 million for information regarding his whereabouts.

BBC and *AFP* reported on April 24, 2024 that Argentina asked Interpol to issue an arrest notice for Iranian Interior Minister Ahmad Vahidi regarding the July 18, 1994 bombing. Vahidi visited Pakistan in mid-April 2024 as part of an Iranian delegation which then went to Sri Lanka. Vahidi had led the overseas operations arm of the Islamic Revolutionary Guard Corps (IRGC) at the time of the attack. On April 11, 2024, Argentina's Court of Cassation ruled that Iran had planned the attack and that the Iran-backed group Hizballah carried out the "crime against humanity".

September 1, 2022: On June 26, 2024, the federal trial began of three suspects in the attempted assassination on September 1, 2022 of then-Vice President Cristina Fernández de Kirchner outside her apartment building while shaking hands with well-wishers. Brazilian national Fernando Sabag Montiel pointed a gun inches from her face and pulled the trigger, but there was no bullet in the chamber. Fernández served as president from 2007 to 2015. His girlfriend at the time, Brenda Uliarte, was arrested days later. Nicolás Carrizo, the couple's friend and boss, was also on trial.

BRAZIL

March 14, 2018: *AP* reported on March 24, 2024 that Brazil's federal police arrested congressman Chiquinho Brazão and his brother Domingos Brazão, a member of Rio State's accounts watchdog, on suspicion of ordering the killing of Marielle Franco, 38, a Black, bisexual Rio de Janeiro city councilwoman in a drive-by shooting on March 14, 2018. Both were linked to militias. On March 27, Justice Minister Ricardo Lewandowski announced that the Supreme Court had validated a plea bargain for the shooter who was arrested along with the driver in 2019. The shooter, former police officer Ronnie Lessa, signed a plea bargain deal. *AP* and *Veja* reported that Rivaldo Barbosa, the head of Rio's police when the murder took place, was arrested on March 24, 2024 for alleged obstruction of the investigation. Mônica Benício, the victim's wife, told *TV Brasil* that he had ordered the killing.

AP reported on October 30, 2024 that the trial began of two former police officers, the alleged killers of Rio de Janeiro city councilwoman Marielle Franco, 38, and her driver, Anderson Gomes. Ronnie Lessa was accused of firing the gun in the drive-by shooting; Élcio Queiroz was accused of being the driver who pursued Franco. The duo were arrested in 2019. They signed plea bargains confessing their roles. Fernanda Chaves, Franco's assistant, was injured but survived. Rio's public prosecutors' office requested the 84 year maximum prison sentence for each defendant for double homicide, attempted homicide, and driving a cloned vehicle. In September 2024, Edilson Barbosa dos Santos was convicted of dismantling the car used in the shooting. In March 2024, Federal Police detained federal lawmaker Chiquinho Brazão and his brother Domingos Brazão, a member of Rio state's accounts watchdog, on suspicion of ordering Franco's killing. Lessa told police that the two politician brothers hired him and informed him that the then-chief of the state's civil police, Rivaldo Barbosa, had approved. Barbosa was arrested in March 2024.

AP reported on October 31, 2024 that Judge Lucia Glioche sentenced Ronnie Lessa and Élcio de Queiroz to almost 79 years and almost 60 years, respectively. Jurors found that Lessa fired the gun and de Queiroz was the wheelman. Brazilian law does not allow for life imprisonment; each man will serve no more than 30 years and could serve 12 and 18 years in prison, respectively, including time already served. They were fined 706,000 reais ($122,000) in moral damages to several of the victims' family members and provide an allowance to the young son of Gomes until he turns 24.

June 5, 2022: The *Los Angeles Times* reported on January 24, 2023 that Brazilian police said that they planned to indict a Colombian fish trader as the mastermind of the June 5, 2022 murders of Indigenous expert Bruno Pereira, 41, and British journalist Dom Phillips, 57, in the Amazon rainforest. Federal police officials charged that Ruben Dario da Silva Villar provided the ammunition, made phone calls to confessed gunman fisherman Amarildo da Costa de Oliveira, alias Pelado, before and after the slayings and paid the gunman's lawyer.

On May 22, 2023, the *Washington Post* reported that police indicted the former head and deputy head of the country's Indigenous affairs agency Funai for failing to take "necessary measures" to prevent the killings of Phillips and Pereira in the Javari Valley of the Amazon rainforest in June 2022. Pereira had been threatened for his work mapping criminal activity in the valley; the Brazil-based Phillips was a correspondent for the *Guardian* and the *Washington Post*. Brazil's state-owned news *Agência Brasil* said the two officials were Marcelo Xavier, who was president of the Indigenous agency from July 2019 until December 2022, and former deputy president Alcir Amaral Teixeira. *O Globo* reported that the duo became aware of the risk to Funai staff following the murder of agent Maxciel Pereira, who was killed while investigating illegal fishing in the Amazon in September 2019.

December 15, 2022: *CNN, AFP, Reuters,* and *al-Jazeera* reported that on November 18, 2024 Brazilian Federal Police arrested five people, among them a police officer and four military officers with special forces training, including retired general Mário Fernandes, a former adviser to ex-President Jair Bolsonaro, over an alleged Green and Yellow Dagger plot to assassinate President Luiz Inácio Lula da Silva in 2022. The plotters planned to kill the then-president-elect and capture or kill Lula's Vice President Geraldo Alckmin and Supreme Court Justice Alexandre de Moraes. Fernandes was previously the second-highest ranking executive of the General Secretariat of the Presidency during Bolsonaro's administration.

CNN reported on November 21, 2024 that Brazilian Federal Police indicted 37 individuals including, ex-president Jair Bolsonaro, accusing him of "full knowledge" of a 2022 plot to kill Luiz Inácio Lula da Silva and overturn the results of the presidential election.

COLOMBIA

February 27, 1980: On October 6, 2024, *CNN* reported that Pope Francis named 21 new cardinals, including retired Vatican diplomat Monsignor Angelo Acerbi, 99, who was once held hostage in 1980 for six weeks in Colombia by leftist 19th of April Movement guerrillas who had assaulted the embassy of the Dominican Republic in Bogota. He was one of the last released in Havana on April 28, 1980.

March 5, 2020: *Stars and Stripes* reported on May 30, 2024 that in January 2024, Colombian Jeffersson Arango Castellanos, alias Harry Potter, 36, pleaded guilty to kidnapping, conspiracy to kidnap, assault, and conspiracy to assault internationally protected persons by kidnapping two unnamed U.S. soldiers on assignment in Bogota, at a bar in Zona T, an upscale entertainment district, on March 5, 2020. A U.S. federal court in Florida sentenced Arango to 48 years and nine months in prison. He targeted the soldiers along with co-conspirators Kenny Julieth Uribe-Chiran and Pedro Jose Silva-Ochoa, who also were named in the indictment. The soldiers were watching a soccer game and dancing when the trio drugged their drinks with benzodiazepine tranquilizers. They took them to Silva-Ochoa's car, stole their phones, wallets and bank cards, and coerced a soldier into divulging his PIN. The kidnappers dropped off the soldiers at various locations in Bogota. One was found in his apartment with no memory of how he got there. The second was spotted stumbling by a passer-by and subsequently taken to a clinic by police. Evidence suggested that the soldiers were sexually assaulted. Arango Castellanos and Uribe-Chiran were arrested in Colombia in December 2020 for similar crimes unrelated to the soldiers' case. Arango Castellanos was extradited to the U.S. in May 2023.

Stars and Stripes reported on December 13, 2024 that Pedro Jose Silva Ochoa, alias Tata, 47, a Colombian man, became the second person to plead guilty in the case in federal court in Florida. He pleaded guilty to conspiracy to kidnap an internationally protected person. He faced life in prison. Colombian Kenny Julieth Uribe Chiran, the last of the three to be extradited to the United States, was slated for trial in February 2025.

June 15, 2021: The *National Desk* reported on December 5, 2023 that medically discharged former Colombian Army officer Andres Fernando Medina Rodriguez, 39, was charged with a bombing that injured three U.S. Army soldiers on June 15, 2021. He was indicted by a federal grand jury in 2022 on charges including conspiring to murder members of the U.S. Uniformed Services and attempted murder. He was extradited to Miami. The indictment says he and co-conspirators planned an attack at the Colombian 30th Army Brigade Base in Cucuta. He allegedly took photographs and video of the areas where the U.S. Army soldiers were primarily located. A co-conspirator had Medina Rodriguez find and purchase a vehicle suitable for conducting a vehicle-borne improvised-explosive device attack. He and his co-conspirators drove a new SUV to Venezuela where it was outfitted with the explosives. On June 15, 2021, he parked the SUV, pulled the detonation pin, ran away, and escaped on a motorcycle driven by a co-conspirator. Medina Rodriguez, 39, was charged with conspiring to use a weapon of mass destruction, conspiring to murder members of the Uniformed Services, providing material support to terrorists, use of a weapon of mass destruction, and attempted murder of members of the Uniformed Services.

Military Times reported on March 12, 2024 that Colombian man Ciro Alfonso Gutierrez Ballesteros, 32, faced charges in a Miami federal court that he, along with an accomplice, tried to murder U.S. Army soldiers with 1st Security Force Assistance Brigade at the Colombian 30th Army Brigade Base in Cucuta, Colombia, near the border with Venezuela, between April and June of 2021 with a car bomb. A federal grand jury indicted Gutierrez Ballesteros on February 16, 2022. Colombia extradited him on December 1, 2023 to the U.S., where his initial court appearance was March 7. He pleaded not guilty. His detention and arraignment hearing was March 12. Prosecutors said alleged co-conspirator Andres Fernando Medina Rodriguez, 39, "used his status as a medically discharged Colombian Army officer to gain access to the base and conduct surveillance". *Military Times* reported that three U.S. Army soldiers and 44 Colombian military personnel were injured in the June 15, 2021 explosion; *Reuters* reported that 29 were hospitalized. By July 2021, Colombian officials had arrested the pair along with six others. Prosecutors said the duo were working for the 33rd FARC front, a faction of the larger FARC guerrilla group that has refused to abide by a 2016 peace agreement between the group and the state.

Military Times reported that on September 12, 2024, two Colombians were sentenced to prison for conspiring and attempting to murder American soldiers. The U.S. Department of Justice announced that Andres Fernando Medina Rodriguez, 40, and Ciro Alfonso Gutierrez Ballesteros, 31, were sentenced to 35 and 30 years, respectively. The extremist faction of the group Las Fuerzas Armadas Revolucionarias, known as the 33rd Front, targeted American troops. Medina Rodriguez, as a former Colombian army officer, entered the base to conduct surveillance. He then drove a bomb-laden SUV to the installation, activated an explosive, and fled on a motorcycle driven by Gutierrez Ballesteros. The duo were extradited to the U.S.

May 10, 2022: *CBS News* reported on January 23, 2023 that El Salvador handed over to Colombian authorities Colombian woman Margareth Lizeth Chacon Zuniga, 42, who was accused of being involved in the "planning, financing and logistics" of the murder of Paraguayan anti-mafia prosecutor Marcelo Pecci during his May 2022 honeymoon on the Colombian island of Baru. She was the seventh suspect detained in the case. She was arrested on January 17, 2023 with Salvadoran Wilber Huezo, 47, who was accused of hiding her. Salvadoran authorities raided two houses where she was hiding and seized Colombian passports, cellphones, laptops, about 15,000 euros ($16,000), dollars, and Colombian and Mexican pesos. In November 2022, the U.S.

Department of State offered a reward of $5 million for information "leading to the arrests and/or convictions of the as yet unknown individuals who conspired or attempted to participate" in the assassination. Four of the detainees, including the hitman, pleaded guilty and were sentenced to 23 years in prison in June 2022. In December 2022, Venezuela's interior minister released a video in which Gabriel Carlos Luis Salinas Mendoza, a Venezuelan citizen arrested in Caracas, told interrogators, "We rented a jet ski, we went to Baru beach (in Colombia) and we executed" the crime. "I got $8,000 and came to Venezuela."

Cuba

1997: On December 30, 2024, Cuban authorities released Salvadoran man Raul Ernesto Cruz Leon, who was convicted of participating in a string of hotel bombings in 1997, after he completed his 30-year prison sentence. Italian tourist Fabio Di Celmo was killed in one of the attacks. The bombings were allegedly masterminded by Cuban exile Luis Posada Carriles, who sought refuge in the United States in 2005 and died in 2018. He was not prosecuted for the attacks. Posada Carriles told the *New York Times* in a 1998 interview that the attacks were meant to frighten tourists from visiting the island. In a 2011 interview, Cruz Leon confessed to placing a bomb in the Hotel Copacabana that killed the Italian tourist. Cruz Leon said he had received the explosives from Salvadoran mercenary Francisco Chavez Abarca, who was arrested in Venezuela in 2010 and extradited to Cuba, where he was also convicted for his role in the attacks.

Haiti

July 7, 2021: *Al-Jazeera* reported that on January 31, 2023 four more suspects in the July 7, 2021 assassination of Haitian President Jovenel Moïse were transferred from Haiti to the United States to face criminal charges with three other suspects in U.S. custody. Haitian-American dual citizens James Solages, 37, and Joseph Vincent, 57, and Colombian citizen German Alejandro Rivera Garcia, 44, were charged with conspiring to commit murder or kidnapping outside the United States. Haitian-American Christian Sanon, 54, was charged with smuggling ballistic vests from the United States to Haiti for use in the assassination plot. A court hearing in Miami was scheduled for February 1, 2023.

The three charged with the assassination faced life in prison. Sanon faced 20 years for his role in supplying the operation.

Al-Jazeera and the *New York Times* reported that the U.S. Department of Justice on February 14, 2023 arrested and charged four Florida residents of "conspiracy to kidnap or kill outside the United States, resulting in death" in connection to the assassination of former Haitian President Jovenel Moïse on July 7, 2021. They included Antonio "Tony" Intriago, owner of the Doral-based Counter Terrorist Unit Security, an affiliate of Ortiz's CTU Federal Academy LLC; Arcángel Pretel Ortiz, a Colombian and "principal" representative of the firm; and Walter Veintemilla, who was accused of funding the operation through his company Worldwide Capital Lending Group, which allegedly extended a $175,000 line of credit to CTU and sent money for ammunition. Frederick Bergmann was accused of conspiring to smuggle ballistic vests for former Colombian soldiers who allegedly carried out the fatal shooting.

The *Miami Herald* reported on February 16, 2023 that Arcángel Pretel Ortiz met with FBI agents and promoted "regime change" in Haiti before the assassination.

Veintemilla was represented by attorney Tara Kudman; Intriago by Emmanuel Perez.

CNN reported on that on March 24, 2023, Haitian citizen Rodolphe Jaar pleaded guilty in U.S. federal court to three counts of providing material support including personnel and services in a conspiracy to kidnap and kill Haitian President Jovenel Moïse on July 7, 2021. The March 26, 2023 *New York Times* added that Jaar faced life in prison and a $250,000 fine. He was arrested in the Dominican Republic and extradited to the U.S. in January 2022. Sentencing was scheduled for June 2, 2023. A proffer attached to the plea agreement indicated that Jaar provided funds used to acquire weapons, provided food and lodging to five other co-conspirators, and provided funding to bribe Haitian officials responsible for Moïse's security.

Al-Jazeera and the *Washington Post* reported on June 2, 2023 that U.S. Judge Jose E. Martinez sentenced Haitian-Chilean businessman, convicted drug trafficker, and former U.S. government informant Rodolphe Jaar, 50, to life in prison for his role in the assassination of Haitian President Jovenel Moïse on July 7, 2021. He pleaded guilty in March 2023 to several charges, including conspiracy to commit murder or kidnapping outside the United States and providing material support resulting in death. Jaar was accused of providing the money used to buy the weapons used in the assassination and to bribe unnamed Haitian officials who were responsible for Moïse's security, and to have provided his co-conspirators with food and lodging. U.S. authorities arrested and charged Jaar in January 2022 in the Dominican Republic. The *New York Times* reported that Judge Jose E. Martinez of the Federal District Court in Miami scheduled a restitution determination for August 2023.

Ten other defendants, including several Haitian Americans, have been charged by U.S. prosecutors in the Southern District of Florida in connection with the assassination; their trial was scheduled for July.

Reuters reported on February 9, 2024 that Florida man Frederick Joseph Bergmann, Jr., pleaded guilty to submitting false or misleading export information and conspiring to offenses against the United States concerning the 2021 assassination of Haitian president Jovenel Moïse. He was accused of smuggling ballistic vests as part of the plot.

The *BBC* and *AFP* reported the same day that a Miami federal court sentenced former U.S. DEA informant and Haitian-American Joseph Vincent, 58, to life for his role in the assassination. He had pleaded guilty two months earlier to taking part in the plot.

AP reported that on February 19, 2024 Judge Walther Wesser Voltaire indicted more than 50 people, including Moïse's widow, Martine Moïse, ex-prime minister Claude Joseph, and the former chief of Haiti's National Police, Léon Charles, who now serves as Haiti's permanent representative to the Organization of the American States. Charles was charged with murder; attempted murder; possession and illegal carrying of weapons; conspiracy against the internal security of the state; and criminal association. Joseph and Martine Moïse, who was injured in the attack, were accused of complicity and criminal association. Also charged with murder were Haitian-American pastor Christian Emmanuel Sanon, wanted to become Haiti's next president and said he thought Moïse was only going to be arrested; Joseph Vincent, a Haitian-American and former informant for the U.S. Drug Enforcement Administration; presidential security chief Dimitri Hérard; former Haitian senator John Joël Joseph; and Haitian judge Windelle Coq, whom authorities say is a fugitive. Sanon, Vincent, and Joseph were earlier extradited to the U.S.

October 7, 2022: *UPI* reported that on October 24, 2023 U.S. federal prosecutors in the District of Columbia filed a three-count indictment charged Haitian Kraze Barye gang leader Vitel'homme Innocent with ordering the kidnapping for ransom of American couple Jean and Marie Odette Franklin, resulting in one of their deaths. The armed gang forced their way into the couple's residence, fatally shooting Marie Odette Franklin and seizing Jean Franklin, who was released 21 days later after his family made ransom payments to the gang.

Innocent was charged with conspiracy to commit hostage taking resulting in death, hostage taking, and attempted hostage taking resulting in death. He remained at large and was believed to reside in Tabarre within the Ouest department of Haiti. He faced a maximum penalty of life in prison or the death penalty if convicted. A reward of $1 million was offered for his arrest or conviction.

The U.S. Department of Justice charged Innocent in November 2022 following allegations that he was involved in the kidnapping of 17 Christian missionaries—16 Americans, one Canadian—who were held captive for 61 days.

MEXICO

September 2014: *UPI* reported that on January 18, 2023, U.S. officials extradited to Mexico Alejandro Tenescalco-Mejia, 41, who was wanted in connection to the 2014 disappearance of 43 students from the Ayotzinapa Rural Teachers' College after being abducted in Iguala. The individual was apprehended in the United States in December 2022 and found to be undocumented. He entered the U.S. on December 14, 2022 by climbing the border wall near Santa Teresa. *UPI* claimed that the students were detained by soldiers and corrupt municipal police before being handed over to the Guerreros Unidos drug gang before being killed. The town's mayor, José Luis Abarca, was arrested and charged with ordering the attack. In 2015, Mexican authorities officially declared the 43 students dead. In August 2022, authorities arrested former Mexican Attorney General Jesus Murillo Karam in connection with the disappearance.

DW reported on June 27, 2023 that Assistant Interior Secretary Alejandro Encinas tweeted that police arrested eight soldiers the previous week in regard to the 2014 apparent kidnap/murder of 43 students from a rural teacher training college in Ayotzinapa who went missing in southern Mexico while traveling by bus to Mexico City. The remains of only three students had been found by mid-2023. Four other soldiers were in pre-trial detention.

PANAMA

July 19, 1994: *UPI* reported on October 29, 2024 that the U.S. Department of State offered a $5 million reward for information regarding the July 19, 1994 crash of Alas Chiricanas Flight 901 in Panama that killed all 21, including three U.S. citizens and several prominent Jewish businessmen on board. The reward also applies to anyone who aided or abetted the terrorist bombing of the flight that was en route to Panama City from France Field in Colon, Panama. Passenger Ali Hawa Jamal was identified as the suspect who brought the bomb onto the aircraft. The Ansar Allah Hizballah offshoot claimed credit.

MIDDLE EAST

AFGHANISTAN

June 30, 2009: *AP,* the *Washington Post,* and *Army Times* reported that on July 25, 2023, U.S. District Judge Reggie B. Walton in Washington, D.C. vacated the court martial conviction of Bowe Bergdahl, a former U.S. Army soldier who pleaded guilty to desertion after he left his post and was captured in Afghanistan by the Taliban. Walton held that military judge Jeffrey Nance failed to disclose that he had applied to the executive branch for a job as an immigration judge, creating a potential conflict of interest. Walton added that presidential candidate Donald Trump had strongly criticized Bergdahl during the 2016 presidential campaign. Bergdahl's lawyers argued that the comments placed undue command influence on Nance. Although Walton rejected the specific argument of undue command influence, he added that a reasonable person could question the judge's impartiality under the circumstances. Bergdahl's defense team included attorney Eugene Fidell.

Military Times reported on September 25, 2023 that the Department of Justice was appealing Senior Judge Reggie Walton's July 25, 2023 dismissal of Bowe Bergdahl's court-martial sentence. DOJ asked the U.S. District Court of Washington to "leave intact the orders of the military courts", including a dishonorable discharge, monetary fine, and demotion to private.

Military.com reported on June 6, 2024 that the Justice Department announced that on May 29, 2024, it filed an appeal at the U.S. Court of Appeals for the District of Columbia Circuit of Judge Reggie Walton's July 2023 dismissal of the conviction and sentence of former U.S. Army Staff Sgt. Bowe Bergdahl, who abandoned

his post with 1st Battalion, 501st Parachute Infantry Regiment in Afghanistan and was held by the Taliban for five years.

November 5, 2009: *Army Times* reported on September 12, 2023 that Judge Colonel Tara Osborn announced that the U.S. Court of Appeals for the Armed Forces unanimously upheld the death penalty for ex-Major Nidal Hasan, who killed 13 in a shooting and wounded dozens of others in a readiness processing center at then-Fort Hood, Texas on November 5, 2009.

August 8, 2012: *Military Times* reported on May 24, 2024 that a graphic novel tells the story of Captain Florent Groberg who received the Medal of Honor for tackling a suicide bomber on August 8, 2012 to save the lives of his fellow soldiers. Groberg, born in France, served with the 4th Infantry Brigade Combat Team, 4th Infantry Division, and was the first foreign-born recipient of the nation's highest military award for valor since the Vietnam War. Four soldiers died in the explosion, including U.S. Army Command Sgt. Maj. Kevin J. Griffin, U.S. Army Maj. Thomas E. Kennedy, U.S. Air Force Maj. Walter D. Gray and USAID Foreign Service Officer Ragaei Abdelfattah, and 16 other soldiers were injured. Groberg lost nearly half of his left calf muscle, and sustained nerve damage, a blown eardrum, and a traumatic brain injury. After nearly three years recovering, he medically retired from the Army on July 23, 2015. Then-President Barack Obama bestowed the Medal of Honor on Groberg on November 12, 2015.

In 1996, his uncle was shot, beheaded, and dismembered by terrorists in Algeria.

Five months after becoming a U.S. citizen, Groberg enlisted in the Army.

August 26, 2021: On April 25, 2023, *Military Times, CBS, UPI, USA Today,* and *AP* reported that a Taliban ground assault earlier in April 2023 killed the ISIS-K terrorist who orchestrated the August 26, 2021 suicide bombing that killed 13 U.S. troops (11 Marines, a sailor, and a soldier) and 170 Afghans at the Abbey Gate of Kabul's Hamid Karzai International Airport during the U.S. withdrawal from Afghanistan.

At first, the U.S. and apparently the Taliban did not know that he was dead in the battles in southern Afghanistan.

Fox News Digital added that the U.S. service members killed included Staff Sgt. Darin T. Hoover, 31, U.S. Marine from Utah; Sgt. Johanny Rosario Pichardo, 25, a U.S. Marine from Massachusetts; Sgt. Nicole L. Gee, 23, a U.S. Marine from California; Cpl. Hunter Lopez, 22, a U.S. Marine from California; Cpl. Daegan W. Page, 23, a U.S. Marine from Nebraska; Cpl. Humberto A. Sanchez, 22, a U.S. Marine from Indiana; Lance Cpl. David L. Espinoza, 20, a U.S. Marine from Texas; Lance Cpl. Jared Schmitz, 20, a U.S. Marine from Missouri; Lance Cpl. Rylee J. McCollum, 20, a U.S. Marine from Wyoming; Lance Cpl. Dylan R. Merola, 20, a U.S. Marine from California; Lance Cpl. Kareem Nikoui, 20, a U.S. Marine from California; Navy Hospital Corpsman Max Soviak, 22, a Navy corpsman from Ohio; and Staff Sgt. Ryan Knauss, 23, a U.S. Army soldier from Tennessee.

CNN and the *New York Times* reported that on March 7, 2024 during President Joe Biden's State of the Union address to Congress, Gold star father Steve Nikoui, 51, Kareem's father, was arrested and charged with a misdemeanor for interrupting the speech. Nikoui yelled "Abbey Gate" and "United States Marines" toward the end of the president's speech after Biden said, "America is safer today than the year I took office." The Capitol Police warned Nikoui to stop and removed him from the House chamber when he did not. Nikoui faced a $50 fine. He was a guest of Representative Brian Mast (R-Florida). The *Daily Beast* reported on March 20, 2024 that Representative Darrell Issa (R-California) announced that the Washington, D.C., Attorney General's office dropped the charges.

GAZA STRIP

September 2014: *UPI* and *N12 News* reported on January 16, 2023 that Hamas released a video purporting to show kidnapped Israeli citizen of Ethiopian descent Avera Mengistu, who was missing since he crossed the border into the Hamas-controlled Gaza Strip in September 2014. He said in the video, "How long will my friends and I remain in captivity here after long years of suffering and pain? Where are the state and the people of Israel?" Mengistu was in his late 20s when he disappeared.

IRAN

September 24, 2018: *AP* and *Mizan* reported on May 6, 2023 that Iran executed by hanging Farajollah Cha'ab, alias Habib Asyoud, an Iranian-Swedish leader of the Arab Struggle Movement for the Liberation of Ahwaz who was accused of masterminding the September 24, 2018 attack on a military parade in Ahvaz in Khuzestan that killed 25 people and wounded 60. Iranian media confirmed that Iranian intelligence officers captured him in Türkiye in November 2019.

October 26, 2022: *Al-Jazeera* reported on July 8, 2023 that Iran publicly hanged Mohammed Ramez Rashidi and Naeem Hashem Qatali for attacking the Shan Cheragh Shrine in Fars Province on October 26, 2022. ISIS claimed credit. The government said 13 people were killed and 40 injured when a gunman from Tajikistan fired an automatic rifle at people in the main compound. Iran had arrested several people for allegedly supporting the killer. The duo were believed to be in touch with ISIS operatives in Afghanistan, providing him a rifle and taking him to the site. Three other men received prison sentences. Mohammad Rahmani, believed to be a leading ISIS operative in Tehran, was sentenced to 25 years. Mostafa Jan Amani was sentenced to 15 years for supporting the armed group. Hamidollah Kaboli was given a five-year sentence.

IRAQ

July 3, 2016: *Al-Jazeera* reported on August 29, 2023 that Iraq hanged three prisoners for an ISIS minibus bomb attack on July 3, 2016 that killed 323 people in Baghdad's Karrada shopping area. The government announced in October 2021 that it had arrested Ghazwan Alzawbaee outside the country as the main suspect. *AFP* reported that Alzawbaee was hanged.

March 2021: *AP, Reuters, BBC,* the *New York Times,* and *Corriere della Sera* reported on December 17, 2024 that Pope Francis, 88, noted in his *Hope: The Autobiography,* ghosted with Carlo Musso, that suicide bombers had planned to attack him during his March 2021 visit to Iraq, but were killed before they could mount the assassination. He wrote that British intelligence informed Iraqi police as soon as Francis arrived in Baghdad that a woman wearing explosives was heading toward Mosul and was planning to blow herself up during the papal visit. He added that "And that a truck was heading there fast with the same intention."

November 8, 2022: *UPI* reported on August 31, 2023 that an Iraqi court sentenced an Iranian and four Iraqis to life imprisonment for killing U.S. citizen Stephen Edward Troell in Baghdad in November 2022. The five admitted they planned to kidnap him, but not kill him. Four other suspects were sought.

AP reported on December 20, 2024 that federal authorities in Manhattan federal court charged Mohammad Reza Nouri, 36, a captain in Iran's paramilitary Revolutionary Guard, with murder and terrorism crimes for the murder. Nouri faced life in prison; one charge carried the death sentence. Nouri, in custody in Iraq, was earlier convicted by an Iraqi court for his role in the killing of Stephen Troell of Tennessee, who died in his car when gunmen pulled up to his street where he lived in Baghdad's Karrada district. Troell worked for Global English Institute, a language school in Baghdad's Harthiya neighborhood, which operated under the auspices of Texas-based non-governmental organization Millennium Relief and Development Services. Acting U.S. Attorney Edward Y. Kim said that Nouri orchestrated the killing, adding "Nouri is alleged to have gathered intelligence on Troell's daily routine and whereabouts, procured weapons and vehicles, and provided safe harbor to the operatives who carried out the sinister plot to brutally attack Troell in front of his wife."

ISRAEL

1986: *Al-Jazeera* and *Wafa* reported on April 7, 2024 that the Palestinian Commission of Detainees and Ex-Detainees Affairs announced that Palestinian novelist and activist Walid Daqqa, imprisoned since 1986, who was suffering from cancer, died in Israel's Shamir Medical Center. Daqqa hailed from Baqa al-Gharbiyye, a predominantly Palestinian city in Israel. He was due to be released in 2025. He was arrested by Israel in 1986 for killing an Israeli soldier. In 1999, he married Sana Salameh while behind bars. Their daughter Milad was born in 2020; she was conceived after his sperm was smuggled out of prison. In 2021, he was diagnosed with myelofibrosis—a rare bone marrow cancer. His works included *Melting the Consciousness, Parallel Time,* and the novel *The Secret of the Oil Story,* which received local and Arab awards.

October 8, 2022: *UPI* reported on January 25, 2023 that 300 Israeli forces demolished the home in the Suafat refugee camp outside East Jerusalem of Palestinian gunman Udai Tamimi, who fatally shot Israel Defense Forces soldier Sgt. Noa Lazar, 18, on the night of October 8, 2022. The IDF said masked terrorists threw pipe bombs and Molotov cocktails at them, injuring two officers, and an armed man, Mohammed Ali, 17, was killed after pointing what was believed to be a weapon at security forces. The weapon was an imitation.

Tamimi was killed on October 19, 2022 while conducting another shooting near a West Bank settlement.

LEBANON

October 23, 1983: *Reuters* reported on March 22, 2023 that U.S. District Judge Loretta Preska in New York ordered Iran's central Bank Markazi and European intermediary Luxembourg-based Clearstream Banking SA to pay $1.68 billion to family members of 241 troops killed in the 1983 car bombing of the U.S. Marine Corps barracks in Lebanon for providing material support to the attackers. Clearstream parent company Deutsche Boerse AG (DB1Gn.DE) was considering appealing the decision. The citation is Peterson et al v. Islamic Republic of Iran et al, U.S. District Court, Southern District of New York, No. 13-09195.

March 16, 1985: *CNN* reported on April 21, 2024 that Terry Anderson, 76, former *AP* Mideast correspondent who was kidnapped by Hizballah in Lebanon in 1985 and held captive for nearly seven years, died at his home in Greenwood Lake, New York. He recently had heart surgery. He was freed on December 4, 1991. His autobiography *Den of Lions* addressed his time in captivity.

August 4, 2020: *AP* and *Reuters* reported that on January 25, 2023 chief prosecutor Judge Ghassan Oweidat ordered the release of the 17 suspects detained in the August 4, 2020 port blast that killed 218 people and injured more than 6,000. He also filed charges against Judge Tarek Bitar, who was leading the investigation, including abusing his authority, conducting work contradictory to his prerogatives, and overstepping his authority.

Al-Jazeera reported on January 26, 2023 that family members of the victims of the port blast tried to break into Beirut's Justice Palace to protest against the lack of progress in the case.

SYRIA

May 12, 2007: *Stars and Stripes* reported that on August 30, 2024, U.S. District Judge Reggie Walton awarded compensation and punitive damages of $364 million from Syria to the families of Spc. Byron Fouty and Staff Sgt. Alex Jimenez, two U.S. soldiers who were tortured and beheaded by Damascus-sponsored Islamic State of Iraq terrorists after their capture on May 12, 2007. They were captured with a third soldier during an assault of a military observation post in the village of al-Taqa, near Yusufiyah, south of Baghdad. Walton had ruled in July 2024 that the Syrian government was liable for the deaths of Fouty, 19, of Oxford, Michigan and Jimenez, 25, of Lawrence, Massachusetts. They and fellow hostage Pfc. Joseph Anzack Jr., 20, of Torrance, California, served in the 10th Mountain Division, based in Fort Drum, New York.

Four other U.S. soldiers and an Iraqi interpreter died in the attack. Anzack's body was found ten days later in the Euphrates River. The remains of Fouty and Jimenez were found in July 2008.

2022: *UPI* reported on March 6, 2024 that British military police arrested five serving British Special Air Services soldiers on suspicion of murder by military authorities in connection with the killing of a suspected ISIS member in Syria in 2022. The SAS members said the suspect posed a threat and that they feared he was about to carry out a suicide attack. The *Daily Telegraph* reported that they said they found a live suicide vest nearby, but the suspect was not wearing it when killed.

TUNISIA

February 6, 2013: *AP, AFP, al-Jazeera,* and *BBC* reported that on March 27, 2024 a Tunisian court sentenced four people to death and two to life in prison on charges regarding the murder of leftwing politician Chokri Belaid, 48, leader of the Popular Front coalition, who was shot in his car outside his home in Tunis on February 6, 2013. Seventeen other defendants were sentenced to two to 120 years. Five people were acquitted. One million people attended Belaid's funeral. He had been a critic of the then-ruling Islamist Ennahda Party, which had claimed that al-Qaeda was involved. ISIS-linked jihadis claimed credit.

YEMEN

February 2022: *The Messenger* and *al-Jazeera* reported on August 11, 2023 that Akm Sufiul Anam, Mazen Bawazir, Bakeel al-Mahdi, Mohammed al-Mulaiki, and Khaled Mokhtar Sheikh, all of whom worked for the U.N.'s Department of Safety and Security, were freed after unknown gunmen had held them in captivity for 18 months after being abducted while returning from a field trip in southern Yemen's Abyan Province. AQAP was suspected.

NORTH AMERICA

CANADA

June 6, 2021: *Al-Jazeera* reported on September 5, 2023 that jury selection began in the trial of Canadian man Nathaniel Veltman, who was accused of killing four members of a Muslim family in London, Ontario, by driving his pickup truck into them on June 6, 2021. He faced four counts of first-degree murder and one count of attempted murder at the Ontario Superior Court of Justice hearing in Windsor. Veltman was represented by attorney Christopher Hicks.

Al-Jazeera added on September 12, 2023 that prosecutor Sarah Shaikh said Veltman was inspired by white nationalism, planned his attack for three months, and acted deliberately and with premeditation. Veltman was represented by attorney Peter Ketcheson.

Al-Jazeera reported on November 17, 2023 that at the end of a 10-week trial, Veltman, 22, was found guilty on four counts of first-degree murder and one of attempted murder. Veltman had worn body armor and a shirt bearing a crusader emblem. He killed Pakistani family members Salman Afzaal, 46; his wife, Madiha Salman, 44; their daughter Yumnah, 15; and Afzaal's mother, Talat, 74, who had been out for a walk near their home. The couple's nine-year-old son suffered serious injuries. Veltman faced life imprisonment with no chance for parole for 25 years. A sentencing hearing was scheduled for December 1.

Al-Jazeera reported on February 22, 2024 that Veltman, 23, was sentenced to life in prison. Judge Renee Pomerance of the Ontario Superior Court of Justice said, "I find that the offender's actions constitute terrorist activity."

June 18, 2022: *CBC News, BBC, Washington Post, al-Jazeera,* and *CNN* reported on May 3, 2024 that Canadian police arrested three Indian Canadians—Karanpreet Singh, Kamalpreet Singh, and Karan Brar—in the shooting death of Sikh separatist leader and Canadian citizen Hardeep Singh Nijjar, 45, outside the Guru Nanak Sikh Gurdwara temple by masked gunmen in a busy car park in Surrey, a Vancouver suburb in British Columbia. The trio were accused of conspiring "with others to commit the murder of Hardeep Singh Nijjar" and with using a firearm "on or about June 18, 2023 (SIC)… to commit first-degree murder." The trio are Indian nationals and non-permanent residents of Canada. Authorities were investigating any ties to the Indian government.

AP reported that on May 11, 2024 Peel Regional Police in Ontario arrested Amandeep Singh, 22, a fourth Indian national living in Canada. The BC Prosecution Service charged him with first degree murder and conspiracy to commit murder. Singh was already in custody for unrelated firearms charges. Singh lived in Brampton, Ontario; Surrey, British Columbia; and Abbotsford, British Columbia.

July 14, 2022: On October 21, 2024, *AP, UPI, Vancouver Sun,* and *al-Jazeera* reported that Tanner Fox and Jose Lopez pleaded guilty in a court in New Westminster, British Columbia, Canada to second-degree murder for the July 14, 2022 killing of former Air India flight 182 bombing suspect Ripudaman Singh Malik, 75, who, with co-defendant Ajaib Singh Bagri, were acquitted in 2005 of murder and conspiracy in two bombings that killed 329 and two people, respectively, in Canada and Japan on June 23, 1985. The duo were initially charged with first-degree murder. Sentencing was set for October 31, 2024. Malik was shot to death in his vehicle outside his business in Surrey, British Columbia, on July 14, 2022. He was a supporter of the separatist Khalistan movement in India. Fox and Lopez have previous criminal records.

UNITED STATES

June 5, 1968: *CNN* reported that the California Department of Corrections and Rehabilitation announced on March 1, 2023 that Sirhan Sirhan, convicted of assassinating U.S. Presidential candidate Senator Robert F. Kennedy in 1968, was denied parole for three years.

August 10, 1969: *Al-Jazeera* and *AP* reported that on July 11, 2023 Charles Manson follower Leslie Van Houten, 73, who was serving a life sentence for fatally stabbing grocery store owner

Leno LaBianca and his wife Rosemary in their Los Angeles home on August 10, 1969, was paroled from the California Institute for Women in Corona and moved into a halfway house. She had served 53 years in prison for stabbing Rosemary more than a dozen times. She was represented by attorney Nancy Tetreault. She was 19 when the Manson Family killed seven people; she was the youngest of the group. The parole board recommended her early release five times since 2016, but she was denied three times by California Governor Gavin Newsom and twice by his predecessor, fellow Democrat Jerry Brown. Charles Manson died in prison in 2017 at age 83; he planned to incite a race war. The words "Death to Pigs" and "Healter Skelter" —a misspelt reference to a Beatles song—were scrawled in the victims' blood on the walls and refrigerator. Van Houten earned a bachelors and masters degree in counseling while in prison. She was a high school cheerleader and homecoming princess.

June 26, 1975: *CNN* reported on July 2, 2024 that the U.S. Parole Commission denied parole to Indigenous activist Leonard Peltier, 79, convicted of the murders of FBI agents Ronald A. Williams and Jack R. Coler in a shootout on the Pine Ridge Reservation in South Dakota on June 26, 1975. He had maintained his innocence. The agents were searching for a robbery suspect. In 1977, a court found Peltier guilty of first-degree murder and sentenced him to two consecutive life terms. He was a leader of the American Indian Movement in the 1970s. He was denied parole in 2009, and in 2017, President Barack Obama denied his clemency request. He will be eligible for another parole hearing in June 2026. He was represented by attorney Kevin Sharp.

October 1982: The *Washington Post* reported on July 11, 2023 that the Cambridge, Massachusetts police superintendent announced the July 9 death of James W. Lewis, 76, suspected of committing the seven Tylenol murders in Chicago in October 1982. No one was ever charged. It was the first major American case of product tampering. Someone had laced Tylenol capsules with cyanide. Johnson & Johnson recalled tens of millions of Tylenol capsule bottles. The *Chicago Tri-*

bune reported that Johnson & Johnson had received a letter demanding $1 million to "stop the killing... As you can see, it is easy to place cyanide (both potassium & sodium) into capsules sitting on store shelves… If you don't mind the publicity of these little capsules, then do nothin…" Lewis was found to have written the letter. He was convicted of trying to extort Johnson & Johnson, and served more than 12 years in prison.

October 11, 1985: The *Los Angeles Times* reported on October 30, 2023 that on October 11, 1985, a bomb exploded at the Santa Ana, California office of the American-Arab Anti-Discrimination committee, killing the group's regional director, Palestinian-American activist Alex Odeh, 41. The FBI called it a terrorist attack and suggested the Jewish Defense League was responsible. No one was formally charged, but the key suspects were Robert Manning, an ex-boxer from Los Angeles, and his wife, Rochelle, both JDL adherents. He was convicted in the 1972 bombing of an Arab activist's Hollywood home, and sentenced to three years' probation. Federal authorities considered him a suspect in four political bombings in 1985, including the Odeh attack; one that killed a suspected Nazi in Paterson, New Jersey; another bomb exploded outside the home of a suspected Nazi in Brentwood, New York, and a fourth that injured two police officers trying to defuse a bomb sent to an Arab American group in Boston. He was convicted in 1993 and sentenced to life in prison for a 1980 mail bombing that killed Patricia Wilkerson, a Manhattan Beach secretary. In 1995, a Los Angeles federal jury convicted real estate agent William Ross of paying Manning to carry out the Wilkerson attack. Prosecutors said Ross intended the bomb for Wilkerson's boss, who had sued Ross over the sale of a Manhattan Beach house.

Manning became eligible for parole in 2001, and lost seven tries. On October 3, 2023, an appellate board reversed the decision in accordance with a federal law that mandates parole for inmates who have served 30 years of a life sentence and are deemed unlikely to reoffend. Now 71, he was due for parole in July 2024 from a federal penitentiary in Phoenix. He was represented by attorney Paul Batista. Manning planned to live with his sister and sell his prison artwork online.

Rochelle Manning, whom prosecutors had implicated in the Wilkerson bombing, died in an Israeli prison in 1994 while fighting extradition to the U.S.

February 26, 1993: Among those who survived the bombing of the World Trade Center on February 26, 1993 and 9/11 were Tim Lang and Lolita Jackson, subjects of features on the 30th anniversary of the bombing by the *New York Times* and *AP*, respectively. The 2/26 memorial fountain was destroyed in the 9/11 attack.

September 11, 2001: *ABC News* reported on September 7, 2023 that President Biden rejected proposed conditions—called "joint policy principles"—for a plea deal for five Guantánamo Bay detainees, including Khalid Shaikh Mohammed—accused of aiding in the 9/11 terrorist attacks. The demands included avoiding solitary confinement and receiving health treatment for injuries the detainees claim were a result of interrogation methods.

On September 8, 2023, the remains of two victims were identified.

By September 11, 2023, more than 17,000 World Trade Center first responders had been diagnosed with cancer; 1,650 had died from the disease, according to the Centers for Disease Control and Prevention.

Al-Jazeera and *NPR* reported on September 22, 2023 that Guantánamo Bay military judge Colonel Matthew McCall found Yemeni 9/11 defendant Ramzi bin al-Shibh mentally incompetent to stand trial because of mistreatment in detention; the prosecution of his four co-defendants was to continue without him. Al-Shibh, delusional and lastingly psychotic, believing that the government was torturing him with invisible rays, remained in custody.

A military medical panel in August diagnosed al-Shibh as having post-traumatic stress disorder (PTSD) with secondary psychosis. He was represented by defense attorney David Bruck.

Defense attorneys said two jurors lied during voir dire.

USA Today and the *Florida Times-Union* reported that DNA investigators identified the 1650th victim of the 9/11 attacks at the World Trade Center as John Ballantine Niven, 44, of Oyster Bay, New York, a senior vice president at Aon Risk Services, an insurance firm on the 105th floor of Tower Two. He was survived by his mother, brother, two sisters, wife, and a son, who was 18 months old when John died.

CNN reported on February 5, 2024 that Bob Beckwith, 91, the former New York City firefighter who, then 69 and a retired grandfather from Long Island, stood alongside President George W. Bush atop a charred fire truck in the rubble of the 9/11 terrorist attacks, died. The cause of Beckwith's death was not immediately released. He had malignant skin cancer, along with other health problems. One of his colleague's sons was among the hundreds of firefighters missing.

CNN, New York Times, USA Today, and *BBC* reported that on July 31, 2024, after 27 months of negotiations, the U.S. reached a pretrial (plea) agreement with alleged 9/11 mastermind Khalid Sheikh Mohammed and fellow accused plotters Walid Muhammad Salih Mubarak Bin 'Attash and Mustafa Ahmed Adam al-Hawsawi that takes the death penalty off the table. The trio agreed to plead guilty to all charges, including the murder of the 2,976 people listed in the charging sheet, in a hearing that could come in early August 2024. In 2008, KSM was charged with, inter alia, conspiracy, murder in violation of the law of war, attacking civilians, attacking civilian objects, intentionally causing serious bodily injury, destruction of property in violation of the law of war, and terrorism and material support of terrorism.

The *New York Times* and *CNN* reported that on August 2, 2024, Defense Secretary Lloyd Austin revoked the plea deal with the three al-Qaeda 9/11 plotters, and relieved of duty Brig. General Susan K. Escallier, the convening authority for military commissions who runs the military courts at Guantánamo Bay, regarding the case. She was still to oversee the other Gitmo cases. Austin said that responsibility for a case of this magnitude should rest with him. Family members of the victims and members of both parties in Congress had criticized the July 31, 2024 plea bargain. KSM was represented by attorney Gary D. Sowards.

AP, New York Times, and *al-Jazeera* reported on November 7, 2024 that Guantánamo Bay military judge Air Force Colonel Matthew McCall ruled that plea agreements struck by Khalid Sheikh Mohammed and co-defendants Walid bin Attash and Mustafa al-Hawsawi are valid, voiding an August 2 order by Defense Secretary Lloyd Austin to throw out the deals, which took the death penalty off the table. On December 30, 2024, a military appeals court ruled against Defense Secretary Lloyd Austin's effort to throw out the plea deals for Khalid Sheikh Mohammed, Walid bin Attash, and Mustafa al-Hawsawi in the 9/11 attacks.

August 28, 2003: *CNN* and *AP* reported that on November 25, 2024 British authorities arrested animal rights extremist Daniel Andreas San Diego, 46, one of the FBI's most wanted fugitives, in a rural area near woods in Conwy, northern Wales. He was ordered held in custody after appearing on November 26 in Westminster Magistrates' Court and faced extradition on charges of planting two bombs that exploded an hour apart in the early morning of August 28, 2003, on the campus of the Chiron biotechnology company in Emeryville, California. He was also accused of setting off another bomb with nails strapped to it at the Shaklee nutritional products company in Pleasanton, California, a month later. The bombs caused no injuries, but authorities said the second bomb was intended to harm first responders. A group called Revolutionary Cells-Animal Liberation Brigade claimed responsibility for the bombings, citing the companies' ties to Huntingdon Life Sciences which animal rights extremists claimed worked with experimental drugs and chemicals on animals while under contract for pharmaceutical, cosmetic, and other companies. Chiron Corporation has since folded into Swiss pharmaceutical corporation Novartis and Huntingdon Life Sciences has since folded into life sciences company Invotiv.

He was indicted in 2004 in a Northern California district court for damaging property with explosives.

FBI Director Christopher Wray noted that in 2009, San Diego became the first person suspected of domestic terrorism to be added to the FBI's Most Wanted Terrorist List. A reward of $250,000 was offered for information leading to his arrest. He was featured on "America's Most Wanted" several times. He was raised in an upper-middle class suburb of Marin County north of San Francisco. His father was the city manager of nearby Belvedere. San Diego had worked as a computer network specialist, was a skilled sailor, and carried a handgun. The *Washington Post* added that his distinctive tattoos included a round image of burning hillsides in the center of his chest with the words "It only takes a spark" printed in a semicircle below; burning and collapsing buildings on the sides of his abdomen and back; and a single leafless tree rising from a road in the center of his lower back.

May 21, 2009: On January 19, 2024, U.S. District Judge Colleen McMahon granted James Cromitie, 58, compassionate release from prison six months after she ordered the release of his three co-defendants, known as the Newburgh Four, for similar reasons. The four men were convicted of terrorism charges in 2010. The judge criticized the FBI for relying on an "unsavory" confidential informant, Shaheed Hussain, for a Bureau-invented conspiracy to blow up New York synagogues and shoot down Air National Guard planes. Cromitie served 15 years of his 25-year minimum sentence. She ordered Cromitie's sentence to be reduced to time served plus 90 days. Cromitie was represented by attorney Kerry Lawrence.

April 15, 2013: The *New York Times* on April 16, 2023 ran several articles on the tenth anniversary of the Boston Marathon bombing, including interviews with victims Dave Fortier, 57, of Newburyport, Massachusetts; Marc Fucarile, 44, of Belton, Texas and Boston; Audrey Epstein Reny, 58 and Gillian Reny, 28, of Boston; Chris Tarpey, 63, of Braintree, Massachusetts; and Allison Elliott, 35, of Taunton, Massachusetts. As of that writing, convicted bomber Tsarnaev was in the second appeal of his death sentence.

AP and *NPR* reported that on March 21, 2024 a three-judge panel of the Boston-based 1st U.S. Circuit Court of Appeals ordered the judge who oversaw April 15, 2013 Boston Marathon bomber Dzhokhar Tsarnaev's trial in 2020 to investigate the defense's claims of juror bias and reevaluate Tsarnaev's death sentence.

June 12, 2016: The Orlando city council agreed on October 23, 2023, to purchase the Pulse nightclub property for $2 million. The city planned to create a memorial to the 49 people who were killed and 53 who were wounded in a mass shooting by Omar Mateen on June 12, 2016. The nonprofit onePulse Foundation scaled back its plans for a $100 million memorial.

October 31, 2017: *USNWR* and *Reuters* reported on January 9, 2023 that the trial presided over by Judge Vernon Broderick of the U.S. District Court in Manhattan began of Sayfullo Saipov, 34, who pleaded not guilty to a 28-count indictment that charged him with murder and for providing material support to ISIS after he used a Home Depot rental truck to kill eight people on a Manhattan pedestrian and bike path along the West Side Highway on Halloween 2017. The U.S. Department of Justice said that it intended to seek the death penalty for the Uzbek national. He also planned to strike the Brooklyn Bridge. He killed five Argentinian tourists and one Belgian tourist and severely injured more than a dozen other people. The dead Argentinians were Hernán Diego Mendoza, Diego Enrique Angelini, Alejandro Damián Pagnucco, Ariel Erlij, and Hernán Ferruchi. Americans Nicholas Cleves, 23, from New York, and Darren Drake, 32, from New Milford, New Jersey, were killed. Belgian woman Ann-Laure Decadt, 31, was a mother of two young sons, and on a trip to New York with her two sisters and her mother. Marion Van Reeth, a Belgian tourist, lost both of her legs.

CNN reported on January 26, 2023 that a federal grand jury found Sayfullo Saipov guilty of all 28 counts, including eight counts of murder in aid of racketeering activity, 18 counts of attempted murder, assault with a dangerous weapon and attempted murder in aid of racketeering activity, attempted murder in aid of racketeering activity, provision of material support to ISIS, and violence and destruction

of a motor vehicle. He had pleaded not guilty. He was represented by defense attorney David Patton.

Saipov came to the United States on a diversity immigrant visa from Uzbekistan in 2010 and was living in New Jersey with his wife and three children.

CNN reported on May 17, 2023 that federal district Judge Vernon Broderick sentenced Sayfullo Saipov to eight consecutive life sentences, a consecutive term of 260 years, and two additional concurrent life sentences. The Uzbek-speaking defendant spoke for nearly an hour to defend his actions, showing no remorse. Some 21 survivors and victims' family members entered victim impact statements.

His attorneys said he was expected to serve his life sentence at the Federal Bureau of Prisons ADX facility in Florence, Colorado, in solitary confinement at least 22 hours/day.

2018: On March 14, 2019, the *Washington Post* reported that federal prosecutors charged Jany Leveille, 36; Siraj Ibn Wahhaj, 40; Hujrah Wahhaj, 38; Subhanah Wahhaj, 36; and Lucas Morton, who were arrested in the summer of 2018 living with 11 neglected children on a New Mexico compound. A superseding indictment said that the group was gathering weapons and training to kill FBI and military personnel, and conspired to provide material support to terrorists. The indictment said the group talked of engaging in jihad and dying as martyrs. Officials found 11 guns on the compound. An earlier indictment said Leveille, an undocumented immigrant from Haiti and the group's leader, wanted to perform an exorcism on the child. Amy Sirignano served as Morton's attorney. On March 22, 2019, the group pleaded not guilty to planning to attack the FBI.

On October 21, 2023, *CNN* reported that on October 17, 2023, a federal jury convicted a father, Siraj Ibn Wahhaj, and several of his family members in a terrorism and kidnapping case in which the decomposed body of his son, Abdul-Ghani Wahhaj, 3, was found on a compound in Amalia, New Mexico. The father had kidnapped his son from his wife in Georgia.

Jurors convicted Siraj Ibn Wahhaj and his brother-in-law Lucas Morton on charges including conspiracy to provide material support to terrorists, providing material support to terrorists, and conspiracy to murder an officer or employee of the United States. Morton was also found guilty of conspiracy to commit kidnapping resulting in death and kidnapping resulting in death.

Hujrah Wahhaj and Subhanah Wahhaj—sisters of Siraj Ibn Wahhaj—were found guilty of conspiracy to commit kidnapping resulting in death and kidnapping resulting in death. They were acquitted of conspiracy to provide material support to terrorists and providing material support to terrorists. Ryan J. Villa and Billy Blackburn served as attorneys for Subhanah Wahhaj.

Jany Leveille agreed to plead guilty to conspiracy to provide material support to terrorists and being in possession of a firearm while unlawfully in the United States.

The prosecutors said the group took the child to New Mexico, withheld his anti-seizure medication, and conducted "an exhausting regimen of daily spiritual exorcisms". The boy died less than two weeks after the kidnapping. His body was found in an underground tunnel.

Prosecutors said the defendants "established a community centered on the belief that Abdul Ghani would return as Jesus Christ to pass judgment on corrupt institutions". They built "a fortified base" featuring an extensive collection of weapons where members practiced tactical training, they said. The group believed that the FBI was watching them and was training to kill those who refused to share their beliefs.

The four convicted defendants each faced up to life in prison. Leveille faced up to 17 years in prison.

Some of the child abuse charges brought by the state were dismissed by a state judge in 2022 due to the prosecution's procedural error.

October 27, 2018: *AP* reported that on May 2, 2023, U.S. District Judge Robert Colville ruled against a defense motion to take the death penalty off the table in the federal trial of Robert Bowers, charged with 63 criminal counts in the killings of 11 worshippers at the Tree of Life synagogue on October 27, 2018.

CNN reported on June 16, 2023 that a federal jury in the U.S. District Court for the Western District of Pennsylvania found Bowers, 50, guilty on all 63 counts for the mass shooting in Pittsburgh's Squirrel Hill neighborhood during which he killed 11 worshippers and wounded six people, including four police officers who responded to the scene. He was eligible for the death penalty. He was convicted of, inter alia, 11 capital counts of obstruction of free exercise of religious beliefs resulting in death, 11 capital counts of use of a firearm to commit murder during and in relation to a crime of violence, and 11 counts of hate crimes resulting in death. The jury had deliberated for five hours. Bowers was represented by defense attorneys Judy Clarke and Elisa Long.

CNN and *AP* reported that on July 13, 2013, a jury found Bowers eligible for the death penalty. He had planned the attack for six months and expressed regret that he did not kill more people.

CNN reported that on August 2, 2023, a jury, after deliberating for 10 hours, unanimously determined that Robert Bowers, 50, should receive the death penalty due to all five of the prosecution's aggravating factors put forth during the sentencing phase of the trial. The defense put forth 115 mitigating factors. U.S. District Judge Robert Colville formally sentenced Bowers to death on August 3, 2023.

Those killed by the anti-Semitic white supremacist included Joyce Fienberg, 75; Richard Gottfried, 65; Rose Mallinger, 97; Dr. Jerry Rabinowitz, 66; intellectually challenged brothers David Rosenthal, 54, and Cecil Rosenthal, 59; Bernice Simon, 84, and her husband, Sylvan Simon, 86; Dan Stein, 71; Melvin Wax, 87; and Irving Younger, 69. He also wounded two worshippers and five police officers.

August 3, 2019: *CNN* reported on February 8, 2023 that Patrick Crusius, 24, pleaded guilty to all 90 federal charges, including hate crimes resulting in death, use of a firearm to commit murder during and in relation to a crime of violence, hate crimes involving attempt to kill, and use of a firearm during and in relation to a crime of violence, regarding the 2019 mass shooting at a Walmart in El Paso, Texas in which he killed 23 people, including eight Mexican citizens. The prosecution recommended 90 consecutive life sentences, not the death penalty. He also faced state charges, including capital murder.

CNN and *AP* reported that on July 7, 2023 U.S. District Judge David Guaderrama sentenced Crusius to 90 consecutive life terms for hate crimes, firearms offenses, and murder. He was represented by Joe Spencer, Jr. State prosecutors were seeking the death penalty.

CNN reported that on September 25, 2023, gunman Patrick Crusius agreed to pay $5,557,005.55 in restitution to claimants in the federal case. Federal Judge David Guaderrama approved the agreement.

December 6, 2019: The *USA Today Network, Pensacola News Journal,* and *Florida Times-Union* reported that on May 2, 2024, federal Judge M. Casey Rodgers dismissed the lawsuit filed against Saudi Arabia for the 2019 terrorist attack at Naval Air Station Pensacola by a Royal Saudi Air Force 2nd Lieutenant training at the base that killed sailors. The families of Ensign Joshua Kaleb Watson, Naval Aircrewman 3rd Class Mohammed Sameh Haitham and Naval Aircrewman 3rd Class Cameron Scott Walters appealed the decision to the Eleventh Circuit of the United States Court of Appeals.

2020: On October 25, 2023, *Military.com* reported that in 2020 Liam Collins, a former Marine lance corporal stationed at Camp Lejeune, North Carolina, was initially charged with two other conspirators and indicted in connection to a neo-Nazi white supremacist plot to target energy facilities in the northwest U.S. The infantryman was thrown out of the Corps. *WGHP* reported that Collins pleaded guilty to interstate transportation of an unregistered firearm on October 24, 2023. By 2021, there were five defendants, including an Army National Guardsman, Joseph Maurino; and two other former Marines, Justin Hermanson and Jordan Duncan. Court records indicated that Collins discussed recruiting veterans into "a modern day SS" on the now-defunct neo-Nazi message board Iron March, stole military equipment, including magazines for assault-style rifles, asked others to buy explosives, and discussed with his co-defendants plans to manufacture firearms. He initially had pleaded

not guilty to destruction of an energy facility and other weapons-related charges. Duncan, who became a defense contractor, allegedly gathered information on firearms, explosives, and nerve toxins. The indictments added that by 2020, the group was considering having every member purchase 50 pounds of an explosive and creating thermite. In October 2020, a handwritten list of around a dozen locations—transformers, substations, and other components of the power grid—in and around Idaho was discovered in a suspect's possession. *Newsweek* reported that Collins served for three years in the Corps before his separation and was on active duty when he made the Iron March message board posts. He often used the aliases Disciple and Niezgoda. Collins was set to be sentenced on January 23, 2024 in Wilmington, North Carolina. Hermanson and Maurino, who took plea deals in 2022 and 2023, were awaiting sentencing.

September 2020: On January 25, 2023, *AFP* reported that French-Canadian woman Pascale Cecile Veronique Ferrier, 55, pleaded guilty to federal charges of sending letters containing ricin to former president Donald Trump and to eight Texas law enforcement officials. Her plea deal called for her to serve 262 months in prison for violating laws on possession of biological weapons. In September 2020, she mailed an envelope from Canada to the White House addressed to then-president Trump containing ricin. The letter contained "threatening language" and called on Trump to withdraw from the upcoming election. "I found a new name for you: 'The Ugly Tyrant Clown' I hope you like it... If it doesn't work, I'll find better recipe for another poison, or I might use my gun when I'll be able to come. Enjoy!" She also tweeted for someone to "shoot Trump in the face". She mailed similar letters with ricin and threatening language to the Texas officials. In 2019 she was detained in Texas for 10 weeks for weapons possession. She tried to enter the United States at an official crossing in Buffalo, New York, where she was arrested after officials found a gun and hundreds of rounds of ammunition in her car.

Al-Jazeera reported on August 18, 2023 that U.S. District Judge Dabney Friedrich, approving a plea agreement, sentenced Pascale Ferrier, 56, to 262 months. She had pleaded guilty to violating biological weapons laws. She was represented by attorney Eugene Ohm. Ferrier had earned a master's degree in engineering and raised two children as a single parent.

October 2020: *CNN* reported on September 15, 2023 that a court in Michigan acquitted Eric Molitor and brothers William and Michael Null on one count of providing material support for a terrorist act and possessing a firearm when committing or attempting to commit a felony in the 2020 plot to kidnap Michigan Governor Gretchen Whitmer from her northern Michigan vacation cottage.

AP reported on December 7, 2023 that Judge Charles Hamlyn sentenced the last defendants in the October 2020 plot, sending Shawn Fix to state prison for three years and putting Brian Higgins, a resident of Wisconsin Dells, Wisconsin, on three years probation. Higgins had spent 217 days in jail after his arrest and was addressing mental health needs. He had pleaded guilty to attempting to provide material support for terrorism. Fix, a suburban Detroiter, had pleaded guilty to providing material support for terrorism.

CNN reported on May 19, 2024 that Eric Molitor, 40, of Cadillac, Michigan, filed to run in the August Republican primary to unseat incumbent county sheriff Trent Taylor, of deep-red Wexford County in Northern Michigan. Molitor previously worked as a subcontractor in the security field.

The Michigan Democratic Party added that Michele Lundgren, one of the 16 people facing charges related to the 2020 election subversion plot in Michigan, was running in a Republican primary for a state House seat.

January 6, 2021: *Reuters* reported on January 5, 2023 that the estate of U.S. Capitol Police Officer Brian Sicknick, who died at age 42 from a series of strokes on January 7, 2021 following the Capitol riot, sued former President Donald Trump in U.S. District Court in Washington, D.C., for wrongful death, claiming that he incited his supporters to commit violence that day. The lawsuit argued that "Defendant Trump intentionally riled up the crowd and directed and encouraged a mob to attack the U.S. Capitol and attack those who opposed them… The violence that followed, and the injuries that violence caused, including the injuries sustained by Officer Sicknick and his eventual death, were reasonable and foreseeable consequences of Defendant Trump's words and conduct." The lawsuit also accused Trump of violating Sicknick's civil rights, assault, and negligence, and sought $10 million in damages. Two January 6 rioters were also named in the complaint.

On January 7, 2023, Derrick Evans, 37, of West Virginia, who had served three months in prison after pleading guilty to a felony civil disorder charge for his role in the riot, announced that he would run for the House of Representatives in 2024.

On January 12, 2023, the trial began of former Proud Boys leader Enrique Tarrio and four lieutenants—Ethan Nordean, of Auburn, Washington, a PB chapter president; Joseph Biggs of Ormond Beach, Florida; Zachary Rehl, president of the PB chapter in Philadelphia; Dominic Pezzola, a PB member from Rochester, New York—for seditious conspiracy. *AP* reported on August 18, 2023 that the Justice Department sought 33 years in prison for Enrique Tarrio, the former Proud Boys national chairman convicted of seditious conspiracy in May 2023, and for Joseph Biggs of Ormond Beach, Florida, a self-described Volusia County Proud Boys organizer. DOJ also requested 30 years for Zachary Rehl, who was president of the Proud Boys chapter in Philadelphia; 27 years for Ethan Nordean of Auburn, Washington, who was a Proud Boys chapter president; and 20 years for Dominic Pezzola, a Proud Boys member from Rochester, New York, who was acquitted of seditious conspiracy but convicted of other serious charges. Attorney Norm Pattis was among the defense team who argued before U.S. District Judge Timothy J. Kelly in Washington's federal court.

CNN reported on May 4, 2023 that a jury in Washington, D.C. released a partial verdict in which it found guilty of seditious conspiracy four Proud Boys—Enrique Tarrio; Ethan Nordean; Joseph Biggs; Zachary Rehl—for their roles to forcibly prevent the peaceful transfer of power from then-President Donald Trump to Joe Biden after the 2020 election. They had been charged with three separate conspiracy counts, obstructing the Electoral College vote, and tampering with evidence. Five defendants were also found guilty of obstruction of an official proceeding; conspiracy to prevent an officer from discharging any duties; obstruction of law enforcement during civil disorder; and destruction of government property and aiding and abetting. The jury did not reach a verdict on seditious conspiracy against Dominic Pezzola, not a Proud Boys leader and inactive in PB chats. The jury did not reach a verdict with regard to some defendants on charges of assaulting, resisting, or impeding certain officers, destruction of government property, and aiding and abetting, but returned for further deliberation.

On September 5, 2023, District Judge Timothy Kelly sentenced Tarrio to 22 years in prison for seditious conspiracy and leading a failed plot to prevent the transfer of power from Donald Trump to Joe Biden. Judge Kelly noted that Tarrio had shown no remorse. Tarrio was represented by attorneys Sabino Jauregui and Nayib Hassan. DOJ had requested 33 years.

CNN reported on August 31, 2023 that Judge Kelly sentenced Joe Biggs to 17 years in prison.

NBC News reported on August 31, 2023 that Zachary Rehl was sentenced to 15 years.

The *Washington Post* reported that on August 31, 2023, Judge Kelly sentenced Nordean, 33, to 18 years and Pezzola, 46, to 10 years. After the hearing, Pezzola yelled that Trump had won the election.

Daytona Beach News-Journal, MSNBC, Florida Times-Union, and *USA Today* reported on November 12, 2024 that several individuals, including Volusia County, Florida Proud Boys leader and Ormond Beach, Florida; resident Joe Biggs, 40, convicted of crimes in the riot, were planning to seek a pardon from President-elect Donald Trump. U.S. District Judge Timothy Kelly sentenced Biggs to 17 years in prison in August 2023 with a release date from the Talladega Federal Correctional Institute in Alabama of January 6, 2036. Biggs was represented by attorney Norman Pattis. Biggs was convicted of seditious conspiracy, conspiracy to obstruct

an official proceeding, obstruction of an official proceeding, conspiracy to use force, intimidation, or threats to prevent officers of the United States from discharging their duties, interference with law enforcement during a civil disorder, and destruction of government property.

CNN reported on January 20, 2023 that the FBI had arrested three active-duty Marines who work in intelligence for breaching the U.S. Capitol. One allegedly espoused support for a second civil war. Cpl. Micah Coomer and Sgts. Joshua Abate and Dodge Dale Hellonen faced several charges, including disorderly conduct in a Capitol building. Coomer had posted selfies inside the Capitol on *Instagram*, and had written messages that "(E)verything in this country is corrupt. We honestly need a fresh restart... I'm waiting for the boogaloo... Civil war 2." Coomer is an Intelligence Surveillance Reconnaissance System Engineer based out of Camp Pendleton in California. Abate is a Special Communication Signals Analyst with the Marine Corps Cryptologic Support Battalion at Fort Meade in Maryland. Hellonen is a Special Comm Signals Analyst at Camp Lejeune in North Carolina.

CNN reported that a Washington, D.C. jury on January 23, 2023 convicted Joseph Hackett, Roberto Minuta, Edward Vallejo, and David Moerschel—three members of the Oath Keepers and a fourth person associated with the far-right militia group—of seditious conspiracy. Judge Amit Mehta placed them under house arrest until sentencing. Minuta is an Oath Keeper from New Jersey. Hackett was alleged to be a Florida Oath Keepers recruiter. Moerschel was an alleged part of the stack formation that prosecutors said acted as a "battering ram" that pushed through the mob and into the Capitol. Vallejo was one of the alleged leaders of the armed quick reaction force, who prosecutors said called for "guerilla war" the morning of January 6. The four were also found guilty of conspiracy to obstruct an official proceeding, obstruction of an official proceeding, aiding and abetting, and conspiracy to prevent a member of Congress from discharging their official duties. Hackett was found guilty of tampering with documents or proceedings. Hackett and Moerschel were found not guilty of destruction of government property. Minuta and Moerschel were found not guilty of tampering with documents or proceedings.

ABC News added on June 2, 2023 that co-defendant Joseph Hackett, a former Florida chiropractor, was sentenced to three years and six months. He was found guilty in January 2023 of conspiring to commit sedition against the United States. That jury convicted both men of three additional felonies, finding they had plans to disrupt the Electoral College certification. Hackett told the judge, "I regret ever joining the Oath Keepers" and that his wife and young daughter had received threats since he was first identified as someone who breached the Capitol.

CNN reported on June 1, 2023 that Judge Amit Mehta sentenced Roberto Minuta, one of Oath Keepers leader Stewart Rhodes's "most trusted men", to 54 months in prison for seditious conspiracy, conspiracy to obstruct an official proceeding, obstruction of an official proceeding, aiding and abetting, and conspiracy to prevent a member of Congress from discharging their official duties. He was acquitted of one charge of tampering with documents. Minuta was not initially at the Capitol but sped over in a golf cart, and was a part of a security detail on January 6 for Roger Stone. Minuta told the judge that he grew angry over Covid-19 restrictions in New York, and claimed he and his family received "in person death threats by Anitfa".

Prosecutors asked for 10 years for Oath Keeper David Moerschel. *CNN* reported on June 2, 2023 that Judge Amit Mehta sentenced Oath Keeper David Moerschel, alias Hatsy, a neurophysiologist, to three years in prison. He was a member of the "stack formation" that served as a battering ram against police defenses of the Capitol, contributed AR-style firearms to the militia's cache of weapons staged outside Washington, D.C., and was part of a group looking for House Speaker Nancy Pelosi inside the Capitol during the riot. Mehta noted that Moerschel dropped out of the Oath Keepers on January 7, 2021.

CNN reported that on January 23, 2023, a Washington, D.C., jury convicted Richard Barnett, 62, alias Bigo, of Arkansas, who had been photographed putting his feet on a desk inside House Speaker Nancy's Pelosi's office during the riot, on eight federal counts, including entering and remaining in a restricted area with a deadly or dangerous weapon and obstructing an official proceeding. He was released on home detention with a GPS ankle monitor until sentencing in early May. He faced 20 years in prison. He was represented by attorney Joseph McBride. Barnett claimed he was pushed inside the Capitol and was just looking for a bathroom. *CNN* reported on May 24, 2023 that District Judge Christopher Cooper sentenced Richard Barnett to four and one half years in prison. He said he would appeal.

CNN reported on January 27, 2023 that D.C. District Judge Thomas Hogan sentenced Julian Khater, who assaulted United States Capitol Police Officer Brian Sicknick with pepper spray on January 6, 2021, to 80 months behind bars. Khater pleaded guilty in September 2022 to two counts of assaulting, resisting, or impeding officers with a dangerous weapon. Khater was also ordered to pay a $10,000 fine and $2,000 in restitution. Co-defendant George Tanois pleaded guilty that summer to disorderly conduct and entering and remaining in a restricted building. He was sentenced to time served and one year of supervised release. He had spent more than five months behind bars. Sicknick died on January 7, 2021 after suffering several strokes attributed to the riot. Khater had sprayed several officers, including Sicknick, with bear spray.

CNN reported on February 9, 2023 that D.C. District Judge Trevor McFadden sentenced Kevin Seefried of Laurel, Delaware, to three years in prison. Seefried pleaded guilty in June 2022 to the five charges he faced, including obstructing an official proceeding, disorderly conduct in a Capitol building, and entering and remaining in a restricted area. He had carried a large Confederate flag inside the Capitol during the riot and was part of the mob that chased U.S. Capitol Police Officer Eugene Goodman, jabbing the base of the flag pole toward him multiple times to try to push him away. Goodman testified that Seefried "was saying things like F**k you, I'm not leaving, where are the members at, where are they counting the votes… You can shoot me, man, but we're coming in." Hunter Seefried, his son, had joined his father in the

Capitol, and was convicted of several charges and sentenced in October 2022 to two years. Eugene Ohm served as Kevin Seefried's attorney.

Newsweek reported on March 27, 2024 that four Supreme Court justices agreed to review *Fischer v. United States*, which challenged the Department of Justice's "obstruction of an official proceeding" charge, which has been used against January 6 defendants for allegedly disrupting the Electoral College certification. Several defendants filed for release pending the final ruling. Among them was Kevin Seefried. On March 26, 2024, Judge Trevor McFadden ruled that Seefried could be released from his prison sentence awaiting the court's decision.

USA Today, the *Florida Times-Union*, and *Sarasota Herald-Tribune* reported on February 12, 2023 that self-identified Proud Boy Daniel Lyons Scott, alias Milkshake, of Bradenton, Florida, pleaded guilty on February 9 to charges related to the riot. He was arrested in early 2021. In video of the riot, he was wearing a black ballistic vest, yellow goggles, and a hat with the words "God Guns & Trump". He was charged with obstruction of an official proceeding, assaulting, resisting, or impeding certain officers. He faced 20 and eight years, respectively, on those charges. Sentencing was scheduled for May 23.

UPI reported that the FBI in Lecanto, Florida on February 26, 2023 arrested Jesse James Rumson, alias Sedition Panda, a man accused of storming the U.S. Capitol wearing a giant costume panda headpiece. He was charged with, inter alia, assaulting a law enforcement officer, entering a restricted building, and an act of physical violence on Capitol grounds.

CNN reported on March 6, 2023 that District Judge Carl Nichols issued a bench warrant for the arrest of Florida woman Olivia Michele Pollock, who did not show up for trial in a Washington, D.C. court on federal charges related to the riot. She had been missing since late February. She was represented by attorney Elita Amato. Jonathan Pollock, Olivia's brother, evaded authorities since he was first charged in July 2021. The FBI offered a $15,000 reward for information on his whereabouts. Another bench warrant was issued for codefendant Joseph Hutchinson.

On January 6, 2024, *CNN* reported that in the morning, the FBI arrested three people in Florida—Jonathan Daniel Pollock, Olivia Michele Pollock, and Joseph Daniel Hutchinson, III—who were charged in connection with the U.S. Capitol attack and were considered fugitives after fleeing from law enforcement. They were scheduled to appear in federal court in Ocala, Florida, on January 8, 2024. Olivia Pollock was set to go to trial on federal charges in March 2023, but did not show up to court in Washington, D.C. Her brother, Jonathan Pollock, had evaded authorities since he was charged in July 2021. The FBI had offered thousands of dollars for information on his whereabouts. Prosecutors accused Jonathan Pollock of punching two officers in the face, kneeing a police officer, dragging an officer down stairs, charging at law enforcement with a flag pole, grabbing an officer's neck and pinning them to the ground, and ramming a police shield into an officer's neck. Hutchinson and Olivia Pollock pleaded not guilty. Jonathan Pollock did not enter a formal plea.

The *New York Times* reported on March 12, 2023 that a federal jury in Washington, D.C. found retired NYPD officer Sara Carpenter, 53, guilty of seven felony and misdemeanor charges that included civil disorder, obstruction of official proceeding, and entering or remaining in a restricted building or grounds. Prosecutors said she pushed against and slapped the arms of police officers, yelled "I'm an animal", and wielded a tambourine. She was represented by attorney Michelle Gelernt. Sentencing was scheduled for July 14, 2023.

AP and *Air Force Times* reported on March 17, 2023 that retired Air Force Lt. Col. Larry Rendall Brock, Jr., 55, of Grapevine, a Dallas, Texas, suburb, who was dressed in tactical combat gear and carrying zip-tie handcuffs on the Senate floor, was sentenced to two years in prison. He graduated from the Air Force Academy and flew combat missions in Afghanistan. He was on active duty until 1998 and retired from the Air Force Reserve in 2014. U.S. District Judge John Bates also sentenced him to two years of supervised release and ordered him to perform 100 hours of community service. Bates convicted Brock in November 2022 of all six counts in his indictment, including felony obstruction of an official proceeding, and five misdemeanors, after a trial without a jury. Brock had posted on *Facebook* on November 9, 2020, "When we get to the bottom of this conspiracy we need to execute the traitors that are trying to steal the election, and that includes the leaders of the media and social media aiding and abetting the coup plotters." On Christmas Eve 2020, he told a *Facebook* contact of a "plan of action if Congress fails to act" on January 6, a "main task" of which was to "seize all Democratic politicians and Biden key staff and select Republicans... Begin interrogations using measures we used on al-Qaeda to gain evidence on the coup." He called for a "general pardon for all crimes up to and including murder of those restoring the Constitution and putting down the Democratic Insurrection... Do not kill LEO unless necessary." Brock was represented by defense attorney Charles Burnham, who called it "inconceivable that (Brock) was motivated by anything other than genuine concern for democracy". Brock was employed as a commercial airline pilot on January 6. The Federal Aviation Administration revoked his licenses after his January 2021 arrest.

Military Times reported on March 1, 2024 that the U.S. Court of Appeals for the D.C. Circuit upheld retired Air Force officer Larry Brock's conviction but ordered a new sentence. Brock, of Grapevine, Texas, stormed the U.S. Capitol dressed in combat gear, including a helmet and tactical vest. Brock picked up a discarded pair of zip-tie handcuffs and was photographed holding them on the Senate floor. The court said a judge wrongly applied an enhancement that lengthened the recommended prison sentence range under federal guidelines. U.S. District Judge John Bates sentenced Brock in 2023 to two years in prison after Brock was convicted of a felony charge of obstruction of an official proceeding and misdemeanor offenses.

CNN reported on March 20, 2023 that six Oath Keepers were convicted of various charges related to the riot. Sandra Parker, Laura Steele, Connie Meggs, and William Isaacs were found guilty on all of the charges related to entering the Capitol during the riot and attempting to make their way to the Senate chamber before being deterred by pepper spray and police officers in the building. Michael Greene, a military veteran accused of being the Oath Keepers "operation leader" on January 6, and Bennie Parker, the husband of Sandra, were convicted of entering and remaining on restricted grounds but acquitted of conspiracy to stop Congress from certifying Joe Biden's electoral victory. The jury was deadlocked on two counts for those two defendants and continued to deliberate. District Judge Amit Mehta rejected the defense's request for a mistrial. The defense team included attorney William Shipley, Eugene Rossi, and Juli Haller, the latter who had served in the Trump Administration.

UPI reported on March 23, 2023 that federal District Court Judge Amy Berman Jackson sentenced Capitol rioter Riley Williams, who led a mob to the office of House Speaker Nancy Pelosi, to three years in prison. Williams was convicted on six counts in November 2022 relating to storming the Capitol. She was convicted on two felony charges: interfering with law enforcement officers during a civil disorder and resisting or impeding law enforcement officers; and on four misdemeanor offenses. She stole Pelosi's laptop and gavel, but the jury deadlocked on whether to charge her for aiding and abetting the theft of the laptop. She was represented by federal public defender Lori Ulrich.

The *Daytona Beach News-Journal* and *USA Today Network* reported that federal prosecutors asked federal Judge Beryl A. Howell in Washington, D.C. to sentence Howard B. Adams, 62, of Edgewater, Florida, to a year and a day in prison, three years supervised release, $2,000 restitution, a $900 fine, and a special assessment of $100. Adams pleaded guilty on January 26, 2023 to obstructing, impeding, or interfering with a law enforcement officer. He faced five years in prison, three years of supervised release, and a $250,000 fine. He was first charged with six counts related to the riot. He was represented by attorney Gregory Smith. Adams had skipped two court appearances in November 2022. He ran High Rise Caulking LLC, and had no previous criminal record. He had moved to Florida in 2002 to open a since-closed skydiving instruction firm. He was a believer in the "sovereign citizen" movement, declaring himself a "Georgian" in an August 4, 2022 letter disputing jurisdiction.

Military.com reported that on April 2, 2023, the FBI arrested active-duty Navy petty officer first class David Elizalde in Arlington, Virginia, on four federal misdemeanor charges, including disorderly conduct inside the Capitol building. The aviation structural mechanic was the fifth active-duty service member to be arrested for the riot. He drove from Norfolk, Virginia, where his aircraft carrier, the *USS Harry Truman*, was docked. The Naval Criminal Investigative Service approached him in December 2021 and interviewed him in April 2022. He was currently stationed at a maintenance department in Rota, Spain. After enlisting in June 2007, he served on the aircraft carriers *USS Eisenhower* and *USS Harry Truman*. He earned four Navy and Marine Corps Achievement medals and five Good Conduct Medals, plus several unit awards.

Military Times reported on April 18, 2024 that Leading Petty Officer 1st Class David Elizalde, 46, an active-duty service member who was convicted for his participation in the riot, pleaded for two weeks of home confinement plus community service and restitution, vice probation, so that he could remain in the Navy working during the week. He was represented by attorney Stephen Brennwald. Elizalde served in the Navy for 17 years. He was convicted in 2023 of one count of parading, demonstrating, or picketing in a Capitol building, a misdemeanor that carries a sentence of up to six months in prison and a fine of up to $5,000. The Department of Justice recommended that he be sentenced to three years of probation, 60 hours of community service, and 30 days of intermittent confinement, meaning he would be incarcerated during nights, weekends, or at other intervals. *Military Times* reported on April 19, 2024 that a judge sentenced him to 30 days of home detention and a $2,500 fine.

CNN reported on May 2, 2023 that authorities in Oregon had arrested Jared Wise, who was a special agent and supervisory special agent with the FBI from 2004 through 2017, on charges related to the attack on the U.S. Capitol. Wise was charged with four federal crimes, including illegally entering and remaining in the Capitol building. Investigators said he confronted officers and encouraged other rioters who attacked law enforcement. After he moved to the Capitol's Upper West Terrace, he told police officers, "You guys are disgusting. I'm former—I'm former law enforcement... You're disgusting. You are the Nazi. You are the Gestapo. You can't see it... Shame on you! Shame on you! Shame on you!" Prosecutors said he shouted to rioters attacking police in front of him, "Kill 'em! Kill 'em! Kill 'em!"

CNN reported that on May 2, 2023 the FBI arrested Daniel Ball, 38, of Homosassa, Florida, for setting off an "explosive device" in the U.S. Capitol tunnel during the insurrection. Ball was arrested in late April 2023 by the Citrus County Sheriff's Office for allegedly assaulting seven people including two law enforcement officers in unrelated charges in Florida. Some police experienced impaired hearing for months. He was charged with assaulting police officers, engaging in physical violence at the Capitol, and entering a restricted area with a deadly or dangerous weapon.

CNN reported on May 5, 2023 that District Judge Amit Mehta sentenced Peter Schwartz, 49, of Pennsylvania, who threw a folding chair at law enforcement and repeatedly used pepper spray on police during the riot, to more than 14 years in prison. In December 2022, a jury found Schwartz guilty on 10 charges, including four felony charges of assaulting, resisting, or impeding officers using a dangerous weapon. His rap sheet included 38 felony convictions dating to 1991 and was a significant factor behind his sentence. Schwartz was on probation on January 6, 2021. He had at least one firearm in his possession at his residence in Pennsylvania. He had two prior convictions of possessing a firearm after being convicted of a felony. Prosecutors had requested a $70,000 fine. He was represented by attorney Dennis Boyle.

CNN reported on May 5, 2023 that prosecutors asked federal Judge Amit Mehta to sentence Oath Keepers leader Stewart Rhodes to 25 years in prison for seditious conspiracy and to apply the enhanced terrorism sentencing penalties. Sentencing was scheduled for May 25.

CNN and *Military Times* reported on May 25, 2023 that District Judge Amit Mehta sentenced founder and leader of the Oath Keepers Stewart Rhodes, 58, to 18 years in prison. It is the first handed down in over a decade for seditious conspiracy. Rhodes expressed no remorse. Mehta ruled that Rhodes's actions constituted domestic terrorism. Rhodes was also found guilty of obstructing an official proceeding and tampering with documents. His deputy Kelly Meggs was sentenced to 12 years. On July 12, 2023, *AP* reported that the U.S. Department of Justice was appealing the 18-year-prison sentence, as well as sentences of other far-right extremists. Rhodes's sentence was below the recommended range under federal guidelines and less than the 25 years the Justice Department had requested. Rhodes's attorney, James Lee Bright, called the appeal "surprising". DOJ intended to appeal the sentences of other Oath Keepers, including Florida chapter leader Kelly Meggs.

Naples Daily News and *USA Today* reported on May 17, 2023 that U.S. District Judge Royce Lamberth on May 12, 2023 convicted East Naples, Florida Proud Boy Christopher Worrell, 52, on seven of 19 counts, including:

- Obstruction of an official proceeding

- Entering or remaining in a restricted building or grounds with a deadly or dangerous weapon

- Disorderly or disruptive conduct in a restricted building or grounds with a deadly or dangerous weapon

- Engaging in physical violence in a restricted building or grounds with a deadly or dangerous weapon

- Act of physical violence in the U.S. Capitol grounds or buildings

- Civil disorder

- Assaulting, resisting, or impeding certain officers using a dangerous weapon

Lamberth scheduled sentencing for August 18, 2023. Worrell had waived a jury trial. He was represented by William Shipley and court-approved custodian Trish Priller, 52.

CNN reported on August 19, 2023 that Proud Boys member Christopher Worrell, 52, who was convicted in a bench trial on seven charges and was scheduled to be sentenced in federal court in Washington on August 18, 2023, had gone missing. The FBI issued a wanted poster noting that Worrell "violated conditions of release pending sentencing". A federal arrest warrant was issued on August 15, 2023 in the United States District Court, District of Columbia, Washington, D.C., after he was a no-show at his hearing.

Naples Daily News, *USA Today*, and the *Florida Times-Union* reported that on January 5, 2024, U.S. District Judge Royce Lamberth sentenced Worrell, 52, an East Naples, Florida, Proud Boy (a member of the Hurricane Coast Zone 5 chapter), to 10 years in federal prison followed by three years of supervised release. Authorities said Worrell pepper-sprayed police. Prosecutors had requested 14 years and a larger fine ($2,000 in restitution, $181,000 fine, and $610 in mandatory special assessments), after he fled and faked a drug overdose. He had cut off his monitoring ankle bracelet in a Walmart parking lot on August 14, 2023, four days before his original sentencing date. He remained at large for six weeks before being re-arrested by the FBI and the Collier County Sheriff's Office Counter Terrorism Intelligence Unit at his girlfriend's home on September 28, 2023. He was unconscious on the kitchen floor.

CNN reported on May 26, 2023 that Judge Amit Mehta sentenced Jessica Watkins, a transgender Army veteran and member of the far-right Oath Keepers, to 8.5 years in prison for participating in a plot to disrupt the certification of the 2020 presidential election. Watkins founded and led a small militia in Ohio. Watkins was acquitted of seditious conspiracy, but convicted of conspiracy to obstruct an official proceeding and other felony charges.

AP reported on May 30, 2023 that prosecutors were aiming to seize $390,000 donated to 21 rioters by requesting heavy fines. The Department of Justice hoped to claw back more than $25,000 raised by Texas resident Daniel Goodwyn on his website, one of dozens of fundraising sites set up by J6 defendants. Many of the sites were hosted on GiveSendGo, self-proclaimed #1 Free Christian Fundraising Site. Markus Maly, scheduled for sentencing in June 2023 for assaulting police, raised more than $16,000 online by claiming to be a January 6 POW. Nathaniel DeGrave, who was fined $25,000, had raised $120,000; he was represented by attorney William Shipley.

ABC News reported on June 7, 2023 that Illinois native and actor Jay Johnston turned himself in to the FBI to face charges of having confronted Capitol police. His acting credits include *Anchorman, Arrested Development, Mr. Show with Bob and David, Men in Black II, Bob's Burgers,* and *The Sarah Silverman Program,* inter alia. He was accused of unlawfully entering the Capitol complex and disorderly or disruptive conduct in a restricted area. He allegedly used a stolen police riot shield to push back against police multiple times in the tunnel that led into the building.

CNN and *BBC* reported that on July 8, 2024, Jay Johnston, 55, pleaded guilty to a felony count of obstructing officers during a civil disorder. Sentencing was scheduled for October 7 before U.S. District Judge Carl Nichols. Johnston faced five years in federal prison.

The Hill reported on October 28, 2024 that Judge Nichols sentenced Johnston to a year and a day in prison for his connection with the attack. The judge added 40 hours of community service and fined him $2,000 in restitution. His attorney, Stanley Woodward, claimed his client was "blacklisted" by Hollywood since the riot. He worked as a handyman for the last two years.

Federal Times and *AP* reported on June 14, 2023 that U.S. District Judge Colleen Kollar-Kotelly sentenced former National Security Agency information technology specialist Paul Lovley, 24, of Halethorpe, Maryland to two weeks in prison for storming the Capitol alongside four fellow followers of the white nationalist American First movement, co-defendants Joseph Brody, Thomas Carey, Jon Lizak, and Gabriel Chase. He was also given three years of probation. In February 2023, he had pleaded guilty to parading, demonstrating, or picketing in a Capitol building, a misdemeanor punishable by a maximum term of six months. The AF movement's leader, Nicholas Fuentes, promotes white supremacist and anti-Semitic views on his livestreams. His followers often call themselves "Groypers" or members of a "Groyper Army." Lovley was represented by defense lawyer David Benowitz, who said Lovley had graduated from California State University, San Bernadino. Carey, from Pittsburgh, Lizak of Huntington, New York, and Chase of Gainesville, Florida, all pleaded guilty to the same misdemeanor offense as Lovley. Kollar-Kotelly earlier sentenced Carey to three years of probation, including 14 days of jail time. Chase was scheduled to be sentenced in July. A sentencing hearing for Lizak was set for October. Charges against Brody, of Springfield, Virginia, were to be resolved.

CNN reported on June 21, 2023 that Daniel Rodriguez, 40, who attacked then-Washington, D.C. police officer Michael Fanone with an electroshock weapon in the neck, was sentenced to 12 and a half years in prison. In February 2023, Rodriguez pleaded guilty to four counts, including conspiracy, assault with a dangerous weapon, and obstruction of an official proceeding.

On June 29, 2023, *CNN* reported that Washington Metropolitan Police arrested Taylor Taranto, who had an open warrant for his arrest for the riot, who had numerous firearms and materials to make an explosive in his van in former President Barack Obama's Washington, D.C. neighborhood. He claimed on an Internet livestream that he had a detonator. In July 2023, Shane Jenkins and 11 other inmates at the jail in Washington assaulted another Capitol riot defendant, Taylor Taranto, in a TV room. Taranto had been saying derogatory things about Ashli Babbitt, the rioter who was fatally shot by a police officer inside the Capitol, and Babbitt's mother.

On July 12, 2023, former actor James Beeks, a Florida Oath Keeper associate who played Judas in a traveling company of Jesus Christ Superstar, was acquitted of conspiring with members of the group to obstruct Congress in the Capitol attack. Beeks, a Michael Jackson impersonator, represented himself at trial. U.S. District Judge Amit Mehta convicted Beeks's co-defendant, Ohio State Regular Militia member Donovan Crowl, of the same charges. Crowl was represented by attorney Carmen Hernandez.

On July 12, 2023, *al-Jazeera* reported that former Marine and Trump voter James Ray Epps, who was at the center of the conspiracy theory that he was an FBI agent who intentionally spurred on the mob, sued *Fox News* for defamation. He alleged that the rumors provoked death threats and harassment against him and his wife Robyn, and that the couple had to sell their home and business and move into a trailer.

On July 19, 2023, *Military Times* and *AP* reported that U.S. District Judge Christopher Cooper sentenced Maryland resident and tow truck driver Christopher Michael Alberts to seven years in prison for using a wooden pallet as a makeshift battering ram against police officers. Alberts was sporting a concealed loaded 9-millimeter pistol, metal-plated body armor, an extra magazine of hollow point and high-pressure ammunition, a gas mask, a two-way radio, an earpiece, a throat mic, bungee cords, binoculars, a ski mask, and two knives. Alberts was the first rioter to reach the northwest steps outside the Capitol. Alberts later urinated on a wall of the Capitol. Cooper also sentenced Alberts to three years of supervised release after his prison term. Alberts said he served in the Virginia National Guard from 2005 to 2011 and was deployed to Iraq for one year in 2007 and 2008. In April 2023, a jury in Washington, D.C., convicted Alberts of all nine counts, including a felony charge of assaulting, resisting, or impeding police. Alberts was represented by attorney Roger Roots.

The *Daytona Beach News-Journal, USA Today,* and *Florida Times-Union* reported that on July 21, 2023, Anthony L. Sargent, 47, of St. Augustine, Florida, pleaded guilty to felony civil disorder and misdemeanor charges of destruction of property, entering and remaining in a restricted building or grounds, disorderly and disruptive conduct in a restricted building or grounds, engaging in physical violence in a restricted building or grounds, disorderly conduct in a Capitol building, and an act of physical violence on Capitol grounds or in buildings. He faced five years in federal prison. He was arrested on September 21, 2021. On December 15, 2023, U.S. District Court Judge Dabney Friedrich sentenced him to five years in federal prison, 36 months of supervised release, and to pay restitution of $2,980.

Sargent had twice thrown a softball-sized object at Capitol doors, separated an officer from a rioter he was trying to detain, and pushed the officer into the mob. Before the attack, he had posted on a Proud Boys messaging platform his support for a riot and civil war.

BBC and *CNN* reported that on July 24, 2023, Judge Rudolph Contreras sentenced Conway, Arkansas truck driver Peter Francis Stager, 44, who beat a Metropolitan Police officer with a flagpole, to 52 months in jail. Stager had pleaded guilty in February 2023 to a felony charge of assaulting police with a dangerous weapon.

The *Lakeland Ledger, Florida Times-Union,* and *USA Today* reported that on July 25, 2023, Carolyn Stewart of Plant City, Florida, attorney for retired Lakeland firefighter Brian Boele, 60, filed a motion with U.S. District Judge Richard J. Leon of the District of Columbia to dismiss charges of entering and remaining in a restricted building or grounds, disorderly conduct, and disorderly and disruptive conduct in a restricted building or grounds. Boele was indicted on May 2022 with four other defendants, including Alan Fischer, III, of Tampa, Boele's son. Fischer was allegedly a member of the Proud Boys, although Stewart said her client was not a Proud Boy "during the events". Stewart in her earlier defense of Paul Hodgkins claimed that his signature on a plea agreement had been forged.

CBS-Chicago reported on July 26, 2023 that former Illinois National Guardsman Joseph Bierbrodt, of Sheridan, Illinois was arrested for breaking into the U.S. Capitol with his brother William and assaulting a police officer inside. Joseph Bierbrodt was charged with eight federal counts, including entering a restricted building; disorderly and disruptive conduct in a restricted building; physical violence in a restricted building; disorderly conduct in a Capitol building; parading, demonstrating, or picketing in a Capitol building; physical violence in a Capitol building; assault on a federal officer; and obstruction of law enforcement. The Illinois National Guard said that Joseph retired in 2018. William Martin Bierbrodt, of St. Cloud, Florida, was charged with seven federal counts, including entering a restricted building; disorderly and disruptive conduct in a restricted building; physical violence in a restricted building; disorderly conduct in a Capitol building; parading, demonstrating, or picketing in a Capitol building; willfully injuring property of the United States; and obstruction of law enforcement. William breached a locked fire door.

WLS and *ABC7 Chicago* reported on October 28, 2024 that Joseph Bierbrodt pleaded guilty to attacking the U.S. Capitol. Sentencing was set for February 2025. He initially faced eight federal charges, among them entering a restricted building, causing physical violence, and disorderly conduct in a restricted building. Joseph clashed with several police officers, was pepper-sprayed, and left bloodied before leaving the Capitol with his brother. Joseph Bierbrodt was earlier arrested in late October 2021 in Sheridan, Illinois.

CNN and *AP* reported on August 1, 2023 that Justice Department special counsel Jack Smith charged former president Donald Trump with conspiracy to defraud the United States; conspiracy to obstruct an official proceeding; and obstruction of and attempting to obstruct an official proceeding. Trump was the only person charged in the indictment, which mentioned six co-conspirators, identified by *CNN* as Rudy Giuliani, John Eastman, Sidney Powell, Jeffrey Clark, Kenneth Chesebro, and a political consultant. *CNN* reported on August 27, 2024 that Smith filed a superseding indictment in the election interference case against Trump, in light of the Supreme Court's "official acts" immunity ruling. He retained the four charges but dropped some mentions of Trump's interactions with senior Justice Department officials and added language describing Trump acting as a candidate and not the president.

The *Florida Times-Union* and *USA Today Network* reported on August 21, 2023 that U.S. District Judge Thomas F. Hogan sentenced Bradley Weeks, 45, of Baker County, Florida to 10 months in jail, an additional year of home detention, and a $2,000 fine for the felony charge of obstructing an official proceeding, along with several misdemeanors. He was found guilty in December 2022 following a bench trial in which prosecutors showed a video of him saying, "We've had to climb scaffolding. We've had to

climb ladders. We've had to break things to get through, but we've gotten through. We've gotten through, and we are taking back the Capitol."

CNN reported on September 12, 2023 that D.C. District Judge Timothy Kelly sentenced Owen Shroyer, a right-wing conspiracy theorist and *InfoWars* host, to 60 days in jail. He had pleaded guilty to one misdemeanor count of entering and remaining on restricted grounds in June 2023. He did not enter the Capitol building itself.

NPR and *AP* reported that U.S. District Judge Amit Mehta on October 6, 2023 sentenced Shane Jenkins, alias Skullet, 46, of Texas, who carried a metal tomahawk during the Capitol riot, and now promotes J6 merchandise (T-shirts, hoodies, hats, tote bags, and other merchandise) calling jailed rioters "political prisoners", to seven years in prison. He tried to smash a Capitol window with the tomahawk and threw makeshift weapons at police officers, hurling a desk drawer, a flagpole, a metal walking stick, and a wooden pole with a spear-like point. He was represented by defense attorney Dennis Boyle. Prosecutors had requested 19 years and eight months and a fine of at least $118,888, equaling the money Jenkins has publicly raised. Mehta refused to impose a "terrorism" enhancement that would have significantly increased his sentencing guidelines. In March, a jury convicted Jenkins of civil disorder and obstructing the joint session of Congress for certifying the presidential election victory of Joe Biden.

In 1997 at age 20, Jenkins shot to death his stepfather in self-defense after the man pointed a shotgun at him and made death threats. His criminal record before January 6 included assault convictions. In July 2023, Jenkins and 11 other inmates at the jail in Washington assaulted another Capitol riot defendant, Taylor Taranto, in a TV room. Taranto had been saying derogatory things about Ashli Babbitt, the rioter who was fatally shot by a police officer inside the Capitol, and Babbitt's mother.

The *Washington Post* reported on October 16, 2023 that the government filed notice that it was appealing the sentences of the five members of the far-right Proud Boys group convicted in the January 6 attack. The government had filed in July a similar challenge to the punishments handed down to five members of the Oath Keepers for their role in the riot.

CNN reported on November 3, 2023 that Federico Klein, a former State Department Trump appointee and former Marine, was sentenced by Judge Trevor McFadden, also a Trump appointee, to 70 months in prison on multiple counts, including assaulting multiple police officers on January 6, 2021. Former U.S. Capitol Police Sgt. Aquilino Gonell testified before the court that Klein had attacked him multiple times with a police riot shield. Klein was represented by attorney Stanley Woodward, who also represents Trump's co-defendant Walt Nauta in the classified documents case in Florida. Woodward noted that Klein had worked on Trump's 2016 campaign.

On November 7, 2023, Daniel Paul Gray, 43, of Jacksonville, Florida, pleaded guilty to obstructing an official proceeding and assaulting or resisting officers. He struggled with police, one of whom fell down a flight of stairs after Gray seized a baton she was holding, upsetting her balance. She suffered a pinched nerve and chronic back pain. Prosecutors dropped seven other charges at a plea hearing on October 24, 2023 in Washington's U.S. District Court. Sentencing was set for February 16, 2024. Federal guidelines called for 41-63 months, although U.S. District Court Senior Judge Amy Berman Jackson could enhance the penalty because of the permanent injury. The legal maximum is 20 years for obstructing a proceeding and eight years for assaulting officers. Gray's attorney said a police officer had grabbed his cell phone and Gray followed the officer inside to retrieve it.

The *Jacksonville Florida Times-Union* and the *USA Today Network* reported that on February 16, 2024, Judge Jackson sentenced Gray to 30 months after saying "I am devastated that I am guilty of assaulting a female officer" during the Capitol riot. Sentencing guidelines suggested 41-51 months; the prosecutor asked for the maximum sentence, saying Gray's conduct "embodies a total disrespect for the law". Gray was a former mixed martial arts fighter and instructor.

ABC News reported on November 10, 2023 that the FBI announced that Gregory C. Ye-

tman, 47, subject of a manhunt in New Jersey, turned himself in to Monroe Township police. He was charged with several offenses, some felonies, related to the insurrection, including assaulting officers; obstruction of law enforcement during civil disorder; entering and remaining in a restricted building or grounds; engaging in physical violence in a restricted building or grounds; and act of physical violence in the Capitol grounds or buildings. He was scheduled for an initial court appearance on November 13, 2023. An arrest warrant was issued for him on November 6, 2023. Yetman was a military police sergeant in the New Jersey Army National Guard, serving from September 2008 to 2022, and was honorably discharged in March 2022. He deployed to Afghanistan from September 2012 to May 2013 and to Guantánamo Bay, Cuba, from June 2015 to March 2016. Authorities had offered a $10,000 reward for his capture. *Stars and Stripes* reported on April 29, 2024 that on April 25, Gregory Yetman, 47, had admitted to pepper spraying police with a 20-inch-tall MK-46H chemical spray canister, and pleaded guilty in federal court to one felony charge of assaulting, resisting, or impeding officers with physical contact. Sentencing was scheduled for July 22, 2024. He faced four years in prison. Four other charges were dropped.

The *New York Times* reported that on July 23, 2024, Judge James E. Boasberg of Federal District Court in Washington, D.C., sentenced Yetman, of Helmetta, New Jersey, to two and a half years. Judge Boasberg also sentenced Yetman to 18 months of supervised release and fined him $2,000 in restitution. Prosecutors had sought a 45-month prison term. Yetman's lawyer, Nicholas D. Smith, had asked for 17 months.

UPI reported on November 14, 2023 convicted Capitol rioter Jacob Chansley, 35, known as the QAnon Shaman, notified the state of Arizona that he is running for the U.S. House of Representatives as a member of the Libertarian Party in 2024 in Arizona's 8th District, which includes several Phoenix suburbs. Incumbent Representative Debbie Lesko (R-Arizona) did not seek re-election in 2024. Chansley served 27 months of his 41-month sentence for felony obstruction of an official proceeding. He was transferred out of federal prison to a halfway house in Arizona in March and released in May. *CNN* reported on July 12, 2024 that the Department of Justice wanted to retain as evidence the horned helmet and flag-pole spear that Chansley had at the riot. He tried to challenge his conviction in light of the Supreme Court ruling in *Fischer v U.S.* of June 2024 limiting obstruction charges against January 6 rioters.

The *Charlotte Observer* and *Military.Com* reported on November 20, 2023 that former Marine Lee Stutts, 46, of Terrell, North Carolina, wore a black helmet with a Marine Corps logo sticker on the back while assaulting at least seven officers during the Capitol riots, according to an FBI affidavit. Stutts was charged with assaulting, resisting, or impeding officers with a deadly or dangerous weapon, and obstruction of law enforcement during a civil disorder, both felonies. He also was charged with the misdemeanor offenses of entering and remaining in a restricted building or grounds, disorderly and disruptive conduct in a restricted building or grounds, and engaging in physical violence in a restricted building or grounds. He was the 31st North Carolinian to be charged. He was accused of pushing and shoving officers with his hands, a barricade, a battering ram, and a bike rack as he helped lead the Capitol breach. He lives in a split-level home built in 1975 on Clement Circle, according to Catawba County property tax records, which shows the house and its half-acre lot, about 33 miles northwest of Charlotte, valued at $866,600. Stutts was scheduled to make his initial appearance in a U.S. courtroom on November 24, 2023 in the Charlotte-based Western District of North Carolina.

Salon and *AP* reported on November 21, 2023 that U.S. District Judge James Boasberg sentenced New York massage therapist Frank Giustino, who joined Trump-supporting rioters, to three months in jail after he skipped court hearings, insulted a prosecutor, and verbally attacked the judge who punished him. Giustino pleaded guilty in February 2023 to a misdemeanor charge related to the insurrection but was arrested in October after failing to appear in court for a previously scheduled sentencing hearing. Prosecutors initially requested a 21-day

sentence but pursued a longer term of incarceration after he defiantly disrupted a June 23 court hearing.

The *New York Times* ran a 3-page article on November 19, 2023 that examined the relationship between father and rioter Brian Mock, 44, and his son, A.J. Mock, 21, who tipped off the FBI about Brian's activities. Brian was transferred from Minnesota to a jail in Washington, D.C. In July 2023, a federal judge convicted Brian of 11 charges, including four of assault against law enforcement officers, stealing riot shields, and obstructing an official government proceeding. Sentencing was scheduled for January 2024. Brian had yelled at law enforcement officers, "Get out! Go!" while he threw a broken flagpole at a police officer, tried to kick another, and shoved a third in the chest.

CNN reported on December 7, 2023 that earlier in the week, a federal grand jury found New Yorker Philip Sean Grillo, 49, guilty of five charges, including felony obstruction of an official proceeding, during the attack on the U.S. Capitol. Grillo had filed in May to run for the House of Representatives New York 3rd Congressional District seat of ousted George Santos (R-New York).

CNN reported on December 7, 2023 that U.S. District Judge Royce C. Lamberth sentenced Alan Hostetter, 59, a retired La Habra, California police chief who brought a hatchet to the Capitol on January 6, 2021, and gave prior speeches calling for the execution of his perceived political enemies, to 135 months. In July 2023, Hostetter was found guilty of conspiring to obstruct an official proceeding, obstruction of an official proceeding, entering and remaining in a restricted building or grounds with a deadly or dangerous weapon, and disorderly or disruptive conduct in a restricted building or grounds with a deadly or dangerous weapon. The Department of Justice added that he had spread several conspiracy theories about the 2020 presidential election. He co-sponsored a pro-Trump rally a day before the Capitol riot. He brought tactical gear, a helmet, hatchets, knives, stun batons, pepper spray, and other gear to the Capitol, and met up with other members of a group known as the "DC Brigade," before joining the "Stop the Steal" rally. The FBI arrested him on June 10, 2021.

The *Daily Beast* reported on December 14, 2023 that Anthony Alexander Antonio, 29, from Delaware, whose attorney claimed he was infected with "Foxmania" or "Foxitus" after watching *Fox News* nonstop for six months, pleaded guilty to felony charges that included obstruction of an official proceeding. Antonio faced between 33 and 51 months in prison; sentencing was scheduled for 2024. Video showed him charging into the Capitol with a stolen police riot shield, yelling at police, "You want war? We got war. 1776 all over again." He wore a bulletproof vest with a far-right "Three Percenter" patch and a camouflage shirt.

USA Today and the *Florida Times-Union* reported that on December 14, 2023, FBI, U.S. Marshals, ATF, and Metro-Dade Police authorities arrested Barbara Balmaseda, 23, of Miami Lakes, Florida, for felony obstruction of an official proceeding and four misdemeanors. She was an acquaintance of Gabriel Garcia, a Proud Boy found guilty of two felonies. They were seen together in security footage from the Capitol. She was represented by attorney Nayib Hassan. She was in the federal Quiet Skies program for a year, subjecting her to extra airport screening procedures. The *Miami Herald* said the Southern District of Florida set bail at $100,000. Her case was transferred to the District of Columbia. She is a former director at large for the Miami Young Republicans and interned for U.S. Senator Marco Rubio in 2018-2019.

CNN reported on December 19, 2023 that Judge Timothy Kelly sentenced Charles Donohoe, 35, former Marine and the first of the Proud Boys leadership to enter a guilty plea and assist the prosecutors in their case, to 40 months in prison. His testimony helped in the conviction of several leaders in the group of seditious conspiracy. He had pleaded guilty to conspiring to obstruct an official proceeding and assaulting an officer by throwing two water bottles at police during the riot. Donohoe had served nearly 38 months of his sentence. He was represented by attorney Ira Knight.

WUSA9 reported on January 2, 2024 that U.S. District Judge Royce C. Lamberth convicted Marine Corps veteran Alex Kirk Harkrider, of Carthage, Texas, of multiple felony counts for carrying a tomahawk to the U.S. Capitol on January 6, 2021. Harkrider was found guilty of seven counts following a brief stipulated bench trial, in which both the defense and prosecution agree on a set of facts to submit to the judge, who then determines if they are sufficient for a guilty verdict. Harkrider was found guilty of obstruction of an official proceeding and entering and remaining in a restricted building with a dangerous weapon, inter alia. He was indicted in early 2021 alongside his friend and fellow Marine, Ryan Taylor Nichols, of Longview, Texas. Nichols carried a crowbar to the Capitol and assaulted police with pepper spray; he pleaded guilty in November 2022 to two felony counts. Under the terms of his plea agreement, Nichols faced 78-97 months in prison. He was permitted several times to participate in emergency response efforts after major catastrophes. *Marine Corps Times* reported on May 28, 2024 that on May 23, 2024, a federal judge sentenced Harkrider, 36, to two years in prison. Harkrider was convicted in a bench trial on January 2, 2024 of felony charges of civil disorder and entering a restricted building with a deadly weapon, and misdemeanor charges of theft of government property, disorderly conduct in a Capitol building, and parading or picketing in a Capitol building. Harkrider wore body armor and carried a tactical tomahawk during the riot when he and Nichols, 32, entered the Capitol through a broken window. Harkrider traveled from his home in Carthage, Texas, to Washington, D.C. FBI agents arrested Harkrider on January 18, 2021, in Carthage, Texas. The lance corporal served as a rifleman from 2008 to 2012 and deployed twice. He received the Combat Action Ribbon, National Defense Service Medal, and Global War on Terrorism Service Medal, among others. He was also a two-time recipient of the Navy Unit Commendation and Sea Service Deployment Ribbon. He was last assigned to the 3rd Battalion, 9th Marine Regiment, 2nd Marine Division at Camp

Lejeune, North Carolina. He was represented by defense attorney Kira Anne West, in the District Court for the District of Columbia.

NBC News reported on May 2, 2024 that U.S. District Judge Royce Lamberth sentenced Ryan Nichols to 63 months in prison and a $200,000 fine for assaulting police officers with pepper spray and calling for additional violence after the Capitol attack. Nichols did not cooperate with a financial evaluation, ergo, there was no evidence that he could not pay, Lamberth said. A crowdfunding account for Nichols and his family raised more than $235,000 since 2021. Nichols's attorney planned to appeal the fine. Assistant U.S. Attorney Douglas Brasher had requested 83 months. Nichols was represented by attorney Joseph McBride, a former Tucker Carlson guest who had often spouted conspiracy theories about the riot. Nichols is a military veteran with post-traumatic stress disorder.

ABC News reported on January 5, 2024 that Harry Dunn, who resigned as a Capitol Police Sergeant in December 2023 and struggled to defend the Capitol on January 6, 2021, announced that he was running for Congress as a Democrat to represent Maryland's 3rd Congressional District, which includes several Maryland counties outside Baltimore. He is running to replace Democrat Representative John Sarbanes, who is stepping down. Dunn explained, "I got called a [N-word] a couple dozen times today protecting this building... Is this America? They beat police officers with Blue Lives Matter flags. They fought us, they had Confederate flags in the U.S. Capitol." He said the January 6 "terrorists...tried to disrupt this country's democracy—that was their goal ... And you know what? Y'all failed because later that night, they went on and they certified the election." He joined the Capitol Police in 2008. He said he suffers from PTSD from 1/6. He authored *Standing My Ground: A Capitol Police Officer's Fight for Accountability and Good Trouble After January 6th*. Hachette Books, 2023.

The Hill reported on January 13, 2024 that Proud Boys member and Army veteran William Chrestman, 51, from Kansas was sentenced on January 12, 2024 to 55 months in prison with 36 months of supervised release and was ordered

to pay $2,000 in restitution. In October 2023, he pleaded guilty to obstruction of an official proceeding and threatening a federal officer. He wore a tactical vest and protective gloves and carried a gas mask and a wooden axe handle with a flag attached to it to the Capitol and bragged about harassing police. He said, "We had the cops running through the f— State Building... dude, trying to slam the emergency doors, like, the big garage door-type ones that segregate off the rooms, and we were throwing f—ing chairs under there to block it dude, to keep going down... The cops were legitimately scared for their f—ing lives." Chrestman gestured toward the police officers with his axe handle, shouting "If you shoot, I'll f—ing take your ass out." He was represented by attorney Michael Cronkright. He was arrested in February 2021.

USA Today and the *Florida Times-Union* reported that on January 17, 2024, U.S. District Judge Jia M. Cobb sentenced Miami Proud Boys chapter member Kenneth Bonawitz, 58, to five years in prison for assaulting at least six officers, including U.S. Capitol Police Sgt. Federico Ruiz, who suffered serious injuries to his neck, shoulder, knees, and back and was forced to retire. Bonawitz had pleaded guilty in August 2023 to three felonies: civil disorder, obstruction of an official proceeding, and assaulting a law enforcement officer during a civil disorder. He had thrown himself at officers, tackled then, placed one in a chokehold, and lifted one up by the neck. He also was sentenced to three years of supervised release and ordered to pay $2,000 in restitution and fines. Prosecutors said he brought an 8-inch hunting knife in a sheath attached to his belt.

The Daily Beast reported on January 25, 2024 that immigrant Duong Dai Luu, 47, of Texas, who was arrested in Houston for storming the Capitol, told the FBI he had no idea what kind of business went on in there. He took cell phone video of ransacked offices in Room S132 (the Senate Parliamentarian's office) and MAGA-hatted selfies. He faced four misdemeanor counts: knowingly entering or remaining in any restricted building or grounds without lawful authority; knowingly, and with intent to impede or disrupt the orderly conduct of government business or official functions, engaging in disorderly or disruptive conduct; disorderly conduct in a Capitol building; parading, demonstrating, or picketing in a Capitol building.

MilitaryTimes.com reported on January 30, 2024 that Chief Judge James Boasberg ordered jailed former U.S. Army soldier Edward Richmond, Jr., 40, of Geismar, Louisiana, on charges that he, while dressed in tactical gear, used a metal baton to assault police officers in a tunnel on the Capitol's Lower West Terrace during the insurrection. Prosecutors deemed him a danger to the community. A federal magistrate judge in Baton Rouge, Louisiana initially released Richmond after his January 22, 2024 arrest. FBI agents found an AR-15 assault rifle—registered to his ex-wife—in Richmond's closet. He pleaded guilty to assault in August 2024. He is prohibited from possessing firearms after his 2004 voluntary manslaughter conviction for fatally shooting in February 2004 in the head handcuffed Iraqi cow herder Muhamad Husain Kadir near Taal al-Jai, Iraq while serving in the U.S. Army. He was sentenced to three years in military confinement at Fort Sill, Oklahoma and dishonorably discharged. Richmond is the sole caregiver for his son, 16. Richmond was represented by Louisiana-based attorney John McLindon. *Military Times* reported on November 18, 2024 that U.S. District Judge John Bates sentenced Richmond to four years and three months in prison.

The *Florida Times-Union* and *USA Today Network* reported that on January 30, 2014, Marcus Smith, 47, of Clay County, Florida, was indicted on a federal felony charge of causing more than $1,000 damage to government property (an interior door). He was arrested on January 27, 2024 in Fleming Island, Florida on seven counts returned by a federal grand jury in Washington, D.C. He faced 10 years in prison. He was also charged with entering restricted grounds, disorderly conduct on restricted grounds, and engaging in physical violence on those grounds, plus three misdemeanor charges.

On March 18, 2024, the *Florida Times-Union* and *USA Today* reported that North Carolina-based public defender Kevin Tate for Marcus Smith, of Fleming Island, Florida, asked for a change of venue from Washington, D.C. to Jacksonville, Florida because he would "face a biased jury" in his trial for damaging government property during the riot. Tate worked for a public defender's office in Nevada. The damage to an interior door at the Capitol exceeded $1,000, making it a felony. Smith also was indicted in January 2024 on six misdemeanor counts.

USA Today and the *Florida Times-Union* reported that on October 1, 2024, a jury in Washington, D.C. convicted Marcus Smith of destroying government property as part of a crowd that broke open a door to Room S-131 of the Capitol. He faced ten years in jail because the damage to the 1850s door was $21,000. U.S. District Judge Dabney L. Friedrich scheduled sentencing for January 10, 2025.

AP reported on February 28, 2024 that U.S. District Judge Tanya Chutkan sentenced former Marine Corps officer Michael Joseph Foy, 33, of Wixom, Michigan, who assaulted police officers with a hockey stick and a sharp metal pole, hitting them 11 times in 16 seconds, then climbed through a broken window and walked around the Capitol building, to three years and four months in prison. Judge Chutkan also oversaw former President Donald Trump's election interference case in Washington, D.C. Prosecutors had requested eight years and one month. Judge Chutkan convicted Foy following a stipulated bench trial of two felonies—assaulting a police officer and obstruction of an official proceeding. Foy served in the Corps from 2015 until June 2020, working as a heavy equipment mechanic. He was honorably discharged as a corporal. He served as a supervisor on a North Carolina base.

The *Washington Post* reported on February 29, 2024 that U.S. District Judge Trevor N. McFadden sentenced Brandon Fellows, 29, a tree cutter and chimney repairman from Upstate New York who smoked marijuana in the office of Senator Jeff Merkley (D-Ore.), to 3½ years in prison after interrupting and challenging the sentencing judge. A jury in U.S. District Court in D.C. in 2023 convicted Fellows of obstructing an official proceeding, entering a restricted building, and disorderly conduct. He was found in contempt at his trial after he called the judge a "modern-day Nazi" running a "kangaroo court". He tried to hide from the FBI by wrapping his cellphone in foil and wiping his data. The judge sentenced Fellows to 37 months for his insurrection-related convictions and five months for contempt related to his courtroom antics.

The Hill reported on March 1, 2024 that a federal jury in Washington, D.C. convicted Kentucky resident Michael Sparks, 46, the man accused of being the first rioter to enter the U.S. Capitol, on all six charges he faced, including two felonies of civil disorder and obstruction of an official proceeding. U.S. District Judge Timothy Kelly scheduled sentencing for July 9. Sparks jumped through a broken window just after another rioter smashed it open. Once inside the building, he and others chased a police officer up a flight of stairs. He was represented by attorney Scott Wendelsdorf, who conceded that his client was guilty of four misdemeanor counts, including trespassing and disorderly conduct. Sparks was arrested on January 19, 2021, and indicted on February 5, 2021, followed by a superseding indictment in November 2021. *CNN* reported on August 27, 2024 that the U.S. District Court for the District of Columbia sentenced Sparks to 53 months in jail.

AP and *NBC News* reported that on March 18, 2024, the Supreme Court rejected an appeal from Couy Griffin, a former Otero County, New Mexico county commissioner and cofounder of Cowboys for Trump, who was kicked out of office over his participation in the insurrection. He thus remained disqualified from public office under Section 3 of the 14th Amendment designed to prevent ex-Confederates from serving in government after the Civil War. He continued to be the only elected official thus far to be banned from office in connection with the Capitol attack. The Republican had received a 14-day prison sentence after his conviction in federal court of entering a restricted area on the Capitol grounds. The sentence was offset by time served after his arrest in Washington. He was represented by Florida-based defense attorney Peter Ticktin. *The Hill* reported that on October 22, 2024, a District of Columbia Circuit Court of Appeals panel upheld the 2022 misdemeanor trespassing conviction of Couy Griffin.

Newsweek reported on April 6, 2024 that inmate Edward Jacob (Jake) Lang told the con-servative cable channel *Real America's Voice* that some 78 January 6 defendants filed a class action lawsuit against 21 Capitol Police officers and officials for "millions of dollars in damages." Lang calls himself a "January 6 political prisoner" who was arrested soon after the attack for wielding a dangerous weapon against Capitol Police officers and obstruction of an official proceeding. He lived in Newburgh, New York, and was 25 at the time of the riot. Lang claimed to be represented by conservative attorneys Stefanie Lambert and Russell Newman. On November 19, 2024, U.S. District Judge Carl Nichols postponed the trial of Lang.

Politico reported on April 9, 2024 that Judge Cornelia Pillard announced that a three-judge panel (including Bradley Garcia and Michelle Childs) of the D.C. Circuit Court of Appeals upheld in a unanimous 27-page ruling a statute that criminalizes "parading, picketing or demonstrating in a Capitol building, thereby tossing John Nassif's challenge to his 2022 conviction for "demonstrating" inside the Capitol and ruling that the building itself—vice the parkland outside—is not legally a "public forum" for protest activity. Nassif was among the hundreds chanting "Whose house? Our house!" Nassif, 57, from Winter Springs, Florida, was convicted following a bench trial by U.S. District Court Judge John Bates.

CNN reported on April 16, 2024 that the Supreme Court was scheduled to hear arguments that day in *Joseph Fischer v. U.S.* from a former Pennsylvania police officer who stormed the Capitol in a case that could undermine federal charges of obstructing official proceedings against more than 350 rioters.

The Hill reported that on April 19, 2024, U.S. District Court Judge Royce C. Lamberth sentenced four "Three Percenter" militia members Erik Scott Warner, 48; Felipe Antonio Martinez, 50; Derek Kinnison, 42; and Ronald Mele, 54, all from California, to 21 to 33 months for conspiracy to obstruct an official proceeding and obstruction of an official proceeding, both felony offenses. Warmer and Kinnison were also convicted on felony charges of tampering with documents or records. The four were also found guilty of misdemeanor offenses of entering and remaining in a restricted building or grounds and disorderly and disruptive conduct in a restricted building or grounds. Judge Lamberth ordered each defendant to pay $2,000 in restitution and complete 36 months of supervised release.

AP reported that on April 22, 2024 Chief Judge James Boasberg sentenced Bonnieville, Kentucky man Isreal Easterday, 23, who was 19 when he stormed the U.S. Capitol while carrying a Confederate battle flag, to two years and six months in prison for pepper spraying in the face two police officers guarding the East Rotunda Doors, partially blinding them for hours during the riot. Easterday was homeschooled by his mother while living on an Amish family farm. Prosecutors initially recommended a sentence of 12 years and seven months in prison. He was arrested in December 2022 in Miami, where his boat was docked. A jury in October 2023 convicted Easterday of nine counts, including charges that he assaulted Capitol police officers Joshua Pollitt and Miguel Acevedo with pepper spray that he acquired from other rioters.

The Hill reported that on April 26, 2024, John Earle Sullivan, 29, a Utah man in a ballistic vest and gas mask and carrying a bull horn, who filmed the fatal shooting of Ashli Babbit, was sentenced to six years in prison for his role in the riot. On November 16, 2023, he was found guilty of obstructing an official proceeding, including possession of a dangerous weapon on Capitol grounds. U.S. District Judge Royce C. Lamberth also sentenced him to 36 months of supervised release and ordered him to pay $2,000 in restitution. Sullivan was arrested in Salt Lake City on January 14, 2021. The *Washington Post* reported that he was paid more than $90,000 for his riot videos.

The *Daily Beast* reported on April 26, 2024 that retired police officer Michael Fanone, who became the face of D.C. Metropolitan Police brutalized in the riot, launched a private security business, Lower West Terrace LLC, in August 2021, four months after his retirement. Among his clients was Representative Eric Swalwell (D-California), who paid $49,057.50 between August 2023 and February 2024.

UPI reported that on May 2, 2024, U.S. District Judge Rudolph Contreras sentenced

Jack Wade Whitton, 33, a former personal trainer from Locust Grove, Georgia, to 57 months in prison, fined him $2,000, established three years of supervised release, and ordered mental health treatment for assaulting Capitol police in the lower west tunnel with a metal crutch in some of the most brutal fighting that took place at the Capitol that day. Sentencing came 19 months after his plea deal, when he agreed to testify against his eight co-defendants. Former romance novel cover model from Michigan, Logan James Barnhart, 41, was sentenced in April 2024 to 36 months in prison for helping Whitton drag the officer into the crowd. Five men were charged in August 2021 for assaulting the officer. Federal prosecutors had requested more than eight years for Whitton and a fine of $61,685, which he had raised via *GoFundMe*. He was represented by attorney Komron Jon Maknoon.

On May 17, 2024, U.S. District Judge John Bates sentenced Leo Brent Bozell, IV, 44, of Palmyra, Pennsylvania, son of a prominent conservative activist, to three years and nine months in prison on ten charges for his "relentless" assault on the Capitol. His father, L. Brent Bozell III, founded the Media Research Center, the Parents Television Council, and other conservative media organizations. Bozell IV was arrested in February 2021 after a tipster told the FBI he recognized him in part from the Hershey Christian Academy sweatshirt that he wore during the riot. Bozell used a metal object to shatter the windowpane of the Senate Wing Door. He and other rioters chased Capitol Police officer Eugene Goodman up a staircase. Bozell entered then-House Speaker Nancy Pelosi's office and made off with an unidentified object. He later entered the Senate gallery and spent several minutes on the Senate floor. He was represented by attorney Eric Snyder.

On May 24, 2024, U.S. District Judge Trevor McFadden sentenced North Brunswick, New Jersey electrician Christopher Joseph Quaglin, 38, to 12 years in prison for six separate attacks on police. The Judge called him "a menace to our society". Quaglin argued with and insulted the Judge before and after the sentencing. Quaglin told the judge, "You're Trump's worst mistake of 2016." Then-President Donald Trump nominat-

ed McFadden to the court in 2017. Quaglin injured a police officer when he choked and tackled him to the ground. He assaulted other officers with stolen police shields, metal bike racks, and pepper spray. He wore an American flag-themed "Make America Great Again" sweatshirt. McFadden had convicted Quaglin of 14 counts in July 2023 after a stipulated bench trial. Among the injured police was Capitol Police Sgt. Troy Robinson. Quaglin was represented by defense attorney Kristi Fulnecky, who claimed that one of Quaglin's former attorneys coerced him into accepting a stipulated bench trial instead of a contested trial.

On May 30, 2024, Benjamen Scott Burlew, 44, of Miami, Oklahoma, pleaded guilty to assaulting a Metropolitan Police Department officer during the riot. He was also charged with assaulting an *AP* photographer by grabbing, dragging, and pushing him over a low stone wall outside the Capitol. He had skipped several court appearances in Washington, D.C. in 2023. Authorities re-arrested him on May 13, 2024 in Tulsa, Oklahoma. U.S. District Judge Randolph Moss was scheduled to sentence him on September 20, 2024. The estimated sentencing guidelines recommend a prison term ranging from 30 to 37 months. He was represented by defense attorney Robert Jenkins.

Marine Corps Times and *AP* reported that on May 31, 2024 U.S. District Judge Beryl Howell sentenced U.S. Marine Corps veteran John George Todd, III, 34, of Missouri to five years in prison for injuring a police officer's hand. Todd showed no remorse. Prosecutors had recommended a prison sentence of 12 years and seven months. He had carried a fiberglass pole attached to a flag. When a Metropolitan Police Department officer Noah Rathbun tried to confiscate it, Todd and the officer wrestled for control of the pole until it splintered and cut the officer's hand. The officer needed seven stitches and missed nine days of work. In February 2024, a jury convicted Todd of six counts, including obstruction of the joint session. Todd was a Marine from 2009 to 2013 and served in Afghanistan, receiving an "other than honorable" discharge from the military related to his abuse of alcohol.

Separately, retired New York Police Department officer Thomas Webster was sentenced to 10 years in prison for attacking Rathbun outside the Capitol, swinging a flagpole at Rathbun and then tackling him and grabbing his gas mask.

CNN reported that on June 28, 2024, the Supreme Court ruled that the Department of Justice overstepped by charging hundreds of Capitol rioters with obstruction in a decision that could force prosecutors to reopen some cases. However, the court held that the charge could be filed if prosecutors could demonstrate they were attempting not just to push their way into the building but rather to stop the arrival of certificates used to count electoral votes and certify the results of the election.

Action News Jax reported that on July 15, 2024, the FBI arrested Garth Nathaniel Walton, 32, of Yulee, Florida, on seven counts, including felony offenses of civil disorder and assaulting, resisting, or impeding certain officers. He was also charged with several misdemeanors. He made his first appearance in the Middle District of Florida court. *USA Today* reported that he faced eight years in prison.

CNN reported that on July 19, 2024, U.S. District Judge Beryl Howell sentenced active-duty Marine Tyler Bradley Dykes, 26, of South Carolina, who attacked the Capitol and apparently flashed a Nazi salute in front of the building, to four years and nine months in prison. Dykes pleaded guilty in April 2024 to assault. Dykes was convicted of a crime stemming from the August 2017 white nationalist Unite the Right rally in Charlottesville, Virginia. He served a six-month sentence in a state prison, then was transferred to federal custody in 2023.

CNN reported on August 21, 2024 that attorney Kellye SoRelle who volunteered for Lawyers for Trump in the 2020 election challenge, pleaded guilty to charges including tampering with evidence by instructing members of the far-right Oath Keepers to delete their text messages after the Capitol riot on behalf of its leader Stewart Rhodes. She was first charged in 2022, but the judge overseeing her case temporarily ruled that she was incompetent to stand trial and sent her to a federal facility for mental health treatment. She faced 20 years in jail. Sentencing was set for January 2025. The former girlfriend of Rhodes has claimed to be the general counsel for the militia.

On August 21, 2024, U.S. Capitol Police Sergeant Aquilino Gonell, who medically retired after being injured during the riot, addressed the third evening of the Democratic National Convention.

The *Independent* reported that on August 22, 2024, authorities arrested Marine Corps veteran Nathan Thornsberry, 42, of North Branch, Michigan, on felony charges of obstruction of law enforcement during a civil disorder and assaulting, resisting, or impeding officers. He allegedly used his body to ram a police barrier separating the rioters from the Capitol. The Flint, Michigan, FBI field office got a tip he was behind *January 6: A Patriot's Story*, a self-published book on Amazon about the insurrection. He used the nom de plume Nathaniel Matthews.

The *Florida Times-Union* reported on August 29, 2024 that the previous week, authorities arrested Putnam County resident Dylan Swinehart in Palatka, Florida, on four misdemeanor counts, ten months after he acknowledged to an investigator that he had been inside the Capitol. He was charged with entering and remaining in restricted grounds, disorderly conduct, and demonstrating in the Capitol. He was to appear for a video teleconference with a federal judge in Washington on August 29. He faced a year behind bars on the charges.

CNN reported on August 29, 2024 that the criminal case of former Pennsylvania officer Joseph Fischer, whose initial charges of obstruction of an official proceeding went up to the U.S. Supreme Court, was scheduled by District Judge Carl Nichols for hearing in federal district court in February 2025. The Court sent his case back to lower courts with instructions about how to assess the charge in light of its June 2024 ruling. Fischer faced six other charges related to the riot, including assaulting law enforcement officers and civil disorder.

CNN reported on September 4, 2024 that the J6 Awards Gala, hosted by First Class Label Group and Vote Your Vision, initially scheduled for September 5 at Trump National Golf Course in Bedminster, New Jersey was postponed indef-

initely. The gala was for those incarcerated for their participation in the riot. Trump had earlier said that he would pardon the rioters in an interview in July 2024 at the National Association of Black Journalists conference. He often refers to those jailed as "hostages".

Military Times reported that on September 4, 2024, U.S. District Judge Christopher Cooper reduced the sentence of Virginia resident Thomas Robertson, an Army veteran and former policeman who was convicted on six charges for his participation in the mob. He was sentenced in 2022 to seven years in prison for interfering with police officers during a civil disorder and entering a restricted area with a dangerous weapon. Cooper dropped the sentence to six years after he dismissed Robertson's conviction of obstructing the congressional certification. Robertson served four years in the U.S. Army from 1991 to 1994, and then joined the Army Reserve in 2001. He deployed to Iraq in 2008 and was injured by gunshot and mortar shrapnel in Afghanistan in 2011. He underwent ten surgeries for his injuries. He joined the police department in Rocky Mount, Virginia, rising to sergeant. He was off duty but still working for the police department when he joined the riot. He was fired after his arrest.

Military Times and *AP* reported that on September 10, 2024, authorities in Hawaii arrested Alexander Cain Poplin, 31, of Wahiawa, Hawaii, at Schofield Barracks, an Army installation near Honolulu, on charges that he repeatedly struck a police officer with a flagpole during the riot. He was charged with five counts, including felony charges of interfering with police during a civil disorder and assaulting, resisting or impeding police with a dangerous weapon.

CNN posted a long article on September 20, 2024 that John Banuelos, now 39, brought a .38 revolver to the riot, standing on a scaffold above the west plaza and twice pulling the trigger. Banuelos had stabbed to death Christopher Senn, 19, on July 4, 2021 in a Salt Lake City incident authorities deemed self-defense. The FBI arrested him on March 8, 2024 near Chicago on charges including discharging a firearm on Capitol grounds. Prosecutors said Banuelos was the only known rioter to have fired a gun. *CNN* cited a litany of 20 arrests in Illinois. He was represented in the insurrection case by attorney Michael Lawlor. Banuelos faced by videoconference U.S. District Judge Tanya Chutkan on May 20, 2024. He was indicted on six criminal charges and was held without bail. He appeared a second time on August 21, 2024. The trial was tentatively scheduled for February 2025 after a grand jury indicted him on new charges regarding illegal use of a firearm.

CNN reported that on January 15, 2021, FBI agents visited Gary Wickersham, 81, an Army veteran who entered the Capitol during the riot. He was arrested in May 2021, and by late 2021, he was sentenced to three years' probation.

CNN added that Rebecca Lavrenz, 71, a Colorado woman known as the "Praying Grandma," spent 10 minutes inside the Capitol on January 6, 2021. She was charged in late 2022, convicted in April 2024, and sentenced in August 2024 to a year of probation, including six months' home confinement, and fined $103,000.

The *Kansas City Star* and *Military.com* reported on October 22, 2024 that Judge Ana C. Reyes in the U.S. District Court for the District of Columbia sentenced U.S. Marine Corps veteran Chad Dustin Suenram, 44, of Wichita, Kansas, who entered the Capitol wearing a patriotic face mask with an American flag painted on his head to two years of probation and fined him $500 for restitution for damage to the Capitol. Suenram pleaded guilty in April 2024 to entering and remaining in a restricted building or grounds, a misdemeanor. He faced a year in prison and a $100,000 fine. The government requested a sentence of 90 days incarceration followed by one year of supervised release, 60 hours of community service, and $500 restitution. He was one of ten Kansas residents charged in the riot. He was arrested on July 17, 2023 in Haysville, Kansas, charged with four misdemeanors: knowingly entering or remaining in any restricted building or grounds; disorderly and disruptive conduct in a restricted building or grounds; disorderly conduct in a Capitol building; and parading, demonstrating, or picketing in a Capitol building. The government dropped three of the charges in exchange for his guilty plea. He received a bad conduct discharge from the military in 2002, for his wrongful use of a controlled substance; he served 60 days in the brig. In 2005, the self-employed single father of five was convicted of sale or possession with intent to sell a controlled substance (cocaine); convicted in 2006 of driving under the influence for a second time; and convicted in 2007 for driving with a suspended license. He was represented by attorney Michael Studtmann.

On November 6, 2024, the day after the presidential election victory of Donald Trump, attorneys for Christopher Carnell of Cary, North Carolina, who was convicted of obstructing Congress, argued that he was "expecting to be relieved of the criminal prosecution that he is currently facing when the new administration takes office." U.S. District Judge Beryl Howell denied the request and scheduled sentencing for December 13. Carnell, 18 at the time of the riot, was convicted of five misdemeanors, including disorderly conduct.

On November 7, 2024, attorneys for Brandon Heffner, of Harford County, Maryland, request a pause in his case. He was charged with civil disorder and disorderly conduct. U.S. District Judge Amit Mehta denied the request on November 11, 2024.

On November 7, 2024, Zachary Alam, of Centreville, Virginia, earlier convicted of assaulting officers, destroying government property, and disorderly conduct, requested a pardon at his sentencing hearing. Instead, U.S. District Judge Dabney Friedrich sentenced him to eight years in prison.

On November 8, 2024, attorneys for Terry Allen, 65, of Spring Hills, Pennsylvania, requested a postponement of his sentencing. Allen was convicted earlier of assaulting police with a wooden flagpole. Judge Mehta on November 12 sentenced him to two years in prison.

On November 9, 2024, William Alexander Pope, representing himself, filed a motion to delay his trial, originally scheduled for December 2, 2024. He was charged with civil disorder and obstruction of Congress. U.S. District Judge Rudolph Contreras set a December 13, 2024 hearing to consider a new trial date.

CNN reported that on November 14, 2024 former NFL linebacker Antwione Williams, 31, who was drafted by the Detroit Lions in 2016 and later played for the XFL's DC Defenders, now part of the UFL, was arrested in Savannah, Georgia, and charged with assaulting law enforcement during the riot. He was alleged to be among the first rioters to breach the restricted perimeter of the Capitol during the attack. Charges included assaulting and impeding officers, civil disorder, entering restricted grounds, and disorderly conduct within a Capitol building. He was released on bond. His next court appearance was scheduled for November 21 in Washington.

On November 21, 2024, authorities in Chicago arrested freelance photographer and local government official Patrick Gorski, 27, on charges including felony obstruction of law enforcement officers during a civil disorder. He told federal agents that he had worked as a photographer for the Chicago Fire Department and for Donald Trump's 2020 presidential campaign. Gorski's resume says he works as a building commissioner for the Village of Norridge, Illinois, and graduated in 2024 from Southeastern Illinois University with a master's degree in public administration.

On December 13, 2024, U.S. District Judge Dabney Friedrich sentenced Army veteran Kevin Loftus, 56 of Dallas, to six months in prison for violating the terms of his probation for his involvement in the Capitol riot. He was arrested at his Wisconsin home several days after the riot. He pleaded guilty in October 2021 to a misdemeanor count of parading, demonstrating or picketing in a Capitol building. Loftus, while on probation, was arrested in December 2023 and charged with driving while intoxicated in Richardson, Texas. He had tried to fly overseas to join the Russian military and fight against Ukraine, but was stopped from boarding an October 28, 2024 flight from Dallas to Tbilisi, Georgia, by way of Istanbul, Türkiye, when Turkish Airlines identified a "security flag" associated with him. Loftus didn't have the court's permission to travel internationally or to drive from Texas to Iowa, where the FBI arrested him. He was represented by attorney Benjamin Schiffelbein. Loftus had served in the army for six years.

CNN reported on December 19, 2024 that Judge Tanya Chutkan, who oversaw the federal election subversion case against former President Trump, authorized Eric Peterson, of Missouri, who pleaded guilty in the fall to "entering and remaining in a restricted building or grounds" during the riot, to travel more broadly within the Kansas City metropolitan area. Peterson will be allowed to attend Trump's inauguration on January 20, 2025. Sentencing was scheduled for January 27, 2025. As part of his plea agreement, Peterson was to pay $500 in restitution to the Architect of the Capitol. He was represented by attorney Michael Bullotta, who noted that Peterson is a military veteran without prior criminal history.

WOKV reported that on December 19, 2024, Joel Linn O'Donnell, 44, of Clearwater, Florida, was arrested and charged with assaulting law enforcement with a weapon related to alleged conduct during the riot. The criminal complaint filed in the District of Columbia listed felonies:

- Assaulting, resisting, or impeding certain officers with a deadly or dangerous weapon.

- Assaulting, resisting, or impeding certain officers.

- Obstruction of law enforcement during civil disorder.

- Entering and remaining in a restricted building or grounds with a deadly or dangerous weapon.

- Disorderly and disruptive conduct in a restricted building or grounds with a deadly or dangerous weapon.

- Engaging in physical violence in a restricted building or grounds with a deadly or dangerous weapon.

His two misdemeanor charges were:

- Disorderly conduct in a Capitol building.

- Act of physical violence in the Capitol grounds or buildings.

CNN and *AP* reported on December 20, 2024 that federal Judge Amit Mehta sentenced military veteran and former Oath Keepers leader Joshua James, 37, of Arab, Alabama, to three years of probation. James was the first J6 defendant to plead guilty to seditious conspiracy. James expressed contrition. He was set to serve six months at a residential reentry facility and another six months on home confinement. Prosecutors noted that James had cooperated extensively with the government, particularly in the trial of Oath Keeper leader Stewart Rhodes, whom Mehta sentenced to 18 years.

March 2021: The *Washington Post* reported on January 30, 2024 that the Department of Justice charged alleged Iran-based narco-trafficker Naji Sharifi Zindashti, 49, and Canadians Damion Patrick John Ryan, 43, and Adam Richard Pearson, 29, in a 2021 murder-for-hire plot against two Maryland residents, a man and woman, after one of them defected from Iran. One of the Canadians was a member of Hells Angels. Court documents indicated that Zindashti offered to pay $370,000 for the murders in Sky ECC encrypted messages exchanged among the co-defendants between December 2020 and March 2021. Ryan and Pearson remained incarcerated in Canada on unrelated offenses.

The U.S. Department of the Treasury imposed sanctions on Zindashti, whom they accused of targeting Iranian dissidents at the behest of the country's Ministry of Intelligence and Security.

The maximum penalty for federal "murder-for-hire" offenses is 10 years in prison and a fine, with that penalty extending to 20 years when personal injury results and life imprisonment or execution when the plot leads to death.

A Minnesota federal grand jury charged the trio in December 2023 with conspiracy to use interstate commerce in the commission of a murder-for-hire plot. Pearson was also charged with two counts related to unlawful possession of a firearm.

March 22, 2021: *CNN* and *AP* reported on October 7, 2023 that Colorado District Judge Ingrid Bakke ruled that Ahmad Al Aliwi Alissa, 24, accused of opening fire on March 22, 2021, at a King Soopers grocery store in Boulder, Colorado and killing 10 people, was fit to stand trial, and will remain in custody at a state hospital to ensure he takes medication to maintain his sta-

tus. Alissa faced 54 charges, including ten counts of murder and one count of attempted murder. Alissa's evaluators diagnosed him with schizophrenia. He was represented by state-appointed defense attorney Kathryn Herold.

August 18, 2021: *CNN* reported on September 15, 2023 that Judge Rudolph Contreras sentenced North Carolina man Floyd Roseberry, who live-streamed threats in 2021 to detonate alleged explosives in his truck parked on a sidewalk blocks from the U.S. Capitol, to five years probation. The judge found that Roseberry had bipolar disorder and was suffering from a significant psychiatric episode at the time due to incorrectly prescribed medication. During his one year in prison in D.C., Roseberry intervened to protect a prison guard who was attacked from behind by a fellow inmate.

November 30, 2021: *CNN* reported on September 29, 2023 that Oakland County Circuit Court Judge Kwamé Rowe ruled that Ethan Crumbley, now 17, who was 15 when he killed four students and wounded seven people, including a teacher, at Oxford High School on November 30, 2021, was eligible for life imprisonment without parole, Michigan's harshest punishment. He had pleaded guilty to one count of terrorism causing death, four counts of first-degree murder, and 19 other charges. He was represented by defense attorney Paulette Loftin. On December 8, 2023, Judge Kwamé Rowe sentenced Crumbley to life without the possibility of parole.

March 5, 2022: *KLAS* reported that Nika Nikoubin, 22, was charged with attempted murder, battery with a deadly weapon, and burglary in March 5, 2022 for stabbing her online date in a Nevada hotel-casino in retaliation of the January 2020 death of Iranian military leader Qassem Soleimani, commander of Iran's Quds Force.

KLAS-TV reported that she met a man on a dating website and the two rented a room together at the Sunset Station hotel. While having sex, she blindfolded him, turned off the lights, and allegedly stabbed him in the neck. He ran out of the room and called 911. She also ran out of the room and told a hotel employee she stabbed a man. She pleaded not guilty to charges in connection with the stabbing and posted bail.

Fox reported on February 16, 2023 that the Texas woman was banned from attending classes at the University of Texas in Dallas while on house arrest.

March 13, 2022: *Marine Times* reported that agents of the FBI and the Naval Criminal Investigative Service on June 14, 2023 arrested Tibet Ergul, 21, of Irvine, and Chance Brannon, 23, of San Juan Capistrano, on federal charges of firebombing a Planned Parenthood clinic in Costa Mesa, California at 1 a.m. on March 13, 2022. A security video showed two people in hoodies and face masks conducting the attack. The duo were charged in federal court in Santa Ana with using an explosive or fire to damage real property affecting interstate commerce.

The *Daily Beast* reported that on November 30, 2023, former Marine Chance Brannon, 24, pleaded guilty to firebombing a Planned Parenthood clinic in Costa Mesa, California. He was on active duty at the time. He was one of three defendants. Tibet Ergul, 22, of Irvine, California, and Xavier Batten, 21, of Brooksville, Florida, were scheduled to go to trial in March 2024. Brannon said he selected the target to "scare pregnant women, deter doctors and staff from providing abortion services, and encourage similar violent acts." No one was injured but the clinic was damaged and rescheduled 30 appointments. Federal prosecutors said Brannon had considered attacking the Anti-Defamation League in San Diego and planned a second hit on a different Planned Parenthood clinic with Ergul and "starting a race war by attacking an electrical substation" with the intention of disrupting the power grid in Orange County. Brannon and Ergul were arrested in June 2023. Two days later, an LGBTQ Pride night celebration at Dodger Stadium was scheduled. The duo had allegedly researched how to attack the event "including by using a remote-detonated device" and Brannon allegedly shared a "WW2 sabotage manual" with Ergul. Brannon pleaded guilty to conspiracy, malicious destruction of property by fire and explosives, possession of an unregistered destructive device, and intentional damage to a reproductive health services facility. Two of the counts carry mandatory minimum sentences of five years in federal prison. A sentencing hearing was scheduled for April 2024.

BBC reported on April 16, 2024 that former U.S. Marine Chance Brannon, 24, pleaded guilty in November 2023 to conspiracy, destruction of property, possession of an explosive and intentionally damaging a reproductive health services facility regarding the March 2022 firebombing attack on a California Planned Parenthood clinic and plotting other attacks against Jewish people and an LGBT pride event taking place at Dodger Stadium in Los Angeles to spark a race war. The neo-Nazi was sentenced to nine years. When arrested, he was on active duty with the USMC.

Co-defendants Tibet Ergul and Xavier Batten earlier pleaded guilty to similar charges and were scheduled for sentencing in May 2024.

May 14, 2022: *CNN* reported on January 12, 2024 that federal prosecutors will seek the death penalty against Payton Gendron, 20, who killed ten Black people at a Buffalo supermarket in 2022, the first capital case authorized by the Biden administration. He faced several hate crimes and firearms charges. He already was serving a life sentence after pleading guilty in 2023 to New York state terrorism and murder charges.

July 4, 2022: *CNN* reported on June 26, 2024 that Robert Crimo, III, 23, accused of killing seven people and injuring dozens when he fired from a rooftop onto Fourth of July 2022 parade revelers in Highland Park, Illinois, two years ago, backed out of a proposed plea deal during a court hearing. Prosecutors said that under the agreement, Crimo would plead guilty to seven murder counts and 48 counts of aggravated battery, one for each named victim in the indictment. He would serve life in prison and other charges would be dismissed. The judge set a trial for February 25, 2025. He had killed Katherine Goldstein, 64; Irina McCarthy, 35; Kevin McCarthy, 37; Jacquelyn Sundheim, 63; Stephen Straus, 88; Nicolas Toledo-Zaragoza, 78; and Eduardo Uvaldo, 69.

July 26, 2022: *CNN* reported on March 18, 2024 that the Bernalillo County District Attorney's office announced that Afghan immigrant Muhammad Syed, accused of killing three Muslim men in Albuquerque, New Mexico in 2022, was found guilty of first degree murder of Aftab Hussein, 41. *KOAT* reported that prosecutors said the killer hid behind a wall and some bushes to shoot Hussein nine times with an AK-47. Syed was represented by attorneys Megan Mitsunaga and Thomas Clark. Syed faced life in prison. He was to be tried separately for the murders of Muhammad Afzaal Hussain and Naeem Hussain. The summer 2022 spree killings included:

- Aftab Hussein was found dead with multiple gunshot wounds on July 26 lying next to a car.
- Muhammad Afzaal Hussain, 27, was found on August 1 with multiple gunshot wounds after witnesses called in a drive-by shooting.
- Naeem Hussain, 25, was shot to death in his car before midnight on August 5, according to authorities. He had recently become a US citizen. He had attended a funeral for Aftab and Muhammad hours before his death.

As of March 19, 2024, no arrest had been made in the possibly related November 7, 2021, murder of Mohammad Ahmadi, an Afghan man who was found with a gunshot wound in the parking lot behind the business he ran with his brother.

August 12, 2022: On July 2, 2024, Hadi Matar, 26, of Fairview, New Jersey, who was held without bail since the August 12, 2022 stabbing of author Salman Rushdie, rejected a plea deal in Mayville, New York, that would have shortened his state prison term but exposed him to a federal terrorism-related charge. Rushdie was stabbed more than a dozen times and was blinded in one eye just before he was to speak at the Chautauqua Institution in western New York. Matar was represented by attorney Nathaniel Barone. Under the agreement, Matar would have pleaded guilty in Chautauqua County to attempted murder in exchange for a maximum state prison sentence of 20 years, down from 25 years. He would also plead guilty to a federal charge of attempting to provide material support to a designated terrorist organization, which could result in an additional 20 years. Matar was born in the U.S. and holds dual citizenship in Lebanon, where his parents were born. Jury selection was scheduled for October 15, 2024.

On July 24, 2024, *UPI* and *AP* reported that a new three-count federal indictment unsealed in U.S. District Court in Buffalo charged Hadi Matar with attempting to provide material support to Lebanese Hizballah, committing terrorism transcending national boundaries, and providing material support to terrorists. He was represented by attorney Nathaniel Barone.

October 28, 2022: *CNN* and *NBC News* reported on November 16, 2023 that a jury in federal court found Canadian citizen David Wayne DePape guilty on one count of assault on the immediate family member of a federal official, and a second count of attempted kidnapping of a federal official in the violent attack on Paul Pelosi, 83, the husband of former House Speaker Nancy Pelosi, on October 28, 2022 in the couple's San Francisco home. He could face a maximum sentence of 30 years and 20 years on the charges, respectively. He was represented by attorney Jodi Linker.

Paul Pelosi eventually underwent surgery to repair a skull fracture and injuries to his hand and arm.

DePape earlier pleaded not guilty to state charges including attempted murder, burglary, assault with a deadly weapon, elder abuse, and false imprisonment. A trial date was expected to be set later in November.

On May 17, 2024, a federal judge sentenced David DePape to 30 years in prison for assault and 20 years for attempted kidnapping, which will run concurrently.

On May 18, 2024, *CNN* reported that the judge granted a motion to reopen the sentencing because DePape did not get a chance to speak during his sentencing hearing. The judge set the sentencing portion of the case for May 28 at 9:30 a.m.

CNN and the *New York Times* reported that on June 22, 2024 a California jury convicted DePape of state charges of first-degree burglary, false imprisonment, threatening a family member of a public official, aggravated kidnapping, and preventing or dissuading a witness by force or threat when he violently attacked Paul Pelosi with a hammer. He faced a 30-year sentence from his federal conviction in November 2023 for assault on the immediate family member of a federal official and attempted kidnapping of a federal official in connection with the attack. Judge Harry M. Dorfman had dismissed charges of attempted murder, assault of an elder, and assault with a deadly weapon, after DePape's defense team argued that would amount to double jeopardy. He was represented inter alia by attorney Adam Lipson.

On October 30, 2024, San Francisco Superior Court Judge Harry Dorfman sentenced DePape to life in prison without the possibility of parole.

November 19-20, 2022: *AP* reported that nonbinary Anderson Lee Aldrich, 22, accused of the mass shooting at the LGBTQ+ Colorado Springs Club Q nightclub in Colorado Springs that killed five people—Ashley Paugh, Daniel Aston, Derrick Rump, Raymond Green Vance, and Kelly Loving—and wounded 17 on November 19-20, 2022, was expected to take a plea deal to state murder and hate charges and accept a life sentence. He faced more than 300 state counts. The next hearing was scheduled for June 26, 2023.

CNN reported on June 27, 2023 that Aldrich pleaded guilty to five state counts of first-degree murder and 46 counts of attempted murder. On June 26, 2023, Judge Michael McHenry of the Fourth Judicial District sentenced Aldrich to five consecutive life sentences without the possibility of parole and another 2,208 years for the attempted murder charges, plus a four-year sentence on bias-motivated charges (similar to hate-crime charges). Colorado had abolished the death penalty in 2020.

AP and *USA Today* reported on June 18, 2024 that Anderson Lee Aldrich, now 24, pleaded guilty to federal hate crime charges. U.S. District Judge Charlotte Sweeney, the first openly gay federal judge in Colorado, sentenced him to 55 life terms in prison and 190 years on gun charges and other counts. He did not apologize or say anything to the victims' families. He was represented by attorney David Kraut.

November 28, 2022: The *New York Times* reported on January 22, 2023, that on November 28, 2022, the trial in Manhattan's State Supreme Court began of Abdullah el-Faisal, 59. The UK

earlier imprisoned him for inciting hatred and soliciting murder before expelling him to Jamaica. The NYPD noted he promoted jihad and encouraged the murder of Jews, Hindus, and Americans. He also allegedly helped a woman who wanted to marry an ISIS fighter. His lawyers included Alex Grosshtern.

December 2022: *ABC News* reported that in December 2022 federal prosecutors in Brooklyn charged four defendants with crowdfunding support for ISIS using cryptocurrency, Bitcoin wallets, GoFundMe, and PayPal to collect what they termed "blood money."

December 31, 2022: The *Florida Times-Union* reported on January 12, 2023 that Trevor Thomas Bickford, 19, was charged with federal terrorism counts for his jihadi plot to attack U.S. government officials and attacking three police officers in Times Square on New Year's Eve 2022. He faced a life sentence.

ABC News reported that a court on May 9, 2024 sentenced Bickford to 27 years in federal prison and a lifetime of supervised release for a "brazen" 2022 New Year's Eve knife attack near West 52nd Street and Eighth Avenue in Times Square that seriously injured three New York City Police Department officers. Prosecutors said he arrived from Maine intending to conduct a jihadist attack on officers in uniform with a "machete-style knife"—an 18-inch kukri knife. Bickford pleaded guilty in January 2024 to three counts of attempted murder of government officials and three counts of assault on government officials. Bickford faced up to 120 years in prison. The government asked for at least 50 years in prison. He still faced more than a dozen state charges in connection with the attack, including three counts of attempted murder in the first degree in furtherance of an act of terrorism. He was scheduled to appear in court on May 22, 2024 in the New York state case.

BIBLIOGRAPHY

GENERAL

Harrison Akins *The Terrorism Trap: How the War on Terror Escalates Violence in America's Partner States* New York: Columbia University Press, 2023, 362 pp.

Dan Ariely *Misbelief: What Makes Rational People Believe Irrational Things* Harper Collins, 2023, 304 pp.

Irina A. Chindea "How Violent Nonstate Actors Adapt" *Rand Review* July-August 2023, p. 5.

Kenneth Christie and Haval Ahmad *Radicalization, Terrorism, and Countering Extremism: Theory and Practice* Rowman and Littlefield, 2024, 180 pp.

David Miller and Tom Mills *The Politics of Terrorism Expertise: Knowledge, Power and the Media* Routledge, 2023, 224 pp.

EUROPE

Emmanuel Carrere *V13: Chronicle of a Trial* Farrar, Straus and Giroux, 2024, 304 pp.

Rory Carroll *There Will Be Fire: Margaret Thatcher, the IRA, and Two Minutes That Changed History* NY: G.P. Putnam's Sons, 2023, 416 pp.

Pau Caruana Galizia *A Death in Malta: An Assassination and a Family's Quest for Justice* Riverhead Books, 2023, 304 pp.

Henry Hemming *Four Shots in the Night: A True Story of Spies, Murder, and Justice in Northern Ireland* Public Affairs, 2024, 368 pp.

Ben McIntyre *The Siege: A Six-Day Hostage Crisis and the Daring Special Forces Operation That Shocked the World* New York: Crown, 2024, 365 pp.

MIDDLE EAST

Tom Blanton *Afghanistan 20/20: A History of the U.S. War in Declassified Documents* The New Press, 2023, 384 pp.

Jack Carr and James Scott *Targeted: Beirut: The 1983 Marine Barracks Bombing and the Untold Origin Story of the War on Terror* Atria, 2024, 432 pp.

Ferdinand J. Haberl *Jihadi Intelligence and Counterintelligence: Ideological Foundations and Operational Methods* Springer, 2023

Ari Harow *My Brother's Keeper: Netanyahu, Obama, and the Year of Terror and Conflict that Changed the Middle East Forever* Bombardier Books, 2024, 262 pp.

Martha Hodes *My Hijacking: A Personal History of Forgetting and Remembering* Harper, 2023, 367 pp.

Sally Lane *Reasonable Cause to Suspect: A Mother's Ordeal to Free Her Son from a Kurdish Prison* Dundurn Press, 2023, 360 pp.

Melvyn P. Leffler *Confronting Saddam Hussein: George W. Bush and the Invasion of Iraq* New York: Oxford University Press, 2023, 368 pp.

Pardis Mahdavi *Book of Queens: The True Story of the Middle Eastern Horsewomen Who Fought the War on Terror* Hachette, 2023, 288 pp.

Colum McCann with Diane Foley *American Mother* Etruscan Press, 2024, 256 pp.

Jessica Roy *American Girls: One Woman's Journey into the Islamic State and her Sister's Fight to Bring Her Home* NY: Scribner, 2024, 341 pp.

Mitchell Zuckoff *The Secret Gate: A True Story of Courage and Sacrifice During the Collapse of Afghanistan* Random House, 2023, 336 pp.

North America

Thomas L. Ahern, Jr. *"Nothing if Not Eventful" - A Life's Journey in CIA* 2023

Kevin Cook *Waco Rising: David Koresh, the FBI, and the Birth of America's Modern Militias* Henry Holt, 2023, 288 pp.

Julie Farnam *Domestic Darkness: An Insider's Account of the January 6th Insurrection, and the Future of Right-Wing Extremism* IG Publishing, 2024, 298 pp.

Bruce Hoffman and Jacob Ware *God, Guns, and Sedition: Far-Right Terrorism in America* New York: Columbia University Press, 2024, 288 pp.

Santi Elijah Holley *An Amerikan Family: The Shakurs and the Nation They Created* Marine Books, 2023, 306 pp.

Steven Johnson *The Infernal Machine: A True Story of Dynamite, Terror and the Rise of the Modern Detective* NY: Crown 2024, 368 pp.

Wesley Lowery *American Whitelash: A Changing Nation and the Cost of Progress* Mariner, 2023, 272 pp.

Shahan Mufti *American Caliph: The True Story of a Muslim Mystic, a Hollywood Epic, and the 1977 Siege of Washington, D.C.* NY: Farrar, Straus and Giroux, 2022, 367 pp.

William Nester *World of War: A History of American Warfare from Jamestown to the War on Terror* Globe Pequot/Stackpole Books, 2024, 472 pp.

Betsy T. Phillips *Dynamite Nashville: Unmasking the FBI, the KKK, and the Bombers Behind Their Control* Third Man Books, 2024, 240 pp.

Ryan J. Reilly *Sedition Hunters: How January 6th Broke the Justice System* Public Affairs, 2023, 480 pp.

Salman Rushdie *Knife: Meditations After an Attempted Murder* NY: Random House, 2024, 224 pp.

Jeffrey D. Simon *The Bulldog Detective: William J. Flynn and America's First War against the Mafia, Spies, and Terrorists* Prometheus, 2024, 288 pp.

Jeffrey Toobin *Homegrown: Timothy McVeigh and the Rise of Right-Wing Extremism* New York: Simon and Schuster, 2023, 432 pp.

U.S. Secret Service *Mass Attacks in Public Spaces: 2016—2020*, Washington, D.C.: January 2023, available at https://www.secretservice.gov/ntac/

Susan Weis *An Assassin in Utopia: The True Story of a Nineteeth-Century Sex Cult and a President's Murder* Pegasus Crime, 2023, 341pp.

John Wigger *The Hijacking of American Flight 119: How D.B. Cooper Inspired a Skyjacking Craze and the FBI's Battle to Stop It* Oxford University Press, 2023, 304 pp.

Brandon J. Wolf *A Place for Us* Little A, 2023, 221 pp.

Responses

Richard J. Chasdi *Corporate Security Surveillance: An Assessment of Host Country Vulnerability to Terrorism* Springer, 2024, 472 pp.

Adam Gamal and Kelly Kennedy *The Unit: My Life Fighting Terrorists as One of America's Most Secret Military Operatives* New York: St. Martin's, 2024, 304 pp.

Huda Mukbil *Agent of Change: My Life Fighting Terrorists, Spies, and Institutional Racism* McGill-Queen's University Press, 2023.

John Ryan *America's Trial: Torture and the 9/11 Case on Guantanamo Bay* Skyhorse, 2024, 240 pp.

Michael G. Vickers *By All Means Available: Memoirs of a Life in Intelligence, Special Operations, and Strategy* NY: Knopf, 2023, 576 pp.

Internet

Hamas.com, an anti-Hamas propaganda website

Hamas.ps, website of Hamas

Hamas-massacre.net shows graphic videos and images to "document the horrors of that day"

oct7map.com, an interactive online map of where Israelis were killed or kidnapped

Fiction

Johannes Anyuru, translated by Saskia Vogel *They Will Drown in Their Mother's Tears* Two Lines Press, 2020, 272 pp.

Ray Collins *The General's Briefcase* Koehler Books, 2023, 334 pp.

V.V. Ganeshananthan *Brotherless Night* New York: Random House, 2023, 348 pp.

Maxim Loskutoff *Old King* Norton, 2024, 283 pp.

Javier Marias *Tomas Nevinson*, translated by Margaret Juli Costa NY: Knopf, 2023, 641 pp.

OTHER BOOKS
BY EDWARD MICKOLUS

TERRORISM

Terrorist Events Worldwide, 2022

Terrorist Events Worldwide, 2021

Terrorist Events Worldwide 2019-2020

Terrorism Worldwide, 2018

Terrorism Worldwide, 2017

Terrorism Worldwide, 2016

Terrorism 2013-2015: A Worldwide Chronology

Terrorism 2008-2012: A Worldwide Chronology

Terrorism, 2005-2007

with Susan L. Simmons *Terrorism, 2002-2004: A Chronology* 3 volumes

with Susan L. Simmons *Terrorism, 1996-2001: A Chronology of Events and a Selectively Annotated Bibliography* 2 volumes

with Susan L. Simmons *Terrorism, 1992-1995: A Chronology of Events and a Selectively Annotated Bibliography*

Terrorism, 1988-1991: A Chronology of Events and a Selectively Annotated Bibliography

with Todd Sandler and Jean Murdock *International Terrorism in the 1980s: A Chronology, Volume 2: 1984-1987*

with Todd Sandler and Jean Murdock *International Terrorism in the 1980s: A Chronology, Volume 1: 1980-1983*

Transnational Terrorism: A Chronology of Events, 1968-1979

with Peter Flemming *Terrorism, 1980-1987: A Selectively Annotated Bibliography*

The Literature of Terrorism: A Selectively Annotated Bibliography

Annotated Bibliography on International and Transnational Terrorism available in *Legal and Other Aspects of Terrorism*

International Terrorism: Attributes of Terrorist Events, 1968-1977, ITERATE 2 Data Codebook

ITERATE: International Terrorism: Attributes of Terrorist Events, Data Codebook

Combatting International Terrorism: A Quantitative Analysis

with Susan L. Simmons *The 50 Worst Terrorist Attacks*

with Susan L. Simmons *The Terrorist List: North America*

with Susan L. Simmons *The Terrorist List: South America*

with Susan L. Simmons *The Terrorist List: Eastern Europe*

with Susan L. Simmons *The Terrorist List: Western Europe*

with Susan L. Simmons *The Terrorist List: Asia, Pacific, and Sub-Saharan Africa*

The Terrorist List: The Middle East, 2 volumes

INTELLIGENCE

Spycraft for Thriller Writers: How to Write Spy Novels and Movies Accurately and Not Be Laughed at by Real-Life Spies

More Stories from Langley: Another Glimpse Inside the CIA

Stories from Langley: A Glimpse Inside the CIA

The Counterintelligence Chronology: Spying by and Against the United States from the 1700s through 2014

The Secret Book of Intelligence Community Humor

Two Spies Walk Into a Bar

The Secret Book of CIA Humor

INSPIRATION

Harlan Rector and Ed Mickolus, eds. *I Still Matter: Finding Meaning in Life at All Ages*

Harlan Rector and Ed Mickolus, eds. *I Matter Too: Finding Meaning in Life at All Ages*

Harlan Rector and Ed Mickolus, eds. *I Still Matter: Finding Meaning in Life at All Ages*

His Words: Inspirational Quotations from Jesus Christ

EDUCATION

The Creativity Sourcebook

Briefing for the Boardroom and the Situation Room

with Joseph T. Brannan *Coaching Winning Model United Nations Teams*

HUMOR

More Funny COVID Memes

America's Funniest Memes: Coronavirus Edition

Food with Thought: The Wit and Wisdom of Chinese Fortune Cookies

FICTION

with T.S. Tripp *White Noise Whispers*

MISCELLANY

with Bill Wildey *Trivia Matters: A Trivia Host Sourcebook*

with Joe Rendon *Take My Weight, Please; Head-to-Toe Fitness for Seniors—The Cowboy Joe Way*

COMING SOON

Famous Last Meals

and others *Naked Came the Spy*

and others *Moscow Syndrome*

and others *Stories by the Side of the Road*

All the Presidents' Heroes: Inspirational Stories from the State of the Union Addresses
    Volume I: Ronald Reagan

Volume 2: George H. W. Bush

Volume 3: Bill Clinton

Volume 4: George W. Bush

Volume 5: Barack Obama

Volume 6: Donald Trump

Volume 7: Joe Biden

and Tracy Tripp *…And Presumed Dead*

Beyond Authorship

WANDERING
WOODS
PUBLISHERS

Find the Author at:

Books: EdwardMickolus.com

Terrorism Data: VinyardSoftware.com

www.ingramcontent.com/pod-product-compliance
Lightning Source LLC
Chambersburg PA
CBHW052109020426
42335CB00021B/2686